TOWARDS A HISTORY OF CONSCIOUSNESS
Space, Time, and Death   Vwadek P. Marciniak

E R R A T A

The notes for Chapter One, 13–70 as they appear in the text should be numbered 82–139. The correct endnotes for Chapter One, 13–81 are as follows.

13. Adam Parry, "The Language of Achilles," *Language and Background of Homer*, ed G. S. Kirk, (Cambridge: W. Heffer, 1967), 4–5.
14. Rollo May, *Man's Search for Himself*, (NY: Signet Bk. New American Library, 1967), 28. See also Hunter, 212.
15. Lucien Levy-Bruhl, *The Notebooks on Primitive Mentality*, trans. by Peter Rivière, (Oxford: Basil Blackwell, 1975), 79. Also see the movie *Zardoz* (1973), directed by John Boorman.
16. Lieberman, 67.
17. Lieberman, 65.
18. Lieberman, 65–66.
19. Lieberman, 76.
20. Lieberman, 162.
21. Walter Kaufmann, *Religions in Four Dimensions: Existential and Aesthetic, Historical and Comparative* (NY: Reader's Digest Press, 1976), 24.
22. Lieberman, 161.
23. Levy-Bruhl, 14–15.
24. Karl R. Popper and Sir John C. Eccles, *The Self and Its Brain*, (NY: Springer International, 1977), 153–54.
25. Julian Jaynes, *Origins of Consciousness in The Breakdown of the Bicameral Mind*, (Boston: Houghton Mifflin, 1976), 136
26. John Pfeiffer, *The Emergence of Man*, 2nd ed., (NY: Harper & Row, 1972), 192.
27. May, 28.
28. Kenneth R. Pelletier, *Toward A Science of Consciousness*, (NY: Dell Publishing Co., Inc., 1978), 216.
29. John Eccles, Sir and Daniel N. Robinson, *The Wonder of Being Human: Our Brain and Our Mind*, (NY: Free Press, Macmillan, 1984), 25–26.
30. Popper, 554.
31. See Chapter Eleven.
32. Jerry Fodor, "You Can't Argue With a Novel," *London Review of Books* review of Dan Lloyd, *Radiant Cool: A Novel Theory of Consciousness*, (MIT, 2000), 4 March 2004, 30–31.
33. James Earl Deese, *Thought Into Speech* (Englewood Cliffs, NJ: Prentice-Hall, Inc., 1984), 10.
34. Deese, 129.
35. Ong, 30.
36. Popper, 554.
37. Elisabeth Kubler-Ross, *Death. The Final Stage of Growth*, (Englewood: Prentice-Hall, Inc., 1975), x.
38. Gregory Bateson, *Steps to an Ecology of Mind* (NY: Ballantine Books, 1972), 465. See also Jean Delumeau, *Sin and Fear: The Emergence of a Western Guilt Culture 13th–18th Centuries*, trans by Eric Nicholson, (NY: St. Martin's Press, 1989), 37.
39. Delumeau, 37.
40. Eccles, 175.
41. Jaynes, 136.
42. Jaynes, 136.
43. Levy-Bruhl, 79.

44. Ong, 35.
45. Ong, 30.
46. Ong, 32.
47. Popper, 153.
48. Gottfried Richter, *Art and Human Consciousness*, trans. by Burley Channer and Margaret Frohlich, (Spring Valley, N.Y.: Anthroposophic Press, 1982), 111.
49. Daniel Goleman, *Vital Lies, Simple Truths: The Psychology of Self-Deception* (NY: Simon and Schuster, 1986), 237.
50. Michael Sprinker, "Gerard Manley Hopkins on the Origin of Language," *JHI*, 41, 1 (Jan–March 1980), 117.
51. Hawkes, 108.
52. Lieberman, 38.
53. Richard E. Leaky and Roger Lewin, *Origins,* (NY: E.P. Hutton, 1977), 180–81.
54. Jaynes, 132.
55. Noam Chomsky quoted in Richard Lederer, *The Miracle of Language*, (NY: Pocket Books, 1991), 17–18.
56. See Robin Dunbar, *Grooming, Gossip, and the Evolution of Language,* (Harvard University Press, 1996).
57. Ong, 31.
58. Ong, 32.
59. Eccles, 114.
60. Leaky, 180.
61. Hawkes, 639.
62. Hawkes, 634.
63. Hawkes, 634.
64. Stephen Kern, *The Culture of Time and Space: 1880–1918*, (Cambridge: Harvard University Press, 1983), 139.
65. John McCrone, *The Ape That Spoke: Language and the Evolution of the Human Mind.* (NY: William Morrow and Co., Inc., 1990), 204.
66. Charles L. Barber, *The Story of Speech and Language,* (NY: Thomas Y. Crowell Co., 1965), 47.
67. Barber, 47.
68. Ong, 30.
69. Kaufmann, *Religions*, 25.
70. Richter, 39.
71. Kaufmann, *Religions*, 56,
72. Kaufmann, *Religions*, 57.
73. Kaufmann, *Religions*, 57.
74. Kaufmann, *Religions*, 57.
75. Fred Alan Wolf, *Star Wave: Mind, Consciousness, and Quantum Physics*, (NY: Macmillan Publishing Co., 1984), 72.
76. Steven Roger Fischer, *A History of Language,* (London: Reaktion Books, 1999), 97.
77. Whittemore, *Whole Lives*, 2.
78. Kern, 139.
79. Whittemore, *Pure Lives*, 2.
80. Owen Barfield, *Saving Appearances: A Study in Idolatry*, (London: Faber and Faber, 1957), 105. There is some evidence of the idea of privacy in a non-negative manner as early as the eighteenth century in Patricia Meyer Spacks' recent work, *Privacy: Concealing the 18th-Century Self,* (Chicago: University of Chicago Press, 2003).
81. Popper, 154–55.

Chapter Eight, endnote 41 should read "Allison, 52." All subsequent endnotes are off by one.

Necessary corrections will be made in subsequent editions.

Towards a History of Consciousness

american
university
studies

Series V
Philosophy

Vol. 199

PETER LANG
New York • Washington, D.C./Baltimore • Bern
Frankfurt am Main • Berlin • Brussels • Vienna • Oxford

Vwadek P. Marciniak

Towards a History of Consciousness

Space, Time, and Death

PETER LANG
New York • Washington, D.C./Baltimore • Bern
Frankfurt am Main • Berlin • Brussels • Vienna • Oxford

Library of Congress Cataloging-in-Publication Data

Marciniak, Vwadek P.
Towards a history of consciousness:
space, time, and death / Vwadek P. Marciniak.
p. cm. — (American university studies. Series V, Philosophy; v. 199)
Includes bibliographical references and index.
1. Consciousness—History. I. Title. II. Series.
B105.C477M37   126.09—dc22   2005037051
ISBN 0-8204-8167-X
ISSN 0739-6392

Bibliographic information published by **Die Deutsche Bibliothek**.
Die Deutsche Bibliothek lists this publication in the "Deutsche
Nationalbibliografie"; detailed bibliographic data is available
on the Internet at http://dnb.ddb.de/.

The paper in this book meets the guidelines for permanence and durability
of the Committee on Production Guidelines for Book Longevity
of the Council of Library Resources.

© 2006 Peter Lang Publishing, Inc., New York
29 Broadway, New York, NY 10006
www.peterlang.com

All rights reserved.
Reprint or reproduction, even partially, in all forms such as microfilm,
xerography, microfiche, microcard, and offset strictly prohibited.

Printed in Germany

Table of Contents

Preface vii

Introduction 1

I: The Pre-Modern West
    One: Beginnings: Pre-History to Antiquity 9
    Two: Medieval Persistence of Classical Antiquity 53

II: Entrance into Early Modern Europe
    Three: The Renaissance: Altered Space and Time 95
        From Re-Birth to Reform
    Four: The Reformation of Early Modernity 137
        From Reform to Re-order
    Five: Scientific Revolution and Detachment 179
        From Re-Order to Restructure

III: Early Modern Definitions
    Six: Descartes and Consciousness 223
        From Doubt to Certainty
    Seven: John Locke and the Language of Consciousness 267
        From Faith to Self-Identity
    Eight: Enlightenment and the Birth of Modernity 309
        From Thought to Sentiment

IV: Modernity and Beyond
    Nine: Romantics, the Self and Individualism 357
        From Reason to Feelings
    Ten: The Fractured Age: Twentieth Century Transformation 401
        From Order to Disorder
    Eleven: A Time and Space for Consciousness 445
        From Disorder to Creativity

Conclusion 491

APPENDIX I   Quasi-Essentialistic Characterizations 495
APPENDIX II Contrastive Terms 497
APPENDIX III Cross-References 499

NOTES 505
BIBLIOGRAPHY 555
INDEX 587

Preface

This search for an historic context regarding the appearance and meaning of consciousness began more than thirty years ago when the topic of our split brain, the right and left hemisphere, came to light. From the beginning the subject proved both challenging and significant if not revolutionary. It became clear that the issue of consciousness would soon dominate a great amount of our intellectual and scholarly attention, which it has.

A great many scholarly disciplines had taken up the subject with books and articles appearing expeditiously but offering a less than satisfactory understanding of this remarkable term. Only after years of reading, studying and thought followed by the gathering of data, was it obvious that there was a vacuity in the world of scholarship confronting the issue of explaining the appearance of a conscious self. Because my discipline as an historiographer has been so conspicuous in its absence it became clear that someone had to step into the breech. The following is such an attempt.

A note of appreciation must be made to my former undergraduate mentor, Dr. Windsor Hall Roberts, for illuminating the way of Western history and political thought. Special thanks must also be expressed to J. T. Ferguson for her outstanding editing and assistance and without whose contribution this work could not have been completed.

As for all ideas, as well as errors that appear here, this author and this author alone must take responsibility.

INTRODUCTION

> A single author cannot speak with the high authority of a panel of experts, but he may succeed in giving to his work an integrated and even an epical quality that no composite volume can achieve. . . . [The specialized historian's] work can be of the highest value; but it is not an end in itself. I believe that the supreme duty of the historian is to write history, that is to say, to attempt to record in one sweeping sequence the greater events and movements that have swayed the destinies of men. The writer rash enough to make the attempt should not be criticized for his ambitions, however much he may deserve censure for the inadequacy for his equipment or the inanity of his results.[1]

This historical survey of our Western history has a very unique theme driving the narrative and analysis. While it does not, "…attempt to record in one sweeping sequence the greater events and movements that have swayed the destinies of men," it does attempt to offer a small clarification of a neglected topic that could enlighten us on the historic background and context for both the introduction and the growth of our capacity for creating a conscious self. The metaphor offered to dramatize the assumptions inherent in this endeavor, one that has grown out of more than sixteen years research and twenty-five years teaching an integrated Humanities program, will be organic. Any study of where we come from is a necessary prerequisite in explaining where and who we are.

In the history of ideas, no aspect has been more neglected than that of consciousness. Historians discuss in depth the great thinkers, their contributions to the world of ideas, but rarely, and only as an aside, our consciousness. They discuss and dissect postmodernism, fascism, humanism and even multiculturalism, but on the whole they remain indifferent to what has become one of the most significant topics for neuroscientists, psychologists, philosophers and cognitive researchers. Part of the problem is that this is the most ambiguous of terms, playing a plethora of roles as a qualifier: "Black Consciousness," "Bourgeois Consciousness," "Feminine Consciousness," "Gay Consciousness," "Double Consciousness," *ad nauseam*.[2] Many writers perceive consciousness as simply too obvious in meaning and application for a definition to be of any particular concern. For many it has become little more than part of a useful social science jargon while at the same time too subjective to admit existence except as a literary convenience. Others would even go so far as to deny that the mind itself exists. It is little wonder that a discussion of the historic development and evolution of the various degrees of modern consciousness would prove for many a conspicuous waste of time.

Compounding this difficulty, there is the historic question of the development of an inner self, one's own distinct individuality, as both part of a personal identity and the development of thoughtful choices. In an expanding world of existential attitudes, the implication of a self and individuality for consciousness is too ambiguous without considering the full breadth of its historical background. This simply exacerbates the complex problem of defining consciousness, especially for the historian seeking causation, relationships and development. Since consciousness is perceived an inclusionary term containing many aspects and components, this survey will use sources from a variety of disciplines. How and where did consciousness come from is an extremely complex issue begging for detailed examination.

From its beginning, consciousness is seen as a biological and organic phenomena growing out of opportune soil; from the earliest where we find nothing that could be considered modern consciousness, then growing slowly through centuries into maturation. Questions arising from this analysis have proven revealing, instructive and often problematic—some suggested here: What should be considered as the most fundamental root that made possible the creation of our transformation into self-conscious beings with a private reality? What are some of the fundamental characteristics of the soil conducive for the growth of evolving consciousness that can be identified and examined? And what has proven to be a necessary fertilizer in our common historic past among thinkers and cultures that make for enhancement and expansion of what we refer to as a modern self? Could it also be that there are associations between our development into modern consciousness and the appearance of the contemporary existential attitudes now increasingly appearing among certain thinkers and artists? Finally, is it possible that we are organically structured to evolve into even higher and more complex states of consciousness than already realized?[3]

There have been a number of themes that have also grown within this work, some of which may be problematic for students of the subject. I have already implied that we have not always been conscious, that when consciousness appears it is in degrees and it only appears as we approach our own era. There may be exceptions to these patterns, some noted in the last chapters, but they too will only be suggestive. The themes themselves will be discussed briefly regarding the orientation of the chronological and scholarly materials.

When this work began it was assumed that consciousness was a singular issue. The companion ideas of self and individuality, however, made their presence central. There are other themes that are indispensable for understanding the forces that transformed us from non-conscious to conscious beings and which may also appear for some rather odd: death and with it the beginning of the idea of certainty were two (certitude in religion). To trace the beginnings of an inner life requires some understanding of our relationship with this fundamental idea of certainty. Death and a desire for alternative certainties has proven to be a necessary *alpha* and *omega* for humanity and this study.

There are other relevant themes, particularly those growing out of the plastic arts and literature, our cultural and literary history. Artistic themes will appear occasionally, while the exploration of the dynamics of our changing language, especially literacy and our sense of space, will also prove indispensable for understanding such unique modern terms. As we alter our cultural sense of space with the expansion of our language we also construct the discipline of history which gives context for those changes that enlarge both our sense of our world and ourselves.

Scientific history will also be given serious attention in order to expand our understanding of the technical side of time, space and the methodologies for investigation that have played such an important role in our transformation from believing to reasoning beings. Political and economic history will be given some minimal but significant consideration in explaining changes in popular societal and cultural assumptions that contributed to the development of the conscious self. The relatively new field of social history will also find some application as we examine our social identities altered by cultural changes.

Since so much analysis for intellectual history is deductive and relatively new, the defining of terms will naturally be of paramount concern. But this is not a work meant to reach conclusive definitions. It is rather a matter of suggesting indicators and pointing in a direction for enlarging contextual understanding. The offering here is more in line with a listing of what could be called quasi-essentialistic characterizations applicable to consciousness. Listed corollary terms and appendices suggest further noteworthy and applicable concepts.[4]

As a methodology, this is a contribution to the History of Ideas, a subsystem of historiography. While it may seem odd that an historian of ideas will be discussing language, it is well to remember that, "...methodologists of the history of ideas usually agree that semantics is relevant for it." As a contributor of *Journal of the History of Ideas* agreed, "...the history of ideas to some extent is the history of words."[5] And the father of the history of ideas, Arthur Lovejoy, also pointed out that any study of ideas should also include the study of "...some parts of the history of language, especially semantics."[6]

Because of serious misunderstandings of our past, and particularly a given period's limited uses and meaning of their language and terms, it will necessitate examination of errors in translations since they too often represent a more modern mentality, one that would be neglectful an understanding of the past within it's own context. The concern, therefore, will be to attempt, where possible, the review of past meanings and understanding rather than adding confusion that might be drawn from an inappropriate modernization of that language. As the above implies, this is a work conducted in a chronological manner although it is appropriately topical as to given themes where indicated.

There has developed more recently, especially among French scholars, a sub-system of intellectual history known as the History of Mentalities. These two fields are not a difference in type but emphasis. The specific study of ideas is best exemplified by the discussion of significant philosophical thinkers and their systems, the two most important reviewed here being René Descartes and John Locke. Because of their significance for consciousness, their contributions will be extensively and systematically studied. Additionally, this is such a lengthy and broad historic period that necessity dictates the use of many scholarly monographs.

Postmodern is a term, which while unpopular with historians, and at best ambiguous, began finding a voice, limited though it may be, in my early rewritings. This will be used cautiously because this is not employed here as occurring after the age of modernity. As expressed here, "post-modern" will be treated as a part or branch of the modern Western mind. As an abstract concept it is much like post-impressionism, suggesting that while the plastic arts continued its pleasures in realism, another aspect began to appear: An art that steps outside the frames of that tradition. The Theater of the Absurd with attempts at post-systematic plots could also be seen as an expression of this post-modern mind. Even physicists entertain such ideas as chaos not being necessarily abnormal. This raises a third point where modern has become enamored if not enslaved to a world of systems, techniques and materialism, while the post-modern could be said more interested in an alternate approach to living as expressed, for example, by surrealism, futurism, modern poetry, jazz and film which reside outside the typical modern establishment schema.

Nationalism is being replaced by globalism and a personal identity. The term *existential* is one major indicator of these changes. Perhaps *post-lineal* would be more accurate although not an issue here, only an explanation for its occasional usage.

The first section reviews pre-historic, Ancient and Medieval contributions in the creation of the earliest hints of an inner voice for consciousness to eventually find a home. The second section, the Renaissance, Reformation and Scientific Revolution, examines the early interior voice finding an outward expression. The third section deals with the birth of the term consciousness and its place among some early modern thinkers. The final section takes us into the voice of an inner, conscious self and individuality that marks the world for many today.

… I ∞

THE PRE-MODERN WEST

CHAPTER ONE

BEGINNINGS: PRE-HISTORY TO ANTIQUITY

The expansion of consciousness is a main theme of history. Nothing has greater significance than the development and exercise of the combined mental powers of intellect and imagination, the two springs of human greatness.[1]

Being conscious is more than being aware. It is being integrated with and beyond our experiences. It is the mark of our unique development and death is the base upon which all else must rest. Consciousness—as a phenomenon—has a history and heritage whose roots have been long neglected. For those who claim to have conscious experiences: self-conscious mental activity and even continuous states of consciousness and for those who actively perceive and introspect their experiences and are more than simply aware, consciousness could be perceived as a normal mental state, an inherent by-product of the further development of the modern sense of self and individuality. This process of the development of the phenomenon of consciousness took many centuries in western history from our pre-historic beginnings to the matured ontology we now experience. To reach this plateau upon which we now stand required an historic transformation where people, like societies, are perceived not as static but dynamic with an expansive understanding of time and space.

Death is the most certain, the most absolute circumstance that humans have had to learn to live with. The awareness of this most fundamental reality highlights both the presence and significance of the life-cycle. There is nothing more central to our existence: rich or poor, powerful or weak, famous or unknown. This is the one certainty that has been a driving force, either directly or obliquely for both our culture and our psyche. It is this certainty that has, in part, helped guide our evolution into the fully mature self-conscious reflective individuality that confronts us today.

It is not only that we know we are terminal but rather that we can speak of, and eventually write about and even create an art around this most necessary of our defining human condition. Any study of the history and evolution of consciousness therefore must begin at this root with an analysis of collective memory and our language representing space.

It was in the early nineteenth-century that a major and rather impenetrable German philosopher addressed this issue of the importance of our knowledge of our terminal condition:

> In Hegel, man is not distinguished from other animal species by being an *animal rational* but by being the only living creature that knows about his death....In the anticipation of death, the will's projects take on the appearance of an anticipated past and as such can become the object of reflection; and it is in this sense that Hegel maintains that only the mind that 'does not ignore death' enables man to 'dominate death,' to 'endure it and to maintain itself with it.' [2]

Our discovery of mortality and with it our unique earliest evolutionary steps have been given shape through a variety of excellent scholarship and research which offer an understanding of the earliest beginnings of our pre-history. This is partly a matter of biology: "...unlike any other creature on earth, man is equipped with a neocortex which enables him to know that he will die. We have never really adjusted ourselves to this absolute bad news. In our art, in our religions, our cultures, our moral codes, our institutions, our architecture and design, we have found ways to let ourselves live on beyond the moment of our own individual extinction."[3] And discussing the earliest chronological periodization that deductively can be studied, *The Universe Within* by Morton Hunt is a worthy beginning:

> This most recent and most significant evolutionary development made all the difference. Modern humankind appeared only 40,000 years ago...In less than 1 percent of the time since our ancestors stood up on two feet, humans learned to make all sorts of new and complex tools and weapons, build shelters, design and construct boats, travel across the sea, domesticate animals, paint and draw and, later, write; finally, transform the entire nature of society and daily life through technology and science.[4]

Our understandings of the remarkable evolutionary beginnings of humans are often ignored or so taken for granted that it seems churlish to remind readers. Yet what we are discussing is the framework for the eventual evolution of our ontology, particularly that aspect dominated by the psychological transformations that brought us here. As Hunt further offers:

> Somewhere along this course of evolutionary development, we acquired one other special trait: self-awareness. Animals are aware of their environment, but not of themselves in the sense that we are. No animal except a chimpanzee or an oran-

gutan, seeing itself in a mirror, knows whose image it is seeing....But we not only know who it is that we see in the mirror, we actively think about ourselves and about our own thoughts; there's no evidence at all that the chimpanzee or orangutan, though it knows itself in a mirror, does anything of the kind.[5]

While the story of mirrors and the self is necessary for our discussion, it will be confronted in a later chapter. The historian must make do with what evidence is available when exploring the pre-historic period.

The study of history is an analysis of our cultural and psychological evolution. Put bluntly, if there is no evolution there is no history, no memory and no consciousness. When looking back far enough into a world where the scholarship is governed by anthropologists and the more technical sciences it becomes very problematic for the historian since it is our proclivity and desire to hold solid evidence, i.e., written documentation. When dealing with the earliest of undocumented time, the anthropologist must dig deep and reach very generalized and cautious conclusions around an assumption. One commonly accepted assumption suggests that humans originally functioned much as pack animals where if one member of the pack falls dead, the others will perhaps stop to smell the corpse, but after a brief moment they will continue their nomadic journey. One of the most significant pre-historic moments arguably occurred when we not only went beyond simple animal curiosity and began burying one of our own.

> Death, and presumably life, had become something special. No comparable evidence appears in earlier records, and as far as we know, men and the ancestors of men had always died like other animals before Neanderthal times, being abandoned when they were too weak to keep up with the band or wandering off to wait alone for the end to come. Burial implies a new kind of concern for the individual and, according to one theory, it arose as part of a response to bitter glacial conditions when a people needed one another even more than in less demanding times and formed more intimate ties and cared more intensely when death came.[6]

As has been expressed, now "...we have evidence of deliberate burial—burial sites in which two or more bodies were placed together and sites in which an assortment of flowers was evidently placed in the grave."[7] This act of recognition of death implies a special occasion: one of the members of the pack no longer is actively engaged within and in motion with the group. This can be considered a primitive but significant evolutionary development. This at least implies a growing recognition of death, its finality and its implication for those still living. It is understandable that we find our "...customs generally reflect an awareness of death as a recurring event...[and] there is reason to believe that the Neanderthals had developed a mythic account of death."[8] There is evidence also, that suggests that "Neanderthal people deliberately placed the skulls and long bones of cave bears in arrangements that may have had some symbolic significance."[9] This was the first and most formidable step in the realization of our human potential through the knowledge of our terminal condition. The next step was the creation of meaningful creative sounds.

For the beginnings of the use of language there are deductive reasons to suggest that there was a certain logic to its development, since "...vocal language represents the continuation of the evolutionary trend toward freeing the hands for carrying and tool use that started with upright bipedal hominid locomotion."[10] This would suggest that there was a fundamental utilitarian as well as entertaining reasons for both the invention and evolution of linguistic sounds. Moreover, there is this bio-chemical proclivity towards language, one which should be considered indispensable, since "...the contribution to biological fitness is obvious. The close relations of hominids who could rapidly shout 'There is a lion behind the rock!' were more likely to survive, as were hominids who could convey the principles of toolmaking in comprehensible sentences."[11] These sounds became a weapon for the survival of our ancestors, a survival larger than simple warnings and an important concept explored in later chapters. Furthermore, aspects of the formal structure necessary for an oral culture has been advanced by Walter J. Ong, "...an oral culture uses formulaic structures and procedures to sustain communication continuity. They use proverbs and other fixed sayings, epithets: 'the sturdy oak,' 'the brave warrior.' They use numerical sets: 'the three graces,' 'the seven deadly sins.' They use balance and rhythms, anything to give fixity and stability to what Homer calls 'winged words.'"[12] It is the nature of structures both to precede and follow action.

While it may be dangerous to project into a pre-historic and pre-written period what language may have been like, there are writers who in agreeing with Ong would suggest further that "...speech is a form of action, and, since the economy of the formulaic style confines speech to accepted patterns which all men assume to be true, there need never be a fundamental distinction between speech and reality; or between thought and reality—for thought and speech are not distinguished," and he adds, "...or between appearance and reality—for the language of society is the way society makes things seem."[13] The issue, of course, remains that of confronting death. Language is a useful defense mechanism and can be seen as a tool that could counter any possible desire for an individuality or self. Language is collectively comforting, for we all know the same facts of our mortality and in this we can avoid the feelings of becoming isolated: "Figuratively speaking it is the specter of death they are trying to appease—death as the symbol of ultimate separation, aloneness, isolation from other human beings."[14] While it may be impossible to imagine humans who would not know that they are terminal, "…the feeling which they have of their own existence is based on the feeling of their belonging to this group: their effort at self-preservation is therefore at the same time an effort for the preservation of this group."[15] In other words, the group is supportive even in the face of, and partially because of, our terminal condition; thus there is a mitigation in just the act of communal belonging. In Egypt there was a tradition long before the Greeks to make a point to remember the deceased and to mention their name often in order for them to continue to live in the mind of the community.

The question being asked, especially for historians who are always looking for antecedents, who and what put us on this road to language and when? One scholar who has attempted to offer some insights is P. Lieberman. One of the more prominent choices has been Neanderthal since there is evidence that they practiced burial rites. On the other hand it could very well be correct to state as Lieberman does that "…Neanderthal hominids…did not have human speech, because they did not have a human vocal tract."[16] But elsewhere he does suggest that they may have had an early or limited form of speech since it would appear that there were only certain sounds that they were unable to reproduce sounds that we today take for granted. As he stated his case: "The Neanderthal vocal tract could not form the configurations that are necessary to produce [i], [u], and [a] vowels. Neanderthal speech is also nasalized and therefore would be subject to higher phonetic errors. At another point in his discussion, using computer modeling, he also indicates that it, "…does not show that Neanderthal hominids totally lacked speech or language; they had the anatomical prerequisites for producing nasalized versions of all the sounds of human speech save [i], [u], [a], and velar consonants and probably had fairly well-developed language and culture…"[17] This is extremely specialized and must not distract from the subject at hand which is the correlation of the discovery of death and its possible relationship to the creation of language and a necessary social order. However, this speech impediment may, he suggests, have had something to do with their demise as a group. He grants that, "…it is probable that Neanderthal hominids had a fairly advanced culture in which elderly, infirm individuals could survive," and that gave them an edge, at least over the "...present-day chimpanzees, who do not aid infirm members of their group....Complex stone tools and the use of fire were other features of Neanderthal life."[18] What minimal speaking abilities Neanderthal hominids had may have resulted in a "...less efficient vocal communication—more confusable speech, and perhaps a very slow rate."[19] Whatever may be the case regarding the quality and quantity of their speech, there remains this recognition of life as a terminal experience.

A rather standard interpretation of ritual burial, for example, offers that "...although elaborate burials with clearly defined grave goods are comparatively recent, belonging to the Upper Paleolithic (about 35,000 years ago), the first evidence for burials with ritual grave goods occurs with the anatomically modern humans who lived 100,000 years ago."[20] This should be acknowledged as a significant point for there is often not a direct chronological tie between events that are in fact inter-relatable. History of one's own life is never neat and events sometime lag between later recognized correlative events. This phenomena only multiplies when dealing with various peoples and cultures. As one scholar put it: "What makes the study of history fascinating is, among other things, the perception of discontinuity in the context of continuity. The historically ignorant believe in absolute novelty; those with a smattering of history are apt to believe in no novelty at all; they are blinded by the discovery of similarities. Beyond that, however, lies the discovery of the small, but sometimes crucial differences."[21] And even if death were recognized much earlier than has been noted, there remains the singularity of the addition of decoration and ornamentation which in "Western Europe appears about 35,000 years ago in association with modern human fossils....Decorative beads made of shells were often transported hundreds of kilometers and then painstakingly worked into their final form."[22] While this is hardly enough evidence to argue for the appearance of individuality, it is enough to suggest here, a beginning of some delineation between varied members of a tribe even as the tribe was the fundamental group identity that all members possessed. "The representation of a separate individual, which seems to us so simple and so natural, is nevertheless not a primitive one. It occurs only secondarily and never alone: without doubt there are individuals—people who belong to the group—but as there are fingers or toes which form part of the hand or foot which in turn forms part of the man who himself forms part of the social group while it above all forms part of the totemic essence."[23] While these feelings of social isolation do not introduce for us any example of a conscious being, it does suggest that there may have been some possibility of a sense or awareness of an afterlife as early as the Neanderthal:

> From the old customs of burial, reaching back to Neanderthal man, one is led to the conjecture that these people were not only conscious of death, but that they also believed in survival. For they buried their dead with gifts—most likely gifts they thought useful for the journey to another world and to another life. Moreover, R. S. Solecki reports that he found in the Shanidar cave in northern Iraq the grave of a Neanderthal man (perhaps of several) who apparently had been buried on a bed of twigs, decorated with flowers. He also reports that he found the skeletons of two old men, one them 'a very handicapped individual' the other 'a rehabilitation case'....It appears that they were not only tolerated, but helped by their family or group. It seems that the humane idea of helping the weak is very old, and that we must revise our ideas of the primitivity of Neanderthal man, supposed to have lived in the period from 60,000 to 35,000 years ago.[24]

Indeed, when dealing with these early dates, conjecture dominates rather than solid historical evidence. Still, could there have been a sense of some after-life so early? Possibly there was, but 'probably' may prove to be too strong a word.

The psychologist, Julian Jaynes, who has offered some unique thoughts on the subject of consciousness and its origins has also suggested that the earliest humans, "…like other primates, had probably left his dead where they fell, or else hidden them from view with stones, or in some instances roasted and eaten them."[25] Since cultures do not condemn any behavior unless it actually may have occurred and since cannibalism has long been a serious taboo, it would follow that at some period it may have been practiced, and it follows that it is possibly relevant as evidence demonstrating again the struggles that early humanoids may have had confronting death. The issue here centers more as to how "death, and presumably life, had become something special." This same writer continues, "…no comparable evidence appears in earlier records, and as far as we know, men and the ancestors of men had always died like other animals before Neanderthal times, being abandoned when they were too weak to keep up with the band or wandering off to wait alone for the end to come."[26] The logic of burial certainly encourages a collective mentality as well a means of finding support for coping with a uncertainty that instills fear. Where there is knowledge of death, fear itself takes on a new edge. "The fear of being alone derives much of its terror from our anxiety lest we lose our awareness of ourselves." And, "…if people contemplate being alone for longish periods of time, without anyone to talk to or any radio to eject noise into the air, they generally are afraid that they would be at 'loose ends,' would lose the boundaries for themselves, would have nothing to bump up against, nothing by which to orient themselves."[27] Solitude and its enjoyment in a more early modern and secular environment can be possibly found in the work of Montaigne although that early example won't be seen until the end of the sixteenth century. While this work is not prepared to use the particular term *individual* so loosely, the cultural impact of death and burial is more than adequately supported by a variety of writers. Knowing one will die could be suggested as the first and necessary step in the creation of the self and thus consciousness.

This understanding is a recent one, however, since, "...it was not until Herman Feifel's classic work, *The Meaning of Death* (1959) that researchers in psychology seriously considered death and dying as significant factors in the comprehension of human behavior."[28] Two well-established scholars, Karl R. Popper and Sir John C. Eccles, have supported this position. Unfortunately, they take this view further than this book is willing to go. As an example, Eccles stated that he found an author who he believes "...expresses well the extraordinary emergence of human self-consciousness," in this case, called self-awareness:

> Self-awareness is then, one of the fundamental, possibly the most fundamental, characteristic of the human species. This characteristic is an evolutionary novelty; the biological species from which mankind has descended had only rudiments of self-awareness, or perhaps lacked it altogether. Self-awareness has, however, brought in its train somber companions—fear, anxiety, and death awareness....Man is burdened by death awareness. A being who knows that he will die arose from ancestors who did not know.[29]

Popper added that "I am quite sure that you...are right in stressing that the realization of death—of the danger of death and of the inevitability of death —is one of the great discoveries which led to full self-consciousness."[30] While death is central concept at the beginning and will make more than a few appearances during the centuries of transformation, any leap from a limited argument regarding this discovery of our terminal condition, to suggesting the birth and development of consciousness and self-consciousness, is at best extreme. As will eventually be demonstrated, self-consciousness is a very recent development[31] and was preceded by individuality and self.

It is in such a context that a question is posed that reveals one of the more important problems in dealing with the issue of consciousness today: what is it that we mean when we speak of the self? While one can add to this the questions: what is self-consciousness; in addition, what is it to be conscious;

how does this apply to what we call individuality; and when do we first find any authentic sense of being an individual? Moreover, what purpose does being conscious have? Is everyone conscious? One recent scholar has even suggested that as far as the presence or absence of conscious states of mind, "...it seems to be among the chronically unemployed."[32] This remains a contemporary question.

This study is dedicated to the principle that from the perception of death to the development of the individual and self which leads to the possibilities of consciousness there is a necessary connection of language. Another student of the subject has noted: "...consciousness and language are closely intertwined in defining the special qualities of human mentality. Through the history of modern philosophy one or the other (sometimes both) has been used as the criterion of humanity, or of the human mind."[33] That language is a mark of our humanity is but an introduction to the inner self that can be built around that frame of meaningful sounds. Even Freud appreciated this relationship:

> It may well be, as many psychologists including Freud have speculated, that consciousness arises both phylogenetically and ontogenetically with the onset of language. However, it is also possible to argue that consciousness arises with the generation of the high degree and unique character of the motor skills of human beings. It is just as plausible to argue that language is a by product of that conscious control. The view that consciousness and language arise out of motor skill is even more plausible when one considers the question of the lateralization of the cerebral hemispheres. Any complex skill that requires the coordination of the two forelimbs, something that must have evolved very early in humanoid species, would require that one hemisphere become dominant over the other. The hand that helps must be controlled by the same source that controls the master hand.[34]

The issue of language is thus again reduced to motor skills: to making meaning by way of sounds as well the inner resonance, the interior vibration felt inside when making sounds—all aspects of the same phenomena. The key is that language is not static, and it is here suggested that, by extension, consciousness should not be perceived as static. The discussion is very problematic, of course, in that one is speaking of something that is in motion. Ong illustrates the concept of fluidity of language:

> Now I want you to think of the word 'necessary' for two minutes, 120 seconds, and never have any letter at all connected with that word occur in your consciousness. You can't do it, there's no way you can do that. Now if you asked a person from a primary oral culture to think of the word 'necessary,' what would he or she think of? He'd think of the word. Those letters are not the word. The word is the sound.

> Sounds exist only when they are going out of existence. When you get to the 'sary,' the 'neces' has to be gone. The oral person would think of something like a bar of music: da da da....We cannot recover that primary innocence of people without writing.[35]

One cannot stop speech and still retain that sound, for it is in the oratorical motion and not the simple meaning of words or syntax that makes language so powerful. Along this line, Popper makes a critical argument when he equates consciousness as a growing, evolving process that can be compared to the evolution and development of a child. Here he states that if we grant a relationship between death and self-consciousness, "...then we can say that self-consciousness arises to full self-consciousness only slowly in a child, because I don't think that children are fully self-conscious before they are fully consciousness of death."[36] This interpretation demands that our awareness of death grows slowly from a non-existing phenomenon into an eventually (at least potentially) full-blown understanding of our mortality and what that can mean; the same position that can be said for the beginnings of consciousness, the sense of self and individuality in an even slower process of maturation. After all, the knowledge of mortality is considerably more fundamental than consciousness.

The idea of a child not understanding what it is to die may best be demonstrated by a simple story, a contemporary myth as it were, about Jimmy and Kitty. It seems that one day after Jimmy had lunch, Mother found Kitty dead. When Jimmy found out and saw Kitty, he did not understand. In order to help the child through this unique experience mother made the following suggestion: "Why don't the two of us take Kitty out into the backyard and bury him?" This seemed like an interesting idea to the three-year-old and so Jimmy agreed. They prepared the cat, put it in a shoe box (yes, Kitty was a small kitten) and took him out to the back of the yard for burial. They proceeded to dig a hole and with a few kind words added they then buried Kitty. After this very special afternoon's experience, Mother brought Jimmy into the house for milk and cookies. After Jimmy had finished, he looked up at his mother who was washing dishes and asked: "Mommy, can I go out and play with Kitty now?"

It is not easy to understand death, and there are those even today who still find it very difficult to come to terms with this absolute fact, the ultimate phenomenon of life. "Death, is a subject that is evaded, ignored, and denied by our youth-worshiping, progress-oriented society."[37] It wasn't so different in our pre-historic past:

> It is understandable that, in a civilization which separates mind from body, we should either try to forget death or to make mythologies about the survival of transcendent mind. But if mind is immanent not only in those pathways of information which are located inside the body but also in external pathways, then death takes on a different aspect. The individual nexus of pathways which I call 'me' is no longer so precious because that nexus is only part of a larger mind. The ideas which seemed to be me can also become immanent in you. May they survive—if true.[38]

It is worth considering that the idea of somehow surviving beyond death other than bodily would eventually appear, although ancient Egyptians did come to the conclusion eventually that the body could somehow also survive. Of even more interest regarding denial is the issue of an after life with a world of ghosts. In a brilliant study of sin and fear, Jean Delumeau concluded that:

> Any historical study of death must, in fact, pay due attention to the ethnographic aspects of dying....Like the members of many other civilization, our ancestors found it difficult to accept the abrupt disappearance of those with whom they had shared their lives. Hence they believed in ghosts, which testify to the continuing presence of the dead—at least for a certain time. In other words, the dead took a long time to actually pass away....Innumerable examples of belief in ghosts can be found the world over, not to speak of the European versions...[39]

What is of equal interest is how this denial of the absolute termination that death holds for each of us is not uncommon in those early stages of civilization where again we find this serious commitment to denial; although this is not always done with pleasant results, as Eccles has pointed out: "Belief in some life after death came very early to mankind, as is indicated by the ceremonial burial customs of Neanderthal man. In our earliest records of beliefs about life after death, however, it was most unpleasant. This can be seen in the *Epic of Gilgamish*, in the Homeric poems, and in the Hebrew belief about *Sheol*."[40] While Eccles is addressing this issue in antiquity and Delumeau's study dealt with the medieval period, these assumptions regarding death and ghosts have not changed that much from their earliest historic developments, at least for those great numbers of people who still believe in ghosts and spirits.

The difficulty in confronting death can be traced throughout most of our history and can be demonstrated when it comes to the naming of children, for under normal circumstances and until recently we did not name children at birth but instead waited long enough, perhaps several years, to see if the child would survive. What is also important is that the act of naming of a child introduces an important issue of early language, and therefore, it could be suggested at the very least that there was a relation between the process of naming and the birth of a very specific being for language, at least an early language whose purpose is simply to register fear, joy, safety and a permanent place in the tribe. Julian Jaynes carried this principle of naming so far as to argue that "…just as a noun for an animal makes that relationship a much more intense one, so a name for a person. And when the person dies, the name still goes on, and hence the relationship, almost as in life, and hence burial practices and mourning."[41] Henceforth we all take part in our own immortality by being remembered by both our name and our namesake. In other words, "…once a tribe member has a proper name, he can in a sense be recreated in his absence. 'He' can be thought about, using 'thought' here in a special nonconscious sense of fitting into language structures."[42] Furthermore labels for animals makes relationships more intense, naming intensifies it even more so. While Kitty may be dead for little Jimmy he lives on in the word—his name 'Kitty.' Consider the choices Socrates was given when he was convicted by his fellow citizens in Athens: the choice was really no choice at all, for the slow death outside Athens would have appeared far worse than a simple physical demise where his name would always be remembered as one of the citizens of Athens. His willingness to die for his belief in philosophy makes him, however, even a more memorable historic figure and thus, in this sense, immortal. This idea has been further developed in the writings of Lucien Levy-Bruhl, specifically in his *The Notebooks on Primitive Mentality*.

> One understands, then, that for these 'primitive men,' as I have shown, death may be only an event of secondary importance,…the passage to elsewhere, a change of residence. What would be tragic and dreadful would be if the new conditions of existence were to prevent the deceased from continuing to belong to his group: it would be something very different from isolation and solitude; it would be the hideous menace of annihilation, the impossibility of continuing to exist as an individual, who is nothing if he ceases to belong to the social body.[43]

What is suggested here is that what we can call our modern mind is comprised of a sense of self, individuality, privacy, reflection and the forces that hold it all together, along with our personal consciousness which possesses a history, one, like all history, rooted in language. While this also applies to the specific concept, consciousness, this must be a history by way of conjecture given the limits of the pre-historic and, to lesser extent, the ancient world. The first historically documented expression of what we call consciousness, as we generally understand it, will have to wait until the seventeenth century, the century of the Scientific Revolution that we still live with. What have been the most important changes, transformations, alterations, and simple discoveries, when added together that created the foundation for our modernity? We now seek to answer questions undreamed until this past century, a century where the issue of consciousness dominates so many thinkers and scholars. Its historical antecedents are searched for in order to establish the roots of such a tremendous transformation of our being—call it a dynamic ontology—that survives through adaptability. This does not, however, make the Neanderthals before and after the development of language any more conscious than to suggest that watching a flight of birds would make one a pilot. To trace the necessary changes one must continue to look at antecedents.

The first major change beyond the discovery of death and oral communications occurred with the creation of the written word, for this is the format that can lead to an interiority exclusive the collective, contributing to an interior ontology. Death and language were important steps but so too was the concretization of language. As Ong put it, "…once the word is technologized, there is no effective way to criticize its condition without the aid of the technology you are criticizing. In other words, as technology is applied to the word, the technology is vulnerable only from the inside."[44] The very act of becoming literate through the power of the written word, an ability that was extremely rare until the early modern world, offered the possibility for some early first steps toward the creation of an inner being. Ong says it well: "Without writing, the literate person would not and could not think as he or she does, not only when engaged in writing, but also when one is composing thoughts in oral forms….functionally literate persons…are not simply thinking and speaking human beings, most recently conditioned also by print and electronics."[45] This is not to say that language is not drastically changed with the arrival of writing since "…it is clear…that writing is an intrusion into language."[46] Once a word (or thought) is concretized it is dramatically altered in its relationship with oral language. While this is a long road to be reviewed, these early primitive steps are important for the actual development of this phenomenon of the power of writing since its most significant impact historically appears rather late in the ancient world. All this raises the question of the use of language, specifically written language, and how it may inform us.

Language is the doorway through which one must first step in order to arrive at the world of abstract thought. Perhaps that is why several serious thinkers have suggested that language is one of the most important if not one of several of the greatest developments that has made humans into what we have become. It could even be argued that it is language that makes us human, especially if we are speaking of an interior identity, since rhetoric in general and written language in particular divides our history; if nothing is written, there is no history and no way for a certainty of consistent meaning. For example, one writer has noted that "...the greatest achievements of humanity lie in the past. They include the invention of language and the use of artificial tools for making other artefacts; the use of fire as a tool; the discovery of the consciousness of self and of other selves, and the knowledge that we all have to die." Most importantly this particular study continued, suggesting that "...the last two of these discoveries seem to depend on the invention of language, and so perhaps may the others. Language certainly looks the oldest of these achievements, and it is the one most deeply rooted in our genetic make-up..."[47]

Language, consciousness and self are the handmaidens that appear out of the potentials of writing. One way to appreciate this relationship between language and death is by way of the observation that "...the nature of the new human experience that characterizes a particular culture shows up...in what kinds of objects it chooses to depict. Egypt, with its written language, chose only *graves* and *temples*. Greece with a more sophisticated tongue included something new: the *theater*."[48] In other words, there is no sense in coming to accept death, with our many temples to death, without also coming to grip with our most out-standing positive abilities, specifically a temple to language in the form of a theater for the rhetorical arts and written words that still educate us. The power of language beyond the spoken, the concrete and transcending, will arrive with the power of the dramatic moment when the ego of the *persona* finds itself challenged and exceeded which will be confronted when discussing Shakespeare. For here, one could also add that written abstract words as they developed with philosophy also note the central importance of our mortality: "The Greek philosophers, of course, had much the same sense of the nature and function of insight. Plato defined the philosopher's task as *melete thanatou*—mindfulness of death—a task that requires an unflinching awareness of life."[49] Socrates died for his love of ideas and demonstrated the greatness of philosophy since it alone was the preparation for the world of ideas, the world beyond our senses, everyday experiences and our immediate.

The one single problem with this discussion is that the student is still left with the question: whence comes language? It has been suggested by a variety of authors that language in part may have been related to the discovery of death, as in naming and as a form of survival, at least within the clan or tribe. Truth be told, however, there is no agreed upon explanation as to its beginnings. There is little reason to reiterate some fascinating theories from the 'bow-wow' through the 'pooh-pooh' and the inclusive 'yo-he-ho' theories. It is likely, however, that the first sounds were little more than "…grunts uttered when men got together to accomplish tasks."[50] One theory that is fairly popular is the view that there is not only a relationship between death and language but one between language and physical gestures. As one author having looked at this question has stated: "The most coherent account of the origin of spoken language which has been devised claims that the first symbolic sounds were uttered as the accompaniment of gestures, particularly of gestures of the hand. The supporters of this theory point to the sympathy existing between land and mouth which shows itself in such things as the movements of a child's tongue during writing, or gesturing as an accompaniment to talking."[51] The sense of this can be dramatized when one considers that the early pre-cursors for us as hunters living in a world where silence is not only golden but can be necessary for survival, sound has to be cautiously exercised. However, with the invention of tools, especially those that facilitate survival, we again find language not only increasingly useful, but perhaps even necessary we recognized that in the shouting that there may be a lion hidden behind a rock or crocodile in the water.[52]

This silence early in our evolution starting with the age of hunting begins to be altered in a major manner with the first stages of the agricultural revolution and the need for more complex relationships. Language like hunting and the growing of crops was and remained a collective activity within the framework of group survival which since the recognition of death and the art of naming was increasingly one of the more singular and fundamental criterion for vocal action, although even in our own time, watching tribal women working and communicating around the encampment, one is impressed by the musical sounds of their voices. It is perhaps even more important that, "…language, tool making, and social organization become entwined in an evolutionary complex responsible for and a consequence of the emergence of the special features of the human brain."[53] It is possible that, as Julian Jaynes, suggests the growing complexity of the sounds necessary for survival may have come from these changes: "An imminent tiger might result in 'wahee!' while a distant tiger might result in a cry of less intensity and so develop a different ending such as 'wahoo.' It is these endings, then, that become the first modifiers meaning 'near' and 'far.' And the next step was when these endings, 'hee' and 'hoo,' could be separated from the particular call that generated them and attached to some other call with the same indication."[54] Whatever the origins, the significance of the evolution of language cannot be overrated. Even the famed linguist Noam Chomsky has maintained that "...when we study human language, we are approaching what some might call 'the human essence,' the distinct qualities of mind that are, so far as we know, unique to man."[55] One could suggest, therefore, that another entirely different scenario for origins could be suggested and that perhaps this had more to do with entertainment, much like musical sounds (and theater), as well offering an aid for group labor, as when many tribal people, as they perform a task requiring a large number of participants, will make rhythmic sounds tied to the labor they are performing. This keeps them both in vocal and physical harmony, as well as giving some pleasure to their toil. Additionally, there is a very unique theory that further suggests that language came about in part as a need to strengthen the clan with gossip, stories and collective memories, not unlike certain species that would groom each other to further strengthen a sense of group camaraderie, loyalty and friendship.[56]

This view could be used to support the position that the very invention of language itself creates the discipline of history in its most primitive form. After all, the concept that the idea expressed as Jimmy or the word Kitty only occurs because of the constant meaning of these sounds in designating what is meant throughout time. Jimmy is always Jimmy and not Jerry and Kitty is always Kitty and never Fido. It is the reliability of a sound to always mean what it means at all times, for today, yesterday as well as tomorrow that is inherent in language. In other words, the sound applies to space, as in 'look over there,' while the consistency of that sound will always mean some reliability out of the past, of the same thing, reflecting the very root of history. A specific sound for a specific meaning over a given period of time is the primal essence of history. One cannot separate the two, language (space) and time (history) which raises the interesting question when addressing the issue of writing. We date history with the beginning of writing but in fact at its root, we find all language is in itself an expression of history at its earliest presence. This should not discourage us from looking at the beginning of history with the beginnings of the written word, for there are other complex components that also will have to be considered.

It is clear from the variety of assumptions regarding the origins of language that both the beginnings and specific causes pose the conundrum where theory will always out-distance the limitations of facts. Writing, on the other hand, by its very nature, has a permanence. Just as the origins of language are lost in pre-history so writing is understood by way of historical evidence. Writing is a young development and even a younger discipline.

> Our literate world of visually processed sounds has been totally unfamiliar to most human beings. Few languages have been written. The oldest script, Mesopotamia cuneiform, is less than six thousand years old; the alphabet is less than four thousand. Of all the many thousands of languages spoken in the course of human history, only about 106 have ever been committed to writing to a degree sufficient to have produced a literature. And most have never been written at all.[57]

Visualizing in our mind's eye is a relatively recent event. It is Ong's explanation, also, of the limits of writing: "Homo sapiens has been on earth for around 30,000 to 50,000 years, to take a very conservative estimate, but writings came along only 6,000 years ago, after thousands of languages had gone down the drain. And of the estimated 3,000 languages around today, there are only 68 or 78 that have a literature."[58] That the written word came about so late and that so many languages that we now know have never been put in written form must mean that writing is and has been a very unique and rare activity. This is all the more significant when one considers that most estimates regarding the spoken word can be dated as early as some 80,000 or even 100,000 years ago.[59] Whatever dates are chosen by whatever school of thought, the issue here is both of the beginnings and evolution of language and its relationship with the birth and development of consciousness. As for evidence, "…the only direct evidence of language is writing, and the earliest signs of it that we know appeared among Sumerian farmers, who about five thousand years ago, recorded their stock holdings on lumps of clay."[60] Even here there must be caution, however, since the writing to which we are addressing ourselves is not to be confused with modern script:

> In the early part of the third millennium B.C. the Sumerian system of writing consisted of a syllabary containing some five hundred to six hundred signs. Most of these still served as ideograms…However necessary syllabic signs might be, the need for them was limited.…When, however, the Babylonians took over the Sumerian script they were obliged to develop further the syllabic system because their inflective language could be expressed only by the help of phonetic signs…[61]

What is of particular interest about the technique used in transferring sound to images is the stimulating theory that "…has been propounded that the idea of making the picture signs represent sounds instead of the objects pictured was first suggested by the existence in both the Sumerian and the Egyptian languages of 'homonyms,' that is, of words having the same sound but different meanings. If we accept the theory, then we must admit that the art of writing could have been invented independent in both countries..."[62] This early use of homonyms, i.e. same sound and/or spelling but different meaning, has suggested opportunities for early thinking regarding sound, writing and the nature of life versus death. As has been pointed out, at least in one sense, the space between birth and death is life, and here lies the very root for all eventual concepts of time, change, evolution and space. As an example, we have here from the work of J. Hawkes and Sir L. Wooley a significant interpretive perception:

> The earliest known example quoted as illustrating this method of extending the range of pictorial signs comes on tablets found at Jamdat Nasr, a site on the personal name En-Lil-ti, which in Sumerian means 'Enlil [the god] causes to live.' The word-sign TI is the picture of an arrow, but in the spolien language the sound 'ti' is a homonym, meaning both 'arrow' and 'life'; the latter would be difficult to represent pictorially and therefore, according to this theory, the scribe uses the arrow sign, which could be drawn to mean 'life.'[63]

This "arrow of life" is an ancient example of what we later think of as a metaphor for the time we have, the space we live in and the changes and evolution we live by. As this arrow moves from its beginnings (birth) through the dynamics of space and time, it must eventually terminate as we all eventually must.

The significance of this space for an arrow resides in that, "...the Egyptians conceived of space as a narrow path down which the individual soul moves to arrive at the end before ancestral judges."[64] What is significant here is that they are not only dealing with death by creating an afterlife but one created which is drawn from the judgement of our living, a powerful controlling force. While this may be an interpretation it is appropriate to remember that the beginning of a written language included numbers which existed at the very beginning of a civilization. In its importance, it was a key factor in the creation of writing since "...writing and mathematics existed at the dawn of civilization. As soon as man settled in villages supported by farming and trading, he needed some crude form of documentation, and early civilizations came up with a variety of ways of counting and recording."[65] The early mastering of agricultural created something unheard of, a surplus of the basic needs for life, which in turn created the foundation for a third way of life, that of the village or urban community for those who would live off the work of those in the fields and hunters. Since there were storage issues as well as trade, a code system was indispensable for the workings and expansion of these early civilizations. If surplus goods were to be preserved, especially for a time when the crops failed, there needed be enclosed pottery to hold the grain and other such basic food stuffs and a means to know what was inside. One such early example is where "...symbols come to represent single words...: for example, four semicircles and the picture of an ox's head would read 'four oxen.'"[66] To take this invention to its purposeful conclusion, it would seem "...that writing arose to meet the needs of the highly centralized city state, and the first writings are records of payments to the temple or city treasury, and similar transactions."[67] This explains the priestly class, those scribes who could decipher the symbols, the writings on jars and pieces of wax, at least until the arrival of parchment. A whole new form of thinking was being created, one that we might today call utilitarian as we began to enter into the world of history. "Without writing, the literate person would not and could not think as he or she does, not only when engaged in writing, but also when one is composing thoughts in oral forms... functionally literate persons...are not simply thinking and speaking human beings, most recently conditioned also by print and electronics."[68] We cannot separate our thinking, our ability to think or what we think from the methods we use.

Nature was not a given until it was given a new concrete place with writing. The after-life component, or mystical component of these scribes developed, in time, something more than our physical being, specifically that something needed for defeating the certainty of death and which would contribute to a sense of something of an interior (or unobservable) being. In the earliest days, especially in Egypt, there was a thought for a time that somehow the body would in some transcendent manner continue beyond death, although this has not always proven an appealing approach. It may be more than coincidence that those capable of knowing the secrets of those symbols—being the first readers—were also as scribes considered to be priests of the faith of the community and thus the first to preserve this idea of an interior being. The social glue as we evolved became written language even though there was only a small elite who could decipher the symbols. Survival in bad times could well depend upon the surpluses and their intelligent use, a form of limited certainty against death now in the hands of the holy ones.

It is no accident that the writing we know something about today is specifically directed to book-keeping symbols on pots and clay tablets in order to hoard for a period of drought and starvation as well as religious purposes. "In Egypt, man's concern with the *life after death* was as intense as it ever was anywhere: the pyramids were tombs; the finest paintings and many of the most remarkable sculptures were found in the tombs in the Valley of Kings..."[69] When they wrote stories they spoke of a pre-occupation with death and also of immortality. One of the very earliest works was the Mesopotamian *Epic of Gilgamish* (?2000 B.C.) and which influenced other works, especially the story of the Great Flood mentioned of their lack of permanence, noting that even the houses we build are not built to stand forever. The story of Gilgamish is also the story of the reality of dying: "...those cultures are also beginning to sense the bitterness of death. This is the message of the powerful epic of Gilgamish..."[70] The Code of Hammurabi of the seventeenth century B.C. was a code of laws that was tied to his sun god Shamash. Governance in both this and the after-life were tied to the laws that were assumed valid for both here and the after-life. *The Egyptian Book of the Dead* (?1200 B.C.) which preceded the much later *Tibetan Book of the Dead* (?8th century B.C.) demonstrates this early orientation of the written word; like the testaments to follow these were guides for living, one that especially takes us beyond the ineluctability that inheres in living because of death.

There are also the stories of the vegetative gods who like the sun will always return with the spring. The setting sun at the end of the solar year is very frightening since everything seems to be about to die. With the sun rising in the spring into the warming heavens again and spring planting arrives, a new world, quite literally, is born. Some cultures would so despair with the circumstance of a disappearing sun that human sacrifice to the gods were not unknown. These are usually referred to as the vegetative or born-again deities for obvious reasons. One of the earliest and more significant prophets was the famed Persian, Zarathustra (Zoraster), who lived somewhere around the early sixth century B.C. His significance was a singular thought that reduced all the world into a simple and to-be classic form of dualism, one a divinity of goodness and the other of evil: He lived at the "...dawn of an age of unprecedented syncretism."[71] This was a world where religious ideas from India were interwoven with ideas drawn from Persia, ideas that would create a beginning for dualistic deities and forces that would also be in opposition to each other. This form of dualism resulted in the conclusion that "...there are two kinds of people, and the prophet calls himself an 'enemy of the followers of the Lie [*druj*] and a powerful support for the followers of the Truth [*asha*]'.... Ahura Mazda commands to 'do evil of the followers of the Lie'..."[72] Additionally, two kinds of deities existed: "...Zarathustra's *ahuras* and *daevas* correspond to the Vedi [Indian] *asuras* and *devas*....the English word 'divinity,' the Latin *deus*, and Greek *theos*, as well as 'theology' and 'theosophy,' 'theism' and 'deism,' all come from this same ancient root."[73] It is this dualism, these two contrary and incompatible forces, one dedicated to evil and the other for good in constant and incompatible conflict that would dominate most of western humanity with a theological theme of eternal struggle to find a way of coping with the ultimate certainty of death. The problem occurs because "...precisely this simplicity has proved irresistible to simple minds. It hallows hatred, glorifies an inhumane self-righteousness that denies the enemy all moral qualities, and assures those who oppose the wicked of a glorious final triumph."[74] This will continue to be an issue, a solution and danger along with a variety of other theories of certainty that will be explored throughout this study. There will also be the inherent problem of resolving the issue of the certainty of our death by methods that can result at first with what seems to be a new counter, certitude of salvation that will be followed by further uncertainty. This was only one of two roads, however, leading to our world, for there was another discovery and development that would become an alternate means of dealing with death and its uncertainty, one of reasoned thought.

One of the earliest examples of this new approach can be garnered by contrasting religious blind faith against this alternative of reason first found in the ancient Greek method of looking at motion in space as opposed to the 'narrow space' with a fixed arrow as imagined by the Egyptians. This can be credited, in part, to the last in the line of the great ancient Greek thinkers, Aristotle:

> How things moved and what caused them to move was for Aristotle no real problem, for there was, for him, a natural order to the five elements: Earth below water below air below fire below ether. Things moved when anything was out of its natural element. Thus water rose in the air when it was 'mixed' with fire. The more fire the water held, the more that fire was out of its natural elemental place. This pushed the water up until the fire left it, so that it would fall to earth once again.[75]

The Greeks were remarkable not only for the breadth but also for the depth of their unique language. They stretched the potentials of not only the spoken but also the written word. Perhaps this occurred in part because of their unique and creative technical contribution, the reintroduction of the vowel into their more complex syntax and alphabet, the vowel which only appeared in very limited sense before the development of the Greek alphabet. It was their genius to realize that "...something had to be done to create an alphabet that was readable for both the writer and reader of Greek. This 'something' effected the greatest development since the emergence of writing itself: the Greeks introduced vowels into the Levantine consonantal alphabet, thereby completing whole new class of writing. The Greek alphabetic script has, since this time, essentially remained the same but for external appearances: nearly 3,000 years."[76] While it is for the scholars of linguistics to study and explain how the vowel may have played an evolutionary role in this remarkable culture and its contribution to the creation of the basis of what we think of as our Western intellectual heritage, there is no doubt that much like the appearance of language itself, writing now with a vowel in the hands of the Greeks altered the direction of that metaphoric arrow. The Greeks were the first ancient civilization to offer a potential for an emphasis on dramatic living with a hint of singularity which contributed to their unique contribution to both epic poetry and classical theater.

The Greek contribution to the theater was revolutionary. In offering us both comedy and tragedy, they presented to their community a didactic experience that by its very nature implied an expectation of change. As Aristotle pointed out, there was an intended impact upon the audience that could and should alter their thinking. The transformation of serious cultural topics of the Golden Age (c.500 B.C.–c.400 B.C.) that can be traced through the developments in theatrical characterization as they became more and more humanized. This humanization process is simply an extension of the psychological potential growing out of the discoveries of death, language and writing already mentioned. In this, the Greeks present us with the first stages of introspection. In the plays of Aeschylus—chronologically, the earliest of the three major playwrights—individual characters were limited in both development and significance because the chorus was given the role of explaining the theme—that is, the expression of the community's attitudes. If you knew the language and didactic point of that chorus, the voice of the community, you knew drama and its lessons. By the middle of the fifth century B.C. the next new giant of playwrights, Sophocles, was winning awards for such masterpieces as *Oedipus*. He increased the number of characters present on stage at one time and allowed them carry the dialogue and theme on a more individualized basis in expressing both entertainment and instruction, consequently decreasing the role of the chorus. In addition to creating more work for more actors, (only men were allowed on stage) and as only freemen were allowed in the audience, an actor's singular voice was slowly becoming the voice of the plot. This is not to say that we have entered the modern world of psychology, for there is no sense of biographic identity: "...the authors of early lives had a different sense of their mission than do modern authors. The cultures of Greece and Rome produced a few works in which private affairs were seriously studied—think of *Oedipus*—yet the Oedipus of Sophocles has little in common with Freud's interpretation. The Oedipus of Sophocles is ruled by forces outside himself, while Freud's Oedipus rules, though subconsciously, his own fate."[77] Still, with Euripides, the final playwright in this triune appearing at the end of the century of Pericles, the chorus could be ignored and the thrust of the plot and didactic lessons would be driven home entirely by his characters. There was no doubt that Euripides' *Medea* spoke her own words, explaining her own cause in place of the collective voice of the community. What had been the voice informing the audience and acting for the society as a whole, the chorus, now became little more than instructor's pointer. Additionally, the character of Medea represents a neglected group, women, who suffer because their only social role was their dedication to the family and by extension, the society, with the sorrow that could follow. This was more of a character study than an archetype, with a singular individual struggling with their own existence. This is not to say that the community had something other than the traditional communal voice, for this was only a hint of a singular, primitive individuality hidden behind the curtains, a voice that would be barely a whisper and remained undeveloped at least until the plays of Shakespeare.

If consciousness can be seen to exist in degrees from very little to optimized, so too it must be considered that the same could also apply to the rise of both any individuality or self. A city-state community is a closed system where belonging meant being born into that community, Otherwise one is always an outsider. The stage was something of a metaphor for the fixed space of community. And the theatrically visual artistic sense of space also reflected the community's best understanding of that space.

> Greek space was dominated by a sense of nearness and limit. The universe was a cosmos, a 'well-ordered aggregate of near and completely viewable things' covered by the corporeal vault of heaven. Its government was a clearly circumscribed city-state; its temples, finite structures formed about a center, enclosed by a colonnade. Classical art had 'closed' figures with sharply bounded surfaces, and the predominance of the body brought the eye from the distant to the 'near and still.' Its statues, like its buildings, were clearly delimited, with no suggestion of the infinite or unbounded, and it produced a geometry of regular, closed figures that were the ideal forms of earth and heaven.[78]

As is noted by art historians, a Greek temple such as the famed Parthenon of Athens had no straight lines, for the tilt of columns allowed for any perceptive distortion, particularly up close. This was not architecture for the gods with columns pointing straight up to their abodes; the Acropolis is an aesthetic and human experience, not a tomb. It was the human component and an understanding of space combined in the talents of the Golden Age of Athens that made possible a new attitude towards our human condition, one where western humanism eventually could be given form and action, a necessary prerequisite for any eventual creation of a modern sense of self.

This humanization process grew from the ancient Greek world's ability to transcend the limits of previous cultures which were not so motivated by a desire for the well-being of their citizens; The Greeks will always be known for the beginning of this revolutionary perspective in their language of their art and thinking. In a sense one can also conclude that in art and theater the Greeks created for the first time a topic that could be called 'the art of being human.' This not to say that we should be using their word 'I' the way we do today unless we want to commit the ultimate crime of those historians who would project into the past any of our contemporary concepts. To say something like, 'I will work with this,' meant that we as a community will work on this together with only an indication toward the speaker's voice, the one making the statement. If you add to the Greek linguistic contributions the later Latin term *ego*, which while rarely used, also works again only as something implying the speaker, the 'I' that is indicated, the singularity of the voice speaking, is given at most a minor emphasis, at least by way of implication, and should not be seen as indicative of the modern notion of our own 'I.' As one scholar put it: "…the ancients had wildly…quaint notions of the uses of the first person. It also shows us that ancients' odd disposition simply to deny that the self is significantly private."[79] Clearly there was something of a limited potential for these changes to point to creating the modern sense of a singular 'I' even if it will be many centuries before this psychological phenomenon would appear. As for privacy, we will have to wait until the modern world for it to make any meaningful appearance.

> When we consider…the evolution of consciousness as the progressive decline of participation, the emergence of the Greek from the ancient oriental outlook is a fact which we can contemplate without being unduly troubled by the absence of biographical details about Pythagoras. Anyone who has struggled for a few pages with the *Vedas* in translation, will know that in their language the entanglement of subject and object, of psychology and natural history, of divine and human, of word and thing, is such as to render the thought virtually unintelligible to a modern reader.[80]

This is not to suggest that consciousness is found alive, active and well in ancient Greece but rather that there are some very important indicators, hints perhaps is a better word. Hints of a beginning, yes, but it would be an extreme exaggeration to take our modern conscious condition back to antiquity even allowing for those indications that may be considered as an early pointer.

This principle, of course, would also apply to Ancient Rome, although in far less didactic manner and driven more by the pleasures of entertainment. Romans were far less interested in the pursuit of culture or education other than preserving what the Greeks had created. Theirs was a society of generals and diplomats. The Roman writer Juvenal referred to it as *panem et circunese*, the bread and circuses of the coliseum, where the concern was more in placating Romans than in making them better citizens. From a political philosopher's point of view, the issue may have been in part the results of the difference between the small and relatively intimate democracy of Athens and that of the massive Republic, and later Empire of Rome. Additionally Rome was a society that evolved with an extremely large and varied population from many differing religions, languages and customs, unlike the more unified and smaller city-states of the Aegean. In time other peoples, 'foreigners,' from all other parts of the world could eventually become full citizens of Rome, an idea Alexander the Great explored but was not one appropriate for Greek city-states. Here the 'I' existed in the form of 'ego,' again only as an emphasis of the subject since Rome had no more use for an individual—as we now know the term—than did Athens. It is an interesting aside to this subject of individuation and Rome that while a citizen of Rome had many duties, he did not have any civil rights (although there were legal rights) as we understand today. Rights, like individuality, are a very recent development belonging, along with privacy, to modernity. The Romans, like the Greeks, continued to find their personal identity within the community. (*Persona* is an ancient Latin term meaning *mask*.) A Roman was a Roman first and for all time and that was more than adequate as a personal affirmation of one's own being. Ontology was exclusively based on citizenship which was a duty.

The Greeks, on the other hand, had used their new-found linguistic inventiveness in other varied and humanizing ways, again adding to our literary heritage and foundation for consciousness. The epic has remained to this day one of the greatest of all literary achievements, and arguably for some, among the Greeks' singularly finest works. Whatever the reader's preference, whether it be drama or epic, masterpieces such as *The Iliad* and *The Odyssey* remain a remarkable reminder of how strong the collective identity originally was. The

Greek's fame rested in part upon their taking a more rational and humanized approach to life in their epics than had ever been seen. This was a totally unique way of looking at the world, playing down, as it did, the role of divine intervention. This is rather surprising in a world of religious forces as established in Homer as well as in the writings of Hesiod. Should one be impressed with gods and goddess who were portrayed as believing in the 'good' life of partying, getting drunk and having fights, followed by unlimited amounts of sex? This appeal may be a popular approach for some college undergraduates on a Saturday night, but hardly something that would act as a potential guide for human behavior. This was not the religion that would be found in other ancient cultures. The unique quality of the Greek religious culture centered on a love for their own language functioning with little or no mystery, offering as it did a reasonable approach to life, a reasoning that raised the question as to why have any gods. This is not to say there were no mysteries. The Greek myths of Homer did have a unique way of looking at life as more than just the physical (material) in addition to the exercise of political power, even if it doesn't always appear so blatantly in the writings of either Homer and his wars or Hesiod and his values. And while the Greeks give us this new concept of rationality they are not afraid to confront the unknown: specifically what it is that continues when the body meets its termination. "Of the foremost importance in Homer is *thymos*, the stuff of life, the vaporous breath soul, the active, energetic, feeling and thinking material related to blood. It leaves us when we faint or, with our last breath, when we die. Later this term is often restricted in meaning, so as to mean courage, energy, spirit, vigor." This contrasts sharply with the "…*psyche* in Homer (although sometimes used as a synonym of *thymos*)" which is

> …hardly a principle of life, as it is in later authors (Parmenides, Empedocles, Democritus, Plato, Aristotle). It is, in Homer, rather the sad remainder which is left over when we die, the poor unintelligent shade, the ghost that survives the body: it is 'not concerned in ordinary consciousness;' it is that which 'persists, still without ordinary consciousness [or ordinary life] in the house of Hades,…the visibly but impalpable semblance of the once living' body. Thus when Odysseus in the eleventh Book of the *Odyssey* visits the underworld…he finds that the shades of the dead are almost completely lifeless until he has fed them with blood, the stuff which has the power of restoring a semblance of life to the shade, the *psyche*.[81]

There was one very significant and specific divine mystery that had been reduced to one and only one characteristic of the gods, one offered to them but not to mortals, the certainty of immortality. It would be natural to wonder at this point: if these are a people who make rationality such an important tool in approaching the mysteries of life, so much so that they absolutely stand out in all antiquity, how is it they have gods that enjoy immortality? Even here, however, Greeks and their growing love affair with rationality cannot resist the temptation to offer a thoughtful explanation rather than simply accept this mystery of immortality, a rather simple exercise at that: Greek deities ingest (eat and drink) ambrosia and nectar and it is this food and liquid that makes them different, i.e., immortal. If we could but find this food and drink, these remarkable ingredients, we too could be, in theory, immortal. It is also true that this could be considered as possibly the first hints of the coming world of chemistry which of course seeks even to this day the resolution of pain and defeat of death by the magic elixir of some drug, some fountain of youth. The beginnings of the excellence of Greek thought therefore does not reside in emulating gods but rather rests within the Homeric story of one hero—Achilles.

The concept of the hero is very significant for this study since it is not a god but a person, a mortal Greek, who acts as the role model in place of these rather prosaic deities, offering a guide to what is admirable and worthy of being emulated. The early developing years of the Greek hero is best expressed in Homer's *The Iliad*. The key to this epic is when Achilles leaves the battlefield in anger but returns after the death of his friend Patrocolus demonstrating the basis of a true hero: someone for all of his greatness, making a very costly error of judgement, admits to it and finally returns to the battlefield. The concept demonstrated here one of *aretē* (roughly translated as 'excellence'). The irony is that it is not the hero's perfections but his imperfections that make him a role model for later Greeks. There is no divine way to be good and noble, for it is only by striving for *aretē* that one fulfills their obligation as a Greek. He is a hero because his perfections are tested by his faults: he pouts and quits the field of battle because of his 'wrath.' But by admitting his error and returning to the field and eventually dying even though he is nearly immortal (human) he achieves the status of hero. The lesson here is that a hero most have some weakness, for why pay attention to the achievements of a Superman without kryptonite? No matter how great, one must be able to identify in some way with that hero, and it is the imperfections that make him relatable, i.e., human. Most importantly, however, the hero is a hero because the community states you are so. Like Mersault in Jean-Paul Sartre's *No Exit*, people must think of you as a hero otherwise you are not. The idea of a lonely, alienated and estranged hero appropriate for our own era, whether in the form of the lonely cowboy riding into the sunset or the private detective sitting in his dilapidated office, only applies for our own era, the age of the lonely individual where consciousness can be a worn as a singular marking, even in pain. This is not, of course, the hero of antiquity. In Greece the badge of heroics resided within the thoughts, judgements and memories of the community. Additionally the language used is one that is closed and simple, a language that offers Aeschylus few options, unlike the broad and deep syntax of our own world. As a study of the language of Achilles it has revealed:

> Homer in fact, has no language, no terms, in which to express this kind of basic disillusionment with society and the external world. The reason lies in the nature of epic verse. The poet does not make a language of his own; he draws from the common store of poetic diction. This store is a product of bards and a reflection of society: for epic song had a clear social function. Neither Homer, then, in his own person as narrator, nor the characters he dramatizes, can speak any language other than the one which reflects the assumptions of heroic society, those assumptions so beautifully and so serenely enunciated by Sarpedon in Book 12. [82]

The further back we look the smaller the vocabulary and the less dynamic and more limited the syntax. For it is in the very formula of language that the foundations for the thoughtful understanding as well as the creation of great literature is to be found. Achilles' "…tragedy, his final isolation, is that he can in no sense, including that of language (unlike, say, Hamlet), leave the society which has become alien to him."[83] While this is a comparison between an ancient model and modern one, a great deal still can be deduced by way of Achilles' own speech seen when he grows angry (wrathful) with the king, Agamemnon: "Passionate, confused, continually turning back on itself, it presents his own vision with a dreadful candour. And what this candour is concerned with is, precisely, the awful distance between appearance and reality; between what Achilles expected and what he got; between the truth that society imposes on men and what Achilles has seen to be true for himself."[84] For Achilles—and by extension, ancient society—there can be no personal road away from society without being ostracized and thus Achilles can no longer be a hero (or a citizen), a lesson that he eventually learns. Again Greek masterpieces are invariably more than entertainment, they are didactic experiences.

The Romans also had their great epic in the *Aeneid* by Virgil, which was very unlike Homer's work. The Romans out of necessity were more political and polemic, interested in suggesting that they, the Romans (guided by Aenaeus) were the great builders while the Greeks were simply destroyers as was demonstrated at Troy. There also was something of a redemptive complex when Virgil, in another work, spoke of the coming of a savior child, (who some early Christians attempted to adopt as anticipation of the coming of the Christ child), one that Virgil actually intended to reflect the Emperor Augustus' own child. These differences are important, for however far we push the envelope of a sense of self growing in Greece, it certainly did not mature to any noticeable degree within the walls of Rome.

It should not be surprising that the writing of history was first practiced by a people who had a special admiration of their own language and their desire to apply reason to understanding society and life. Where they had been as a people became very important for the collective memory and the significance of an historic record that began as a literary art with the histories of Herodotus (c.485–425 B.C.) who recorded the wars with Persia that began the Golden Age.[85] As a discipline, this new art form was continued by Thucydides who recorded the Peloponnesian War at the end of the century.[86] This era, the fifth century B.C., was dominated by the brilliant political figure, Pericles. The Greeks were obviously aware that they lived in a time of great significance, one that needed to be recorded and remembered. To create history as distinct from collecting data, to look for causal relations and accept achievements of all sides in battle, even your enemies, proved to be one more example of the creative nature and revolutionary mentality of the Greeks. To put all things into a time frame (history) and into specific space (language) made for another form of immortality, the eternal place of a given culture. Herodotus gave us history as narrative, Thucydides as scholarship.

The Greeks almost appear compulsive in their desire to achieve a new plateau. When discussing the evolution of Greek sculpture, we see the pattern again, beginning by drawing from the early Egyptians with stiff figures presented in terms of frontality, beaded hair and bulging eyes. This eventually evolved into an idealized humanized figure, less than realistic and referred to as 'mature classical' and which was finally followed by a very humanistic and realistic rendering in the Hellenistic era. These humanized aesthetics from the Greeks in drama and sculpture will dominate western thought both in interpretation and aesthetics. Their understanding may appear ancient but still influential beyond compare even now.

These mental achievements will also apply to their attempts to further understand and express what could be called the human condition, especially in the case abstract thinking. With only one exception (East Indians), the Greeks were the only people "…in the history of the world which developed a complete scientific and philosophical terminology entirely in its own language and almost free from any foreign influence."[87] As for the abstraction that they eventually developed, beginning as they did with the concrete make-up of the Homeric world of physical images. This would change with the abstraction found within certain writings of several of the pre-Socratics and eventually in the writings of Plato (427–347 B.C.) and Aristotle (384–322 B.C.). This transformation of thinking while important for many categories of study today also applies to our own discussion of consciousness, self and individuality since these abstractions owe their modern interest and importance to the Golden Age of creative Greek originality. The story centers from its beginnings in the work of several Ionian thinkers, one of the earliest being Thales of Miletus (c.620–c.555 B.C.), followed by Anaximander (611–547 B.C.), Anaximenes (c.500 B.C.), followed by Heraclitus of Ephesus (d.460 B.C.) and Parmendies of Elea (c.515–445 B.C.) with their respective views as to the nature of reality growing from the first, water, to the 'indeterminate' (boundless), to air (vapor), to fire and finally to some sort of a singular, entire, unchanging, perfect and eternal equilibrium, the most abstract thinking at the time. Although there may have been a clear lack of agreement among these earliest pre-Socratics, they proved that disagreements did not contradict their sense of community as they continued to add to a growing body of systematized thinking about the basis of life and nature. These thinkers are seen today as a prelude to the well known giants of Socrates, his student Plato, followed by his own student, Aristotle. Before attending to their thoughts, however, it would be appropriate to again address the subject at hand: where if at all in all of this is there consciousness, and its companions of self and a sense of individuality?

There has been a rather interesting and controversial study that has suggested that consciousness should be recognized as making its first appearance in the world of the Greeks. In *The Origins of Consciousness in the Breakdown of the Bicameral Mind* by Julian Jaynes, the theory is offered that by the time of the Greek philosophers, playwrights and artisans, consciousness must have made something of an appearance. While this theory can be drawn with some complexity, for our purpose, brevity is attempted without distortion. His basic premise, for the idea of an agreed upon basic definition of these three terms, *self*, *individuality* and *consciousness* is still more of a theory than a reality even in our own time. With this in mind, Jaynes begins cautiously enough, suggesting that before there was consciousness the earlier mind was given to bicamarality, by which he meant that within the two halves of the brain, left and right hemispheres, one side would sometimes communicate with the other as a voice of a god, deceased relative or the voice of an earlier tribal leader. We now find

Antiquity | 39

ourselves immersed in divine intervention as a resolution to the uncertainty that death interjects into living. This could be considered a primitive form of schizophrenia that was in Jaynes' judgement, the basis for leadership decisions and, of course, where it existed, there would be no self or conscious beings, only alternate voices. While an interesting theory, it has little to do with our work except to support the idea that there was a time when people were not conscious. Jaynes further suggests that consciousness is not a particular necessity, but more often than not, a possible hindrance to much of human activity. As he stated it: "…we are constantly reacting to things without being conscious of them at the time."[88] While this may seem a relatively safe statement for many observers, there are those who would find this a difficult concept since they may have a very large interest in the idea that consciousness as both a constant and an absolute. Moreover, Jaynes would suggest that "…the seeming continuity of consciousness is really an illusion…"[89] This statement could appear to be obvious to many, including this writer, although again, there are those who would in good conscience truly object. While it is true that Jaynes reaches some interesting conclusions, his more interesting ideas are based upon theories with little or no evidence. Any attempt to find in an ancient setting what we understand today as a sense of self, individuality or consciousness would be contradictory and ahistoric. Still, Jaynes does offer food for thought.

One of the more interesting hypotheses of his is that the pre-conscious mind was very like that of the schizophrenic:

> The voices of schizophrenia take any and every relationship to the individual. They converse, threaten, curse, criticize, consult, often in short sentences. They admonish, console, mock, command, or sometimes simply announce everything that's happening. They yell, whine, sneer, and vary from the slightest whisper to a thunderous shout. Often the voices take on some special peculiarity, such as speaking very slowly, scanning, rhyming, or in rhythms, or even in foreign languages. There may be one particular voice, more often a few voices, and occasionally man. As in bicameral civilizations, they are recognized as gods, angels, devils, enemies, or a particular person or relative.[90]

What is even more curious is where Jaynes also holds that this early mind is where "…the gods take the place of consciousness."[91] It is for this reason that the pre-consciousness mind is thus a bicameral mind, at least "…before its weakening by writing about 2500 B.C." He then follows this with the suggestion "…that there was no hesitancy in the hallucinated voice and no occasion for prayer. A novel situation or stress, and a voice told you what to do.

Certainly this is so in contemporary schizophrenic patients."[92] While this is certainly an interesting if not compelling theory, there is too much conjecture tied with too little documentation to be anything other than an interesting thought exercise. While it is not difficult to accept that "...consciousness emerged in evolution," the problem as he notes is "...when? In what species? What kind of a nervous system is necessary?" He is right, therefore, to argue that "...what is wrong about emergent evolution is not the doctrine, but the release back into old comfortable ways of thinking about consciousness and behavior, the license that it gives to broad and vacuous generalities."[93] This summarizes, at the least, one of the many problems with contemporary theories of consciousness: broad generalizations and a lack of historic context.

It is a valid thesis that consciousness is not universal or eternal unless you make consciousness little more than being awake. Again Jaynes anticipates this argument when he suggests the meaninglessness of the phrase 'to lose consciousness' after receiving a blow on the head. He continues, "...if this were correct, we would then have no word for those somnambulistic states known in the clinical literature where an individual is clearly not conscious and yet is responsive to things in a way in which a knocked-out person is not."[94] Moreover, does any animal that is knocked-out for a moment, or asleep for that matter, living without consciousness, and then awake, regain consciousness? To argue this is to argue that all animals are, when awake, conscious. "In what species" must be taken seriously for if we have a problem attempting to define the historic presence and an understanding of the meaning of consciousness in the human species, looking to make this complex issue more confusing by introducing other species makes little or no sense. At least Jaynes recognizes that this is a complex and evolving concept in need of new thinking.

One of Jaynes' strong points is his recognition that such a complex term may require the recognition of several components for us to understand its operation. Since, as the thesis goes, we are not always conscious,[95] and the "...seeming continuity of consciousness is really an illusion,"[96] one can understand how he could argue that perhaps "...there is no such thing as a complete consciousness..."[97] or that he is "...convinced that a civilization without consciousness is possible."[98] When we discuss in detail his analysis in defining this most ambiguous term we discover that he considers at least six components of a conscious mind: spacialization; conciliation; excerption; narratization; metaphor 'me;' and analog 'I.' This at the least, is a presentation of a very complex scheme. And while his understanding of the complexity of the issue is clear, for here and now the issue is whether there is a presence of this very complex consciousness within the walls of antiquity.[99]

He argues that, "…each age has described consciousness in terms of its own theme and concerns. In the golden age of Greece…Heraclitus…called it an enormous space whose boundaries even by traveling along every path, could never be found out…"[100] is interesting but unsupported and unfortunately lacking a concrete basis since the etymological root of the term is more Medieval Latin and not Greek. While this does not clarify very much, it may have been intended to convince us that consciousness has been present even if only relatively. But in what manner is there this relative consciousness? Jaynes is on sounder footing when he announces that "…there is in general no consciousness in the *Iliad.*"[101] True, he does attempt to offer some exceptions but they are not convincing since some of the translations are questionable and of little merit in helping us to understand any nuance of this term. As an example, Jaynes suggests that "…the word *psyche*, which later means soul or conscious mind, is in most instances life-substances, such as blood or breath…"[102] Breath yes, and in time, some time later in the Roman Empire, soul does begin to appear after the impact of the Stoics and Christians filter into the Roman culture, but consciousness is too much a leap if one is comparing it to an even more problematic term, i.e., soul. If you were to equate psyche with consciousness why not equate psychology with consciousness? His discussion of the *Iliad* is interesting but not demonstrative of consciousness which even he admits since this epic, "…is about *action* and it is full of action—constant action," and therefore, "really is *about* Achilles' acts and their consequences, not about his mind."[103] It is a somewhat different story with Homer's second great epic, *The Odyssey,* for here he perceives that "…Odysseus of the many devices is the hero of the new mentality of how to get along in a ruined and god-weakened world."[104] This definitely indicates a more open thought pattern but again not consciousness the way he himself defines it. True, there is more of a sense of space in the *Odyssey* than in the *Iliad* and thus it may offer, "…an increased spatialization of time in its use of time words, such as begin, hesitate, quickly, endure, etc., and the more frequent reference to the future."[105] Again, even when the interpretation is generally an accepted one, it does not offer any evidence of the presence of this very modern concept.

There are other intriguing examples which the reader of Jaynes should approach cautiously. One example is regarding Aristotle where he offers that "…the Aristotelian writings…located consciousness or the abode of thought in and just above the heart, believing the brain to be a mere cooling organ since it was insensitive to touch or injury."[106] Again, he simply states that where thought occurs, in Aristotelian thinking, there must also follow something to be labeled consciousness. This observation is not inconsistent because later we will find a potential and partial agreement (see Chapter Seven) but consciousness is not, again, an ancient Greek term and his interpretation is not to be found among an audience of classical scholars. Additionally, the sense of self which is indispensable for the rise of modern consciousness is not present since, "...for the Aristotelian grave spirit the model self was always, properly, working to purify itself *of* self, not only by disciplining the beast, but also by being public spirited—that is, by joining the purifiers. Not to discipline the self-life by means of public service was, in essence, evil."[107] Aristotle came rather late in the Hellenic world as it was in a transition to the more syncretistic Hellenistic one, although he appeared to remain true to the city-state (*polis*) concept of human identity.

One other serious attempt to place consciousness into antiquity centers on an unusual interpretation of Aristotle. Found in *Aristotle: The Power of Perception* by Deborah K. W. Modrak, this is an attempt to put consciousness into the writings of Aristotle. It is her position that: "...some commentators deny that Aristotle has any conception of consciousness at all; others attribute a concept of consciousness to him but not a Cartesian concept; still others would attribute a Cartesian conception to him."[108] These various views, it should be added, are all recent and probably reflect the growing post-World War II interest in the subject more than any hard beliefs in consciousness appearing in Aristotle's thinking. Philosophers, after all, are no less likely than historians or scientists to jump on whatever is the most recent and engaging intellectual band wagon. This is not to negate the subject, it is meant only to remind the reader of the context of the discussion. Moreover, Modrak does make it clear that, "Aristotle's conception of consciousness must be gleaned from his analyses of particular types of cognition since his analytic approach to psychology leads to the investigation of specific cognitive activities and not to the systematic study of consciousness, which requires a synthesis of the various aspects of 'mental' life."[109] When Aristotle thinks of those who could possess some quality of independence he did not mean as we would that your dealing with a private independent self. As another scholar noted:

> This is where Aristotle's upper-class perspective entered. In his conception of self such a leader—that is, a being 'highly renowned and prosperous,' and possess of clout—was the only sort of person with a potential for being meaningfully pure. Only great beings like that could even *have* character, since character, he said flatly,

'is that which achieves moral purpose.' And by moral purpose he insistently did not mean private purpose like the saving of a solitary soul; he meant purpose that influenced, carried over into, the lives of others.

Plutarch followed this Aristotelian gospel steadily in his *Lives*. So, if we can believe his, did most of the noble Grecians and Romans he wrote about, certainly the good ones.[110]

The aim of this book is to offer an historic background for consciousness on the basis that once we were without consciousness and only in time did we slowly develop an ever growing and maturing consciousness. While the historic development of consciousness requires an equally parallel appearance and development of a modern self and individuality that characterize our world, there is the additional difficulty of creating a meaningful agreed upon definition and history. While it is not the intention of this book to offer a definitive definition of any of these terms, it will prove necessary to offer a review of what can be considered historically as a foundation for anyone seeking to establish such an ultimate definition. Additionally, the self, individuality and such varied parallel terms as *perception, reflectivity* and *introspection* must equally be confronted. The purpose is to clear away that which is not historically valid, allowing for what might be a more promising approach in understanding the roots of such difficult terms.

It is here, in the world of definition, that Modrak has a serious problem. Modrak states, without reservation, that:

> ...a consensus seems to be emerging among specialists in ancient philosophy that Aristotle has a theory of consciousness and that the key concept for understanding his theory is the concept of the common sense. Kahn originally stated the argument. He concluded that direct self-consciousness of thinking as well as perception is the work of the sense faculty (i.e., of the common sense). Hardie distinguished between general consciousness and reflexive consciousness, the two components of the Cartesian concept of consciousness, and he found both notions in Aristotle's conception of human consciousness.[111]

It may not be uncommon for students of philosophy to project into the past a circumstance appropriate for the future, but for an historian this unacceptable since every era is perceived as having its own reality and sense of unity and substance that makes comparisons let alone projections difficult and often impossible. One can certainly accept common sense as Aristotle's sixth sense which makes it possible to combine any of the other five senses with little difficulty. When we see fire we come to know that it hurts and that flesh smells when you put your hand in it, and thus, we know the potential results to the two other senses when we 'see' fire. But so do some animals, and would this not be better defined as a primitive form of simple pragmatism? Even here, Modrak has to admit that there are limits to this argument. "There is also no question that many modern philosophers from Descartes to the present have denied that animals possess consciousness."[112] And again, "Hardie emphasizes the differences between human and animal consciousness; Kahn minimizes them."[113] At the least what this has to do with consciousness is beyond this writer's understanding and Modrak, as well as two other authors she sites, Kahn and Hardie,[114] offer no answer as to why we should accept this as consciousness except in order to push this seventeenth century and its modern variations back to the fourth century B.C. As has been said, this is an interesting philosophical exercise but should hardly be considered historically accurate.

To further confuse this picture, Modrake offers another definition that could be used to argue that our modern consciousness began with Aristotle when in a footnote she states: "I use *consciousness* in what Landesman calls the 'broad use to designate any mental state or whatever it is about a mental state which makes it mental.'"[115] Now we have the pleasure of understanding consciousness as any thinking process whatsoever. This raises the interesting question as to why bother with consciousness when we already have the word 'thinking?' As will be shown later, this is a similar to a definition offered by John Locke in his attempt to come to grips with this elusive term, but simply to state it as thinking is a great convenience for a philosopher writing a book on Aristotle but not enlightening to those of us trying to delineate between what it is that specifically makes consciousness and its origin and not simply a word for another process or activity which is already named and delineated. True, at one point Modrake does offer a little more clarity when she suggests, "Aristotle's conception of common sense was his device for accounting for the central features of human consciousness as we understand it. I set out four features of consciousness that modern authors have taken to be definitive to consciousness, namely, unity, reflexive awareness, intentionality and apperceptual relations, and I found that Aristotle invoked the common sense to explain all four."[116] There are a series of problems with defining consciousness as being a simple matter of the appearance of *unity, reflexive, awareness, intentionality,* and *apperceptual relations.*[117] Of these five terms, *awareness,* a very ill-defined term for ill-defined consciousness, has been consistently confused with consciousness in contemporary literature and for this we will lay the responsibility at the feet of Descartes.[118] This leaves us with the problem of defining two terms—*consciousness* and *awareness*—to resolve the issue, leaving us as confused as before. Defining an ill-defined term with another ill-defined term does nothing to clarify our understanding.

There simply is no evidence of the existence of this Latin-rooted term to be found earlier and Modrak has to admit this. She states: "…my project rests on the assumption that the psychological theses found in *Parva Naturlia* and the *De Anima* can be profitably viewed as a continuous exposition of one psychological theory."[119] These are not assumptions that a historian of ideas would be willing to make unless there was an extremely good reason to do so. This also demonstrates the fundamental difference between historians and philosophers since the former are more interested in the historic impact while the philosopher is more interested in the actual systems. In any historical study of ideas the impact either on the future of ideas or the effect of given ideas on later events is the focus, while for philosophers, the system, its roots as a system and the later application of that system, is of primary interest. While these are not differences of type but rather of emphasis, they are fundamental. Since no one has offered an agreed-upon system for consciousness, the impact of this term as well as its earliest appearance appears to be an appropriate approach for the discussion of this concept, at least for the historian of ideas. Modrak et al. certainly offer food for thought, but some of their conclusions leave us with more questions than answers. An example of such a statement occurs when she quotes the pragmatist Richard Rorty who writes that "…in Aristotle's conception intellect is not a mirror inspected by an inner eye. It is both mirror and eye in one. The retinal image is *itself* the model for the 'intellect which becomes all things,' whereas in the Cartesian model, the intellect inspects entities modeled on retinal images."[120] The conclusion reached that "…the Aristotelean conception leaves no room for a homunculus who receives the reports of the various faculties and is the ultimate source of consciousness,"[121] is fine as far as it goes, but the inner being in contrast to an outer reality is not recognized in the ancient or, for that matter, the pre-modern mind. That it may even be appropriate to offer as Rorty does that "…at the 'I' of modern epistemology and philosophy of mind is a philosopher's myth, we will be pleased that Aristotle propounded a psychological theory that makes self-contained psychological activities the basis of consciousness," even though it does not alter the situation.[122] But for those looking for the beginnings and evolution of two components for the development of consciousness, a sense of self with any meaningful recognition of interiority and a growing sense of the 'I' that marks off the parameter of individuality, these mental exercises offer food for thought but not an historical meal. That there is not an interiority as we understand it in Aristotle's thinking means that those who are looking for the beginnings of the subjective experience of consciousness will have to look elsewhere.

This is not an attempt to denigrate Modrak's stated desire for a charitable reading. As she puts it: "It is often not immediately obvious in which sense Aristotle is employing a given term, and in many instances, the present included, a harsh critic may object to the charitable reading and choose a reading that makes Aristotle's position untenable. To such a critic, there is often no further answer except the advocacy of charity."[123] Even then she has to admit that this is an extreme reading since "...Aristotle did not posit a faculty for consciousness; he posited a perceptual faculty and assigned the lion's share of the activities belonging to consciousness to the perceptual faculty; he also posited a noetic faculty for thinking and may have included the reflexive awareness of thinking among its functions."[124]

So what is to be concluded from reading this interesting work on Aristotle and consciousness? First, it is clear that a good philosopher has the ability to take a limited amount of information and create a very fascinating, if not equally extreme, conclusion. It should be recognized, secondly, that systems building in the hands of a thoughtful and well-informed scholar can be made into most whatever the scholar may want, even if its conclusions are tenuous. And finally, the subjectivity of consciousness requires some historical context for explaining its evolution as well as giving it something of a cogent understanding and evolving framework rather than simply offering a philosophical creation that supports presupposition, whatever the conclusion. Actually, one of Aristotle's most informative works is his *Poetics* where the issue of language plays a larger part than in his more metaphysical works.

> His *Poetics* has been a purification bible for centuries, and is relevant for biography as well as tragedy. Aristotle posited a hero who was a model human—that is, a superior being by reason of his character and position in life—who was nonetheless possessed of an impurity (his 'flaw,' his manifestation of the beast) that needed to be purged.... By that action the hero was in effect sacrificed to his own impurity, and the *audience* was vicariously purified as a result. Aristotle described the rite as an imitation of real human actions, an indication of how deeply rooted in human nature was the impulse to imitate....'Through pity and fear,' he said, the action effected 'the proper purgation of these emotions.'[125]

The didactic, the community's educating its populace, was extremely important, perhaps more important than any other aspect of his thinking and is reflected in his *Politics* as well his more than 100 studies of various constitutions to establish the best society for the best human beings. Aristotle, it could be argued, is more of a social than psychological thinker. In any case, his psychology is still primitive.

This presents us with the next stage in the evolution for a modern ontology, one where there is at least an early beginning of an interior world for consciousness to eventually find a home. This evolution occurs within the new world of Hellenized Greece and its impact up the Roman Empire and involves a major break from the exclusionary nature of citizenship in the *polis* into which one was born. This new perspective appeared with the movement known as Stoicism which was created in the expanding diversity of an Hellenistic Greece and Roman Empire and where a synthesizing occurred within the powerful and eventually successful Christian movement in Rome. The operational basis for judgement slowly shifts from the reasoning found in Athens to the faith that came to dominate the Roman Empire. This was the byproduct and extension of a deity. The world of a localized order—the *polis*—had collapsed in the hands of a growing and diverse population dominated increasingly by a faith replacing the certainty of death with the certitude of eternal life.

In the eclectic world of the Roman Empire there were a variety of early significant thinkers and ideas on the road to St. Augustine. The rhetorician Cicero, Quintillian the educator, who found some agreement with Aristotelean ideas, the neo-Platonist, Plotinus, the Christian Clement of Alexandria and Lucretius, the Epicurean (c.99–55 B.C.), were some of the more prominent thinkers of the late Republic and Empire. The Greek philosopher Epicurus (c.341–270 B.C.), held a fourfold prescription for a healthy life suggesting that gods are not to be feared, death is of no concern, good can be easily attained, and evil can be easily endured. "The Epicureans held to the mortality of the soul, which is an atomic structure, dissolved with the body. They denied that the gods reward the righteous or punish the wicked."[126]

However, the most influential body of ideas arose from the earlier teachings of Hellenic Stoicism which offered a comprehensive life-guiding scheme. It was established by Zeno of Citium (c.334–c.265 B.C.) at a time when divisiveness, uncertainty and fear grew at a rapid rate in the far-flung and complex empire of Alexander the Great. People are never comfortable with the unknown which is where fear can breed freely. Thus the key was to establish a new means of functioning in order to cope with an expanding and ever more complex and chaotic world. Without becoming overly engaged with the issues of Stoicism, it can be summarized as a system that divided all knowledge into one of three groupings: physics, logic, and ethics. Because Stoic literature is so diverse and disparate depending upon the thinker, it should be sufficient to explain that there was some organic unity assumed that would give coherence to these diversities. The first key is that everything in Stoicism is inter-relative and what is of significance is that through the proper training of reasoning abilities organized into harmony with nature one could make peace with the travails of daily life. As Friedrich Nietzsche once observed, it isn't the bad breaks that you suffer that is most terrifying; for most people the far greater pain centers on the question 'why me?' Stoics believed that they offered an ethical base in order to come to grips with any potential fear by the simple act of acceptance, the familiar Stoic attitude being "uncomplaining endurance of hardship" which could not be "…adequately grasped without reference to their physical and logical basis."[127] The literature is slim and lacks an organized structure which makes much of our understanding dependent upon those varied thinkers and their known works following in what they thought of as a Stoic tradition. Especially of interest for its spread was its introduction and influence in Rome, the Empire that spread much farther and was greater than anything ever dreamed. But unlike Epicureanism which entered Rome through the writings of Lucretius, Stoicism had a far wider and deeper following among both leaders and citizens. From Cicero to the last of the good Emperors, Marcus Aurelius, the influence is clear. It even impacted on the most significant movement that offered an adjustment to a growing world of uncertainty and fear—that of Christianity. The idea of a soul, for example, a piece of the divine spirit which is to be found in each of us, in all humanity, was an idea that came originally from the teachings of Zeno. While no soul existed for Epicureans the Stoics made it central.

When a soul is tied to the born-again deities, the vegetative gods, the basis for a religion is created that is a major break from the traditions of the Hebrews and Egyptians. Jesus Christ was one of many ancient vegetative deities where the issue of re-birth was not only inherent but central to this religion of renewal. There were a multitude of the earlier versions of vegetative deities, from Osiris in Egypt to Mithraism in Asia Minor. Death occurs in autumn but with the arrival of spring a re-birth and life continues and fears are abated. But there is a more important contribution that a figure like Jesus of Nazarene offered to the creation of the self. The idea of one person, a teacher or rabbi, speaking so often and in his own name was unheard of in the Hebrew tradition. About forty percent of the New Testament is about one voice and only one, Jesus. This offended the traditional rabbis, the Saduccees and

Pharasees, who stood with the Old Word where there were many prophets who had spoken in terms of the law and tradition. Now we have this singular voice speaking in his own name and dominating the scene from the Sermon on the Mount to the Garden of Gethsemane. This was clearly a step towards the positioning of a singular individual, especially if one thinks of him as only a teacher and not a deity.

In the end this will prove to be little more than the creation of a personal perspective in order to accommodate a peace of mind in an era of stress and uncertainty. How, for example, does one make sense of the unique creation of a city of a million people as had occurred in ancient Rome at its peak? The mistake that should not be made, however, is to suggest that somehow this was the beginning of the appearance of modern individuality as has been suggested, unfortunately, in a relevant section of the multi-volume *Dictionary of the History of Ideas*: "By cutting through the barriers of birth and wealth, and by emphasizing the autonomy of the individual, Stoic ethics did much to liberalize and humanize the social practice of the Roman empire. In the second and third centuries A.D. writers as different as the Christian, Clement of Alexandria, the Aristotelian scholar, Alexander of Aphrodisias, and Plotinus attest to its influence."[128] It also should be noted that Stoic reasoning which was so indispensable for adjusting one's everyday life to accommodate the difficulties inherent in both nature and society was actually reduced to a piece of ultimate rationalization: place all in God's hands. "Man, like all things, is pervaded by God, but he possesses a special status. The *pneuma* which gives coherence to a stone and life to a plant manifests itself as reason (*logos*) in mature men." It is through the reasoning power of God that we partake in what makes life bearable and virtuous. "The natural life for man is 'rational' life and this makes him a partner of God, or universal Nature. As Epictetus, the Stoic slave, puts it (*Discourses* I. i, 12): 'We [i.e., the gods] have given you a certain portion of ourselves, the faculty of choice and refusal, of desire and aversion; that is, the faculty to make use of the impressions presented to your mind.' Natural events are outside human control, but man has the power to evaluate them and adapt his life accordingly."[129] This philosophy makes each of us part of a divinely individualized being by way of the greater God or the wholeness of the universe and as such should not be referred to as "the autonomy of the individual," since the only self here is that by way of God.[130] An autonomous individual is without any ties to anyone or anything and that would have to include any dependency upon any deity, or for that matter upon any society. While it is true that this represents a more individualized approach to living than what had preceded the Stoics, we must again avoid that most common error of projection from here into the past. True, there are historic precedents, but they should always be properly qualified. The context of any period in history is too unique for a simple one-to-one transference of either behavior or attitudes over many centuries. History never offers a simple construct with patterns that are discovered by the historian since the patterns are actually a creation rather than a discovery. History as a discipline is an art and not a social science. The intent should be to see the small beginnings of what may become a great change but not to place undo emphasis on any one particular event or condition that would distort that particular past being studied.

It is with this caveat that a discussion of the unique contributions to the early hints of some primitive form of consciousness and of the self within the historical event of Christianity can be studied. Specifically, a unique moment of the second century A.D. can and should be given credence, a moment centering around the writings of Marcus Aurelius, the last of the good Emperors, who lived and died in this period (121–180 A.D.). As a Stoic he wrote in his *Meditationes*: "…nowhere can a man find a quieter or more untroubled retreat than in his own soul."[131] This is a man whose thinking could have been confused with those Christians that were in Rome at the time. While simply a Stoic, however, he does demonstrate the close proximity between Stoics and Christians. However, the man who is most often called the first founder of Christianity, St. Paul noted that the Christian religion stands or falls on the belief in first, the crucifixion and then, most importantly, the resurrection. Here the Stoics can no longer be confused with these believers and in that there is an interesting transformation of a perception which allowed for at least some exercise of reason by someone overwhelmed by faith. In both Stoicism and Christianity, the issue is to make an accommodation with necessity, for Stoics living a difficult and often lonely life and for the Christians, a life of faith, living with the fear of death and the unknown but also with the promise of the resurrection. What is revolutionary is that this new concept may have offered some hope for those seeking certitude in an uncertain world, especially in the avoidance of death, which, as will be seen, will in the long run introduce a new problem, the rather unique and future problem of the concept of sin and damnation. It was St. Paul who "…gave a structured character to the doctrine of sin. After Adam's crime, man, cut off from Redemption, is 'sold under sin' (Rom. 7:14), certainly still able to desire the good but not to 'perform' it (Rom. 7:18). Man is inevitably bound unto eternal death, the 'wages of sin' (Rom. 6:21; 7:24 LE)."[132] The dread of death had not been abated but only mitigated.

Quintus Septimus Florens Tertullianus comes from the same era. He was born in Carthage in c.160 A.D. (the last year of Aurelius' life) and died c.220 A.D. He was a significant theologian and early writer in Latin for the Roman Church. His contributions include his concept of hell—one of fire and brimstone. Of hell, Tertullian "...wrote that 'its nature is incorruptible, by a property for torture given to it by God' and that it 'does not consume that which it burns, but mends it.'"[133] His uncompromising attitude towards faith is demonstrated by his famous line regarding the incarnation of Christ: *Certum est quia impossible est*, i.e., "it is certain because it is impossible."[134] Added to the fear of death there was now a new fear of sin, and Tertullian is clear about what he meant when sin was the issue. Since he offered a "...list of sins whose remission could be obtained only by public penance: idolatry, blasphemy, homicide, adultery, debauchery, false witness, and fraud."[135] One had not simply to make peace with the Lord, it was now also necessary to avoid sin at all cost. "Whether one is appalled by Tertullian's inhumanity and by the whole idea of eternal torture..."[136] this fear can lead great numbers of people to attend to their fearful condition, clearly marking the expanded power of Church's teachings for salvation. This also partially explains the rationalizations, denials and rituals regarding death that appeared so early. There is little doubt that one of the most wide-spread pastimes centered around denial: "The different forms of death denial share a common structure. The life-in-death paradox is converted into life-and-after-life, an altogether more comfortable and consistent proposition, but one that dangerously obscures the choice of living out our span in this life. We shall survive death, we say, in heaven, on war memorials, in the annals of romantic love, the future of the corporation, in some final 'fix,' in deathless art or prose."[137]

Where reason had once reigned, faith began to take hold. It was in this context that at the end of the classical world and Roman Empire, Augustine, Bishop of Hippo (354–430 A.D.) was the culmination of classical values on one hand and an arrow in the direction of the next era, that of the medieval world. It would be a mistake, however, to think that the world after Rome, that of the Middle Ages, will be somehow dramatically different from the ancient, for in one sense "...the ancient and medieval worlds saw nature and mankind as part of a cosmos in which the human being had a proper place—one participated as part of a larger whole. The goal was to conform to this pattern of nature..."[138] To be of the cosmos or nature is to be also of society and to be of society is not to be some stranger in the land of order and familiarity. Certainty was discovered with our realization of being terminal. What was also necessary was the extension of the family into larger communities by way of oral and written language. Additionally, there was public control now through the power of shame since it has been rightly suggested that shame and death are handmaidens:

> ...there is a more intimate connection between shame and death than simply the violation of an individual's experience. Shame seems to have a primordial relationship with death. Common expressions describe this connection: 'I was so ashamed, I could have died'; 'I could have sunk into the ground and disappeared'; and 'I was mortified.'[139]

This suggests that if one is to grow into an independent individual struggling for an inner self and thus become conscious, shame may need to be transcended, an issue to be discussed later.

All of this hints at a term conspicuous in its absence in antiquity yet possibly of some significance to the rise of consciousness: curiosity. The discovery of death, the creation of language followed by writing and the ordering of the universe, both by rational and by religious means, reflect well on the inventive nature of humanity while raising an unanswerable (at least here) question: Is there a correlation between the human drive of curiosity and an evolving development of a conscious self? Whatever the answer, the ancient world ended without a true sense of self, individuality or activated consciousness.

CHAPTER TWO

MEDIEVAL PERSISTENCE OF CLASSICAL ANTIQUITY

Reading, like any human activity, has a history.[1]

Uncertainty and curiosity should be considered a driving force for human development at the end of the classical world. Since fear inheres in uncertainty which in turn can lead to doubt, the confrontation with one's own death, with the termination of not only the present but also any possible future, created a morbid condition for our early but talented, fumbling and stumbling ancestors. It was neither sought or wanted but it was certain: death spares no one. It was the Medieval world that carried this tradition of uncertainty and curiosity to new and increased levels of recognition and inventiveness, patterns of coping followed eventually by confusion. In establishing a spoken language, however, there was an organization of the community support of like-minded sound-makers both as an action for defense and for the pleasures that would extend beyond those fears. Even today, the collective creation of sound retains its power to comfort and give pleasure whether it is in the form a choir or an orchestra. In fact one of the characteristics of a child is its joy at making noise, since this is one serious means of asserting one's presence (ego), and this, even before the comprehension of terminality or recognition of the self. Even adults in the right context can practice the same behavior believing that if they were to make enough noise during holidays with guns or fireworks or at a sporting event it might somehow keep the doors of death closed. Uncertainty must be kept at bay.

While in one sense antiquity metamorphosed into the Medieval world, it could also be considered to be little more than a distraction since in both eras the results are the same—keep death from one's door. The world of Antiquity continued in some ways well into the Medieval especially in the history of ideas. "For the history of the mind—above all, when it is treated as a history of consciousness—the periods into which it is most convenient and most significant to divide the past history of mankind, will not be those familiar ones which are adapted to a more superficial record. From the former point of view, the Graeco-Roman period is seen as extending, practically unbroken, to the end of the Middle Ages."[2] The Middle Ages was also, in some aspects an extension of the Roman Empire, especially in an altered form of the Holy Roman Empire. Once writing began, it was unknown how far the narrative and poetic forces could take the Western mind. What began as the power of organized sound was followed by the power of icons of those sounds—the written word. Language became more permanent than living memory and somehow more immortal, especially with what was considered the sanctity of 'The Word' from the New Testament. From this and other contributions to our cultural heritage the Greeks also created a basis for both our transcendent and institutional thought. There was no turning back to a simpler world after the gifts of Hellenic and Hellenistic cultures and the Roman preservation of them. Christianity presented a culmination of what had gone before.

The traditional gods that guided the Greeks and later the Romans gave way to the reasoning that began in the Hellenic and Roman worlds, eventually contributing to the scholastic mind associated with the Medieval world. In the end, Antiquity became dominated by hope in a new universal order of one supreme savior, one who would remove the burden of doubt and offer mankind certitude. Unfortunately, there would be a new fear to highlight the certainty of death, one growing behind the curtain of salvation: that of sin and damnation. What was needed at the end of Antiquity was a new, more secure ordering of knowledge, a clearer but more systematic construct for our understanding of what it meant to be human, one that would relieve us of some of the inherent burdens and pains of living with any remaining doubts. This was the historical, social and psychological contribution of the newly forming Christian communities that would replace the remnants of the *Pax Romana* with a divine guide. This is not to say that those living in these circumstances saw a dramatic change in their world. For the average members of such a large and divergent community of tribes and those with something of an understanding of their classical heritage, there was in their mind a continuity. The old Roman Empire now metamorphosed into the Holy Roman Empire with a sanctified Emperor of the one true faith. This was an idea concretized in the writings of St. Augustine, specifically in his classic, *The City of God*.[3]

It was the genius of St. Augustine of Hippo, that established a new and comforting order for confronting our terminal condition. In this study, however, it must be understood that, when looking at some of his summations of classic thought and his inventiveness in transforming classical thinking into an reasonably ordered structure for the coming age, 'self' is still not present although nascent. Augustine was a student of the ideas of Plotinus (c.205–270 A.D.), the founder of Neoplatonism. As such, Augustine always possessed a certain empathy for Platonic ideas, which he converted into the official theology of the Medieval establishment. He was also the most complete thinker summarizing the classical mind of his own time. In addition, his writings have acted as a pointer that aided in creating our modern world-view. Some of his contributions will be found significant, ironically for the Protestant Reformation. Caution should be advised, however, on avoiding misreading his thoughts: some commentators will attempt to perceive a very modern 'self' and very defined 'individuality' in his writings. While extremely important and a worthy comparison, even if limited to some later Cartesian thought, Augustine remains the one who summarized classical thought as he organized the base for Medieval philosophy. Naturally, there will be serious caveats offered to our understanding of Augustine's contribution to the creation of a modern self. For the history of ideas, there is no way to undertake such a study as this without this remarkable thinker, notwithstanding the tendency of a few scholars to suggest more modern interpretations.

There are massive problems in turning to the deep past for both clues as well as examples of a serious change in mentality when we study ancient sources. First is the problem of acquisition. So many works we know of antiquity were destroyed: fire and water take their toll over the centuries. Secondly, what we do have besides occasional references regarding these early writings, are later copies, specifically translations or translations of the translations of the originals. Translations always have serious limits that must always be kept in mind. (None of these are more problematic than those important sources here referred to and all varied translations where they exist.) We should first attempt to be as true as possible as to what was meant in a specific text. This would include not only its meaning for the ancients, but also being attuned to their context. This position cannot be overstated since this is where the first and most common mistakes often occur. By attempting to enter the context of their world and their own words in a time long gone—their vocabulary, syntax, assumptions and culture—only then can we be as true as possible to the ancient world-view and meaning. We must attempt to read their world, not project our own upon theirs, especially in that we, with our much larger, even massive vocabulary and complex syntax, have a very different way of thinking. It is always very difficult, if not impossible, to understand the thinking of those in a linguistic world that is almost beyond our comprehension. This is only highlighted when comparing the closed universe of the ancients to the openness of our own world. What was meant—rather than our perception of what they meant—is not an easy task to discern and should be one of our primary concerns, difficult as that may be. Reading requires that we should attempt to avoid becoming locked into a given assumption or preconceived meaning, especially one that we find so very personally satisfying and therefore more appealing than what may have in fact been the original thoughts of the writer. Today we live with the most sophisticated, complex and open language schema that has ever existed. The depth and breadth of our contemporary English would be beyond comprehension in many, many ways only a century ago. We 'e-mail,' are 'cool' and 'dig' while we 'blow' and 'flow.' We as a people have not caught up to our own language or the implications of some of our own changing words and syntax which go well beyond yesterday's assumptions, a condition that always occurs in times of dynamic change. Albert Einstein once noted that last thing to change in a world of change was our assumptions.[4] It should not be surprising therefore that everything we read or hear has to be translated, i.e., interpreted. "Indeed, we have to remind ourselves of what interpretation has always been: an act of translation."[5]

As a suggestion, therefore, a reexamination of the translation of the title of St. Augustine's most personal work, *The Confessions* would appear in order. Specifically, it has long been held that this famous work never genuinely fits our traditional context of being a simple confessional.[6] The implication has been that this is a work that appropriately should be regarded as part of the genre of biography and particularly autobiography. As one student of the subject has gone so far as to note:

> Anyone writing about him-or herself is bound to be a truth-selector, and few who have done so have rushed to present themselves as irremediably mean. Saint Augustine...in his *Confessions*—frequently cited as the first 'true' autobiography—did not omit his own early meanness...he was only a few pages into his life when the tributes began. Did it matter that he described his grave virtues as gifts of the Lord? Did it matter that he had learned 'to delight in truth...hated to be deceived, had a vigorous memory, was gifted with speech, was soothed by friendship, [and] avoided pain, baseness, ignorance' by virtue of the fact that he had put himself in the hands of the Lord?[7]

When the writer refers to an autobiography as a 'truth-selector' it is accurate since we now understand that the life led by the author is one life, and the life spoken of, as in an autobiography, is another, offering two different lives, one of experience and one of memory. That this is such a very recent recognition further demonstrates how very modern the idea of autobiography is since it is only in our own world that there has been enough research into the working of our memory and therefore enough light brightening our understanding of this unique activity. In contrast to the more traditional interpretation that Augustine had written an autobiography as we understand it today, a more recent reinterpretation has now been offered, one that suggests that this historically significant work should be given a new, but perhaps more accurate, English title calling it a *Testimony*[8] rather than a confession. Since in a very real sense the issue being discussed here is first and foremost a matter of keeping clear specific terms and their meaning, the question of accuracy of translation will be one that must be constantly addressed. If we must admit that the very term *consciousness*, as we will see, has had more than one historic meaning, as do the terms *self* and *individuality*, and since their meanings are inherent and relevant to when, how and by whom they were used, the term *autobiography* should also be treated with great caution.

It was no less a literary critic than Harold Bloom who once observed that "'Interpretation' once meant 'translation,' and essentially still does."[9] To translate any term and interpret its meaning is to attempt to take part in the world of that word. When we read Augustine, or Marcus Aurelius for that matter, we enter a linguistic world that while once alive in action and words (classical Latin), is now long gone, and since it has expired there is no immediate and exact component to our own world of meaning. The famed nineteenth century translator of *The Meditations* of Emperor Marcus Aurelius Antonius, George Long, stated in his 1873 preface that there still remained "…difficulties which I cannot remove, because the text is sometimes too corrupt to be understood, and no attempt to restore the true readings could be successful."[10] This is a statement with which most translators of any work would today agree. To attempt to travel to the ancient world particularly poses problems since the ancient Greek and Latin syntax is only remotely part of our contemporary structure or lexography; the changes to that lexography have been significant. We have already noted, for example, the ancients "…had wildly…quaint notions of the uses of the first person in antiquity and an "…odd disposition simply to deny that the self is significantly private."[11] Self and privacy are both modern concepts. The act of interpretation and translating are at best an art, not unlike the re-creations of historians.

It is a necessary condition of scholarship to always point to the importance of definitions, translations, interpretations which will be at best approximations. As one student of this issue has observed: "Each interpretation transposes something into something else. We should therefore shift our focus away from underlying presuppositions to the space that is opened up when something is translated into a different register."[12] While this should not be surprising, it is unfortunately all too often overlooked by either readers or translators. To read is to interpret as well as to translate even if the writings are in your own native language. Most people tend to assume that to read means understanding the words and syntax and simply turning the pages, but that is simply the introduction to reading and not the art of reading itself, understandings that have come about only recently. This can be illustrated by examining interpretations of the classics—Homer, Aurelius, Plato, Augustine—by various scholars. A famous case in point would be the translation of Plato's works by the Victorian scholar, Benjamin Jowett (1817–93). For him, the Greek use of the singular for god, now understood to have meant Zeus, was translated to mean the God of the New Testament. This is simply an error of fact.[13] Assumptions, prejudices and ignorance all can lead us to many errors, especially when dealing with the intention of disputed words. Perhaps we could have recognized for ourselves that the very idea of subjective interpretations is itself a modern condition since the term *subjective* that is used today is also of modern origins. Moreover, it is generally agreed today that the act of projection is one of the more common psychological habits for people who perceive in others what they do not want to admit about themselves. If "...translation, then...is a form of transcription and reading of texts, creates a difference,"[14] as stated by Willis Barnstone, then we must accept the massive difficulty we have in attempting to avoid placing our own values and pre-judgements into a vat of very unique expressions. The resolution to accept is the need to attempt to determine the meaning meant as opposed to the meaning we would prefer to understand or would most favor.[15] While this is a rather lengthy explication of a particular aspect regarding primary sources it is necessary for this and later chapters in order to establish that much of what is read must be admitted to being at best an approximate meaning and intent.

If Augustine wrote an autobiography it would follow that he had a powerful sense of self and pride therein and could not be considered a Medieval Christian, pride being the deadliest of the sins. Since translation is interpretation, his confessions can be reviewed more as a testimony than an autobiography in any modern or even post-Rousseaun tradition. It is in a study by Gary Wills that this point is appropriately drawn out: "...the English word has anachronistic connotations of criminal or sacramental confession. Augustine uses *confiteri* to mean 'testify,' and *confesio* as a synonym for *testimonium*. Thus he can 'confess' that time is measurable (*Confessiones*) 11.35. Even inanimate things confess—testify to—their Creator: 'Their beauty is their testimony' (*Pulchritudo eorum confessio eorum, Sermones* 241.2). So I translate *Confessiones* as *The Testimony*."[16] While there are those who would wish to use the term *confession*, it should be seen as an extreme exaggeration to state, as another modern writer has, that, "Augustine's *Confessions*...constitutes the foundation of the Western introspective autobiography."[17] The fact is that the term *autobiography* appears to find its origins in the nineteenth-century "...when the Romantics fought off the Deists by asserting the reality of the inner life, the values of the self, the significance of the individual."[18] The same problem applies to the scholarly use of the term *biography*, "...at Carleton College there was a department of biography, and the College boasted that it was the very first department of biography in the whole academic...world. It has been started in 1920 by one Andrew Vernon, whose theme about biography as that '[it sent] the student forth with the richest human material within reach.'...then moved to Dartmouth to start a department of biography there."[19]

When attempting to trace the history of a concept—in this case, consciousness—it would be appropriate to approach the history of the concept of autobiography with a similar caution and reserve. It is not difficult to find studies regarding various cultures of antiquity and applying the term *biography* to them, even in ancient Mesopotamia.[20] True, while Augustine was willing to speak of his life from his early childhood to adulthood in less than a complimentary manner, this does not make for an autobiography.[21] It is not inaccurate, however, to conclude that while, "Augustine also was a launderer,...he traveled a different route entirely. He did not leave himself out when considering the lusts in need of laundering..."[22] But these are not acts of biographic revelation but rather what one offers the priest in the confessional in order to be free of God's wrath. While Saint Augustine "did not omit his own early meanness," it took a very little time for his tone to change as, "...he was only a few pages into his life when the tributes began. Did it matter that he described his grave virtues as gifts of the Lord? Did it matter that he had learned 'to delight in truth,...hated to be deceived, had a vigorous memory, was gifted with speech, was soothed by friendship, [and] avoided pain, baseness, ignorance' by virtue of the fact that he had put himself in the hands of the Lord?"[23] It is equally true, however, that while he was willing to confront that which was good and that which was evil, and more the former than the later, he did look at himself in a way that would be foreign to the earlier Stoics as, "he was attentive to his own 'I,' for which he spoke often—so often that a stoic Roman would probably have been annoyed and contemptuous."[24] And although the *Meditations* has also been considered something of a auto-biographic piece, "Aurelius provides a particularly useful contrast to Augustine, not only because he lived two centuries earlier, but also because the two men were a religion apart; and at the core of their religious difference was the self, the 'I.'"[25] This could be attributed in part to the nature of the Christian religion, the foundation that Augustine is addressing since the idea that all Christians now have is of a specific and unique soul, the 'I,' which must be considered originating with God. This was definitely a step further into the self than the limited condition of the Stoics even if it is still not much like the modern use of this personal 'I.' Moreover this could be seen as an obvious conclusion since the Christian world was much more specific than the Stoics regarding life after death and the banishing of fear with eternal hope. The Stoics were mostly interested in making peace with life here and now, in harmony with nature and their circumstances, rather than turning to some after-world filled with eternal bliss. It is this difference—death and an afterlife—that made the rise of the Christian religion such an important force contributing to the introduction of both the self and individuality. This was a personal God where the myth of the resurrection implied eternal bliss for all individual believers. When turning back to the classical world of Rome there is, through the influence of Stoicism, a picture that is somewhat similar but also clearly different. "Aurelius's thought about service to society and the subordination of self have a Plutarchian ring throughout. They are grave, virtuous thoughts, but conspicuously unbiographical thoughts."[26] This Stoic and Roman idea of duty can also be found in an altered fashion in Augustine's concept of the Christian duty that one has to the Lord while Aurelius wrote of the classical role model and how to be a good Roman citizen by fulfilling one's duty. Again, as long as the issue centers around the outside world of politics these were citizens and not individuals or even selves. Put another way, it was not the "I" *per se* that was unique to Augustine and the Christians, but that this same "I" was an immortal soul.

Julius Caesar had earlier laid something of a groundwork for this viewpoint in his *Commentaries*, which although "written by the man himself, were characteristically in the third person and endlessly devoted to military campaigns."[27] In addition, "the ostensibly private *Mediationes* of Marcus Aurelius (121–180 A.D.) were private for the first chapter only. After that they were about men in general, good men, and how they should conduct themselves to be good." There was no chronology, no life story. "Aurelius's classical self proved to be self-reticent."[28] There is far too little in the way of precedence for the creation of what we think of as a biography here. And while it is true that Plutarch wrote what must be considered his most famous work, *Lives of the Noble Grecians and Romans,* in a model not unlike biography, again should we consider it biographic as we mean the term? One student of the subject has suggested that it comes close even if historians are not so generous. He begins with the agreement that, "…modern biographers speak condescendingly of Plutarch.…He was too anxious to assess his subjects ethically, they feel, to have had a clear view of them. He was not disposed to be objective about them, or to plumb the depths of that mysterious entity, character…" The idea of *objectivity* in antiquity is simply too difficult to comprehend since if a distinction between objective and subjective were normal then the history of that world would have been more modern than ancient. *Subjective* and *objective* in the Ancient and Medieval worlds were simply grammatical terms. The same commentator continues by suggesting that, "Modern historians have not been kind to him either. They like to quote him on himself at the beginning of his life of Alexander: 'My design is not to write history but lives.' In Plutarch's time the word biography was waiting to be born, but his remark is still taken as proof that he was a biographer, not an historian." The nature of these two disciplines make them very different intellectual genres and no doubt Plutarch's work possesses a plethora of information for the historian but not much in the way of a story of the private lives of the parties written about. Finally he offers that, "The obvious fact about it—and about Plutarchian lives even are sharply shaped by moral values—is that it straddles history and biography."[29] A moralizing tale is precisely that and suggests nothing more than that the reader should follow the author's lead in appropriate behavior.

The fact remains that the ancient world, as noted, was not a world with any concern for individuality as it is in the case of the modern world, for as has been correctly pointed out: "…ancient biography was handicapped, I believe, less by ignorance of the nature of self than by conventions within which the genre worked, conventions of social observance that kept its practitioners from exploring many of the ramifications of self-meaning that were open to them."[30] Even now, we work by way of the conventions within which we "…in many corners of the genre, think of individuals as being perfectly approachable as social figures first, and as individuals," after the fact.[31] The idea of only speaking of those who are most important to society as well as an idealization for proper behavior can be traced back to Aristotle: "In his conception of self such a leader—that is, a being 'highly renowned and prosperous,' and possessed of clout—was the only sort of person with a potential for being meaningfully pure. Only great beings like that could even have character, since character, he said flatly, 'is that which achieves moral purpose.' And by moral purpose he insistently did not mean private purpose like the saving of a solitary soul; he meant purpose that influenced, carried over into, the lives of others."[32] In antiquity, a self, by its very nature, would be an ostracized being, someone without a country or kin. The story until very recently has been the story of one's social or community definition of "success"[33] and not the interior life of an expanding self. Even in those earliest of notes pointing to the rise of biography in Plutarch's writings, the "...ritual had been largely one of identifying biographies with groups, and attaching relevant group standards to the lives."[34] To even think independently of the group was foreign enough to pose great a danger for such figures as Socrates and is seen in his trial and subsequent drinking of hemlock. Another famous Roman writer, Sutorius (c.69–c.140 A.D.), author of *Lives of the Caesars*, who although born after Plutarch, "...may well be the classical biographer most modern historians would choose over Plutarch..."[35] Moreover, Sutorius took on "... Plutarch's ethical approach to character. Such lines as 'this was the noblest Roman of them all,' and 'Then must you speak of one that loved not wisely but too well,' may be mint Shakespeare, but they had deep roots in Plutarch's view of biography."[36]

'Objective,' like 'biography' would wait for the modern world to offer a meaning which our deep past could not. It was not just Plutarch who possessed a "relative lack of interest in the self." It was a characteristic in the classical world where people were "the product of an attentiveness to public lives—that is, lives dedicated to public, social service." For his contemporaries as well as Plutarch, it was normal to render the self as incidental, as well as the kind of domesticity that we may now find central to any biography and autobiography.[37] In light of this attitude, even Aristotle argued on behalf of this sense of community rather than in defense of a self.

> Aristotle posited a hero who was a model human—that is, a superior being by reason of his character and position in life—who was nonetheless possessed of an impurity (his 'flaw,' his manifestation of the beast) that needed to be purged....By that action the hero was in effect sacrificed to his own impurity, and the audience was vicariously purified as a result. Aristotle described the rite as an imitation of real human actions, an indication of how deeply rooted in human nature was the impulse to imitate...'Through pity and fear,' he said, the action effected 'the proper purgation of these emotions.'[38]

From early Antiquity to its conclusion with the words of St. Augustine, the collective social good was always far greater in importance than any part or sum total of the parts. "The climate that produced Plutarch's *Lives* ... was most obviously different from ours with respect to the individual, the self."[39] This attitude did not disappear with the end of the Hellenistic age and the rise of a Roman World where the sense of duty dominated the citizen's life. For "...much more directly than Plutarch, Aurelius was a public relations man for the classical ideals of discipline, moderation, uprightness, right-thinking, and avoidance of the trivial (to the classical mind most matters of self were at least officially trivial)..."[40]

The differences between the classical thinkers and Augustine were much further reaching than so far indicated since their words differed from each other not only philosophically but culturally as well. As one commentator put it:

> For Aurelius and Plutarch were indeed from a different world than Augustine. Plutarch was a rich, gregarious, patrician citizen of the Roman Empire; and habitué of Athens, Alexandria, Rome; and insider known to emperors. Marcus Aurelius was even richer, more worldly, more patrician, more everything, being himself an emperor. In contrast, Augustine, though an intellectual, was middle class (his father was a burgess in a North African town, the one later named after Constantine), and thoroughly removed from the Empire machinery that created, for noble Romans, their official conscience.[41]

Again, a difference in culture also means a difference in language which again means a difference in thinking. The world being born on the ashes of the Empire was to be similar on the surface but a very different world beneath the labels and titles was beginning, for this was now a land without prosperity, without urban living, without an effective legal system or an organized military or the brilliant engineering for which the Romans were rightly famous. As for the influence of Augustine on the writings of important lives that would follow, they would now be of a new and different class, a world of "...monks before and after Augustine whom we call the hagiographers [who] were further removed."[42] For a time there will be little or no centralized government and each and every one of the members of the Christian communities will be reduced to much smaller organized groups. This transformation is dramatized when we consider that most experts suggest that Rome at its peak had a population with a centralized government of about one million people, a situation not matched until the modern world.

To speak of the self in antiquity and in the middle ages is an extreme anachronism which is further confused by a diversity of tongues. Community, social standards of honor—what the Greeks had called *aretē*—and the power to belong and be a part of such societies were the driving forces contributing to creativity. In a very real sense, for the Aristotelian tradition, "...the model self was always, properly, working to purify itself of self, not only by disciplining the beast, but also by being public spirited—that is, by joining the purifiers. Not to discipline the self-life by means of public service was, in essence, evil."[43] When one compares the ancient lives with the lives of a Friedrich Nietzsche or later someone like an Andy Warhol, it is obvious that these lives could only have been written at the end of the nineteenth and the middle of the twentieth centuries respectively. One scholar has offered an 'anthropological guess' as to why the primitives and ancients were adverse towards any sense of self: "...the constraint can be traced back to the most primitive human taboos, back to when group solidarity began to question individual deviance. Stamping around tribal fires, muttering incantations, slaughtering sheep (or deviants), the purifiers began to cleanse us of our private selves and make us theirs. In most cultures they still do, and the part of our private selves that is most in need of purification is usually the beast."[44] While somewhat hypothetical it would not be inappropriate to note that there is a tendency for some to assume that the self was the original natural order as distinct from the view here held that the collective and cooperative nature of humans was dominant and natural.

In contrast to the ancients who had avoided the subject of the self, there was another difference to be found comparing Aurelius to Augustine since, "...unlike Augustine, who had at least to own up to his early sins to arrive at his purities, Aurelius was pure from the beginning."[45] Whereas the public determined the honor of their chosen hero, such as Achillius (or Aurelius), for Augustine the determination of any honor or virtue was established by the absolute of God's power over eternity. Paul, the conservative Hebrew and father of Christianity, made that point in defending belief in the resurrection. Easter, the only truly important day of remembrance for this faith, was and is marked by the joyful shout "Christ has risen." This, it could be argued, is the seminal issue for being a Christian, i.e., salvation from certain death. This placed a very different weight upon behavior, and gave Augustine, in an interestingly ironic manner, a more direct relativeness to our own world. The issue which had been one's duty and the honor of serving the Empire which was a public activity for the good of the community now shifted in the direction to a more personal commitment to the salvation of a singular soul. On the surface, while this was certainly more an individual issue, it was nevertheless an issue driven by the forces of divinity, of God's will, rather than the forces of a lone self and an inner drive. The situation simply shifted the determination from society to that of God. As Augustine makes clear, you cannot get to heaven without significant help, which he labeled as grace and that only comes from the Lord through the Church. Additionally, Augustine helped give shape to the new rules to guide human behavior in a Christian rather than Jewish world, not the ten commandments, of course, but rather the Seven Deadly Sins and Seven Cardinal Virtues. The sin that Augustine studied as the one that is most deadliest was that of pride that is common in all self-driven people. "And again, discussing the sin of pride: 'I cannot easily tell how far I am cleansed of that pollution, and I greatly fear my secret sins, which are known to your eyes, God, though not to mine. In other kinds of temptation I have some sort of ability to explore myself, but in this one, hardly any at all.' (*Confessions* X, 36) Passages of this sort are characteristic of Augustine, and illustrate a realistic appreciation of the difficulties of self-knowledge."[46]

While this may be antithetical to the modern notion of pride, Augustine did offer a hint of early modern ideas when he wrote his *Soliloquy*. This reminds us of an earlier contemporary of Descartes, William Shakespeare, who came much closer, even radically so, to the modern mental world in his transcendence of the simplistic Medieval morality plays of his day.[47] Another commentator observed further that since Augustine in his *De Trinitate* made it clear "that 'nothing can be more present to the mind than the mind itself,' asks rhetorically, 'what is so intimately known as the mind, which perceives that it itself exists and is that by which all other things are perceived?'" Again, Augustine is the tradition upon which Descartes would build,[48] but a tradition that will be greatly altered. The evidence is at best, of course, mixed since Augustine neither speaks nor thinks in modern terms. Another author, for example, would go so far as to argue that "it was Augustine who introduced the inwardness of radical reflexivity and bequeathed it to the Western tradition of thought."[49] How valid is this statement? It should be considered at best as very questionable, especially in using such modern terms as *reflexivity* let alone *radical* for in another passage on the subject there is a qualification offered that would lead to a more cautious conclusion: "…for Augustine, the path inward was only a step on the way upward."[50] To make one the self of selves, a modern viewpoint held by some, was clearly yet a foreign concept: God is at the center of Augustine's thoughts, and not Augustine, and with good reason if the point is eternal life. The intent makes for a serious distinction all too often missed. Here it is instructive to remind ourselves, again, of the differences of purpose between the Emperor Marcus Aurelius and Augustine, Bishop of Hippo. The development and growth of the Christian religion was revolutionary because it placed the burdens primarily on the single individual instead of exclusively the community as in the case of the Jewish and pre-Christian religions of the Empire. This must be considered, therefore, a notable if small step on the road toward the modern condition of a self-conscious individual.

It is true, however, that Augustine did occasionally write and develop his thoughts like Descartes from a first-person viewpoint[51] and that he had asked pointed questions such as 'what is the self?' and 'What am I' as if he was working in the context of a psychological autobiography. But it is clearly more than a little tenuous to offer, as one author did, an Augustine who had "…clearly recognized the power of childhood experience in the shaping of personality and identity; the uniqueness and loneliness, indeed the estrangement, of the self; the epigenetic nature of self; and the role of unconscious ideation and affect, which are, for the first time in the Western tradition, explicitly discussed."[52] To tie Augustine to modern psychological theory is more than a stretch, it is more like projection. True, this description will certainly find an application much later within the thinking of someone more like a Rousseau, but it is hardly appropriate for a classical figure like Augustine. If we disregard, for example, the modernity of some of these terms as *identity, uniqueness, loneliness, estrangement* and *unconscious*, we find that the author does agree that Augustine felt an incompleteness since he needed a 'relatedness,' which, in his case, is a relatedness to God. "'I am not at one complete until I am one with Thee,' says Augustine…"[53] Augustine did not write an early version of the unique art form of a confession[54] and did not pursue the burdens of the existential self alone in a world, alienated and estranged. There is no discussion of privacy or individuality except in the tradition of man's weakness, which Dante will document in a much more poetically creative manner some nine hundred years later.

Augustine was a child of God, through and through, and everything about him, from time and space to life and death were, in the end, the purview of God. The secularization of space, time or nature will take a great deal of time to evolve beyond Augustine before seeing the light of a thoughtful and reasoning day. The Socratic idea that "the unexamined life is not worth living," a philosophical position, was now moved transferred to role of God and one's own soul, the avoidance of damnation and the reward of eternal life. It was Quietus Tertullian (c.160–c.220 A.D.) who "…cleverly closes the *De Testimonio Animae* by harping on the fears of mankind. The soul will stand before God on the Day of Judgement." That judgement would determine one's relationship with God and eternity. "Will it have proclaimed God or disdained him, abominated demons or adored them, expected or disbelieved in the judgement to come, predicated the torments of hell or failed to escape them, will it have embraced or persecuted the name of Christians?" Needless to say the position for Tertullian was simple: "The prospect must terrify all who do not believe that the soul dies with the body."[55] This made for a very serious difference from the worlds of Aristotle, Plutarch and Aurelius whose intellectual framework did not include an after-life filled with the potential of damnation and pain. The issue now had become faith rather than reason. As we noted before, the famed line from Tertullian is that the truth is certain now not because it makes sense but because "it is certain because it is impossible."

Augustine, whose creations were intended to benefit future sinners, a synthetic culmination of so many of the earlier creative thinkers' works, offers a powerful force for the new Medieval world. It was through his own genius as the second founder of the Christian faith, and as one who clearly spoke for a reality beyond the classical Platonic idea or ideal, that he aided in making possible a new structure for a Christian reality, a new concept of what it meant to be 'real,' one that came to dominate Western thinking. This was especially true concerning the institutionalization of his ideas within the walls of the official theology of the church for centuries to come. This new view of a moral life and ontology, of course, had a new label: the immortal soul. It dwelled in our very own interior place where God could speak to us in the form of our conscience which would soon dominate organized Western Christian Europe. What makes this internalization, this inner soul, so distinct from the later work of Descartes is that it "…does, in a very real sense, place the moral sources within us.…An important power has been internalized."[56] And the emphasis by Augustine is "…the importance of the cogito, the central role of a proof of God's existence which starts from 'within,' from features of my own ideas, instead of starting from the external being, as we see [later] in the Thomistic proofs…"[57] There are certain assumptions within Augustine that anticipate "Descartes's internalism as a rejection, on philosophical grounds, of the appeal to outside authority."[58] Augustine sought certainty within by way of a divine presence while Descartes will seek certainty by way of his own reasoning. In both cases the key to certainty was an interior state, a guide born within for the former or developed within for the later. This turning to an interior self for certainty is at least one serious result of the changes that we have briefly mentioned: From the discovery of life's termination as a natural condition, to the creation of a language, spoken and then written, to abstract thought in the Hellenic world followed by the examined life and then the Stoic interior soul followed by the religious context of the Roman church. But the modern implication of this interior life would have to be suppressed by those who would follow in Augustine's footsteps, those who would become martyrs and saints for their faith while free from any pride. This altered the literature that followed Augustine from the forms of antiquity into a new modality, one known as hagiography, or the lives of the saints. The hagiographers of the Middle Ages would have to pay obeisance to Augustine's *Confessions*.[59] Moreover, the later Christian writings of lives, while having been somewhat influenced by the Augustinian model as they understood it, were not prepared to be as personal as his own writings. The early "...martyrs' rebirths, as described by the early hagiographers, remained conspicuously impersonal. Each Christian convert's greatest mission was to relinquish [their] individuality, abandon the selfness of soul, with the result that hagiographic 'lives' had as little in them of private life as the pagans.'"[60] Moreover these lives could be put into a categorical collection of lives as a group of saintly types, archetypes if you will, in order to preach a moral lesson on living in the now Holy Roman Empire. This had been demonstrated in the writings of the Benedictine monk Aelfric, coming somewhat later (c.955–1020 A.D.) and who was famous for his homilies, i.e. sermons, on the various lives of some twenty-five saints.[61] This was in some ways much more of a step away from the beginnings of the creation of the self and a step towards the creation of a collective spiritual archetype.

But the problem appears because the extension of the classical world into that of the Medieval Christian world occurred in such a manner that it made it possible for these Medieval citizens to accept their own way of living without granting much to their heritage except for the anticipation of the coming of the savior. Not only do we find a decline in literacy but we also find a decline of historical understanding or knowledge of cultural precedents. This was a serious break from the early beginnings of what little historical thinking the ancients had created. Hagiography reflected this ignorance of philosophical roots upon which the nascent Medieval world was being built: "Indeed, the ignorance of most early Christians about the great heritage of Greece and Rome was one of the conspicuous manifestations—almost as conspicuous as the fall of the Empire itself—of the cultural throwback we call the Dark Ages. Accordingly, the hagiographer's notion of the proper ingredients of a self—and how the truth of a self was to be laundered—was much more foreign to the virtue-notions of Plutarch and Aurelius than might first appear."[62] Whatever nascent sense of self that may have been developing, even if only minor remained too extreme a position for this Christian community. This position of the classical version of pride demonstrated in the works of Sutorius, Aurelius et al., was all too un-Christian and too secular to be applicable to these writers of the saintly as well as those given to martyrdom. Since the self is of so little consequence as to not apply to this early period, this raises a fundamental question regarding what in the evolving Medieval mind may have contributed to a new mentality, the necessary contributions for the self and of conscious development.

It is appropriate that Augustine acts as both a transition and a conduit for classical views. His (very important) addendum is the development of a certitude of an after-life with its accompanying fear of damnation. It is a realistic —if only theoretic—conclusion that fear might have been more applicable for most of those in this age than the simple hope of eternal life: we have seen that part of the psychology of Christianity is driven by the fear of damnation. Our understanding as well as our insights into this topic has been greatly aided by the work of the French scholar, Jean Delumeau, in his *Sin and Fear*. Contributing to one of today's more recent sub-disciplines of historiography, the history of mentalities, he offers a clear picture of the dilemma for those who were striving for some peace in an after life along with the fear of perdition if one dies in a state of sin. In the theology of the Roman Church, it is accepted that one can and will sin. But through God's infinite mercy offered by that grace created by God's sacrifice of "his only begotten son," it is possible for anyone, at anytime and with any sin to still be saved by way of Divine forgiveness and gain salvation. This is a legacy that becomes central in further expanding the historic role and the cultural power of the exclusive institution for salvation, the Church of Rome. And while life after death became the watchword for the new faith there was this new person concept of our conscience that was eventually tied to the sacrament of confession.

A central idea of importance for us in Delumeau's study was the extent of dependence now placed upon the role of the church for the exercise of our conscience and the cleansing of the soul. Augustine must be given the credit for beginning to explore what became very important for this topic: the internalization of sin.[63] With a personal conscience and a church offering forgiveness on behalf of the Lord through the sacrament of confession, it was made possible for a Medieval soul to still discover eternal bliss and avoid the massive fears inherent in the prospect of eternity in Tertullian's fire and brimstone. It is the legacy of the early church fathers such as Tertullian and Augustine that offered to the Western world this important new concept, conscience, a term that grew in popularity, particularly after the thirteenth century.

Because literacy was a rare phenomena in the Medieval world, it was the oral tradition of antiquity that would be continued and expanded in part through sermons. This became a nearly exclusionary practice and activity of the church, the only home for certainty from death and damnation. Orality was an ancient and fundamental form of exchange of information, and, as in the past, continued for the listeners in the Middle Ages who considered it reliable and trustworthy. What if what is written is unclear and in need of explanation, how can this be done without the writer there to do so? One of the reasons that Socrates, according to Plato, opposed writing was his complaint, "…that written text is basically unresponsive. If you ask a human being to explain his or her statement, you can get an explanation or at least an attempt at an explanation. If your ask a text, you get nothing except the same, often stupid, words that called for your question in the first place."[64] How can one trust something written? Who actually wrote it? Is it a lie? How can we know? If it is spoken and we can hear the speaker we at least know the speaker said what was said. Augustine, it should be remembered, was a rhetorician first, a writer second. There is no way to ensure that the written word was written by the claimed perpetrator of those words except by way of one's own ears. Moreover, what does a world dominated by agriculture need with written words? Literacy remained rare throughout the Medieval world. For the peasants there was a literal word, but not one as we would think of it today. The word that was seen and made concrete, much like a heard sermon would be 'seen,' appeared in the architecture of the Romanesque churches, followed in the High Middle Ages by the Gothic cathedrals and, more importantly in the sculptures that they could witness, admire and then hold fixed with their eyes. A statue of Christ, the risen, could be see on a tympanum for example and thus would be considered literally true. Literacy is not as common or even as natural as many may like to think even today and there still is very little or no need for literacy for so many in so many parts of the world. "The emblems of the mnemonic system gave to an orally delivered text a visual representation that Roman scripts without word division could not provide. The practice of speaking from notes or an outline, which emerged in the late Middle Ages, was totally absent from the Roman world."[65] A fair number of significant changes in literacy in the Western world, those that will seriously alter our perceptions, attitude and activities, only appeared when we passed beyond the end of the Middle Ages.

The crisis that had struck the remnants of the Roman Empire was of such proportion that one could wonder if the heritage of the great ancient civilizations that had preceded could have possibly vanished. Would there be continuity? Could there be a Western World without the creative gifts of these earlier civilizations' arts, their developments of languages and their histories? There was a very real potential for the beginnings of a Western heritage to stagnate and eventually disappear down the slippery slope of growing barbarism and illiteracy. Vandals, Visi-Goths, Franks, Osto-Goths and many other illiterate tribal peoples moved from the east into the remnants of what had been the most impressive culture and empire in all the ancient world. Yet a limited but indispensable salvation from the 'Darkness' (later called the Dark Ages) of those early years after Augustine finally arrived in the form of a political transformation within the congruence of two great contributions: one the genius of a people, the other the genius of a leader. These were the gifts that arrived from the linguistic abilities of the Irish monks, while the man, Charlemagne (747–814), created a new order which established the roots of a Western Europe. These two gifts would follow ancient traditions and bring a revitalization to the evolving languages of the West, especially those gifts of the art of writing, reading and learning, a gift of a new linguistic architecture.

When we think of the Italian Renaissance we think of a giant leap forward, especially into the basics of our modern Western society. We are far less likely to think such thoughts regarding the Carolingian Renaissance, or even think of it at all. This was a barbarous age when Charlemagne was crowned Holy Roman Emperor. It is difficult to imagine our world without the added significance of the Renaissance of the twelfth century and its ushering in the High Medieval world and its eventual offspring the Italian Renaissance without the small but significant changes that occurred during the Carolingian Renaissance.[66] Charlemagne was responsible for several significant changes, the first of which was the preservation and retention of what was known of our heritage. This occurred in part by way of the psychological and cultural ties to Roman antiquity. Until his time, the Papacy of Rome had retained a certain dependency upon the Eastern Empire, the power of Byzantine, for its security.

To have been crowned by the Pope as Holy Roman Emperor on Christmas day, 800 A.D., was a very important symbol but it was not enough to raise the flag of the moribund empire. With Charlemagne's reign, however, there was a difference of the first order. It was his policy to establish an empire built in part upon the strength of its bureaucracy, something which had been missing since the demise of ancient Rome. For the Emperor to rule, even if only a comparatively small empire, there was a need for permanence, something more than simply the power of a founding and charismatic personality. This had been demonstrated again and again when contrasting the success of the Roman Empire with the talents and forceful attempts of an Alexander the Great or later Clovis, neither of which had created an institutional basis that would live long after their own time. Something of the political creative forces of such leaders had to be retained after their death, and this was what the bureaucratic institutions could do. For the Holy Roman Emperor to rule, he must also govern, even in the most distant lands under his sway. For this, Charlemagne created the *missi dominici* as agents of the central government, to continually go into the hinterland, into the smallest villages, to make certain that the central laws of the Emperor and not just the whims of the local lords were being obeyed. Two agents were sent together to each location, one to be a check on the other, and to set up a review court, insuring that the laws of the palace were being exercised, while they also heard disputes as a court of law, demonstrating how much Charlemagne realized that creating a centralized government would be extremely difficult and replete with problems of loyalty. This was a first and very early step, however, in the creation of a central European government, or at least the basis for what would eventually be a French government, acting as a continental basis for political maturation. The Carolingian Renaissance may not appear as a gigantic event, but its impact has and continues to be rightly recognized. The key foundation for the growth of Western knowledge as well as any creative thinking and development of independent ideas is to first possess stable and reliable political and social institutions.

To govern as Holy Roman Emperor with an effective central government, however, meant there was another need that must also be filled if success was to be realized, a need that was satisfied in such a unique way without a break, that it led to modern languages and eventually self-conscious readers. That need was for a revitalization of literacy—specifically for those who governed—and a coherent future political and social order. The issue was then to fill the need for more competent literate agents of the crown. The lands that Charlemagne inherited from the Merovingians and acquired by conquest were dominated by Germanic tribes and illiteracy. What was needed and would be created was a school, a Palace School as it was known, that would train the future governors of this unique and disparate political entity. With so many languages brought together as various tribes gathered under the Emperor's wing and so little in the way of an agreed upon official language it could appear to be a formidable if not impossible situation. Even Charlemagne who appreciated the importance of literacy in particular and learning in general worked a lifetime attempting to learn how to write his own name. But if illiteracy was the norm on the continent and even more common than disorder, where would the basis for this educational transformation come from? Here the congruence of geography came to play in Ireland and the many nearby inaccessible islands where a tradition of learning had been kept alive within the protection of the isolated monasteries. It has been said with only something of small exaggeration that it was Ireland that saved Western culture. There can be no doubt that Western culture does owe a great deal to the literacy that had been preserved among the Irish monks.[67] It was those from the more remote areas who had preserved and expanded writing and grammar books and made the Palatine school at Charlemagne's court possible.[68]

One of the first serious contributions for the creation of a Western mentality after Augustine, therefore, would occur in the realm of literacy and, with it, the first Western renaissance. This was anything but an insignificant or minor event. First there is the creation of a modern written script which we still use, the Carolingian minuscule. Finding an agreed upon form of written letter style was serious work given the tower of babel that was the remnants of competing ancient styles. What was also needed was an architectural structure of language that would make it more accessible not only as a rhetorical tool but also readily readable. This also introduced, in addition to expanded clarity, the "dual alphabet" with the combination of capital letters and small letters in a single system. Thus from the creative act of preservation grew the creative act of innovation. Concrete language was taking on a form more familiar to the modern reader and thus more accurate in the eventual reflection of the modern mind.

Along with this new development of a Western Europe, a term that could be used with the arrival of Charlemagne, there still was an occasional thinker keeping the fires alive that would point to a latter High Medieval world of ideas, one building a foundation for later revolutionary thinkers. One early influence was that of Boetheus (c.475–524 A.D.), and, especially what would be of great aid for later thinkers, his *Consolation of Philosophy*. This work along with Augustine's continued the preservation and expansion of classical thought. And the working with this expanding language made possible another early example for knowledge that would be "…conceived of as the perfection or completion of the 'naming' process of thought. In ordinary thinking or speaking, as in perception, the participation was a half-conscious process." Language connotes knowledge, and the seventh century intellectual, John Scotus Erigena (c.810–c.877 A.D.) understood that "…knowledge was an actual union with the represented behind the representation. 'The knowledge of things that are, is the things…'"[69] he said quoting Dionysius. John Scotus knew what Boetheus knew, that the literacy and knowledge are hand-maidens.

It is these and writings by others that led to what flowed from the new Carolingian Renaissance where we discover another very significant creative development, one that is as important if not more so than conscience and one that would significant aid in building an interior self. This was arguably a most indispensable step towards the creation of an interior identity and thus a framework for our own modern consciousness: the appearance of silent reading, a skill that was rare if not unheard of, especially in the ancient world where there was little or no purpose for such a methodology. One can return to early ancient Athens and find warnings against the very act of reading and writing, again as Plato notes in the *Phaedrus* from a Socratic conclusion, writing that it "… is inhuman. It pretends to establish outside the mind what in reality can only be in the mind. Writing is simply a thing, a manufactured product, something inhuman you can manipulate. It is artificial."[70] The opposition to writing and reading centers upon the desire for an oral order of knowledge. Socrates could have no idea that the activities of the mind could and would extend from silent reading to the printing press.

There was a very famous historic confrontation at the end of the Roman era, one that further dramatizes the rarity of reading silently. This confrontation is recorded in Augustine's *Confessions* and dramatizes the strangeness of such an activity. "When he [St. Ambrose] read, his eyes scanned the page and his heart explored the meaning, but his voice was silent and his tongue was still." The significance of this cannot be overstated since Ambrose was Augustine's mentor. He further adds that: "All could approach him freely and it was not usual for visitors to be announced, so that often, when we came to see him, we found him reading like this in silence, for he never read aloud. We would sit there quietly, for no one had the heart to disturb him when he was so engrossed in study."[71] Silent reading was not a practice in the ancient Graeco-Roman world.

For a beginning of this remarkable development, there has been some very recent scholarship offering what occurred in early Roman writing and its limitations. "[P]aleographic evidence offers a partial explanation of why silent reading was an uncommon practice in classical antiquity. On the whole, the books of the ancient Romans were highly unsuited to private visual reading and study."[72] What posed a most clear and serious problem was "...the fact that the typical Roman book contained neither punctuation, distinction between upper- and lower-case letters, nor word separation."[73] Therefore, language built of words and ideas had yet to be made common place in the written text. This analysis has been given us by way of the fine study of silent reading by Paul Saenger who noted that: "Latin writing, which consisted of undivided rows of capital letters or their cursive equivalents, was entirely phonetic and had no ideographic value."[74] This was still an oral age and writing was still subordinate to the sound of the letters strung together, and is best exemplified by the dominance of poetry, specifically in theater where plays were sung as were the great epics from Homer to Virgil. Sound always precedes the concretization of written language. We find, therefore, that "...in ancient books verbal concepts were not represented by recognizable images, the Romans developed no clear conception of the word as a unit of meaning. Instead, Roman grammarians considered the letter and syllable to be basic to reading."[75] While this may appear a rather foreign concept it also contributes to making it more difficult to understand the mentality of those who read by deciphering a string of unbroken letters. The oral tradition, the need to speak what is read, to comprehend aurally, can be seen as a necessary requirement for someone reading any text in a traditional manner. As has been observed, "...the Roman reader, reading aloud to others or softly to himself, approached the text syllable by syllable in order to recover the words and sentences conveying the meaning of the text."[76] Besides being laborious it is obvious that it was also lacking anything that could be considered a flow of set sounds since there can be no heightened sense of importance of one set of letters or lines or words compared to others without a developed architecture that would make these delineations for the reader. This may be why someone the stature of Quintilian would have "...considered it a special facility of a scribe to be able to glance ahead as he read to see the end of a phrase before articulating it."[77] The very act of reading must have taken so much mental and physical effort that there may have been little if anything left for reflective thinking. As the author of these insights further elaborates: "For all Romans, the proper coordination of the eye and the tongue was an indispensable part of the activity of reading."[78] It is tempting to compare this kind of reading with that of music and poetry in that "...a written text was essentially a transcription which, like modern musical notation, became an intelligible message only when it was performed orally to others or to oneself."[79] Even today it is natural for young children learning how to read to do so in a group setting and to do so reading aloud.

There is an architecture of sound and there is an architecture of words; when both are tied together in harmony, one can find security in meaning and intent. Tying together the *Sermons* and the *Books* into a support system, for the state of immortality, required the word written, something more than the transience of a rhetorical language. To put ink to parchment is to become permanent. To become permanent is to become immortal and who is more immortal than Jesus of Nazarene and his words? The expression of rhetoric is represented by space while the written word acts as the columns of the temple. Words expressed only as sound can only represent space while the writing of concrete words is fixed. The Acropolis of Athens may be fixed but you can move around and through much of its space and thus alter the sense of fixity. Space changes as you alter your relationship with it because motion offers different aspects and implications. Together they can give shape to the abstraction of ideas. Limitations were common in the writings of ancient Rome:

> The difficulty of reading, writing, and revising Roman scripts without word separation made autograph composition slow and tedious work. Cicero, who strongly counseled the prior writing out of orations, himself employed a recording secretary, Tiros, to take down his orations in shorthand, a practice which clearly suggests that Cicero's speeches had not invariably been oral presentations of a previously handwritten text. When Cicero composed letters, he also used dictation, pronouncing each syllable separately to his scribe. Saint Augustine, who professed that certain religious thoughts were so private that they could not be confided to a scribe, nevertheless regularly used secretaries to record his sermons, letters, and biblical exegesis. Many other Roman authors including Caesar, Galba, and Pliny the Elder composed their works by dictating them to secretaries.[80]

Dictation had been the normative approach to putting thoughts into a permanent form. The scribe alone needed the knowledge of how the particular structure worked, the architecture of the language, and thus the demands for a more accessible written language would have to wait for the appropriate historic and creative circumstances. Arguably one of the most significant contributors to this change was St. Benedict, the man responsible for the rules of Benedictine monasteries, especially the rule of silence. With the 'word' expressed in the sacred text and used as a basis for sermons, the scripture became very important both in being read by specialists but also by being copied—especially with a growing population in need of guidance. While it is true that "…oral reading, dictation, and self-dictation were inherent features of ancient book culture, reference reading, which required more extensive ocular manipulation than narrative reading, was not entirely lacking in antiquity, particularly among the early Christians."[81] The cultural place for sacred Scripture was established by the ancient Jews since "…the exegesis of the Old Testament formed part of a body of oral rabbinical learning, predating the development of writing, which was not set down as the Talmud until late classical times."[82] While the ancient Jewish tradition was originally an oral one, the actual "…evolution of Christianity from a predominantly Hebraic to a predominantly Gentile religion left later Christians of non-Jewish ancestry unprepared to master the Bible in the traditional manner. To compose their sermons and letters, Gentile Christians who had been reared as pagans tended to go directly to the written text of Scripture, especially the text of the four Gospels."[83] All this made it that much more a matter of concern that the written word "…was important to Gentile Christians in a way in which it had never been to Jewish rabbis and rarely even to pagan literati." In other words, in order to "…facilitate consultation of the New Testament canon, Christians, at an early date, divided their texts into chapters and paragraphs, a custom not unknown to the textual tradition of the Torah but little exploited by the pagan classics. These divisions, although unstandardized, may well have aided Christian authors to peruse the Bible and find the passages of Scripture which they incorporated verbatim into their compositions."[84] What became important for the later Christian writers was established somewhere in the seventh century when "…in order to facilitate consultation, Christians at an early date favored the use of the codex text, whose frequently numbered leaves provided early reference points and whose margins afforded the possibility of notations to help the reader to find his place in the text." There also appeared at this time the separation of words, and "…in the seventh-century, a two-column format, which made it easier to find one's place in the text, became characteristic of the Christian codex book."[85] But there were several other factors that made reading more accessible and private, just as there were other reasons for the development of silence besides the rules of monasteries where specific rooms for copiest scribes to perform their holy deed had been created. These rooms would, in time, be referred to as "mumbling rooms." There, monks could be heard mumbling the words to be copied since even then the idea of having these words noted silently inside one's head was still too unusual an activity let alone a viable concept.

One of the more important reasons for this change was the idea of a personal or a 'private' relationship with God. "Saint Augustine, in the *Soliloquies*, clearly stated that certain thoughts intended for God were too private to be shared with a secretary."[86] This reminds us of Socrates' argument that writing destroys memory. Moreover, there had not been much of a drive for reading and writing until religious words took hold as seriously significant for an entire culture. The act of writing had to evolve into a form conducive for the development of silent reading in order for early modern literature and reading to evolve, and with it, birthing of an inner life. The first purpose of an agreed upon language for a given region was to organize its people under a single governance, whether it be the Church of Rome or the Empire. This created a paradox since what was being created was a readily acceptable collective language where an individual could eventually develop a personal and singular social and religious relationship. With the expansion of this fundamental change, not only would an inner self come to the surface but it would also, at the same time, add to social and political stability.

The earliest textual evidence for documentation of the practice of silent reading in the scriptorium dates mostly from the British Isles. It was in these relatively isolated lands that the creation of word-blocks as well as word divisions became increasingly common in Insular manuscripts. Moreover, in order to avoid censure, Irish monks would also write messages, silently, to each other in lieu of speaking out loud. From the British Isles to the continent, "…silence was compulsory in the monastic scriptoria on the continent at Tours in the ninth century, when texts there were also regularly being copied either in word-blocks or with word division." It was not until the late eleventh century, however, "…when the separation of words was universally practiced throughout France and silent copying of manuscripts was considered a normal part of a monastic life."[87] The time lag should not be surprising since such historic changes can and often do take a great deal of time before any meaningful impact can be seen. With this new activity, for example, performed at the Abbey of Saint Martin of Tournai, a visitor would "generally see a dozen young monks seated on chairs, silently writing at desks of careful and artistic design."[88] Somewhat later, in the twelfth century, "…Peter the Venerable praised Benedictine scribes who, without opening their mouths and violating the rule of silence, spread the word of God by copying texts. In this way, the silent scribe could speak through the voice of the Creator and murmur in the ear of the solitary servants of God."[89]

This is not to say, of course, that silent reading had become a clearly established norm at this early date, for as Paul Saenger has noted: "In spite of the clear impact of word division on the silent copying by scribes, all reading in the twelfth and early thirteenth centuries was clearly not silent. As Peter the Venerable's remarks suggest, outside the scriptorium reading was still oral in character. Most twelfth and thirteenth century miniatures continued to show people reading in groups."[90] Nevertheless, he also notes that:

> ...composition is not a silent process but one of oral self dictation. In a low voice, the author articulated to himself the phrases he composed as he set them down on wax tablets or in cursive writing on membrane codices which the Romans used as notebooks. If the author was preparing a speech, he was encouraged to memorize the oration by first writing and then reading and rereading it aloud to himself. Quintilian disapproved of quiet memorization because it encouraged the mind to wander.[91]

The interior mind, while slow to develop, would not only change monastic life but contribute to changes associated with other transformations and contribute to the creation of both a Renaissance and a Reformation set of radically new values, causing a dramatic alteration of our Western culture. The simpler ancient writing style of antiquity would not serve those significant transitional thinkers who would pursue new intellectual activities in the High Medieval world which had appeared by the time of the twelfth century. First there was trade that had begun to expand and with it villages growing into cities, where written records were needed as an aid for expanded governance, politically and economically. The singular event for Saenger was the necessary creation of a system of word separation in place of the more traditional running on of undifferentiated letters. Saenger's analysis is most clear in his major study although he states it also in an article where he suggested: "...word division began as an aid to oral reading, but, paradoxically, it provided the *sine qua non* for the silent copying of texts by Medieval scribes, The rule of Saint Benedict had set forth the ideal of silent labor, but early monastic scribes, like their pagan predecessors, had been forced by the undivided written lines to enunciate as they copied."[92] Silent reading is in some ways an accidental by-product of this facilitator. Additionally, this condition would only be tolerated by the Christian world as long as the 'Word' was spread throughout the world, for this was an evangelical religion and the 'Word' was their sword. What is most interesting here is that the new architectural forms from Gothic cathedrals to the newly formulated texts alter not only our views of culture and writing but also alter the availability of the changes that Saenger considers most important and which occurred, as so much did in the seventh century, when

> ...scribes began to divide lines of texts into word-blocks of ten to fifteen letters, Gospel books in particular were copied in such units to form texts of extremely short lines. Modern research in the psychology of reading has shown that a space of fifteen

characters constitutes the approximate physiological limit of the eye's ability to grasp a section of a text as a single visual limit. Texts that were written in blocks of fifteen letters or fewer, therefore, could be easily retained visually and copied without the enunciation and ensuing aural recall employed by scribes in antiquity. Placing spaces after every word made visual retention even easier. The eyes of the reader moved along a line of written text not in a steady progression but in jumps called saccades. While the eye focused on one section of text, peripheral or paravoleal vision prepared the eye for the section of text to be focused upon in the next saccade. Without word-blocks or word separation, saccades were more frequent and the amount of text which the eye could maintain within paravoleal vision was much reduced.[93]

The end result of this newfound ease was that, "…the author achieved a new sense of intimacy and privacy in his work."[94] What this offered was nothing less than the ability to creatively write some of the most significant and sophisticated works that would come to mark the High Medieval culture. For example, the depth and breath of the writings of Thomas Aquinas (1225–74), who many would suggest was arguably the most brilliant Christian theologian of his era and perhaps ever since, was dependant on the newer and more complex structures of written communication in order to examine implications of earlier Aristotlean assumptions. Again, according to Saenger, it was not monastic silence that pushed for these changes but rather "…the increasingly complex body of thought known as scholasticism that came to dominate education in the twelfth and early thirteenth centuries. Reading aloud, even for the reader, made the comprehension of complex ideas slow and difficult."[95] While scholasticism is a complex and difficult term with at least three distinct meanings, the one here to be noted was the ability to bring to faith a certain harmony with reason. The discovery of the brilliant thinking of authors such as Albert Magnus and Thomas Aquinas was that "…they could no longer formulate and organize their exceedingly complex thoughts within the limited space of wax tablets."[96] The traditional and simple system of the past no longer proved adequate, certainly not for Aquinas who is famed for his contribution of bringing together, beyond a harmony faith and reason, a method of teaching at the University of Paris which offered another definition for that form of Medieval scholasticism—an academic methodology. His impact is demonstrated in that he has become the official theologian of the Roman Catholic church in our own era.

This problem of writing and reading was recognized as early as the seventh-century when Isidore of Seville, "…remarked that reading in a loud voice interfered with comprehension, and he recommended that the tongue and lips be moved quietly."[97] Not moving the tongue or lips and making noise while reading was not an easy task and proved to make such an activity a slow process in comparison to the new methods of silent reading that were increasingly popular. Its appeal, after all, was that it was more efficient than traditional dictation, copying or oral reading of holy script and essays. With the creation of universities in the twelfth century Renaissance there were required ever increased reading speeds, comprehension and absorption in order to grasp more and more sophisticated ideas, whether dealing with the large and ever growing corpus of glosses on Scripture or the commentaries on canon law which were replacing letters and sermons as the literary genre of the day. That there was an increase in private reading did not mean the end of all dependency upon the oral tradition, however, for while it is true that "...private silent reading became more pervasive in the fourteenth and fifteenth centuries, public lectures continued to play an important role in Medieval university life." We must not assume that these changes affected a great number of people, for there was little recognition let alone participation in such changes. As Saenger points out:

> The transformation from an oral monastic culture to a visual scholastic one between the end of the twelfth and the beginning of the fourteenth centuries in the world of Latin letters had at first only a limited effect on lay society, particularly in northern Europe. Until the mid-fourteenth century, French kings and noblemen rarely read to themselves but were read to from manuscript books prepared especially for this purpose. When princes such as Saint Louis could read, they read aloud in small groups. In addition to liturgical texts, the literature read to princes consisted of chronicles, *chansons de geste*, romances, and the poetry of troubadours and *trouvères*. Most of these works were in verse and were intended for oral performances. Thirteenth-century prose compilations, such as the *Roman de Lancelot* and the *Histoire ancienne jusqu'à César*, were also composed to be read aloud. The nobleman was expected to listen to the feats of his predecessors or ancient worthies.[98]

The access to books was still as rare as were the books themselves. Even at the height of the High Medieval culture there were serious limits even among academicians. For example in "...thirteenth- and fourteenth-century Oxford and Cambridge Colleges, and at the Sorbonne and other Paris colleges, libraries were installed in central halls and were furnished with desks, lecterns, and benches where readers sat next to one another. Important reference books were chained to the lecterns so that they could always be consulted in the library."[99] Originally the student at a monastery had no access to books other than in the copy room until enough copies were made that would create an increased availability, and even then the "…technique of visual reading was essential for the comprehension of public lectures, for while professors read aloud from their autograph texts, students followed the lectures by silently reading from their own books, This was a change from the monastic schools of the early Middle Ages when one monk read aloud and others, without books, listened."[100]

In both quantity and quality the written word played a greater and more extensive role in Medieval thinking in general and scholasticism in particular than any writings of antiquity. "Because of the greater freedom it afforded to movements of the eye, silent reading favored the perusal and reference consultation of books."[101] By this time writers had made wide use of intricate symbols that were the direct ancestors of our modern footnotes which in turn aided the "…reader's eye in glancing back and forth between the text and the appropriate gloss."[102] And glosses, the addition of notes in the margin offered as clarification of some difficult passage of a work, continually increased as copiests expanded their understanding, literacy and insights regarding what was being copied. Glosses were a form of editing where the earlier copiest made notes in the margin. Oftentimes a later copiest would then put the gloss into the body since he would decide that it was too important to be not be in the text. He then would proceed to often add his own gloss for a later copiest to add to the body. Aside from corruption of the text, this led to a new case in writing, with the copiest and author achieving a sense of both intimacy and of privacy in his work. It was now possible for the author to work in solitude, without scribes or copiests cluttering their newly found private space. This is not to say there was an interest in privacy at this time for this is but a rhetorical way of pointing out what was a very early beginning. The writer or copiest would be "…personally able to manipulate drafts on separate quires and sheets. He could see his manuscript as a whole, develop internal relationships, and eliminate redundancies common to the dictated literature of the twelfth century. He could also, at his leisure, easily add supplements and revisions to his text at any point before forwarding it to a scriptorium for publication."[103] The depth of thought, the breadth of ideas, and the readability of texts reached new heights in the revolutionary and creative thinking that we associate with the great scholastic and artistic minds at the end of the Medieval world. Alighieri Dante (1265–1321), a poetic genius, in many ways was the culmination of this Christian Medieval transition. His poem, *The Divine Comedy*, an Italian vernacular epic masterpiece was probably meant to be read silently by the newly literate aristocratic class.[104]

In addition to the creative impact on the mentality of the scholars, thinkers and aristocrats, silent reading also introduced enough of an interior and private world that thoughts considered heretical at the time would find it easier to develop and spread. Authority, which had been the exclusive purveyance of the public institutions inherent in public lectures, readings, conversations and governance began to shift to that of individual conscience. This shift would, in time, contribute negatively on the traditional establishment of the church. An information revolution began to impact with the chained libraries and increased availability of books that could be copied so much more quickly in silence than in the monastic mumbling rooms. This resulted in a new kind of reader, a reader who was psychologically, 'emboldened' because the ability to read silently. Now the reader had

> ...placed the source of his curiosity completely under his personal control. In the oral world of the twelfth century, if one's intellectual speculations were heretical, they were subject to peer correction and control in the very act of their formulation and publication. Dictation and public *lectio*, in effect, buttressed theological and philosophical orthodoxy, Twelfth-century heresy had popular origins and reflected collective spiritual needs rather than individual intellectual curiosity. The teachings of the heretics such as the Cathars were not based on any corpus of forbidden writings but were communicated orally.[105]

The world of orthodoxy was no longer a secure place. Silent reading was not only an act of privacy but also a potential for undermining the authority of the Church of Rome. "Reading with the eyes alone and written composition removed the individual's thoughts from the sanctions of the group and fostered the milieu which the new university heresies of the thirteenth and fourteenth centuries developed. These heresies were spread by the privately read *tractatus*, which increasingly replaced the orally presented *quodlibet* and *lectura* as the preferred vehicle of intellectual expression."[106]

The power of the written word was also a power dependent upon interpretation, and as one recedes into something of a private life of reading they also enter the opportunity to find their own religious frame of reference, their own interpretations. This did not necessarily mean that only heretical thoughts would follow, however. On the contrary, there is evidence enough that this practice could also keep people in line with their spiritual commitments.

> Gerhard Groote looked upon private visual reading as the highest form of spiritual exercise. Sermons composed by the learned were regarded as an inferior substitute for the illiterate. The very wanderings of the mind which had made silent study

suspect to the ancients endeared it to the adherents of the *Devotio moderna*. Wanderings of the mind when accompanied by the reading of Scripture were first steps toward mystical spiritual experience. It was in his private reading that Gerhard Groote, through free association, discovered the hidden and mystical meaning of the Bible. The light of Divine Radiance visited Florentius Radewen while reading the Bible. Thomas à Kempis recommended isolated silent reading, meditation, and prayer as the means of achieving an intimacy with the Divine which was only to be found hidden within oneself.[107]

The power of the collective while still great was finally finding the first chinks in its armor. There was no doubt that as the High Medieval world evolved, it did so with a growing religious revival, one that may have been aided significantly by both the new and more readily availability of literature and ideas. Thomas à Kempis (1379–1471) wrote *The Imitation of Christ*, which was very popular with the layman as well as the clergy.[108] Problems for traditional religious authority as well a potential for political implications was clearly evident, however, with the arrival of the Lollards of the fourteenth century in England and it became a crime of heresy to possess any Lollard writings. As the fourteenth-century ended, the "…theologian Alphonse de Spina, in the *Fortitudenum Fidei*, attributed the origin of heresy to the private and unsupervised reading of Scripture."[109] While the printing press will play an important role in the rise of alternate views of theology, it wasn't alone in breaking the traditional monopolistic control. It is not simply having alternate ideas, however, since heresy had always been a problem from the earliest days of the church and is exemplified in the Church's creation of the Nicene Creed (325 A.D.). The threat of an inner self and an inner conscience will prove to be a far greater threat to the Roman Church, curia and local clergy than that from alternative interpretations of orthodoxy, at least in the long run. When we reflect on the later writings of Descartes and Locke we do well to remember that they were the beneficiaries of the varied aspects of this new form of reading and writing.

If it has been a long difficult road to get observers to appreciate what one scholar has called "The Unacknowledged Revolution."[110] For all the importance placed on the significance of the printing press in encouraging personal instead of collective readings and its accompanying heresy with the rise of the Protestant Reformation, the expansion of a personal and inner relationship with the holy writ should not be ignored. From the *Devotio moderna* on the edges of the official church to the Lollards well outside, silent reading played a significant role.[111] It may have also been in part the practice of silent reading that contributed to the earliest sense of isolation, alienation and uncertainty.[112]

> Isolated private reading and prayer as the pathway to salvation, in turn, may have fostered insecurities about the worthiness of each individual's faith and devotion and thereby stimulated zeal for religious reform. Indeed, the reformed mendicant orders found their strongest supporters among the urban merchant families and the aristocratic families who silently read vernacular religious manuscript books. Three generations later, these same families would become the supporters of John Calvin. On the eve of the Protestant Reformation, the mode of the dissemination of ideas had been so revolutionized that laymen, like university schoolmen, could formulate dissenting views in private and communicate them in secret.[113]

The "…printing press played an important role in the ultimate triumph of Protestantism, but the formulation of reformist religious and political ideas and the receptivity of Europe's elite to making private judgments on matters of conscience owed much to a long evolution, beginning in the twelfth century and culminating in the Fifteenth-Century, in the manner in which men read and wrote."[114] Obviously the greater number of choices one can make regarding intellectual conclusions the larger the opportunity for diversity.

This diversity, we will see later, may have been a factor in Descartes' desire to establish a certainty as to what should be labeled existence and Locke's attempt to establish what is meant by personal identity. Certainly the increased climate of questioning in this new environment of silent reading created a potential for unique intellectual stimulation, raising the questions that especially grew out of the extensive use of the confessional as the church entered the Renaissance and Reformation. The development of an interior conscience may have also contributed to the growth of an anti-cleric and anti-confessional attitude among Protestants who defended their right to possess a more personal conscience, an interior space, with their own understanding of God. With a growing urban and merchant society of tradesmen, with increased availability of money and the opportunities to become increasingly independent and isolated, such a movement could only expand given the limited defenses that the Church could marshal. Moreover, the growing complexity with the beginning of a High Medieval world, a necessary prerequisite for the great changes of the following centuries, placed more pressures on the church and her attempts to hold onto exclusive authority, i.e., orthodoxy. For example, the understanding of space was being altered not only in the format of letters and words but in the development of the great cathedrals of the Gothic era. What was to be called the "up-rush of stone" of the 140-foot high nave of these cathedrals was also the space that offered a sense of divine presence rather than a cocoon to hide seen in the smaller and darker Romanesque churches. Space literally expanded as the Medieval cathedrals grew in popularity. These cathedrals were God's space in a universe that was God's place, all belonging to God's time. Today, even the non-religious must be impressed with what many would consider a divine presence when entering a Gothic cathedral such as that of Chartres, for the experience is one that is transcendent even for a rational and empirical atheist.[115]

The Gothic cathedral is but one innovation of this twelfth century Renaissance since cathedrals were a response to the new phenomenon of the expansion of cities which was itself a response to the serious growth of trade and new economics, hence the impact of the reintroduction of money. Money, cities, growth of trade, Gothic cathedrals, the increased appearance of the vernacular along with the creation of the mendicants (the Fourth Lateran Council, 1214 A.D.), a preaching order of clergy that was not cloistered like traditional monks but created as 'shock troops' for new communities that were without churches, were hand-maidens to change in general and growing literacy specifically. The High Middle Ages also included the universities at Paris, Oxford and Bologna in order to satisfy the rising tide of literacy, learning and theology that were by-products of a major population expansion.

We should remember that to speak of a Dark Ages is somewhat inaccurate. To say the twelfth century Renaissance and its legacy was considerably greater in breadth and depth than that of the Carolingian would have to be considered an understatement. But if the cathedral represented God's place and the universe, His space, the Medieval soul was still in a quandary as to what would happen when they would die, i.e., what would be their place in God's time? This certainly was not a world dominated by the inner voices of an individual pursuing the personal self, rather, the forces of divine presence were the crux of faith and the final arbiter in all decisions. And in this faith there was only mitigation since for even the most devout, the additional unknown, the fear of whether they would end in hell rather than heaven still loomed. It was this conundrum that one of the greatest of all popes, Innocent III (1160-1216), would confront if in only a limited way at the Fourth Lateran Council offering the rule that would institutionalize another form of interiorization to run parallel to silent reading, a means of matching the human condition with divine space—the institutionalization of one's own conscience—the annual confession.

Space as was demonstrated by the Gothic cathedrals was a divine space, psychologically. Time, as the word was partially used, meant time in 'The Word,' God's word, which naturally implied that language itself was divinely inspired. It was a sacred act to write and it seemed logical for monks to be allowed the holy role of scribes. Upon entering the cathedral, you 'knew' God for you participated in 'His' space. But with trade, money and the rise of cities as trading centers, a new space was appearing, a space that was the first step that moved the Western world more to a set of secularized values, human places for those money changers returning with an ever greater presence. There were, additionally, the Crusades starting in the eleventh century which were the result of a growing population, with extra sons born to the nobility who could not inherit land set aside for the eldest. The ownership of land became an issue and in some cases even a crisis, notwithstanding the First Crusade which was concerned with the spiritual obligatory needs of the penitent warriors; this was the only one of the crusades that was not concerned mostly with acquiring feudal kingdoms. Add to this the growing popularity of universities, vernacular literature, glosses and new techniques of coping, and we find the sacred mumbling rooms losing their exclusionary hold on the mentality of the late Medieval mind. The increased technique here as well as with the new 'sciences' from such thinkers as a Roger Bacon and the brilliance of such others as William of Ockham and Thomas Aquinas aided in a transformation that would explode first, with the Italian Renaissance then followed in time by the Northen Renaissance. While a more secular view may have only been on the other side of the door of what was then assumed to be reality, it nevertheless proved to be only a matter of time for a small crack to develop into an opening. True, there remained the world of a Medieval normative, of group readings which could be found in the court of Eleanor of Aquitaine where courtly love evolved and the guide book by Andreas Capellanus, *De amore* (*The Book of the Courtier*) of the late twelfth century found an harmonious audience.[116] Both the lack of literacy and the need to associate in and with groups compelled this idea of a collection of noble women at the court of Eleanor to spend leisure time listening to the tales of adventure and courtly love and to seek to establish a more civilized pattern of social behavior. The idea of the collective still reigned supreme over the individual. The seeds of serious change were being planted but any new set of assumptions would take a great deal of time before any impact would be seen. Signs of the first appearance of private bedrooms for the prosperous, for example, were just beginning to make some headway.

This was the time of a political order associated with feudalism where the experience of death was great enough that burial rituals as we enter the High Medieval World were being concretized, especially for the nobles that had acquired power out of the Carolingian changes. Death was never far from the minds and rituals for those important enough to have a tomb to mark their presence was of central concern. Many of these tombs, especially in the Gothic cathedrals, were and are very impressive.

> Needless to say, they had a different attitude toward death than we do today. For the vast majority of us in the modern Western world, it would be utterly inconceivable to pay for the privilege of having ourselves carved on our memorials (should we choose to have one) as a desiccated, rotting corpse. Why bury the dead, only to have the tomb throw up our remains in all their hideous, gruesome deformity for all to see? Even in the Middle Ages, the thirteenth-century theologian St. Thomas Aquinas asserted that burial is 'for the sake of the living, lest their eyes be revolted by the disfigurement of the corpse.' But unlike medieval men and women, we in the modern West studiously avoid all unpleasant reminders of death. [117]

Yes, there appeared to be more of a willingness to accept the realities of death and thus face it more readily than many, even today. The reason for this can be anything from the belief in an afterlife stronger than the reality of one's personal mortality to general acceptance of necessity. Whatever the reasons, with the Great Plague of the mid-fourteenth century killing perhaps more than half western Europe's population and the 100 Years' War from the middle of the same century until the middle of the following, death was more a normal fact of existence that demanded acquiescence. As one scholar of the subject has noted: "From illuminations and other depictions of the Fourth Rider of the Apocalypse to portrayals of interactions between death and man, to the enshrinement of cadavers in the transi-tombs, these expressions of mortality are all closely dependent on each other."[118] The resurrection of the spirit was sought until the later Medieval years when the body was beginning to be assumed to somehow also be able to rise, at least by the time of 1424–1425 when the Archbishop Henry Chichele, English diplomat and friend of Henry V had the first double tomb made as his resting place.[119] The desire for salvation, redemption and eternal life can be seen in these double tombs where the lower sculpture renders the deceased as a rotting corpse while the upper rendering has the same figure in all its youthful glory. Even the body should be able to somehow defeat the certainty of death. As the scholar quoted above further observes:

...the tomb proclaims a hope in the resurrection of the body at the Apocalypse, not just a morbid meditation on the theme of corruption and decay. In this dialogue between two bodies, one of the deceased as a living, resplendent effigy, and the other as a rotting, naked corpse, one is tempted to 'read' only downward, from the effigy to the cadaver, and see the end of man as nothing but 'dust, worms, vile flesh.' But for medieval patrons like Chichele, death was not the end. Rather, it was the beginning, the gateway to a better world. Death, who triumphs as the Fourth Rider of the Apocalypse, now at the Last Judgment bows down in defeat before the triumph of the resurrected body. We must read upward in the two-tiered tombs, not to a *representacion du vif* (representation of life), but to a *represenatcion de l'apres-vif* (representation of the afterlife). The upper effigy is a pristine body resurrected out of the mere skin and bones lying underneath. Thus, as Chichele read down his tomb, he viewed his humility before God: the corruption and decay that would come upon all earthly status and goods. But when he read back up, he saw his reward: his restored body, around thirty years of age, dressed in his pontifical vestments, rising up like a phoenix out of his ashes below. Two angel supporters on either side of his head, and angels bearing heraldic shields in the canopy, escort him upwards to the heavenly host, to rejoin his beloved king.[120]

How to take advantage of this sculptured reality was simple—head to the confessional.

The confessional had not been given a serious and consistent role as a sacrament within the church until Innocent III. With annual confession and communion made mandatory, the role of the clergy became increasingly powerful since it was the members of the cloth that would guide you into your conscience thus aiding both the remembering and admitting of sins, a necessary act for salvation. The church could cure you of your spiritual disease and remove the fear of damnation if you could only bring to the fore through the power of your conscience, the sources of your committed sins.[121] Conscience, the precursor and father of consciousness, now becomes a central power of the church and later the hated enemy of the Protestants. These beginnings of a transformed language, along with silent reading and a more personal relation with the word, while inherently significant for the birth of a modern self, as well individuality and the development of a self-consciousness, was only that —no more than a beginning. The idea of privacy was yet relatively unknown, except in the act of reading. For even in the great houses and palaces in the cold of winter the custom had been for all members, including animals, to sleep together in the great room with the master fire-place. Such fundamental functions as sex or defecation which we think of as being extremely private and personal were, in fact, still not private acts. Even students in the fourteenth century at Oxford University when taking an evening walk should never be seen doing so alone, since "...walks should be taken with others, never alone."[122] It is not surprising, therefore, that privacy, a handmaiden to individuality, has proven to be an historically late concept not yet to appear until the establishment of a more modern sensibility. The end of the Medieval world was more in tune to antiquity in so many fundamental ways and was still a stranger to our modern psyche. Hints were only beginning to appear by the fourteenth century.

The modern mentality that we now possess began during the seventeenth century, the time that consciousness, began. As must be reiterated, any discussion of either the development of the term or activity of consciousness must also note the importance of the development of a sense of self as well one's individuality as active and necessary corollaries. Introspective capacity would have to wait for a more modern mind to develop. There is some general agreement that the Renaissance played a key role in the early stages of this transformation, from the changes of a community-driven psychological framework to one that began to be increasingly more personal. And notwithstanding the beginnings of some sense of individuality in the Renaissance—that which Burckhardt described—will be shown to apply more to late nineteenth century German society within which he lived than to the much earlier Italian Renaissance. The influences that did contribute to any limited sense of an early stage of individuality has and is increasingly being well-documented. The key for the reader is to remember that all the changes that include the language we use and the meaning intended, move very slowly into our own age where we can bear witness to a significant revolution in mental processes.

In the world of letters, the Renaissance humanists will continue to make the serious contributions that have increased our understanding of syntax and meaning. Here, "...the scribe's most original contribution was the use of the parenthesis, a mark specifically employed to give a graphic representation of the aside..." The ancients of course had no need for such punctuation.[123] When they read Cicero, they read him aloud. Saenger makes very clear in his *Space Between Words* that not only is there a massive significance in word separation for the creation of silent reading but he also offers a detailed discussion of the use of various punctuations.[124] In addition, another scholar on this subject has offered a relative aspect of the world of punctuation and silent reading when he stated that:

Punctuation remained unreliable, but these early devices no doubt assisted the progress of silent reading. By the end of the sixth century, Saint Isaac of Syria was able to describe the benefits of the method: 'I practise silence, that the verses of my readings and prayers should fill me with delight. And when the pleasure of understanding them silences my tongue, then, as in a dream, I enter a state when my senses and thoughts are concentrated. Then, when with prolonging of this silence the turmoil of memories is stilled in my heart, ceaseless waves of joy are sent me by inner thoughts, beyond expectation suddenly arising to delight my heart.' [125]

If we move further into what is referred to as the early modern world, this phenomena of the parenthesis became very significant, specifically by way of the writers associated with fifteenth century humanist and their texts, further permitting the private silent reader to recreate a vicariously oral experience. This invention of the parenthesis spread quickly throughout Italy, and at the end of the fifteenth century it was one of the humanistic innovations in graphic language which was most readily received in northern Europe.[126] When it was used in scholastic texts, it could develop nuances which had no direct equivalent of the rhetorical.[127]

But for all of the Renaissance contributions to the interior voice of the self, the Reformation will be equally remembered for placing the issue of our relation to God on an even a more personal basis, one drawn from personal readings of the Word that made it possible for one to worship their God without doing so exclusively in public. The Roman church began losing its monopolistic institutional control as a gate keeper to the Lord. If you could read, you could know the word, thus having a direct link to God. One need not confess to a cleric to open one's soul to heaven; read His word and speak your conscience directly to Him without the aid of a middle man. In time most Christians could put the Bible between them and God and even support a private relationship since no one else could hear your heart, or your mind for that matter, when reading the sacred text.

There are other serious physical and psychological changes that will have to be confronted, however, before we can understand the massive alterations that make possible the Renaissance, Reformation and Scientific Revolutions that allow the doors to open enough for Descartes and consciousness to enter.

II

ENTRANCE INTO EARLY MODERN EUROPE

CHAPTER THREE

THE RENAISSANCE: ALTERED SPACE AND TIME

Petrarca's contribution to the forming of the mind of modern man can hardly be overestimated.[1]

FROM RE-BIRTH TO REFORM

The new geography of the age of discovery, the economics of mercantile trade, the governance of sovereign states, reflective arts of perspective, independent city-states, the newly established political independence from the Roman Catholic Church, the recent appearance of vernacular and the printing press, increased literacy and silent reading were some of the many changes that impacted the beginnings of the Italian Renaissance.

This transformation from a classical and medieval psychological orientation to that of the early modern was gradual and remarkable. There was a time not long ago when the argument was made suggesting that historic events occurred because of "Great Men" who make history. This idea, associated with the Victorian writer Thomas Carlyle, was one of the earliest precursors advocating the modern cult of personality that dominates a great deal of today's popular explanation of historic change. This is a simplistic explanation because historians know it is first and foremost circumstances that demand and create opportunity for leadership, if and when it can be found; otherwise, as it is in most cases, societies simply keep fumbling along. Historic significance does not result, moreover, from a unique and specialized divine power that intervenes in our daily life, a position generally held by the pre-modern mind. History is simply marked by change if nothing else, much like music, for it has the nature of the rhythm of a given time, not unlike the creation of a personal memory, an interior rhythm. You can read a Renaissance text, for example, Machiavelli, and also learn something of his world as well as deducing something of the issues he confronts. The creations of historians are narratives that demand loyalty to all pertinent facts as well as offering evidence and documented sources when reaching any conclusions or offering any hypothesis. The problem is that varied occurrences at any given time are often collectively unintentional and undifferentiated, often random pieces left for the historian to organize and construct. This can often appear to be a massive task. Trapped by this certainty of uncertainty, the historian is left to shape meandering events and peoples into something of a coherent whole.

The Italian Renaissance is, in retrospect, not what was necessarily experienced by the participants. This is one of the reasons that writing history is primarily a matter of re-construction which makes the writing and interpretation resemble a creative act and should not to confused with a simple regurgitation of chronological data. This activity has many limitations all of which enlarge the challenge for the researcher. The historian's advantage, however, is also the historian's disadvantage. It is an advantage to not be personally and subjectively involved in those issues of the period studied, without any vested interest in a particular position and therefore potentially be able to offer more objective conclusions. On the other hand, to not be a party of the events and people means to not have had any close or intimate contact with the subject and thus inherently it will lack, at least to some extent, a subjective communion that only a contemporary of the period could possess.

If history is the study of a particular time and the processes of a particular set of dynamics and changes appropriate to that particular era, then its modern aspect can first be found in the Italian Renaissance. In this regard, the most significant discovery of the Renaissance would have to be the discovery of different historic cultures; i.e., the discovery of unique, distinct historic periods in the Western world, prior to the Renaissance. The writers of the Renaissance began to offer a new and altered perspective in the way we look at our past, our lives and the universe that we live in. The beginning of the early modern world was one with a constant increase in more pluralistic views of existence. The West was beginning to put its toe into the doorway of a more open society with an increased although limited freedom, a world with hints of consciousness. There can be no arrival of privacy, self, individual or consciousness in our world without this series of changes in the north and south that characterize the Renaissance and the subsequent and overlapping Reformation. This story of the appearance and early beginnings of freedom and primitive expressions of a self proves to be complex and heady.

The Renaissance and Reformation are particularly difficult historical periods for a variety of complex reasons. The earlier southern Italian Renaissance, a massive transformation, stands alone as a historical event and has offered interesting difficulties in interpretation. The very subject of the Renaissance involves more than any one event and is of such a proportion that it stands alone. Modern historiography can itself be traced as part of that studied; the problem of a subjective transformation being objectively examined. Additionally, the Reformation is equally complicated—given modern prejudices—for historians to clarify. However, the significance of these two dynamic periods makes the understanding of their key ingredients seminal since they specifically relate to the foundations for the modern mind. In other words, components of the psychological complexity of our world begin in the fifteenth through seventeenth centuries.

One of the more significant results has been a transformation of our sense of space and time. In the Medieval world, God was always and everywhere; all space and time was under His omnipotence, omnipresence and omniscience. His presence was clearly established in the concretely fixed churches, cathedrals and heavens which made Him visual by way of His guidance of the hands of artisans and craftsman who were thus able to produce fine art. After all, God dictated and thus controlled the word along with space and time. Divine presence would remain dominant in somewhat altered forms with the Catholic Reformation, the Protestant Reformation and the Counter-Reformation. But beyond every day living, serious thinkers would begin developing new and revolutionary attitudes outside this tradition. The changes that did take place would alter the landscape of the relationships of God, man and nature in such a way that a relatively secular world of new economics, politics and, most importantly, the Scientific Revolution, would be given an early but solid foundation.

The development of the Renaissance and its new sense of time can be highlighted with a contrast between the writings and thought of two contemporary giants: the epic poet Dante Alighieri (1265–1321) and the creative writings of his younger contemporary, Francesco Petrach (1304–1374). They were both citizens of Florence where the first seeds of the Italian Renaissance began to take root. Dante represented the culmination of the Medieval world much as Augustine had done for the Classical. By contributing to the creation of a psychology of sin and virtue, a study of sinners and their place in his contrived underworld he continued the tradition of divinely-driven universe. Those souls confined within Dante's *The Inferno*, the first of the three parts of his epic, only reinforced for some, the sense of despair that some could still feel, notwithstanding the principle of salvation, the 'Christ has risen' syndrome. His hierachalized levels of Hell where he placed very specific and well-known historic figures, including a Pope, which only made the picture that much more bleak and certain for those who would not appropriately follow their church doctrine and their conscience and properly participate in the confessional, at least according to the creative ideas of Dante. The varied sins and their respective punishments were, as one would be inclined to agree even today, a frightening tableau for believers. It was a literate poem and a poetic continuum rooted in antiquity adding to his own contemporary world with the only real difference being the arrival of Christ. For the great majority of people, the illiterate peasants, this book would of course mean very little; after all, their fundamental fears were simply of daily survival, especially during the Great Plague. However, as an abstraction of eternity, this picture of pain versus bliss did have a great impact on the powerful and the literate. This was, after all, a unique project: it was written in the Italian vernacular, a beginning for the Italian literati. But it was also appropriate to the age since it was written, as a typical Medieval work, as an allegorical poem rather than as a literal narrative. It also qualifies as an epic, great enough to be placed along side those of Homer, Virgil and the later Goethe, arguably one of the greatest masterpieces of all times.

The High Medieval world was one with high art, great masterpieces and historically significant intellectual transformations from scholasticism to both great poetry and a beginning of a reconsideration of early classical science. But the people portrayed in these transformations, even if they are literary figures from the likes of Tristan and Isolde to those in the *Chansons de gestes*, were still more archetypes than unique flesh and blood figures. Dante was interested in the stereotypical traditions of sin from the avaricious to the prideful, rather than strong-willed independent selves. The seven deadly sins and the seven cardinal virtues dominated his thinking. It remained in this realm of the classical style as a study not of real people but rather a study of sinful acts, the perpetrators of those acts, now also to be known as vices. Moreover, rather than speaking in the present or future tense it tended to be trapped by actions of the past but not as a work in recognition of a unique historical heritage. Like all great epics it possessed doors, but only those that were closed. Writing of the archetypal rather than a very unique and specific individual was common even to that which was somewhat more modern seen in Geoffrey Chaucer's *Canterbury Tales* (1397–1400) which clearly demonstrate this archetypal characterization. Chaucer, also writing in the vernacular—early English—did offer a great many more social 'types' than had ever been seen in the earlier days of the High Middle Ages. But it is also true that the context of the work, although unquestionably a masterpiece, still had most of the characteristics of a medieval story rather than that of the individual living a singular life, since the plot centered on a journey that was a holy pilgrimage. The power of the singular which was hinted at in some of Augustine's writings was still too foreign a concept to explore until we enter the High Renaissance. It should be observed, as a counterbalance, that Dante's work, and even more so Chaucer's, did go beyond the Medieval world in their use of a vernacular mode. As both a part and a culmination of what went before, the genius of Dante did travel beyond his own culture, for his writings and political views reveal someone on the cutting edge of the world he lived in and the political conflicts that existed between the Roman Church and Holy Roman Empire, a conflict where the secular will eventually be victorious, a position he himself anticipates.

Participating in the political conflicts of the Florentine parties of Guelfs and Ghiblines, Dante was enough of a late medieval Florentine political actor to imply support for a future that was just in its infancy, for it was the secular politics of Florence that was the new wave of political reality that would replace the political power of the Church. Dante has occasionally been considered a man representing that which was to come—the Renaissance even while using the medieval/scholastic form of poetry. It is in this one sense that he was something of a transitional figure. When he places himself on the journey, a pilgrim throughout the Divine Comedy, traveling through Hades, he is led not by a medieval saint but by the Classical genius, Virgil. Reminding us of Augustine, he records honestly his own sins, including the ultimate of deadly sins, the sin of pride. But this component of a personal identity hardly should be compared to modern individuality since this is a Christian rather than a personal psychological journey. Very few scholars would suggest that this should be considered even a Renaissance piece. Every part of this epic masterpiece, was a typical medieval allegory to be decoded. Virgil is Virgil, true enough, but he also represents the original trip to the underworld which appeared in the Aeneid, a world of the Roman Empire (pre-Italian), and he, like Dante was a poet. Here is Dante's sin of pride, for he is comparing himself to Virgil who he uses less as a classical figure and more because he is a Latin poet, not unlike Dante. One could go on with at least four levels of meaning of hell, purgatory, heaven and earth and its various figures. The point is that the work does not speak to us and our world. It speaks to the brilliance of the High Medieval scholastic mind and, of course, the role of sin in the very value structure of that world, all allegorical. It mattered not if he spoke of ancients or medieval, sin was the issue: "…we only have to think of the entirely different picture of the past in the Divine Comedy, where Dante usually couples ancient and mediaeval figures in his representation of the various vices and virtues of man."[2]

This story of an historic transformation within the confines of the Italian Renaissance is the story of a completely new perspective regarding both our sense of space and of time, and it is here with the work of Petrarch that the building of modernity finds its foundations. When we speak of time and space of Petrarch it is more as a matter of cultural perceptions rather than the context of a more technical or scientific approach. People's views of time will historically change but few will recognize that change because it is based on assumptions rather than cognitive decisions.[3] "Whatever may have been the assumptions of the Italian peasants of this period, the evidence from the towns suggests that much more precise attitudes to time were widespread, like the mechanical clocks which both expressed these new attitudes and encouraged them. From the late fourteenth century, mechanical clocks came into use; a famous one was constructed at Padua to the design of Giovanni Dondi, a physician-astronomer who was a friend of Petrarch, and completed in 1364."[4] That the mechanical clock should be used in this manner, almost as a necessary natural element in such a short time since its creation, demonstrates the ease that this culture had in adjusting to a new convenience. The first clocks arrived at the time of the Great Plague, mid-fourteenth century, in part because there were too few peasants and thus too few bell ringers to let people know of time for rising, prayer, lunch and the ending of the day. "About 1450, a clock was made for the town hall at Bologna; in 1478, another for the Castello Sforzesco in Milan; in 1499, another for Piazzo San Marco in Venice, and so on. By the late fifteenth century, portable clocks were coming in."[5] All this led to a more mechanical view of time and space, and therefore,

> There is an obvious parallel between the new conception of time and the new conception of space; both came to be seen as precisely measurable. Mechanical clocks and pictorial perspective were developed in the same culture, and Brunelleschi was interested in both. The paintings of Uccello and Piero della Francesca (who wrote a treatise on mathematics) are the work of men interested in precise measurement working for a public with similar interests. Fifteenth-century narrative paintings are located in a more precise space and time than their medieval analogues.[6]

Whether cultural or mechanical, the changes in our understanding of space and of time had altered our perceptions of our world and of ourselves. Time in this cultural context becomes the phenomenon of history in a public context. Space, on the other hand, is a term that can be best correlated with language, in particular and with the written word, a literacy which, in a sense, expands the horizon of our sense of space. One way to observe what is being addressed here is to remind ourselves that a word is a word only because of its history, i.e., its consistency through time. It is the consistency of the sounds to fixed meaning, the historic repetition of that sound which always implies a specific meaning that makes language work. As has been noted, Jerry is Jerry is Jerry and in this the clan or tribe can keep 'Jerry' for as long as there is some memory and until eventual writing makes it more concrete. When the consistent historic sound becomes fixed in a written form, language acquires a new and meaningful presence throughout time—or history. Space is thus part of time, as when we say 'that cat' pointing to the cat by the fireplace versus 'that cat on the mantel,' and again when at a large meal one can control the space of the table by asking for the salt. Language transcends space while it lives in time.[7] Additionally, it has also been argued that, "...interior space was not really achieved until the beginning of modern times."[8]

It is the changes regarding the view of the historic cultural past and the sources of our varied writings that further contribute to a transformation of mentalities. At this point Petrarch plays a very significant role. For example, when we review Dante and his Italian heritage we find that the "...visible relics of the ancient greatness of Rome left Dante indifferent, just as the new humanist rhetoric passed by him entirely."[9] Moreover, Dante possessed a perception of time and space that was both consistent to classical thought and in harmony with the traditional Christian view: "Changing views of time and space seem to have coexisted with a traditional view of the cosmos. This view, memorably expressed in Dante's *Divine Comedy*, was shared in essentials by his sixteenth-century commentators, who drew on the same classical tradition, especially the writings of two Greeks, the astronomer-geographer Ptolemy and the philosopher Aristotle. According to this tradition, the fundamental distinction was that between Heaven and Earth."[10] This was not a position subscribed to by Renaissance figures who had static views of time. Petrarch "...complains bitterly that the contemporary Romans know nothing about Rome and things Roman."[11] Unlike anyone we know of before him, Petrarch was enraptured with antiquity, so much that, "...when in 1337 he came to Rome for the first time and actually saw the remains of her ancient grandeur, he was so overwhelmed by the impressions he received that he was unable to express his feelings in words."[12] And yet it was 'words' that were the basis for his understanding of time. It was language that drove him to understand some of the unrecognized contrasts between his own era and that of antiquity.

When he discovered that for all of his knowledge of Latin he still could not understand a recently acquired work of Cicero's because the ancient Latin and the Latin of his own day, what we now know as Medieval or church Latin, were not, in fact, the same. The times and thus the language had changed over those nearly thousand years and it was Petrarch who was the first to appreciate this fact and start the development of historic periodization. Petrarch and those who followed formed a love affair with that long-neglected antiquity as it was, not as its later Christianized version which had left Dante so indifferent.[13] As for Petrarch's love of books, especially the classics, as well as what would soon become classics, the evidence of his commitment is clear from his statement that he had possessed some "...sixteen or more of Plato's books alone,"[14] a remarkable achievement given that we were still decades away from the incursion of the printing press. He possessed what is assumed to be the first serious private library, an important step in creating a basis for the rise of the self without the necessary suffix to make it a selfless act. It is said even today that to know someone well, examine their library. It was in August of 1362 that Petrarch "...entered into negotiations regarding his library with the government of Venice....In a proposal...he declared his wish 'to have Saint Mark the Evangelist as [my] heir of those books, unknown in number, which [I have] now or will have in the future.'"[15] His coronation as Poet Laureate of Rome, earlier in April 1341, had given corroboration of his worth as a lyric poet for himself and for those humanists who would follow. And as a collector as well as a brilliant poet, he spent time in France, Flanders, and the Germanies looking for manuscripts. He found two unknown orations of Cicero as well as a collection of his letters in Verona, and in Florence, an unknown portion of Quintillian's writings. Known as the first Renaissance humanist, he sought to bestow his personal library on Venice in order to build a public library, or as one scholar put it, "...he wished to do this...because he hoped 'that later from time to time this glorious city will add other books at public expense and that also private individuals noble and patriotic minded citizens, as well as perhaps even foreign born persons...in this fashion it might easily be possible to establish a large and famous library, equal to those of antiquity.'"[16] This reference by Petrarch to the libraries of antiquity was to encourage the development of public libraries and implied something of a beginnings of philology[17] as well as a demonstration of his interest a in revitalization of what he considered the greatness of the classical world. All this leads to our appreciation of his transformation of our understanding of both language and history.

Since the Medieval world had thought of itself as a continuance of antiquity with the only difference being that it now was the Roman Empire with God, it followed that, "…the Middle Ages did not envisage classical antiquity as a different civilization or a lost Paradise. Despite the differences in religion between the pagan and Christian, and until the writings of Petrarch, medieval men failed to notice a fracture between the classical age and their own times. To them Frederick Barbarossa was as much a Roman Emperor as Augustus or Trajan…"[18] The very new language for addressing this altered historic view, this original and unique Petrarchan sense of the past, was also a gift of this 'Prince of Humanists' and most likely his greatest gift to posterity. It was his historic achievement to recognize and assert regarding the era before his own medieval world that: "…amidst the errors there shone forth men of genius, and no less keen were their eyes, although they were surrounded by darkness and dense gloom."[19] While he does not mark the world from whence he came as the 'Dark Ages,' his words do mark, as one scholar has noted this was,

> …'the moment at which the metaphor of light and darkness lost its original religious value and came to have a literary connotation.'…Men like Boccaccio, Filippo Villani, Ghiberti, and others contrasted the 'rebirth' of the arts and letters which, they held, had been effected by Dante, Giotto, and Petrarch, with the preceding period of cultural darkness. With this change of emphasis from things religious to things secular, the significance of the old metaphor became reversed: Antiquity, so long considered as the 'Dark Age,' now became the time of 'light' which had to be 'restored'…[20]

The view of the past that Petrarch and these early modern Renaissance thinkers subscribed to as well those who followed is an extremely different idea of the historic past since it is in clear contrast to the earlier, that of a "Medieval historiography [which] was based on essentially different principles.…the medieval historians almost without exception wrote universal history…"[21] In the words of the modern Italian historian, Benedetto Croce, medieval historiography became, "…a history of the universal, of the universal by excellence, which is history in labor with God and toward God."[22] Any sense of time was dominated by God's order and will and thus, like God, it was fixed. It was well articulated by Thomas Aquinas who, being influenced by ideas associated with Aristotle, referred to his deity as the "unmoved mover." The Medieval mind, therefore, perceived:

> …universal history was divided up into the succession either of the four world monarchies or of the six ages. These two patterns were first drawn up by Jerome in his *Commentaries* on Daniel's famous prophecy on the statue composed of different

metals and on the four beasts; and by Augustine in the *City of God* (XXII). Both schemes had in common the conception of the world and its various countries and peoples as a unity, which implied the notion both of universality and of continuity in history. This idea originated in Hellenistic times, and later on was taken over by the greatest of the early Christian historians, Eusebius of Caesarea. [23]

This pre-Christian pagan view of our historic background remains active through an act of metamorphosis that would make it palatable to Medieval theologians. In the end, "…the four world monarchies and the six ages became the models of almost all the mediaeval universal histories, those of Isidore of Seville, Bede, Otto the Freising, Vincent of Beauvais, to mention only the great names."[24] Mathematical order tied to the numerology of the universe was a typical pre-occupation for those looking to explain the world they lived in and also reminds us of the power of allegory so well represented by Dante.

What was remarkably important for the Renaissance was that "…by setting up the 'decline of the Empire' as a dividing point…Petrarch introduced a new chronological demarcation in history. This scheme has been distinguished…by the name 'humanistic.'"[25] Thus Renaissance Humanism was based in part on the transformation of our understanding of the past and thus our understanding of time; becoming humanized rather than divinely controlled. History could not be divided into three distinct periods to be known as the 'Ancient,' the 'Mediaeval,' and the 'Modern' worlds as yet. that is to say, the "…traditional division that still prevails in most European countries' *histoire moderne* commences with the Renaissance or Reformation and finishes with 1789 whereas *histoire contemporaine* still begins with the French Revolution."[26] It is of some additional interest to note that "…the first written proofs of the expression 'Middle Ages' used in the technical sense, date from the middle of the fifteenth century…"[27] While it is true that Petrarch didn't directly create this distinction, he did offer hints, stating in a work he considered his greatest, *Africa* (his epic poem): "My fate is to live amid varied and confusing storms. But for you perhaps…there will follow a better age. This sleep of forgetfulness will not last for ever."[28] In addition, it was, "…in one of his *Epistles*, in which he complains against Fate for having decreed his birth in such sad times, and …'there was a more fortunate age and probably there will be one again; in the middle, in our time, you see the confluence of wretches and ignominy.'"[29] While one should be restrained from making him one of the very first Early Modern European men, it is impossible to find anyone else coming any closer at this stage of historic or present-day scholarship. As for those who followed, it can safely be said that "If there is one thing that unites the men of the

Renaissance, it is the notion of belonging to a new time."[30] "New time" may be a rather extreme expression even as those following Petrarch knew that theirs was somehow a new world, a time very different from what had gone before. This has become a critical scholarly issue, however, since there have been some scholars who have gone so far as to deny the Italian Renaissance occurred,[31] even though there were those at the time who saw themselves as strikingly unique, a perspective to be considered as an historical component for something that was refreshingly and definitely new.

This alteration, or humanization of time, through our sense of history, was only part of the revolution creating this new humanistic world. For additionally, Petrarch had come across a word in Cicero well known in his own day that changed the way the thinkers and artists would look at their own world and work. That word was *virtue*, which, within the confines of the Medieval culture of Christianity, had acquired a passive meaning: it was the Lord that entered into the hearts of thinkers and artisans that made success possible in their moral and creative endeavors just as He guided the hand of Moses and the writers of the Gospels. As sinners, it would have been impossible to do such divinely inspired work as the Bible or the building of great cathedrals by ordinary artisans who were technically inadequate in and of themselves. "The medieval mind could not as yet accept one Virtue, which amounted to a perfection attainable in this world by the efforts of man, but only a plurality of virtues derived from the reflecting that perfection which is Christ."[32] The change would not be complete but rather it would be indicative, for now, "…one of the aspects of Petrarch's thinking as well as of that of the generation following him: the demand that every man, on reaching in his life the fateful point of the parting of the ways ought to choose, as Hercules had done, the right path, that of *virtus*, through which he will obtain fame."[33] This idea of being totally responsible for whatever virtue was achieved through one's actions, personal excellence, manliness and obedience to duty, was a classic idea that would return after about a thousand years of religious influence. From political leaders to artists, writers and thinkers, each would have to actively become people of virtue without a deity entering their soul giving them that quality. This large and activated component of the human condition would continue to effect all walks of life and thinking throughout the Renaissance, the Reformations as well as the Scientific Revolution and Enlightenment, eventually finding fertile ground in a peculiar modern Western attitude: a new way of thinking that would lead us to our own world of action for action's sake. This was anything but a passive point of view. As Eric Fromm put in *Escape*

From Freedom, "Activity…assumes a compulsory quality: the individual has to be active in order to overcome his feeling of doubt and powerlessness."[34]

One must learn to participate in their own virtue and not simply rely upon a divine guidance that would drive the sinner in the proper direction. One would also have to take a more active part in their personal salvation as they were beginning to learn to participate more actively in the new economics and Italian city politics. This is not to say that Petrarch was prepared to be the first to genuinely understand virtue as an activity in the Cicerionian sense of the term, however. Notwithstanding his newfound and unique perception of periodization and understanding the differences between Classical and Medieval thought, he was not prepared to cross over into a classical or new version of a classical mind, for "…although Petrarch held to both the medieval and more modern view, he was able to see some of the classic view, as when he recalled Cicero's statement that the word *virtus* is derived from *vir*, that is to say that *virtus* is that quality which makes a human being into a man in the fullest sense."[35] Perhaps the most famous story of this duality in his understanding of the term could best be told with the legendary story of Petrarch's hike up Mount Ventoux. Petrarch could possibly be called the first alpinist when he climbed this mountain to gain new heights and achieve a far greater and panoramic perspective. However, when he arrived at the pinnacle, the glory that was not in the view but in his experience reading passages of St. Augustine's *Confessions* which he had brought with him. You could take this revolutionary figure out of the Medieval world, but you could not take all of that same Medieval world out of the man. Pride was still the greatest of the deadly sins, at least for this friend of the writings of Augustine, for it has rightly been said that when one examines one of Petrarch's more intimate works written at a time of personal crisis, *The Secret Conflict of My Cares* (*De secreto confictu curatum mearum*), he demonstrates his sincere dependence upon Augustine. There is plenty of reason to believe that "…selecting Augustine as the other interlocutor seems to suggest, however, that a guilty Petrarch wishes to listen to his conscience."[36]

For a conscious mind to appear we would have to wait for it to develop since it had to grow out of and to compete with conscience, and religion was still too central for the Humanists in their daily lives. It is true that the humanists in the next century would light candles on a Saturday evening at their statues of Socrates, Plato, Cicero, etc. But we should also remember that these same humanists would the following morning again light additional candles at Sunday morning mass. Even if some of these humanists were to return to that time prior to the rise of the Christian religion to the age of paganism, there would be more than a few theologians and church leaders who would attack these new humanists for encouraging such ideas. After all, this dabbling with pre-Christian forms and ideas was more a matter of historical analysis by devout Christians and anything but a rejection of the church or her teaching.[37] The Church, moreover, had too many developing problems to do much other than encourage the Renaissance artists and sculptures as long as they appeared faithful.

It is an irony of history that the man responsible for contributing the most to the theory of this creation of a modern cultural event labeled the Italian Renaissance did not appear until the late nineteenth century. Emile Burckhardt (1818–97) wrote the seminal work on the subject overstating his case for the existence of a modern individuality beginning in Italy. It was his thesis that they not only created the historical period known now as the Italian Renaissance, he also posited that it was at that time that the Italians developed the independent city-state form of governments (there were five significant ones) and offered a basis in doing so, for the creation of what is called intellectual history. There is clear evidence to support the argument that the Italian cities were developing primarily because of expanded trade and population growth after the end of the fourteenth century. But there are those who hold to another position like that of the well known scholar and historian, Lynn Thorndike, who upon writing extensively about science in the Medieval world, would correctly point out that any intellectual history regarding the sciences in the Renaissance was less than impressive.[38] This could be an example, again, of the historian's dilemma: to paint an accurate picture of a given past without projecting one's attitude and assumptions on that distant past. This may explain why there are those who would argue that Burckhardt did not discover but rather invented this historic period. Reading the individualized components of *The Civilization of the Renaissance in Italy* (1860) one finds it closer to an explication of Burckhardt's own contemporaries rather than reflective of the mind of fifteenth century humanists. There is a great deal of truth to the comment made by Eric Fromm: "Medieval society did not deprive the individual of his freedom, because the 'individual' did not yet exist."[39] And even the brilliant Burckhardt had to admit something of the same for the Middle Ages when he noted that "…man was conscious of himself only as a member of a race, people, party, family, or corporation,—only through some general category," which is equally an accurate evaluation.[40] While not present at all in the Medieval world, it was different for the Renaissance since there certainly was the appearance of some small but unique increase of a sense of individuality—with the reservation that a small increase does not make for a completed independent self. As for Burckhardt's position, he later qualified his position when he observed that "… you know, so far as individualism is concerned, I hardly believe in it any more, but I don't say so; it gives people so much pleasure."[41] The question that could also be asked here is whether it could be that the ultimate historical development of a beginning sense of self, as now expressed in our own era of the twenty-first century, is the end of that development, or are we still only expanding ever more this sense of self and consciousness? A question we will return to later.

In the end the pull towards the early modern psychology of self would be far too great to turn back, especially in the arts, and the evidence indicates that Petrarch may have understood this, at least in part. For example, "…in 1370, [Petrarch] expressed the belief which Boccaccio had expressed even earlier, that Giotto's art appealed primarily to the 'intelligent' and not to the 'ignorant'"[42] Genuinely original art requires a liberation from what was considered an inherited presumed order. And at the time of Petrarch, that meant letting go of divinely defined space. In other words, the Renaissance artist would have to do for space what the humanists had done for time: emancipate it. When looking to the past, "Petrarch's whole creative work was marked by a conscious effort to unite classical content and its form and expression. The poet was more advanced in this regard than the contemporary artists."[43] Accepting a more accurate phrase of 'aware of their effort,' and what the artist Giotto was doing at the same time as Petrarch, the point is well taken that the poets and artist were the earliest to understand the ties between the classical world and their own since the written word remained a primary force for historic change. This also introduces reservations regarding nineteenth century attempts to qualify individuality in the Renaissance with such terms as *self-assertiveness* in place of *self-consciousness*[44] while at the same time offering that "…the idea of the uniqueness of the individual goes with that of a personal style in painting or writing…"[45] This only means what it says, the talented and—even more so —the genius as artists, were unique as they always have been and still are. Moreover, there is no evidence of any one having had an inner space to be explored as we would and do expect of a modern self working within their own state of consciousness.

It is in the realm of the Renaissance that the idea of a new reality of space took on a new meaning. In attempting to clarify how artists contributed to a transformation of our visual perspective, a brief review of an artist or two will illustrate. For painting, this transformation began with Giotto di Bondone (?1266–1337) who was the first to offer a more realistic renderings of his figures. As an introduction to this tradition a brief explication of a late Romanesque structure, the Mary Magdalen Church in Vézelay (Bourgogne), is instructive. Located on a high and magnificent hill, this twelfth century Benedictine abbey had an important history: it was a major pilgrimage church where St. Bernard preached for the Second Crusade (1146) and where King Louis VII took up the cross. In 1190 Richard Cœur de Lion and Philip Augustus started from here the Third Crusade. Upon entering through the central doorway into the narthex but not yet inside the interior and sacred space of the nave, one discovers over these inner doors a very imposing tympanum of a relief sculpture with Christ seated in the center, in the midst of a great nimbus, a symbol of his power and glory, and representing the symbolic liturgy of Christ's words, "I am the Door." The subject here is Christ, the Risen, sending out the Apostles on their mission and is based on passages from the Gospel according to St. Mark and the Acts of the Apostles. Since the body of Christ is elongated, almost Byzantine in style, with his feet pointing downward but touching nothing, the symbolism is clearly of the rising Christ. This is not realism but allegory, a representation in reference to the New Testament. Figuratively, for the illiterate feudal peasant, Christ is 'real' and 'present' because they can 'see' Him not as human but as God in stone on the tympanum, much as you can 'hear' someone's words. Although late Romanesque, the church indicates changes that are part of the later Gothic formula since the nave is not as dark as one would expect. Moving into the nave with its high Gothic ceiling, the interior space possesses larger and lighter clerestory windows with flying buttresses and pointed arches, a great monument to Gothic engineering. The space with its up-rush of stone clearly represents God's world from the magnificent rose windows to the integrated capital sculptures. The combined Romanesque and Gothic art is given an heightened sense of divine allegorical presence in contrast with the later early steps of the Renaissance artists' pursuit of realism and specifically with Giotto, the revolutionary new idea of foreshortening.[46] There is a lack of interest in realism, i.e., the human dimension that was not natural but sacred because the view is Divine and the artistic creation was a by-product of Divine intervention. With the Renaissance, we begin to have human dimensions with which we can personally identify.

There were some contemporaries who believed that perhaps Giotto simply could not paint or perhaps that he even was not mentally sound. Of course petty jealousies were not uncommon at this time. What is true is his concern for depth-of-field (or foreshortening), for making clear which figures were to be dominant from a perspective that allowed the viewer to see the subject; this was unheard of prior to his work. One of his works should suffice to demonstrate the point: *The Bewailing of Christ* (also known as *The Lamentation* or *Pietà*, c.1305). This masterpiece demonstrates why Giotto was rightly famed for the beginnings of a rationally organized painting. Christ and his mother are in the center of this moving scene. The faces of the women express despairing grief while the two nearby disciples, mourning quietly, have resigned themselves to the cruel fact of their master's death. There is an extremely heavy, earthward pulling atmosphere about the scene that heightens the human condition. Although there are angels who share this grievous moment, they, through their weightlessness and placement on the top half of the painting, balance the heaviness of the lower half of the fresco where the story is told. The hopelessness of the situation is further underlined by a tree which stands between the lower weight of earth and the upper space of the heavens and which is barren. What is arguably the most striking aspect of this work is the composition not simply of the fresco's theme, heightened by using the lower half to tell the tale, but the method of drawing our eyes again and again to that point: the top left has three angels each moving to the right while another two angelic figures act much like a pointer, looking down and to the right, drawing our attention to the tree on the top of the hill, a tree that is shorter than its actual size to allow for the illusion of foreshortening. Then from the right side high point where the tree sits on top of the hill, the eye is drawn to the left and to the bottom of the fresco into an ever tighter scene of figures around the limp body of Jesus who is embraced in the arms of his mother. The anguish is palpable. One of the figures at right of center along the rock formation has his arms drawn back while his head is pointing, again acting like a arrow and looks forward drawing our attention to the critical scene. This is a highly contrived and is clearly a rationally organized composition that demands the observer to pay attention to what Giotto would have considered as both the central theme and its point: the ponderous body and death of Jesus. While clearly a religious theme, still using the medieval halo to mark the holy characters, it is highly humanized, and takes the observer into account. Here lies the beginning of a revolution of both artificial perception and aesthetics, a revolution now known as a product of the Italian Renaissance and what it was to become. This preoccupation with realism will dominate from this point until the end of the nineteenth century.

David (Florence, 1430–1432), by Donatello (1386–1466), also captures this humanized sense of realism that expanded Giotto's inventiveness into the new realm of realistic sculpture. Breaking from a tradition of placing sculpture as embellishment within architecture, we have the first free-standing life-size bronze since antiquity marking the revival of the classical nude, one that is to be seen from all angles and not just from the front. Lyrically fluid, with its delicate and youthful features, the boy David only wears a hat and boots which only heightened his rather sensuous innocence. With the *Equestrian Monument of Gattamelata* (Padua, Piazza del Santo, 1445–1450), again by Donatello, we witness the first equestrian statue since the ancient rendering of Marcus Aurelius. Besides being a massive work, the face, body, armor and horse of this recently deceased commander of the Venetian armies reveal a fine dramatic attention to the smallest detail and arguably should be considered one of his mature works. The face is something to behold, a man who is used to giving orders and being obeyed, while the quality of the bronze on the horse flesh is distinct enough from that of Gattamelata to be recognized as such while the horse appears to be moving at a brisk pace. Understanding the achievements of the classical art was inherent in someone who had traveled to Rome to study classical art (one of the West's earliest tourists) revealing his understanding to faithfulness to realistic detail. As an example of this Renaissance uniqueness, one can compare Donatello's work with the earlier statue of St. Theodore in its niche at the medieval Chartres Cathedral. Theodore was an officer in the ancient Roman army who was converted to Christianity during the reign of Diocletian after which he set fire to the temple of Cybele and suffered martyrdom for his offence on 9 November 300 A.D. While the work, both as an embellishment and as part of the great Gothic (scholastic) synthesis, is very mature for an early twelfth century piece, it stands out in striking contrast to the Renaissance understanding of our past and of the historical changes that have taken place. The body of this ancient Roman soldier is clothed in medieval chain-mail holding a medieval sword and shield: truly an historic anachronism. It was through the eyes of the Renaissance artist that the ancients would return, but now in a more humanized and realistically accurate form.

Along with Donatello on his trip to study the antiquities of Rome, there also traveled the brilliant architect, Brunelleschi (Felipe Brunellesco di Brunelleschi, 1377–1446). When we think of the Renaissance we think of Florence and when we think of Florence we think of La Cupola of Santa Maria del Fiore. Studying the ancient architecture of Rome, and understanding the creation of the potential uses of the arch that could be extended into a dome, Brunelleschi reintroduced the idea, using eight skeleton ribs that can be seen rising from an octagonal base, and 16 interior ribs not seen, two between those visible from the exterior, to tie the whole together at the top and creating the spaces in between to be embellished. In 1436 the Cathedral was dedicated, a date that was consequently considered the official beginning of the Renaissance. The visual certainty of the Renaissance was given concreteness. What is special for the topic at hand is that the domed building has a very unique feeling upon entering. In a Romanesque church the weight of the darkness can sometimes be psychologically overwhelming, and with the Gothic cathedral, space is everywhere, posing an omnipresence and clearly implying the divine. With the experience of a dome, you need not look up to know that you have actually stepped into the center of that space, that you are in the center of the dome (cupola) and have entered into what could be considered the center of the universe. Here the human psyche is satiated with the certainty that existence, one's own being, occurs at that very specific moment, and not some sort of eternal moment as would be the case in the spacious heaven of the medieval cathedral. Space retains its grandeur but also is made identifiable to the human psyche. The compatibility of both space and humanity is given concrete fixation. This also gives additional reason for people like Burckhardt who sought to find whatever evidence possible for individuality, not only in the politics of the city-states, but also in the poetry and now the visual arts.

Artists for the first time now signed their paintings, carrying their pride, their sin of pride if you will, into the public realm. Portraits become very popular, especially in the hands of those names associated with what has been called the Age of Genius: Leonardo da Vinci (1452–1519), Michelangelo (1475–1564) and Raphael (1483–1520). From the *Mona Lisa* to the self-portraits of Michelangelo on the Sistine Ceiling and *The Last Judgement* as well as Raphael's *The School of Athens*, which happens to offers us a portrait rendering of both Leonardo and Michelangelo, visual arts would never be the same. The nineteenth century philosopher, John Stuart Mill once observed that if you see a genuine individual you are also looking at a genius.[47] This may not be the world of individualism, but it was a world where the artist began to express something of the individual choices and uniqueness that make for a characterization of the self and each of these artists is clearly singular.

The Venetian mastering of mirrors made self-portraiture possible and offered new aesthetic understanding. As one student of the subject has noted, "Generally, the Renaissance portrait does not intend to show us a person, but a kind of person. This might even be considered an elaboration of the ancient Egyptian emphasis on the subject's trade, so that we see him not as a person but as a scribe, baker, fowler, and so forth."[48] Even in a world where a more realistic rendering is offered, it still remained a world where one's name was derivative of one's occupation. Standing alone without a defining function was yet to appear. Even the third member of this Age of Genius, Raphael, in his famed *The School of Athens*, portrays all figures within their philosophical orientation, either on one side in the camp of the idealists (Apollo in the niche with a portraiture of Plato standing) or on the other with the realists (Athena in the niche with Aristotle standing). This is a brilliant philosophic statement notwithstanding, the portrait of Plato is based on the face of Michelangelo while Leonardo's face was used for Aristotle: allegory and metaphor remained pertinent.

There were, of course, many other transformations of thinking, especially in the arts, from Holbein to El Greco and Titian to the Flemish brothers, van Eyck who created a personal relationship in some of their work as in the case of *The Madonna and Chancellor Rolin* (also known as *The Virgin of the Donor* or *The Madonna of Autun*, 1234–1235). The scene is that of Nicholas Rolin, the donor in Autun, who had been Chancellor to Duke Philip the Good of Burgundy. You, as the audience of the painting, are also positioned by the artist within the scene, since you note that you are standing (sitting?) in a Romanesque palace where the Chancellor is in worshipful pose facing the Madonna and the sacred Infant. There are no saints present and the only other figure present in the foreground is an angel hovering over Mary's head holding her crown. The room is virtually bare of furniture except for a chair upon which the Virgin is seated and a reading desk with a ledge for kneeling that is occupied by Rolin who is praying. Both the faces of Mary and the Chancellor have been painted against a darker background while the head of the infant Jesus is painted against the much lighter background, the halo which highlights the city behind him , further implies this divine presence. Beyond the donor—who paid for the work—and the balcony beyond, is an arcade. Through the arcade can be seen a flower garden with birds. Lilies are in the center and beyond the garden is a walk, a wall and one of the two men present is seen gazing through the crenelation into the valley beyond and below. It is obvious that we are within this church looking at a valley with a village beyond that is divided by a river with a bridge bringing the two sides of the community together. There are about 30 figures recognizable on the bridge, and further beyond this there is a castle before coming to the peaks of mountains in the background. All this is done in a space of only 26 x 24 inches. Here is an example of new and challenging techniques. Van Eyck has also been given credit for the invention of oil painting.[49]

Arguably the most clear expression of individuality made at this time, one that could make us possibly think in terms of our own world, was that offered by the neo-Platonic Renaissance philosopher, Pico della Mirandola (1463-94) who wrote *On the Dignity of Man*. In it he states that the most positive belief in the human capacity was to realize the highest achievement of one's own existence. Put bluntly, he offered that man, constrained by no limits, shall ordain for himself the limits of his own nature, a rather radical and equally very unusual statement at this time. There were other notable humanists who while not in the same philosophical camp as Pico, also expressed this new sense of singularity. One such example is Coluccio Salutati (1331–1406), a neo-Aristotelian who, as chancellor of Florence, demonstrated that there were new career opportunities for the Renaissance intellectual and humanist. This also highlights the lack of a dominant Renaissance philosophy—neither Platonic nor Aristotelian. There was, however, a serious change in the academic curriculum which was different from the scholastic trivium (grammar, logic and rhetoric) and quadrivium (arithmetic, geometry, astronomy and music) that had been required at the Universities of Paris, Oxford and Cambridge. The trivium and quadrivium begin to find competition with a new curriculum founded upon the early writings of the ancient rhetorician, Marcus Fabius Quintilianus (c.35–c.100 A.D.) This new curriculum can be found at the Renaissance school founded in Mantua by Vittorino da Feltra (1378–1448) with the new subjects of history (concrete perspectives), eloquence (getting the point across), ethics (moral philosophy) and poetry (the least utilitarian). This emphasized teaching how to live well rather than solving the mysteries of God's universe. One of the most famous students of this school who would teach anyone who wished to learn was the humanist who later contributed to the rise of critical humanism and historical documentation, Lorenza Valla (1406–57). He analyzed the document known as the *Donation of Constantine* and made public in 1440 that it was a forgery because the Latin was not of the period (it was closer to a ninth century document). The Church didn't much care for this because it contradicted the traditional argument that when Constantine died he left his Empire to the Church of Rome. There were other discoveries but this particular example indicates the appearance of both critical thinking and a skeptical and rational approach to important topics. This is what a fine revisionist scholar of this period refers to as the age of *studia humanitatus* (study humane).[50]

While the sciences as a matter of abstract thought did not dominate during the Renaissance, it was an inventive period in those techniques applicable to aesthetics. It was also a period when our understanding of physical space began to be challenged. The world had been physically expanding with a deeper and wider knowledge not only regarding aesthetic space but equally in terms of a new space, the discovery of the New World. The explorations of Columbus literally altered our understanding of the relative nature of physical space. As in art, so to in the physical world, our traditional assumptions were being challenged: "Views of time and space are particularly revealing of the dominant attitudes of a particular culture, precisely because they are rarely conscious and because they are expressed in practice more often than in texts."[51] What is also significant, and is demonstrated in the case of Columbus, is that any discovery of new worlds and the consequent expansion of our knowledge of that world can often be a result of errors of fact. The irony is that Columbus made his trip based on the assumption that the circumference of the planet was 12,000 rather than the 24,000 miles that it is. Space was not only becoming rational, the errors of judgements, whether from the ignorance of space as was expressed in late Medieval art or that of our physical world, needed reexamination, a challenge to the human psyche.

Just as the painters and their paintings possessed a new sense of action, realism and space, so too did new ideas confronting the concept of virtue. Without a sense of interior space, a personal sense of virtue cannot be achieved. Painting itself was subsumed under the heading of expressing this renewed sense of virtue. The Renaissance sense of virtue possessed a dimension that offered a more humanized characterization in the arts, in painting, sculpture and architecture, as well as in the willingness of those who were now risking much for discovery, looking at both our planet, a new world and the revolutionary vision of the universe around us. It is common knowledge that notwithstanding Leonardo's successes, especially with his murals, most famously the *Last Supper*, which was somewhat experimental and has had to be restored regularly in order to give us an idea of what the original looked like, da Vinci offers, again, evidence that the presence of errors at any given time can often aid in creating serious contributions to our mental development. Leonardo's mistakes are in their own way as much a contribution to the revolutionary changes as are his successes. This was a virtue, a very unique virtue, that was not present in the monasteries, but rather drawn from the re-birth of the classical mentioned earlier. This was virtue defined as action even if sometimes in error. Rather than a world with answers, it was now a world where knowledge was to be discovered by activated curiosity. As Petrarch stated in his *On His Own Ignorance and of Many Others* (c.1363), "I have read all Aristotle's moral books if I am not mistaken." He then follows with: "I see virtue, and all that is peculiar to vice as well as to virtue, egregiously defined and distinguished by him [Aristotle] and treated with penetrating insight. When I learn all this, I know a little bit more than I knew before, but mind and will remain the same as they were, and myself remain the same."[52]

The assumptions of earlier centuries had been that all questions had been answered. Medieval scholastics constantly attempted to give those answers various forms and details. As things turned out, however, we didn't acquire all the answers with either the coming of the Christ figure or an institutional church. We now return to an earlier period in the search for answers as well as recognizing that 'virtue is its own reward,' i.e., seeking even if the results may be wrong is not to be neglected. Knowledge was certainly achievable but only by clearly moving away from the pessimism of sin and replacing it with an optimism in human capacities. It was the Renaissance humanist Pietro Pomponazi of Mantua (1462–1525) who recognized 'an entirely different conception' of knowing. "He denies that there is any direct insight of a spiritual character, since all our knowledge is based on our sense. The end of human life is moral virtue. This is its own reward; and it can be attained by every human being during his earthly existence."[53] His position was to simply argue from *De immortalitate animae*: "…the essential reward of virtue is virtue itself, which makes man happy." It follows for him that, "…for human nature can possess nothing greater than virtue itself, since it alone makes man secure and removed from every perturbation."[54] The issue of fear, as in the fear of death, or "perturbation," has not, of course, left our psyche through all this. We need only turn to northern Europe during the first two centuries of the Italian Renaissance to acquire a different picture from that of the growing discovery, knowledge, and optimism in the south. There is an irony in that as optimism grew in the south pessimism grew in the north, helping to explain the later development of the northern Renaissance and the sources and power associated with the Reformation. The basis for a great deal of pessimism occurred when in 1348, Black Death found its way to Western shores. Within the next two years nearly all of Europe lost almost half its population.[55] This undermined the old social order to such a degree that anyone with skills became extremely marketable due to the shortage of workers. Social stability had become a fragile commodity.

Little wonder that virtue as action was taking on a deeper significance in daily lives, especially considering that "…even before the plague, …bad weather and bad harvests brought devastating hunger to northern Europe during a Great Famine that lasted from 1315 until 1322."[56] The idea of death was still a central concern at the end of the Middle Ages and beginning of the Renaissance. The Great Plague also became a central theme in art and culture. We have spoken of tombs and how death was given very high ritual treatment. Its impact can be found in the rise of the flagellants, those who would travel from village to village beating themselves with whips and begging for forgiveness and redemption from the Grim Reaper.[57]

> Visual images of this period just after the Black Death were the 'dance of death' and the *'memento mori'*—the dancing skeletons beating drums, leering, shrouded in black or carrying a spear. These images were ready at hand, going back to the early thirteenth century when the orders of friars had developed them, in mural paintings, as a form of illustrated sermon. But now they took on a grimly humorous and satirical spirit. In Italy in the fifteenth century the skeletons are friendly and jovial while the living are reluctant and demure; there were often darkly comic captions ('come, fat Bishop'); at Grossbasel one artist of a Dance of Death included himself and his family among the victims. Displayed bones or a skull, the skull and crossbones worn sometimes in jewelry as a reminder of the imminence of death, or represented in painting and sculpture, are traditions that date from the fads of this period.[58]

To say that England and Western Europe were entering a crisis of unheard proportion is itself almost an understatement for next event on the horizon arrived the so-called Hundred Years' War between France and England that would rage intermittently from about 1337 to 1453. It was the great scholar of the Medieval mind, J. Huizinga, who "…has called attention to the obsession with death and the physical corruption of the body which runs through so much of the literature and art of the fourteenth and fifteenth centuries and also to what he has called 'the extreme saturation of the religious atmosphere.'"[59] Again we have pointless slaughter and misery. Little wonder that "…and above all, there loomed the image of Death, ever present and unconquerable, a constant figure in much of the art and literature of the Middle Ages."[60] There was a serious difference in the northern cultures with an increase of a sense of doom, fear of death, and the terror and the power of a growing uncertainty. When we review northern literature and compare it to that of the Italians, we find "Products like these [allegories] would seem to betray mere decadence and senile decay. Thinking of Italian literature of the same period, the fresh and lovely poetry of the quattrocento, we may perhaps wonder how the form and spirit of the Renaissance can still seem so remote from the regions on this side of the Alps."[61] Huizinga was so committed regarding this topic of death at the end of the medieval age that in his *Waning of the Middle Ages*, he titles his chapter eleven, "The Vision of Death."

These and other crises were, however, also opportunities if not necessities in altering our perceptions and thus our view of life, our values and assumptions. In Italy, Pomponazzi may have something of this in mind when he offered that "…every virtuous man is rewarded by his virtue and happiness." This revealed his thoughts regarding "Aristotle, in Problemata 30, problem 10, when he asks why rewards are set for contests, but not for virtues and knowledge…"[62] These accumulating crises—among other changes during what has been called the waning of an era—brought about the following conclusion:

> The fifteenth century in France and the Netherlands is still medieval at heart. The diapason of life had not yet changed. Scholastic thought, with symbolism and strong formalism, the thoroughly dualistic conception of life and the world still dominated. The two poles of the mind continued to be chivalry and hierarchy. Profound pessimism spread a general gloom over life. The gothic principle prevailed in art. But all these forms and modes were on the wane. A high and strong culture is declining, but at the same time in the same sphere new things are being born. The tide is turning, the tone of life is about to change.[63]

Meanwhile, the Italian Renaissance city-states possessed what should be considered roughly the largest urban population in all Europe.[64] Morever the recent prosperity drawn from the newly established trade with the Levant and Asia Minor further contributed to the explosive growth of economic support impacting on the Italian culture. Demographics, economics and the fact that the Medieval feudal system never became established in Italy as it had in the north leaves little doubt as to which lands were most ripe for these dramatic changes, especially with the rediscovery of the ancient worlds of the Aegean and Mediterranean area, the city-states of Greece and Rome ushering in the beginnings of early Modern European. In Florence and Venice "…an interest was taken in statistics of imports and exports, population and prices. Double-entry book-keeping was widespread."[65] Little wonder that the Italian Renaissance was less an event and more a process impacting on the European mental make-up, an impact that accumulatively conspired to bring about these changes in the Western world. Double-entry bookkeeping, after all, is a method of tracking one's profits which Thomas Aquinas had condemned. The economic and political changes in Italy that impacted on Europe altered more than economics or politics, however, since the world of ideas, aesthetics and eventually our psychological attitudes were forever changed. As one Renaissance scholar has put it: "...viewing the European scene as a whole, it cannot be said that the Renaissance saw transformations in institutions which matched in anything like the same degree those in the history of ideas."[66]

For novice students of history still finding their way in the maze that makes history so fascinating, there is a tendency to think of history as a series of important dates and singular facts as well as important personalities. Perhaps this may explain why it is that so many students prefer the historic subject of inventions, from clocks to compasses, as their model of history, whereas the more traditional historian is interested in the longer view of cultural and political impact and their implications. While Petrarch along with Giotto were the early arrows to the new perceptions, this transition would lead to even greater giants, the Michelangelos, the Machiavellis and Shakespeares, the artists themselves would be the precursors of what modernity was to become.

Serious problems of study for this period centers around those amorphous words like *individuality* since this is the period when this term became something of a catch-all with the odor of historical inexactitude. It is this lack of an exact and clear meaning of such terms that are for the historian a topic the greatest concern: The view of history by the Medieval mind and that of our own have little to do with each other. The historian can ill afford that "...very phrase 'to commit an anachronism,'" since it is a "...reminder of the extent to which we think of the concept in pejorative terms."[67] Or to be more thorough, as the scholar Myron P. Gilmore stated it:

> We are today so accustomed to applying the test of anachronism to our reconstructions that we take if for granted. Every schoolboy know that Roman senators did not smoke cigars and that Napoleon's troops did not fight with machine guns. The wide diffusion of knowledge about what belongs in particular historical periods does not of course prevent the frequent occurrence of amusing mistakes. The historical novelist who described a moving scene of farewell between father and son in 1356 when the latter declared his intention of going 'to fight in the Hundred Years' War' forgot that the war could have been so christened only by a later generation. But on the whole we are more conscious than any previous civilization of the succession of historical epochs and of the differences between them.[68]

This same scholar who gave us some of the finest studies in revisionist Renaissance scholarship also contributed to the recognition of the inherent presence of anachronism in historical scholarship in general and the Renaissance in particular, further noting, "...we must in the end recognize that there have always been and always will be human anachronisms and this is in fact one the conditions which prevents the course of history from being as determined as some philosophers have supposed."[69] Part of the problem is that history is replete with missing the more important element in the story. For example, the significance of the date 1492 when it was in 1491 and the end of the domestic conflicts in Spain that made what followed possible. While effects cannot be diminished the causes should be placed in proper perspective. Moreover, we have noted that mistakes can make an important historic difference and consequently an anachronism of understanding can actually move history forward. Gilmore offers another interesting thought when he continues with the observation that, "...this over-developed modern consciousness is the product of a long evolution which may be said to have begun with Petrarch and those of his followers who shared his attitude towards the past."[70] While it is understandable that a Renaissance scholar might wish to use the term *consciousness* for *aware* in the modern sense, it is still problematic for the thoughtful student of consciousness to make some sense of what this actually meant, because this could be labeled another type of anachronism. The term consciousness only first appears in the seventeenth century, and today continues to have an amorphous meaning as we find revisionists regarding the Italian Renaissance who wish to qualify some of Burckhardt's more extreme anachronisms, also experiencing the same problems.

Since the use or misuse of the term *consciousness* appears all too often, what can we say about the term *individuality*? One suggestion is, "...like the portrait painting of the time, the biographical literature reflects the so-called individualism of the period, that is, the importance attached to personal experiences, opinions, and achievements, and the eagerness to see them perpetuated in a distinguished work of art or of literature."[71] Others have made similar suggestions: "The most direct evidence of self-awareness is that of autobiographies, or more exactly (since the modern term 'auto-biography' encourages an anachronistic view of the genre) of diaries and journals written in the first person, of which there are about a hundred surviving from Florence alone..."[72] While the argument for awareness is not the issue here, the word *self* as used today is not inherently applicable to the above quote and should be looked at cautiously since it is such a very modern term. However, that same sense of a self could be found having a limited presence and that the writing of personalities exists in biographical form, is not being disputed. But spiritual attainment does not apply for the self in this study in that this act of faith is guided by God and not by personal or private reasoning, guided more by an inner divinely-driven self is not modern but more an act of selflessness. An inner state of consciousness will begin elsewhere.

The writer, Giorgio Vasari (1511–74), for example, is well known for his study, *The Lives of the Most Excellent Painters, Sculptors and Architects* (1550), while "…cheerfully admitting to being modern himself."[73] But this is not to say that the writings regarding other artists were any more accurate a rendering of some inner being than were the portraits. It has been rightly observed that these works were in general more a matter of rendering a topographical structure. For example, "… one reason for this topology is that the Renaissance had no psychology, so that people were not seen in their complexity, but in their accomplishment or their role in society. They might even be seen through allegory, as in the fifteenth-century Italian paintings, which often place the head of the artist's subject on the body of some figure in classical mythology or biblical story."[74] Again this represents more a Classical and Medieval position than modern. Declaring that the writing of biographies is modern does not inherently make for a modern study although it is a helpful reference for Renaissance scholars and has rightly been associated with the idea of being Early Modern. The issue is and remains the same; at best these are exercises in ego gratification which can be traced back to the listings of heroic deeds of past cultures. If these bits and pieces, and even copious works qualify, then the word *modern* has less than a clear meaning. Still, this is an indicator, and as such, it is pointing towards the eventual rise of the individual; but finding a door does not a room make. Moreover, there are even statements that those knowing little of this history would have to wonder about. As an example, it has been argued that the "…feudal age abounded in rugged individualists, but the individualism of the feudal nobles was circumscribed by the traditions and inherited status of their castes. It meant little more than the free play of ego and arrogance."[75] Here the emphasis for the reader should center entirely on the limits, the traditions and inherited status of their castes. That has been the central point of the earlier chapters regarding antiquity: there can be no individuality in a world dominated by group identity. We do have the individual as ego today, but that is not the subject here, since it is the individual as an inner self that creates the foundation for a self-conscious being. When the perception is an agreed upon perception for all, the individual cannot possibly be a reality. Part of the problem occurs as a legacy of the nineteenth century scholar who created the issue: "…there were many factors in the urban society of fourteenth and fifteenth century Italy that not only made possible a more autonomous assertion of individual personality, but also gave it positive encouragement. Burckhardt noted particularly the incentive given to individualism by the hectic political life of the city-states, both despotic and republican."[76] This, in retrospect, is an honest but confusing expression: politics is public and self is private.

The names of the famous mentioned are real and each have a portion of some unique characteristics from Petrarch to Machiavelli (as well as Pericles to Caesar). But the question is when does this become a matter of projection: Burckhardt's rhetoric sounds more like his own age than that of Renaissance Italy. Twentieth century writers have often continued this language of individuality. Thus a limited degree of a sense of individuality along with an early expression of some sense of self can be deduced from the use of Venetian mirrors that were popular with the artists and their very realistic self-portraits, much as were the early attempts at qualified biographies, signed works of art and secular honors such as when Petrarch was made poet laureate. Demonstrating the significance of mirrors, one Renaissance figure, Giambattist Gelli offered a song "...for the mirror-makers of Florence, 'A mirror allows one to see one's own defects, which are not as easy to see as those of others.'"[77] In a Christian world finding one's own defects hardly qualifies as a revolutionary idea. Introspection may not have become something common but there is a basis for its later development which is mostly beginning to appear around one's faith. Added to this, one can include the newly created phenomena of limited privacy with the early appearance of private bedrooms. As small as these beginnings were, they are still important steps giving life to what is of central importance to many today, our own private and inner life.

This sense of varied and limited meaning for these important, contemporary terms is recognized, if only in a rather limited manner, with the following observation:

> ...the moral thought of the Renaissance was fundamentally individualistic in its outlook. Of course, the term individualism has several meanings, and its applications to the Renaissance have aroused a good deal of controversy among historians.... Renaissance individualism, a term should be understood in a different way. Above all, Renaissance thought and literature are extremely individualistic in that they aim, to a degree unknown to the Middle Ages and to most of ancient and modern times, at the expression of individual, subjective opinions, feelings, and experiences.[78]

This at least grants that the term *individuality* should be used cautiously since there are degrees as well as different meanings and it is more a matter of using the term in a comparative manner rather than as an absolute. This is appropriate since these three terms that concern this work are not perceived as absolutes but rather as contextually relative. Was there more of a sense of individuality in the Quattrocento compared to the age of Innocent III, for example? Speaking historically, the answer is probably, if not more likely! The tendency is to use the terms *individuality*, *self* and *consciousness* as absolutes, with no possibility for the existence of degree. To argue as an historian that there are no intellectual and mental degrees is anti-historical. This is not only a fundamental error of reasoning, it is a rhetorical trap from which there is no escape. When we say someone is tall or short, fat or skinny, smart or dumb, are these absolutes or are these relative terms? Is there not always someone taller, shorter, fatter or skinnier, smarter or dumber than someone else? It makes no sense to not be able to say that someone is becoming their own self, or more of an individual, and actuating more in the acquisition of their interior conscious state. And what of the term *subjective*? Kristeller suggested, "…when we come to the end of the Renaissance, this subjective and personal character of humanist thought finds its most conscious and consummate philosophical expression in the *Essais* of Michael de Montaigne."[79] Two points need be drawn here: first, the term *subjective* as applied to Montaigne (1533–1592) is being applied at the end of the French Renaissance and second, *consciousness* here applied is actually not an established defined term that can be found in use in the sixteenth century. The term *subjective* which did not mean then what we take it to mean in modern lexography. At the least, this use of these terms could be considered a distortion of the thinking at the time, one where the modern meaning is forced into an extremely limited strait jacket of understanding as the next chapters will attempt to clarify. Regarding the writings of Montaigne, there sometimes appears to be a compulsion to make him a prototype of the ideas of a modern European man: "In my opinion, the problem of immortality became of such pressing importance within the framework of Renaissance theology and metaphysics as a result of the individualism of the period, that is, of its tendency to attach very great importance to the concrete and individual qualities and experiences of each human being, a tendency which we encounter in all humanists of the period and which finds its culminating expression in Montaigne."[80] While this particular viewpoint has its appeal and was made by a well-respected Renaissance scholar, it offers us the problem of suggesting there is a singular voice for modern man. Additionally there is the suggestion that Montaigne somehow by implication was the one to discover the terminality of our existence. The issue of mortality, which has been a serious concern for more than just the past four hundred years, should not be placed on the back of this very interesting and important writer. The burden of the quiet life and thoughts devoted to life and death questions had been given shape by the Benedictine monks long before Montaigne's solitary if more secular journey. Humanism may have altered some of our basic assumptions, but the power of salvation from death still was very applicable to all members of the Christian community. When discussing these three correlated terms, it has become all too uncommon to seek a more subtle understanding of their meanings within a particular historic environment.

It has been a fundamental thesis here that the functioning of a singular consciousness as is now understood to have developed fairly late in Western history, and not meaningfully until after the beginnings of the modern world. Additionally, its development and evolution ran parallel with the rise of a sense of self and individuality. The contemporary phenomenon of a capacity for a serious self-reflective conscious individuality did not make any meaningful appearance that can be documented until after the end of the Renaissance and Reformation and not until the Scientific Revolution. While there have been earlier partial steps and necessary components that have grown out of our pre-modern background, the actual inner life had yet to make any noticeable mark. We must remember that "…the intellectual revolution [of the Renaissance] was profound, and was both cause and consequence of the enormous extension of knowledge and experience in time and space. Greek and Roman history and especially the latter came into ever clearer view and the increasing knowledge of classical civilization posed anew the problem of the relationship between classical and Christian values."[81] These changes occurred in generally small increments that eventually lead—combined with other historic changes —to a large impact. This is not a history of the mind but rather of the mental assumptions that dominated at any given time and as it applies to the birth and development of consciousness. Here the anachronisms are plentiful.

Having said that, what do we do with such a term as capitalism? For even here the revisionists wanting to avoid falling into the linguistic trap that plagues the history recorded in Burckhardt's masterpiece, still seem again to fall into it themselves. An example of this view regarding changing economics can be found in the following:

> Capitalism acted as a solvent on the corporate forms of medieval urban society and furnished a powerful incentive to autonomous individual enterprise. If a new spirit of individualism characterized the upper classes of Italy in the fourteenth and fifteenth centuries, it was as clearly manifest in the calculating audacity of the entrepreneur, whose success in a highly competitive business world depended solely

upon his knowledge and judgment, as it was in the self-reliance of the despot, the demagogue or the condottiere.[82]

To use the term *capitalism* within the structure of this era requires at the least something of lip service to the classic studies of Max Weber (c.1904) and R. H. Tawny (c.1925).[83] There is no doubt that one can make a case for the first baby steps of capitalism within the space of the Reformation even more so than the Renaissance, although the beginnings of mercantilism are clearly established in the Italian city states. Mercantilism, a more accurate term for the new economics, will dominate for at least the next two centuries. These new economic patterns and activities certainly did bring about some small increase in the pluralism of social types as well as contributing in a limited manner to more independence from the traditional closed socio-economic system, particularly when compared with the stringent restrictions inherent in feudalism and manorialism.

If we were to consider the Protestant movement's successful beginnings with Martin Luther we would note that three of his contemporaries included the Renaissance artists, Leonardo, Michelangelo and Raphael, as well as the significant literary figures, Machiavelli, and more devout, Erasmus and Sir Thomas More, each a genius in their own right notwithstanding their contributions to the Reformation while also running parallel to the Renaissance. Additionally, Michelangelo will live long enough (d.1564) to have become a contemporary not only of Copernicus (1473–1543) and Tycho Brahe (1546–1601), but will also die the year that Galileo was born. Three historic movements now overlap: Renaissance, Reformation and Scientific Revolution. Europe was moving in sundry directions: new expressions of institutionalized faith, new understanding of governing as well as new models and new perceptions of what it meant to live in Early Modern Europe and a studied universe. Machiavelli (1469–1527) was the Renaissance man who offered in his writings a new view of governing based upon his understanding of that classic term, virtue, influenced as he was by what had become something of a tradition of the Italian Renaissance contributing to our new sense of space and time, specifically political time. Machiavelli had a great deal to say about the political animal of his own day as well for the those who would march across future political stages. His three most important works were first, his polemic *The Prince* (1513), next the more philosophical, *Discourses on Livy* (c.1518) and although not his last work, his important political ideas regarding what must all too often have occurred, *The Art of War* (1521). While very controversial, and for some, too cynical, his writings for others would eventually contribute in the modern university to our idea of contemporary Political Science departments, while his thoughts have proven to possess great weight, both for the world of politics as well as very early psychology.

The most misunderstood thought associated with Machiavelli is that he supposedly advocated the 'ends justifying the means.' Since political success, what was later to be called *raison d'état*, was what he in fact advocated, he did not intend that any means would be justified since some means may not have a positive impact for the safety and security of the state. As a forerunner of *realpolitik* he had a clear understanding of what virtue for a political leader was; i.e., knowledge. The purpose of this virtue or knowledge was, of course, the survival of the state: "...for where the well-being of one's country is at all in question, no consideration of justice or injustice, of mercy or cruelty, of honor or shame must be allowed to enter in at all. Indeed, every other consideration having been put aside, that course of action alone which will save the life and liberty of the country ought to be wholeheartedly pursued."[84] This knowledge, this 'virtue,' was of two distinct types. The first knowledge was that which embraced the nature of being human of which he found to be less than complimentary: "For this can be said about the generality of men; that they are ungrateful, fickle, dissembling, anxious to flee danger, and covetous of gain. So long as you promote their advantage, they are all yours, as I said before, and will offer you their blood, their goods, their lives, and their children when the need for these is remote."[85] While this would strike many as very cynical, for political historians, this is a far less startling picture. Of more interest, perhaps, is the second category of his virtues or a different type of knowledge: a knowledge of history. Influenced by the classical Greek historian Polybius (c.205–c.123 B.C.), he concluded that every political system is either on an incline or a decline. All the political leader can do is either slow the decline or, if expanding, encourage growth, attempting to speed up and further encourage the country's development. The reason for this historic sense—that all good leaders must possess—is that all societies fluctuate between growing and dying. Societies, he suggests, begin in virtue, move on to political stability, then experiment with innovation and finally and eventually must experience instability. Therefore, how well the leadership understands the historic place of the kingdom determines in part the level of political success. As for what the average member of the political community perceives, it is best that the leader be perceived as a charitable, humane, humorous, imaginative and that he is someone who possesses integrity and most importantly, be a man of piety. This impression should not interfere, however, with the actual activity of governance even if contradictory to perceptions. As for the people's responses to, as well their regard for their prince, it is best that they both love and fear their leader; if only one of these two psychological responses is to apply, then let it be fear since it is more important to be obeyed than loved. As Machiavelli put it, "…men are less concerned about offending someone they have cause to love than someone they have cause to fear. Love endures by a bond which men, being scoundrels, may break whenever it serves their advantages to do so; but fear is supported by the dread of pain, which is ever present."[86] And if that was not clear enough, he adds, "…still a prince should make himself feared in such a way that, though he does not gain love, he escapes hatred; for being feared but not hated go readily together."[87] Again, is this cynical or realistic? The important point for the historian of the Renaissance and Reformation remains that he was anticipating the politics that were just being born—the politics of the nation state. In fact there is no way to get to the birth of a strong sense of self without a driving individuality that separates you from mankind and society leaving you alone with your own inner ontology. This can only be done by letting go of the inherent assumptions of a fixed social and political order. Most liberties are in the beginning liberty from, while only in time can it later become freedom to and of.

Perhaps one of the best early examples of this combination of Renaissance humanism and religion during the Catholic Reformation occurred with the rise of the modern political state in Spain when Ferdinand and Isabella finally unified their lands in 1491 with the help of the Church of Rome, suppressing Moors and Jews with the religious leadership of Cardinal Ximenes (1436–1517). Religion was a very useful political tool, even before the rise of Protestantism. Meanwhile, throughout Europe, Calvinism spread quickly, especially in the Germanies, Switzerland, England and Scotland as well as somewhat in France (Huguenots) and within the borders of what would eventually be Holland. All this reflects the power of the religious movements, their ties to the new politics of bourgeoning nation states, the inadequacies of Rome in satisfying the needs for certainty, a hunger to end all doubt, and the development of silent reading tied to the recent influence of the printing press. These changes, especially in the north, were far more extensive beyond those within the Italian city-states. Christianity had, in the beginning, offered answers to the dilemma of death—the faithful's sword of an eternal life. However, as these changes occurred they brought an expansion of living and a transformed reality of death, for the sword appeared to be two-sided, offering eternal salvation on one side and the possibility of damnation on the other.

The psychological crises of the later Middle Ages has been documented by John Aberth when he speaks of the Apocalypse: famine, war, plague and death became commonplace, and "...plenty of chroniclers of the plague accused their contemporaries of moral turpitude."[88] Unbelievable burdens of life and death, righteousness and condemnation along with fear and despair marked the same chronological period as humanistic optimism; it was just a matter of when and where you lived, with the south more optimistic and the north enduring more trepidation.

With the appearance of the nation state and a 'Machiavellian' sense of political order, a rationalized, humanized and systematized means of governing was beginning to replace the outdated medieval feudal-church schematic and organic fixed hierarchy of governance. By the end of the sixteenth century the French political philosopher, Jean Bodin (c.1530–96), was actively thinking through the modern concept of sovereignty, one that allowed for the power of the state to be within the state with a limited monarchy, leaving behind the fixed heavens of the Great Chain of Being with a divinity and then monarchs at the top. The state and not a personality would be the basis for laws. These changes, these beginnings of the rise of secularized European states, are but a few of the many that made for the possibility of the individual to begin growing into an eventual central force; first with emancipation from the historic social constraints followed by an expansion of political space which will eventually begin to be filled with a growing number of individuals.

The economics of opportunity also gave the nascent individual more room to flex. Arguably, one of the many famous example is the story of Henry VIII's financial and dynastic needs. At the time, wrong though it may have been, it was believed that the burden for the sex of a child was on the woman and since Isabella, Henry's wife, had a daughter, he believed he needed another wife to give him a male child. From this arose England's break from Rome. This move enabled him to confiscate church, and particularly monastic properties which would help fill his depleted coffers. From Spain, as another example, the great wealth from the New World poured into the homeland and led to comfort, complacency and lack of initiative that contributed eventually to Spain moving from being the first great power in Europe under Phillip II to a backwater in the centuries to come. Holland took advantages of the new trading opportunities to become an important part of the wool industry, especially in processing and exporting. Under Cosimo De Medici, Florence became the financial center of Europe with its golden florin, which was, for a time the most trusted coin of Europe. Additionally, there is the appearance of double-entry book-keeping, indicating profit was becoming a key component of the new economics, notwithstanding the traditional condemnation of usury by the Church. Each country had somewhat different experiences in their economic and political evolution moving into the seventeenth century where modernization was increasingly becoming the rule. Thus, these new states were creating needed new economies in order to operate their new and experimental political structures, creating mercantilism, a system which would be more attuned to supporting the state and encouraging the exercise of opportunists.

The institutional changes that would create national monarchies in place of medieval systems nevertheless continued for a time supporting the authority of the Divine Right of Kings which was part of the larger theory of the Great Chain of Being. However, there were new economic structures where trade would come to dominate. Additionally, many of the northern religious reformers began returning to older practice of mysticism, moving in the direction of the earlier post-Roman world of the extremely devout, the hermits and saints who were significant in the earlier church. The Black Death, not surprisingly, offered fertile ground for the spread of these movements with the a sense of the mystical and immediate communion with God. The addition of the Hundred Years' War between France and England only further exacerbated an already difficult sequence of crises. The Church contribution to this disillusionment, after political choices coincided with the arrival of political instability and grew so extreme and threatening in Rome that it decided to move its center of operation from Rome to southern France, a period known as the Babylonian Captivity (1309–77). One can only imagine the horror for those so concerned for their soul's salvation, attempting to follow Church doctrine and remain in harmony with the one and only true Church of Rome. An additional mistake in judgement occurred when it appeared that the papacy had taken sides in this centuries-long conflict between England and France by moving its headquarters to France. How should the English and non-French continentals (devout men like Thomas à Kempis from a small Rhineland town, Kempen) subscribe to such a politicized church? This was followed by the Great Schism beginning in 1378 when the papacy moved back to Rome and the French cardinals and clerics, having grown accustomed to the pomp and power of a 'French Church' created their own Papacy and College of Cardinals at Avignon. During the time of this dualistic church with a monolithic belief, until its end at the Council of Constance (1414–1417), the crisis of salvation reached epidemic proportions: it was the Fourth Lateran Council that established that eternal life and salvation was dependant on being in harmony with the one and true church of Rome. This was part of a larger theological orthodoxy which created, arguably, the church's greatest weapon, the requirement annual confessions. But to what church does a penitent confess: Rome or Avignon? To this day the church has not declared directly or indirectly which of the papacies were the one and true. But perhaps, rather than an issue of politics and theology, it was the crisis of the plague more than anything that drove many towards an alternative and a more personal relationship with God. At least that is one interpretation:

> In the face of plague, it seems, medieval man was powerless. The Black Death of 1348–49 can now be said to have carried off at least half of England's and Europe's population, but his was merely the beginning of a century and a half of recurring epidemic disease. During the later Middle Ages, death was, sometimes quite literally, always in the air. Even so, a remarkable resilience can be detected in the flowering of mysticism that occurred throughout England and the Continent as this time. Both men and women sought a closer, more personal rapport with God, perhaps in part because they wanted to better understand his will, even if that meant death on an unimaginable scale. But if God's ways remained mysterious, it was enough to know that a supremely wise and benevolent deity was fulfilling his own plan for the history of the world and for man's place within it.[89]

A young Europe was under great threat and the Church appeared to be too often part of the problem and not the solution. While the north enjoyed the growth of new national political entities with great suffering from multiple wars, the south experienced their own crisis of conscience with many Renaissance artists and humanists responding by creating a new psychological art form, braggadocio. Where Augustine would make pride the deadliest of all sins, the Italians were, in the form of becoming braggarts, resurrecting an ancient social activity and treating it as a virtue. It was a crisis of conscience when conscience meant everything.

The psychological structure of the Western mind had gone through a series of constructs and collapses, each moving our thinking processes and assumptions to new levels of self-revelation as we moved further from Antiquity. With the end of the Ancient world there evolved a unifying set of mental systems, in which the Western mind entered a fragile and tenuous union dedicated to the day after death: a singular Christian union with a singular god and faith given daily support by the actions of both an inventive feudal and manorial system where monotheism and social order had fused. The Church sustained order and contributed to innovation. However, the diversity of economics and political orientation were clearly beginning to impact the city-states of Renaissance Italy. The Medieval world gave way to the weight of a Church and social problems that had left the church, as an institution for guidance, discredited and a feudal order that had increasingly no role in the coming of such developments as the use of money and trade, and the rise of universities with expanded curriculum choices. Tied to the Italian states, along with the discovery of a once viable and unique historic Antiquity, there were added technical changes that would imply different thinking processes and sets of assumptions, some belonging to the cultural impact of the compass, gun powder, mechanical clock, spinning wheel, treadle loom, windmill and water mills and most importantly, the printing press. The old world had to give way since the new world had no room for it. It is with these developments that the Protestant Reformation began, ironically, from Antiquity and its own Medieval roots. Pluralism, secularism, diversity and the development of modern science find their foundation here.

What is loosely termed the Protestant Reformation is less an event and more a series of accumulative occurrences. Once begun, they were followed by the Roman responses which were known as the Counter-Reformations. The result was a tower of babel, more confused than ever with a Christianity filled with violence and a decline of all generosity. Luther's impact in the Germanies, or Calvin's influence in Geneva and in southern France with the rise of the Huguenots, or Henry VIII's Anglican Church, is here of less interest than the encouragement of an even more personal relationship with faith, or at least the faith subscribed to by one's family. This was a step into further personalizing a relationship with God. The increasing privacy in religion would in time become increasingly normative and had to be one of the more important contributions to our understanding of some of the earliest expressions of a sense of self. Combine the expansion of silent reading and the availability of books—thanks to the printing press—with this more personal deity and certainly there is a guarantee of a Europe never seen before.

When the Protestant movement arrived it settled on a soil rich with the compost of a decaying church, corrupt feudal rule and an opportunism born of a series of crises. It is generally too often thought that the printing press was the most powerful singular invention in the history of man's cultural evolution. But reading remained as public an event as it had always been. The printing press unto itself would not have altered the picture of a family reading together that Rembrandt (1606–1669) portrayed in his painting, *Holy Family* where the father reads the Good Book to his family, a common Protestant activity. The family and the Bible replace the Roman Church as the intermediary to God.

Remember, Rembrandt as a Protestant artist painted some 62 self-portraits, a grand example of a sinner in Augustine's book, again practicing that deadliest of the seven sins: pride. While he was an extremely talented and religious artist of the Protestant movement, he was also an 'individualized' artist of the Baroque period that grew out of the Renaissance artists. As one commentator has noted, he "...deliberately used Dutch realism to explore man's inner life, especially the world of religious feeling, mystery, and destiny."[90]

The Renaissance artists did not disappear with the arrival of the Reformation but rather some of them became part of that next artistic movement first known as Mannerism then followed by the Baroque, all leading into early hints of the Enlightenment. With the traditional economic and political order in various states of turmoil, people increasingly found themselves looking at a narrower community, the family, and even in a few cases, as with mystics and later thinkers like Montaigne, turning inward. Somewhere in all this, one can sense the beginning of the modern notion of the individual, an attitude nascent in the writings of both Thomas Hobbes and René Descartes.

This is a story where countries become increasingly independent of Rome and their own neighbors, with Spain, England, Holland, France and regions within the Germanies becoming increasingly linguistically self-contained, having their own trade, understanding their own (vernacular) language and their own concept of what it means to be a Christian. The Reformation movement and the progress of nation states grew in a parallel manner. When the earlier wars of religion, those between German princes who joined Luther in opposition to the (Spanish, Catholic) Holy Roman Emperor ended at the peace of Augsburg in 1555, the principle established was *cuius regio, eius religio*—the religion of the prince would be the religion of the people, "...a revolution of the first magnitude."[91] In time, of course, the people would choose for themselves, but it can be seen, just as double-entry book-keeping records the value of profit which encourages the 'individual' to maximize personal gain, so too, opening the door to eternal salvation meant that the individual, or at least some, would eventually be encouraged in time to find their own way. As for the relationship between the changes in religious passions and interpretations and of the political and social organizations, they would remain problematic throughout the sixteenth century, not to be resolved until the next. This immediate crisis between states—the defining of religion within the new walls of these nations—was not resolved until the end of the Thirty Years' War (1618–1648). This war was fought in four stages, with varied alliances between different newly-formed national governments and German principalities. The first three periods of fighting were followed by short truces, respite and adjustment of alliances. The treaties brought allies together by way of their respective religious persuasions, Protestant countries in opposition to those that were Catholic. During the fourth and last period of warfare, the alliances and battles fought were not based on religious alliances but along national lines, with an alliance of several Catholic and Protestant countries fighting against another alliance of several other Catholic and Protestant countries. What started as a religious war had become a national or secular conflict. Machiavelli's secular argument for defending the good of the state, not what was good for the soul, had survived.

Reading and the printing press, however, has had a more subtle and far more reaching impact upon our psyche. Before turning toward literacy and silent reading, however, it would be appropriate to first end this area of study as we began, discussing the transformation of language. We began with the writings of Dante and Petrarch and will finish chronologically with that of Shakespeare's dramas, for one of his many particularities was his ability to end a plot with a completed a circle, ending his plays with a final scene reminding us of its beginning scene: a creative closed world. Specifically, two points are appropriate here to our discussion of the rise of the individual and sense of self and the power of our awareness of death. These points have, independently of each other, been studied and discussed in some very fine works regarding Shakespeare's art.

The first issue to comprehend is that the tragedies of Shakespeare exist to a great extent because of the open space that had become a condition between man and his God. As long as there is an immediacy of divine presence whether it is in the Gothic cathedral, the role of the Roman church in every day living through the sacraments, or the power of the system to make a significant difference in daily living, there was no room for tragedy. How can there be tragedy with God in all His eminence? We recall that a peasant in the High Medieval period 'knew' God by observing Him in the cathedrals, in the statuary, the stained windows and on the cross. He was there because He was seen. Where there is an efficacious divine power there can be no tragedy. This strength of His presence through the exclusive door of the Roman Church was receiving less and less unqualified and blind support, however. The appearance of heresies and their suppression was only becoming more common that by the end of the fifteenth century religious questions and doubts were beginning to expand. Vernacular bibles were appearing, making it possible for the local literates to find their own way. Henry VIII had left the Church only after having been given by Rome the title 'Defender of the Faith,' a title, *Fidei Defensor* still worn by today's English monarchs. Arrows of contradictions appeared to fly in various directions.

Shakespeare's England was, therefore, a land that pointed to salvation without a powerful ancient church positioned between man and God and instead placing the more personal Bible in that crucial position, despite Henry and his theologian, Thomas Cranmer (1489–1556), retaining a remarkable similarity in theology to that of Rome. In a very real sense this genius of a playwright did the same, pointing to the future while holding onto the past. The implication for us today has been illustrated by Harold Bloom in his *Shakespeare. The Invention of the Human* where the "Player King" in *Hamlet* states:

> Our wills and fates do so contrary run
> That our devices still are overthrown,
> Our thoughts are ours, their ends none of our own. [92]

The power of the past and ties to the future can also be found in another study, *Hamlet in Purgatory*, where Steven Greenblatt has suggested that the late-Medieval Catholic notion of purgatory is still found in the Protestant Reformation of sixteenth century England: a half-way house between damnation and salvation.

In a world of the Armada of 1588, religious wars and massive continuous transformations, death retained a powerful force on the psyche.[93] A simple but clear example from Shakespeare can be drawn from a medieval art that deals with death, and where it has been observed that, "Of all the cadaverous art and literature produced during the later Middle Ages, that of Death dancing with a series of partners culled from the whole range of the medieval social hierarchy was perhaps the most popular. Texts and images of the Dance of Death, or *Danse Macabre*, penetrated nearly all countries of Europe and inspired some of its most famous authors…it appeared in Shakespeare's *Measure for Measure*…"[94] The audience for his plays understood the meaning of these dances, which was perhaps one of many ways to work the issue of death into a ritual that would put a distance between the living and that fear.[95] As for purgatory, there remained this issue of some form of transition between the laws of hell and eventuality of heavenly salvation as well as a debt to the 'faithfully departed' in Protestant England. Today we note that the burden for those who live as survivors from an accident are simply not that they lived but that they lived while others died, leaving feelings of guilt for the survivor. Put more directly, death is not a burden for the dead but for the living.

It is this and much more about Shakespeare's *œuvre* that is significant for our study, for it is this giant dramatist who was the first to introduce a modern notion of self, of our very humanity, as Bloom has suggested. Ironically, we should not consider that the dramatist's work is only to be known on the stage, seen and heard, but not necessarily read, for reading the play closely is indispensable not only for the director, actors and production crew, but also for the audience. Words worthy of production are worth reading and in the Reformation, the word takes on a new importance that has led us to our own world.

This will become clearer, however, as we enter into era so dominated by religious Reformation movements.

CHAPTER FOUR

THE REFORMATION OF EARLY MODERNITY

It is generally acknowledged that the sixteenth century represents the watershed in the transition between traditional and modern European societies.[1]

FROM REFORM TO RE-ORDER

The Early Modern period of European history is so significant that trying to separate its Reformation from its Renaissance aspects can inevitably lead to distortions. The creation of historical periodization, silent reading and a new excitement regarding the vernacular languages as well as the applications of varied mechanical marvels and scientific thought had a great deal more impact on society and ideas and the way we think of ourselves than is always properly noted. There are varied reasons for this historic attitude, one summarized here states part of it succinctly:

> Not because social institutions begin around that time to evolve in a more rational direction, but because somewhere in the course of this century there appear in recognizable form many of the institutions we have come to take for granted as dominant features of the modern age: administrative bureaucracies, professionally staffed armies, the massive intervention of the state in economic life. By necessity or accident, the religious division of Europe and the discovery of the new world coincide in time with the legitimization of practices which our era accepts as the criteria of effective government.[2]

What is problematic in integrating this period into a cohesive whole is that the Reformations, which began well before the end of the Renaissance continued into the period of the Scientific Revolution and the next stage of modernism and evolving secularism. That this is not an easy era to either cover or to clarify, especially when considering the changes that have occurred psychologically in the West and must not be underestimated. Thus, again what follows must remain tentative.

The psychological structure of the western mind had gone through a series of constructs, alterations and collapses, each moving our thinking processes and assumptions to new levels of self-discovery. One example of this is that with the movement from Antiquity to the Renaissance we witness increased heresies beginning in the second century and the church's response with the creation of the New Testament, the fourth century Nicene Creed and the thirteenth century's offering of the Fourth Lateran Council. The pressure of heresies was a critical problem for the Church. With the evolution of the Italian states as well the (re)discovery of a once viable Antiquity adding to the technical changes that would imply different thinking processes that effectively undermined traditional assumptions, the world of Medieval thinking lost its ability to enclose those assumption as the startling cultural changes of clocks, optics, vernacular and most significant, the printing press changed our way of thinking. Pluralism, secularism, diversity and the rise of modern science all find their early expressions here.

Because the term *Protestant Reformation* refers mostly to a series of accumulative occurrences that offered a set of responses to what was seen as a negative and corrupt Roman church, we will work cautiously. The hunger for freedom from doubt had now grown into a demand for a new order of faith. This was followed by the response to these protests of the Roman Church's Counter-Reformation. Western religion was growing increasingly confused with a Christianity often filled with violence, sometimes reactionary, and for a time, devoid of common or moral sense. Thus, a personalization of religion would increasingly be the normative Western approach to faith and would be one of the more important contributions of our understanding of the rise of an early expression of a unique and clearer sense of the self. And yet, rather than finding a great deal of movement towards the independent self, the opposite in some ways occurred:

> This solitary and silent reading was a very Protestant and potentially seditious experience, for there is no control over the imaginings, speculations, and impertinences of the silent reader as there would be in public readings. The invention and spread of movable type is probably the most important mechanical contributor to the idea of the unique self, but other forces—religious and political revolutions, and rediscovery and admiration for classical models of being—retarded the assertion of the self.[3]

Combine the expansion of silent reading, the availability of books and this more personal deity and you receive a guarantee of a significant alteration of the European mind, assumptions and relationship to belief, although these possibly radical transformations were tempered by political upheaval.

While it cannot be denied that the printing press was one of the important contributions to literacy, it also remained an important stimulant for the growing ability to read silently. The printing press, on the other hand, did not change that picture of a family, led by the father, publicly reading the Bible which can be seen in Rembrandt's painting, *The Holy Family*. But this early silent reading contributed less at this time to the century of a self since its driving force was meant to expand spiritual dimensions. It was still too early for a secular world with room for a secular self.

Rembrandt was not the only Protestant artist to work in defense of this new version of an old religion. Another fine artist in this new tradition deserving mention was the master of the broadside propaganda pieces for the Protestant cause, Albrecht Dürer (1471–1528). Using block printing he could produce a plethora of pieces to paste on walls as propaganda to further encourage the Protestant cause. Another unique and interesting artist of the time, one we know so little about was also from the Netherlands and witnessed much of the religious confusion in the earlier years of the conflict between Protestants and Catholics; this was the rather enigmatic Pieter Bruegel (c.1520– 1569). Among his many works some of the most interesting dealt with the lives of peasants, a not particularly popular topic of the times. In addition to these Protestant artists there were those of Catholic persuasion who also used art to explore and popularize their own religious point of view. For example, in the seventeenth century, religious conviction and concern in the arts can be found in Bernini's mystical *Saint Teresa*, a work of a genuinely devout Catholic. Another Catholic artwork is the remarkable tableau called *The Triumph of the Eucharist*, by Peter Paul Rubens.[4] While both Bernini and Rubens demonstrate the overlap between the Renaissance artists and the impact of the Reformation, they are, of course, worth enjoying for their fine art in the Renaissance tradition with or without a consideration of religious persuasion.

Renaissance artists, Protestantism and the rise of individuality have a significant relationship in the turmoil regarding the traditional economic and political order where people found themselves increasingly looking at a narrower community, that of the family. There were, additionally, a few who turned inward in a revival of varied mystic and religious movements. And more importantly, there appeared certain significant thinkers like Michel Montaigne (1533–92) who began to move toward a more secular inwardness.[5] In this and so much more, one can sense the beginning of the modern notion of individuality and the corollaries of self and consciousness that will receive their first serious expression in the thinking and writings of René Descartes. The Reformation movement, however, needs explication and understanding for it did and did not contribute to the modern mind.

In the year of 1517, Martin Luther (1483–1546) posted his 95 theses to be debated on the doors of the Wittenberg church in his attempt to correct what he thought were mistakes in church theology. His personal crisis has led at least one writer to suggest that this was the beginning of the appearance of a singular self and at the least, this argument attempts to distinguish "...the 'inner' man from the physical one."[6] This was a crisis of the spirit much like Augustine had suffered, however, it is not valid view of the modern secular self. Moreover, the concept of grace and therefore the central role of divine intervention for the certainty of eternal bliss which was first articulated by Augustine now reappears in an altered form at the hands of Martin Luther: "Luther, therefore, developed a new conception of grace which, he believed, did not operate magically and mechanically through the sacraments, but directly, as a constant, dynamic, ethical force in the individual, enabling him to combat sin, which is always present until death, and to fulfill the law, which requires righteousness. God had made this possible by sacrificing Christ on the cross."[7] This is, after all, the story of Luther's personal spiritual crisis, or series of these crises and not a philosophic analysis. In a very fine study of Luther's hunger for feelings of salvation, R. H. Bainton offers a very good beginning.[8] Simply put, Luther felt he could not be certain he was saved from damnation and was therefore trapped between eternal life and damnation. How did he know that he confessed ALL his sins? Had he committed any sins since his last confession but yet before going to communion? These questions led this Augustinian monk to visit Rome, the seat of his faith. But he received no lasting satisfaction from the experience and so his chief abbot suggested he teach at the local university in order to find some merit of salvation. It was here that he found what he believed to be his answer: salvation by faith alone. This simply meant good works do not make a good soul for one is saved because of the generous grace God has offered through the sacrifice of his son. Luther places salvation on acceptance not on man's but on God's actions. "Luther's emphasis upon the omnipotence of God and the importance of man is reflected in his doctrine that God draws man into fellowship freely, even giving him the power to believe. Thus he disregarded the nominalist doctrine that God considers the works or merits of man acceptable and on the basis of these imputes righteousness to him through grace. Not even faith should be considered a merit."[9] Little wonder that the spiritual crisis he personally felt and which was resolved at first by the Pauline doctrine of 'salvation by faith alone' proved lacking since he had several later spiritual crises—as he referred to them. Nevertheless, he had faith and grace now to guide him since he could simply lean very "...heavily upon the letters of Paul and the Gospel of John…" His immediate guides, however, were in his discovery that there were "…mystics [who] had opposed the intellectualism of the scholastics and stressed the importance of man because of original sin, man's inability to merit forgiveness, and the necessity of believing and trusting in salvation of Christ." Their mistake was that "…they had not developed the Pauline doctrine of justification."[10] While this was a position not unlike Augustine's, it was even more so for Luther since he had a very deep sense of a more extreme Tertullian concept of being unworthy and thus damned, although, through the miracle of divine grace, salvation could be achieved. A good person naturally does good works while good works do not make a good person thus allowing God to make salvation possible.[11] Again, not surprisingly, there is this sense of an Augustinian approach in Luther who although an Augustinian monk, could not understand or appreciate his problems with the church hierarchy. After all, Luther was a thoughtful student who had been influenced by several Renaissance writers: "[He] also showed considerable interest in the New Learning. He made use of the Biblical scholarship as Valla, Pico, Lefèvre d'Etaples, Reuchlin, and Erasmus; joined the humanists of his day in their assaults upon scholasticism, sympathizing openly with Reuchlin in his conflict with the theologians of Cologne; shared their demands for reform; and enjoyed their support during the first critical years of his activities as a reformer."[12] Because Luther understood that he could not find justification on his own or by his own acts, he eventually argued for the "priesthood of all believers." Who needs the church? With his singular act of 1517 the basis for the Reformation that would impact throughout most of Europe had begun. This was not what he had wanted, but opening the door, even if a crack, created unintended consequences with many subsequent reformists.

Luther is supporting a perspective that points backward, turning to the early traditions that had been the practice of, specifically, going directly to God, without either middle-men or a meddling Church. The first reappearance of this simpler exercise of faith occurred in the High Medieval world. The immediate roots for Luther's approach, therefore, was a result of a movement that appeared in the previous century, the mystic movement that attacked the church for becoming more and more worldly. Luther had come to gradually "…interpret the entire Bible in the sense of the Pauline conception of justification and how he found support for his views in the works of Augustine and Dionysius and the medieval mystics, St. Bernard, Master Eckhart, Tauler and Gerson. He was particularly influenced by a book of an unknown author of the fourteenth-century circle of mystics in western Germany called the 'Friends of God.'"[13] This was one of many groups, mostly in the north, that belonged under the general rubric of *Devotio Moderna* and was a non-institutionally driven spiritual revival. This more recent mystic attitude was demonstrated by those who "…sought religious satisfaction primarily by stressing pious living and proximity to God. This was a religious approach favored especially by townsmen, who found scholastic subtleties beyond them and preferred a simple, practical and intuitive theology. The movement was strongest along the Rhine River in Germany and the Low Countries during the fourteenth and fifteenth centuries."[14] One of the earliest of these mystically inclined thinkers, one with a lasting impact in the north, was the German thinker Master Eckhart (1260–1327), who as a Dominican scholar was to develop a speculative theology where man had the ability to become one with God.[15] Further west, another very influential mystic who helped create this northern *Devotio Moderna* made his appearance:

> It was inspired by Gerard Groote (1340–84), a wealthy canon lawyer who had become a Carthusian monk and devoted the rest of his life to reforming the clergy and teaching the young. His followers, called the Brethren of the Common Life, constituted a semimonastic order of layman who took to irrevocable vows but sought to live lives of piety according to the ethics of the Sermon on the Mount. In seeking to carry out their ideas into practice they cultivated the inner live, lived by the work of their own hands, cared for the poor, and educated the young.[16]

This was a movement for those seeking spiritual support and who were looking for a more direct and personal sense of salvation than they felt they could find among the scholastics and members of the church hierarchy. The people in this northern movement were mostly laymen, not part of the institution of the church and dissatisfied with the rituals of faith in place of a simple sense of satisfaction that arises from a simple act of faith. The traditional scheme for finding certainty was clearly losing some of its comforting paradigm. The group known as the Brethren of the Common Life was one of several of the more significant and popular movements satisfying a hunger for a certainty in an after-life with their Lord. Arguably, of the varied members, Thomas à Kempis may be the best known. As the author of *The Imitation of Christ* he personalized religion and minimized the importance of formal Christian rituals. He emphasized peace of soul, purity of thought, and simplicity of life, making his work one of the most widely read books of his day.[17] This book was and has remained a very significant and popular hand-book for those mystically inclined on how to behave if eternal life is the goal. This type of personalization particularly impacted upon a great number of Christian humanists, mostly in the north, with one of the most famous northern writers and reformers being Desiderius Erasmus (c.1466–1536). As an intellectual writer who sought to stay within the church, he sought reform within rather than in breaking away. This explains why he could be an original supporter of Luther, i.e., as a reformer, but no longer so when Luther found himself excommunicated. In fact, Luther's original positions "…were similar enough to those of the Brethren that his opponents accused him of Hussite doctrines immediately after the publication of his Ninety-five Theses in 1517."[18] The Hussites had been condemned for heresy earlier and were one of those groups advocating the creation in the vernacular of what they considered to be a corrected Bible. Silent reading and the printing press only exacerbated the attempt to contain heretical thought.

Erasmus was a practical man of letters, a northern humanist also known as "the Christian humanist" who had married the tradition of a humble striving after the virtuous life, as recommended by Thomas à Kempis, with that of the knowledge and eloquence learnt from the Italian humanists. Erasmus went, of course, much beyond that in his writings, especially his very famous *Praise of Folly*, a lampoon written when ill and as a guest of his good friend Sir Thomas More. More is of course well-known for his opposition to Henry VIII when, as the Archbishop of Canterbury, he refused to support the King's desire for a Papal dispensation to divorce and remarry. The flexibility and fluidity of the new politics and economics of these changing times were too overwhelming for any one person or any institution to control. The concept of an evolution by way of a cultural natural selection clearly was operational if not understood. Perhaps it should not surprise us that Sir Thomas More's most famous writings happen to be his *Utopia*, a word he coined meaning *nowhere*. What one notes when reading it is that it is in fundamental ways a reactionary and idealistic piece, attempting to create a mythic past of an ideal world. Such an important work that is more reactionary while claiming to point to the future will not appear again until the nineteenth century. This is a story, in part, of those countries that became increasingly independent of Rome and its traditional role as a political power-broker. The nascent nation states, exemplified by Spain, England and the Netherlands became increasingly self-contained with their own languages, their own commitment to trade, national economies and the growing variations of their understanding of what it meant to be Christian. France along with Spain remained in the Catholic fold while England and Holland moved away. Religious wars and the rise of the nation states grew together. Whether one were Catholic or Lutheran was not a personal choice but that of the prince of the lands wherein they resided. There is no doubt that this was, "a revolution of the first magnitude,"[19] as noted, and insofar as this marked an end to the Roman Catholic Church controlled hegemony, it could be in retrospect even more significant for the psyche of the average faithful.

People, in time, would choose for themselves, but, as double-entry bookkeeping introduced the efficacy and power of profit which encouraged families (and individuals) to maximize their personal gain, so too opening of doors to external salvation meant that the individual, or at least those so inclined, would eventually be encouraged to find their own way to certainty rather than rely upon being told what road to take. This process would take centuries for the full impact to make its presence fully appreciated. As for the relationship between the changing religious passions and interpretations with the political needs of various states, this situation would not be resolved until the end of the Thirty Years' War. This is part of the fascinating story of the rise of a secular approach, perhaps in part out of pure necessity, in an extremely conflicting set of countries (politics) and religions (theologies) and which would eventually contribute to opening the door for a non-religious approach to an inner identity. By the end of the seventeenth century these confusions and conflicts were becoming clearer while hostility was simply diversifying.

> This is not surprising, since the seventeenth century was a period of great contrasts, even of polarities. Catholic and Protestant Europe, now permanently divided; mystic Spain and the down-to-earth Dutch Republic; 'classical' France and 'baroque' Italy; a dismembered and distracted Germany, its intellectual life dealt a severe blow by the Thirty Years' War; and Bourbon France, successful in its search for unity, law, and order; English empiricism and continental rationalism, not to speak of the eternal feuding among the sects, religious, philosophical, and political.[20]

The problem for those who dealt with the disparate phenomena of a changing world was where to place one's loyalties in order to know salvation. Added to the religious fanaticism of the Thirty Years' War was the War of the Three Henries in France at the end of the sixteenth century where the conflict between the Catholic and the Protestants (Huguenots) ended when the Huguenot leader, Henri of Navarre (1551–1610), became King Henri IV, the beginnings of the Bourbon reign until the French Revolution. In this process, Henri IV agreed to convert to Catholicism, followed by the implementation the Edict of Nantes (1598) which gave Huguenot villages and towns independence from Catholic Paris. Another example of secularization of government is found in England after the famed bloody revolution of 1648, the beheading of Charles I, followed by a decade of rule by the extremist Puritan

Oliver Cromwell and then the restoration of a more rational and legitimate governance in 1660 with the return of another Stewart, Charles II. The Glorious Revolution of 1688 simply made concrete the combined rule of parliament and monarchy, a genuine rationalization of English governance. *Raison d'état* and secularization were finally coming to dominate in England and France.[21]

These conflicts, wars and slaughter raise an interesting observation regarding a most peculiar phenomena which had been occurring, a phenomena where the Catholics killed Lutherans who killed Zwinglians who killed Calvinists who killed Anglicans who killed Catholics, who killed…! The point is clear: for a time it could be said that a Christian was defined as one who killed Christians in the name of Christ. This was clearly unsustainable. Thus, a gigantic shift from the religious wars to a national (and more rational) identity can be found in these years of upheaval. Secularism was almost a necessary approach given the religious madness. Stability was needed, if for no other reason than it was good for business. From 1648, onward, the issues would be primarily political and economic with a continuous decline in theological influences. Machiavelli's demand for the working of an intelligent prince who was dedicated alone to the good of the state was beginning to dominate the social structures. Again history caught up with genius.

This is not to say that the Church of Rome was not aware of the need for reform, if for no other reason than to maintain Roman control over Christian Europe. The church did attempt to improve its image, and attempted to make it more attuned to the devout and their spiritual needs. One way the Church of Rome addressed these spiritual needs was by controlling the Bible. Spain of the fifteenth century with Ferdinand and Isabella acquired the aid of Cardinal Ximenes who cleared the Spanish universities of any heresies and created a newer polyglot version of a the New Testament, a Greek text tied next to a Vulgate (Latin), and called it the *Compultensian* which was eventually published in 1520. Thus even Church leaders could and did become involved fairly early with the opportunities of the printed word and the creation of newer studious editions of their sacred writings. Even Erasmus produced a Greek version in 1516 and a Latin version in 1519. An interest in the Bible did not necessarily alienate one from the Roman church.

In response to the Protestants themselves, the Church used two tools, the first, a major gathering at the Council of Trent (1545–1563) that would articulate for the faithful what it meant to be a Catholic, establishing further definitions and clarifications of orthodoxy as well as the basis for further definition of heresy. It was here that the concept of transubstantiation, a theological theory where the priest is actually converting the host, the bread and the wine into the body and blood of Christ, was established as orthodoxy. This was intended to give the church increased power over the laity, specifically through clerical control of the Seven Sacraments, the primary doorway to God's grace and thus salvation. Confession and communion are the only two sacraments that establish and support the believer's ties to Christ that can be regularly repeated. These adjustments ran counter to Luther and the other reformists, such as Calvin in Geneva who rejected a variety of these Roman sacraments, especially the confessional.

One other weapon in the arsenal of the counter-reformation was the creation of the Society of Jesus (S. J.), or Jesuits, a kind of shock troops of the Roman Church. Saint Ignatius of Loyola, a one-time soldier turned pious, was responsible for the creation of his own spiritual warrior group, an "army of Christ." Their most important weapon was a "spiritual exercise" which would guide them in their committed obedience to the Papacy. Their successes were numerous, including the recapturing of Poland as well as southern Germany (Bavaria) from the Protestants. They were also effective in keeping France in line but failed in England where Queen Elizabeth firmly re-established the Anglican church. The Calvinists of France (Huguenots), especially in the south eventually would leave France for the New World in the following century after the Edict of Nantes was revoked.

What the varied reformist movements and the appearance of increasingly diverse numbers of Protestants as well as a Catholic Counter-Reformation could not stop was the increase in cultural pluralism expanding throughout Europe, in both the western and the eastern areas. The Catholic Spanish, Philip II, sought to expand his claims to the English throne and suppress the Dutch independence movement that William the Silent (d.1584), Prince of Orange, had led, for William had used his conversion to Protestantism (Calvinism) as an aid in breaking from the Catholic control of Spain. The Spanish Armada was meant only in part to exercise Philip's claims in England: it was also meant to suppress the rebellion in the Netherlands, which not only failed, but many interpreted as God siding with the Protestants.[22] Elizabeth I, who for political reasons had supported the Dutch rebellion, had no choice after her Catholic sister, Mary Tudor, died (1558). She had to return England to the Anglican Church if for no other reason than to establish her legitimacy since she would have been considered a bastard in Catholic theology as she was born after her father, Henry VIII, had broken from Rome and remarried. England, therefore, returned to an Anglican persuasion where it has remained.

These were leaders beginning to use *realpolitik* as a guide for action rather than acting on behalf of classical and medieval theological interpretation.

An interesting and significant phenomena in this reforming revolution, specifically regarding Elizabeth, is the role and nature of another sectarian group named after its founder, John Calvin (1509–64). Calvin, like so many reformers, was trained in the Renaissance humanist tradition, learned Greek, eventually edited a work of Seneca and acquired a law degree. Calvin—and the impact of his thinking—is one of the more significant of reformist leaders with ideas that in some ways turned traditional Christianity and values on its head even while opening the door wider for the appearance of a new degree of individuality, its companion, decentralization and new levels of diversity. He broke from Rome in 1534 and two years later produced one of his most significant works, *Institutes of the Christian Religion*. As was becoming more common, Calvin turned to the word instead of an institution, making the point that the true word of God cannot be found in any church but only in the Bible. This was appealing to those he was preaching to, specifically, the business community of Geneva. Given their growing economic opportunism and belief in profit which was so important for their nascent banking system, Genevans had found Roman positions untenable—at least those articulated by Thomas Aquinas. Thomas had held to the position that those who profited from such questionable activities as usury were damned. In this, Thomas was following the moral guidance of the Seven Deadly sins that operated in Christian communities throughout Medieval Europe. What was needed for the new economics was a justification for being a profit-driven merchant and banker while also finding salvation. Not surprisingly, some Protestants leaders will begin to emphasis the Hebrew Ten Commandments in place of the seven deadly sins, especially that regarding greed, in order to avoid restraints on profit.

Calvin was the right theologian at the right time for this new economic class. His approach was simply an extreme extrapolation of the Lutheran view regarding the certainty of salvation since for him all that was needed was absolute faith in Jesus Christ as savior. Agreeing with Luther, Calvin argued that good deeds did not make for good souls; rather, he held that good people perform good deeds because of inherently divinely-guided goodness. This was significant since one element of the Church's activity that particularly offended him and Luther was the selling of indulgences where the penitent need only pay for grace to acquire it from the Church. But Calvin went further than most when he took the step of announcing that all mankind is damned for the sins of Adam and Eve and no one deserved salvation no matter their actions. The key for Calvin, therefore, was that human nature was completely corrupt. God in His infinite mercy and for reasons that we cannot fathom however, will choose some to be saved but most are probably damned, or at the least should be. The diversity of theory regarding the two-sided sword, damnation and of salvation, now came to complete the subversion of any certainty of salvation from death. The problem was, he noted, that people suffered as a matter of a defect of understanding. Naturally everyone wanted to believe that they were one of the saved, and in this a construct of behavior was drawn, one associated with what would later become known as the blue-laws. The theory went that if you were saved, if for reasons that only God knows, then you would obviously be blessed and therefore it would follow that besides eventual liberation from death, you would be a community member of social stature, prosperous and filled with righteous behavior. After all if you lived a miserable life in poverty it made no sense that God was shining his countenance upon you. You, the favored of the Lord, would become a role model since everyone would want to believe that they too were one of the elect, and those most likely the elect would be the model to emulate. This was not far from a theocratic leaning and economic opportunism where outward conformity became increasingly expected. Not surprisingly, even the Anglican, Elizabeth I, only required outward conformity, which in her case required her subjects to appear each year at an Anglican service (even if you were a surreptitious Catholic). In the end, an unintended consequence (U.C.) was to contribute to increased secularism, even for those who would regularly attend church services. The role of faith was being compartmentalized, separated from the way one made a living and any secret life one might actually live. What was being created was a religion for opportunists where an increased secularism was finding a space and what had been an organic understanding of the world was slowly shifting into one that was more mechanical.

 The idea of a faith and a divinity that not only allowed for profit but also very successful profit (greed) changed the rules of what had been an otherworldly belief. This conceptual change was making Christianity into a new religion for those who were dedicated to profit and gain here and now: a this-worldly faith. Not surprisingly it took very little time for the idea to appear that those who are saved are blessed and if blessed, it should be evident in this world by way of wealth and status. This contrasts with the earlier model of a righteous Christian, St. Francis of Assisi (c.1181–1226) who gave his inherited wealth away to the poor and then entered into the market place to give away his last possessions, the clothes he was wearing, announcing he would pursue his mistress—poverty. The Franciscans carried on charity and good works but the Protestants in general, and Calvinists in particular, would have none of that Romanism. Max Weber posited the theory in his now classic work, *The Protestant Ethic and the Spirit of Capitalism* that this economically-driven religion was the basis for the beginnings of capitalism. This work has only acquired further support and corroboration through time.[23] Now, the two-sided sword had struck and would lead to the idea that people are only good because of God and for reasons that could never be understand. Moreover, being chosen would also at the same time mean that one was technically independent of any church and thus capable of moving into a new cultural and psychological direction while overtly retaining faith. Historically, of course, this argument has proven to be more appropriate to than just the deeds of capitalist Christians since it also implies a psychological independence.

Before turning to the bellwether writer of this era of change, William Shakespeare, it should be noted that a change in manners and behavior was also an inherent by-product of this transformational age. The social status structure like so much else at the time was unstable if not under attack by new ideas and functional realities. The Great Chain of Being into which all are born and which gave everyone a specific niche from the lowest—the feet or workers, middle—the sword or fighters, and the highest—Kings who rule and Popes who pray, was no longer sacrosanct, especially in the city-states of Italy where it never did take on such a strong hold: "Awareness of differences in social status seems also to have been unusually acute in Italy; at least, the vocabulary for describing these differences was unusually elaborate. The medieval view of society consisting of three groups—those who pray, those who fight and those who work the soil—was not one which appealed to the inhabitants of Italian cities, most of whom performed none of these functions."[24] One of our best sources for this creation of a new set of behavioral and social standards was *The Book of the Courtier* by Baldasar Castiglione (1478– 1529).[25] It was published in 1528 with an English translation in 1561, which gives evidence of its popularity. The idea of a handbook for appropriate behavior of the more affluent is in itself also telling. Dante and Chaucer created role models from a Christian point of view, Castiglione created a secular guide, a beginning of how-to books. It also demonstrates the confusions arising out of the social changes for those who were the noble-born and the new merchant class. The style of writing in *The Book of the Courtier* is reminiscent of a Platonic dialogue while the suggestions made are remarkable for their demand in the creating of a good appearance, an image rather than a reality. First, Castiglione argues that nobility is determined by birth, an important argument since the first signs of the purchasing of noble titles was beginning to appear as a means for the rulers to raise funds for the running of the new national governments. Those who were noble, like the saved in Calvin's world who behave morally, appear so in their talents and their beauty. The men are bold and strong but in a social context can be very gentle, modest and reserved without any ostentation or self-praise. Braggadocia was not found among the truly noble. Moreover, nobles were the truly gifted in the world of letters, especially in Latin and Greek. They can be seen as affluent, confident and assured in their splendor. They studied the *studia humanitatus* of the Renaissance rather than the old trivium and quadrivium. In addition they are known for their musical skills both for relief of tedium and for the pleasure of the ladies. The view was that the world was made of music, i.e., a matter of harmony. From this there would follow good habits of mind. Learning to paint was also encouraged since it would bring one into contact with God's own creation, nature. Exercise was recommended but not wrestling since one could lose and that would be unbecoming. It would be better to play tennis, and for grace, to take up dancing. Clearly what was sought was a self-assurance with a certain degree of humility. For the lady it is important that she appear in public as dainty, soft and proper. Social graces had not been introduced or encouraged until the twelfth century under Eleanor of Aquitaine (1122–1204); in Castiglione we find the more early modern version of these social graces. Ladies should always appear pure of heart in public, quickly given to blushing at anything slightly off-color even if she could swear like a sailor in the privacy of her own rooms and with her companions. Platonic love is approved of, sex is also supported but for the young. A new order was seeking expression in social activities but the changes would remain disturbing to the older order. At the same time there were many more opportunities for those not of nobility to become very wealthy, as was so clearly demonstrated in the case of Spain and the wealth of the New World.

Silent reading and the impact of the printing press worked together in supporting these and other changes as well as having a much more subtle but more far reaching impact upon our psyche. These and the growing confusion of the changes we have discussed contributed significantly to the removal of an absolute centering of all truth into a single institution which turns out was itself riddled with problems of its own. The traditional world of monolithic certitude was sliding over the horizon's edge of modernity. From Copernicus

Descartes and Galileo to Locke, those who were literate enough to read, especially in a silent mode, would eventually lead to the creation of revolutionary concepts. But before turning to the early modern implications of both literacy and silent reading, it would be appropriate, as we began, to review a sampling of the literature that eventually followed the revolution associated with the Renaissance. We began in the last chapter with representational writings of Dante and Petrarch and will finish in the seventeenth century with the revolutionary art and language associated with Shakespeare.

We have noted that Shakespeare could take his reader and members of the audience to the end of his tragedies with a plot that completed a circle since the end could be found at the beginning, creating his own orderly universe. This ability to come full circle would also take us through a life's circle, not unlike the natural movement from birth to death. Hamlet would begin with death and ghosts and end carried off the stage, dead.[26] Before discussing the humanism of Shakespeare's characters, however, we should note his contribution to the English language, coining eighteen hundred new words, many still in common use.[27] Moreover, when we place his works in a more modernized setting, it is not because he necessarily addressed questions three hundred years earlier but rather that his works sometimes lend themselves to interpretations that clearly possess implications that closely resemble contemporary thinking especially regarding our sense of individuality.

The first issue to comprehend is that the tragedies of Shakespeare make sense to a great extent because of the open space that now existed between man and his God. The appearance of vernacular Bibles only increased opportunities for literates to find a personal road in the domestic translation free from the exclusive Roman Vulgate. When the first Stewart, James I, became King of England in 1603, he wasted little time in commissioning the creation of an English Bible, the King James, which is still highly regarded for the quality of its language.

Shakespeare's England was, therefore, a land that pointed to salvation without a powerful ancient church positioned between man and God. In its place stood the personal Bible. Henry VIII had retained a theology remarkably similar to that of the Roman Catholic Church and which exists even today. It was Shakespeare's talent to be attuned to the changes occurring as well as to offer characters, plots and ideas that would prove to be such insightful masterpieces that many of his works, especially the tragedies, pointed to a mastery of a language that will aid in the creation of a more literate future. This picture of a future anticipated by the playwright has been noted most clearly by

Harold Bloom. He offers some remarkable insights and suggestions that demonstrate that the best thinking at the time was both confusing and promising, especially for the appearance of a nascent individuality and an eventual need for what we now think of as consciousness.

While we consider the presence of any individuality or consciousness, assuming any appearance at all, it is premature for it to be a meaningful topic for study by the historians of mentalities or ideas. While Bloom makes an excellent case for the appearance of a clear outline of a modern being it should be qualified, especially with Shakespeare's deep and abiding commitment to English history and his consideration of the subject of death. In a world of the Spanish Armada (1588), of religious wars and massive continuous transformations, death retained a very real presence. The new artistic term applied to this period is *Baroque*, and can be seen in the architecture of Bernini or paintings of Rembrandt. Even the treatment of death, or at least funerals, had changed somewhat since the horrific years of the Great Plague, being: "…less a baroque procession, and more a social display."[28] What is critical is that the "…sentimentalization [of] death for the benefit of the bereaved now displaced rituals for the dying."[29] The growing uncertainty that had developed through the centuries of crisis, and the new approaches of adapting to such major changes may have impacted on the idea of death itself. It had always been a uniquely singular force but by the time we enter the seventeenth century the certainty of knowing that death might be defeated was not so clear for some: "…death became a greater threat, stripped of the prospect of any relief beyond time. The helpless grief of those left behind expressed a sense that death was now the ultimate barrier which could no longer be overcome."[30] In time, holding picnics in graveyards became rather popular. A simple but clear example of the images of death drawn from medieval art that then reappears in Shakespeare, and can be seen in his masterpiece, *Measure for Measure*.[31] The audiences of his plays understood the meaning of the *Danses Macabres* which was perhaps one of many ways to work the issue of death into a ritual that would put a distance between the living and their fear.[32] As for Purgatory, that Catholic issue discussed by Stephen Greenblatt, there remained the question of the form of salvation as well as any debt owed to the 'faithfully departed' which had not completely disappeared in Anglican England. As has often been documented and already noted, today the burden of the survivors, is not simply that they lived but that they lived while others involved in the same event nevertheless died—a feeling of guilt. To put it even more directly, death is not a burden for the dead but for the living. It is this and more that is of significance for us in

Shakespeare's *œuvre*. And it is this genius who was the first to introduce the earliest signs of a modern notion of the self, being an individual and of what makes us humane, as Bloom suggested. We have here the basis for contemporary English, one of the most singularly dominant languages in the world already taking form and acquiring its modern implications.

It is not an accident that the dramatist's works were known more than just on the stage, or that they are to be seen and to be heard. It is an error, as earlier noted, to think that these plays were not necessarily read privately. After all, any play that is a work of art and worthy of being seen more than once is definitely worthy of being read, or better still, should be required to be read, which Bloom has suggested in regard to Shakespeare in general and *Hamlet* in particular.[33] This raises a very important issue that cannot be ignored. How did this written language come about, especially a language that can be read silently? The story of the evolution of this language and what it took to reach the Shakespearean stage has received a great deal of attention and is very pertinent, especially for the creation of modern English, our sense of space and in many cases our very thinking processes, especially these thoughts regarding individuality. The reader should keep in mind how successful Shakespeare really was, "The critical reading of Shakespeare, not by academics but by the authentic enthusiasts in his audience, had to have begun as contemporary concern, since those early quartos—good and bad—were offered for sale, sold, reprinted. Eighteen of Shakespeare's plays had appeared in separate volumes before the First Folio of 1623, starting with *Titus Andronicus* in 1594, the year of its first performance and Shakespeare turned thirty."[34] His plays were read as well as observed and thus only further added to our literate capacities. As with so many other factors regarding language, this was just one more step in the literary contribution to the creation of a modern mind, but what a contribution. And since Shakespeare was so popular in his day, it is a possibility that high-culture can come from what at the time could be considered as popular culture, and the printing of books must certainly have played some part in this transformation.[35]

It wasn't the printing press alone, of course, that broke the monopolistic hold of Rome over the theological thinking of the day. This break could also be attributed, in part to the growth of an interior place for thought of God that became increasingly private and trusted in place of dependency upon the community of the church. When we reflect upon the writings of Descartes and Locke we do well to remember that they were the beneficiaries of the varied aspects of architectural changes in their languages, new forms of reading and the evolution of expanding vocabularies. It was the combination of these factors which contributed to the impact of the printing press making it possible for these thinkers to more readily acquire books and even accumulate private libraries. For a large number of people to read and study the writings of Locke or Shakespeare or Descartes at their own leisure, was a significant component in the changes that created the early stages of modern life. It was a long and difficult road to impress upon observers that one scholar we noted labeled, "The Unacknowledged Revolution." For all the importance placed on the significance of the printing press in encouraging personal instead of collective readings, the rise of heresy and the eventual appearance of the Protestant Reformation, it is the culmination of varied factors that spoke to the impact of printing that made a massive contribution to creating our inner self where consciousness could reside. From the *Devotio Moderna* on the edges of the official church to the heretical Lollards, well outside, silent reading cannot be overrated as a significant causative role, It may also have been the part of silent reading that in part contributed to our earliest sense of isolation, alienation and uncertainty.

The printing press would, of course, also expand a negative side inherent in the new reading techniques:

> Isolated private reading and prayer as the pathway to salvation, in turn, may have fostered insecurities about the worthiness of each individual's faith and devotion and thereby stimulated zeal for religious reform. Indeed, the reformed mendicant orders found their strongest supporters among the urban merchant families and the aristocratic families who silently read vernacular religious manuscript books. Three generations later, these same families would become the supporters of John Calvin. On the eve of the Protestant Reformation, the mode of the dissemination of ideas had been so revolutionized that laymen, like university schoolmen, could formulate dissenting views in private and communicate them in secret. [36]

While it is an established theory that the printing press was important in the ultimate triumph of Protestantism, it was only one factor since the "…formulation of reformist religious and political ideas and the receptivity of Europe's elite to making private judgments on matters of conscience owed much to a long evolution, beginning in the twelfth century and culminating in the fifteenth century, in the manner in which men read and wrote."[37] The problem for the historian in attempting to understand the impact of both silent reading and the printing press is that the full measure must be deduced with a cautious sense of uncertainty as one attempts to make an allowance for its accumulative growth and impact. Elizabeth Eisenstein's copious two volume study of the printing press was published in 1979 while Paul Saenger's book on silent reading was published in 1997. The impact on scholarship and thinking of both of these fine works has yet had enough time to fully be integrated and included except in a small number of very specialized monographs. Additionally there is the question of the impact of these two technical changes on the creation and development of a sense of self and reflective consciousness which was even more difficult to qualify. The old certainties were in decline, true, but in some cases they were bent into a new pattern while in other cases they were simply broken. This may have been a factor in Descartes' desire to deal with his doubt and to establish some certainty as to what should be labeled existence. Additionally Locke will follow with an attempt to establish what he understood 'personal identity' to mean. Serious fundamental questions would eventually grow out of the extensive examination of the inner life in the confessional, especially the challenges and dynamics of the Renaissance and Reformation that were increasing for the Church. Protestants now defended their right to possess their own personal conscience, that new interior space where their personal God could reside upon which no church structure could impinge. With a growing population, developing urban and merchant societies with increased availability of money and the opportunities to become increasingly mobile, independent and isolated, such a movement could only expand into the unknown given the limits in defenses that Rome could marshal. That words took on new meaning and new words had a fruitful soil to grow in because of these changes, cannot be denied. Even orthography began to make itself felt because printers had to know and agree on how to present given words and sentences. And it cannot be avoided that Shakespeare took the English language, that printed and theatrically enhanced set of words, poetry and meaning, well beyond anything ever dreamed, and arguably, quite unlike anything ever done since.

It is here that the impact of printing within the development of writing, and increased vernacular literacy that the forces for an interior and secular self clearly began to take shape. That Shakespeare was one of the earliest and most prominent practitioners of these changes is extremely significant for the English language. As a result of the many years of researching this book, and with an appropriate caution regarding a degree of certainty, a thesis has here taken shape suggesting that if it were possible to give a date for the undatable, the earliest moments of the appearance of something of a modern self and the individual and with it, the basis for consciousness that would follow, it would have to be somewhere around the beginning of the end of the Renaissance, with a parallel entrance into the concluding years of the Protestant Reformations and finally, the first steps taken into the Scientific Revolution, i.e., somewhere around the beginning of the seventeenth century. Of all the great artistic voices that touch upon these changes, the one very singular voice for this period, one that created a massive revolution of language and thought, as well as offering a key component to our personal and interior in the blackened room of certain death, the voice that finally reaches us as an introduction to an absolute of our own modernity would have to be that of William Shakespeare.[38] He more than any of his contemporaries or predecessors pointed in the direction of our own modern psychology. This was the language of the nascent self expressed especially in Hamlet's soliloquies, the language of the deep inner drive of a personal identity that transcended public circumstances, demonstrating a hunger for an ontology that went beyond both one's birth and the community's expectations. These, it is suggested here, were very possibly the very first hints of even something so modern as to be qualified as an existential self, for there is something very modern about this young man, Hamlet. After all, there is residing within the burden of knowing and doubts that your uncle killed your father, married your mother and you are obliged to reap revenge, a great conundrum that allows for a very wide opening to a varied set of responses even in a contemporary Western society, including such ideas as 'accidently' killing, ending a life with the idea of a modern villain. It is no accident that many scholars of this play question Hamlet's sanity, something very contemporaneous for our own psychology.

While we humans have been around for some time, the consciousness that we associate with our own era does not make any consequential appearance until the end of the nineteenth century. The voice that is extremely early in beginning this sense of a reflectiveness and anticipation of these changes and can arguably be found in some of the creations of Shakespeare as has been properly noted by Harold Bloom who so eloquently stated:

> Literary character before Shakespeare is relatively unchanging; women and men are represented as aging and dying, but not as changing because their relationship to themselves, rather than to the gods or God, has changed. In Shakespeare, characters develop rather than unfold, and they develop because they reconceive themselves. Sometimes this comes about because they overhear themselves talking, whether to themselves or to others. Self-overhearing is their royal road to individuation, and no other writer, before or since Shakespeare, has accomplished so well the virtual miracle of creating different yet self-consistent voices for his more than one hundred major characters and many hundreds of highly distinctive minor personages.[39]

A great deal of credit for that move in the direction of a more dynamic characterization must go back not so much to the appearance of the printing press but rather to a new set of attitudes arriving under the influence of new scientific and technical answers that increasingly replaced what had been the exclusive property of religion and theology. Shakespeare was a consummate genius in tying together well-known stories in unique ways with startling language. It may help to remember the powerful alteration of assumptions and perceptions that arrived with the mechanical clock and movable type which will eventually extend and contribute to the laws of motion articulated by Sir Isaac Newton.

Changes in our understanding of science began, however, before the traditional dating of the Scientific Revolution, well within the walls of the late Medieval world. For example, it has been observed in pre-early modern Europe that "…operating in instinct, insight, trial and error, and perseverance, the craftsman and craftswomen, the entrepreneurs, the working monks and the clerical intellectuals, and the artist-engineers all transformed the world, on balance very much to the world's advantage."[40] From a practical point of view, those changes that occurred at the end of the medieval world include two items of great impact upon our perceptions of space and time; the compass and the mechanical clock which, when combined, revolutionized travel and thus space. It is not enough to observe profound mechanical changes without also noting that things do not hang in a vacuum but often do eventually alter our very way of thinking. This transition received serious encouragement when the Western mind discovered:

> Natural history and scientific biology are both modern creations, stimulated indeed by the rediscovery of Greek sources in the sixteenth century. But this was not the only fruit of the Italian Renaissance, for naturalism is older in art than in science.…It is fairly clear that the medieval draughtsman was not simply incapable of attaining realism, e.g. in matters of perspective, but was not interested in perfecting direct representation. The element of symbolism was as important to him as it has been in the twentieth century.[41]

The foreshortening of the Renaissance artists, like all those technical changes, were part and parcel of a larger alteration of our view of life and even death; for to change our assumptions of time and space, to first humanize and then study them, is to equally offer opportunity for new ways to perceive our lives as well as our live's limitations. It is the transition from the end of one world, the High Medieval world, and with that the ending of a set of assumptions regarding our heritage, followed by the creation of a more accurate picture to match that of linguistic transformations and a new sense of time, especially when we mean memory, history or even the clock that makes the old rules appear irrelevant. When we look back at the attitude regarding any standards for either art or science we discover, "...there is no absolute standard. All that can rightly be said, when we have understood that medieval men had prejudices, purposes and hopes totally different from our own, is that they were less inquisitive and self-critical than they might have been. They were less interested in natural philosophy, for to them it was but a step forward to higher things. Science was a means, not an end."[42] For this to occur and a new science to appear it will be necessary to create our own modern sense of objectivity.

The original meaning of the Latin root for the word *science* is simply knowledge. It was very limited because of the mind-set of the Middle Ages was innumerate as well as illiterate. How much reckoning could be done in a world with no uniformity of measurement?[43] One could add, other than divine measurement. A new language not mentioned yet, that of modern mathematics, will need to replace the long outdated Euclidean systems and offer a higher level of certainty, for only then would the dramatic changes in methods of thinking be enough to create new perspectives. There was very little compulsion to create any other order since the Medieval world had the ultimate order in a fixed universe of the Lord. Almost all of the "...scientific books printed before 1500 contained material which was familiar two centuries earlier." There was little reason to depart from what was assumed to be a fixed truth of understanding from the original sources that were clearly articulated as late as the early sixteenth century with, as for example, the *Margarita Philosophica* of Gregorius Reisch (d.1525), published in 1503 which was a "...an attempt at an encyclopaedia survey, perhaps rather conservative, certainly immensely simplifying the best knowledge of the age, but useful as a conspectus of scientific knowledge at the opening of the sixteenth century."[44] This sort of cataloging with the aid of printing, expanded throughout the century into a new industry, a knowledge industry that would, ironically, be completely foreign to the scholastic mind. No one had doubted that the concreteness of the universe was certain and unchanging, controlled by the divine and orderly forces and governed all of life. These ideas were rooted in antiquity and also appealed to students of the Holy Word in their seeking a congruence between this understanding of the universe and of scripture, of church doctrine and what was considered scholarly knowledge. This mechanism was clearly "...described by Aristotle; the complex form, capable of accounting for more involved planetary motions, was due to Ptolemy. The former was a physical rather than a mathematical doctrine, the latter was mathematical rather than physical…"[45] In this universe, movement only occurred when there was a given cause. There were eleven concentric spheres progressing outwards from the sublunary region, the place where sin had alone occurred, the Earth being at the center. These were first the moon, followed by Mercury, Venus, the Sun, Mars, Jupiter, Saturn followed by the Firmament (Fixed Stars), the Crystalline Heaven, Primum Mobile and finally the Empyraean Heaven where God and all the Elect resided[46]—the place where those who have defeated death and enjoyed the fruit of their faith and their actions.

How positive for the Church to have this construct as first articulated by Aristotle where motion only occurs with a given cause. It followed therefore, that when one throws an object into the air and then watches it fall to the Earth, you have the 'proof' that as decedents of Adam and Eve, humans are at the center of the universe since all objects seek their inherent and natural resting place which is the Earth where sin was begat. Thus Earth is proven to be the center of that divine order according to both Aristotle and the Bible. God made Earth for man, a place where the Garden of Eden exists and consequently where sin and disaster were introduced and within which we can witness the imperfections around us from storms to droughts. The universe itself remains perfect. And since nothing moves without a mover, we now have a purpose for angels—pushing the heavenly objects that move around this unmoving Earth. Think not we are fixed? Do we not say the sun is rising, or the sun is setting? Besides, if we were moving would we not all fall off just as we would from a wagon barreling down a hill? Aristotle and the Holy Word in the hands of Thomas Aquinas, who tied them to common sense, congeal into a logical and scholastic order where we can see that the universe has motion only because God says it should occur. There was a problem however, for "…this simple theory did not allow of prediction, it did not take into account the motion of the moon's modes, causing the cycle of eclipse, nor the variations in brightness (i.e. distance) and velocity of the heavenly bodies."[47] As we move through the later medieval centuries the argument for this faith-based and rationalized universe became increasingly problematic, so much that even in a Holy Roman Empire there was an increasing need for new explanations of the workings of the universe. One of the earliest to make this effort is found in the writings of Roger Bacon (1214–1294) who was one of the first to argue for a new methodology, one called empiricism. In chapter two of the sixth part of his *Opus Majus*, "On Experimental Science," Roger Bacon summarized his view:

> The experiment science has three great prerogatives with respect to the other sciences. The first is that it investigates by experiment the noble conclusions of all the sciences. For the other sciences know how to discover their principles by experiments, but their conclusions are reached by arguments based on the discovered principles. But if they must have particular and complete experience of their conclusions, then it is necessary that they have it by the aid of this noble science. It is true, indeed, that mathematics has universal experiences concerning its conclusions in figuring and numbering, which are applied likewise to all sciences and to this experimental science, because no science can be known without mathematics. But if we turn our attention to the experiences which are particular and complete and certified wholly in their own discipline, it is necessary to go by way of the considerations of this science which is called experimental.[48]

But he does not press the issue or develop the idea of experimental methodology beyond the general idea that this has merit. Even today, there are those who would preach the oxymoron 'creation science,' negating this important scientific concept. But we should not neglect the significance of this new and still developing direction in our search for knowledge. The experimental method is more complicated than many might believe and this will be demonstrated in the following chapter. For now, however, Roger Bacon was not alone in this era that has so often been unfairly maligned as being 'dark.' Another figure to keep in mind of serious significance in this regard was William of Ockham (c.1284–1349), whose "…importance in the history of science comes partly from some improvements he introduced into the theory of induction, but much more from the attack he made on contemporary physics and metaphysics as a result of the methodological principles which he adopted."[49] Here was a thinker whose genius and creativity comes to us through "Ockham's Razor." Much later the well-known phrase, *"Entia non sunt multiplicanda praeter necessitatem,"* was introduced in the 17th century.[50] That Ockham advocated the creation of a particular method that would need be developed and used, will be appreciated only later.

This body of breakthrough thinking based on only a desire for new methods and solid evidence was building and eventually would peak in the seventeenth century. Perhaps the most profound development centered around time, space and motion with the last term being the dominate in this instance. Was there an alternative to the first cause of motion and the unmoved-mover of Aristotle and Thomas Aquinas? It was from the thinking within the camp of Ockham where a continuous development of an alternative theory of motion would rise. "It has been claimed by some historians that by rejecting the basic Aristotelian principle expressed by the phrase *Omne quod movetur ab alio movetur*, Ockham took the first step towards the principle of inertia which was to revolutionize physics in the 17th century." In a footnote regarding this past statement, the medieval science historian, A.C. Crombie succinctly explained this new physics: "According to the principle of inertia a body will remain in a state of rest or of motion with uniform velocity in a straight line unless acted on by a force. This conception was the basis of Newton's mechanics....The principle of inertia was thus directly contrary to Aristotle's principle according to which motion was not a state but a process and a moving body would cease to move unless continuity acted on by a moving force."[51] But this idea of inertia that must be developed before any sense can be made of the later work of Newton and his laws of motion was not left unattended after Ockham's original suggestions. On the contrary, it was carried on by a somewhat younger contemporary, Jean Buridan (c.1295–1358). As Crombie continues: "In the event it was not Ockham who produced the most significant and influential new dynamic theory in the 14th century, but a physicist whose outlook was profoundly opposed to that of the 'terminists,' Jean Burdin, [sic] twice Rector of the University of Paris between 1328 and 1340. Buridan discussed the classical problems of motion in his *Quaestiones super Octo Libros Physicorum* and in his *Questiones de Caelo et Mundo*."[52] It is important to draw a clear explication of the distinction we use to explain the phenomena of motion by way of impetus as opposed to the later theory of inertia. Impetus, unlike inertia, is an ancient idea. Inertia, on the other hand, belongs to the first of the laws of motion that will be established at the end of the seventeenth century.

> The theory of impetus by means of which he explained the various phenomena of persistent and accelerated motion was based, like the earlier theory of *virtus impressa*, on Aristotle's principles that all motion requires a motive power and that the cause must be commensurate with the effect. In this sense the theory of impetus was the historical conclusion of a line of development within Aristotelian physics, rather than the beginning of a new dynamics of inertia, of which, since it lay in the future, Buridan himself naturally knew nothing.[53]

This is not to say that the idea of a first cause as articulated by Aristotle had disappeared, however for "…Buridan concluded that the mover must impress on the body itself a certain impetus, a motive power by which it continued to move until affected by the action of independent forces. In projectiles this impetus was gradually reduced by air resistance and natural gravity downwards; in freely falling bodies it was gradually increased by natural gravity acting as an accelerating force which added successive increments of impetus, or 'accidental gravity,' to that already acquired."[54] In other words, just as we can alter our view of our death, a great transformation of perception could and was beginning to take place regarding motion. For those with an historical bent, these changes included the discoveries of lost classics begun by Petrarch as well the new perceptions of space and time in the literary and philosophical sense impacting on artistic constructs. The Renaissance re-discovery of the classical world contributed to a new understanding of so much that many thinkers now take for granted while history, like memory, can lead to further knowledge. Even for the religious there were the new theories, especially among the more reform-minded, of what the intentions and thus the orthodoxy of the first Christians and their Holy Writ actually was. Curiosity was clearly being stimulated.

It was within this context that a new theory of the movement of planets by the Polish thinker Nicholaus Copernicus (1473–1543) would develop. The difficulty since antiquity had been in explaining and defining the objects within the universe, their motion and symmetry, an issue centering around the question of how it could be possible that a given motion at a given time was not only a constant from one point to another, but could on occasion actually turn in opposite direction of what would be expected. When observing Mars, one can see it moving from east to west while at a different time, one would note that it was moving in reverse. How to explain this anomaly within the Ptolemaic system? Were the angels doing the pushing occasionally confused, or perhaps, ingesting some strange celestial drugs? The answer that had long been offered was labeled epicycle, a solution that grew more and more convoluted as the Western mind moved into the aesthetics of the Quattrocento and the subsequent religious crises and upheavals that followed. What was troubling for increasing numbers of interested students, including young Copernicus, was the idea that this conundrum was resolved by simply adding more and more complex configurations, whether circles, ellipses or just plain confusion into the heavens. As Crombie put it, eventually "...it was left for Nicholas Copernicus...to elaborate a system which could replace Ptolemy's as a calculating device and yet represent physical 'fact,' and also 'save' additional phenomena, such as the diameter of the moon, which according to Ptolemy's system should have undergone monthly variations of nearly a hundred per cent."[55] In confronting this complexity, he simply suggested that one answer to the problem would be to simply place the earth not at the center, but rather put our sun there, an ancient Greek concept first articulated by Aristarchus. The logic is so simple and yet so profound. There are, after all, some problems that are not to be solved, but simply out-grown by thinking 'out of the box,' i.e., outgrowing traditional paradigms. "Copernicus not only gave the earth a daily rotation but made the whole planetary system, including the earth, revolve round a static sun in its center. His reluctance to publish this theory, of which the manuscript was completed by 1532, seems to have depended largely on the fear that it would be considered absurd."[56] To put his achievement into a clearer context, it was by way of "...postulating the annual motion of the earth that Copernicus made his great strategic advance in theory over the medieval discussions of a reformed astronomy, and opened the way for the full mathematical development of a new system."[57] Much of this work waited for the more concrete discoveries, documented theories and coherent alternatives to the traditional views regarding motion that were brought forward by Galileo Galilei. His fame was only further heightened by way of his infamous line regarding motion which he whispered on leaving the church court that convicted him for heresy. Galileo successfully applied fresh thinking and techniques, especially with new inventions such as the telescope and microscope, that were part and parcel of a longer and larger movement that brings us to the culmination of some very important earlier inventions.

We are at that point where mental changes include not only offers of constructive alternatives but also the rejection of old paradigms and the confrontation of the implications of letting go of familiar, traditional, comfortable and often outmoded realities that had become habitual. That this occurred in this era of transformations is given support with one of the more enigmatic and interesting thinkers and teachers of the age, Paracelsus, a.k.a. Theophrantus Bombastus von Hoheneim (c. 1493–1541).[58] It has long been held that Paracelsus, who was both something of a mystic and a physician as well as a revolutionary defender of the new sciences (natural philosophy), was supposed to have taken certain classic works of medicine for study, from Aristotle to Galen, et al., out of his classroom and demonstrated for his students what it is that they should really be learning of the physical body and its health by proceeding to burn those classics. He held that it is necessary to clear the field of the old in order to make room for the new. As one historian of science stated: "It is true that Paracelsus is supposed to have burnt the books of the masters before his inaugural lecture at Basel in 1527, and that he declaimed against official medicine..." It was Paracelsus who best expressed his perception when he noted that, "I will not defend my monarchy with empty talk but with arcana. And I do not take my medicines from the apothecaries. Their shops are but foul kitchens from which comes nothing but foul broths.... Every little hair on my neck knows more than you and all your scribes, and my shoe-buckles are more learned than your Galen and Avicenna, and my beard has more experience than all your high colleagues."[59] To build anew, first bring an end to the outmoded. Going beyond just the book is not only what we today would want from our personal physician but also it has been further suggested that "...perhaps this lesson was the most enduring contribution made by Paracelsus to true science."[60] That the thoughtful Renaissance humanist and mystic could also be drawn to a more mystic orientation can be found among a variety of thinkers and writers at the time as in the case of the very interesting Agrippa von Nettesheim (1486–1535) who could defend in court someone charged with being a witch, write a history and decide that all knowledge was unattainable.[61]

This destruction of certain traditions, however, was much more extensive than a symbolic gesture for there were other and more powerful destructive forces at play beyond the symbolic acts of a Paracelsus. True, one does not think of inventions as destructive, but some are more clearly so than others, as is the obvious case of gunpowder. This was an old invention appearing for the first time in China, somewhere around the early ninth century.[62] While its destructive component is self-evident, there is another that specifically contributes to the separation of the actions of a warrior from the warrior as an actor. In other words, war was becoming and eventually will become almost completely dehumanized since it will be possible to destroy an enemy without direct contact. In modern wars, the force of violence is depersonalized when for example, the bomber drops their payload on the enemy, whoever that may be, some thousands of feet below, and then returns to have lunch at the base. This is an example of later stages of alienation and estrangement that scholars eventually will confront as we become industrialized as well as more individualized, and potentially, increasingly more detached not only from others but possibly from our own behavior, especially our destructive behavior. To carry the logic to its conclusion, it has been correctly pointed out that "...as with all the inventions that have increased the gap between man and the rest of creation—speech, writings, fire, the wheel, the magnetic compass and gunpowder—nothing is known for certain of the inventor...."[63] What is known is that this will prove to impact significantly on some of our later perceptions. It is an irony that as we become more individualized and self-conscious selves we also can achieve a more detached attitude to all that surrounds us.

For the world of motion—of time and space—a more immediate and significant impact arrived with the introduction of two specific inventions —the compass and the mechanical clock. Like moveable type, we are dealing with both an effect and a cause in the service of motion. These contributions to technical knowledge were recognized from an early date, when "…in 1550 Italian physician and mathematician Jerome Cardan wrote that the magnetic compass, printing, and gunpowder were three inventions to which 'the whole of antiquity has nothing equal to show.'"[64] And these were not the only remarkable contributions that altered daily living, for there was what "…most modern textbooks include in their history of invention the medieval discovery or adoption of the heavy plow, animal harness, where open-field agriculture, the castle, water-powered machinery, the putting-out system, Gothic architecture, Hindu-Arabic numerals, double-entry bookkeeping, the blast furnace, the compass, eyeglasses, the lateen sail, clockwork, firearms, and movable type.[65] Most of the years associated with the Renaissance and Reformation were filled not with abstract science as has been rightly noted, but they were years full of applied science in the form of variety of inventions and their implications. All of these are well worth studying but our concern centers on those two altering forces of the natural (divine) order, the compass and mechanical clock. While the compass is another Chinese invention, it proved to be very important for the Europeans as they began to learn how to conquer global space; as they perfected this new tool and added the clock, space shrunk and became humanized. The road to the globalization of cultures began with such creations. And it is precisely the clock that contributed to this shrinking of our world and the expansion of Europe, contributing to mastering and humanizing time, at least in the earlier years. The Reformation and national politics would further divide the West while the technological changes would bring us closer together and in some cases eventually dehumanize us. These are the many paradoxes inherent in our inventive abilities. As Lewis Mumford has put it "…by its essential nature, [the clock] dissociated time from human events," while simultaneously, "…helped create the belief in an independent world of mathematically measurable sequences."[66] We should also note that this "dissociated time" only occurred after it came to first define our mechanical and human events with a unification that it also helped create and out of this would come a belief in an independent world of mathematically measurable sequences that became the special world of science.

The development of the mechanical clock is one of those remarkable stories that impacts on the theme of this book and has been told innumerable times.⁶⁷ One such study, for example, actually titles a chapter, "The Attack on Tradition: Mechanics." Since the issue here is that of space as well as time and the innovations in mechanics, it is worth noting that once again it was the "…astronomers [who] were the first to want to measure time in seconds and fractions of a second…"⁶⁸ As for the impact on history this mechanism was a necessary door that leads us to eventually participate in the larger historic event of the industrial revolutions, since, "In the fifteenth century, observers began using time as a coordinate of location of celestial bodies, and where the indicators on clock dials could not furnish sufficiently accurate information, they counted the teeth of the turning wheels. The larger the wheels, the more the teeth and the finer the divisions."⁶⁹ The improvement of gears meant the road taken for true mechanization and the new order of time would lead eventually to time efficiency. "It is the mechanical clock that made possible, for better or worse, a civilization attentive to the passage of time, hence to productivity and performance."⁷⁰ The appearance of more sophisticated time pieces when combined with the compass meant improvements in shipping and trade. With the pendulum clock of the seventeenth century "…it was possible for the first time to build timepieces accurate to less than a minute a day. A century later, observatory clocks could keep time within a fraction of a second a day, and by the end of the nineteenth-century this variation had been reduced to a hundredth of a second or less."⁷¹ How much the world had been transformed in time and place can be demonstrated by the following thought exercise: Picture the incongruity of a fundamentalist evangelic attempting to proselytize you on your front porch while constantly looking at the digital watch on his wrist. That which had belonged exclusively to God and divine control now was being mastered by man. As has been pointed out, "…go back to the mechanical clock in medieval Europe. This is one of the great inventions in the history of mankind—not in a class of fire and the wheel, but comparable to movable type in its revolutionary implications for cultural values, technological change, social and political organizations, and personality."⁷²

This is not so much a matter of keeping time but rather another method of living in a mechanically-driven framework of time instead of a divinely-driven world. The serious causal contributions to this marvel were many and diverse from the appearance of the escapement in the fourteenth century to the demographic altering Great Plague of the same century and its accompanying labor shortages. With the oscillator, the ability of making this specific motion into something less divine, humanized action was becoming clearly appropriate for daily experience. Here is the paradox inherent in these changes being discussed, for the bells are to be rung by machines and not by human hands and yet the shortage of workers due to the Great Plague helped to bring about the demise of the feudal order. Machines can liberate and they can enslave and the human condition is seriously altered. A new language of knowledge in science and of technology and its impact on every day living exploded in the world of Luther and Galileo. It is not an accident that a new college, Gresham College, was founded in London at this time (1598) since the rising business class wanted their children to learn practical arts appropriate to business rather than the scholasticism of Oxford and Cambridge. Trade and business, language in general and vernacular in particular revealed a new early pragmatic mind-set being born.

The evolution of the nation state dictated a unique political identity for its citizens in place of the universal membership of the Catholic Church. This was a major change since the word *catholic* means universal. For regions establishing their own identity, one of the first and clearest expressions of that identity was the vernacular unique to those areas. When Luther attacked his enemy, the Catholic Church, he attacked it not simply as a corrupt institution, but rather as the corrupt a Roman institution, separating him and those of a Germanic language from foreign influences. Luther's attack of 'Romanist' in his writings, therefore, is also understood to mean those who speak and write Latin. The alternative tongues and writings of varied regions help solidify the early political independence of both nation states and the new mercantile and trade economies, as well as bring an end to the unity of a world so long associated with the Hellenistic, Roman and Medieval heritage. It should not be surprising that the Roman Church restricted publication of books in lands they controlled through the *imprimatur*, a label stating that the Church had given her approval for publication. Censorship was an obvious corollary to the introduction of the printing press and the growing diversity of various unique 'national' cultures.

While the language of motion changed in order to set up a language for the Scientific Revolution, the language of the living was also going through a change in a way that offered a transformative construct of what it meant to be human, and therefore the ways of confronting death. When we study the earliest results of that power inherent in the movable type, we find ourselves within the thoughts of a genius like Machiavelli and his contributions to political science, i.e., the rationalizing of governance. We must also consider the contributions to religious humanism and language of Sir Thomas More and

Erasmus. For both Machiavelli and More, it is noteworthy to look at the brilliant piece by J. H. Hexter where both these giants of the Renaissance and Reformation era were capable of creating language in new ways that the best minds would not catch up to for a century or more.[73] As with Plato and Aristotle, great ages can produce great strains on the limits of the contemporary tongue. As for the new craft and art of printing and publishing one could do no better for the occupations of writer and printer then to read *Praise of Folly* which made such brilliant observations as "…speech is the least deceptive reflection of the mind."[74] To say that the printed word was not a trusted for many decades after the arrival of printing would clearly border on an understatement. But in the new professions of writing and publishing, it is relevant that at such an early age someone of Erasmus's stature already understood and was willing to make public its shortcomings:

> In the same realm are those who are authors of books. All of them are highly indebted to me, especially those who blacken their pages with sheer triviality. For those who write learnedly to be criticized by a few scholars,…seem to be more pitiable than happy to me, simply because they are continuously torturing themselves. They add, they alter, they cross something out, they reinsert it, they recopy their work, they rearrange it, they show it to friends, and they keep it for nine years; yet they still are not satisfied with it. At such a price, they buy an empty reward, namely praise —and the praise of only a handful, at that. They buy this at the great expense of long hours, no sleep, so much sweat, and so many vexations.[75]

He recognized that the down side of printing in making more and more books readily available also meant more nonsense would make their way into libraries. He also noted the rise of vanity with his critique:

> It is worth one's while to observe how pleased authors are with their own works when they are popular and pointed out in a crowd as celebrities! Their work is on display in bookstores, with three cryptic words in large type on the title page, something like a magician's spell. Ye gods! After all, what are they but words? Few people will ever hear of them, compared to the total world population, and far fewer will admire them, since people's tastes vary so, even among the common people.[76]

It is tempting to continue quoting someone possessing such perspectives, but for brevity sake, let us finish with the following prescient comments: "The most touching event is when they compliment each other and turn around in an exchange of letters, verses, and superfluities. They are fools praising fools and dunces praising dunces."[77] And, as he adds further: "Or sometimes they will choose a competitor and increase their reputation by rivaling themselves with him."[78] One can only wonder what Erasmus would have to say of the 'talking-heads' in our electronic media?

There were additional revolutionary contributions made by others to these types of alternate perceptions, all of which lead eventually to a future that no one could anticipate. Those who lived along the border of the Renaissance and the Reformation, those overlapping of two powerful revolutionary changes, the one giving birth to the idea of classical studies through a new historiography, i.e., a new sense of time and space, and the other taking the advantage of that view by applying the new understandings of history and language to the question of biblical accuracy as well theological correctness, were left without traditional underpinnings. But for this study the more significant transformation would be built around the heart and soul of language, a language that did not belong to God but was a construct of our own humanity. For if one should seriously change the language used, the way people perceive, assume, think and relate will also change. In other words, there are certain types of changes that will seriously alter our understanding and definition of what it means to be human.

With this in mind, we return to Shakespeare, that voice so reflective of and that contributed to these changes and which is found clearly in several of his creations, as Harold Bloom has elucidated. It is his thesis regarding Shakespeare's characters who we (the audience or reader) perceive *overhearing* themselves and who represent a significant presence of individuality.[79] The inner intimacy of the spoken word clearly was present in some of his speeches, especially in the monologues where the character speaks his inner voice aloud so the audience can hear what he would possibly be stating within and to himself. This was a language that took a giant leap forward to a yet undiscovered future, if not of our own world with our own psyche, at least in so far as it applies to the English we now use.

It is within the realm of language and the transformations of sound, a written tone framed from a growing vernacular literature, along with an historical sense, that was arguably the most important phenomenal transformation that brought about the modern mind and with it the first expressions, primitive though they may have been, of something that resembles a rough and early introduction to being conscious. This new linguistic exercise marked the rhetoric found in the age of Queen Elizabeth I, the early years of James I and the years of Shakespeare. Having been well educated in the arts as well as the sciences, Elizabeth knew her language and audience and once gave such a powerfully moving speech to parliament, often with tears, that it gained her some very needed support for her financially desperate government. Never perhaps since Cicero was a language so forcefully presented as a powerful drive to legislative action. Language had developed both in substantive and methodological expression in Shakespeare's England while it added to and remains part of one of the key factors in the evolution of early consciousness, including eventually the English word consciousness itself. The thesis here remains that language and history, a humanized understanding of space and time, were prerequisites for the development of the modern self and with it our consciousness. When we speak of history we are always speaking of some form of memory and some foundation for a sense of self. When speaking of language we confront some understanding of space and perception. It is in these terms of self and perception, and their new meanings in this early modern world, that we find the very foundations for a radical transformation of the mentalities of those more educated and literate artists and thinkers to contribute to the creation a Western vision.

It can be argued, therefore, that the single most important event in the rise of a sense of self, individuality and consciousness could be found rooted in many of the dramatic renderings of Shakespeare. The first issue regarding any consideration of contributions from Shakespeare at this point is the question mentioned earlier of the contrast between reading and performance. If his work is only to be seen and heard, what do the issues of expanding literacy, the appearance of vernacular and the printing press, as well as the growth of silent reading, have to do with the appearance of an individuality and a sense of self? True, a contemporary critic, Charles Lamb, has apparently been denigrated in this century for insisting that it was better to read Shakespeare than to watch him acted.[80] If this appears to be too contemporary an observation directed at so early an age as Shakespeare's, there is the fact that "Lamb was amiably seconded by Rosalie Colie, who reminded us of the advice given by the editors of the First Folio, Shakespear's fellow actors, Heminges and Condell: 'Read him, therefore, and againe, and againe.'"[81] As anyone who has participated in the life of the theater will attest, "...when you read, then you can direct, act, and interpret for yourself....In the theater, much of the interpreting is done for you, and you are victimized by the politic fashions of the moment."[82] The following quote according to Bloom, was drawn from "a wise book," *Imaginary Audition* (1939), by Harry Berger, Jr. and offers, "a fine irony." He notes, "It is no doubt perverse to find that desire of theater burning through Shakespeare's texts is crossed by a certain despair of theater, of the theater that seduces them and the theater they seduce; a despaire inscribed in the auditory voyeurism with which the spoken language outruns its auditors, dropping golden apples along the way to divert the greedy ear that longs to devour its discourse."[83] Live stage performances are a singular creation within the confines of a very unique audience experience that is very distinct from that found within a movie theater or a group sitting around a television set. The passion of the audience becomes part of the performance, even to a point that there are not only bad productions but it can also occur that there can be, as any performer knows, a bad audience. For the thespians this is already recognized, for there is a dramatic if not overwhelming difference between the dress rehearsal and an opening night performance—one with a live audience where "auditory voyeurism" becomes part of the production.[84] Only with a live performance is there a collective personality of an audience whose identity can change the event emotionally and psychologically. This is the nature of the rhetorical arts. Reading is private while performances are public. As another Shakespearian scholar has made clear, there is much of Shakespeare's language that is very special, one especially that increasingly grew beyond the general audience's capacity for understanding.[85] And Bloom adds: "The point is that Shakespeare knew he had early readers, less numerous by far than his audience, but more than just a chosen few. He wrote primarily to be acted, yes, but he wrote also to be read, by a more select group. This is not to suggest that there are two Shakespeares, but rather to remind us that the one Shakespeare was subtler and more comprehensive than certain reductionists care to acknowledge."[86] Reading is not something undone when speaking of a play as opposed to a novel. To read in the modern sense requires a private act of personalizing the words of the writer (rhetorician). How many people, sitting alone in their abode, have quietly read the Gettysburg Address or even Pericles' funeral oration even though they are two very public works?

But in Bloom's studying and thinking about and writing on Shakespeare's works, the birth of the modern self simply inhered in some of these characters and their language. As he stated it: "I go on insisting that Shakespeare invented us (whoever we are) rather more than we have invented Shakespeare."[87] Thus as brilliant and original as the language may be, as creative as the thoughts are and as compelling as the stories are, there is something far more important for the human condition in all this, for "...to call Shakespeare a 'creator of language,' as Wittgenstein did, is insufficient, and to call Shakespeare also a 'creator of characters,' and even a 'creator of thought,' is still not enough. Language, character, and thought all are part of Shakespeare's invention of the human, and yet the largest party is the passional."[88] Where were the great characters that the modern mind can identify with? It is of interest that the characters of Shakespeare's dramas were like the classical Greek models in one very important sense, that they were important figures of their day, which as Aristotle had noted, accounts for the significance of their fall. It means little to see the collapse of a drunk or bum, something not unpopular in the pop kitsch of movies and television today. Yet how do we identify with Hamlet, the Prince of Denmark? It may very well be this point that another scholar, Frank Kermode, in a discussion of the language of Shakespeare, was indirectly addressing when he stated that: "Following the story, understanding the tensions between characters, is not quite the same thing as following all or even most of the meanings. Even modern editors, surrounded by dictionaries and practised in the language of the period, cannot quite do that, as almost any Shakespeare edition shows. There are passages, especially in some of the later plays, which continue to defeat learned ingenuity."[89] This language could often go well beyond the understanding of the common man. Shakespeare was pushing the envelope beyond the frontiers of everyday meanings, even to the point of occasionally offering to our own contemporary minds similar if occasional conundrums. It is not an accident that the great changes in the mentalities in the Western world run parallel to those great changes in language. When Plato wrote he was forced to invent and combine new words that were unique and indispensable for his students to move well beyond their old paradigms of thought.[90] The same happened in the Renaissance with both Sir Thomas More and Machiavelli. And we will find that Descartes and Locke will do the same, particularly regarding the term *consciousness*. Thus it is through the history of the Western world of ideas that we find the roots, both linguistically and mentally of the meaning of the new and extremely complex early modern word, consciousness. The importance, again, is demonstrated as to how we personalize those words for ourselves by means of the act of reading and reflecting on those words.

As for those who have spent a career teaching the humanities it is not unusual to suggest to students that when they read their Homer, Virgil, Dante, Chaucer, Shakespeare or Goethe, they should first read aloud; for both poetry and theater are rhetorical arts and deserve to be discovered by way of their original intention—by way of sound. Today, there have been such dramatic changes with complexity, flux and dynamics where the best minds find it possible for themselves and some of the best students to both read silently and hear publicly the sounds, cadence and multi-meanings implicit within a work even on a first reading. The ability to hear without humming a musical note, another form of silent sight reading, is another example of a language, musical notation in this case, that is internalized, as professional musicians know. The same would also have to be said for pure mathematics. This same principle also applies to one's own reading of the classics. When re-read for a second or third time will often offer a new rendering, a new vision and a new understanding because of the changes and growth of the reader. We can understand today in ways and in depths never dreamt. The beginnings of this more modern perspective and capacity, this transformation of understanding, can and usually is traced to the so-called Romantics and Post-Romantics in the nineteenth century, especially in the writings of such figures as Nietzsche. Bloom also ties him to his own study with the following observation:

> Nietzsche ambiguously followed Hamlet in telling us that we could find words only for what was already dead in our hearts, so that there was always a kind of contempt in the actor of speaking. Before Hamlet taught us how not to have faith either in language or in ourselves, being human was much simpler for us but also less interesting. Shakespeare, through Hamlet, has made us skeptics in our relationship with anyone, because we have learned to doubt articulateness in the realm of affection.[91]

There are very few thinkers and writers who could more qualify as early as Nietzsche for this modern attitude, and in this it is also true that in some ways Hamlet is a modern man. Bloom is convinced, however, that it is not only Hamlet that walks in many ways the streets of the modern world, for "…in vitalistic self-awareness, Falstaff truly is the Wife of Bath's child."[92] Falstaff is the man of humor while Hamlet is that of tragedy; these are two necessary companions. That Hamlet should be so noted is not surprising for students of another great work of very contemporary and existential modern (post-modern) world, the musical *Hair*, with its remarkable quotation drawn from Hamlet regarding the wonder of "What a piece of work is man…" And in this as well as in Bloom's Shakespeare we perceive a common thread where "…most human beings are lonely, and Shakespeare was the poet of loneliness and of its vision of mortality. Most of us, I am persuaded, read and attend theater in search of other selves. In search of one's own self, one prays, or mediates, or recites a lyric poem, or despaires in solitude. Shakespeare matters most because no one else gives us so many other selves, larger and more detailed than any closest friends or lovers seem to be."[93] The question of multiple selves will be discussed later, but for now it should be recognized that this is a very unique and modern idea. Here again the issue centers upon the use of language to delineate oneself, and as Bloom states it, "…as much a creator of selves as of language, he can be said to have melted down and then remolded the representation of the self in and by language. That assertion is the center of this book…"[94] Of course language is inherently central when taken with the action on stage as in life where words are words but the measurement is actually in the actions of the participants. After all, "…it is most possible that Shakespeare was unaware of his originality at the representation of human nature—that is to say, of human action, and the way such action frequently was antithetical to human words."[95] The emphasis here is on action, that Renaissance discovery of a virtue reintroduced by Petrarch and, as will be seen later, will be typical of a post-Nietzschean understanding.

This tendency to project upon such a distant figure, even that belonging to the world of Shakespeare, and such a monumental figure as Hamlet, requires that he still should be treated with caution for while there may be some validity in Bloom's interpretation, it should not be considered the one and only position to subscribe to. Moreover, when one considers the role of humor in a world driven by annihilation as exemplified by our own twentieth century of world wars it is of note that Bloom must return to that one character comparable to the stature of Hamlet, to his pantheon of modern (post-modern) figures —Falstaff. As he put it: "Our ability to laugh at ourselves as readily as we do at others owes much to Falstaff, the cause of wit in others as well as being witty in himself. To cause wit in others, you must learn to how to be laughed at, how to absorb it, and finally how to triumph over it, in high good humor."[96] To draw on self-mockery and take one's own being as something that can be laughed at is a necessary characteristic, as we will later see, of a mature self-conscious individual as opposed to the immature self-consciousness of an ego-driven psyche. Such an attitude can be found with many followers of the Surrealists, Beats and the humor of luminaries like Lenny Bruce, et al. Self humor will become a significant tonic in a world where *One Flew Over the Cuckoo's Nest* makes sense. And if one is to speak of a self, then one must speak of a reflection that is demonstrated by way of that same self-humor.

Questions regarding the issue of our own humanity, its understanding and meaning, are beginning to become central in their confusions, uncertainties along with the eventual machinations of a self-reflective and conscious life, one where the choices are not simply choices, but conscious choices which can occasionally be discovered in some Shakespearean writings, exists without any major extension of interpretation. Granted, this is most clear in the characters of Hamlet and Falstaff: "…in Shakespeare, there is always a residuum, an excess that is left over, no matter how superb the performance, how acute the critical analysis, how massive the scholarly accounting, whether old-style or new-fangled. Explaining Shakespeare is an infinite exercise; you will become exhausted long before the plays are emptied out."[97] This we can find is a typical comment applicable to the deeply thoughtful individuals and artists of our own world (again the genius). As for religion and death, the conclusion is self-evident: "Almost the only lasting human concern that Shakespeare can be said to have not affected is religion, whether as praxis or as theology."[98] Perhaps it was his good sense regarding religion as a subject that was increasingly less applicable to the corpus of his work of art that led Shakespeare to see even death in a different context, as has been interpreted by Bloom's own comment:

> His tragicomedies—or romances, as we now call them—treat death more originally even than do his high tragedies....Death's ambassador to us uniquely is Hamlet; no other figure, fictive or historic, is more involved with that undiscovered country, unless you desire to juxtapose Jesus with Hamlet....his peculiar distinction prevails: he teaches us the nature of dying. Some have said this is because Shakespeare approximates a secular scripture. It does seem more adequate, to me, to take Shakespeare (or Montaigne) as such a text than it would be to take Freud or Marx or Franco-Heideggerians or Franco-Nietzscheans.[99]

How far could one take this analysis? Bloom has no hesitancy to reach for an alternative to a death driven by the answers of salvation, heaven and hell, and instead offers the idea that "...a substantial number of Americans who believe they worship God actually worship three major literary characters: the Yahweh of the J Writer (earliest author of Genesis, Exodus, Numbers), the Jesus of the Gospel of Mark, and Allah of the Koran." He continues that he does not "...suggest that we substitute the worship of Hamlet, but Hamlet is the only secular rival to his greatest precursors in personality."[100] Again this may seem not only an overstatement but even border on hyperbole; but it is true that the adaptability of his plays' sounds make them more modern than even some of our own contemporary works. The fact is that when you read, study or witness the road from *Hamlet* to *Hair* it is difficult if not impossible for many to agree. This of course only dramatizes the power of language, the life of history from our beginnings to our emancipation into the nightmare of the burden of our own consciousness.

Language, the crutch, tool and force in these plays that Bloom and others have been so impressed remains central. No electronic gimmicks. Here the audience attempted to grasp the overwhelming ingenuity of the language. And language works to a great extent because of the sense of the unknown carried by those moments of power called silence. As another Shakespearean critic has noted, "...such essentially dramatic silences are impossible in earlier drama that depends wholly on florid speech. Much has come to depend on everything not being said, and this is essential to the later Shakespearian development of character. At such moments silence and speech are complementary. We recall that the soliloquy, brought to perfection in *Hamlet*, is speech in silence, the speech of silence."[101] It takes very little imagination to understand this fundamental truth of sound—its impact is built by way of not just what is said but also, and this is the important component, what is not said. It reminds us of the adage regarding the question of how to listen to modern progressive jazz—the answer usually associated with the jazz pianist, Thelonius Monk (1917–82)—to listen to jazz (or Monk) you must learn to listen to the silence, the spaces in between the notes. This has been brilliantly dramatized in a film by Michelangelo Antonioni, *Blowup* (1966). Is reality what we hear or see, think we hear or see or something entirely different? It is not a surprise, therefore, for the Shakespearean critic Kermode to make the following observation:

> Transformations from early work...might after all be expected in drama as well as in others arts—in music, for instance. We do not need to cite such exceptional instances as Beethoven, marked by the contrast between the first quartets and the last; musicologists chart this contrast confidently, deploring what they think is the momentary regression of Opus 74 to the manner of Opus 18 before progress towards the last quarters is resumed. They don't deny a relation between early and late, but they affirm an unpredictable profundity in those final works and might not object to its being represented as gesturing towards silence.[102]

There is thus support for the idea that the soliloquies in *Hamlet* can also be seen as a loud form of silence, the inner voice, and the earliest proof of an individual's actual mental concentration and action, an interior state both as a subjective experience and as an inner but public expression. This is a miracle on a human, not a divine level. For today's scholars who are concerned with and interested in consciousness, a major problem has been (and remains) how do you discuss something unrevealable since it is but a purely interior experience? Is it not possible that this "To be or not to be," is a first expression of the quiet inner self at work?

This is in some ways the language with which we now live: A language of silence which is eternal and the opposite of sound, noise and society. Where the sound ends, whether rhetorical or written, so too ends external life, while the issue of immortality now becomes one of a sound, the name that lives in memory, articulated by others, as in Shakespeare, whose words yet live every time they are read or an actor walks on stage to interpret his lines. This offers one aspect of the ultimate power of language, the source of the self and a form of immortal certainty, at least for an historical genius.

The legacies of the Protestant movements were several, starting first with the replacement of the seven deadly sins with the older Jewish tradition of commandments as they turned their backs on Rome. The commandments had the advantage of not condemning the new activities of working for a profit, living by way of greed and holding onto one's pride that made possible a more secular religion much as turning away from the virgin birth made Jesus more of a human. Secondly, religion was now further personalized and made more a family event rather than being part of a larger community. Third, this event created a religious Tower of Babel—the beginning of the end of unity, as in someone today stating that, 'I'm a Christian' with the response being, 'what kind?' Fourth, the process also undermined what little homogeneity that had once existed in Europe—divisive, with disparate regions, religions and languages rather than a singular unified community. Fifth, the changes in the printed word, silent reading and vernacular made for a new world that now had at its base a more personal and somewhat private existence outside the traditional literacy that had existed within the monastic walls. Sixth, there was an expansion of Western dualism, from Zoroastrianism to Christianity, from Platonic idealism to Protestant faithism and from Catholic universalism to Reformer particularism, which would continue in a new guise of the Scientific Revolution and its secularism. Fresh answers in the search for certainly will appear after we travel beyond religion.

CHAPTER FIVE

SCIENTIFIC REVOLUTION AND DETACHMENT

Men fear death, as children fear to go in the dark
                                                    Bacon

FROM RE-ORDER TO RESTRUCTURE

In a real sense, the story we tell of history is the story of necessity and the inventive nature of our ancestors was never more evident than in the age associated with natural philosophy, that is, the Scientific Revolution. There was an explosion of diversity and change as we have noted: popularization of vernacular languages; birth of the nation state and national economies; discovery of the past in place of myths; beginning of an opening of physical space and mechanization of time; radical inventions like the compass, gun-powder, mechanical clocks, printing press etc., as well as the expansion of silent reading. The classical and medieval world could only wither.

Because history is also the story of cause and effect compounded by unintended consequences (UC), it also concerns those changes that impact on both our actions and thinking. Institutional adjustments to changing circumstances are at best a problem and for the Church of Rome, during the Renaissance, it was an impossibility. The Church continued but in a truncated form. Changes can often appear as a paradox, as when Erasmus attacks publishing in his own published book, *In Praise of Folly*. Change can manifest as an adjustment to stress and fear, after which it can create something so new that it too becomes a new unknown, as in weapons of war. It is in this context of change that the scientific revolution and its step-child, the Enlightenment, took form. As one student of this period has made very clear:

> Never was there a greater contrast, never a more sudden transition than this! An hierarchical system ensured by authority; life firmly based on dogmatic principle—such were the things held dear by the people of the seventeenth-century; but these—controls, authority, dogmas and the like—were the very things that their immediate successors of the eighteenth held in cordial detestation. The former were upholders of Christianity; the latter were its foes. The former believed in the laws

of God; the latter in the laws of Nature; the former lived contentedly enough in a world composed of unequal social grades; of the latter the one absorbing dream was Equality.[1]

Whether one would consider these changes as gigantic events, creating a chasm between two worlds is, nevertheless, not totally unusual. The historian responsible for this analysis, Paul Hazard, is convincing when suggesting that the eighteenth century was both an extension and a distortion of what preceded, evolving into something that was so unheard of or unseen that it is unlike anything experienced in Western history—what we label the Age of Reason. Morever, the larger question of when modernity should be associated with the Western world, is also worth considering since the thesis here is that the self, consciousness and individuality are modern creations. As an example, another respected scholar has suggested:

> The old division between medieval and modern history in 1492, in particular, has very little meaning. The great change in outlook, the great change in intellectual climate, the change which ushers in the modern world, comes not with the Renaissance or the Reformation but with the Scientific Revolution of the seventeenth century. The modern history of Europe, in other words, starts not in 1485 or 1492 but between 1660 and 1680. In fact, it might be argued that there were only two great breaks in European history: the one at the end of the eleventh century when Europe, which had been hemmed in from all sides by the Saracens, the Vikings and the Magyars, broke out and began to expand. The second came at the end of the seventeenth century when the scientific spirit, which was the mark of Europe in modern times, really took shape.[2]

It is valid to raise questions regarding this idea of historic traditions once the driving force of "controls, authority, dogmas," by which people lived so long were expiring, leaving the door open not only for a new and revolutionary language exemplified by Shakespeare, but a new approach to nature as well. This clarifies a key point in history which states that for a new certainty to appear the old must prove to be inadequate or false.

It should be understood that what had happened to the well-established certainty based on the various classical ideas and assumptions was that, whether in intellectual or political systems, supportive institutions were being replaced with new ideas and creations that were represented by a variety of equally new understandings drawn from the Renaissance and Reformation. As important as Roger Bacon, William of Ockham, Copernicus, Paracelsus, et al., were for this change in the world of natural philosophy, it was the works of others such as Giordano Bruno (1548–1600), Galileo Galilei (1564–1642), and Sir Francis

Bacon (1561–1626), that capped this transformation of thinking regarding our understanding of space, time and nature; i.e., what we mean when we speak of being human. The explosion of religious confusion and options that developed in the Reformation creation of Christian pluralism had left Europeans with more questions than answers. People were not yet given the opportunity to decide something so fundamental for themselves as their personal road to the removal of doubt regarding salvation. Therefore the question was: Who decides? At one point during the Schism, the problem had been that there were too many Popes; now there were too many Christs to establish certainty. The new basics in thinking as well as the underlying assumptions meant that the days of an absolute domination of faith were numbered.

This was a period of increased questioning of beliefs and as well as an introduction of increased doubt that attended the already well-established historic uncertainty. If you are uncertain you may well make a choice and live with it; but how to choose when you are in doubt of everything, and perhaps even have grown more than simply frightened and perhaps actually entered paranoia? As for any appearance of unbelief, it did manifest itself at least by the time of Blaise Pascal (1623–62) who "…had first-hand knowledges since he numbered among the friends of his 'worldly period' such *libertins* as Damien Mitton, who doubted the immortality of the soul, and the Chevalier de Mère, a gambler and man-about-town." This made it possible for Pascal to "…put himself imaginatively in the position of the more serious libertine," and to state that "I look everywhere and everywhere I see only darkness. Nature offeres me nothing that is not a source of doubt and anxiety.…Seeing too much for denial and too little for certainty, I am in a state which inspires pity, and in which I have wished a hundred times that, if there is a God who preserves it, it should reveal him equivocally…"[3] The unifying wholeness of God, of nature, as well as the universe, man and society had been slowly slipping through the fingers of observers of contemporary events, creating intellectual instability and a lack of comprehensive understanding. It is a piece of irony that the very thinkers that were so important for the development of the Scientific Revolution during the age of the Bourbons in France and the Stewarts in England would create some of the greatest difficulties when attempting to speak with authority of a universally accepted and understood God alongside their discoveries in natural philosophy. The divisions were serious and expanding, which was surprising and not fully appreciated for another two centuries. In this sense, the community of thought was dividing among various interests and becoming specialized in different categories of study, although some leaders, such as

Cardinal Richelieu in France, attempted to keep the ties between church and state and faith and reason on behalf of and in favor of the Church. Obviously this did not work since each traditional cultural unit would continue, with the state and the church, the arts and the sciences, the families and new economics continuing divisively while increasingly evolving and developing their own divergent methods and goals, with hints of expanding specialization making itself felt. This was partially a continuance, in part, of the rise of heresies even in Protestant lands:

> Heresy was no longer a solitary, hole-and-corner thing. It made conquests, it gained disciples. Flown with insolence and pride, it came out into the open, it flaunted itself for all to see. Reason was no longer synonymous with sober good sense, with serene and benevolent wisdom. It became critical, aggressive. The most widely accepted notions, such as deriving proof of God's existence from universal consent, the historical basis of miracles, were openly called in question. The Divine was relegated to a vague and impenetrable heaven, somewhat up in the skies. Man and man alone was the standard by which all things were measured. [4]

This was an age where on the one hand they were burning witches while on the other we witness, through the scientific revolution, a growing faith in man's ability to apply reason to his world. The Thomistic division between faith and reason was disappearing and so too, a traditional sense of order.

This is not to imply that at this time there were no serious faithful believers. On the contrary, for most people, faith was overwhelmingly the only road that made sense and would continue to be their guide, not unlike our own era. An example can be found among the growing mystic movements, some that originally appeared historically in the age of magic, witchcraft and ghosts in both ancient 'rational' Greece and in the 'practical' Roman Empire.[5] The curiosity and hunger for answers in such an age of dramatic changes was expressed either by those who would lean on faith (the past) or those who were beginning to lean on reason (the future). The Western world was clearly beginning to divide between the thinkers and believers. The crisis of conscience and an exasperation of faith was a byproduct of those religious upheavals where "…the religious protest against the Renaissance and Humanism, which Reformation and Counter Reformation share, intensified otherworldly beliefs. The revival of religion strengthened a fierce moral fanaticism often culminating in arid dogmatism and intolerant persecution, in superstition and violence."[6] It was not simply religious reform and reaction but rather more importantly, the creation of other modes of thought and action that made for the first hints of the creation of new patterns of thinking, moving closer towards that of the modern mind. Part of the period's unique quality can be summarized around one word: Baroque, a word that is usually associated with the arts but which for historians of ideas and mentalities is seen as a worthy term for explaining the nature and character of an era, one which, in this case, is rather ambiguous.

Baroque, it can be argued, blends in with many definitions, some even contradictory. The style itself is often dated chronologically from about the middle of the sixteenth century until somewhere around 1660. While it may not be unlike some other styles in not being easily defined, there are several components that reveal not only some of its character but can also be used to reflect this historic period, offering clues to its definition. Perhaps one of the better offers is it being "...described in analogy to two magnetic poles operating within a common field of ideas and feelings. This common field of feeling was focused on movement, intensity, tension, force, Baroque art found its richest fulfillment in the castle and the opera..."[7] This was an age where the term *power* would become more and more commonly used—from the new developments on the stage, with the arrival of opera, to such massive building projects as Versailles. An interesting thought regarding opera is that it could be interpreted as a secularization of the performance of a Catholic High Mass in a Gothic cathedral which was a great theater in itself, a stage where Medieval society would experience specific theatrical productions, particularly morality plays. It is clear that there was a slow, limited but definite sense of increasing secularism seen parallel with this new-found turn towards reason and new forms of aesthetics, while at the same time there was still retained a strong desire to seek from the realm of faith the answer for big questions (certainty). "The extremes of mysticism and rationalism which divided religious feeling in this period were reflected in baroque style."[8] Some, like the Baroque artist Rembrandt, as noted, worked their Protestant themes artistically, while others like Bernini, who was responsible for artistic achievements inside St. Peter's Basilica with his *Baldacchino* and *Cathedra Petri*, were more interested in the active orientation of style in sculpture and architecture, that is, the technical qualities. "The baroque delighted in curves, movement, tension, expansive spatial effects—in a word, dynamism—as in the great churches of Bernini and Borromini in Rome. As we have seen, empiricism, and its ally experimental science, was similarly dynamic, at least in its conception of knowledge."[9] This new era was exercising a sense of motion and power, activity and action, in art as well as politics, economics and varied religious revivals. The rational and aesthetic along with this new religious attitude were exemplified in the technical skills of such Baroque artist as Francisco De Zurbaran (1598–1662), Diego Velazquez (1599–1660), Peter Paul Rubens (1577–1640) and Jan Vermeer (1632–75) all of whom could practice their faith and yet cultivate their rational thinking through their artistic skills. Albrecht Dürer had been called the "Leonardo of the North"[10] and was famed for his engravings and graphic arts. While Rembrandt's work portrayed the importance of light and Bernini is overwhelmed by the sense of motion, two compatible thoughts notwithstanding their religious and aesthetic differences, they were inherently attracted to a growing interest in the new science of motion and light that were being explored by the natural philosophers. These artists like those three 'Age of Genius' artists felt their own significance and power; some sense of their own genius now clearly individualized. This is natural in the arts where one most finds the clearest expression of the Baroque mind; and as has been noted, this art also meant "…something more subtle, of which one becomes acutely aware from looking at contemporary art and architecture." It is the sin of pride that was being discarded with the coming of the Renaissance braggadocio while even moving towards vanity: "Consider, for instance, the *vanitas* motif in seventeenth-century painting, strong not only in Spain of the Counter Reformation where it might be expected but in Holland where the new still lives glorifying the senses did not succeed altogether in elbowing it out…"[11] To accept pride is one thing but to also allow for vanity further demonstrated the change in attitude. The traditional rules of morality were not only shifting but in some cases, losing ground to new ideas and perspectives. The ancient (active) virtue was put into new use in encouraging action, which could mean pride in what one does and devoid of humility. But then, for Protestants the commandments had become more important than the seven deadly sins which meant that one could ignore the condemnation of pride even those who favored being as Augustinian as Luther.

Art is inherently universal. Louis XIV's Versailles demonstrates the new economic wealth and the significance of royal families: the feelings of power were ever-present. The sense of power must have been, as it may still be for many, euphoric, and central as a title for a section of a book on the Baroque style well states: *The Common Ground: The Restless Search for Power.*[12] After all, the literature of Shakespeare and Cervantes (1547–1615) went well beyond the Renaissance and thus can also be associated with both the Baroque and the modern.[13] Writers, like visual artists, were beginning to see an alternative way to organize their world view, a new way to witness the world. As one observer has noted, this was "…literary work as an expression of the 'spirit of the age.'

The sense of power in all its forms, spiritual and secular, scientific and political, psychological and technical is the only common denominator which enables us to conceive of them as varied expressions of a common view of man and the world."[14] And this attitude of power as well as a sense of both being of and in the world which was now about to be deconstructed, offered new and various approaches to art and religion. One statement that captures this new perspective among writers, especially in the seventeenth century offers that:

> The startling achievements of man led to a sense of potential might which alternated with a crushing realization of human limitations in the face of an infinite world created by a remote and all-powerful being transcending all human comprehension. The inherent drama of such a view provided a magnificent setting for the poets of true grandeur. It is the glory of the baroque age that everywhere men rose to this unique challenge. Milton and Vondel, Corneille and Calderon, Lope de Vega and Grimmelshausen—they all spoke the language of an age when man's dignity was his most prized possession in the face of the powers of this earth and those of the beyond.[15]

Beyond this, religious fanaticism also played a key role in holding onto a past, even if mythical, while the Western world and new mentality kept pointing to tomorrow.

Of course the real power would turn out to be something very special, that is the power of the human mind to explore the nature of the universe and what it means to be human. And there are many more writers, some to be discussed later, who belong to this post-Renaissance and post-Reformation world and, "…sum up the literary work as an expression of the 'spirit of the age.'" Perhaps this was partially a result of an interesting irony in that there was now a growing tendency at this time to begin thinking in terms of "…having rather than being,"[16] while at the same time there was still a powerful tendency pulling some toward religious and political extremism. If we look back far enough we find that the mind of those preceding this period was one of need, one that "…loves stability, nay, if it could, it would be stability."[17] Just because doors of a newer and wider space as well as a more open sense of time were beginning to appear does not mean everyone will walk through or acknowledge them. On the contrary, "…what men craved to know was what they were to believe and what they were not to believe. Was tradition still to command their allegiance, or was it to go by the board?"[18] It was not that which was new that was embraced but rather the old, the familiar that was being clung to: "Under the Feudal system the predominant social control had been that of tradition. This prescribed a man's status and the roles he had to play as the various departments of life. Economic life was static and secure, regulated by the guild system which blocked undue competition and self-assertion. There was little social mobility."[19] The new forms of an inherent Western dualism would now become that much more extreme, those turning to faith and religious revival and those towards reason and secularism, resulting in divisive approaches and conflicting values that will only continue to increase both in depth and breadth.

There are periods in history when events change more rapidly than the mind set; that is to say, assumptions, attitudes and values no longer apply to developments within that traditional societal order. The end of the Hellenic, Hellenistic, Roman Republic, Empire, early Medieval, the High Medieval periods, and onto the modern, all participate and become dramatic examples of this transformation of assumptions. While some changes are more significant than others in their impact, the period from about 1600 to 1700 was one of the most significant. There are some who would even suggest that the end of the twentieth century could very well be another example of extreme transformation; only historical judgement will reveal if this valid. In the end, in all cases, the old views cannot withstand the challenges, the new crises, the altered realities and the basic conflicts that now stand with little or no immediate precedent. Arthur Schopenhauer once observed, "…those who do not remember the past are doomed to repeat it." We could add: Those who do not adjust to the ending of one period will not partake in the birthing of what is coming. Thinkers like Bruno, Galileo, Bacon, Harvey, Hooke, Boule and Willis, not to mention Descartes and Locke contributed early to this era of dynamic changes and can claim to have stood on the cutting edge of both a new understanding and form of certainty that has continued to act as a foundation for our own world. These thinkers may have acknowledged the past but chose to go beyond.

The remarkable phenomena of this era of the birth of modern rationality was the addition of new religious forms. The monolithic Western world that had existed at least since Alexander the Great had lost its efficacy. But faith still remained a dominant component in the struggle to understand contemporary circumstances at a time of unprecedented confusion. There was little in the way of dispute regarding an agreed upon deity, the biblical Jesus, who was first and lastly the source of all values for living and dying, although Bloom would now add Hamlet to the pantheon of "precursors in personality."[20] But by the time of the seventeenth century, there developed a view suggesting that even if God's essence was unknowable, one could know perfectly as Locke noted, "…the precise real essence of the things moral words stand for." Not knowing GOD did not mean we did not know His Word, making it clear that: "...what man's mind was fitted for, not for the 'niceties' and 'notions' of theological speculation but for moral knowledge, which, Locke concluded, was 'the proper science and business of mankind in general...'"[21] Disputes over the question of who was the 'correct' Jesus, whether Anglican or Catholic, Lutheran or Calvin, was a waste of time since it was believed that He had left words that fit our best nature. It was this fact in Locke's view that this subject "...if properly pursued, could enable men to agree tolerably well and live in peace with one another."[22] Descartes somewhat earlier suggested a similar conclusion, and used a rather well-established ontological argument in order to prove the existence of God. As he saw it, the very idea of God 'is in us.' While this was an extremely weak argument, he nevertheless suggested that God's presence is innate in the sense of being evident to our minds simply as an *a priori*, a well advanced knowledge inherent and that clearly precedes 'any sense experience.'[23] Some thinkers were prepared to move away from an institutional church and literal biblical Lord—only one of several disagreements—turning instead to one of a more personal nature; one way to a new sense of toleration and peace. The overwhelming power expressed as a hunger to know, to truly understand, had genuinely expanded since the Italian Renaissance and was further enlarged by both those driven by faith and those new souls who were driven by reason; it is accurate to note that the "...spirit of curiosity regarding nature and man, a distinctive trait of the Renaissance, was too strong to permit an entirely unbroken acquiescence in ancient learning."[24] The issue now became how to go beyond the past and also retain and feed one's curiosity.

The reasons for a growing doubt regarding traditional answers during this period are as varied as the multiplicity of events that offered contrary and differing roads to salvation and made for a growing need for more rational explanations. The strange new worlds being first discovered and increasingly explored added to this confusion since there was no biblical guide for these remarkable phenomena. Exploration and eventual colonization is, of course, a subject for another study, although the question of what it means to be human certainly can in part be attributed to the discovery of these new societies on the American continent and elsewhere. The impact can be found rather early historically since the appetite and fascination with these 'savages' was insatiable: "Although the first-hand accounts by travelers were often sober and factual, it did not follow that belief in the fabulous disappeared. Popular travel books embroidered the tales—describing, for instance, the inhabitants of the New World as 'blue in colour and with square heads.' One of the most successful of these collections, the *Cosmographis* (1544) by Sebastian Muenster, presented an indiscriminate mixtures of the old 'monstrous races' and the newly discovered 'savages.'"[25] Confusion as to what or who was discovered only grew in time, although they did quickly become both something of an appealing mental exercise for those who possessed a mystical bent and an issue for study and understanding for others. As has been noted, those "... 'monstrous races' gradually sank down to survive as mere popular superstitions, while the 'savages' became an important concern of philosophers and theologians."[26] The ultimate question was, of course, that of explaining these new peoples, these 'savages' in the tradition of placing all humanity into a context of types and origins. For the religious there were potential challenges to the biblical story of the descent from Eve and Adam.[27] Columbus started this whole issue by bringing natives back to the Spanish court. There was one scholar from Italy who "...studied their language and questioned them about their way of life. He came to the conclusion that it was like the Golden Age, when people were simple and innocent. This foreshadowed the eighteenth-century picture of the 'noble savage,' and swings in polarity between the 'good' and the 'bad' savage."[28] While an interesting theory it was more mythical than rational.

Three of the more famous interpretations on the discovery of the natives of the Americas were first that of Paracelsus, another by Sir Walter Raleigh (1552–1618) and last, from Jean Bodin, all offering a representation of interesting if differing positions. The importance of this topic is revealed by the fact that until we can accept that all people are in some very fundamental way different from all others there is no room for the appearance or acceptance of a self. Paracelsus' understanding was not that unusual in holding to a somewhat contemporary view: "...the newly discovered remote peoples were so strange that they could not be the offspring of Adam and Eve; thus they were not truly human." In 1520 he further suggested that: "It cannot be proved that those men who inhabit the hidden countries are descended from Adam...in speech they are like parrots, and have no souls..."[29] That these beings were not human as was understood by Christians had the advantage of allowing the enslavement of these "lesser beings;" good for European economies but bad for the so-called savages. The second position offered was by Sir Walter Raleigh who retained the most popular position at the time, the unity of human nature. Sir Walter Raleigh's *History of the World* (1614) is of particular interest in the present context, since it was based upon "...the assumption of the uniformity of the human mind and the likeness therefore of past to present historical processes."[30] The idea of uniformity will remain dominate for some two more centuries since the idea of a cultural anthropology must wait in the wings for some time. Until one can move beyond this position and grant fundamental differences inherent in varied peoples there can be no true individuality nor a sense of what we think of as a self and therefore no real expression of consciousness as we now would use the term. This was a difficult concept to grasp and for many, even today, the idea is anathema. Jean Bodin, a Frenchman and contemporary of Raleigh but also well known at the English court of Elizabeth I, was more complex in his judgement. He was politically adept and a thoughtful participant of his times, including arguments for religious toleration. He also was a more radical thinker regarding the creation of differing peoples as used in his *Of the Laws and Customes of a Commonweale* (1557): "Essentially an environmentalist, he believed in an interaction between a people's disposition (their 'humors') and climatic and geographical factors." Additionally, Bodin "…also placed great emphasis on migrations, with the consequent mingling of peoples giving rise to new institutions." Therefore, with "…the minimum necessary bow in the direction of orthodoxy, Bodin explained human diversity in largely naturalistic terms."[31] This was a rather remarkable position for its time, and would remain so, eventually becoming less unacceptable by the nineteenth century. Today the debate has shifted to the question of nurture versus nature with nature coming to dominate. For now, however, the West was not yet ready for such a breakthrough. The pull between the long, evolved and complex sets of theological arguments of differing sects would begin to face more powerful problems, namely, approaches dominated by reason and newly discovered scientific facts.

The philosophic issue of belief and the individual made its appearance at this time. There was an alternate position regarding oneself existing within a society that went beyond the circumstance of birth and which was tied increasingly with the new economics. Bodin was not the only one addressing the issue of developing nation states and the potential for new mercantile economies. In fact, it was Hobbes, not Bodin, who would create a construct for the state as the arbiter regarding all human activities, a position that the church had once possessed. Hobbes is also part of that larger change as well, the rise of a scientific approach. Additionally, there were new theoretical views regarding both cosmology and the question of a methodology of reasoning that now made an appearance along with those changes that were slowly unseating such classical giants as Aristotle. Interestingly enough it was less Copernicus than Bruno and Galileo who were making the largest waves, the kind that create new and sometimes even frightening questions. Of course modern science is as much if not more predicated on the questions rather than specific answers. Today we accept that scientific questions increase as part and parcel to any breakthrough. But in these early years, *science* was not even the term used. What we now call science was actually referred to in the older tradition of natural philosophy, and of some note, Bruno never was a scientist as we understand the term but rather a professional philosopher. As a precursor to Hobbes, he has been listed as one of the most significant philosophers of the Italian Renaissance, and, whether one agrees with this view or not, it is a position that has good reason as the *Encyclopedia of Philosophy* makes clear. Since "Bruno was no scientist, ... his impact, his historical importance, his ultimate influence upon the development of non-scientific attitudes to science, were all the more startling..."[32] While he continued an interest in "...the scholastic discussion of plural worlds and the infinity of space," he also had "...realised that Copernicus, in making it plausible to take any point as the centre of the universe, had abolished absolute directions." What he had done was to popularized the "...idea that space was actually infinite and therefore without favoured natural directions."[33] The universe that had been guided by Divine intervention was a closed, contained and controlled entity. Now we find an attitude suggesting an infinity to space raising serious questions regarding God's role. Specifically, however, Bruno did not turn his back on his religion or the classics as he made clear in his *De l'infinito universo e mondi* (1586), for he did not rely on Copernicus primarily but rather culled from a variety of philosophical materials, including the *Timaeus* of Plato and the writings of Nicholas Cusanus, Lucretius, and Democritus. His religious and traditional view-points are revealed in his expression, "Thus is the excellence of God magnified and the greatest of his kingdom made manifest; he is glorified not in one, but in countless suns; not in a single earth, a single world, but in a hundred thousand, I say in an infinity of worlds."[34] This is still a form of conformity, ignoring the question about what happens to the human thought process in a time of great change when the very assumptions by which we live are first challenged and then have been drastically altered from our earlier and familiar modes of thinking.

The greatest change in the universe historically is within the universe itself, for we have been pompous as well as humbled in her overwhelming power which we have been forced to honestly witness after we experience a necessary cultural change. It was Bruno's suggestion, "Therefore the earth and the ocean thereof are fecund....For from infinity is born an ever fresh abundance of matter."[35] This was a much more extreme position than that of Copernicus who also did not exercise scientific methods and was more conventional in his thinking. Copernicus, who gained fame for his construction of a more updated heliocentric theory replacing the earth with the sun at the center of the universe offered no evidence for his suggestion. While this may sound somewhat extreme it was, after all, an idea that had been posed (and rejected) in antiquity. As one scholar put it: "The Conservatism of Copernicus."[36] As for his contemporaries, again he does not come across as a daring thinker. A significant contributor to this revolution, Kepler, "…said that Copernicus failed to see the riches that were within his grasp, and was content to interpret Ptolemy rather than nature."[37]

There was in these dynamic years of re-birth, reform and revolution a period of transition where one may look somewhat forward but only through a fog. Since the Church took the position that the once existing garden of innocence was here on Earth along with hell in the center of the Earth, and finally that God made us his most important creature, it must follow that the Ptolemic system had to be the truth. Not by any research but by a simple mind exercise, Copernicus had suggested a sun-centered system which ended the problem of epicycles. This was theorizing in the medieval tradition and was offered in his published work in 1543 only after he had died, which may account for his surviving the Inquisition. In other words, he tinkered with Ptolemy but he was no threat to the Church's position since he offered no scientific evidence. Moreover this was only revolutionary in a very limited sense, that is, "Copernicus, by making the earth a planet, and ultimately applying terrestrial dynamics to the heavens, reduced all nature to one system, homogeneous in substance, and subject to the same laws. They dismantled Aristotle's 'Sky,' which, unlike 'Nature' below the moon, was supposed to be inalterable, immutable, and immortal."[38] This had deep implications for the future not just the Ptolemic system but the Christian view of the universe, as well, if only by implication, since it also began altering our view of space which if changed would have, by necessity, also rearranged our view of time. Space and time are completely tied together and the idea of the universe as infinite cannot but alter our sense of time.[39] As noted, however, "Bruno did not merely move the fences of man's cosmos farther out; he tore them down and filled up the universe beyond with a plurality of worlds."[40] This was heady stuff when witnessed from the expanding reality of sixteenth century Europe. These thinkers including Bruno and those following, from Descartes to the Cambridge Platonist Henry More and Fontenelle (author of the popular *Entretiens sur la Pluralité des Mondes*, 1686) as well as others were correctly described as destroyers of "…the finite world of the Middle Ages, the world in which Dante and Shakespeare lived, not to speak of Aristotle, and projected a radically different sort of infinite universe."[41]

When our entire physical world could be and was completely rewritten, it should not come as any surprise that we would find an improved understanding of ourselves as part of the beginnings of a continuum of revolutionary changes, sociological, psychological, cultural and intellectual. That this arguably is one of the more if not most profound times in our history has been noted: "...the so-called 'scientific revolution,' popularly associated with the sixteenth and seventeenth centuries,...outshines everything since the rise of Christianity and reduces the Renaissance and Reformation to the rank of mere episodes, mere internal displacements, within the system of medieval Christiandom."[42] To change our views so completely regarding space, whether because of the introduction of the New World or of the New Art of the Renaissance or the writings of Bruno, simply helped to create the foundations for modern man as both a reality and a dilemma. It is valid to state that "Bruno got drunk on space, or, to use his own metaphor, he felt released from prison," which is also to state that human potential was yet untapped, for he understood that the "Ptolemic universe had shut the human mind up in 'a most narrow kingdom,' like a parrot in a cage." Humankind was only just learning how to be free to explore this world of ours, for as Bruno put it:

> Henceforth I spread confident wings to space,
> I feel no barrior of crystal or of glass;
> I cleave the heavens and soar to the infinite. [43]

In these times of trouble there was glimmer clearly visible of optimism, a source for the eventual idea of progress.

All this leads to a very important question: if the world was being turned up-side-down, no longer possessing the certainty of antiquity and its immediate legacy, how do we reestablish certain knowledge? Interestingly, the answer came from a younger contemporary of Bruno, Galileo Galilei. This new order of space could never have been imagined since the structural changes should be traced as follows: "The new nature also involved a drastic rearrangement of the heavens and a new conception of space. This space revolution, as we may call it, is usually described as coming in two phases, the first or Copernican phase, and the second, proposing the infinity of the universe, spearheaded by the Italian philosopher Giordano Bruno."[44] True, the basis for this new sense of space can be traced as far back as Giotto and the foreshortening of subsequent Renaissance artists. But the cutting edge of this post-Bruno thinking can be found in the writings of Blaise Pascal (1623–62) who also found infinity a revolutionary and meaningful approach to understanding our universe. "Blaise Pascal's response was more extreme, and less typical. Reacting more to the new notion of infinity, than to the Copernican hypothesis (which in fact, he did not accept), Pascal felt lost in nature's immensity."[45] The Copernican revolution was both a lot less and a lot more than the simple theory that Copernicus articulated. As Pascal saw it, "Nature is an infinite sphere, the center of which is everywhere, the circumference nowhere.... What is man in this Infinite?...We sail in a fast sphere, ever drifting in uncertainty, driven from end to end."[46] Here there is a sense of being capable of accepting that something inherently unknown, and that a phenomenon is uncertain. Perhaps this can explain his conclusion regarding the issue of God: as a mathematician like his father, he eventually contributed in 1654 to the foundations of today's probability theory based upon his wager theory regarding the existence of God.[47] To wager on the existence of God is a form of rationalization regarding one's beliefs and could also even be considered a form of secularism in the service of one's own faith, a secularization of belief.

This was the land that Galileo entered and helped transform not by way of simple theories, but as a matter of the New Science, or natural philosophy. There are two very important issues that Galileo would have to confront, one being epistemological, where we have to question how we know that we know, the other, equally important for Galileo, was that of motion. The first is ancient but equally seen as a relatively germane question as early as the fourteenth century by contemporaries of Dante, Giotto and Petrarch. Two distinct voices can be found, one, Jean Buridan, the other, Nicole Oresme. Buridan who was born and died in the fourteenth century was concerned with motion. He was a student of the brilliant William of Ockham who was famous for, among other things, his Ockham's Razor—which could be considered a rule of ontological economy to the effect that "entities are not to be multiplied beyond necessity." Buridan addressed the issue of our knowing the correct path in an equally rather unique way. His theory, remembered in history as "Buridan's Ass," states that an ass faced with two equidistant and equally desirable bales of hay will starve to death because there are no grounds to preferring one bale to the other. Choices have long been a serious burden that humanity has been able, through the community, to ameliorate. As community loses its hold, more and more one finds themselves left to their own devices.

The other issue, motion, can also find its roots in this period.

> ...an alternative theory of motion was put into a definitive, and to some extent mathematical, form in the fourteenth century, principally by two masters of the University of Paris, Jean Buridan and Nicole Oreseme. The principle they adopted, but did not invent, was that though rest is the normal state of matter, movement is a possible but unstable state. They illustrated this conception by analogy with heat: bodies are usually of the same temperature as their neighbourhood, but if they are heated above that temperature, the unstable state is only gradually corrected. A moving body acquired impetus, as a heated body acquired heat, and neither wasted away immediately. The impetus acquired was the cause of the result of the residual motion; and only when the store was exhausted did the body come to rest.[48]

In the Aristotelean world, which would include the brilliant medievalist Thomas Aquinas, motion occurred because of given reasons causing that motion to happen. This made sense on a certain level as we only experience things moving if they appear to have a cause. If Aristotle believed in anything, it was in causation. The traditional order was "...to conceive of force as producing motion from the state of rest, and as the invariable concomitant of violent motion. Within itself inert matter could have no potentiality for any other than its proper natural movement: and though Aristotle never explicitly formulates the proposition that the application of a constant force gives a body a constant velocity, it is implied in the whole of pre-Galilean mechanics."[49] Moreover, the Roman Church, as has been noted, had a vested interest in employing its angels in such an Aristotlean idea as causal motion: for an object to move it needs a mover. With the concept of impetus that Galileo contributed to by way of his observations, however, the rules of motion began to change since impetus suggested there were natural reasons for motion. "The impetus theory contained the first tentative outlines of the explanation of all changes in nature in terms solely of matter and motion which was to figure so prominently in the scientific philosophy of the seventeenth century."[50] The new understanding regarding motion had provided a new basis for the functioning of science in general and specifically for what would become the discipline of physics.

Galileo is historically an extremely significant figure for a variety of reasons, including supporting the concept of an infinite space as the epistemological answer of using observation. But more applicable to our study would be first, his mathematics and then his announcement that his studies (observation) led him to conclude that the universe is mostly a vacuum, a great deal of empty space. The thought that God created nothing in creating the universe was, of course, more than just a little unnerving for contemporary clerics. Even today such ideas, along with that of evolution for some who are driven by faith, are seen as untenable. The new order, which was just beginning to replace the old medieval perspective was still not acceptable to many. At the same time, Galileo deserves a great deal of credit for offering increased evidence for a more rational and secular view of our universe. As an example,

> Galilean mechanics was thus the necessary complement to Copernican astronomy, and though it is true (as Professor Heisenberg has remarked) that nothing could have been more surprising to the scientists of the seventeenth century than their discovery that the same mechanical laws were appropriate for celestial and terrestrial motions alike, on the smallest and largest scale, the coincidence was not fortuitous, for it followed from Galileo's conscious endeavour to interpret Copernicus' mathematical model in terms of natural philosophy. [51]

It now became something beyond a new hypothesis. A new mechanics with new mathematics was now beginning to be explored as an alternative salvation, at least intellectually, to that of the risen Christ. By way of developing rational explanations of our world and eventually of our physical being, the door was opened for an alterate explanation for our psychological and intellectual condition, even though it was but a beginning. What may be most important, however, for the topic of the appearance of consciousness, and with it a discovery of the self and sense of individuality, was the corollary development, again, of a new understanding of space and time. As a point of reference, there was even with Pascal an unwillingness to accept the implications being discussed here. In regard to the self and individuality, Pascal was clear: "'*le moi est haissable*'" [the self is detestable].[52] Additionally, it is clearly stated in his major work, *Pensées*: "'I am nothing but an unimportant thing in the abyss of time and space'—and this is the limitation of the self as determined by Destiny."[53] Though apparently fixed by way of destiny, that which is within was detestable rather than simply fixed. The whole of the universe could still be perceived as a fixed entity but now questions were raised about the motion inside the universe or even inside our very being. There was a need, now, for a new mathematical means of expression and understanding, one that would point towards the revolutionary work of Newton. As for the implications of Galileo's mathematical physics, they

> ...were set forth by Newton's teacher Isaac Barrow (1630–1677)....If time is defined and measured by motion, we are in danger of a logical circle, for the rate of a motion involves the idea of time. But Barrow said that space and time are absolute, infinite and eternal, because God is omnipresent and everlasting. Space extends without limit continuously, and time flows for ever evenly and independently of sensible

motions. Here we meet the first clear formulation of the ideas of absolute time and space as held by Newton. Time and space are represented by Barrow as being independent of human perception and knowledge, existing in their own right, save in their relation to God.[54]

Any idea of a time and space beyond our everyday experiences of an omniscient deity where nature is humanizing because there is now no need for a God to be involved in every part of human and natural existence, meant there was also no need of some sentient being that directs all and is engaged in everything. While this view was slowly taking hold and changing the views of at least a small supportive minority, the implications for humanity living in nature, a natural being, were not yet comprehended although the aspects of nature and man's place in it will eventually become the focus of study for natural philosophers and scientists. Galileo stated it clearly in *The Assayer* (1623), a work referred to as his scientific manifesto:

> Philosophy is written in this grand book, the universe, which stands continually open to our gaze. But the book cannot be understood unless one first learns to comprehend the language and read the letters in which it is composed. It is written in the language of mathematics, and its characters are triangles, circles, and other geometric figures without which it is humanly impossible to understand a single word of it; without these, one wanders about in a dark labyrinth.[55]

This remark is neither outside of nor a denial of the historic context of the presence of mathematics rooted in antiquity since it reflects the rediscovery of ancient mathematics in the Renaissance, specifically Archimedes of Syracuse whom Galileo had studied. The Renaissance artists' work on perspective and the practical geometrizing of thinkers such as Niccolo Tartaglia, one of the first translators of Archimedes was further aided by the new-found philosophizing of Leonardo da Vinci.[56] The Renaissance artist, Leonardo, was after all, an engineer, a master draftsman and an inventor with creative ideas regarding canons, submarines and the helicopter. Leonardo, although rightly thought of as an artist, clearly was attracted to both motion and mathematics and was committed to their application. Unlike most of the philosophers of the day who were to develop their ideas almost entirely outside academic circles, "…Galileo had taught mathematics at the universities of Pisa and Padua and was knowledgeable of new world where navigators, merchants, and princes were calling for a more quantitatively exact treatment of their practical problems."[57] Diversity of capacities clearly was representative of the Renaissance mind. The divine immutability of the universe, its fixity, its certainty and its absolutes derived from divine energy and His creativity in all of nature was a given that Galileo, who, while religious, was not prepared to grant. One of the more remarkable aspects of Galileo's personal view was his preference for alterability, as compared to inalterability.

> I cannot without great astonishment—I may say without great insult to my intelligence—hear it attributed as a prime perfection and nobility of the natural and integral bodies of the universe that they are invariant, immutable, inalterable, etc., while on the other hand it is called a great imperfection to be alterable, generable, mutable, etc. For my part I consider the earth very noble and admirable precisely because of the diverse alterations, changes, generations, etc., that occur in it incessantly.[58]

The age of the fixed universe was slowly coming to an end and the idea of life and nature as dynamic was beginning to be recognized.

The idea that the world was becoming a mechanism in motion led Leibniz to describe the "Great Clock." And like those ideas developed most recently from the experience of the clock, the compass and the printing press as well as the telescope that Galileo used so effectively, machines were now seen as not fixed but rather as mutable tools. This meant that what was important was not inventions like the telescope and microscope but rather the attitude held by those using these instruments. What was beginning to appear was what has been referred to as an attack on tradition by way of a growing preoccupation with mechanics. Space and time may have retained some aspects of fixity, but the mechanics within this realm remained subjects of manipulation and study as something of a changing phenomena, much as the earth moving around the sun could be understood as objects of scientific observation. Galileo had to retract the statement that his evidence supported Copernicus regarding the motion of the earth when he went on trial for heresy in 1633 since the church had concluded that his position was a threat. There is little wonder in this. Some church leaders refused even look through his telescope. After all, Galileo had looked closer than anyone ever had at the moon and found its surface to be pock-marked (with blemishes). If God was perfect, how is it that all his creations were not perfect? The imperfection of the earth was a by-product of the sin of Adam and Eve, in that space that is known as Earth and where there was justified fire and plague and the sorts of horrors that followed. Evil existed because of the failures of mankind. God did not create imperfections, which raised an interesting and very problematic question: How could a god in all his perfection create a moon that had what appeared to be acne? Finding a plurality of satellites around Jupiter, or finding that falling bodies do not fall proportionality by way of their size, did not help his situation. The commitment of this Italian genius is demonstrated by the well known event right after he was forced to recant his views on the motion of the earth. As he was walking out from his inquisition, conceding that the earth is not moving, he was supposed to have quietly whispered: *"Eppur si muove"* (but it moves). But then, it is never easy to be a genius. He recanted not because he was wrong and the church was right but because he valued his own life since only a few years earlier (1600) the church burned Bruno at the stake for his heretical ideas, particularly his public agreement with Copernicus. First we stand on this moving object the Earth, and we then find that all planets like Earth experience decay. The logical question is then whether there is anything beyond death that is fixed and certain. This query is still too early and too problematic.

A very important English contemporary of Galileo, Francis Bacon added his own contribution to the transformation of thinking that marks the creation of this revolution in natural philosophy. What was slowly being recognized was that there were two elements to making these changes meaningful. The first was data and the second, methodology. Herbert Butterfield insightfully observed that "It could not be very long before it was realized that certain forms of scientific knowledge gained something by the very lapse of time, whether by the accumulation of data—the sheer increasing aggregation of observed facts —or by the continual revision of the results and the improvements in actual methods."[59] This was partially recognized in the writings of Francis Bacon who aided the birth of natural philosophy in that he, like Bruno, was not a scientist or natural philosopher, but a remarkably successful propagandist for his cause—science. Unlike others convicted of heresy and burned at the stake, Bacon was able to successfully make his argument, perhaps in part, because he was an established English writer, one who was first and foremost a master of the King's own. We are speaking of the time of Shakespeare and the *King James Bible* and the impressive developing language which he used as literary propaganda for the coming Scientific Revolution. It was Bacon who "…inspired in his followers such complete confidence in his ideas, that they were stimulated and incited to carry on experiments with an intensity hitherto unknown, so much so, in fact, that Sprat was moved to call his times 'this age of experiments.'"[60] He and others had a powerful fascination regarding their sources of knowledge in that they "…never tired of contrasting the two sources of information, as the antitheses which the contrast suggested testify: nature versus books, works versus words, laboratories versus libraries and closets, industry versus idleness."[61] One of his most famous achievements is the attack on errors regarding the application of language and the assumptions that can be explained by both his public role in society and his scientific literature:

> Bacon's courtly allegiances were unquestionable. Son of Elizabeth's Lord Keeper Nicholas Bacon, Francis was born in 1561 within 'the shadow of the court.' Under Elizabeth, he endured slow advancement, rising only to the level of Queen's Counsel. Bacon's political career took off under James I, and he advanced beyond the titular position of his father when he became Lord Chancellor in 1618. Bacon often served as a liaison between the king and Parliament, attempting to settle conflicts to the Crown's benefit. His scientific ideas were shaped by his own political and legal interests as a court official. Once James came to the throne, Bacon forged a scientific program that he hoped would gain intellectual acceptance and financial support from the reigning monarch.[62]

This was a practical man of government and the new natural philosophy. As will be explored later, it was this type of attitude that was a critical component for the creation and development of the French *Encyclopédie* in the following century. There were precedents for his ideas, of course, especially his idea of the importance of empirical knowledge that had been articulated some several centuries earlier by Roger Bacon. While modern empiricism as a philosophical position is attributable to John Locke, the nascent idea can be found in the writings of Roger Bacon, that of the High Medieval mind that remains rather odd but brilliant. He wrote commentaries on Aristotle, was known as Doctor Mirabilis ("Wonderful Teacher"), anticipated later arguments for mathematical proofs and experimentalism along with developing speculations about lighter-than-air flying machines, mechanical transport on land and sea, the circumnavigation of the globe, and the study of optics including the idea of creating both a microscope and a telescope.[63]

All this discussion has centered on the development of secular reasoning either on behalf of faith as with Pascal's wager or equally remarkable, clearly setting the subject of faith aside. Religion, however, was not irrelevant for the vast majority. Francis Bacon remained committed to the world of faith and he offered the following caveat: "…give to faith no more than the things that are faith's."[64] In Bacon's system, theology, though still dominant, had lost its hold over science,[65] but the desire for a teleological explanation of man and nature was not about to disappear. Notwithstanding the traditional Aristoteleans and Platonists, so numerous and hostile to mechanistic presupposition, there would be great many with a significant new attitude, those in the next century referred to as "progressivists." These progressivists, thinkers who would be part of the Age of Reason, included philosophical materialists like Bacon who demanded a "rigid separation between theology and natural philosophy" as well as suggesting we know our nature by way of God,[66] the power and wisdom of god being found in nature as well as the Bible. "Like the Virtuosi of the Royal Society later on, Bacon thought of the scientist as studying the bible of nature, and of science as having religious overtones, that is, as revealing God's power in his created works."[67]

Whatever faith that may be found in the heart of Bacon, it was in the mind that he sought to find a certainty that he appeared not to find elsewhere. In his classic, *The New Atlantis* (1626), he offered, in extremely clear and brilliant Elizabethan English to popularize a definition of natural philosophy which meant to find, "…the knowledge of causes and secret motions of things, and the enlarging of the bounds of human empire, to the effecting of all things possible."[68] Again the phenomenon of motion, from the compass to movable type, was central to the thinking of Francis Bacon. If it is not in the divine that we must search for the origins and understanding of motion, then we must turn to natural philosophy and the impact of technological changes.[69] This was more than new thinking, it was a new attitude and most importantly, new perspectives and understandings of what is implied in these perceptions. When we think of scientific knowledge we think first of observation, i.e., objectivization of data, followed by analysis, i.e., developing an analytic mind, and finally the theorizing that is the creation of an hypothesis or axioms. At the time of Bacon, the work of both Tycho Brahe (1546–1601), using non-telescopic observations, and Johannes Kepler (1571–1630), who determined the elliptic movement of Mars and established the first of the three laws of planetary motion, began to appear in public, along with the thoughts of Galileo. The ability to step back, to observe and to make judgements, first introduced by Giotto with foreshortening, was clearly expanding. It could be suggested, now, that the great discovery was one of a new attitude beyond religiously-driven faith. The expanding curiosity of those attracted to this new natural philosophy found opportunities in rational searching. While this phenomenal transformation of understanding took root with the early stages of the continuous process we think of as the "scientific revolutions," this is one movement that should be thought of as multiple or plural, since it has technically continued to this day.

There were other barriers besides religious inhibiting explanations of nature, the universe and humankind. Those which preoccupied Bacon were what he referred to as his four "Idols." The first, he called "The Idols of the Tribe which have their foundation in human nature itself, and in the tribe or race of men." As he put it, "...human understanding is like a false mirror, which, receiving rays irregularly, distorts and discolors the nature of things by mingling its own nature with it."[70] Additionally, there is a paradox between understanding and nature. As he stated it, "...there are Idols which have immigrated into men's minds from the various dogmas of philosophies, and also from wrong laws of demonstration." It is this tendency towards conformity that he called the Idols of the Theater, "...because in my judgement all the received systems are but so many stage plays, representing worlds of their own creation after an unreal and scenic fashion."[71] When we discuss the human dimension of our understanding, the problem that will occur does so because we are "...prone to suppose the existence of more order and regularity in the world than it finds. And though there be many things in nature which are singular and unmatched, yet it devises for them parallels and conjugates and relatives which do not exist."[72] Here Bacon recognizes something that is more appreciated today than at any other time. It may very well be, after all, that there is enough diversity in nature that it can eventually be argued that there may in fact be degrees of chaos inherent within what once was assumed to be an entirely ordered universe.

For all his contributions to this creation of a systematic critique and methodology and the changes necessary for the beginnings of a modern natural philosophy, Bacon also gave to us two other innovations, the first, his contribution to the new language of science, and the other, is a corollary rise of individuality. First, as to language, he stated that

> There are also Idols formed by the intercourse and association of men with each other, which I call Idols of the Market Place, on account of the commerce and consort of men there. For it is by discourse men associate, and words are imposed according to the apprehension of the vulgar. And therefore the ill and unfit choice of words wonderfully obstructs the understanding. Nor do the definitions or explanations wherewith in some things learned men are wont to guard and defend themselves, by any means set the matter right. But words plainly force and overrule the understanding, and throw all into confusion, and lead men away into numberless empty controversies and idle fancies.[73]

This, his Third Idol, makes clear that words and syntax are not neutral but rather loaded with values, assumptions and prejudices. This was one of the reasons why Bacon placed so much stock on a new language, specifically that language that was considered to be more neutral and thus honest, the language of mathematics. This would have to be considered to have been one of the few commonalities he shared with his contemporary, the political philosopher,

Thomas Hobbes.[74] The power of the word had long been accepted, of course, with the words of the bible and its varied political interpretations. This point was significant enough for Rome to disapprove of lay-people reading the bible since the language and interpretations could lead to more confusion than enlightenment, as evidenced in the Protestant Reformation. While this has been discussed earlier, it is important to note that the rise of an objectification of the study of nature required not only a new method, but equally a new more neutral language which mathematics now offered. One could argue, as occurred in scholasticism, how many angels can sit on the head of a pin or how many Marys are to be found in the New Testament, but about 2+2 making four in the ten decimal system there can be no argument. By rejecting religious scholastic foundations as he defended the idea of a new scientific method and his new language, Bacon was seeking a certainty of knowledge. It may well be no accident that modern mathematics with all its certainty appears at the same time that uncertainty regarding what we can know made itself so very strongly felt.

Language, as has been noted throughout, is, among other things, the key to coping with death, with the uncertainty of living and with the fear of all that is unknown. A name gives permanence and writing concretizes that permanence. It is in this transformation that we reach a certain sense of individuality as was demonstrated by Shakespeare. As the excellent scholar on orality and language, Walter J. Ong, has noted, "…without writing, the literate person would not and could not think as he or she does, not only when engaged in writing, but also when one is composing thoughts in oral forms."[75] It is in the construction of our thoughts in a concrete form that creates a very strong sense of one's own singular sound, the interior sound of our voice resonating within our heads that gives parameters to the evolving individual, the idea of being one of a kind with one's own unique sounds and written words. What had been given substance through religion in Genesis, "In the beginning was the word," now was to become substantial for the beginning of the individual. When the sound of the word could only belong to the lexography of God there was an agreement for all that the word was all-inclusive. When the sound shifted to the speech and writings of a particular individual who through that language itself was significant, the word of God had to allow for a new word, the word of humanity. The addition of printing and silent reading only heightened that very nascent sense of an individual self.[76] Bacon was one of the earliest to appreciate some of the elements of this more modern perception as well as to entertain some of the implications of such a voice. He stated his position on the tie between the sense of individuality and language with his remaining Idol, his Fourth:

> The Idols of the Cave are the idols of the individual man. For everyone (besides the errors common to human nature in general) has a cave or den of his own, which refracts and discolors the light of nature, owing either to his own proper and peculiar nature; or to his education and conversation with others; or to the reading of books, and the authority of those whom he esteems and admires; or to the differences of impressions, accordingly as they take place in a mind preoccupied and predisposed or in a mind indifferent and settled; or the like.[77]

The humanity and thus implications of individuality that Bloom suggests existed in the works of Shakespeare, now found additional support from a different author and orientation, in the *New Organon* (1620), one of Francis Bacon's masterful philosophical essays. Additionally, the inherent presence of misjudgements, pre-conceived perceptions and prejudices as well their roots are finally being laid open for readers of the seventeenth century to finally observe. Since language was beginning to be more and more a personal language, as can be seen in Shakespeare's plays, there is an increased opportunity for this expanding vocabulary to begin expressing those thoughts that are not colored by traditional truths but by inner viewpoints. It would be the later works of Descartes and Locke that gave shape to these early transformation of thought and psyche with an even newer and more modern language. If language can expand so can thought.

This new concept of knowledge and understanding was being born out of a "…dynamic conception, consisting above all in a shift from a contemplative to a utilitarian and activist goal." Bacon had "…called for a conjoining of contemplation and action, and was always talking about knowledge for 'the relief of man's estate,' and for 'the enlarging of the bounds of human empire, to the effecting of all things possible.'"[78] Knowledge was being suggested as the true source of power rather than in its traditional residence, nobility and/or church hierarchy. His concerns centered around the dangers of self-deception, one of the most powerful inhibitors to the growth of any knowledge of nature as well as the development of an authentic self. Self-deception is not being directly confronted here, although opportunity for its discovery and the problems commensurate with such deception does make an appearance. To be honest raises so many questions today that it is difficult if not impossible to comprehend the sensation of possessing an orthodox certainty of a world that a thoughtful and reflective person could subscribe to. This creation of something of a new psyche raises serious questions about our grasp of knowledge especially in that the modern psyche itself was not yet understood. If language can be varied so it eventually followed that human nature could vary. As for the subject of the mind or psyche "...there seems to be no fundamental difficulty with regard to 'mind' as long as one thinks of it broadly as the key feature of 'human nature.'...For in spite of the fact that the term itself dates back only to the late sixteenth century,...authors usually have no compunction in tracing origins back to Antiquity."[79] Like those central terms, *consciousness*, *self* and *individuality*, *human nature* is used freely and without regard to its etymology. One must be cautious since "...another leap forward came with the scientific revolution of the seventeenth century which, by the threshold of the eighteenth century, had brought about a transformation of ideas about nature and human life."[80] The tendencies are to "...'project back' the subject as if it is at present rather than portraying it as the meaningful activity it was in the past."[81] Thus, as we use these terms there will continue to be a concern with original meanings as delineated from what can be described as 'projected meanings.' Bacon was inherently correct regarding the idol of the cave.

What happens when the most fundamental and most often asked constructive questions begin with the *how* rather than with the traditional *why*? The new view of life and death had changed into an open question, one without the certainty that had survived for some eight hundred years. The problem for the old order, the one that held sway for so long, now became a problem of time, even an anachronism, with the appearance of a world increasingly dominated by commerce and trade, a world that would become the basis for both the nation state and the appearance of the new mercantile economics. This is what would replace feudalism as well as manorialism and its antiquarian language. Uncharted territory, especially that which was acknowledged by the appearance of the compass and the clock, was an inherent contradiction of the assumptions of the traditional mind with the new, unknown and unestablished phenomena. The problem becomes a matter of how much freedom of thought can be experienced? When Luther defended his 'Here I stand' and thus his freedom to interpret holy writ he opened the door for himself and followers to move away from Rome. However, when you knock down something so fundamental to the old order you cannot expect minor alterations since a plethora of beliefs and perceptions can quickly make their case and fill any vacuum that remains from such revolutionary activity. Selective openness does not have sustaining power in a world that grows larger, more varied and offers an enlarged set of more diverse possibilities. Once the universe was opened, it remained open even to the students of nature and science, that is true even for us in the here and now. A new set of paradigms were filling the void of the inadequate old ones, an alternative to the bankruptcy of the scholastic order, which at one time was the exclusionary source of all truth. Now it is replaced by an openness and an opportunity without any fixed limits, opportunities opened with no certainty regarding the potential for something new. While the best minds may not yet be future-oriented, they are beginning to lean in that direction.

The road that began with Petrarch and Giotto opened vistas and opportunities, not by looking back, but rather by creating a base for a modern historiography and thus a more humanized time with an equally new understanding of language, a new sense of space, while, at the same time, helping to knock down the old unchangeable order. First we must embrace a more honest view about our historic past as we would with our own memories, then, and only then, can we look to and work with the potentials of the future. As one scholar so well put it:

> ...the Renaissance, centering in the new sort of humanism, and the Reformation, defiant of traditional doctrines and authorities, were mighty movements in thought, or that they had important implications for modern ways of thinking. Psychologically, however, these movements tended to look to the past for inspiration and guidance. This was not true of the Moderns of the seventeenth century who looked more to the future and present. Sir [sic] Francis Bacon,...a product of the Renaissance and Reformation, but also of the scientific revolution, was both prototype and epitome of this new sort of modernity.[82]

This transition in the Western mind in these several centuries altered not only the Western world, it has also changed the entire order of our understanding of what it means to be human. True, this period of Bacon, Galileo, Descartes, Locke and Newton was only the beginning, but one whose unprecedented ripple effects are felt to this day. The early stages of development of the individual are but part of the larger transforming phenomenon which includes that of the birth of consciousness. As Ong stated it: "The meaning of individualism is quite varied..." But, he continues, "I believe that you can say that the rise of individualism over the centuries is simply the history of human consciousness."[83] If the history of individuality is in fact a branch of the history of consciousness, and the former is less problematic than the latter, then our understanding and ability to trace it through time would demand we be prudent in our struggle for an understanding of the latter and to at least wait upon a clarification of our understanding of the meaning of being an individual.

The subject of the individual is much more dominating in the nineteenth century, during what is called, for good or ill, the age of Romantics, than at any other earlier time. It is then that we are able to establish something in the way of an hypothesis for a definition, or at least a delineation, of the individual separated from the community that dominates societies from which we have evolved. One such commentator dealing with the issue of this more modern individuality was the popularizer of that new philosophy called Utilitarianism, John Stuart Mill (1806–73). The question he addressed, if indirectly, was, what is individuality? His answer was to equate it with what society refers to as a 'genius.' "Persons of genius are, *ex vi termini*, more individual than any other people—less capable, consequently, of fitting themselves, without hurtful compression, into any of the small number of molds which society provides in order to save its members the trouble of forming their own character."[84]

Because it is not the intention of this work to confuse a difficult term with another difficult term, it is not the intention here to argue that an individual is a genius or a genius is an individual, *per se*. Rather, the intent here is to point out the singular uniqueness of the individual as contrasted to those conforming to social mores. When the community speaks of one as an individual, as someone who introduces what could be considered a major positive contribution to that community, it is impossible to comprehend the actual meaning since the order of social purpose and action, as Mill rightly observes, is contradictory to the basic understandings of what is immediately good for that society and what is the interest of that one person who follows their own mind, voice and unique abilities. The individual must decide for themselves what they consider good in themselves, notwithstanding the very judgements of that social collective. When the Athenians decide that Aeschylus is an individual in being a hero this is a collective judgement rather than the modern sense of our own psychology. Standing alone is part of being an individual (genius) Perhaps this is a case one could make for Homer given the effect of his epics. Moreover, in stating that they are "more individual than any other," Mill recognizes that individuality, like a sense of self and the exercise of consciousness, exists as a matter of degree since no one can argue they know what a perfectly formed individual, self or conscious being is. This reflects an historical evolution of the development of this unique phenomena where the belief in the importance of the individual has become for many in the West the ultimate achievement in realizing the potential of one's humanity. Whatever a genius may be, the issue of uniqueness cannot be denied. The individual, like a genius, is one of a kind which is something that very few people would ever seek as their own personal road. Again, as Mill insisted:

> If from timidity they consent to be forced into one of these molds, and to let all that part of themselves which cannot expand under the pressure remain unexpanded, society will be little the better for their genius. If they are of a strong character, and break their fetters, they become a mark for the society which has not succeeded in reducing them to commonplace, to point at with solemn warning as "wild," "erratic," and the like; much as one should complain of the Niagara river for not flowing smoothly between its banks like a Dutch canal. [85]

It is precisely the rarity of the person who chooses to or is able to exercise their individuality that makes them so special, and those who would achieve consciousness, as will be suggested, may also be rare. Harold Bloom has stated in his book on genius that "...consciousness is what defines genius..."[86] Again we are speaking of consciousness and not awareness. "Persons of genius, it is true, are, and are always likely to be, a small minority; but in order to have them, it is necessary to preserve the soil in which they grow. Genius can only breathe freely in an atmosphere of freedom."[87] To be free is different than seeking to be free, concepts that will take time to be explored. In fact, personal freedom is more important to the individual than is social liberty. This can be demonstrated beginning with Socrates and ending with Malcolm X, both exercising freedom while incarcerated. As an utilitarian, Mill was very unusual in being more concerned with the value to the society of the unique few than the inverse. Here, the issue is tracing the rise and evolution of early examples of those who possess the greatest opportunity to realize and express their own individuality, thus achieving a high level of personal consciousness. If we remember that consciousness first appears in the form of conscience, we often find examples of those, even in the religiously driven world of the Middle Ages, who were without any conscience, for in some cases their interest centered upon the achievement of power, a social and not a spiritual construct. As Machiavelli made clear, for society, the thinking of the group is more important than the thoughts of one citizen. Political science is not interested in the individual, its interest is in the political collective. It seems reasonable to assume that there are people, perhaps many, that never really achieve either individuality or consciousness. And again, freedom is a term more appropriate to the next centuries than even in this age of new science.

It could be suggested, however, that Socrates, as best we can determine, was actually following his own conscience and thus was something of an individual. He certainly appears to be a genius and in that aspect, would satisfy Mill's judgement.[88] Those condemning him could not tolerate, let alone understand, such independent thinking. Is it not true that we still admire this Greek for being the father of philosophy? Is it not also true that we hold him in such high regard because of his willingness to give up his life in order to honor his quest for truth? And is not his value partially accrued because of the impact of his thought, honesty and commitment on such intellectually giant figures as Plato and Aristotle? Perhaps he has been acquiring a new significance beyond those mentioned, the significance of living and dying for his unique individuality. In any case, if we were to look for examples of those individualized, self-driven, and perhaps earliest examples of hints of early consciousness, we certainly could not do not much better than Socrates or any other genius for that matter, assuming we would be willing to admit at least a suggestion or even beginnings in that person.

This raises questions regarding others who perhaps should be included in a pantheon of pre-cursors of our own world of contemporary self-reflective conscious individuals. Those Mill (and Bloom) would call 'genius' and we would call intellectual and cultural molders of our present world and potential future, may be more genius than we would think, if we could only think in a different manner regarding our past heritage and its forming of character. From the Millian point of view, society "…might possibly learn something from them."[89] When defining genius Bloom suggested that "…there are common characteristics to genius, since vivid individuality and speculation, spirituality, and creativity must rely upon originality, audacity, and self-reliance."[90] As though to give merit to these thoughts of Bacon and Bloom, Mill continued with the following observation:

> It will not be denied by anybody, that originality is a valuable element in human affairs. There is always need of persons not only to discover new truths, and point out when what were once truths are true no longer, but also to commence new practices, and set the example of more enlightened conduct, and better taste and sense in human life. This cannot well be gain-said by anybody who does not believe that the world has already attained perfection in all its ways and practices.[91]

The major problem with this approach is in finding some sort of evidence of individuality and the potential for consciousness in historically significant political figures. According to Bloom the genius here is thought of only in a cultural form leaving the issue of politics for others. For us, Bach and Telemann, both brilliant composers, have swapped historic significance. There are trends and there are preferences that ever color the community's definition of a genius. Certainly contemporary conservatives would not consider Mill a genius while liberals would. Is it that they are so tied to the inside of the social and community's milieu that they should not be counted? Are Pericles, Alexander the Great, Augustus Caesar, et al., to be disregarded as too involved within the very systems that inhibit personal, private and individualized thinking?

All societies at best tolerate and at worst attack that which is perceived as less than appealing or, more importantly, dangerous, i.e. those challenges to community standards. Individuality with a sense of self and a basis for consciousness develops in degrees, from little or none to increased amounts in the direction of completeness; at least this must be considered as the a possible scenario. There are some who are very unique in possessing a greater degree of this singularity, genius if one will, while there are others who while rather distinct are not as singular in consciousness or individuality. One means of deducing who is most likely to possess the sense of self at the greatest level, perhaps, is to note who is the most on the outside or despised and frightening to the community. But would we wish to make Hitler an example of the fully developed conscious individual self? I think not. This would be more applicable when the society and citizen mutually dissolve its relationship, making the individual free from a community definition. Montaigne sought his own isolation in contradiction to society and the Church. How would we make a judgement in his regard? Bloom suggest that of his hundred brief biographies of genius in action that he surveyed literary figures because they made the biggest impact upon the thoughtful, reflective and singular reader. Thus the answer is subjective. Galileo was fortunate not to suffer what Socrates had. Is he less a genius or even an individual? Then there are others who were mocked but never put on trial. This is not a certain test case but an indicator, and perhaps not necessarily a very appropriate means of singling out a true self. For this topic, Bloom is certainly worth reading. Even with this suggestion as to how one could determine who should be considered truly expressive or indicative of individuality within these walls of history, at least prior to the modern world, there are few agreed upon parameters. Who is it that should be placed on such a list and on what basis? Socrates, Plato and Aristotle have already been suggested. But what of possible others—Dante, Chaucer or Shakespeare? Bloom makes Shakespeare primary since this playwright "…like his Hamlet, exceeds us in consciousness, goes beyond the highest order of consciousness that we are capable of knowing without him."[92] But being an original is potentially another slippery slope that could prove more confusing than enlightening for our discussion. And even if granted, somehow, the problem of the quality or quantity of that originality adds further difficulties. Should we consider Michelangelo more of an individual than say Leonardo or Picasso? Should we consider the potential for individuality to be greater in Thomas Aquinas than in Augustine? These are impossible questions at this juncture and thus of little help except in the general sense, again, as indicators that perhaps more importantly demonstrate how impossible it is to create a standard of measurement. Granted, generalities are the bane of scholarship, still they play an indispensable role. It was the prolific historian, Peter Gay, who observed that while it may be hard to live with generalizations, it is inconceivable to live without them.[93] So, it is best here to simply note that there have been early examples of individuality even if primitive, at least under the rubric of genius. Those we find historically significant do prove one theme of this study: there is a relationship between cognitizing one's demise and finding an effective means of defeating it. This is the immortality of the individual genius throughout history. One could take the position of Professor Bloom that "...the dead genius is more alive than we are...vitality is the measure of literary genius. We read in search of more life, and only genius can make that available to us."[94] This should at least be a consideration.

Did Jesus rise to heaven and did martyrs follow? The Church of Rome says yes with certainty. Here and here alone is immortality—according to Rome—at least the immortality of Jesus. But since the beginning of historical development and for the more critically minded, this has proven to be an unsatisfactory conclusion. There has grown now, in an age of geniuses, another approach to defeating death, or at the least to make it less immanent. This is more than the having one's name remembered by family and friends. When Jimmy remembers Kitty, that is a first principle of language. For all its utilitarian value, quality language gives a small victory over death since it may last longer than that which is simply remembered. The name after all is only representational. Giving greater solidity to that name is often offered in the form that can give it a greater significance, that is by tracing the family tree, the attempts to make memorable one's heritage, a not unpopular pastime. Now we can perceive even a far greater way of overcoming the inevitable, i.e., the immortality that the historian bestows because of the contributions made to humanity, whether a Columbus or a Petrarch, an Ockham or Tertullian, a Jesus or an Einstein. Like it or not, there are those who while now physically dead continue to live on not only in memory and a family tree but by way of historic studies. Today we could also add film to this collective memory. Who is remembered the longest, and who will live the longest may well depend on what one has done with their life.

The problem with this approach is that what is remembered is not necessarily who actually existed and not what they necessarily did but rather the present perception of that person or event. Bloom implies that there are many who have been a genius but only a few that make a mark in the world of remembrance. Not surprising, history gives us an alternate view of a phenomenon rather than the actual event. Just as one's memory is not an accurate rendering of what actually happened so too what historians write is not necessarily what actually happened. History—by necessity—may be further from the events, people and phenomena discussed in order to achieve Baconian objectivity. But we now know that such circumstances when they occur are much more complicated and varied with a great deal more grey than simple black or white. Distance allows for the acknowledgment of a complexity which is far more accurate than any one contemporary account of events or people. Of course what has happened was equally not accurately known by anyone at the time of the event. As the brilliant Latin American writer Jorge Luis Borges (1899–1986) has observed in one of his wonderful short profiles: "History is the mother of truth!—the idea is staggering. Menard, a contemporary of William James, defines history not as a delving into reality but as the very fount of reality. Historical truth, for Menard, is not 'what happened'; it is what we believe happened. The final phrases—exemplar and adviser to the present, and the future's counselor—are brazenly pragmatic."[95] It is precisely in this desire for accuracy in any historical interpretation as well clarity of language that must be emphasized in this panorama of a growing sense of Western individuality. But it is an interpretation, an art, that attempts an approximation since we do not have first-hand knowledge. Perception is what determines truth and our understanding and that is all we can be sure of. Accuracy is the effort to acquire as close a rendering of those forces and events as can be determined to actually have happened; that is our past. This is a two edged sword since it also implies that we have the advantage of distance in time and language that separates us from and can give us a much more objective understanding of events, circumstances and changing mentalities. Historic narrative is a very difficult art and the more it is personalized the more problematic it becomes.

Looking to the past to name those who are worth remembering was a beginning of the collective memory associated with the genre of biography and autobiography, although this particular genre did not develop in some mature fashion until fairly recently, again being a very modern phenomenon. There were earlier examples, of course, some of which are mentioned here, but that genre has been quite different as has been demonstrated by the Medieval version, hagiography. In a non-collective sense, of course, we are speaking of the personal act of memory, something of such significance that eventually there will be those writers as early as John Locke who would on occasion, not only equate memory with personal identity, a sense of self and individuality, but more importantly, with consciousness itself. Thus the road from classical and Medieval to early-modern was one of significant changes of our views of the *persona*, the ancient Latin mask, becoming more, as Shakespeare would suggest, "a piece of work is man." These are the immediate precursors of a very modern idea, that humanity can be seen as a work in process.

As for the transformation from medieval models, there is one other that greatly impacted upon the nascent sense of personal self and individuality. Again, reaching into the nineteenth century to the age of Mill, we also find a Karl Marx (1818–83) who carried on a tradition first articulated the century before, in the writings of the English humanistic philosopher, Adam Smith (1723–90). This was the creation of *homo economicus*—human being defined as driven by economic desires—a revolutionary theory, in contrast to that specific lineage in the earlier anti-profit writings found in the High Medieval works of Thomas Aquinas. It was he who created for Rome a theology that was eventually adopted at the end of the nineteenth century when he was declared its official theologian. His position on economics and the marketplace was unequivocal and appropriate for a church that produced St. Francis of Assisi and the seven deadly sins. This change can be found (as noted) in leaving the world of Aquinas and entering that of the Reformations, specifically the ideas expressed in Calvinism. Gresham College in London acknowledged this new economic opportunism as did the growing banking industry, the newly founded insurance industry which aided in sharing risks in shipping and finally the new market economics, exemplified by the wool trade. Bacon knew Gresham and encouraged its creation as he also knew that the influences of the Royal Great Chain of Being were no longer in exclusive control.[96] Oxford and Cambridge and the University of Paris continued the old scholastic order but their days and the days of the old physics were clearly numbered. The idea of a Great Chain of Being that had been around since its roots in Aristotle would become by the eighteenth century an anachronistic view of order because societies were increasingly driven by commerce and subjectivized economic identity.

Francis Bacon reflected a new openness for the scientific revolution by contributing to the newly discovered sense of objectivity, the idea of defining some kind of space between the object and the observer. That an object exists independently from that of the observer requires at the same time that the observer exists independently from the object. Since we had lived in the space of God, there could be no space that was not under divine control. Once that order began to collapse, the slippery slope of change began and history shifted. It was in this transformational context that Bacon took what has been suggested as the first steps toward that objectivized view. Each of these contributions are seminal to the early revolutionary mood and for what could be described as the unintended consequences (UC) in our intellectual development. A worthy summation of his views on objectivity is stated as follows:

> Bacon's idea of objectivity—emerging most prominently in his doctrine for evading the 'idols of the mind'—represents a Jacobean counselor's epistemic response to changing relations between king and Parliament, between sovereign and private subject, and between monarch and merchant. Lord Chancellor Bacon's advocacy of cognitive self-distancing is a consequence of his worried fascination with the discreteness of socially differentiated minds at work in the marketplace. He sees the necessity of tapping the intellectual riches produced by subordinate subjects but remains fearful lest these threaten the royal regime. At the same time, the changes Bacon witnessed forced upon him an awareness of the efficacy of private desire and its role within his scientific program. Hence, Baconian objectivity is less a matter of erasing desire than of continually displacing it onto a collective social construct—'the real'—produced in the course of dialogue.[97]

The reason for this radical approach centered not only on something new and fresh as a means for pursuing knowledge, but of equal importance and perhaps more importantly, it centered upon the inadequacies of the old order. After centuries of attempting to control those with differing perceptions and after living with a distortion of so much of the order of the universe, and with a growing independent thinking, possessing a newly found common sense in search for new methodologies, with further complications with the alternatives in art, in literature, religion and science, it may have been inevitable that the term *objective* took on a very new meaning than what it had meant to the Medieval mind. The following makes this clear:

> Bacon's promotion of cognitive self-distancing depended upon the breakdown of Scholastic-Thomist epistemology that led to the proliferation of often conflicting views of knowing in the fifteenth and sixteenth centuries. Indeed, the recent claim that modern Western scientific discourse is 'governed by the demand for legitimation'—for evidence and proof of all knowledge claims—is in part the consequence

of the breakdown of the older medieval episteme and the subsequent need to resolve disputes among competing systems of knowing and knowers.[98]

Unfortunately, the term *objective* remains, much like those of central interest in this work, problematic. Historians have only recently looked at such words as *objective, self, individual* and *consciousness*, as well as any nexus between them.[99] The theory that there is a basis for the modern idea of objectivity can first be found in the work of Francis Bacon where it is documented in a study by Julie Robin Solomon, *Objectivity in the Making: Francis Bacon and the Politics of Inquiry*. Solomon suggests that his act of "self-distancing" represents the beginning act of objectivity. "I start with the premise that the human capacity to engage in self-distancing is only realized through interpersonal intercourse within a particular sociohistorical context. In other words, any regime of disinterestedness is a consequence of the discursive and nondiscursive interactions between at least two social subjects about a posited sociomaterial material world—which in turn shapes the terms of those interactions."[100]

This theory of disengagement was of some significance not only for natural philosophy but also for the application of English law since Francis Bacon was also the Chancellor of the Exchequer and so possessed a professional concern with the application of the law, a subject that was of great importance for the legal activities of a newly developing nation state. Judicial impartiality began to mean a great deal at the beginning of the seventeenth century.[101] In addition to the position of Chancellor which was the highest executive officer of the realm, Bacon also was the keeper of the Great Seal as well as serving as the chief judge of the Court of Chancery. At one point, therefore, Bacon possessed a great deal of power and influence. Part of the reason for mentioning this is that not only because of his contribution to the methodology and literary defense of modern scientific research which made him significant but that he was also a very active political and legal figure as the "…defender of common law and its jurisdiction that he argued for a notion of judicial impartiality that was more in keeping with his experience as Lord Chancellor."[102] The idea of taking what we would call a more objective stance in seeking the truth in nature was also equally applied to the legal system being created at the time. Locke, too, we will see was an English political as well philosophical thinker in this tradition. It should not come as a surprise that these immediate changes which began with the Italians are now dominated by the English from Shakespeare to Bacon since a new center of power was shifting from Italian city-states and the rule of the Spanish. The English will now share center stage especially

Scientific Revolution | 215

in the next century with the thinkers and writers of the French Enlightenment. And when speaking of the French, the term *objective* and its potential meaning will wait for the contributions of Descartes although it should be clear by now that this new thinking was anything but an anomaly.

That scientific and political interests encouraged Bacon's form of thought should not be surprising since the idea of specialization was still a long way off. Thus the reason that Solomon used Bacon as a case study is "…because his discourse of objectivity *avant la lettre* makes apparent what later formulations obscure—the kinds of epistemic and socially systemic tensions and fissures that made the advocacy of philosophic self-distancing compelling to intellectual and political elites."[103] In those early years we saw the assumption that 'the kingdom of God is within' and that the soul, "…the very essence of primitive Christianity was its inwardness."[104] It follows that the most logical historical and evolutionary step would be that an eventual cognitive line would be drawn separating that which is inward from that which is outward. While there is a tradition of basic differences in original thinkers that can be seen delineating divisions between giants like Plato and Aristotle, or Augustine and Aquinas, the level of thinking was much deeper and a great deal broader. Our understanding, our epistemological approach to knowledge, was being continually changed in that period beginning in the fourteenth continuing into the seventeenth centuries in ways not yet fully understood. As has been observed: "Bacon's texts help me uncover some of the sociopolitical, technological, and intellectual determinants of the sixteenth and seventeenth century transition to an early modern scientific episteme. These factors included new ways of conceiving the nature of human knowing in general and natural philosophic knowing in particular, new ways of conceiving the relation between subjects and objects, and new attitudes towards the authority of the material particular."[105] The first rule found in the triadic methodology appropriate for the exercise of natural philosophy is observation. But not just any observation will do since it is clear that it must be disinterested before one can come to a theory. And, ironically, without some limited early sense of a self, the method may have proven too difficult, at first with too much pre-determined subjectivity (or bias), making it that much more problematic for the birth of individualism and its corollary self sometime later. It is far easier to live a prejudiced life than an open and objective one. First was the establishment of a methodology as central, then, and only then will come the turning inward.

Bacon is but an introduction, but a very important one for this new concept of the objective: "Bacon's formulation of a discourse of scientific objectivity is a complex, dialectical, often contradictory, and ambiguous exercise."[106] There are no important historic transformations that do not begin with but small steps, with eventually large effects to follow, at least if they are to become significant and Bacon both proves the adage and demonstrates its impact, especially when considering his tie between the world of politics and that of ideas. "Bacon's formulation of scientific disinterestedness was responsive to contemporary political, social, and legal conditions. By virtue of his prominent political position within the Jacobean court—coupled with his humanist erudition and familiarity with commercial and prudential practices—Bacon was a thinker at a key point."[107] The need for an established political order in place of the decaying medieval order was in its own way as important as understanding the order of the universe, therefore, understanding that our humanity required this new methodology and understanding. At the court of James I, his views were indispensable. "Indeed, Bacon's conception of natural philosophic disinterestedness possesses many of the attributes and tensions that will mark later formulations."[108] The reasons for this are obvious since "…his natural philosophic discourse, which strives to bridge status related, occupational, and other social divides, derives from his attempts to combine the royal interests of the Jacobean court with the prudential styles of knowing prevalent in the world of commerce."[109] For him the methodology of a disinterested approach in the activities of natural philosophy should also apply to that of the governing of the Royal court as well as a basis for judicial decisions and by implication, even economic activities: these were an early attempt to defend systems over values. After all, "…the incipient early modern orthodoxy of scientific objectivity arose in response to growing awareness of competing philosophic views and the cognitive idiosyncrasy of human minds. As we shall see, early modern discourses of scientific objectivity arose to satisfy the demand for legitimacy by deriving knowledge from matter and demanding the knower's disinterestedness."[110] The issues of trust and certainty again appear as central concerns. As Solomon puts it, his "…discourse mediates between the political and intellectual culture of the Jacobean court and the wider commercial culture that both shaped and was shaped by monarchy." His achievement, moreover, was that he acted as a mediator who, "…locates himself—sometimes sequentially, often simultaneously—within each sociocultural subject position."[111] The separation of the observed and the observer in time will produce new conclusions and a new sense of reliability in those same conclusions.

The traditional theory of plenitude from antiquity onwards demands that the there are only so many types and kinds of all living things and beings, and in time, all will make their appearance since the universe was still assumed to be a fixed entity. We all know the story of Noah and the Ark. Thus, the observer and observed remained for Bacon in a static state that need only to acquire understanding with this new methodology. It is here that a friend of Bacon appears to further our understanding and judgements. Thomas Hobbes was born in 1588, the year of the fearful Armada, and died in 1679 the year of the great London fire. Needless to say, he had once observed that he was born in fear, and the fact is his life was dominated by fear, as he put it, "...fear and I were born twins."[112] This should not surprise anyone since Hobbes is the earliest thinker defending what is now considered the modern political philosophy of conservatism. He was also a friend of Bacon, an acquaintance of Galileo, while also held in low regard by his contemporary in France, Descartes. It was Descartes' general view that he would prefer not to have "...any more association with him."[113] Hobbes also has another dubious distinction of being one of the most serious thinkers to offer the classic defense of a new political order, the authoritarian state, as articulated in his classic, *The Leviathan* (1651). Like many other philosophers he concluded that the early state of man was one of self-interest where life is little more than "...solitary, poor, nasty, brutish, and short." This infamous position is somewhat consistent with the Christian notion regarding man, whose life after the fall is sinful. For better or worse, this is a popular tradition of a negative or 'fallen' view of human beings. Contemporary evidence, however, is more consistent to what has been discussed in the first chapter: that man was a pack animal with a group-think that was basic for all their actions. But Hobbes' central issue was the need for an authority of government in opposition to authority of personal choice, for, while still early, the degree of individuality that could be seen in England in the seventeenth century worried him a great deal. What he sought was to counter any sense of individuality with an extremely powerful state, a view that was still held and articulated by the French even into the nineteenth century.

Hobbes' contributions to our topic, however, are not difficult to list for they are remarkably contemporary in many ways. It has been noted, for example, that he gave birth to analytic philosophy, since any analytical method if it is to work, "...is employed when we wish to understand some given phenomenon, we must work backwards from a description of it until we come to what Hobbes called 'primary propositions' from which our description can be logically deduced."[114] He may have contributed to such new forms of reason because of his alteration of the traditional Aristotelean definition of causation, moving to one and only one cause, that of material causation, and dropping the traditional other three, efficient, formal, and final causes. But then Hobbes was an early leader of an extreme materialism, including even the nature of authentic sovereignty. More than just simplifying, he added his vote for a materialist world view. The Western mind had been dominated by the assumption that everything was organic and as such was able to tie heart and soul to all other entities. This worked perfectly well in a god-dominated universe. Classical thinking melded into the Christian without so much as a serious challenge. The world of plentitude and the Great Chain of Being made clear that a rock and an angel and joy and grief were unified. The Great Chain of Being, the great Western pyramid had a place for all known social and political types. It was arguably the ultimate poetic if not metaphoric world. But the metaphor was precisely what Hobbes had no use for. Like Bacon, he wanted the clear and unvarnished truth spoken of directly and preferably mathematically. "This demand for plain speech and the anchoring of terms to palpable things like bodies has been one of the main characteristics of British philosophy since Bacon and Hobbes initiated it..."[115] The plain speech regarding this cause-effect mode was driven by the principle of motion since it was the motion between the two that accounted for them: things in motion interacting, changing one state of affairs into another. It was in this way that he could still offer lip service to the unified theory of the world and fixed nature of mankind even if nondynamic. But, again, the nemesis of tradition appears, with this added view that motion is inherent in cause and effect, a necessary step leading to the uncertainty principle of our own age since the presumption of cause and effect will also be eventually questioned.

As with his friend Bacon, Hobbes appreciated the language of geometry, which is understandable since it appeared to contribute to a particular language appropriate to his materialist views, especially his faith in the senses. As he put it, "...for besides sense, and thoughts, and the train of thoughts, the mind of man has no other motion; though by the help of speech, and method, the same faculties may be improved to such a height, as to distinguish men from all other living creatures."[116] While addressing the knowledge of language, he appears to have preferred the use of speech to writing, which, while it may strike some today a little odd, nevertheless was important for him in its more traditional ability to communicate, something that preceded all other forms, notwithstanding hand signs and drawings, and thus was the first and most important key to the sharing of knowledge. As Hobbes put it: "But the most noble and profitable invention of all other, was that of SPEECH, consisting of names or appellations and their connexion; whereby men register their thoughts; recall them when they are past; and also declare them one to another for mutual utility and conversation; without which, there had been amongst men, neither commonwealth, nor society, nor contract, nor peace, nor more than amongst lions, bears, and wolves."[117] That we are distinct from all other non-human living beings is now argued as a matter of both our abilities and in our act of cultivating language skills, starting with speech. That Hobbes placed such value on this capacity can be demonstrated by a very informing if lengthy passage of the *Leviathan*:

> The use of speech. The general use of speech, is to transfer our mental discourse, into verbal; or the train of our thoughts; into a train of words; and that for two commodities, whereof one is the registering of the consequences of our thoughts; which being apt to slip out of our memory, and put us a new labour, may again be recalled, by such words as they were marked by. So that the first use of names is to serve for marks, or notes of remembrance. Another is, when many use the same words, to signify, by their connexion and order, one to another, what they conceive, or think of each passion for. And for this use they are called signs. Special uses of speech are these; first, to register, what by cognition, we find to be the cause of any thing, present or past; and what we find things present or past may produce, or effect; which in sum, is acquiring of arts. Secondly, to show to others that knowledge which we have attained, which is, to counsel and teach one another. Thirdly, to make known to others our wills, and purposes, that we may have the mutual help of one another. Fourthly, to please and delight ourselves and others, by playing with our words, for pleasure or ornament, innocently.[118]

There is an addendum to his theory of language and its relationship to us in not only making us human, but specifically our inevitable glossing of our own individuality, our sense of self, and mostly our ability to consciously make choices. The role of speech and with it writing has often been given a less than significant role in our evolution since people in general would rather give the emphasis to the invention of the printing press or some other singular material object. It is here that this author does find an agreement with Hobbes who also insightfully observed that "…the invention of printing, though ingenious, compared with the invention of letters, is no great matter."[119] The caveat to this argument, however, is that this implies that the appearance of silent reading was equally of "no great matter" in application to the issues of this study. While this is not a resolvable issue since it is one of weighing differing factors, and thus more a matter of interpretation, there is no question that the transformations being discussed here, especially silent reading, were monumental.

There were other similarities regarding the contributions made by both Bacon and Hobbes, as in, "...like Bacon, he [Hobbes] was to coin some of his most pungent epigrams for the discomfiture of the Aristoteleans; like Bacon, he replaced reverence for tradition by belief in method, albeit a different method and, like Bacon he believed that knowledge was power."[120] They may not have thought alike but they did agree in some of their conclusions.

It has been suggested here that Hobbes was facing, and was one of the first to do so, a serious conflict between individualism and authoritarianism. It is true that the beginnings of the modern state can be traced back to England, France, Spain and the Netherlands in the early sixteenth centuries. It is also correct to note that by the time of the seventeenth century, England had taken the lead in this development. The French thinker, Jean Bodin, of course, had already begun his unique thinking regarding sovereignty which was now seen residing in the state and not in any one person. Hobbes' views also proved to be appropriate if radical in this context. As for individualism, Hobbes was clearly thinking of a series of changes that led to the seventeenth century in England which experienced "...the great period of individualism in England; it was from the various sects and splinter groups which broke away from the Established Church that the Nonconformist movement in this country developed."[121] This is an individualism of type however and not one of singularity, at least not yet.

The problem is that recommending new thinking for old problems and our understanding of nature cannot be limited even by the power of the state, notwithstanding Hobbesian fears. The revolution is only beginning.

III

Early Modern Definitions

CHAPTER SIX

DESCARTES AND CONSCIOUSNESS

The consciousness that reason is 'my reason' is the opening shot of the enlightenment. [1]

FROM DOUBT TO CERTAINTY

The earliest concept of self as a philosophic and psychological term can be traced to the seventeenth century with a certain degree of safety. This is also the same period that gives evidence to the earliest expressions of the term consciousness. This will prove, however, to be only an introduction.

Prior to the seventeenth century the study of consciousness as an interior phenomenon, like the term consciousness itself, was relatively unknown. For the historian of ideas, consciousness did not become an important or a cogent part of any serious discussions until there occurred a growing recognition of the impact of the early steps of a sense of individuality inherent within some of the introspective possibilities and components of the Renaissance and Reformations. It can be stated without exaggeration that "...for the first time in Western history, the individual was freed from the oppressive demands of conscience in his pursuit of manhood: he could accept his own thought and desires —even his passions—without qualm or hesitation, if he but subjected them to methodical self-discipline."[2] If one begins privatizing conscience, the unintended consequence (UC) of the Protestant movement should not be surprising that such secularization could metamorphose into the more modern term consciousness. Only when given an alternative for faith were we forced into developing our sense of being an individual, which would at the least imply an inner self. And it is this self where one must begin to stand increasingly alone, without the certitude of the one and only absolutely true theology and its liturgy and other conforming and comforting support systems. It is here that consciousness can become a new and substantive guide in the nascent methodology of natural philosophy and the comprehension of this new entity, the mind. Protestants turned their back on the confessional and towards a communally supportive conscience leaving room for the eventual transformation from the collective confessional into an inner experience. When faith becomes personal it is far easier to find oneself alone in a social setting than in a divinely-driven one. While the term *consciousness* appeared earlier in the writings of Thomas Hobbes as both term and phenomenon, it made its systematic appearance in the French and Latin writings of René Descartes (1596–1650) and later, in English in the empirical writings of John Locke.

Given the significance of his contributions, it should not be a surprise to discover that Descartes was fully aware of the significant transformations of the world he had inherited as well as changes within himself, although how much he was fully aware of any of the substantive implications of consciousness is questionable. His sensibility to his own era and his place in it partially explains the breadth of many of his contributions not only as a philosopher, scientist and a mathematician, but also as one of the very earliest students of the 'mind.' These activities and achievements are all the more remarkable since they developed within the confines of the antiquated Medieval Latin he learnt from the Jesuits and a very new French tongue that was not yet used in a serious manner by scholars. Descartes contributed to the development of French in the originality of his thoughts and which additionally became indispensably useful intellectual fodder for later generations, especially in the Enlightenment. His contributions to our understanding of several key modern intellectual terms has been significant; those best known being *ideas*, *dualism* and most importantly *consciousness*. Our basic language and assumptions regarding these terms has largely remained centered around Cartesian thinking. As one commentator has characterized it:

> Descartes... generally acknowledged as the father of modern philosophy, could be said to have invented the modern concept of mind, or at least to have given it its decisive formulation. It was he who fostered certain dualisms and conceptions of human inwardness that have permeated much of the philosophical, scientific, and ethical thought coming after him. Consciousness in the Cartesian scheme is conceived of as radically distinct from the material plane of extended substances, a plane that includes the body in which this consciousness is mysteriously housed...[3]

It was in his work as the father of modern science and philosophy centering upon the discoveries of new perspectives, influenced as he was by heliocentrism, gravity, the New World among other issues that made it possible for him to take advantage of linguistic changes, both rhetorical and mathematical to express his revolutionary thinking. This expansive new perspective, growing out of Renaissance artists and thinkers now impacted on a grand scale upon assumptions. Descartes' thinking moved well beyond the traditional and dated presuppositions of those dominated by theology and scholasticism, a scholasticism which he certainly understood from his earlier education in a Jesuit academic environment. In the following century it would be possible for Voltaire to state: "…in eloquence, language, literature, and the arts, the French…'were the legislators of Europe' while he referred to the previous century, that of Locke and Newton, as *'le siècle des Anglais.'*"[4] But Voltaire, while writing in French, was more of a follower of Locke than Descartes which is all the more interesting since Descartes himself wrote his famous *Discourse* in French rather than the Latin of his teachers.[5] Again silent reading, the printing press and the vernacular tongue contributed to this new mode of thinking and his revolutionary ideas and an expansive contribution to his mother tongue.

Descartes benefitted from these earlier intellectual breakthroughs, of course, especially the discovery of inertia, since it had significantly weakened the Aristotelian philosophical arguments about our understanding of motion.[6] The world he arrived in had a new understanding of its heritage, of past frameworks and history, as well as those dramatically reconstructed religious assumptions, all of which made for the creation of an opening for constructing radically new ideas that come closer to our thinking today. Naturally, the term *modern* is often applied to his work. Most essential for future thinkers, however, was the profound change in perception of time and space. This specifically applied because of the arrival of both significantly important technical and geographical changes that had impacted accumulated experiences drawn from inventions, exploration and colonization, as well as the added alteration of space with the impact of printing.[7] The openings provided by the accessibility of books and travel to hundreds of miles of diversity, the differing time zones and experiences had to alter thinking processes and assumptions. This also led the seventeenth century reader to quantify reality in place of the more traditional and religious approach of qualifying the world. In his *The Seventeenth Century Background*, Basil Willey establishes the interesting thesis that a new set of questions now made their appearance because of a new orientation to nature based upon a scientific approach and a declining Church. Willey saw a transition of questions: *how* something either is or is not happening in place of the earlier theological question as to *why* something is or is not happening.[8] Why I am alive is fundamentally a theological question while how it is possible that I live is a question for the scientific discipline of biology. The natural curiosity of a child is demonstrated by taking apart daddy's wrist watch to see how it works and not to ask why there is time. For another perception of the new attitude and views associated with this natural philosophy or science, one would do well to review Alexandre Koyre's *From the Closed World to the Infinite Universe* where he offers a fundamental theory in his observation that "...some historians have seen its [seventeenth century] most characteristic feature in the secularization of consciousness."[9] Secularization yes, but of consciousness is simply too expansive a statement for the available evidence, although the historical direction implied is accurate. Nevertheless, these and a plethora of other works have attempted to do justice for both the beginnings of the Scientific Revolution (natural philosophy) and the new mind-set born out of these changes which creates an introduction to the coming Enlightenment, partially born of the changing assumptions and methodologies that occurred in the seventeenth century. From the roots of the Renaissance, discovery of a more secularized or humanized space and time, through the breakdown of absolute and singular religious doctrines the door had been thrown wide open to a new set of doctrines—political, economic and intellectual—that were based on reason for their definitions and which began to make a serious impact on the creation of modern thinking. No other thinker of the time had a greater impact on our world than René Descartes and while Bloom's book on genius is of literary figures, his comments would perfectly fit Descartes of whom it could also be said: "Talent cannot originate, genius must."[10]

In his youth Descartes was favored with insights of mentors who recognized his intellectual capacity and who indulged him partially because he was a sickly child and partially because of family connections, all of which appear to have contributed to a leisure necessary for youthful reflective thinking or "self-conversing." This idea of such conversations is explored by Bloom as a key component in his study of genius although he expressed it as "self-overhearing" which could be construed as the other side of the same coin and by which he means:

> Is there a difference between hearing and overhearing oneself? When we are surprised at listening to our tape-recorded voices, are we hearing or overhearing? Dictionaries define 'overhear' as hearing a speech or speaker without the speaker's awareness or intention. To overhear oneself is to be initially unaware that one is the speaker. That unawareness is so brief that self-overhearing seems more metaphoric than not, yet the moment of literal nonrecognition is authentic. Shakespeare, taking a hint I think from Chaucer, seizes upon that moment to fashion another version of the human will-to-change.[11]

It is a fair assumption that he probably entertained inner conversations, reflective thinking and introspection which would have also included the new mathematical language that had been expanding since the previous century and to which he also made serious contributions. It is difficult to believe that he did not participate in "self-overhearing" of the inner place called his mind. On the other hand, he was young enough to experience some of the vagaries of the age by serving for a short time in the military during the Thirty Years' War. He certainly understood some of the contradictions pressing upon the opening space of two new worlds then being discovered—the New World across the Atlantic and the other in the world of natural philosophy.

In such an age of increasing uncertainty it is not surprising to find that Descartes' single driving desire was to establish certainty. And in an age of ironies, it should not surprise us that Descartes began his quest from these experiences by adopting the one certain idea he could freely embrace, that of doubt. Thus dualism was now being restructured in modern cloth, on one side the force of certainty and on the other that of doubt, which is correctly associated with the name Descartes, who began his own very personal mental methodological technique by way of contrasting the certainty that he sought with the doubt that he had achieved. This created a massive chasm that broke away from the older dualism of the church in the forms of good versus evil and of heaven versus hell. Little wonder that any discussion of Cartesian thought without at least some discussion of his language would make futile any comprehension of his own understanding. Unfortunately there is a body of literature that does make this fundamental mistake by ignoring his own very creative foundation of linguistic interests, including both that of mathematics and of metaphysical reasoning.

What he suggested is a very simple mind-test: How do I know that I'm not dreaming that I'm here rather than actually, in fact, being here? This is, of course, a mental activity that begins our very sense of what we mean when we speak of the singular idea of our very existence. When we use the modern philosophic term *idea*, its understanding can be traced to Descartes who, "…was consciously giving it a new sense," and we may add, with good reason, since "…it was a new departure to use it systematically for the contents of a human mind."[12] Not simply an abstraction any longer, an 'idea' was something possessing a specific location, held within the interior of the mind, implying a space that could retain its 'contents.' Descartes further noted that of all ideas that we may have there may be none more central to our lives than pain, a position that Rousseau will take up later. Since the ancients, including Plato and Aristotle, had no knowledge of the central nervous system, the introduction of a "Cartesian model of pain that was far from original—implies innovations as far-reaching as…the invention of gunpowder, printing, and the compass."[13]

Pain is known now for its presence within 'the mind.' To know that there is a direct relationship between the physical condition of pain and the idea of pain is to change our understanding not only of the phenomenon of pain but how we come to understand what it is to have an idea. This particular concept also contributed in shifting our perceptions away from an exclusively divine-centered universe that dominated so much of the religious conflicts of the day while offering a more humanistic viewpoint and a more secular attitude—one without an active divine presence. It should not be forgotten that it is also true that Descartes did make a case in support for his belief in a form of divine presence within some of his writings. There were some people in England that were attracted to this new form of thinking which was introduced by Henry More (1614–1687), a clergyman and a philosopher and who was a lifelong fellow of Christ College at Cambridge, a Neo-Platonist and acquaintance of Newton. It is he in particular who was "…credited with having done more than anyone else for the introduction of Cartesianism to Britain. In the first stage of his enthusiasm, he conducted a substantial correspondence with Descartes." However, as the implications of Cartesian thinking began to sink in, he recanted his "…expressions of unrestrained adulation." He then "…later turned into a violent prosecutor of Cartesianism, whose originator," he would later refer to as, "a daring monster." In particular he took exception with Descartes' notion that animals are mere machines and concludes that his own "…spirit…turns…with abhorrence…from that deadly and murderous sentiment…whereby you…withhold life and sense from all animals, for you would never concede that they really live.'"[14] It is true that Descartes had a very narrow and even negative view of life, pain and joys of the animal kingdom, only demonstrating the limits of his own scientific understanding.

That he made such an effort to defend his religiosity also proved a problem since he was not convincing for some later thinkers. This has been dramatized by one writer in particular, Ralph Cudworth, in his *True Intellectual System of the Universe* (1678):

> …which was expressly designed as 'a Discourse concerning Liberty and Necessity, or to speak out more plainly, Against the Fatall Necessity of all Actions and Events.' In this campaign against determinism, Cudworth identified the true enemy in the philosophy of Descartes, a philosophy that he knew well and from which he had benefitted a great deal. Charging the Cartesian deists with having 'an Undiscerned Tang of the Mechanick Atheism hanging about them, in…their so confident rejecting of all *Final* and *Intending Causality* in Nature,' he rejected the notion that all earthly events are exclusively predetermined by an initial set of efficient causes

because that view was in conflict with his belief in an omnipotent God whose freedom of action was unlimited and who directed the fortunes of the world according to his 'providence' as a set of final causes.[15]

This was not the only anti-Cartesian polemic of the day but it does represent what some felt was a dangerous precedent of moving too close to a secular view of the world. Moreover, Descartes was not inclined to write in such a way that inhibited his many intellectual and scientific pursuits. In this his thinking was more inclined towards a mechanistic view, somewhat like Hobbes and his more materialistic attitude, and thus he logically was offering a more direct causal relationship to phenomenal and mental occurrences, contributing to the alteration of the fixed map of inherent knowledge also contributing to the development of our own modern experimental disposition. It was within the confines of the seventeenth century, after all, that the first serious discussions regarding the nature, activity and our understanding of what we think of as consciousness made its earliest appearance. The earlier development of a possible singular self that had been at the least implied in some of Shakespeare's plays was but one step, important though it may be, in the humanizing process, one where the joy and sorrow of being a human being is demonstrated by both the actions and the massive dilemma presented to the analytic mind; Descartes was simply carrying on and contributing to this newly formed tradition.[16]

It was Descartes who first established a serious interest and significant purpose for the term, *consciousness*, making it very much a part of the fundamentals of his own being and his own sense of doubt. Rather than look to the Bible or traditional authority which would not have introduced him to consciousness, he decided that the proper approach to certainty was through the mind, the home of his doubt, and specifically through his own thoughts, or, more specifically, his *cogito*. Seeking certainty in an increasingly uncertain world, Descartes observed how he witnessed "…clearly that there is nothing which is easier for me to know than my mind."[17] Put another way, he began with doubt, found that if he doubted everything, he did prove something: he proved his doubt which he concludes is a form of thinking. To doubt is to think and thus a cogito is, of necessity, inherently present: the more you doubt, the more you are thinking. He suggested, in effect, that he is closest to, most intimate with, and thus more understanding of his own thoughts than anything or anyone else—a truly subjective reality. But it was not simply thoughts that gave rise to certainty since a thought is merely "…everything that exists in us in such a way that we are immediately conscious of it."[18] This he took as one of his certainties, his "clear and distinct idea" of himself as "a thinking thing," i.e., one whose very "essence consists solely in the fact that I am a thinking thing."[19] One commentator has suggested that, in following Descartes "...many in the philosophical and popular traditions since then have readily agreed. While they might not quite regard their belief in their own consciousness as *a priori* knowledge, they would certainly conceive it to be in some analogous way 'incorrigible,' or unrevisable in the light of further research."[20] We would conclude today that he meant 'conscious' thought, that thought one is aware of and which he seems to infer to mean 'consciousness' while keeping it distinct from just the act of thinking which could imply a hint of reflection. In any case, one could go so far as to argue that the source of our essence in a Cartesian world centered upon our own state of consciousness.[21]

There is a sense with Descartes of consciousness being a fixed phenomena still possessing as it does much of this terms earlier roots and meaning, that is, its earlier precursor—conscience, which had been considered fixed and unchanging. And as it has been observed, there have been and still are many scholars today, whether in the philosophical, scientific or more popular fields of study, that have and remain committed to this idea of awareness for consciousness, one that is fixed, and that it is in fact an *a priori* form of knowledge.[22] Whether one agrees that this is a fixed condition or not, Descartes continued by elaborating that thought is, "...thus all the operation of the will, intellect, imagination, and of the senses are thought."[23] For such "...distinguished Cartesian scholars as Gilson, Laporte and Alquie, this definition asserts that thought is simply a synonym for consciousness."[24] It was Descartes' concern with the *cogitatio* as a philosophical problem—with the nature of 'thought'—that remained, then, a concern when dealing with the concept of consciousness itself.[25] This is not to equate, however, *cogitatio* with what Descartes himself generally referred to as *conscientia*.[26]

There are some scholars who have proposed that "Descartes was the concept's discoverer (or inventor). Others return to a much earlier date in attempting to give credit to Aristotle, Plotinus, or St. Augustine," or even see some continuity growing out of antiquity.[27] The evidence is less than satisfactory, however, since the appearance of the root term, *conscience*, existed only within the confines of ancient Latin writers, and not any earlier than the later years of the Roman Empire, i.e., before the time of St. Augustine but after the fall of the Roman Republic.[28] Even then its earliest useful effective appearance cannot be noted until the High Medieval culture, as noted, specifically with the later development of the confessional.[29] Whatever the concept's origin, it should also be associated no earlier than the time of broader cultural developments: "…in [Renaissance] Italy… [where] man became a spiritual *individual*, and recognized himself as such."[30] But if being a "spiritual individual" should only be considered an indicator, then, by way of that reasoning, the argument for a spark of god as expressed by Zeno would also qualify. And to add to this confusion it has also been suggested that beginning somewhere in "…seventeenth-century Europe *Homo sapiens* (the individual) had become…vividly aware of himself as a feeling, perceiving, and thinking person."[31] To call this an 'individual' is, however, an overstatement because 'feeling, perceiving, and thinking' must have been observed a great deal earlier than the century of Descartes and not to be considered as anything particularly unique. The modern self—and with it consciousness—is simply not easily demonstrable at this time. While there is some limited evidence that does warrant concluding that the first appearance of an early beginnings of a modern 'self' was occurring within some of the ideas of Descartes, caution should be used, again, in avoiding too modern an interpretation. This has been done on more than a few occasions with a variety of arguments that would further suggest that at the time of Descartes one could find a person who was "vividly aware of himself" in some unique manner. While this quote is perhaps acceptable for some as a generality, the author of this quote definitely crosses the line when he further suggests that, "…never since the beginning of time was there, that we hear or read of, so intensely self-conscious a Society."[32] At this point one wonders if the author was thinking of the twentieth century since this comment clearly fits many of the modern and post-modern Western citizens of our own day. This characterization of intensity should be viewed, therefore, at the least, as a very extreme exaggeration considering that it is being applied to the seventeenth century and there would need be some very serious documentation by way of proper research that would tie it with a very clear and generally agreed upon understanding of these critical words, *individual, self* and *consciousness*, a position this writer is simply not prepared to take, even if this scholar is so prepared. Moreover, this statement does imply a comparison. It could possibly make sense, however, in a very limited sense, within the context of comparing Descartes' world with that of the Medieval where the self was conspicuous in its absence. If we are speaking in terms of degrees then there is room for limited, and limited at that, agreement that the word individual and perhaps self could be used if qualified, although the language should reflect that it remains a matter of either degrees or as an indicator. The more accepted viewpoint is very qualified by way of "…pointing out that the elusiveness of the self has generated philosophical muddles from Descartes to Hume…"[33] What would be more helpful, and is introduced here, would be an analysis of what history tells us about what was meant and understood when speaking of consciousness, especially when struggling with that period of time that witnessed its earliest appearance.

The earliest significant appearance of *consciousness* in English according to the *Oxford English Dictionary* (*OED*) came from an English contemporary of Descartes, Thomas Hobbes, who stated that "...when two or more men know of one and the same fact, they are said to be CONSCIOUS of it one to another, which is as much as to know it together."[34] Two points deserve attention here. First, it should be noted that while the *OED* does offer a few earlier although oblique poetic citations of the use of *consciousness*, none of them offer any philosophical basis or context for its usage. *Conscious* is listed in the *OED* under some 11 headings including *conscience* while *consciousness* makes its appearance under seven headings with the last under the title of 'double consciousness.'[35] Dictionaries, of course, are not always a good source of understanding for difficult abstract terms. Nevertheless, Descartes was well acquainted with Thomas Hobbes, even responding to some of his "Objections." Descartes was not fond of Hobbesian thinking and made that extremely clear as noted earlier although here we can offer his complete reservations which he stated as follows: "...any more association with him [Hobbes]...We would hardly be able to confer together without becoming enemies.... I do not believe I should ever again respond to what you might send from that man, whom I think I must despise in the extreme."[36] It is therefore possible, although not necessarily probable, that given Descartes' literacy as well as his reading of some of the positions of Hobbes, that this early usage may have influenced him. Second, and of a more serious consideration, is Hobbes' use of the term *conscience* in the context of the use of consciousness. Because of this tie between the earlier conscience and later consciousness, it is necessary that the complete quote from the *Leviathan* should be noted in its entirety:

> When two or more men know of one and the same fact, they are said to be conscious of it one to another, which is as much to know it together. And because such are fittest witnesses of the facts of one another or of a third, it was and ever will be reputed a very evil act for any man to speak against his *conscience*, or to corrupt of force another so to do, insomuch that the plea of conscience has been always hearkened unto very diligently in all times. Afterwards, man made use of the same word metaphorically for the knowledge of their own secret facts and secret thoughts; and therefore it is rhetorically said that the conscience is a thousand witnesses. And last of all, men vehemently in love with their own new opinions, though never so

absurd, and obstinately bent to maintain them, gave those their opinions also that reverenced mane of conscience, as if they would have it seem unlawful to change or speak against them, and so pretend to know they are true when they know at most but that they think so.[37]

While his definition has the ring of its classic Latin roots, i.e., two people having the same secret knowledge, the OED offered as its first definition, "joint or mutual knowledge" in its entry as being obsolete and rare although it is the most literally faithful to the Latin. As for its second meaning, the OED offers the definition of "consciousness to oneself" followed by *consciousness* being "internal knowledge or conviction: knowledge as to which one has the testimony within oneself; esp. of one's own innocence, guilt, deficiencies, etc." Since the first definition of *conscience* is "inward knowledge, consciousness; inmost thought, mind," the relationship of both terms' origins in the common Latin root should be apparent, as even Hobbes implied in his understanding of this relationship. Clearly consciousness arose out of the earlier and more prevalent medieval term—conscience.[38] The primary concern for the student of philosophy, however, is with the working system of a thinker's ideas, their coherence, consistency and meaning. On the other hand, for the historian of ideas, interest centers more on the context and relationship where these ideas developed as well there latter implications. "Historians of philosophy naturally limit their attention to the ablest thinkers," Leslie Stephen observed. "They tell us how the torch was passed from hand to hand from Descartes to Locke, from Locke to Hume, and from Hume to Kant."[39]

Conscience and *consciousness* possess a common Latin lineage, therefore, but with divergent meanings, which is important for the historian of ideas, since the former is inherently judgmental (with moral implications) and the later is not. They both require looking inward, the first meaning coming out of the High Middle Ages and possessing religious connotation, while the second meaning stands within the confines of a more modern secular framework. First given birth in the pagan world of Rome, conscience was nurtured through its maturation within Christian communities where it was tied to the sacrament of penance, while consciousness, as we will see, was a child of the Scientific Revolution and did not become a difficult adolescent until after the Second World War. While given these earliest roots, it is appropriate to note the similarity of both terms, but in actual application, they are clearly divergent. What was significant in their similarities was that both required something of a private inner life in order to function, conscience appearing in the first stages of a developing personal soul dominated by sin and shared in the confessional, while consciousness evolved from a growing sense of a nascent independent self and a maturing individuality. The first serious step toward this inward life, therefore, began very early with the creation of a personal Christian religion, one that stood both separate and distinct from ancient pagan religions and one that broke from the exclusive community oriented, collective and publicly practiced beliefs of its Hebrew and Greek roots. Christianity was unique in offering the beginnings of a personal religion with its emphasis on individual salvation while ironically still being practiced in a public arena as part of the cement that would hold the community together. Once there was a beginning for the development of an interior life with a personal soul (Stoicism), however, the public parameters proved to be less of a central issue for some Christians (mystics), although it remained central to the Roman Church, and eventually, within the confines of what followed in the Reformation, it became less concerned with a dominant collective for the identity of a community and its members. It was this inherent 'inner-directness' that would aid in creating an environment for individuality which would eventually become increasingly fundamental as it ripened in the later Romantic era.[40] The early beginnings of an interior self, after the Reformation, began to evolve, then, as has been noted, throughout the seventeenth century to the Enlightenment. This is what is meant by the earlier quoted statement that "…their own 'consciousness' is believed to be 'incorrigible,' or unrevisable."[41] It is correct, therefore, to state that "…since the writings of Descartes, mentality or consciousness has become the central area of philosophical attention and investigation."[42] Unfortunately this particular quote suggests that its author does not draw a distinction between a specific conscious activity and any mental activity in general, a position which presents us with a great many more questions than answers: for example, are mental and consciousness the same and if so, why two terms?

Perhaps one of the more important contributions Descartes made to this early development and use of consciousness was his placing it at the center of operation of the *cogito*. While his *cogito ergo sum* has been the subject of considerable writing, his contributions to the meaning and use of consciousness has not received that much attention.[43] This is unfortunate since the *cogito* is operational according to Descartes only if and when we are being actually conscious of it. As was noted above, Descartes held that thoughts only exist when we are immediately conscious of them. Moreover, the *cogito ergo sum* contributed to the necessity of consciousness in one other significant way. When we discuss conscious states we know we are discussing an entirely interior phenomenon. To be conscious is to be within a private and subjective state of mind.[44] This is still one of the most serious problems contributing to the confusion and debates surrounding most discussions regarding the term *consciousness*. In fact, there are philosophers, psychologists and neurophysiologists who simply throw up their hands in despair, suggesting that there is no such thing as this subjective state labeled *consciousness*. Why attempt to discuss something that is non-objective and therefore not measurable? This is the price paid for the Baconian idea of distancing onself from what is to be studied. If consciousness exists, then we should be able to agree upon its parameters.[45] But consciousness, as a mental activity that is applied to thinking, like the very act of thinking itself, is an interior operation, something within our own mind, indispensable for the creation of an eventual private self. When we listen to the soliloquies in a Shakespeare masterpiece it can be suggested, as it has, that this was a method for the audience to be privy to an interior and private state of mind. And it has been suggested that "…thought, previously associated with dialogue, begins, with Descartes, to seem a quintessentially private event; and knowledge, previously conceived as a communal possession, comes to be associated with a 'logic of private inquiry.'"[46] What should be added is that this was not considered a passive state now following in the newly established Renaissance tradition of virtue made active, encouraging a more active state of mind. Or as one student of the subject has stated it: "Rationalism from Descartes to Leibniz posited an active mind, which constructed knowledge on the basis of innate ideas." We will find with Locke and his empirical approach to certainty, a divergent construct where "…empiricism from Hobbes to Hume posited a blank mind as passive receptor…"[47] From either side of the coin, Cartesian innate or Lockean sensate, the concept was clearly a presence of ideas and thus the potential for conscious thought. For some today, however, and because of difficulties in measuring the presence of ideas, there have been some theories that would question the existence of the mind itself; the brain can be dissected but the mind can leave us with a question mark. It is little wonder, therefore, that Descartes offered some of his best logical arguments for the existence of the mind, specifically going so far as to argue that the mind possessed a reality that was independent from the body. As has been suggested: "Descartes's rationalist nativism left an imprint on psychological conceptions of humanity. He was a dualist, who regarded the body as essentially a mechanical device, and animals lacking a soul as mere machines. Humans are unique in possessing a mind and a language capable of expressing reflective thought."[48] This inner reflection was indispensable for the occurrence of a conscious state and his reasoning arguments suggest he may have had some understanding of this condition. After all, "Descartes defined a body as something which was (three-dimensionally) spatially extended. Thus extension was the essence of bodyhood or materiality. (This was not very different from Plato's theory of space in the *Timaeus*, or from Aristotle's theory of the first matter.) Descartes shared with many previous thinkers (Plato, Aristotle, St. Augustine) the view that mind and the consciousness of self are non-corporeal." Where he delineates the *cogito* from body is in his acceptance of "...the view that extension was the essence of matter, he was forced to say the incorporeal substance, soul, was 'unextended.'" Or another way to express this distinction would be to suggest that "The essence of the soul-substance was, according to Descartes, that it was a 'thinking' substance. 'Thinking' is here, clearly, meant as synonymous with 'conscious.' The definition of matter or body as *extended* led Descartes direct to his peculiar form of a mechanistic theory of causality..."[49] While this comment implies that there is a direct correlation for Descartes between thinking and being conscious, the delineating lines, as we will see, are not quite that clear.

However one may feel about the possibilities of this modern dualism, if one accepts a *cogito* within the mind, and that this *cogito* must be separate from the body, then the dualism that would follow would not simply be between mind and body, or thought and matter, but between the interior world which is not measurable, and the measurable objective world, thus creating a modern subjective-objective dichotomy. There are two sources for this conclusion, one classical and pagan, the other, religious and Christian. The former was an idea developed by Plato who drew a clear and absolute distinction, supposedly gained from his teacher, Socrates, between a given object perceived and the idea regarding that particular object. And for Plato, his emphasis as to significance was the idea rather than a perceived object. However, Western dualism got its most serious commitment from a different source, that category of religion which grew out of Asia Minor. In this particular case when looking at this dualism in light of Descartes' world one might want to suggest that this was nothing more than a movement toward a secularized version of the long-held and rationally argued theory regarding the existence and separation of body from soul. This earlier interior presence within the unique Christian concept of a personal God with an interiorized Divine presence in the form of a God-given soul, was a fundamental factual requirement subscribed to by a true believer. This new mentality, rooted in Stoic ideas in the Hellenized world, was then transformed with Paul's 'new man Adam,' to an interior existence separated from the public body. Those souls separated from the body tended to be one dominated by God, spirits, saints, angels, devils and general transcendence as well as Tertullian's anti-reason with its immortal soul beyond the prying eyes of either analytic mortals or reason. All one need know is that it if one fails the Lord, it would be a very painful afterlife. This world of a singular divine control began waning as the Reformation expanded into disorder and confusion, the maddening religious wars and destruction in the name of obeying one's own personal conscience. What had been assumed to be a unifying and collective conscience for the religious community was fracturing by way of an extension of a private relationship with God's intent. God's voice exercised within individual men's interior thoughts was increasingly being controlled and manipulated by man himself, from Shakespeare's soliloquies to Cartesian metaphysics. For this spiritual dualism to survive, an alternative world must under no circumstance ever rear its ugly head. It is this conscience, this interior voice of the medieval mind, with its need to appease a sense of Catholic (universal) guilt, that was challenged by a growing Renaissance and Anti-Catholic and anti-confessional Protestant world, occurring at the very time that there was an increased questioning of Christian behavior during religious wars that was referred to later—in the Age of Reason—as the 'Age of Enthusiasm.' It must appear ironic for some that the very reformers and the deeply devout should in the end undermine their own assumptions, but that is what happened, and again demonstrates the power of those historical unintended consequences (UC). Personal shame began to replace collective guilt. How was one to judge a religion, a Christian religion, that implied that a good Christian killed a Christian for Christ and in the process become a very brutal institution? This may appear to be a very irrational position but it was nevertheless a not unpopular one, even subscribed to by great thinkers, for there was "…a sort of seventeenth-century version of Tertullian's *credo quia absurdum* (I believe precisely *because* it is absurd.)…"[50] As an example we have Blaise Pascal who appears "…aware of the fatal effect of letting the cat out of the bag: Men must often be deceived for their own good…the truth about the usurpation of the law must not be made apparent; it came about originally without reason and has become reasonable. We must see that it is regarded as authentic and eternal, and its origins must be hidden if we do not want it soon to end."[51] Also there is the view of "the more cynical Montaigne" who stated that "The Laws of conscience, that we pretend to be derived from nature, proceed from custom."[52] The hold of the past was not broken until the impact of the thinkers in the seventeenth century is absorbed into that of the following. Nevertheless, while sin may have remained, consciousness began replacing conscience as the exclusive interior vehicle for guidance in our search for one's ineluctability if for no other reason than to avoid the insanity of the religious wars that were continuing even during most of Descartes' lifetime.

It is in the realm of sin, guilt, admittance and forgiveness where the act of will is associated with conscience as one would attempt to delineate between good and evil, and thus to choose a life guided by divinely-inspired virtue. This was drawn out beyond religion and into our psyche when Descartes makes our consciousness the necessary ingredient for the effective operation of the *cogito*, this revolutionarily new and now secular guide. Thinking becomes willful only because it is a conscious act: a knowledgeable choice, at least that is the implication of his position although it will take centuries to be understood, embraced and expanded. If thinking would be non-directed, it would then be random and without focus. For Descartes to have a thinking self, he would also have to acquire some sense of a volitional consciousness, as in: "I am consciously choosing!" While this is an 'homoculous' that some speak of as inherently Cartesian, it would perhaps be more accurate to speak of a triune experience, a dialectic combination of mental components that are processed into a new or third idea, conclusion or even mental state. The self and consciousness thus would be perceived as mirrors that reflect and thus expand each other through volition and perhaps create the individual that history will give light to. This process of reflection could be seen as indispensable for the functioning of consciousness (as in self-reflective consciousness).[53] Thinking appears partially an act of focus, therefore, although Descartes wasn't very clear on this particular point.

The implication of an association between thought, consciousness and self was not something that Descartes was prepared to pursue, but it would become more of a central issue for John Locke when he constructed his own view of "personal identity." Nevertheless, thought now had a very specific, identifiable and necessary place to reside; a space to be exercised and measured in the mind. An interior world received a major contribution when not only thought but consciousness was given that rational holding chamber called the mind and it was the first clear expression (rather than a Baconian hint) of an appearance of something now known as a subjective identity (and space) as distinct from a singular objective world.[54] As one student regarding the subject of a private self has noted: "The idea of a 'presentation' within the mind derives from the Cartesian system of thought, in which objects in the external world have a perceptual representation within the self (mind)."[55] When Bloom makes the case that "…self-overhearing is anything but a metaphor in this hearing with only half-awareness and little intentionality…," he could be speaking of the demands that Descartes is making in regard to the inner voice and the perception of that voice when exercising consciousness.[56] This is not to say that a private mental state of mind was making significant impact at this time for the idea of even being in a private place was still seen as an extremely rare if not subversive activity. One scholar regarding the topic of the family and the question of privacy made the following suggestion:

> The historians taught us long ago that the King was never left along. But in fact until the end of the seventeenth century, nobody was ever left alone. The density of social life made isolation virtually impossible, and people who managed to shut themselves up in a room for some time were regarded as exceptional characters; relations between peers, relations between people of the same class but dependent on one another, relations between masters and servants —these everyday relations never left a man by himself. This sociability had for a long time hindered the formation of the concept of the family, because of the lack of privacy.[57]

There are precedents for the introduction of an interior life prior to that of Descartes. Building upon the legacy of Plato, the Stoics and the Pauline Christian concept of an interior soul, we have noted that the writings of St. Augustine could be and have been considered an example that was at the least an anticipation, even if marginal. The problem with any anticipation of something of an early self as here suggested, is that it must rest upon the divine spark known as the soul and the grace that makes any individuality extremely limited especially in expressing any non-spiritual inner self. The implications of an interior life realized in Augustine's writings were only an indicator of what was definitely not anticipated although it will, in retrospect, and in an odd manner anticipate what will be fully developed.[58] Both within a work that anticipates an autobiographical framework as well as in his own recognition that his interior mind (soul?) was of central importance to his salvation, Augustine suggested a place for God to reside—or more traditionally, God created this sense of an interior space for his will and his grace to reside. When Descartes spoke of a knowledge born of the mind being more certain than that of the body, he was carrying on a tradition originating, by implication, at least as early as Augustine who we have noted believed that "nothing can be more present to the mind than the mind itself," and asked, rhetorically, "…what is so intimately known as the mind, which perceives that it itself exists and is that by which all other things are perceived."[59] Augustine unintentionally offered a theory that eventually would become a more modern view although not in the Cartesian manner of having an inner space, the mind, but rather more a soul from the Lord. As a student of the self, Charles Taylor, has clearly put it:

> It is hardly an exaggeration to say that it was Augustine who introduced the inwardness of radical reflexivity and bequeathed it to the Western tradition of thought. The step was a fateful one, because we have certainly made a big thing of the first-person standpoint. The modern epistemological tradition from Descartes, and all that has flowed from it in modern culture, had made this standpoint fundamental....It has gone as far as generating the view that there is a special domain of 'inner' objects available only from this standpoint; or the notion that the vantage point of the 'I think' is somehow outside the world of things we experience.[60]

While there are serious questions as to how much of a personalized and privatized self and "I" that should be granted as having a presence in the writings of Augustine, there is no question of a significant distinction between "…the internalization wrought by the modern age, of which Descartes's formulation was one of the most important and influential,"[61] and that of Augustine's. Moral paradigms remained cardinal within Augustinian thinking, moreover, being operational with divine guidance and thus capable of only independence from those outside social forces that would judge the immoral. And while it is true that an interior ontology was being developed, one that was technically separated from the community of man, it was one still divinely-driven retaining a communal imperative, basing the inner being on some spiritual (or mystical) phenomenon which is hardly the topic of our modern self's condition. Augustine was guided by his perception of God's will and not by his own will: anything less than that would have been sacrilegious and worthy of damnation. He also was not actually that detached from the community since he subscribed to the importance of his attachment to the community of the church in order to acquire the necessary grace for salvation as well as granting him a pulpit from which to preach the Holy Word. Descartes, on the other hand, placed the moral force within the human condition, within an interior certainty, where an "…important power [reason] has been internalized."[62] With Descartes, the arrow pointed clearly toward the human condition rather than to an exclusively divine basis of knowledge. The mind would now become a singular guide. One of the more significant breakthroughs and examples that we have dealt with so far is the well-established theme of Shakespeare's successful tragic masterpieces which would permit his major characters—Falstaff, Hamlet—to explore their inner identity. Professor Bloom correctly noted this radical change that makes clear this new road of thinking that had been delineated from Augustine's thinking even before Descartes put pen to paper. As Bloom offers:

> Is that fashioning of sufficient import to speak of the invention (or reinvention) of the human? In the most famous of his seven soliloquies, Hamlet hears (or overhears) himself contemplate taking arms against a sea of troubles and, by opposing, end them. All of us with literary interests inherit Hamlet's equivocal assertion of the power of the poet's mind over a sea or universe of death. What Shakespeare invents, most supremely through Hamlet is that inward assertion of opposition to what most menaces the ever-burgeoning spirit of self. Hamlet's study of himself is an absolute, and diminishes what is outside the self as a sea of troubles. Incessantly pondering his own words, as if they both were and were not his own, Hamlet becomes the theologian of his own consciousness, which is so wide that its circumference never can be discovered.[63]

The role of God in Augustine, sinners in Dante and social types in Chaucer had been weakened enough that by the time of Descartes that for those thoughtful few who could recognize a developing new world and a potential new paradigm they could also partake in those ideas that were still begging for development. And Descartes was not the only one to recognize these opportunities. The time had arrived for something more than bits and pieces of new thought; what was needed was a new road map.[64] There were clear hints that a new and complete epistemology for arriving at knowledge, not only of nature in general, but also the nature of being human was being established. After the mayhem and slaughter of religious wars, many of the more thoughtful could no longer accept the model of the omnipotent, omniscient and omnipresent god. There was a growing mental void that was in need of attention.

A solo entity, a singularity with a subjective or inner self reflecting a private consciousness, what could be called an individualized modern mind, found its beginnings with such questions as 'what is the self?' and 'What am I?' We sometimes find an early and rough expression of these questions articulated for the first time in a context of psychological autobiography. But as has been noted, Augustine's *Confessions* took one small step in the direction of what could be called a reflective if moralizing autobiography but could hardly be considered more than a primitive beginnings.[65] If one is to theorize about the self one must be prepared to stand alone as a singular being taking one's own compass on any judgements, otherwise one is part of a larger community or of some divine order where there is little or no need for personally drawn conclusions.[66] While it is true that "…Augustine had a keen sense of the incompleteness of the self, of the need for relatedness," it should also be noted that it is only to a very specific and narrow category of relatedness, one "...which, in his case, is predominantly relatedness to God." As he stated: "I am not at one complete until I am one with Thee." It is not extreme to suggest that Augustine could not be "at one complete" with his own sense of self, of individuality or even of self-consciousness, let alone the privacy (and isolation) that is implied in such mental interiority; he was simply too early and too religious on that stage of what would eventually be called an historical self-development.[67]

There is a possibility that Augustine was a willing discoverer of something of an interior life beyond the soul but he certainly was not willing to enter into, embrace or pursue it. This is connected to his thoughts regarding the sin of pride, the deadliest of his seven deadly sins. Only God is both an alpha and omega. It could be that Augustine peeked through the door of individuality and pulled back although this is not a position this writer is prepared to make. We have spoken of how Augustine could only point out the etymological link between *cogitare* and *cogere*, i.e., 'to bring together' or 'to collect,' and to understand thinking as some kind of inner assembly of an order that we construct but only with divine guidance. The operational word here with Augustine is always 'divine.' It would not be until the writings of Descartes that a genuine and unique use for such a revolutionary inner 'bringing together' could be created and given its wings.[68]

This may appear to be somewhat belaboring the question of Augustine's mind and the ancient frame against that of Descartes' but as long as there are those serious and scholarly authors who persist in applying a fifth century mind into the world of the seventeenth century, some effort at reintroducing a more accurate and balanced viewpoint and an explication of an historical context must be seen as a necessity. Any thinking regarding an interior mind was dependent upon divine authority and thus always limited in some way or other to that framework. Descartes, on the other hand, while retaining a Christian God, was able to keep this divine role separated from several key elements of his ontology and thinking, where the earlier constancy of a divine presence, now absent, made it possible to begin an exploration of an interior life which would guide him to a certainty other than that by way of a soul and salvation. As Gareth Matthews in his study of ego in both Augustine and Descartes put it: "...I characterized Descartes's internalism as a rejection, on philosophical grounds, of the appeal to outside authority. In resolving to be his own guide in the search for what he can know, Descartes in effect resolves to make himself his own authority. Augustine, by contrast, never expresses any such ambition."[69] Again, as a reminder, the term *ego*, so freely used, is an ancient one that acts only as an emphasis of the speaker, not someone standing alone with an inner ontology.

It isn't the lack of ambition but rather a lack of capacity that restrained Augustine, even if he was one of the very earliest to willingly make extended use of the first person pronoun, *ego* (I). True, both Augustine and Descartes willingly developed and presented many of their thoughts from a first-person point of view.[70] Along with Shakespeare who in his soliloquies created an illusion of being inside the mind of individual, there was in France before Descartes, Montaigne's deliberate choice of writing in solitude in the pursuit of what he considered to be his own inner being as best he could understand it.[71] Cloistered monks earlier separated themselves from the travails of daily life and Montaigne does with no religious reasons. These steps should be noted but not exaggerated. Bloom notes that in Shakespeare, "…we are thinking of the largest consciousness and most incisive intellect in all literature…," clearly an overstatement.[72] Moreover, Matthews' study makes a case that a personal orientation in Augustine's writings drawn from the ego only further reflects how much, in fact, he was a classical thinker and antithetical to our own mind set. *Persona*, the ancient Latin word which literally means mask, gives us a social sense of the individual—as in look how he is individually dressed—is not a psychologically-driven individuality working from a sense of self but rather is drawn from the social, a stage in a public setting. There is perhaps an ego but not an individualized quality in Augustine when he states that: "For long I had been turning over in my mind many various thoughts," since this does not demonstrate much more than that he could think he exists, ("How can I be mistaken [in thinking] that I am?") a position that is not removed from the classical Greek mind.[73] While it is possible to argue that Augustine may have been the "…first thinker to ask this most famous of 'I' questions,"[74] there is nothing modern in this statement. As a cleric and preacher, he belonged to the very establishment that was contrary to what he was speaking of when defending "his own thoughts." It has rightly been suggested, in fact, that it was not until long down that road that there was an "…historical or evolutionary leap from medieval authoritarianism to the modern discovery of subjective consciousness." Moreover, "…the modern discovery of the 'I' as the center of consciousness," which is philosophically symbolized first, "…by Descartes, is just one of the later in a series of awakenings of the human spirit to the reality of individual consciousness."[75]

Augustine possessed his holy grail within the arms of his Lord. As Charles Taylor articulated it: "Here is what I described as the basically Augustinian demarche: I can only understand myself in the light of a perfection that goes far beyond my powers. How is it that this light is cast upon my thought? It is beyond my powers to have produced it myself."[76] If the self is only knowable by way of an external force (God) then there can be no individuality and no road to any conscious identity. Descartes sought ineluctability much as a modern scientist would; Augustine sought perfection as a Medieval saint would. No philosophical inquiry of Augustine's is "…as broad or as thorough as that which leads Descartes to the rational reconstruction of knowledge found in the *Discourse* and *Meditations*." Descartes's inquiry began from the standpoint of his own inner thoughts, since his thought alone "…calls into question…the very existence of the external world."[77] Therefore any Augustinian discussion of the rise of consciousness would require a relevant discussion regarding the appearance of an interior singular and secular self, something not possible for a mind in the early years of the Medieval world. Descartes belonged to a world so different in just the level of literacy that it is incomprehensible such a mind could be equated at all with that of the fifth century.

In an age of readily available books it should not surprise us that the seventeenth century was also the age of growing linguistic interests. In the sixteenth century we find an expansion of the English and French languages and a new found love for the creation of dictionaries and translations, itself an expanding art form which was partially the home for the thoughts and writings of seventeenth century thinkers.[78] It was a new world that presented those inclined to forging new thinking and fresh ideas with the creation of an unique dilemma, a by-product of this increasing availability of published information: what and where one could publish. Holland became a haven for publishing activity. From the point of view of thinkers, scholars and authors, there was, by the time of Descartes, a plethora of both written information, interpretation and vocabularies in search of publishers. Galileo had two volumes of Brahe and Kepler data that sat on his desk although they appeared to have gone unread. (This, of course, raises the interesting question that if he had studied those volumes it may have been possible that what we call the laws of motion associated with Newton may have rather been known as the Galilean laws of motion.) Information was expanding exponentially. One way of describing this new and readily available information, an unprecedented amount of books and articles, would be to refer to it as an "Early Modern Information Overload,"[79] Personal libraries were expanding and a great deal of information and analysis was being published and a hunger for guides to take the curious through this growing maze of discovery and critical writings was expanding. For example, "…a typical royal magistrate in the late Fifteenth century would have owned sixty books; one hundred years later Montaigne remarked that he owned about a thousand books, in what would have been an exceptionably large private library for the time…"[80] Little wonder that he sought to spend time on his estate alone in his library. By the time of the "…early eighteenth century another famous French provincial magistrate, Montesquieu, owned over three thousand books."[81] What facts were readable, what theories were worthy of serious consideration, who was to be trusted in their examinations and analyses, what were the latest theories and what should be discarded as worthless or a distortion and what criteria should be applied? These and other important questions will plague serious thinkers as the disciplines inherent in modern scholarship slowly evolved into a useful structure.

It is in the confines of this explosion of literary information that the term *conscience* went through its metamorphosis. In English, the term *conscience* enjoyed a rich history as it evolved from early Medieval to modern English. The *OED* states that "In M[iddle] E[nglish], *conscience* took the place of the earlier term INWIT in all its senses."[82] *Inwit* in Middle English appears to refer more generally to "…mind, while conscience, taken from Latin, begins to take on a more common and somewhat more modern connotation."[83] The fourth definition of *inwit* in the *Middle English Dictionary* (MED) offers inwit as an "Inward aware of right or wrong, conscience." The first definition, however, is "Mind, reason, intellect, comprehension, understanding," which in time will become associated with what we will later call a consciousness state of mind.[84] In the MED, *conscience* (also *conscience, conciens, conscientia*) is offered, in its first definition, "…as the mind or heart as the seat of thought, feeling, and desire; attitude of mind, feelings." The entry continues with describing this as "…the faculty of knowing what is right…awareness of right and wrong; consciousness of having done something good or bad," and with "the moral sense," suggested as the second definition where sin and guilt are associated with conscience.[85] Thus *conscience*, although in its Latin roots and origins is a neutral or non-judgmental term, became a moral issue as it evolved within the walls of the Christian world, developing parallel and sometimes interchangeably to the more judgmental and older Greek term *synderesis*. However, "…synderesis…suffered a gradual eclipse, retaining what life it had only with the scholasticism of the universities. It was then that the Medieval association of *synderesis* with two synonymous terms, 'spark' and 'natural instinct,' and with two descriptive biblical expressions, 'the spirit of man' and 'the candle of the Lord,' allowed a metamorphosis to take place."[86] As a living term for moral imperatives, *synderesis* went through a major change that did not alter its sense of the righteous. Additionally, it represented "...an ancient idea that had initially received its definition as a technical term of scholastic anthropology survived in new guises and continued to play a role in late Renaissance thought until the time of Locke and Butler."[87] John Locke in 1695 spoke of the 'spark' in the mind with the 'candle of the Lord' from Proverbs 20:27. In *The Reasonableness of Christianity* (1695), Locke demonstrated his interest regarding the operation of "...the same spark of the Divine Nature and Knowledge in Man, which making him a Man, shewed him the Law he was under as a Man," and asserted that "...he that made use of this Candle of the Lord...could not miss to find...the way to Reconciliation and Forgiveness."[88] The seventeenth century produced not one but two giants addressing this new word and what it might mean. Consciousness in the hands of Descartes followed by Locke was an opening salvo towards our world.

The metaphor of a candle of the Lord had its beginnings in an earlier idea expressed by way of St. Jerome's 'spark of conscience' and makes its return in the early modern tradition of natural law applied in religious and philosophical thinking until as late as Joseph Butler's *Sermons* (1726) and Thomas Reid's *Essays on the Active Powers of the Human Mind*" (1788).[89] The etymological playing field for potential terms that could address the new thinking was left with conscience and the more recent consciousness; *synderesis* clearly appeared less and less frequently, although the metaphor of "spark" and "light" remained active as we know it in later and altered states of usage during the Enlightenment and in some ways by implication even to this day. It should be emphasized, additionally, that the two meanings of conscience—the 'mind or heart as the seat of feeling' and 'awareness of right and wrong'—were concurrently in use partly because consciousness, according to the *OED*, did not make its first developed appearance until the seventeenth century. In its early use, as noted, *consciousness* meant *consciousness to oneself*, or if one will, "internal knowledge or conviction; knowledge as to which one has a testimony within oneself; esp. of one's own innocence, guilt, deficiencies, etc." It is obvious from these early definitions that the two words were close relatives, consciousness evolving from conscience as the latter was increasingly associated with right or wrong, that is, with moral definitions, and the former increasingly observed as a neutral description of some mental activity associated with thinking.[90] The point being drawn here is that an interior mental state was clearly present as the first definition of conscience since it is clearly expressed in the *OED* as an "inward knowledge, consciousness; inmost thought, mind."[91] While this is being repetitive, there is a fundamental reason for this emphasis. It is the thesis here that this is precisely the basic definition of an interior ontology of thought that began to both make itself very clear while being developed and expanded in the writings of Descartes and Locke. In defense of this position it should be noted additionally that even the same Thomas Reid already discussed in his *Essays on the Intellectual Powers* offered understanding of some of those inherent problems with the following observation: "Descartes created a picture of the relationship between the human mind the human body with which philosophy has struggled ever since." When we trace the history of it we are, in the words of Thomas Reid, "…led into a labyrinth of fanciful opinions, contradictions, and absurdities, intermixed with some truths."[92] Needless to say there will follow additional philosophical enlargements and divisions to this issue beyond that of Locke.

One final comment must be made regarding the issue of consciousness within the confines of the seventeenth century. It should be kept in mind that any discussion of the evolution of both the term and activity of 'consciousness' should not be perceived as an isolated phenomenon but predicated on the necessary and equal existence of some sense of a personal and an interior 'self' which it can be argued can also be found, or at the least implied, in the writings of Descartes. Since the theory here is that there is no way for consciousness to exist as an interior reality without the concurrent development of a sense of being a separate and unique self and individual, what Descartes suggests or implies in this regard is of great importance. Thus the self is a key component that Descartes contributed to even if he left later thinkers more problems than answers. As has been suggested:

> The essential implications of Cartesianism for the modern self might be summed up in two words: disengagement and reflexivity. On this account a full realization of one's essential being—which is to say, of one's being as a consciousness—requires detachment from the body and from the passions rooted in it….The achievement of certainty in knowledge also requires disengagement—disengagement from naive acceptance of the existence of the external world in favor of an inspection, by the 'inner Eye' of the Mind, of those 'clear and distinct' ideas that can be found within (this is Descartes's famous method of doubt).[93]

Only with the appearance of something more, the concept of a private self that is expanding and seeking inner understanding with its separate distinct and overt individual expressions of that self, will we be able to appreciate the act of becoming and being conscious. This is a sense of the existence of an individual that is mature enough to exercise an independent reflective conscious action and interior life separate from and yet attached to the world. This is not unlike what the late twentieth century commentator, Abraham Maslow, has called a state of being self-actualized (humankind in the making).

It is generally agreed that the Renaissance played a key role in the early stages in this transformation from a community-driven psychological framework to one that was beginning to be thought of as a more personal and inner-driven frame. But the individuality that Burckhardt described is more appropriate to the late nineteenth century German society within which he lived than to that of the Italian Renaissance.[94] Nevertheless, the influences that contributed to this early stage of individuality have been well documented and debated.[95] From foreshortening to biography, portraiture to the signing of artists' works, the use of the dome with its psychologically centered specificity as well as the development of a somewhat more personalized autobiography (at least secular); with all this and more, a private mentality was being given space for the earliest stage of its birthing, an opportunity that was both advancing and intensifying especially in regard to the very modern word *privacy*. This revolutionary transformation was an eventual threat to the more fundamental sense of the community that consistently dominated our earlier mental patterns and way of life and, of course, added to the creation of the Scientific Revolution

It was in language, however, in the world of letters, that the fifteenth century humanists made a remarkable contribution to the development of the printed word and the expansion of knowledge and interpretations. The printing press' most original contribution, has been noted, was the extensive use of parentheses and when they were used in later scholastic texts, they developed nuances which had no direct equivalent rhetorically.[96] Although we should note that the age of agreed spelling also began at this time.[97] Also, since the twelfth century rag paper had become available which made the potential for the printing press a realizable activity. Reading Cicero was not done silently but rather aloud for the issue had not been one of literacy but of rhetoric,[98] we now have an internal mental vocalization expressing the written word. The theatrical drama of spoken language now could be made a completely individualized experienced within the privacy of a person's mental space. If you could read, you could know the word and have a direct link to God or playwright or author and most importantly, new and revolutionary ideas.

It is inconceivable for a Montaigne to dedicate so much of his life in the privacy of his own space, mastering language and contributing to the art of the essayist without the earlier reformation of the new literacy, the vernacular and printing press and now access to printed materials including on the Holy Word now given new importance and a demonstration of expanded awareness. Even "Luther, himself, described printing as 'God's highest and extremest act of grace, whereby the business of the Gospel is driven forward.'"[99] One need not confess to a clergyman to open one's soul to heaven; one could read His word and speak one's own conscience directly to Him without the aid of an interpretative institution or rhetorical abilities. It may seem a little odd for some observers that the appearance of a conscious self required an opening beyond the pillars of traditional institutions that had control over the exclusive command of all thinking, but in retrospect that is precisely what happened.

Again it must be repeated that we are speaking of a psychological transformation or of a transformation of mental states and assumptions.[100] There is in this transformation an additional philosophical revolution toward the principle that the most important foundation for a full human life is no longer found exclusively in the public theater. The unthinkable was happening: a new mental perception now would aid in creating a foundation where both Romanticism and eventually twentieth century term *existential* and the theater of the absurd would be given birth. The private self can and will increasingly take precedence over that which had been exclusively public. As Charles Taylor stated it: "Strength, firmness, resolution, control, these are the crucial qualities, a subset of the warrior-aristocratic virtues, but now internalized. They are not deployed in great deeds of military valour in public space, but rather in the inner domination of passion by thought."[101] In ancient Greece, the 'hero' was more than simply a hero because of his achievements, his public deeds, but also was seen the hero because his actions were recognized by the agreed conclusions of the community, again that magic word for a collective judgement. Again, a hero is someone that the public labels a hero. Contrast this normative with that offered by one of our own contemporaries, such as Jean-Paul Sartre and his play *No Exit*, and it is most telling, especially when we consider that we now live in the world of the anti-hero.

This contrast between the emphasis that was placed on a public conclusion as opposed to the more modern private world mirrors the contrast between exterior and interior assumptions, and has contributed to a serious alteration of our views of functionality, especially when discussing the significance of and even the need for new techniques in the sciences and mechanics. This modern sense of technique can be found to be useful if not indispensable for the world of problem solving, not only for natural philosophers (scientists), but equally for various cultural and political leaders. And it has been correctly observed that, "...[t]echnique, in its strictly technological sense, involved two factors. (1) There must be a clear and distinct separation of the subjective and objective components in any situation in order for us to take rational hold of the problem. (2) The objective problem, thus isolated, is to be dealt with by a logical procedure that seeks to resolve it into a finite number of steps or operations. Both these conditions were the creation of philosophy."[102] It should not surprise us therefore that Descartes (with Bacon in the background) was the one who "...ushered in the modern age by establishing the primacy of method, in which he fixed the distinction between subject and object as sharply as could possibly be done."[103] Bacon may have introduced the idea of a new method but it was Descartes who was the first to systematically make use of it as well as to systematize it. This is, in other words, one of the activities of the Cartesian mind that gave him for later generations the title of father of both modern science and modern philosophy. Descartes, it is true, may not have been capable of drawing a clear-cut modern distinction between objective and subjective,[104] but, as has been noted, as a critical thinker he was clearly ready to offer "...the world its first secular framework for total comprehension and, concomitantly, the most unequivocally secular conception of human dignity ever asserted in the West."[105] As noted earlier, his defense of the existence of God and God's role, while an interesting essay, actually has little or nothing to do with his philosophy, science or his contributions thereof. If one were to study his arguments for the existence and role of God they would be rather disappointed. As has been noted earlier, the "...understanding of thinking as a kind of inner assembly of an order we construct," will eventually "...be put to a revolutionary new use by Descartes."[106] The word revolutionary is most appropriate here because all scientific and philosophical thinking after Descartes was fundamentally dependent in some way, even if in opposition, upon his revolutionary insights. Another more simplistic way is to think of it as first an Ancient and Medieval world, next undermined by the early modern contributions of the Renaissance, Reformation and then the Scientific Revolution and Descartes as well as those brilliant minds who will follow in the next centuries, culminating with elements of a post-modern world of self-conscious reflective individuality.

This is a by-product of his commitment to doubting everything. Moreover, one can find here the beginning of an interior dialogue, not just a monologue since: "…thought, previously associated with dialogue, begins, with Descartes, to seem a quintessential private event; and knowledge, previously conceived as a communal possession, comes to be associated with a 'logic of private inquiry.'" Additionally, there is the idea from the same commentator, Louis Sass, that offers two important notes in regard to Descartes' use of the idea of an interior space since "…consciousness is assumed to have direct access not to the external world but only to inner 'ideas.'"[107] This introduced both the idea of being conscious of one's own consciousness and that, additionally, of the idea of detachment that was achieved by a certainty in knowing that required some form of disengagement. This idea of detachment is so indispensable for the development of modern science, the disengagement from what has been handed down as the unvarnished truth regarding the world we inhabit allowing for the possibility of introspective observation that would offer an alternative in one's search for certainty. Is such an introspective state required for the activity of consciousness? Julian Jaynes questions this view when he states: "I am not saying that all consciousness is introspection, but rather that it is introspectible (what we have access to in our 'minds,' a definition in absolute agreement with Descartes, Locke, Hume, and the tradition that followed)."[108] There is a difference between being introspective as distinct from what it is to be introspectible even if that distinction is not necessarily clear. The point is that the divisions between an interior self and the outside world were becoming so established that it is hard for us now to imagine a time when we would not be capable, let alone joyous, in living with the inner self: Before 'having perceptions' had become as common in the modern world as having a body, or "…before, that is, the subject-object split that Heidegger talks about in his essay *The Age of the World Picture*, it could be argued that no one 'perceived' anything." This question of perception in the modern world could be compared to a time "…before Saint Augustine worked on the notion of free will, that no one 'willed' anything or, for that matter, before the Greek philosophers had worked out the concept of mind anyone 'thought' anything."[109] Until we replace the old systems of thought and ideas with a new set of assumptions where man's unique interior mental states are accepted as being normal, we speak of such events, if ever, as extremely rare.

The world of that '*idea*' was both transformed and enlarged by Descartes' commentaries, offering it as a word by which "I understand the form of any thought…by the immediate awareness *perception* of which I am conscious of that said thought," and "…in such a way that, when understanding what I say, I can express nothing in words, without that very fact making it certain that

I possess the idea of that which these signify."[110] The first and most fundamental point to be drawn here is that Descartes clearly marks off the space between idea and thought by making an idea simply the 'form' of any given thought. When we experience having a thought we relate within our interior space to the form that the thought takes, and we refer to that form as an idea. If the thought is linguistic then a viewable form would be in letters, words and relationships or even perceived syntax, while if the thought is an image then the form will follow with an appropriate visual construct. The same would, one must conclude, also apply for the thoughts regarding mathematical problems or musical notation. Consciousness, in this process, is that which brings forward into a state of awareness an understanding in the form of an idea of what began as a thought. Since aware and conscious are so often intermingled by Descartes in both meaning and use, this passage inheres with a certain necessary ambiguity if not confusion. What is certain is that Cartesian thought is a step away from the interior phenomenon of idea which stands next to what for Descartes is at the deepest (most subjective?) level of the mind's interior, his consciousness. Put another way, Cartesian consciousness (awareness) gives life to an idea by recognizing it for what it is, an expression of thought. Much as abstract thought developed in the Golden Age of Classical Greece, and interiority cannot be documented as probably existing any earlier than its possible appearance in the writings of Augustine,[111] Descartes and later seventeenth century thinkers introduced us to our modern understanding of *perception*, *thought*, *idea* and, most importantly, *consciousness*. While the language that Descartes uses is limited to his own era, arriving as it does on the back of the earlier medieval and scholastic traditions and which was clearly less than adequate in expressing his thinking, he still contributed to a transformation of a philosophical lexicon, placing it into a frame that was far more modern than ancient and went far beyond where anyone else had ever ventured. This is worth keeping in mind when discussing his comments regarding objectivity: "By the *objective reality of an idea* I mean that in respect of which the thing represented in the idea is an entity, in so far as that exists in the idea; and in the same way we can talk of objective perfection, objective device, etc. For whatever we perceive as being as it were in the objects of our ideas exists in the ideas themselves objectively."[112] To the modern ear this passage sounds odd indeed since objective is used here for an interior state of mind. However, Descartes is clearly thinking of an idea as an 'entity' much like any entity external to our being, and in the thirteenth century scholastic tradition, this usage, while now obsolete (see *OED*), meant certainty, which any reader of Descartes will quickly find to be the central concern of his philosophy. It would appear, then, that Descartes considered an idea and its observer, our consciousness, to belong to the world of certainty, much as he was convinced of the certainty of both the doubt and the existence of God. This supports the view that Descartes possessed both a clear and distinct perception of both his thoughts and his existence as well as the presence of his idea of both which he would consider with this newly formed mental activity to be labeled being conscious thinking, and that somehow literally resided within that inner wall he would call the mind.

After Descartes defined thought as a "...word that covers everything that exists in us in such a way that we are immediately conscious of it," he continued by stating: "Thus in all operation of the will, intellect, imagination, and the senses are thought."[113] Robert McRae has observed that when Descartes discussed the term *idea*, consciousness may very well have become the best contemporary idiomatic expression to convey what he meant when he wished to delineate what he may have also had called his 'thought.'[114] It has even been rightly suggested that "...consciousness has been widely used in this way by philosophers of very different philosophical persuasions."[115] In fact, McRae even suggested that "...those who share this use of the term consciousness with...many others, would...be justified in rendering Descartes' seventeenth century *penser* or *cogitare* into English as *to be conscious of.*" This is less than satisfying since, as McRae makes clear, the "...result would pose a serious problem in translating his definition from Latin into English of the *cogitatio* into thought, it could also be rendered as *consciousness*, making it impossible therefore to render *ut ejus immediate conscii simus* by *that we are immediately conscious of it* for the expression *conscious* would already have been used up.[116] That *consciousness* is often used interchangeably with *thought* is understandable although confusing if not a distortion. This will be one of the positions that Locke later experiments with in his attempt to define the conscious aspect of personal identity. For the student of consciousness one of the most serious difficulties is confusing the act of being conscious with that of thinking, since in today's world computer builders would be, by implication, creators of consciousness, a God-like position indeed. Most ardent materialists, scientists and behaviorists are rarely prepared to make the statement that the computer that defeats a chess master is conscious even though it does possess certain thinking capacities of a type (computation).[117] There are, of course, serious students of the subject who are not convinced that computers can achieve a state of consciousness. For Descartes, however, such modern distinctions were at best primitive.[118] Again McRae attempts to make the case that "...we can say that the difference between thought and consciousness can be expressed in these two kinds of sentences: (a) I think. (b) I am conscious that I think. For the variable 'think,' in both of these sentences can be substituted the values 'doubt,' 'understand,' 'affirm,' 'deny,' 'desire,' 'refuse,' 'imagine,' 'see,' 'hear,' 'feel.' No term other than a synonym can be substituted for 'am conscious.'"[119]

The search for a synonym for consciousness rather than accepting it as a singular and incomparable phenomenon with possible varied aspects of its expression has led a great many thinkers to over-simplify or even to embrace meaningless observations. In addition to the stock terms for consciousness such as awake, aware, group (American consciousness, etc.), and thought there are a great many adjectival alterations for consciousness, literally many dozens of variations and contradictory usage plus those ideas that suggest everything from absolute to ultimate consciousness, a good many of which can be found in Appendix II. One wonders how many books could be published let alone written without this plethora of catch-all terms applied to consciousness. Consciousness is not simply thinking any more than it is any one or simple combination of *doubt, understand, affirm, deny, desire, refuse, agree, see, hear,* or *feel.* Each of these are terms so complete unto themselves that they are in no need of help from another synonym for understanding. Consciousness, which consistently appears out of reach of our definitive understanding, is not helped by using other completely ill-defined, self-contained or confusing terms to elucidate; to be aware must be assumed to mean being aware as when we are thinking we are involved in the act of thinking. But it is hardly the same thing as this very active and complex act of consciousness. Perception is nothing more or less than precisely that —thus we do not say we are conscious of the sunset, we would say we 'see' the sunset. Seeing, like hearing and desire, are at best possible aspects applicable to but never the phenomenon of consciousness in itself. Descartes drew no such distinctions since for him a perception was the foundation of our thoughts which, when existing in the space of the container that he refers to as the mind, could mature into an idea; straight forward, if not simple. Descartes was certain of his perceptions and ideas because of the observational or recognitional power of what he considered to be his consciousness. What I am thinking is not what exists in me, McRae noted; and we would add here, what is conscious is a special form of knowledge, from the original meaning of the Latin term—to have knowledge with one other ('con' meaning together and 'science' from 'scire' meaning to know). So stated, it should be read that "...consciousness is for Descartes the kind of knowledge we attribute to agents. To be conscious is preeminently to know what we are doing or to know what is happening to us." Or, we also could add what McRae suggests:

> There are at least three things related to Descartes' definition of thought, which deserve to be considered. The first is that consciousness would appear by virtue of the word 'immediately' to demarcate for Descartes an area of absolute certitude, one which he totally exempts from hyperbolical doubt. The second is his denial that we can have any thought, in his very wide sense of thought, of which we are not conscious. The third is that being conscious of whatever exists in us is not the same as thinking of what exists in us.[120]

While it is true that I could share my thoughts and my knowledge, I could not share the inner experience of my thoughts or my knowledge or my conscious recognition of those same thoughts, knowledge or my own reflection. That is precisely what some will often attempt, however, as a special activity for the modern poets and artists that will be discussed later.

One place Descartes sought certainty was found in mathematics (extension) as it was provided for him in the infallibility of what he called his consciousness. For Descartes it was this initial certainty on which his whole metaphysics rested.[121] There can be no question as to "...whether I am really doubting rather than, say, affirming, desiring, or denying, or imagining, or perceiving. Each of these is exactly what we are conscious of it as being." Negatively, students of Descartes usually begin with the thought that what drove his metaphysics was his admittance of his own doubt. But this is to imply a non-positive or even a negative basis for his reasoning. It could be countered that instead we would do better to offer an emphasis on what he affirms as a positive, i.e., his striving to achieve a sense of certainty. After all the dependence upon the *cogito ergo sum* rested on this certainty.[122] But all thought is not necessarily a part of some conscious action, however, and Descartes was careful to make clear to what extent his actions were the object of his consciousness. "For if I say I see, or I walk, I therefore am, and if by seeing and walking I mean the action of my eyes or my legs, which is the work of my body, my conclusion is not absolutely certain....But if I mean only to talk of my sensation, or my consciousness of seeing, or walking, it becomes quite true because my assertion refers only to my mind, which alone is concerned with my feeling or thinking that I see and I walk."[123] It is true that Descartes did create a major confusion for those today interested in this topic with his interchangeable use of the two terms of consciousness and awareness (and on occasion even *sensations*). This is a linguistic confusion and thus an equally philosophical and psychological one which has remained an active problem for us.

We should keep central that Descartes was introducing revolutionary new ideas using a very limited vocabulary and syntax compared to our own. Moreover, his inconsistencies were not that unusual when reviewing some of his more fundamental thoughts. His insights are remarkable considering his historical background and linguistic limitations.[124] For example, "When defining 'thought' in *Replies II*, as 'a word that covers everything that exists in us in such a way that we are immediately conscious of it,' he emphasizes that he has said *immediately* in order to exclude those bodily movements which are a consequence of decision."[125] This would seem to rule out both memory (the past) or willfulness (future choices). The implication is that he may have had some sense that consciousness, in our modern parlance and at least for some interpreters, possessed, or at the least, could imply something of an existential parameter. Consciousness is always, then, seen as being immediate. By stating that what is happening is in particular happening because I am consciousness of it happening, "the *me* is finally a person, not just a mind." He could therefore state:

> ...there are certain things which we experience in ourselves, and which should be attributed neither to the mind nor body alone, but to the close and intimate union that exists between the mind and the body....Such are the appetites of hunger, thirst, etc., and also the emotions of passions of the mind, which do not subsist in mind or thought alone, as the emotions of anger, joy, sadness, love, etc.; and finally all the sensations such as pain, pleasure, light and colour, sounds, odours, taste, heat, hardness, and all other tactile qualities.[126]

This "union" could be interpreted as a nascent self-consciousness which could include a possible beginning appearance of the self. This is not to say, however, that the modern idea of a self (or selves) is in fact necessarily a Cartesian creation, since any mature sense of the self will only slowly evolve out of these first steps, early though they be. This idea of a *cogito* as a basis of the self is one that is as static as his consciousness in the tradition of the older conscience. And there is also the problem of the language of his day versus our own language.[127] That the French use the same word for both conscience and consciousness is of little help and potentially confusing for our reading and understanding of Descartes' writings. While it can be argued that through his *cogito* the soil was being created for the seedlings of the self, and eventually an individuality which would be self-reflectively conscious, this appearance was at best only at the earliest stages of a fundamental indication of what would follow. Any complete psychological separation of one individual from another (isolation) will come in the end from each individual's highly developed unique interiorization within their own mind. The creation and acceptance of a fully matured subjectively willful self will wait to arrive for centuries after the creative basics and insightful legacy offered in the seventeenth century. This is significant because there have been attempts to tie our modern sense of self-consciousness to Descartes, especially as it has been used by Jean-Paul Sartre, although the arguments are again a classic example of projecting back into the distant past contemporary assumptions and language. In this particular case, this is a projection that is more than some two hundred years out of historical context where the language, the perspectives and the assumptions do not belong in that world of early beginnings that are associated with the term *Enlightenment*, and is thus inappropriate for our own, modern (and post-modern) world.[128]

Descartes' theories hinged upon the distinction he made, with certain inconsistences, between thought and consciousness.[129] Since he believed, "...there can exist in us no thought of which, at the very moment that it is present to us, we are not conscious," it followed that consciousness was more fundamental to Descartes than thinking since thinking is not what is of note but rather that you are conscious (can know) of your thinking. Locke will also find something rather appealing in this argument. Moreover, Descartes made clear that he had "...no doubt that the mind begins to think at the same time that it is infused into the body of an infant, and is at the same time conscious of its thought, though afterwards it does not remember that," for the rather interesting reason that "...the specific forms of these thoughts do not live in the memory." This becomes much clearer when he tied the idea of thinking and consciousness with that of actualization: "But it has to be noted that, while indeed we are always in actuality conscious of acts or operations of the mind, that is not the case with the faculties or powers of mind, except potentially. So that when we dispose ourselves to the exercise of any faculty, if the faculty reside in us, we are immediately conscious of it; and hence we can deny that it exists in the mind, if we can form no consciousness of it."[130] The presence of consciousness which would bring to light our thought was a 'potential' that only operated 'immediately' (i.e., 'actualized' in Aristotelian terms) when placed in the present tense, and then gives any of our thoughts that are to be known a presence only as they are brought to light.

There is a confused mixing of elements here of *synderesis*, conscience and Cartesian consciousness which further contributes to the difficulties in understanding what it was that should be revealed by his language. Descartes' conception of consciousness included consciousness of the mind's acts, i.e., the consciousness of its own powers when these have once been brought into play.[131] There is residing within this mind-space that something that recognizes the phenomena of perception, thought and idea. What is of interest is the volitional component Descartes attributes to consciousness, in this case reflecting on thought is not necessarily the same thing as consciousness of it if "...thought is not something of which we are *always* conscious. Instead, Descartes is saying here that we can reflect on our thought, or become conscious of our thought whenever it pleases us to do so."[132] We have, in other words, a discretionary ability when thinking. This would explain in part why at times Descartes admitted that consciousness was necessary for thought to be understood and that thought could still exist without consciousness, even if it was not recognized as such. The distinction is not in the existence of thought but in its recognition. "The major premise must be to know prior to the *cogito ergo sum*. As remarked...[earlier], the priority of 'that internal cognition which always precedes reflective knowledge,' while the relation of the general proposition, 'he who thinks exists,' to 'I think, therefore I exist,' is one between what is known implicitly and what is known explicitly."[133] The only place within us, the 'internal' state of cognition that could account for the bringing of knowledge forward and into our understanding would, of necessity, be our consciousness of that which is implicit in order to make it explicit. It is this consciousness then that the infant in the womb does not possess, and while thought for Descartes can be present there is no recognition of that very same thought.[134] It would also account for the contemporary situation where a computer can 'think' (computation) but not in a manner comparable to the functioning of the human brain. "We have implicit knowledge of everything present to consciousness, and any part of this implicit knowledge can be rendered explicitly by the direction of attention upon it."[135] Another way to think of Descartes' meaning is to note a certain lack of unity when he speaks of 'modes' of thoughts since these do not make for a "...heterogeneous collection of things, whose only common denominator is that we happen to be conscious of them." For Descartes, then, his perceptions, his feelings and desires, all his doubts and affirmations were "*modes* of thought" since all these mental states were mentally united.[136] We return again to the interiority of the experience, where a kind of editing of the thoughts that we have must take place. As McRae stated it, when confronting the issue of the relationship between thought and consciousness: "...being conscious of what is occurring in the mind is not the same as thinking of what is occurring in the mind."[137] Since thinking and consciousness are not the same thing, there is a type of dualism within the mind where the thought is occurring and where the recognition of that thought occurring is present in the form of consciousness; there are two distinct phenomenal operations here. This explains how it is possible for what appears to be, to some observers, more than one idea present at a time within the mind: "To be conscious is certainly to think, and to reflect on one's thought, but that this cannot occur so long as the previous thought remains, is false, because, as we have already seen, the soul can think several things at the same time, persevere in its thought, and whenever it pleases reflect on its thought, and thus be conscious of its thought."[138] This raises the interesting idea that it may be possible for some people to eventually have more than one conscious state operational at any given time rather than there being necessarily only one. Is it possible that we can be conscious of thinking our thoughts, what our thoughts are and what someone is saying to us at the same time? This subject that will reappear later with the concept of what could be labeled a poly-conscious mental state.

Much of this results from the standards that Descartes offered for certainty: "In defining clear and distinct perception," Descartes declared, "I term that clear which is present and apparent to an attentive mind....But the distinct is that which is so precise and different from all other objects that it contains nothing within itself but what is clear."[139] Explicit knowledge, that which we get from attending to what we are conscious of as being in ourselves is, then, the "*clear and distinct perception* of what we are pre-reflectively conscious of." Here is where mental mistakes occur: when we in our thinking fail to live up to the structure offered by a Cartesian standard of clear and distinct ideas. "Error can arise, according to Descartes, only when we allow ourselves to assent to what is not clearly and distinctly perceived. Accordingly, it follows that we *can* be mistaken about what is occurring in the mind, in spite of the fact that there is nothing in the mind of which the mind is not conscious. Moreover we can be ignorant or partially ignorant of what is in the mind in so far as ignorance is identified with lack of explicit knowledge."[140] It is this 'explicit knowledge' that leads us away from doubt and to the conclusion where Descartes can say that many men are ignorant of their beliefs. "For since the act of thought by which we believe a thing is different from that by which we know that we believe it, the one often exists without the other."[141] All of this ends with the significance of an application of our mental attention, or as McRae put it, "...that act of thought by which we know that we believe, to which Descartes here refers, is the act of *attending* to our belief, so that we clearly and distinctly perceive what it is, although prior to any such attention we are conscious of our belief or have an implicit knowledge of it."[142] Besides the requirement of a consistency for that which is "clear and distinctly perceived," Descartes spoke for a consistency "in the mind" or the "interior" whenever discussing consciousness. The image is clear; there is no more likely an 'almost thought' existing for Descartes than we could accept as valid any statement regarding 'almost pregnant' or 'almost perfect.' Certainty only exists when we are free from qualifications and for Descartes the *cogito* offers that certainty. After all, if you are doubting you are thinking according to Descartes, you are then proving that something is existing, i.e., the certainty of a *cogito*, in that he considers the act of doubting to be nothing more or less than the act of a type of thinking.

The role of God appears within the realm of a certainty of knowledge of one's own sins when reviewing one's conscience and this is now replaced with a consciousness that resides within the mind that recognizes and acknowledges the veracity of our thoughts with equal clarity and certainty. From the certitude of God in outside space we move to the certainty of consciousness in an inside space, in the land of the mind. Descartes turns to a traditional viewpoint, however, when he agrees that our most certain knowledge is that of God, while our senses are the least certain for our knowledge. Emotions are the primary problem when the certainty of knowledge is the issue. When it comes to such things as "...believing, or desiring, or undergoing certain emotions, people are far from being certain of *what* they believe, or even realizing that they *believe* it, and that the same is true of desires." As McRae argues on behalf of Descartes: "As for the emotions, what can be more puzzling sometimes than what it is we really feel?"[143] Caution is a watch word here, as McRae makes clear and Descartes further states that "...we cannot be deceived regarding the passions, inasmuch as they are so close to, and so entirely within our soul, that it is impossible for it to feel them without their being actually such as it feels them to be." Yet Descartes will later offer, "Experience shows us that those who are most agitated by their passions are not those who know them best."[144] This discussion in an analytic manner of our passions and emotions was radically new and is demonstrative of the willing exploration of what would become very important for later analysis of our psychological pre-disposition. Moreover, this can be related to that term applied specifically to the arts of his time as well as the culture as a whole, the idea of baroque and the power we may feel. As one student of the topic has noted, "...baroque man emphasized having rather than being something, and the passions were believed central to man's essence: Descartes, Hobbes, Pascal, Spinoza all philosophized in terms of the passions and their great power over human destiny; these Baroque philosophers sought to explore and understand them; hence the beginning of psychology in this generation."[145] While this will become primarily an issue in the centuries to follow, for now it is important to acknowledge that it is here that we return to the principle that 'implicit' knowledge can be rendered 'explicitly' by the direction of our attention, i.e., volition.[146] Again we have the implication but not the recognition of will, especially as is often though of today in an existential modality. It cannot be denied that Descartes may not have appreciated much of the implications of his own thinking but the following flow of history will.

Where there is an exercise of asserting choices by way of reason there is freedom from the limits of our passions, an important concept and basis for action in our own era. McRae suggested that "explicit knowledge" is that which we get from "...attending to what we are conscious of as being in ourselves...[and] is, then, the *clear and distinct perception* of what we are pre-reflectively conscious of." The interior presence of a certainty for Descartes, an ability to observe and verify by way of consciousness, became his central assurance in his embracing of a *cogito* as the basis for his philosophy.[147] Again, as he stated it: "I term that clear which is present and apparent to an attentive mind..."[148] His argument for the construction of "the attentive mind," the "interior" space, was an attempt to create the place that could offer a certainty that satisfies Descartes. And this would give meaning to what Descartes intended when he discussed a "potential" consciousness: "...while indeed we are always in actuality conscious of acts or operations of the mind, that is not the case with the faculties or powers of mind, except as a potential. So that when we dispose ourselves to the exercise of any faculty, if the faculty resides in us, we are immediately actually conscious of it; and hence we can deny that it exists in the mind, if we form no consciousness of it."[149] He continued that "...it must be noted that the mind is indeed always actually conscious of its acts or operations, but not always actually conscious of its faculties or powers; for them it is sometimes only potentially conscious." Part of the problem may arise from the fact that "...apparently prior to Descartes, conscience and its cognates were not used in the psychological sense they can have in modern French, but only in a moral sense." The legacy of conscience is only here for the first time being placed behind the wall of secularism that needed to be created for our own sense of consciousness and its parallels to come into maturation.[150] Thus when in the *Second Replies* Descartes defined thought as "…whatever is in be us in such a way that we are immediately conscious of it,"[151] he only spoke of actuality which does not result with thought and consciousness being used interchangeably. There have been those, of course, who have made the attempt to make these two terms synonymous. McRae admitted, as noted, that while some might feel "…justified in rendering Descartes' seventeenth century *penser* or *cogitare* into English as to be conscious of," it "…would produce an awkward problem…"[152] It is little wonder that serious scholars have a problem with defining "the relation between thinking and being conscious" as well the question, "are modes of thinking just ways of being conscious, or are they themselves objects of consciousness?" When it comes to Descartes's own responses to such dilemmas, it turns out that "different passages suggest different answers."[153] The conundrum arose from the nature of the mind where the mind can both think and at the same time be conscious of its thinking and thoughts, raising such questions about the relation between thinking and being conscious. Are modes of thinking just ways of being conscious, or is thinking an object of consciousness? He recognized that moving from conscience to conscious state of mind removed traditional guidance for ethical behavior. He finds a new order not unlike Hobbes in social ethical behavior. And he "…had also held out the promise of social order and harmony: he had proclaimed ethics to be the highest branch in his tree of knowledge. And ethics, as the term has been used throughout history (certainly as Descartes' Enlightenment progeny understood it), places the beholder in a perspective which demands that he look askance at exclusively egocentric behavior."[154] Hobbesian thought placed the burden on a powerful state to restrain the negative aspects of humanity. Descartes, far from being so negative in his views of human nature, took a more social position which can be seen as we move to our own world where the individual becomes more a norm and we find that, "Ethics involves the individual in a relationship of obligation to others; it requires that the subject venture beyond himself in interests and fundamental commitments, that he be genuinely other-regarding."[155] To secularize conscience is to secularize what had been moral imperatives.

Daisie Radner offers a theory of resolution in which she does not claim Descartes ever explicitly acknowledged. Her suggested distinction, while at best only implicit in his writings, offers the advantage that certain problems can be averted by bringing them out into the open. Her theory suggests that "…two notions of consciousness co-exist in his theory of mind, and he does not confuse them. It is always possible to determine which one is being referred to in a given passage."[156] What is particularly appealing to Radner in this deductive process is that her "...analysis of consciousness will be to free Descartes from the theses of incorrigibility and evidence." Her thesis would be to draw a distinction between "...consciousness of thinking and consciousness which is synonymous with thinking..."[157] She continues that this distinction is essential to Descartes' system. "What Descartes is saying, then, is not that one cannot be conscious...of thinking unless one has implicit knowledge that one thinks, but rather that one cannot notice or be conscious...that one thinks unless one has implicit knowledge of what thought is. To have this sort of knowledge means simply that if one considers the question 'What is thought?' one finds that one can 'answer' sufficiently to satisfy himself."[158] This is not unlike the theory posited here that Descartes does in general draw an implicit distinction between the act of thinking and that of recognizing the act of thinking through consciousness. For someone accustomed to the world of modern science and mathematics, this language is at best difficult and at worst distorting of what was attempted to be elucidated. In place of attempting to confuse the already extremely new and difficult term, 'consciousness,' our understanding might be better served by taking the approach that consciousness was a new and unique means for Descartes to explain something never before confronted—the relation of the distinction between the interior and exterior worlds, that of thought and things, and subjective and objective. It is tempting in this manner to see Descartes in a Platonic or Augustinian tradition—the alpha of a new vocabulary. Richard Aquila in discussing Cartesian consciousness, in fact, has made this suggestion, observing that, "As for Descartes in his own right, my proposal simply is that we regard the concept of unity of subject-and-directness, in a single state of 'consciousness,' as at least implicit in his concept of *cogitatio*. But its implications are developed neither by him nor by his immediate successors."[159] Descartes knew the Latin roots of consciousness and certainly understood that knowledge was one of two key components defining the term. As McRae succinctly stated it: "To be conscious is pre-eminently to know what we are doing or to know what is happening to us."[160] The key here is to remember that all knowledge for Descartes occurs within the mind, in the interior 'space' of what had once been the exclusive province of the soul. It was for Aquila to suggest that: "...the 'internal cognition' of concern to Descartes is not a distinct awareness directed toward a second awareness of which it is a cognition. To the contrary, Descartes proposes an *identification* of a certain kind of self- or inner-directed consciousness and a certain kind of cognition or perception of which it is a consciousness. In the case of concern to ourselves, the latter is of course a cognition or perception of something 'external' to one."[161]

Without an interiority where a self can be identified, the patterns associated with modern thought and our understanding of what we think of as contemporary mentally sophisticated conclusions would have been crippled even before beginning down this long developmental road the previous three centuries. As one student of the history of schizophrenia has pointed out: "…it was the rationalism of the seventeenth and eighteenth century Enlightenment that give them their modern stamp."[162] And continuing, he included associating consciousness with the rise of schizophrenia: "Once human consciousness came to be defined by the self-awareness of its mental essence, as in Descartes's famous arguments about the certainty of the *Cogito*…, it seemed especially evident that madness must be understood as a deviation from this condition of self-transparent mentation, that thought and madness must somehow be profoundly antithetical."[163] With the creation of an interior self where one's own madness could exist, he finishes with the following: "At the deepest level, then, all three of these models—psychiatric, psychoanalytic, and avant gardist—share the assumption that schizophrenic pathology must involve a loss of what, in the West, has long been assumed to be the most essential characteristics of mind or subjectivity: the capacities for logic and abstract thinking, for self-reflection, and for the exercise of free will."[164]

For all his insight there is a conspicuous omission in Descartes' treatment of the mind that can be demonstrated anew when his discussion turned to the thinking of an infant and the question of the presence of consciousness: "I do not doubt but that the mind begins to think at the same time as it is infused into the body of an infant, begins to think, and is at the same time conscious of its own thought," but avoids the dilemma of consciousness in an infant by adding, "…though afterwards it does not remember that, because the specific forms of these thoughts do not live in the memory."[165] Descartes simply did not think through the issue of memory. He did distinguish intellectual from corporeal memory and also aligned intellectual memory with ideas in their potentiality. And in his *Regulae*, "…imagination is meant to overcome memory; in his *Meditationes*, imagination and thought are supported by remembering the knowledge we have had." This rather introductory discussion of memory was completed, as Dennis Sepper, in his discussion of Descartes's imagination put it "at the level of the body," where "…the physiological traces of memory in the brain are produced by the actual experiences we have had, and…largely govern our particular associations of images, so that the memory of corporeal images is a key to the reliable functioning of the unified mind and body." Sepper also pointed out "...that Descartes wrote very little about memory, and that little is more enigmatic than clarifying. Descartes thus leaves us in more than one sense on the threshold of memory."[166] Images would become a very important component for later thinkers dealing with the issue of the self, especially that of Hume who "...says that ideas are 'images' of impressions. Descartes, too, speaks of ideas as images: 'Of my thoughts some are, so to speak, images of the things, and to these alone is the title "idea" properly applied; examples are my thought of a man or of a chimera, of heaven, of an angel, or (even) of God.'"[167]

As for this "threshold of memory," it too will not be confronted until later, in this case by John Locke in his continuation of this discussion of consciousness while attempting to avoid some of the Cartesian confusion inherent in the application of his metaphysical dependence on the existence of innate ideas. While Locke's success was achieved with many inadequacies, it still took a second genius in a single century working independently on this problem of an interior life to put the Western mind on the road to a modern mental activity and understanding.

And even then it will still be but a beginning for any self, new ethics and imagination as well as inherent memory to have an impact.

CHAPTER SEVEN

JOHN LOCKE AND THE LANGUAGE OF CONSCIOUSNESS

John Locke is the most influential philosopher of modern times. His Essay initiated the vigorous and lasting philosophical tradition that is known as British empiricism, but Locke's importance reaches far beyond the limits of what has since his time become recognized as the professional discipline of philosophy. [1]

FROM FAITH TO SELF-IDENTITY

Descartes belonged to an illustrious collection of brilliant seventeenth century thinkers who comprised what Alfred North Whitehead (1861–1947) labeled the "Century of Genius." In this century—the seventeenth—he dubbed his "sacred number of twelve:" Sir Francis Bacon, Harvey, Kepler, Galileo, Pascal, Huyghens, Boyle, Newton, Locke, Spinoza, Leibniz and Descartes.[2] The majority of these giants, as can be readily noted, are English, with Descartes the important exception. For those interested in the study of consciousness and its history this is a significant consideration since linguistically the English have not only a different but a less complex relationship than the French to that term *consciousness* insofar as it and conscience are clearly two distinct terms possessing two distinct meanings and understandings that are not as easily confused as the French and Latin meanings. While the moral imperative within conscience was something Descartes had to break from it was not necessary since Locke could use a different term with different implications. These linguistic differences must have contributed to the differences in understandings. And with Locke, empirical methodological approaches highlighted these differences.

John Locke (1632–1704) was an extremely popular gentleman in an extremely unsettling age. "His influence in the history of thought, on the way we think about ourselves and our relations to the world we live in, to God, nature and society has been immense." This particular observer continues his praise with the suggestion that Locke's "…great message was to set us free from the burden of tradition and authority both in theology and knowledge, by showing that the entire grounds of our right conduct in the world can be secured by the experience we may gain by the innate faculties and powers we are born with. God 'commands what reason does'…are the words that best reveal the tenor and unity of Locke's thought."[3] In addition to his varied interests he also possessed an important social standing. As a young man Locke would occasionally read romances and later put his pen to poetry. One of his first loves was that newly revived and expanded language of mathematics, as it had been for Descartes. With this and his interest in both science and philosophy he went on to study for a medical degree although in order to be awarded a medical degree, it was required that he be ordained which he refused.

While Descartes' mathematics abilities were significant enough that he would invent analytic geometry, Locke's talent was best reflected within the more public world of government. It was for the world of politics that he offered his *Two Treatises on Government* (1690) and for philosophy and psychology he produced his *Essay Concerning Human Understanding* (1690). This very popular English genius achieved a significance that would transform several fields of thought and add an alternative to the traditional assumptions which had already begun with the work of the earlier Englishman, Thomas Hobbes. While today, the Hobbesian view is most associated with conservatism, Locke developed an opposite point of view, one of optimism and progress and which helped set England on the earliest road map in a direction that would lead in many ways to what is accepted and unique in the West: a more liberal democracy and open society. Locke was the opposite to the Hobbesian dependence upon fear as a driving force.

There are several Lockean ideas that remain viable and, of course, in need of discussion and debate, significantly his contributions to our modern empiricism. But what makes his work of interest for this review are his contributions to the early development of psychology, especially his willingness to explore the English of his day to accommodate his insights regarding thought, ideas, memory and, most importantly, consciousness. What follows can be little more than an introduction to the most significant of his relevant ideas which will be drawn primarily from *Essay Concerning Human Understanding*. While Descartes had found doubt and then sought a certainty and consistency by way of clear and distinct ideas, for Locke the issue was to establish a certainty and consistency of not only knowledge but also, more importantly, of what it means to have a personal identity. What Descartes had begun with his emphasis on an interior mental space in contrast to the dictates of the outside world, Locke continued with his own exploration of this interior state of mind in its innerrelationship with that very same outside world. Locke began to enlarge—through empiricism—the definition of what it meant to possess an inner consciousness. John Locke, like Descartes, as well as others of Whitehead's "dozen" benefitted greatly from the fruits of the earlier changes contributing to the intellectual life that "...typifies the forward-looking features of that century."[4] The Cartesian basis for the coming Enlightenment and what followed was simply expanded and made more dominant for those thinkers and artists who would carry on these revolutionary changes.

As a transitional figure rooted in the unstable English history of the Stewarts, the Bloody Revolution of 1648 and the Glorious Revolution of 1688 which were important steps in a long democratization process, Locke played a critical role in the necessary "...whittling away at the old sources of truth," in order to finally look "...blankly at the flux of experience." There were serious artists who supported these changes by looking inward to find an alternative to the traditional definitions and expressions of nature's secrets which contributed to the eventual rise of a self-reflective personality: such examples noted being Dürer, Rembrandt, et al., painting portraits with the aid of mirrors.[5] Or we can consider the writings of "Milton turning in upon himself when his blind orbs roll in vain to see the Book of Nature. And, not to be outdone, also Pope manipulating the Augustan machinery of anonymity so that he can publish his own corrected correspondence before his death."[6] Shakespeare had created a great expansion with his portrayal of powerful and singular characters who were some of the earliest representations of the burdens of this newly developing self and whose creation an increasing number of creative writers continued into the Enlightenment.[7] While this was an age of greatness and Locke was a member in good standing, it serves us well to remember that it is not simply the introduction of something new that makes for a revolution, but the additional act of removing the dead underbrush of old methods and traditional perceptions that inhibit any serious original discoveries. Locke professed in his *Essay* that he worked merely as an "...underlaborer in clearing the ground a little, and removing some of the rubbish that lies in the way to knowledge..."[8] While it is common knowledge today to argue that the old must be removed in order to make room for the new, it is truly unique that Locke understood and acted upon this during his own lifetime.

A close reading of the first four books of the *Essay* reveals that Locke threw aside the arguments for innate ideas, which he abhorred, and instead decided, "...to clear my way to those foundations, which, I conceive are the only true ones, whereon to establish those Notions we can have of our own Knowledge."[9] Not wanting to participate in the traditional, metaphysical structure he would later demonstrate to his own satisfaction that experience, our own personal sensations and impressions are the origin for all our ideas, including those ideas that had been held by Descartes and others to have been *"née avec moi."*[10] As Douglas Greenlee put it in his article discussing John Locke's position regarding innate ideas:

> Locke is seeking to discredit a scholastic method of reliance on authority and of disputation in order to replace it with what may be called simply a method of discovery. I use 'method of discovery' to mean, negatively, the avoidance of that order or sequence in inquiry in which conclusions are determined in advance of inquiry, with the reasons or/evidence selected in order to support those predetermined conclusions according to the evidence or reasons encountered—whether the reasons be non-empirical, as in the case of conclusions of mathematical and logical systems, or empirical, as in the cases of the sciences and common sense knowledge.[11]

It also should be added that, "Locke marks the watershed for this change." He "...portrays in great detail what the structure and content of a deductive science of nature would be, from real essences and real necessary connections." However, as the Lockean scholar, John Yolton reminds us, Locke "...also shows that such a knowledge is not possible for humans, urging us to be good observers instead."[12] If man and not God becomes the basis for the determination of knowledge and any absolutes, then religious certainty must come into question with variable degrees of increased doubt in this expanding scientific world. The idea of 'predetermined schemes of thought' increasingly began to be suspect and eventually disregarded. While metaphysics—Descartes' orientation—was now questioned by Locke and beginning to run downhill, empiricism began finding its upward path.

> The seventeenth century introduces the forces which lead to a movement away from metaphysics towards empiricism; from scholastic reliance upon definitions and predetermined schemes of thought, to an impartial phenomenological analysis of knowledge; from a simple, direct form of realism to a complex, representative position embodied in the generally accepted way of ideas; from making theory of knowledge harmonize with the requirements of religious beliefs and theological dogma, to the reverse: to making theology keep in step with the demands of the phenomenological analysis of knowledge.[13]

The description by John Yolton of the movement from divinely-driven to reason-driven reality marked the temperament of thinking in the expanding seventeenth century humanization especially in our perceptions of motion (time), history, space and language and reflects a comment made by Whitehead regarding this change: "The historical revolt was the definite abandonment of this method [scholasticism] in favor of the study of the empirical facts of antecedents and consequences."[14] There was no longer any opportunity for ever turning the clock back from its modernizing direction.

After the weakening of the socially-driven theological threads of the traditional mental web with its concomitant ties to innateness, there was a serious shift in the understanding of what should be considered an altered meaning along with a growing curiosity regarding space. Within the Renaissance prologue, we have noted that the sense of space was permanently revised with the Age of Discovery, the unexplored space of the New Worlds, as well as aesthetic discoveries of foreshortening and spacial realism. Not surprisingly this new understanding of space aided Locke in suggesting that the "...essential, defining characteristic of ideas," as Yolton has pointed out: "...is that they are in the mind,"[15] i.e., within that space we label the mind. Here it is helpful to remember that the definition of the mind from Descartes to Locke is now, in part, one of being this internal space. There are now two new spaces, one internal, and one external both enlarged and expanding as byproducts of the exploration of nature, time and the manipulation of the plastic arts. This outer space was replicated within our interior mental arena, finding some unity at the end of the seventeenth century. This came to dominate many of the future discussions of what we mean when speaking of ideas that live within this inner space of the mind.

This discussion of space, for Locke, was preceded by a discussion of solidity which he believed became the "*Idea* most intimately connected with, and essential to Body." [II.IV.1] As Yolton put it:

> The idea of pure space arises in conjunction with body and solidity as follows: A man conceives of two bodies at a distance such that they could move toward one another and touch edges. This thought gives us the idea of space without solidity by a kind of intellectual operation or experiment. If we then think of one body moving without its place being immediately filled, we have the idea of pure space. Sensation and reflection have been used in the genesis of these two ideas, and sensation and reflection are what Locke means by experience.[16]

Space is a deduced phenomena with a 'place,' as Kenneth McLean suggested, and of necessity left ambiguous "...because we have only a working idea of place for indicating the position of things in this world, and do not know the actual place of the universe 'in the undistinguishable inane of infinite space...'"[17]

MacLean, in discussing Locke's influence on eighteenth century English literature (as well as French thinkers), noted that Locke on the issue of space,

"...denies that we have any real knowledge of place, thereby depriving man of another supposed possession of his mind. This same efficient simple idea of space furnishes all the complex ideas of distance which man has marked with the convenient lengths of feet, yards, and miles."[18] MacLean continued by quoting Locke: "...this Power of repeating, or doubling any *Idea* we have of any distance, and adding it to the former as often as we will, without being ever able to come to any stop or stint, let us enlarge it as much as we will, is that, which gives us the Idea of *Immensity*." [II.XIII.4] This lack of certainty could be a result of Locke's attitude toward the power of the mind to create additional space: "For besides the vast Number of different Figures, that do really exist in the coherent masses of Matter, the Stock that the Mind has in its Power, by varying the *Ideas* of Space; and thereby making still new Compositions, by repeating its own *Ideas*, and joining them as it pleases, is imperfectly inexhaustible: And so it can multiply Figures *in infinitum*." [II.XIII.5]

The key issue remains, however, that Locke, much like Descartes, explored this rendering of the new idea of space. This would include not just in the sense of something outside our identity, but that which resides within our own identity: an interior space where there is this "stock that the mind has in its power," that place where ideas reside. Their understanding of space may have been less developed than our own modern view but then revolutionary geniuses are inherently a beginning. This was the century where the horizon of two ideas regarding space expanded from Giotto, Columbus, Galileo, Brahe and Kepler, along with the interiority created Descartes and Locke. Locke had been given an invitation to come to the New World but rejected the idea even while being aware of the new open idea of space that so excited the imagination of the European and English mind. This was a world filled with an interest in the study of optics (Cartesian as well as Galilean) and where the wonder of perception (distance) was increasingly taking hold alongside that of the experimental method. The issue became a Cartesian one of the relationship between the object outside us (*sum*) and the impact on the interior (*cogito*) of the mind. Locke noted that "...*Our Senses...do conveying into the Mind*, several distinct *Perceptions* of things." [II.I.3] He then further refined, according to Yolton, "...the meaning of 'convey' by offering that the senses 'from external Objects convey into the mind what produces there those *Perceptions*.'"[19] As Yolton elucidated, "...the move from what is present with the mind to knowledge of objects distant from the mind was sometimes made by claiming that a resemblance existed between ideas and objects, without giving much attention to the analysis of 'resemblance.'"[20] There were other occasions when, as Yolton noted, the claim was made "...that ideas carried an internal mark of external causation: when, as Locke said, I am actually receiving sensory ideas, I cannot doubt that there are objects causing those ideas."[21] It is through the combination of "...external sensible objects and internal operations of the mind," that the mind would be "...directed and from which ideas are derived."[22] There was a recognition of a coherent tie between the inner subjective state and objects that impinge upon that state. While Locke, unlike Descartes, avoided the question of the ontological aspect of objective reality, he did offer an unequivocal account of what he meant by the "...notion of 'being in the mind.'" As he stated: "For if these Words (*to be in the Understanding*) have any Propriety, they signify to be understood." [I.II.5] This position had already been suggested by Antoine Arnauld's remark: "I say that an object is present to our mind, when our mind perceives or conceives it." According to Yolton, Arnauld insisted that "...ideas were not real beings and that having ideas and perceiving were virtually the same." In several places in the *Essay*, Locke repeats this linkage between having ideas and perceptions.[23] One such example offered that "...our *Ideas* being nothing, but actual Perceptions in the Mind, which cease to be any thing, when there is not perception of them..." [II.X.2] While, "Descartes spoke of the 'objective reality of ideas,' meaning the reality of objects as they exist in the mind, Locke spoke of *ideas* being in the mind objectively."[24] The issue of objectivity was a difficult one for these thinkers who had just begun down the subjective trail of modernity and were ill-prepared to accept any reality totally based on subjectivity. Discussions of an interior presence of ideas, however, did contribute to a 'de-ontologizing of ideas' in the seventeenth and the eighteenth centuries.[25] The place of an operational god in the mind may have been replaced by an operational 'theater' for Descartes as understood by contemporary thinkers—like Daniel Dennett—and their concept of a "Cartesian Theater,"[26] however valid or questionable that argument may be. Locke could now recognize that the interior space within was a place not only for ideas, but also for perception, conceptions, understanding, knowledge and most especially, consciousness. Clearly, the seventeenth century formulated an interior mental space where it would be possible to create a truly developmental consciousness, and with it the modern self and individuality.

This brings to mind the transformation inherent in Shakespearean 'theater' where room for the exploration of the human condition grew as a divine presence, exemplified in earlier morality plays, moved from center stage. The drama and narrative of the human condition could only exist with the space for the discovery of our mortal existence and emotional perplexity with dilemmas. Secular reasoning demanded secular conclusions which in turn required a place to exist since heaven had already been taken, leaving us the question: what is this idea of interior space? The most common mistake is to argue for a blank slate. But it is not a pure blank slate without any innateness, according to Greenlee:

> For there is 'much in the mind,' according to Locke, if in this 'much' is to be included knowledge in addition to the materials—the simple and complex ideas—out of which it is composed, which was not first in the senses. In fact, the official concept of knowledge introduced at the outset of Book IV of the *Essays* so construes 'knowledge' that there can be no knowledge that was first in the senses. For 'knowledge' is there conceived of in such a way as to be the creation of the mind, or of the understanding, as it goes about its business of relating ideas, the definition of 'knowledge' being 'the perception of the connexion of and agreement, or disagreement and repugnancy of any of our Ideas.'[27]

Thus within the confines of this interior space, there exists ideas, knowledge, and perception. It is here where Locke perceives that simple ideas by way of sensation followed by converting them into complex ideas. Locke may be associated rightly with the idea of a *tabula rasa* or blank slate but there are some important restrictions on all reality coming from the outside. It is this 'internal sense' that is the prerequisite spatial entity for the creation of the complexity of a self which is an interior, and therefore, subjective state of existence. This may prove to be one of the more important legacies of the seventeenth century in general and of Locke in particular, especially when tied to the Lockean conception of consciousness. It was precisely this issue of consciousness and awareness that Locke was at his most original when exploring "Of Identity and Diversity," the title of Chapter XXVII of the second edition of his *Essay on Human Understanding*. It was Locke's analysis that "...encouraged a new intimacy and even inwardness in the conception and portrayal of character that we recognize as an innovative feature of the English novel in the eighteenth century."[28] It was this specific inwardness that would also become, in time, a serious component for the Romantic writers of the nineteenth century.

This interior space of the mind would now have a purpose for Locke; it was to be the residence of the varied components and experiences that would create a basis for our knowledge of the world around us. The clean and definable lines between dualism in Descartes and those in Locke are not as clear as is often assumed. Just as there are Cartesian elements in Lockean thought, such as in his discussion of fixed principles and an interior space that cannot negate as absolute the possible partial existence of something innate, so there are no consistent anti-dualistic arguments to be found in Locke either. Locke, like Descartes, was just as complex in this remarkable era, standing on the edge of one world ending and another, just beginning. An interior life, separate from God and the divine control of divine space, offered a necessary support for freely opened and unencumbered perceptions—a secular source of knowledge. Locke called this "…supposed inner perception, 'reflexion' (our 'introspection'), borrowing the word 'reflexion' from the familiar optical phenomenon of the reflections of faces in mirrors." In other words, the position is stated that "…the mind can 'see' or 'look at' its own operations of the 'light' given off by themselves."[29] This observation was made by the same author who is well known for his condemnation of Cartesian dualism and who has held that this is little more than to argue for some mysterious "Ghost in the Machine," which he suggests is "…one big mistake and a mistake of special kind. It is, namely, a category-mistake. It represents the facts of mental life as if they belonged to one logical type of category (or range of types or categories), when they actually belong to another. The dogma is therefore a philosopher's myth."[30] There are not many such theorists in opposition to this new secularized dualism, but it is true that philosophical dualism has actually been a central theme of the Western mind since Plato, even if some have had very definite reservations. As an historic fact, however, and whether right or wrong, the Western world has been and mostly continues to be a dualistic one.

When we examine Locke's discussion regarding thinking we find that his definition of consciousness is "…the perception of what passes in a Man's own mind."[II.I.19][31] It could be suggested that Locke seems at times to equate consciousness with perception although as we shall see later, Locke, when taken *in toto*, is less than clear—in the tradition of Descartes—as to what specifically is meant. Moreover, according to one of the more interesting and controversial commentators on consciousness, the earlier mentioned Julian Jaynes, there should be added another position regarding the argument for an interior space: "Most people…tend to think of their consciousness —much as Descartes, Locke, and Hume did—as a space usually located inside their heads." This is especially true "when we make eye contact," for, "we tend to—in a subliminal way—infer such space in others." The problem is that it can equally be argued, "…that there is of course no such space whatever."[32] One looks out through what one thinks of as a window of their eyes at another who they assume are also looking out through the windows of their own eyes, each hidden behind the form of a kind of one way mirror while hidden from the other by the reality of their own existing interior, subjective conscious self. That there is or is not an interior space is too subjective a state to lend itself to evidence, at least scientific or empirical evidence. But it can raise all types of interesting questions: for example the question what would have happened to modern radio drama where the reality of the visual action is hidden from view and must of necessity be a product of an interior state of mind where the unseen *Shadow*, for example, comes to life? Does this not conform to the Cartesian term 'image' previously mentioned at the end of the last chapter? Finally, the question must also be raised as to where one finds imagination, assuming such a phenomena exists?

People still tend to believe in this seventeenth century invention of an interior space where, as Locke suggested "…the other Fountain from which Experience furnisheth the understanding with *Ideas* is,— the *Perception of the Operations of our own Minds* within us, as it is employ'd about the *Ideas* it has got…" As he put it,

> …such are, *Perception, Thinking, Doubting, Believing, Reasoning, Knowing, Willing*, and all the different actings of our own Minds; which we being conscious of, and observing in ourselves, do from these receive into our Understandings, as distinct *Ideas*, as we do from Bodies affecting our Senses. This Source of *Ideas*, every man has wholly in himself: And though it be not Sense, as having nothing to do with external Objects; yet it is very like it, and might properly enough be call'd internal Sense. [II.I.4]

For Locke understanding began from those experiences placed upon the "white paper" of our mind, [II.I.2] and began thus with "*our senses, conversant about particular sensible Objects*," and which equally "*convey into the mind*, several distinct *Perceptions* of things, according those various ways, wherein those objects do affect them…" He then concluded that "This great Source, of most of the *Ideas* we have, depending wholly upon our Senses, and derived by them to the Understanding, I call SENSATION." [II.I.3] As can be readily seen, Locke was very comfortable with this new and expanded understanding of the Cartesian modernization of the word *idea*.

There can be no question that the transition from a divine-driven to a reason-driven world view can be readily found in the writings of Locke. It is also true that Locke often spoke, even eloquently so, of the power of the divine, but he does not place any real emphasis on a dependence upon divine forces for his system just as Descartes had not done with his mathematical certainty. He did appear, however, to suggest a limited dependence upon the perfection of God's own certainty and consistency. As a post-Renaissance humanist and Englishman in an age of revolution, Locke after all, was more interested in reasoning rather than in taking religious orders. Whether this was the result of the influence of one of his teachers, Robert Boyle (1627– 91), or the circumstance of his era, he was, in any case, unwilling to participate in the 'enthusiasm,' specifically the Religious Wars, that was anything but conducive for clear thinking. He was not prepared to accept the argument that all was knowable for he saw the limits to human knowledge and that calling on a god would not necessarily change things. After all, it is hard not to believe that there was by now some understanding of the philosophical principle that if God can be used to answer most questions there is no reason why he could not be used to answer all questions which is the same as to offer no answer at all. Conscience, for Locke, the knowledge shared of oneself with another in a theologically-driven value system, was replaced by consciousness, wherein knowledge was acquired and understood within oneself. This was not yet necessarily a valueless system for Locke. There remained something of a moral guide in all of this, for Locke was still a participant in many of the inherited if limited seventeenth century religious assumptions and sensible in understanding that a weakening of religious faith could mean a weakening of moral guidance. What he sought was a less dogmatic attitude toward the acquisition of knowledge. The revolutionary nature and attitude of his thinking made its appearance in the use of a new language, for he was a very early commentator on the nature of language in general. This linguistic interest brought Locke to consider the role of this new found intellectual and linguistic tool of consciousness.[33]

Since England was witnessing the development of a growing technical and spacial sense of reason, Locke's legacies would be immersed in these circumstances. "Locke, and the empirical associationists who followed him, such as Bishop Berkeley and David Hartley, tended to think of the process of the association of ideas in highly mechanistic and even mathematical terms." The scientific developments of the seventeenth century altered their approach so far as "…they replaced the mystical analogical thought of the Renaissance with what they thought were truer and more scientific analogies." As an example, Hartley "…talked about the sensations that men receive as being conveyed by longitudinal vibrations in the bloodstream which conveyed these to the mind, where they apparently piled up like silt and eventually resulted in oral precepts in the higher mind." In the end it was "…such notions which treated the mind more as a file cabinet than a muscle," that "…were widely popular in eighteenth century salons, and the romantic absolutism of these systems often created a reaction which burst through to the other side of certainty, and the result was pietism, Mesmerism, and Gothic horrors."[34] Any study of the transformation from the mind of the Middle Ages to that of the Enlightenment should always note, however, the importance of the mechanical metaphors that began seeping into the language of the day. The age of the clock or a human manipulation of the basis for any conclusions regarding time, or Leibniz's "Great Clock-Maker" universe made for the beginning of man as a mechanistic being with materialistic attitudes. All of man, everything we think of as being human including the very interior world of our consciousness, was now fair game for the newly discovered and developing analytic mind.

From its roots in Latin, *consciousness* was a term that had been equated with knowing. Its origins began, according to C. S. Lewis, with the "Greek *oida* and Latin *scio* mean[ing] 'I know.'" This "Greek verb can be compounded with the prefix *sun* or *xun* (*sunoida*), the Latin with *cum* which in composition becomes *con-*, giving us *conscio*."[35] There is no doubt that the study of classical languages in its relationship to the rise of the vernacular in the seventeenth century made one more aware of both the meanings of these terms as well their roots, for this was the first great age of the publication of a plethora of dictionaries.[36] As C. S. Lewis explained it, "*Sun* and *cum* in isolation meant 'with,' And sometimes they retained this meaning when they become prefixes, so that *sunoida* and *conscio* can mean 'I know together with, I share (with someone) the knowledge that.'" Here we have a collective knowledge, but held in private, i.e., with the implication of being secret knowledge which was always present in the early Latin stages of *conscio*. However, these terms sometimes "...had a vaguely intensive force, so that the compound verbs would mean merely 'I know well,' and perhaps finally little more than 'I know.'"[37] What is important to keep in mind is that consciousness is rooted in the possession of knowledge first, with later accretions, such as 'awareness' added and given significance by Descartes and then Locke. As Lewis put it, "...*conscientia* could be either the state (or act) of sharing knowledge or else simply knowledge, awareness, apprehension—even something like mind or thought."[38] How much Locke understood the roots is not certain, although like most of the educated of his day, he was literate in Latin. However, it is clear that he was able to use it in both the traditional as well as a more modern, i.e., Lockean, sense. It is this compound of construct and meanings that both enlighten and confuse any student of this term.

The first time Locke used the term conscious in his *Essay* was the introduction [I.I.3.] when he stated, "*First*, I shall enquire into the *Original* of those *Ideas*, Notions, or whatever else you please to call them, which a Man observes, and is conscious to himself he has in his Mind..." Here the term *consciousness* could mean to have knowledge "to himself" or that he was aware "to himself." Both *knowledge* and *aware* are easily confused. If one thinks back to the confessional and the necessary review of one's conscience, it is obvious that the act of contrition requires an interior analysis of one's past acts, a bringing up to one's awareness, a need to ac-'knowledge,' what it is that must be confessed. Thus, in that Medieval tradition, the meaning came to include not only the knowledge shared but also the awareness of that knowledge being shared. Put more succinctly, in order to have knowledge of something, it is necessary to be aware of that something that you are knowledgeable about, a position not that far from Descartes. The full impact in Locke's *Essay* in this discussion of consciousness, however, is not drawn from the occasional references to the term throughout the *Essay* but from the curious addition of Chapter XXVII of Book II in the second and all later editions. What makes this chapter remarkable, for one thing, is that the apparent cause for this addition arose from discussions that Locke had had with his very good friend and correspondent, William Molyneux. "Of Identity and Diversity," his title for this chapter, was also remarkable for its extensive use of and interpretations of consciousness. Using the term, or its root, a total of some 102 times in that single chapter more than adequately dramatizes the necessity that Locke subscribed to for its use and importance. Obviously this was the clearest and most complete expression and manipulation of consciousness at such an early date. Appearing as often as it did in a single twenty page chapter[39] and struggling with it as a part of any working definition of identity, it is not surprising that this term proved necessary for the later development of a modern sense of 'self' and 'individuality.'

Locke argued in Chapter XXVII, Book II that personal identity depended upon the same continued consciousness inhering in any "thinking thing." The operational word here was 'same' which he used with great consistency. That he is dependent upon the principle of sameness reveals how he retained a traditional world view as being fixed, even as he participated in the era's significant changes: specifically the idea of motion as natural and, for Locke, the development of a self in its dependent relationship to consciousness and empirical experiences. What he sought was proof of both a person and an individual as being one and the same, possessing one and the same identity consistently throughout one's entire life. This was an issue that hinged in part on the shift to a reason-driven view of the world. God was a fixed framework for any and all realities including an ontological self. The soul was an absolute given without substantive change, much as the constant that was drawn from its creator. In the theological world that followed the collapse of Antiquity this absolute worked well in conjunction with the ancient assumption that nature was inherently fixed rather than changeable. Nature might not be absolutely immutable, but any change that occurred still required an explanation, from the fall of a rock to the movement of the planets. While this Aristotelian worldview remained the norm in the Christian age, it had proven to be increasingly inadequate. Even the Copernican Revolution was little more than an attempt to short circuit the epicycle maze that had grown around the Ptolemaic system. Sir Isaac Newton was not only an acquaintance of Locke but when Newton became the leader of the Royal Society, Locke became its secretary. And although Newton and Locke were contemporaries, it was too early, much too early, for either one or both to rethink the very essence of nature, notwithstanding the new thoughts regarding motion and light.[40] Locke was prepared to confront self, however, when he stated very clearly and directly his position "...that *Self* is that conscious thinking thing,...which is sensible, or conscious of Pleasure and Pain, capable of Happiness or Misery, and so is concern'd for it *self*, as far as that consciousness extends." He then added the following: "...with *self*...not determined by Identity or Diversity or Substance...but only by Identity of consciousness."[41] The last thing to change in a changing world is the assumptions people apply to both everyday living and serious philosophical questions.[42] It is no surprise that while someone like Locke might be more willing to use the term motion in a more modern sense in place of that of the more theological and traditional fixed universe there was, as yet, no general agreement as to what new paradigms this would imply. The acceptance of God as Clock-Maker, uninvolved in our everyday life or the mechanistic universe, may have worked for Newton and Leibniz (and perhaps Locke, much as evolution worked for Darwin and relativity for Einstein) but many people at first found these ideas less than acceptable if not reprehensible. Motion is a rather interesting topic especially after Einstein, and psychologically, it will have an application to the issue of the relationship of space and time and thus its contribution towards full consciousness. Here let us observe that there was agreement with these seminal thinkers that in the newly defined nature of Galileo, Descartes and Newton, both space and time were absolute, in the sense of existing objectively and of being completely independent of any physical content. "Matter, to be sure, occupied and moved in space, but space itself remained, as Newton declared in Scholium II of the *Principia* (*Mathematical Principles of Natural Philosophy*, 1687), 'always similar and immovable.' For that reason, Henry More could describe space as, like deity, 'one, eternal, independent, Being in essence (*Ens per essentiam*), Being in act.'"[43]

A fixed nature was so prevalent that the idea of an unchanging nature in man continued into the literature of the eighteenth century, especially in a variety of novels and early autobiographies.[44] It would take still another century for the more modern and more existential view of constant flux to make an appearance. For Locke's era, a self, like "personal identity," was still defined as fixed and unchanging, the "same" in Locke's theory. As one student of the subject of the origins of the self has put it: "…personal identity is the identity of the self, and the self is understood as an object to be known."[45] The assumption was that to know what we mean by the self was a realistic goal because of its unchangeable nature, not unlike the much earlier soul. This certainty of an unchanging universe and self (always the "same") was linked to the unaltering nature of sin and virtue. It was this placing of fixed values that gave conscience such a central place within those theologically fixed walls of sin that for Locke confirmed the Bible as a fount of truth.[46] He always accepted this inherent value judgement within conscience, at least in the few occasions conscience appeared in his *Essay*, although its appearance was not anywhere as often as consciousness. [II. XXVII.23] As such, conscience could run parallel to consciousness as though, for Locke, it may have been possible that in his thinking they could have been born of different roots. And even consciousness, in Locke's view, could somehow contribute to the continuing meaningful role of God and his values. One Latin-English dictionary made it clear that it is possible historically to associate consciousness directly with conscience when it stated that: "conscientia,…*a consciousness of right or wrong, the moral sense, conscience*."[47] This would tie the rational act of consciousness with the faith-driven morals of the act of conscience. While the Enlightenment will continue this particular orientation, it is the rational side of the issue that drove Locke's thinking both as a process of being and that of action and is what is most historically important. As one Lockean scholar has pointed out: "For Locke, the prime fact about 'person' was that it was conscious of its manipulation of ideas [II.XXVII.9], the building blocks of reason, which accumulated as (analogical) evidence of the existence and nature of God. Being conscious of this thinking process, the 'person' guarantees the self's responsibility for its actions and tends to be regarded as a real agent, or an aspect of one."[48] Locke was replacing conscience with consciousness in so far as we must be conscious of our actions and thus accept our responsibility. He stated the premise as follows: "In this *personal identity* is founded all the Right and Justice of Reward and Punishment; Happiness and Misery, being that, for which every one is concerned for *himself*, not mattering what becomes of any Substance, not joined to, or affected with that consciousness." [II. XXVII.18][49] Locke was acknowledging "in his own way," according to Taylor, the very "...close connection between our notion of the self and our moral self-understanding."[50] This Lockean structure of knowledge was at a very early stage of development in offering a rational basis for moral behavior; a position that would cause Locke to be accused of Socinianism or Unitarianism. While this may have made him less an ally of traditional theology, it did represent the future direction of theological thought, i.e., that one could supposedly create a theoretical reasonableness for any and all religious interpretations without falling back into the dilemma of a scholastic *sic et non*.

The long conflict between reason and faith, first won in Augustine's favoring faith, followed by Averroes' consignment to a rather odd and altered type of Aristotelean categorizations, and finally resolved in the scholastic categorical unity brilliantly articulated by Thomas Aquinas, now moved to a modern commitment to reason. Faith was not to be confused with natural philosophy. What had been a reasonableness of faith now became a faith in reason. And the issue of personal identity and consciousness replaced the Medieval debates regarding substance and faith. If man, not God, were the arbiter of what was rationally valid, then a new attitude with an appropriate change in language would be necessary. As has been succinctly stated: "For a living being, Locke maintained, identity stands independent of the particles of matter that compose the body, and is determined solely by a consciousness of having performed certain actions."[51] And one may add Locke's complete analysis:

> Had I the same consciousness that I saw the Ark and *Noah's* Flood, as that I saw an overflowing of the *Thames* last Winter, or as that I write now, I could no more doubt that I, who write this now, that saw the *Thames* overflow'd last Winter, and that view'd the Flood at the general Deluge, was the same *self*, place that *self* in what Substance you please, than that I that write this am the same *my self* now whilst I write (whether I consist of all the same Substance, material or immaterial, or no) that I was Yesterday. For as to this point of being the same *self*, it matters not whether this present *self* be made up of the same or other Substance...[II. XXVII.16][52]

The confusion of the meanings of self and consciousness in the *Essay* should not be a surprise since that same confusion has not even now been resolved even after all these years of serious thought applied to the differences. Locke was opening a large door to an even bigger set of issues: He used words, sometimes relatively new words, in striving for what in retrospect would be considered a secular approach to the psyche. The developments of groundbreaking ideas are in part a corollary of a shift in language. In this spirit, Locke attempted to define the issue by using the consistency of memory as a buttress against the mutability of time: "…'tis plain consciousness, as far as ever it can be extended—should it be Ages past—unites Existences, and Actions, very remote in time, into the same Person, as well as it does the Existence and Actions of the immediately preceding moment: So that whatever has the consciousness of present and past Actions, is the same Person to whom they both belong." [II.XXVII.16][53]

Locke was committed to the idea of his "*same person*" concept in seeking to establish a single, consistent and unalterable self with the force of a unifying consciousness that would guide it through life. The appearance of the term "same" modifying consciousness, as an example in his chapter "Identity and Diversity," occurs seventeen times, a true commitment to the traditional view of unity and similitude. Still, it is not difficult to see hints of the modern self with a sense of significant subjectivity operating on some interior perch of the mind that nevertheless gives it, for him at least, the resemblance of a consistent identity. And there are some who have suggested, and even exaggerated, this element in Locke: "This radically subjectivist view of the person is defended by Locke through a series of bizarre thought experiments, e.g., of the same consciousness inhabiting different bodies, or two consciousness sharing the same, or bodies exchanging consciousness…"[54] As Taylor stated the issue: "Personal identity is the identity of the self, and the self is understood as an object to be known." Such loose interchanging of terms like personal identity with self can lead to more confusion than clarity, but then, as Taylor has pointed out regarding Locke's own position, "…it has this peculiarity that it [personal identity], essentially appears to itself. Its being is inseparable from self-awareness." If this doesn't leave the student of consciousness confused, Taylor adds that "…personal identity is then a matter of self-consciousness." Whatever confusion Locke may have had in delineating the meanings of *consciousness, awareness, personal identity, self, self-consciousness* and *self-awareness*, contemporary writings have often unfortunately further extended not only confusion but also lead the reader more towards incredulity than clarity.[55]

There have not been more than a few scholars who have studied Locke's discussion of consciousness, but one of the more interesting analyses is that of Richard Aquila who suggested that "...the deeper the significance of Descartes's concern does not lie in his identification of consciousness with a type of self-consciousness. In the context of modern philosophy we might characterize such an orientation as more Lockean than Cartesian." In other words, as the sense of a self developed, it did so along side the growth of consciousness, with the possibilities for the eventual creation of a self-conscious ontology, although limited in its presence and more relevant to Locke than to Descartes. This is because, in part, the "Cartesian notion of consciousness" is more restricted in that it is "...of a single state that is at once self-directed and directed toward what is an external object." For Locke the term *self-consciousness* was used but only in the context and as an extension in further support of the absolute historic consistency of what is always that "same" consciousness.[II. XXVII.16] It should be concluded, therefore, that for Descartes, consciousness is little more than awareness, an undefined term that can be construed as an arrow pointing to an external and recognized object. As Aquila has rightly noted: "...the notion of a single, bi-directional state of consciousness is in turn conceptually connected with a particular development in the modern use of the terms 'conscious' and 'consciousness.' It is connected with their use to signify consciousness of objects and of the world, where such consciousness goes beyond the mere perception, cognition, or even the 'awareness' of objects and the world."[56] Aquila further suggests that the "...evolution of this notion in its modern linguistic setting is mediated by developments in poetic contexts. The upshot is not simply permission to speak of a consciousness of objects and the world," for this contributed to the "...most fundamental mode of 'inner'-directedness," and is a "...matter not of distinctively inner-directed states but of one's mode of awareness of the world at large."[57] Thus, consciousness cannot exist without an interior mental state where the word and action of conscious delineation occurs, notwithstanding the relation that consciousness can have with outside objects. There can be no doubt that the development of modern fictional literature could prove a revealing source of data regarding the maturation of our sense of self.[58]

The argument follows that "...personal identity, the self, is the *I* that accompanies all consciousness."[59] While this is easily offered, it is not easily clarified and thus not easily supported. Even Locke had to agree that this "sameness" may be something of an illusion, when we look at other parts of his discussions. Disregarding the issue as to how one remains the same when new and altering impressions are constantly bombarding our *tabula rasa*, it is extremely difficult to retain the idea of the "same" when our perceptions seem to perish as they occur; indeed, Locke defined time as a "perpetual perishing," which belies a human need for some sort of continuity in time.[60] Identity, used as pointer to the self, depends not only on our perceptions but equally on our consciousness as an ability to recall through our memory—as an act of continuity—what it is that is noted.[61] We know, of course, that we are not always residing in a conscious state. And yet for Locke, it must follow that if there is to be the presence of a self, the *same* self, if one must, it should exist as a continuous conscious activity. So how to address the discontinuities in our experiences? Without being in a constant state of consciousness, there must be something else that would bridge the existence of our self with any of those given moments when we are without our consciousness. Memory became that bridge.[62] When Locke suggested that memory was a part of our consciousness and a component for the continuity of identity, he introduced a new and important idea for later scholars who have wrestled with the modern problem—which Locke neglected—the problem of definitions.

While Locke offered only incremental additions of insight to Descartes' introduction, this one century, with Descartes' analysis and Locke's singular chapter, proved to be the one century where consciousness found a solid foundation that is often confusing but cannot be dismissed. The century of the Scientific Revolution could also be referred to as the century of the Birth of Consciousness. What Descartes had introduced, Locke proceeded to give a new shape. In Book II, Chapter XXVII, section 9, Locke attempted to create a psychological meaning which appears for the first time in the light of the word *knowledge*: "...wherein *personal Identity* consists...which, I think, is a thinking intelligent Being, that has reason and reflection, and can consider it self as it self, the same thinking thing in different times and places; which it does only by that consciousness, which is inseparable from thinking, and as it seems to me essential to it..." Disregarding whether Locke believed that everyone could acquire a personal identity, (considering he did not have a very high regard for the ability of most people to reason, think or reflect) the question of the meaning of consciousness clearly appeared to be one of knowledge: knowing that I am thinking. Does this suggest that for Locke the average person will never know what it is to be conscious? This would be consistent with one of the original meanings of the original Latin term, *conscire* (to know). Defining consciousness as knowledge—to know—does not occur very often, however, since Locke, like Descartes, preferred another synonym, that of awareness, a synonym that still retains a dominant role. Still, we now have both knowledge and memory being offered and added to whatever a conscious state of mind is, and this offers the further possibility of an important indication, moreover, that perhaps not all people are equally conscious or capable of being conscious.

Of the examples of what Locke meant by 'aware' in the context of consciousness, the following is representative: "For to be happy or miserable without being conscious of it, seems to me utterly inconsistent and impossible."[II.I.11] To not be conscious, i.e., aware, of being happy or miserable, makes no sense since it is the awareness that makes such feelings recognizable, if not applicable. In addition, it is this use of 'consciousness' as 'awareness' that may have contributed to the common usage of consciousness being associated with wakefulness; to be awake is to be aware which is to be no longer unconscious (a view popular with many of today's neuroscientists). The full quote may be of some help since it reads as follows: "If the Soul doth *think in a sleeping Man*, without being conscious of it, I ask, whether, during such thinking, it has any Pleasure or Pain, or be capable of Happiness or Misery? I am sure the Man is not, no more than the Bed or Earth he lies on."[II.I.11] The opposite would be unconsciousness which would mean to be unaware, or asleep, or, in the case of a boxer, for example, knocked-out. This would be just one more opportunity for potential confusion, unfortunately, for an already difficult term, for if being awake is being conscious then the question must be asked: what is the problem with the use of the term awake rather than *conscious*? If being awake is being conscious then we should only use that word—*awake*, and discontinue the use of the term conscious. And to add further confusion, Locke sometimes would go so far as to associate being sensible of events as a form of awareness. "But I do say, he cannot think at any time waking or sleeping, without being sensible of it. Our being sensible of it is not necessary to any thing, but to our thoughts; and to them it is; and to them it always will be necessary, till we can think without being conscious of it." [II.I.10][63] There can only be thinking when there is consciousness and there can only be consciousness when we are awake which means that we can thus claim awareness when awake and thinking. He even goes so far as to suggest that when we are awake we are always thinking and, *ex post facto*, we must always be, therefore, either conscious (awake) or unconscious (not-thinking). "I grant that the Soul in a waking Man is never without thought, because it is the condition of being awake: But whether sleeping without dreaming be not an Affection of the whole Man, Mind as well as Body, may be worth a waking Man's Consideration; it being hard to conceive, that any thing should think, and not be conscious of it."[II.I.11] Thinking must be dependent upon consciousness for Locke just as it appears to be for Descartes. But does this mean consciousness is to be understood as knowledge or does it mean simply to be aware that we think—or is it being aware of *what* we think? There is a proclivity in Locke to suggest that what makes us fully human, the person as distinct from the biochemical man, is the presence of this consciousness:

> Or if it be possible, that the Soul can, whilst the Body is sleeping, have its Thinking, Enjoyments, and Concerns, its Pleasures or Pain apart, which the Man is not conscious of, nor partakes in: It is certain, that *Socrates* asleep, and *Socrates* awake, is not the same Person; but his Soul when he sleeps, and *Socrates* the Man consisting of Body and Soul when he is waking, are two Persons: since waking *Socrates*, has no Knowledge of, or Concernment for that Happiness, or Misery of his Soul, which it enjoys alone by itself whilst he sleeps, without perceiving any thing of it; no more than he has for the Happiness, or Misery of a Man in the *Indies*, whom he knows not. [II.I.11]

But this is not only about being conscious, aware or knowledgeable. For if we are without awareness of our actions or our sensations, i.e., what Locke calls consciousness, personal identity is shortchanged: "For if we take wholly away all Consciousness of our Actions and Sensations, especially of Pleasure and Pain, and the concernment that accompanies it, it will be hard to know wherein to place personal identity."[II.I.11] Locke stretched the point here and immediately above as Fraser noted when he explained, "Locke holds that consciousness *constitutes* personal identity, which he has to reconcile with his argument here, that continuous personality is consistent with intervals of unconsciousness—in sleep, &c." a small but important detail that Fraser here introduces.[64] Again we do a disservice to expect brilliant consistency by Locke in his use of consciousness when the best minds today are uncertain.

Thinking may help form the person, but in itself it cannot complete the creation. "To suppose the soul to think, and the Man not to perceive it, is, as has been said, to make two Persons in one Man."[II.I.19] Knowledge precedes memory in the Lockean psychological sequence, and awareness precedes thought and knowledge which is the prerequisite to knowing you are thinking. But perception is what the aware state of mind must also possess in the form of consciousness, which "…is the perception of what passes in a Man's own mind." [II.I.19] Again we find another definition of consciousness, now to be equated with *perception* when defining a 'person,' especially the same person.

This being premised to find wherein *personal Identity* consists, we must consider what *Person* stands for; which, I think, is a thinking intelligent Being, that has reason and reflection, and can consider it self as it self, the same thinking thing in different times and places; which it does only by that consciousness, which is inseparable from thinking, and as it seems to me essential to it: It being impossible for any one to perceive, without perceiving that he does perceive.[II.XXVII.9] [65]

Thus, we recognize that, "To ask, *at what time a Man has first any* Ideas," we would find, "…is to ask, when he begins to perceive; having *Ideas*, and *Perception* being the same thing."[II.I.9][66] To think, to perceive and to be aware of one's own sensations and reflections is to acquire ideas or knowledge, and thus to retain "sameness." "This few would think they had reason to doubt of, if these Perceptions, with their consciousness, always remain'd present in the Mind, whereby the same thinking thing would be always consciously present, and, as would be thought, evidently the same to itself." [II.XXVII] And the "same thinking thing" and "same consciousness" are indispensable ingredients in the creation of personal identity which for Locke is the "same person" and the "same self." Thus, "*Self* is that conscious thinking thing," which he can address, for "…(whatever Substance made up of,…it matters not) which is sensible, or conscious of Pleasure and Pain, capable of Happiness or Misery, and so is concern'd for it *self*, as far as that consciousness extends."[II.XXVII.17][67] Even self-concern is dependent upon our consciousness, although it is hard to image an animal not being "concerned for itself," for animals would also be obedient to Locke's first Law of Nature which was self-survival. "That this is so, we have some kind of Evidence in our very Bodies, all whose Particles, whilst vitally united to this same thinking conscious self, so that we feel when they are touch'd, and are affected by, and conscious of good or harm that happens to them, are a part of our *selves*: i.e. of our thinking conscious *self*. Thus the limbs of his body are to every one a part of *himself*: He sympathizes and is concerned for them."[II.XXVII.11] Our very existence, the knowledge of being affected, as in being "touched," is dependent upon the operation of our consciousness and is why, for Locke, self-survival is a necessary conscious choice. As Locke continued: "Cut off an hand, and thereby separate it from that consciousness, we had of its Heat, Cold, and other Affections; and it is then no longer a part of that which is *himself*, any more than the remotest part of Matter."[II.XXVII.11] Clearly the constant for the same person resides within the actions of consciousness. Additionally, this would apply to the very nature of the self. "Thus we see the *Substance*, whereof *personal self* consisted at one time, may be varied at another, without the change of personal Identity:

There being no Question about the same Person, though the Limbs, which but now were a part of it, be cut off." [II.XXVII.11][68]

While Locke suggested that consciousness existed within every part of our physical being and is dependent upon attachment to the whole being, he did not recognize that our memory was always very selective, being in general emotionally driven and never complete, which is, close to concepts supported by very recent discoveries regarding memory. This could make consciousness incomplete although this does not appear to be what Locke had intended. It may be, in part, because Locke sometimes became fixated on sameness (consistency?). "For the same consciousness being preserv'd, whether in the same or different Substances, the personal Identity is preserved." [II. XXVII.13] That is to say, it will remain the same. A consistency of consciousness, never changing, definitely appears as an odd idea to the modern mind if not to an empiricist, in principle, except in so far as he might imply, as Fraser noted, that memory was the cement for this consistency.[69] But then one must remember that without a consistency, as with an unchanging and fixed conscience, it would be difficult to justify the penitent's relationship to God and morality.

Locke did recognize, however, that there were some difficulties that he simply could not resolve. As he stated at one point in his discussion, "Can another Man perceive, that I am conscious of any thing, when I perceive it not my self?" And further, "…it seeming easier to make one's self invisible to others, than to make another's thought visible to me, which are not visible to himself." [II.I.19] How does one know for certain that one is asleep, aware and thinking?[70] Here, he pushes his thinking towards the Cartesian beginnings of the modern idea of subjectivity as in a central fixed subjective state of mind. And just as modern day neuroscientists, cognitive philosophers and behavioral psychologists reject the notion of a non-perceivable subjective self, so too does Locke wonder out loud that perhaps, "This is something beyond Philosophy…"[II.I.19][71] Locke was right, of course, for it would take centuries of thoughtful study to create alternative philosophical and psychological frameworks for the still problematic discussions of what we could best describe as a subjective mentality and any understanding of our psychology. The jury is still out regarding understanding the self, individuality and consciousness since the interior voice has remained a hidden and therefore a difficult if not questionable phenomenon. We will wait for the modern developments of psychology and psychoanalysis as well as and post-modern artists and writers for eventual useful suggestions if not guidance.

Throughout this discussion Locke continued to use the term consciousness analogous to memory since this is the completion of the process of moving from the perception of sensation and reflection of outside objects of which one is finally aware of thought in the form of ideas which become the home of knowledge and remembrance. The final step of this knowing, therefore, resides in this ambiguous entity we call memory:

> But that which seems to make the difficulty is this, that this consciousness, being interrupted always by forgetfulness, there being no moment of our Lives wherein we have the whole train of all our past Actions before our Eyes in one view: But even the best Memories losing the sight of one part whilst they are viewing another; and we sometimes, and that the greatest part of our Lives, not reflecting on our past selves, being intent on our present Thoughts, and in sound sleep, having no Thoughts at all, or at least none with that consciousness, which remarks our waking Thoughts. I say, in all these cases, our consciousness being interrupted, and we losing the sight of our past *selves*, doubts are raised whether we are the same thinking thing; i.e. the same substance or no. [II.XXVII.10]

Consciousness is not only absent when sleeping, it is also non-continuous, giving us an ability for forgetfulness (i.e., no memory), for no one is always conscious at all times, a view still held today by some, including this writer. Memory is as intermittent as consciousness, which raises the interesting question of whether Locke believed that we were less a self or possessed less a personal identity when not in a fully activated state of our memory (or consciousness) which is not most of the time. To relate meaningfully to this question depends upon our understanding of consciousness as it relates to memory. There can be no doubt that he believed that it was a natural state for a thinking being to have the same consciousness no matter the substance: "Different Substances, by the same consciousness (where they do partake in it) being united into one Person; as well as different Bodies, by the same Life are united into one Animal, whose *Identity* is preserved in that change of Substances by the unity of one continued Life." [II.XXVII.10][72] Locke never tired of making the point: "For it being the same consciousness that makes a Man be himself to himself, *personal Identity* depends on that only, whether it be annexed solely to one individual Substance, or can be continued in a succession of several Substances." He can make this argument because, "For as far as any intelligent Being can repeat the *Idea* of any past Action with the same consciousness it had of it at first, and with the same consciousness it has of any present Action; so far it is the same *personal self.*" [II.XXVII.10] Again the problem for Locke is making an assumption that later studies make untenable; specifically, he assumes that memory is somehow constant, unchanging, always what has been and always the same—again that magic word. We now know that memory is remarkably pliable and therefore is never to be assumed to be a fixed constant.[73]

Because Locke was concerned with knowledge as an interior condition where a subjective state was more a matter of psychology than an issue of metaphysics, he had no intention of being trapped by the medieval question of substance:

> ...as to...Whether, if the same thinking Substance (supposing immaterial Substances only to think) be changed, it can be the same Person? I answer, that cannot be resolv'd, but by those who know what kind of Substances they are, that do think; and whether the consciousness of past Actions can be transferr'd from one thinking Substance to another. I grant, were the same Consciousness the same individual Action it could not: but it being a present representation of a past Action, why it may not be possible, that that may be represented to the Mind to have been, which really never was, will remain to be shewn. [II.XXVII.13] [74]

Whatever exists within substance it is not consciousness since "...personal Identity reaching no further than consciousness reaches," can never reach the object observed.[II.XXVII.14] Fraser offered the following explanation of Locke's view of substance in a footnote where he asked: "How does Locke thus distinguish the spiritual substance from the self that is given in consciousness? Is not a person a spiritual substance manifested?" The answer, as is so often with Locke, depends upon the meaning of his language. As Fraser stated: "Here again he uses words which seem to imply that a substance, material or spiritual, is one thing, and its manifestations of itself another and different thing, by which too the substance is concealed rather than revealed." In other words, Locke is more interested in the operation than in the manifestation, for as Fraser noted, "...is not our idea of personality rather the highest form in which substance can be conceived by us?" Fraser continued by suggesting that what is discussed here is "'Consciousness,' i.e. memory," that includes its "latent possibilities."[75] The potential for conscious perception, thought and memory is always present while its actualization is not, a recognition of an Aristotelian distinction. Consciousness itself can never exist in the realm of substance. Locke stated that "This may show us wherein *personal Identity* consists, not in the Identity of Substance, but, as I have said, in the Identity of *consciousness*..."[II.XXVII.19] Sometimes Locke even goes so far as to speak of a thinking substance as though the mind were itself a substance. But substance is not a material entity while it remains dependent upon the active working of our memory: "For granting that the thinking Substance in Man must be necessarily suppos'd immaterial, 'tis evident, that immaterial thinking things may sometimes part with its past consciousness," after which it could "...be restored to it again, as appears in the forgetfulness Men often have of their past Actions, and the Mind many times recovers the memory of a past consciousness, which it had lost for twenty Years together." He is suggesting here that consciousness appears to be something we can lose and then reacquire by regaining our memory. This creates a condition, however, he already admitted to, of giving a single definition of a personal identity in one and not two people. You could end up otherwise with a form of dualism that Descartes could not imagine: "Make these intervals of Memory and Forgetfulness to take their turns regularly by Day and Night, and you have two Persons with the same immaterial Spirit, as much as in the former instance two Persons with the same Body." This is but one more argument on behalf of the important role that consciousness plays in establishing what we would call a person in possession of a self: "So that *self* is not determined by Identity of Diversity of Substance, which it cannot be sure of, but only by Identity of consciousness."[II.XXVII.23][76] Locke came close here to making even substance dependent upon consciousness just as he also made our own identity a private condition. "Can another Man perceive, that I am conscious of any thing, when I perceive it not my self? No Man's Knowledge here, can go beyond his Experience." The issue again is one of that contemporary conundrum that always appears when discussing a subjective condition as a basis for one's identity. "Wake a Man out of a sound sleep, and ask him, What he was that moment thinking on. If he himself be conscious of nothing he then thought on, he must be a notable Diviner of Thoughts, that can assure him, that he was thinking..."[II.I.19] Locke expanded his position by making an analogy with physical hunger of our bodily substance which he considered not as private as the interior experience of our thoughts.

> If they say, the Man thinks always but is not always conscious of it; they may as well say, His Body is extended, without having parts. For 'tis altogether intelligible to say, that a body is extended without parts, as that anything *thinks without being conscious of it*, or perceiving, that it does so. They who talk thus, may, with as much reason, if it be necessary to their Hypothesis, say, That a Man is always hungry, but that he does not always feel it: Whereas hunger consists in that very sensation, as thinking consists in being conscious that one thinks. If they say that a man is always conscious to himself of thinking; I ask, How they know it? [II.I.19]

One may be able to note something about our body, but they would not be able to know something about our thoughts. "And they must needs have a penetrating sight, who can certainly see, that I think, when I cannot perceive it my self, and when I declare, that I do not; and yet can see, that Dogs or Elephants do not think, when they give all the demonstration of it imaginable, except only telling us, that they do so." [II.I.19]

Any meaningful discussion of this modern concept should not forget, therefore, that the Latin term originally was not used for consciousness but rather for conscience. The significance of this relationship can be found at times in the *Essay* where Locke sounded as though he was discussing the value judgment that inheres in conscience rather than the more neutral consciousness (a position articulated even now). "In this *personal Identity* is founded all the Right and Justice of Reward and Punishment; Happiness and Misery, being that, for which every one is concerned for *himself*, and not mattering what becomes of any Substance, not joined to, or affected with that consciousness." [II.XXVII.18] Happiness and misery are rooted in Hobbes' discussion of pleasure and pain, an issue that would continue throughout the English empirical school of thought in the centuries that followed. The idea of rewards and punishment that we associate with conscience originated within the reflective act of the confessional. As Locke stated, any conflict in consciousness as past action and consciousness of present activity can "…be best resolv'd into the Goodness of God, who as far as the Happiness or Misery of any of his sensible Creatures is concerned in it, will not, by a fatal Error of theirs transfer from one to another, that consciousness, which draws Reward or Punishment with it." [II.XXVII.13][77] It should not surprise us, therefore, that there is this attachment of happiness and misery to reward or punishment since there was in the Lockean schema, an early hint, if not step, towards secularized psychology. Because, in a divinely-centered world happiness occurs only for the blessed and only after death, the idea of seeking happiness parallels with that transition from conscience to consciousness. There is in this period of transition a bridging of the medieval other-world of heaven and hell with the modern sense of this world of pleasures and pain. It is within our memory that we find a key component for an appropriate review of our sins and our virtues. Fraser, in one of his copious notes, offered his own insight into the role of memory, person and the association of consciousness with conscience:

> Throughout this discussion, what Locke means by 'person' must be kept in view. If person means the living agent, or the man, then appropriation of past actions by present consciousness is not necessary to sameness of personality; since they are the

same living agents, whether conscious or not of past and present actions. But a 'person' with Locke means an agent who is *accountable for past actions*. Although present 'appropriation' by consciousness of past actions is not implied in a living agent, it is necessary, according to the *Essay*, to our being persons, i.e. the proper objects of reward or punishment on account of them. If a man is not justly responsible for a past act, he is not the *person* by whom it was done, although he is the *man* or *living agent* through whom it was done; as no man can justly be punished for an action that cannot be brought home to his consciousness and conscience, as in a Book of Judgment.[78]

As conscience should give the penitent a basis for reviewing his life and reviving the soul in its relationship to righteousness as a unity of rights and wrongs under the umbrella of a divine order, so consciousness, it could be argued, can create a wholeness, another kind of unity, for one's varied experiences, one that could imply the possibility of happiness on earth. At least this explanation would give Locke his consistency, his uniformity, in the exercise of consciousness. Any divisions or barriers between awareness and perception, knowledge and ideas, and memory and consciousness would disappear. It is suggested here that through the act of confession and the willful review of our mind (our experiences and thoughts) we create a whole person at a given moment, the moment of judgement. A similar wholeness of person could be created within the psychological characteristics, consciousness rather than conscience, of our being. The difficulty is that on first reading, there is no problem viewing Locke as unable to make up his mind whether he wants consciousness to be exclusively tied to memory, as many have suggested.[79] Fraser is willing, at least, to imply a potential for a unifying ontological explanation when he ties together these two terms as he did above and as he also offered with the following: "We are thus responsible only for voluntary actions which can by consciousness be appropriated to ourselves; consciousness uniting the most distant actions in one and the same personality."[80] The implication is that consciousness is not only the seat of personal identity but it could be additionally argued that it equally could be the unifying force that takes control of all past memories, putting them together into a coherent process that is created by some volitional act. It is the exercise of this consciousness that creates the singularity of person and thus sameness according to Locke:

> For it is by the consciousness it has of its present Thoughts and Actions, that it is *self* to it *self* now, and so will be the same *self* as far as the same consciousness can extend to Actions past or to come; and would be by distance of Time, or change of

> Substance, no more two *Persons* than a Man be two Men, by wearing other Cloaths to Day than he did Yesterday, with a long or short sleep between: The same consciousness uniting those distant Actions into the same *Person*, whatever Substances contributed to their Production. [II.XXVII.10][81]

Locke made the case for the unifying role of consciousness in keeping all of our memories, our knowledge and any awareness or perception we may be having at this moment, tied together into a coherent whole, a tight knot of mental order and unity.

> Could we suppose any spirit wholly stripp'd of all its memory or consciousness of past Actions, as we find our Minds always are of a great part of ours, and sometimes of them all, the union or separation of such a Spiritual Substance would make no variation of personal Identity, any more than that of any Particle of Matter does. Any Substance vitally united to the present thinking Being, is a part of that very *same self* which now is: Any thing united to it by a consciousness of former Actions makes also a part of the *same self*, which is the same both then and now. [II.XXVII.25][82]

The same self and the same person unified by the sameness of our consciousness operates not so much as a repository of that which has happened but as an exercise of the will to put together the reality of our singular and moral existence. This aspect of consciousness recently has been called 'access consciousness' by some of those confronting this "...circle that everyone wants to square."[83] As Locke put it: "Nothing but consciousness can unite remote Existences into the same Person, the Identity of Substance will not do it. For whatever Substance there is, however framed, without consciousness, there is no person; And a Carcase may be a Person, as well as any sort of Substance be so without consciousness." [II.XXVII.23] This "substance" only proves, however, recognition. Locke spent so little time discussing the will and its relationship to consciousness that the combination of awareness, knowledge and memory would have to be deduced. (The concept of a conscious volition remained for later generations to discover.) In effect, then, Locke possessed two states of consciousness: one that is the actual present tense exercise of the function; the other state, which as we noted is more implied, occurs when there is a conscious volitional unification of our present awareness, our knowledge (which could be considered something akin to our short-term memory) and the very memory itself.

There are reasons for us to be cautious in suggesting this idea of consciousness as an exercising, unifying and organizing activity, three aspects of collecting and structuring our personal identity. The implication is that consciousness ties together our awareness of experiences and their reflections regarding our experiences and that such an act is a foundation for perceptual knowledge and eventually a foundation of our memories. The major reason for this caution is because of the language that Locke, much like that of Descartes' had been found insufficient to express these revolutionary new ideas. We should remind ourselves of what Yolton noted about the ambivalence and even contradictions that Locke had to live with: "Locke was the inheritor of two traditions: the one, the new science with its radically new categories, the other, the older scholastic tradition which he in part ridiculed but did not entirely reject."[84] As has been noted, Locke was not only not interested in becoming part of the clergy and its dependence upon traditional approaches to knowledge, he was not interested in taking part in the 'enthusiasm' of the day with its fanatic religious extremism. Locke was far too thoughtful and introspective for that. He had studied with and had been deeply influenced by Robert Boyle, attending some of his scientific lectures. Boyle became a fellow member along with Locke and Newton of the Royal Society. Locke therefore may have been rooted in the traditional academic assumptions in his early schooling but was equally immersed in the scientific revolution as an adult, spending hours and days, immersed in its new, dynamic and experimental activities. His language struggled to find expression for those new thoughts that were forming around this new science. Yolton put it well: "The very newness of the language employed by Locke startled some, convinced others that he was merely using another ruse to attempt to persuade the reader of the novelties to be found within, and led still different readers to distrust the entire position."[85] In addition to consciousness, ideas, and memory "Locke had to struggle" in order to clarify his insights with the development of such confounding terms as *immaterial substances, selves, thinking substances, rational souls* as well as *persons*.[86] As Locke observed: "I know that in the ordinary way of speaking, the same Person, and the same Man, stand for one and the same thing."[II. XXVII.15] The development of his thought required that he draw a distinction between *man* which he used in a substantially ordinary sense and *person* which he sought to use in a sense which would allow the possibility of disembodiment or embodiment in different bodies. Locke possessed a clear vision of the relationship and difficulties of clarifying ideas through language, and, given the language at hand, he was not always as clear either in his meaning or in his intent.

Locke had enough of a concern with the problems of language, that of the four books of the *Essay*, the third, "Of Words," has been referred to as "Locke's logic."[87] To study Locke, then, one must be prepared to not just be concerned with his ideas but equally with his use of language. As Locke stated it so clearly: "...*words in their primary or immediate Signification, stand for nothing, but the* Ideas *in the mind of him that uses them*..."[III.II. 2] And later he continued: "...in the beginning of languages, it was necessary to have the *Idea*, before one gave it the Name..."[III.V.15] He concluded that words have two uses: first, for each of us to record his own thoughts; and second to communicate those thoughts to others.[88] (This is reminiscent of one of the difficulties that Plato had to confront when creating the necessary language to express his original and unique thoughts.[89]) It is little wonder that one of Locke's contemporaries, Henry Lee "...admitted that he had not always been able to follow the language of the *Essay* since it was 'writ in a kind of new Language.'"[90] Yolton added that: "It was not only the term 'idea' which troubled Lee: the entire *Essay* was written in an unfamiliar language."[91] The very word 'idea' often appears to have bothered some more than most of the terms he used:

> John Milner (1700) objects that the frequent use of the term 'idea' confuses the reader, suggesting that 'Mr. *Locke* and others, had done better if they had not amus'd the Word so much with the term *Idea* as they have done.' Like Lee and Browne, Milner contrasts this language with the ordinary language which he prefers, arguing that Mr. *Locke* had made his ESSAY more easy and intelligible to all sorts of Readers, if he had made use of other Terms, and not fill'd every Page almost with the mention of *Ideas*.'[92]

Because of the new role of an interior state of mind in reading and with it an interior thinking by way not only of images but also by language, a private self and language was created, a self that found it more and more difficult to cross the divide from one's own conscious state to someone else's state of mind: For Locke, language is before anything else the means by which the mind makes ideas known to itself. 'Words,' he [Locke] says, 'in their primary or immediate signification, stand for nothing but the ideas in the mind of him that uses them.' Language is the means of self-realization."[93] A clearer statement could be arranged if we were to suggest that it is the interiority of language, a personal tongue as it were, that leads to the possibilities of 'self-realization,' if not also for the development of a private ontology, a personal individuality and eventually self-reflective consciousness. Language could now be used solely to record one's thoughts and experiences for oneself alone.[94] As the public voice in public readings and gatherings declined and with the expansion of personal libraries of finely printed books, there must have occurred more private association with words and ideas. Because ideas can vary

Locke could argue that language was ultimately private: "And every Man has so inviolable a Liberty, to make Words stand for what *Ideas* he pleases, that no one hath the Power to make others have the same *Ideas* in their Minds, that he has, when they use the same Words, that he does."[III.II.8][95] We are witness to the early steps in the development of a modern linguistics and even more so, a psychology often described in our own world as that of isolation, just as specialization eventually will contribute to this growing separateness from community and eventually from society.

Notwithstanding the dilemma of working with a language still rooted in a scholastic and feudal order, Locke was not only capable of clarifying some of his points, even if he did confuse us regarding others, he was insightful enough to anticipate a couple of contemporary commentators on the issue of language and its workings. It has been observed, for example, that: "We can very well imagine Locke to agree with speculations to the effect that a universal grammatical structure underlies all languages and that this structure is present in human nature in the form of innate dispositions to pick up linguistic rules of various sorts. Locke could be expected not to take issue with this speculation because his real objective in Book I is not to attack an innateness concerned with *meaning* but rather with *truth*."[96] Locke created in his own language from the past while at the same time pointing to the future, as so many of the great minds do, repeatedly asserted, especially in Book III, that words became signs of ideas "...not by any natural connexion, that there is between particular articulate Sounds and certain *Ideas*, for then there would be but one Language amongst all Men..."[III.II.1][97]—a claim postulated by an "Adamic"(or "angelic") language. For Locke, a language works only by the tacit consent among its speakers to respect the familiar use of words, that is, by agreement (contract).[98] He had tied this notion to his use of the social contract which was fundamental for his writings in philosophy. What makes language is history, i.e., convention, or an agreement over time. When someone steps out of the circle of time it is either a mistake or a revolution, (something witnessed in 1688) and perhaps for some, both. There is no doubt where Locke stands on language, especially looking at his philosophic contributions to the rise of modern historiography. It has been suggested further that: "...the beginning of language confirms the core of Locke's philosophy: the rejection of innate ideas and the rehabilitation of sensation. The conclusion was also just one step from saying that the genetic epistemology or progress of the mind is recorded in words." It is little wonder that, "Locke's section [Book III] became the rationale for using etymology to reveal the trains of thought that had been in the minds of speakers in the course of the progress of the mind."[99] The interior existence of a thought in words replaced here the simple external and rhetorical meaning of words. As Aarsleff put it: "From having been the history of things, etymology became the history of thought. The section that Locke had subtitled 'words ultimately derived from such as signify sensible ideas' became the most quoted and pervasively influential passage in the *Essay*."[100]

It should be pointed out, nevertheless, that Locke would appear to be only a qualified friend of the discipline of history since he was more preoccupied with being a student of all things scientific when not involved in political activities along with general and political philosophy. It will be some time before the Enlightenment will make peace with historical scholarship, for as one commentator has offered:

> …to the early Eighteenth-Century scorn of history numerous reasons have been assigned, as explanations also have been given for the return to history that characterized the latter part of the century. [And one can also list]…among the causes for the early unpopularity of this study, it seems reasonable to suggest that the sheer inaccuracy of the subject, implied in Locke's statement that history is altogether a matter of probability, would have made it an undesirable pursuit in an age when thinkers were trying to be very exact and scientific.[101]

Locke stated his position clearly that the certainty of our sources cannot be trusted, and his position should be quoted in its entirety:

> I would not be thought here to lessen the Credit and use of *History*: 'tis all the light we have in many cases; and we receive from it a great part of the useful Truths we have, with a convincing evidence. I think nothing more valuable than the Records of Antiquity: I wish we had more of them, and more uncorrupted. But this, Truth it self forces me to say, That no *Probability* can arise higher than its first Original. What has no other Evidence than the single Testimony of one only Witness, must stand or fall by his only Testimony, whether good, bad, or indifferent; and though cited afterward by hundreds of others, one after another, is so far from receiving any strength thereby, that it is only the weaker. Passion, Interest, Inadvertency, Mistake of his Meaning, and a thousand odd Reasons, or Caprichio's, Men's Minds are acted by, (impossible to be discovered)…[IV.XVI.11][102]

Personal experiences and reflections which are the source of knowledge, a knowledge to be held as secure as that which the Christians once held now becomes personal knowledge. Everything else to be known must be second hand. Others who were anti-historical were even less sympathetic than Locke to tradition for as Maclean noted in his study of Locke's influence on historic scholarship; "…the brief but striking remark of Walpole's father, 'Anything but history, for history must be false,'" was the more typical response. And if this is not enough of a negative attitude towards the discipline of history, Maclean adds that "Johnson is equally prejudiced against this 'shallow' species of writing, because it is so conjectural. 'We must consider,' he says, 'how very little history there is; I mean real authentick history. That certain Kings reigned, and certain battles were fought, we can depend upon as true; but all the colouring, all the philosophy, of history is conjecture.'"[103] As antiquarian information, there is nothing invalid in collecting the dates of battles and monarchies. Beyond that, history was seen to be little more than opinion. But the work of men like Locke on language would eventually alter our view of the study of history. Even the same Samuel Johnson (1709–1784), "…took his basic view of language from Locke and included some thirty-two hundred quotations from him in his famous dictionary, more than from any other source."[104] Etymology was the foundation for this change in attitude, for "…the central conception of these views of the nature of language is the familiar romantic notion that the genius of a nation is expressed and revealed in the genius of its language." It is thus that "…etymology changed our sense of the past not least by making historicism possible because it gave us the means to understand history by entering the minds of those who had lived and acted in it."[105]

This is not to say that Locke represented the beginning of a 'romantic' (individualistic) attitude even if his work offered some creative challenges that help transform philosophy into a more positive and acceptable discipline. It will not be until two centuries later that we find the argument for the beginnings of modern historiography that would expand the Renaissance sense of periodization, notwithstanding Burckhardt's error, since secularism was not yet dominant and made no serious appearance until the late eighteenth century. Without freedom from theologically received truths, no space could be found for modern historiography, just as there is no theatrical tragedy without space between man and heaven. While this is a modern capacity, the modern ability to stand alone, it nevertheless did have some roots in the changes growing out of the Renaissance, Scientific Revolution and Enlightenment. As one of the better Renaissance scholars has noted: "The rise of science introduced a new element into the Renaissance idea of the Renaissance; men became aware of their era not because it was like another period which had died away and was reborn but because it was different from any other era of the basis of its own distinguishing accomplishments. This notion of uniqueness, the result of the rise of science, was converted in the seventeenth century into the concept of modernity…"[106] What could be more unique or more modern psychologically than the appearance of the developed self and interior life defined by a time noted and space accepted? This new perception can be seen in the transformation of the meaning of the term, *revolution* which had once meant the act or state of the overthrowing the established political order and was understood by Locke in his comments regarding the 'Glorious Revolution' of 1688. This is not to say that revolutionary characteristics of political changes were necessarily the only ones occurring, since the additional revolutions in the sciences and arts were equally matched by a revolution in our vocabulary and use of syntax.

"Traditionalism was a new word," equally "as were such otherisms such as 'antiquarianism,' 'classicism,' 'medievalism,' 'orientalism,' and 'primitivism.'"[107] This new science, new politics, new economics and generally new era were equally one of a new language demonstrated by the plethora of dictionaries that previously would have been unimaginable.[108] The old and new would continue for a time to exist parallel to each other, only separated primarily by a difference of attitude regarding time and space. It is natural to see that this could become a basis for describing the eighteenth century as one "…more aware of the radicalism and innovation implied in the act of a political overthrow."[109] But if this form of 'radicalism' is the child of the eighteenth century, we would do well to remember that it was supported in part by the birth of the discussions regarding consciousness in the century before. The term radical must wait in the wings for later meaningful application.[110]

While the English tended to retain a primary interest in the philosophy of politics, there also were significant changes in the philosophy of language impacting upon the understanding of the ontology of psyche and thinking. This was pointing to a world that would eventually be preoccupied with personal identity in its earliest systematic treatment in the writings of John Locke. *Consciousness* and *self* as well as *ideas* were not only being used in new ways for new mental and cultural constructs, they were becoming increasingly important terms for the understanding of the nature of what it means to be human. Unfortunately, these and other terms, would increasingly become more complex and difficult to define. The problem, in part, was that there were at least two very clearly distinct and contrary mental activities striving for center stage in the seventeenth century: on one side of the stage stood traditional and reformative religions with their own languages, on the other the upstart secular and scientific world with newer and in some cases more than just mathematical languages. In itself, this represented an outstanding metaphoric opportunity. New, yes, and yet still maintaining certain traditional aspects: These inherently non-allied characteristics would continue in English life during a period of serious social and political transitions well into the nineteenth century.

'Conscience' continued to be part of both an English and Lockean lexography as a well as a way of self-communion and which remains today an applicable conception appropriately expressed. As has been seen, Locke never was able to use the term *consciousness* "clearly and consistently."[111] There were some fundamental immutable assumptions dividing both camps. A good part of the difficulty centered around the view of man as fixed and unchanging, even if living within this new natural philosophy, granting a divine-driven existence, space and time, in opposition to the view that sees living in flux as more human and a secular-driven one with a more humanized sense of time and space. This confused state of incompatible loyalties would continue to be problematic not only for the subject of history but also for the early beginnings of etymology. Geoffery Barraclough, when once discussing the transition from the mid-century and the writings of Hobbes to the rise of the Royal Society later in the century, noted that:

> Down to around 1650 and 1660 the old confusion, the old interconnection and interrelationship between politics and religion were still very evident in Europe. Hobbes' *Leviathan*, published in 1651, is regarded as one of the foundation stones of modern political theory. But we should never forget that no less than half of Hobbes' book (the half we do not read) is concerned with the 'Christian Commonwealth' and 'the kingdom of Darkness.' After 1660 there was a reorientation and a secularization of thought, of which the writings of John Locke are the clearest evidence. The symbol of this secular change was the foundation in London, in 1662, of the Royal Society.[112]

The mind and its mental experience had become the central guide in searching out answers in place of divine or biblical imperatives for nature's wonder, although religion still dominated the lives of most citizens and retained an healthy and active presence in a variety of ways, even in Locke's world of writings. For secular mental activities to be given their due, more extensive explorations were needed. Those who would follow Locke would look less at heaven above and more at the earth under their feet and would more accurately reflect a growing attitude away from scholastic thinking that was increasingly becoming less and less the normative at the end of the century. As Aarsleff stated, any part of the fulfillment of a position should be reviewed as a whole:

...language confirms the core of Locke's philosophy: the rejection of innate ideas and the rehabilitation of sensation. The conclusion was also just one step from saying that the genetic epistemology or progress of the mind is recorded in words. With this step taken, Locke's section became the rationale for using etymology to reveal the trains of thought that had been in the minds of speakers in the course of the progress of the mind. From having been the history of things, etymology became the history of thought. The section that Locke had subtited 'words ultimately derived from such as signify sensible ideas' became the most quoted and pervasively influential passage in the *Essay*.[113]

This developing rejection of innateness and the embrace of etymology, especially as operational within the mind, was the lifeline to the eventual creation, ironically, of modern historic writings. One fine example offered from the eighteenth century would be the French thinker, Étienne De Condillac (1715–80), who wrote extensively on the new scholarly topic of language. The most famed lines, however, may have come from the sixth volume of the French *Encyclopédie* (1756), under the heading "Etymology":

> ...the young philosopher Turgot, who later became known as a great economist and administrator. Here, saying that he was 'speaking according to Locke,' Turgot called etymology 'an interesting branch of experimental metaphysics,' thus echoing d'Alembert's words about Locke having made philosophy the 'experimental physics of the soul.' Words being like grains of sand that humanity has left in its course, they alone can show us the path the mind has followed in its progress toward the present.[114]

In other words, to know the thoughts of an age, nature as they understood it, or their space and their time, you must first know their language and semantics. Turgot did not stop here, however, since he also argued that "...those who study the march of the human mind in the history of past modes of thought must march with the torch of etymology in hand to avoid falling into a thousand errors."[115] What is interesting in this quote is the use of the torch metaphor. When looking back on the relationship of conscience and *synderesis*, it is notable that the "...metaphor of the torch became a commonplace for celebrating the power and lessons of etymology almost as if we were entering Plato's cave with our own light."[116] The use of light to represent the good, a Platonic as well Stoic and Christian theme, remained something of a commonplace. What is fascinating is the movement towards a unique future with many words born as well as altered out of its traditional past and metamorphosed into the world of the Enlightenment. One clear example of that newborn pattern must be, of course, the term *consciousness* because of its originality and secular tone.[117]

It is a truism that seventeenth and eighteenth century historians lacked objective understanding of other eras much as they had little understanding of the diversity of peoples in other areas of the world. Massive diversity, or diversity at all, was not an understood concept. As they had difficulty comprehending the diversity of values and assumptions of others they "...were unable to penetrate to the specific, changing motivations and mentalities of those other ages."[118] Donald Lowe in his unique study, *The History of Bourgeois Perception*, had suggested that the transformation in mentalities ran parallel to the changes in "...development-in-time despatialized historiography." This occurred in part because "...with the extension of the historical landscape, time now possessed a depth and diversity which it previously had lacked." The moment something as basic as our sense of space and/or time is humanized, diversity is created. With the decline of the certainty in sameness that Locke sought and the beginnings of an interior individuality it is not surprising that Lowe found, "It was now much more difficult to maintain that human nature and reason were constant, universal." This development had already been introduced in the Renaissance with the "...concept of anachronism, i.e., each age possessed its own coherence, integrity." It wasn't until the Scientific Age, however, that the problem of historicism was discovered, "...i.e., how could one age know another," and as Lowe put it, "if each, including our own, were distinct and self-contained?"[119] This is comparable to the question of how could one know another's consciousness since it was 'distinct and self-contained?' Because our relationship to time (history) and space (language) was being totally transformed during that era, is it little wonder we witness the first signs here of the rise of a more personal, interior, and self-driven conscious individuality?

Although there is no evidence that he comprehended any of this, Locke nevertheless did broach this issue not only with etymology but with his emphasis on memory, his touch-stone along with consciousness in the creation of his idea of personal identity. After all, personal memory is much like a nation's memory—(history) writ small. Thus "...the change in approach was not a result of mere accumulation of information," as Lowe noted, "...but the result of the displacement of representation-in-space by development-in-time."[120] Space and time, language and history, and our understanding of these terms were central to Locke's *Essay*, even if much of it may seem unremarkable today. When (time) we have a Lockean experience and where (place) we have it play a significant role in the forming of ideas that follow, i.e., its context. What is significant is that while this change in mentality may have come about slowly, it clearly received a serious and indispensable boost by way of the contributions of Lockean empiricism. "History looked, in the Middle Ages, like a straight line divided into parts, with a beginning and an end." After the seventeenth century and the beginnings of a Lockean psychology, time moved into an what could be considered an "...infinite past and forward into an infinite future." Clearly this is a more modernist view. It is the "...modern habit to see time itself as a process" which was an idea that "...began in the eighteenth century, when people commenced to number years backward from the birth of Christ." The stages of earlier historic writings were not a "...progress or evolution, as we would see them, or even a process; they were cycles, mere repetitions, and anything like a process in them was a process of decline."[121] In other words, time was still perceived to some extent as non-dynamic, more like Locke's view of memory.

A *tabula rasa*, or blank slate, must by definition mean change, even if Locke sought a consistency in his concept of "same." New impressions would imply new data and a changing context. And his legacy, ironically, for all his commitment to sameness, contributed far more to change than consistency. Knowledge was an accumulative process as the eighteenth century French philosopher Fontanelle observed: "...an educated mind is, as it were, composed of all the minds of preceding ages; we might say that a single mind was being educated through out all history."[122] Locke's contributions were, while unintended, nevertheless moving the Western mind toward the creation of a world more secular and linguistically sensitive and which meant, as with our changing understanding of nature, much more fluid and freer than anything ever known. As has been correctly pointed out, the "...meaning of the term 'personal identity' broadened as the concept of freedom developed."[123] Where there is increased freedom, an interior state of mind or psychological condition (unlike liberty, which is an external political condition), there is both the opportunity for a sense of self and an increased arousal of individuality attached to a developing personal consciousness. Many of today's "...historians have been enthusiastic about the Enlightenment 'discovery' of man and its formulation of new, scientific secular concepts of the personality and identity; about the birth of self-awareness and the exhilarating odyssey of individualism that occurred during that period..."[124] Locke was doing a great deal more than addressing the issue of identity or what it might mean for someone to be conscious. He was establishing the foundations for today's debate regarding what makes us human—the very issue of nature versus nurture. From then on, the argument stands that a singular inner space, given a specific outer experiential nudge at a given times makes for a unique individual.

All of this and so much more must be attributable to the transformation of our understanding of the transformed psychological nature of our mentality that arose from a dramatically altered sense of space and time and by extension, our sense of language and history. We first begin by finding "…literary evidence of a modern awareness of interiority while any philosophical conceptions of the individual person that is independent of particular roles does not come to prominence until the eighteenth century." Traditionally, whatever selves did exist they did so only in a public sense, even while we can perceive the first beginnings of some sort of private selves in the writings of these early figures: Montaigne, Descartes and Locke. Today's historians and sociologists have viewed these as "inner deep-seated changes in the psyche" that reflect "the emergence of modern European and American man."[125] In explaining these changes, they point to a number of factors, one of these being the "…pluralization and segmentation of society—the fact that modern society requires human beings to play a variety of different, even mutually incompatible roles in various reference groups." In addition to learning to wear a variety of different hats, there is what is considered the "related factor" of "…increased social mobility [space], beginning in the Renaissance and on the increase ever since." One is reminded of the time Locke spent in Holland where he refused an offer to travel to Colonies. He may not have wished to partake of this enlarged geographic space but he must have considered this factor in his judgements. For, "…this may have encouraged a heightened awareness," of not only his place in the scheme of things but also of the "…possibility of fashioning human identity in an artful, manipulative way…"[126] Determination through one's position, as it were, or a hint of what will become known as a 'Be Here Now' mentality is at least a possible implication.

The modern self like the modern individual can be said to be making their earliest appearance from the Cartesian and Lockean roots growing into the following century where "…something recognizably like the modern self is in process of constitution, at least among the social and spiritual elites of northwestern Europe and its American off-shoots." This growing sense of self was held together while retaining "…two kinds of radical reflexivity and hence inwardness," both of which were rooted in an Augustinian heritage with "…forms of self-exploration and forms of self-control." As Charles Taylor has further suggested, "…these are the grounds, respectively, of two important facets of the nascent modern individualism, that of self-responsible independence, on one hand, and that of recognized particularity, on the other." We might describe this new-found self, additionally, as the "individualism of personal commitment." After all, one of the appeals of the "...various purified ethical visions of Renaissance humanism, of Erasmus, for instance, or the later neo-Stoics, was partly that they offered such an ethic of the whole will against the more lax and minimal rules demanded by society at large."[127] We can attribute this in part to Locke's desire to make personal identity, the person in place of the man, a responsible agent for his actions. This also would account for the secular use of consciousness as still possessing a hint of conscience, and is about as close as Locke comes to implying that there is something called conscious choice, i.e, something that much later will be labeled existential.

One way to look at consciousness at its earlier stages of development is as a conscience without a God. Its presence may be minimal but it is implied nonetheless, and the very nature of modernity, it has been suggested, hinged after all upon the role of consciousness in everyday life: "Modernity is defined by a consciousness of novelty, and it is this awareness that forms the cornerstone of Hegel's philosophy. For Hegel, the most recent stage of history, beginning with the Reformation and continuing with the Enlightenment and the French Revolution, enjoys a special preeminence insofar as the principle that it brings to explicit articulation, freedom is the motor force of history (novelty) itself."[128] But Hegel leads us too far astray from this story and the age of Locke and consciousness although it does demonstrate the extent of Lockean influence. And it may not be an exaggeration to offer that Locke's work with language, consciousness and identity, earned him the accolade of genius, as Diderot would define it a few decades later. "In the article 'Encyclopedia' Diderot wrote that '...man of genius can put a nation in a state of fermentation, shorten centuries of ignorance, and carry knowledge to a point of astonishing perfection.' Geniuses are rare, but among them we will hardly ever 'find any who have not improved language. Creative people have that special quality...It is the heat of imagination that enriches language with new expressions.'"[129] Another Englishman, John Stuart Mill would concur in the nineteenth century for it would be likely he would agree that Locke would qualify for this distinction.

If a genius leaves the world altered, Locke certainly should qualify in the fields of psychology, philosophy, linguistics and political theory. The only downside is that we still live with the view that "Consciousness is the biggest mystery. It may be the largest outstanding obstacle in our quest for a scientific understanding of the universe." And in fact "Consciousness ...is as perplexing as it ever was. It still seems utterly mysterious that the causation of behavior should be accompanied by a subjective inner life."[130]

In the beginning when we first discussed Descartes we acknowledged that the glass was half full with a quote from Paul Churchland; now at the end of Locke we have an alternate view from another contemporary student of consciousness David Chalmers who suggests that the glass is half-empty. Could it be the next genius to come will find that the glass is in fact both?

CHAPTER EIGHT

ENLIGHTENMENT AND THE BIRTH OF MODERNITY

Cultivate your own garden—Voltaire

FROM THOUGHT TO SENTIMENT

What had been an argument for the reasonableness of one's personal faith was now being replaced by a belief in reason. This was clearly demonstrated in 1660 when the Royal Society was founded and then incorporated two years later with Locke a contributing member and Hobbes a contributing non-member. Sir Isaac Newton (1642–1727), as its first president and the creator of revolutionary laws of mathematics of motion, calculus, made a perfect transition from sixteenth century beginnings of the new science to the thinkers and authors of the Age of Reason. In 1687 the Royal Society published the *Philosophiae naturalis principia mathematica* of Isaac Newton. "This epochal work, which was destined to serve as the frame of reference for physics and other sciences for more than two centuries, was itself a synthesis of advances made during the two preceding centuries."[1] The center of intellectual understanding, first regarding the universe and the natural order we live in, followed by attempts to define being human, was clearly shifting, in particular to the new rationalists now appearing in England and in France, those who inherited the thinking of Locke and Descartes.

It was in this new world that both Descartes and Locke had attended to liberating language from the limitations of scholasticism. Even though Descartes had written in both Latin and French, the latter was now the language of the land. In England, "…this demand for plain speech and the anchoring of terms to palpable things like bodies" and which, "has been one of the main characteristics of British philosophy since Bacon and Hobbes initiated it…"[2] The end of the uniform language—Latin—began when the feudal, manorial and localized systems began to collapse. "Under the Feudal system the predominant social control had been the basis of tradition. This system had prescribed a man's status and the roles he had to play as the various departments of life." With this system everyone knew their place and the language that reflected their place. As can be seen with Chaucer's social structure, "...economic life was static and secure, regulated by the Guild system which blocked undue competition and self-assertion. There was little social mobility."[3] Birth almost always dictated social standing and any opportunities that existed to escape were rare. "But in the fourteenth and fifteenth centuries, with the rapid growth of international commerce, a new economic order began to emerge. Large commercial companies were formed." The comfortable and orderly system constructed over centuries from its base in antiquity was dramatically changing. "Work was decreasingly regulated by Guilds and men who had previously worked for themselves had to hire out their labor to the growing class of ambitious employers." Time and space were being removed from the exclusive realm of the divine and given over to the efficiency of human control. "Time became valuable and clock-faces began to show the quarter hours; thrift, efficiency, and hard work became virtues; social life became more and more characterized by acquisitiveness, the desire for power, and desire for honor." The space of the new world and the heavens did not fit any traditional cosmology. This new cosmology only expanded out of the Renaissance and Reformation. For as Hobbes pictured it, the new values were marked by a "...desire for power, and desire for honor....life indeed became rather like a race."[4]

It is within these accelerating times, this opening of space and philosophical opportunities, the changes in political order, the opening of religious diversity and economic opportunism, the discovering of both new worlds and this new consciousness which became the basis of a self, at least a Lockean self, that marks the beginnings of our own contemporary world. If we dramatically change our sense and understanding of time and space not only in the creation of history and expansion of language, but also in the living of our daily lives where the interior begins to compete with the external world —whether dominated by innate ideas or empiricism— then opportunities for individual development truly appear. As one commentator regarding Hobbes has stated so well:

> And just as motion came to be regarded as normal in Galileo's universe, so too was social mobility increasingly taken for granted. Individual effort as well as traditional status were coming to determine a man's place. In the religion of Protestantism all believers were priests: the individual was alone before God; and he had to make his lonely way in the Quest for salvation by his own individual effort. The great gains of this movement were in the field of individual liberty, self-discipline, and personal responsibility. But they were won at a cost, and the cost was the loss of security.[5]

The opening doors of opportunity, the knocking down of social walls and religious limitations and the uncertainty that Descartes and others sought to overcome led to a struggle for a new order, one that was dominated by the new natural philosophy and with it an understanding of our world through the new methodological reason as a means of discovery.

The certainty of the world we live in, the nature of that world and most importantly the relationship between nature and man was now bringing forward important and very complex problems. What is the nature of being a human being? What is it to be alive in a state of nature? What is humanity's appropriate political and social status? And what is fixed and what is variable? The issue then became one of how to study something as central as our very existence without the guidance of the Holy Word, especially if Bacon is correct in arguing for a new method of disinterested observation. What is the role of God in such a Christian world? If the traditional center will not hold then something new must fill the void. As it turns out there were two contrary forces vying for center stage by this time, one a drive towards something of an individual sense that had been developing since the Renaissance, and the other being the issue of a central executive power in the newly developing nation states. Of equal interest was the congruence between these two forces. As one commentator has put it:

> Although these two tendencies, the one toward individualism and the other towards the centralization of executive power, were in a sense complementary to each other, they were also obviously opposed. Direct conflict was partly averted by the king winning the support of the more wealthy of the new middle class. Trade and strong government go well together. Henry VII and Elizabeth, for instance; made great use of this class of new men who made money by ability and achieved social status by buying land with it. Hence the great disposal of Crown lands during the sixteenth century, which admirably met the monarch's need for money and the new men's need for social status.[6]

This should be no surprise to students of Hobbes or those who would expand the arguments for the Divine Right of Kings or the early development of a mercantilistic economy. The forces of singularity in arts, literature and science were marked in contrast by the strengthening of these very centralized governments and new economics. Without the addition of the guilds as patrons of the arts, for example, many of the great Renaissance works of art would not have come into being.

Analytic governance began to replace the traditional, i.e., Divine Right of Kings, as the model of government.[7] The same could be said for our understanding of humanity since in some ways as with the Renaissance humanism, a new cultural man was being added to the newly discovered natural man, which by the eighteenth century was also becoming analytic man. As we have seen in our observations regarding Descartes and Locke, with the earliest stages of self-identity also came an analytically—rather than a spiritually-driven being. The first tool for this change and analysis was a new language drawn from Shakespeare, Montaigne, Descartes and Locke that had taken on a new urgency with many new potential meanings. Whether mathematical or narrative, a new age of rhetorical and written techniques was developing, not only in the sciences and arts but equally in the new and untested politics that were growing out of Machiavelli's insights. For the English this was especially trying. It is little wonder then that the dominating force in the Enlightenment search for understanding was fulfilled by philosophical tomes and narratives in poetic and novel forms were particularly unique and forceful in England.

The term *Enlightenment* is difficult for historians. The idea of people being motivated exclusively or even being dominated by reason is on the surface far less normative than one would anticipate and as in the case of ancient Athens, rational society was more dominant in the rhetorical than the literary mode. It is rather facile to state we had lived in the past with a faith determined reason and were now moving to a faith in reason, although certainly appealing, the fact is that reality was more complex and diverse. In looking at man and nature by way of reason there is as much confusion if not more than there are secured facts and it is in the interpretation where the confusion becomes an even more major problem. The breadth and depth of representative thinkers in this important step toward modernity—the eighteenth century—are impressive if not necessarily the singularly greatest thinkers in the history of philosophy. As has been observed, "…most historians would agree that while such men as Voltaire, Diderot, d'Holbach, and Helvetius were superficially conversant with the major intellectual currents of their time, they were not particularly astute as philosophers; their doctrines are often shallow and unoriginal."[8] And an interesting footnote calls attention to other scholars attending to these philosophers of the eighteenth century as not, "…philosophers in the usual sense, but were primarily combative social and moral thinkers, usually with a strong tinge of scientific dilettantism."[9] This may account for another observation that suggests that some of these writers used philosophy "…as a polemical device—for the Enlightenment was indeed unabashedly polemical. The *philosophes* used reason and empiricism and feeling to construct, at least in theory, a better world, to argue for abandoning the lamentable defects of past and present."[10] Of these social reforming and political philosophers, one that should be considered as an extremely fine example of wearing two hats at the same time, one being a reformer and the other a philosopher, would have to be the Baron de Montesquieu (1689–1755). Here was a political philosopher who not only described the relationship between various climates and the system of political order, he also strongly subscribed to the idea of a more equitable society in his *Spirit of the Laws* (*Défense de l'espirit des lois*, 1748). The idea of 'the people' became increasingly central to these French pre-Revolutionary thinkers[11] as well as some in England. Although it should be mentioned as a caveat that, "modern psychology was as yet unborn, and Montesquieu's scatter-shot efforts in sociology by no means inaugurated a systematic discipline."[12] Nevertheless he was a serious political philosopher who made a very important impact on the fathers of the United States Constitution in his theory of tripartite system of government.

Still, the idea of the 'enlightenment' was eventually given some developmental discussion by Immanuel Kant in his short essay, "What is Enlightenment?" in 1784, which is nearer the end rather than at the beginning of this historic period. This period does reflect a growing conviction that if faith cannot establish a certainty that overcomes death and opens up an opportunity for the life of the individual then reason as a certainty must be the answer. This fact alone justifies the following comments regarding this period: "The *philosophers* of the French Enlightenment represent western man's last attempt to impose ethical coherence upon his life by means of his reason. And though some view this enterprise with misgiving, the general tendency is to treat the *philosophes* with great sympathy and veneration."[13] While this may appear to be worth considering a 'misgiving' for some readers, it nevertheless is a fact that there were many bright stars following in the traditions of Descartes and Locke who attempted taking up the mantel of morality (or ethics) that was felt in decline if not diminished since the Reformation; turning to the new art of reasoning as a basis for morality seemed to many as an appropriate approach. At the same time, as we shall see, there is the irony that the Cartesian unified system began to decline in popularity, for the Enlightenment thinkers were not fond of Desartes' idea of innateness and the metaphysics it implied. Even in France, for a time, there were new attempts to reconstitute a uniform system, more in harmony with the writings of Locke. After the Age of Reason, however, the rest of French history will be dominated by Cartesian thinking, innate ideas and metaphysics.

What turned out to be the major problem with the Cartesian scheme ironically centered upon the very original and also revolutionary idea of the *cogito* (thought and idea without extension in time and space) as distinct from that of matter (material and substance with extension). Put in simplistic terms, the argument runs that if you 'think' your arm should rise rather than some other part of your anatomy, how do you account for this consistency? The idea of the arm rising is only an idea and does not displace space as an object like the arm itself does according to Cartesian metaphysics. Furthermore, the arm somehow will 'tell' you with pain or in some other way to lower that arm and not some other part of your anatomy. There is a direct and a correctly constant corollary for Descartes between that which extends in space (*res extensa*) and that which will not (*res cogitans*). If you are feeling pain sitting on a post you will 'know' (cognitize) to move the body and not, let's say, write a poem. This one-on-one consistent corollary creates a unity between actions and thought, between ideas and matter, between the 'I' and objects. This addition to the Baconian argument on behalf of disengagement offers us the modern distinction and understanding between objective and subjective as we understand it today. But the question remains, if only two phenomena exist, object (matter) and subject (thought), how then, do they remain in continuous and symbiotic contact? Why shouldn't I think that my arm should rise and then I proceed to sit down? There are cases today where the body does not conform to thought as in the case of those who could feel the sensation of the amputated leg or those who would hear someone speaking who is not there. In the former this is not an uncommon condition, one referred to as a phantom sensation, while in the latter, the hearing of voices is usually most associated with schizophrenia, although those same voices can now generally be suggested to be the person's own inner voice.[14] The only answer that Descartes was prepared to offer was what were called 'animal spirits,' which he also referred to as vortices and which he eventually centered in the pineal gland or the 'seat of the soul.' While the idea of an embodied consciousness in this seat of the soul was supposed to resolve the issue, it offers, in the end, more confusion than answers and remains, even to this day, an unresolved enigma. How could there be only two entirely different entities, thought and material object, existing in entirely separate worlds and interacting upon each other? It should be kept in mind that it is this issue more than most any other that drove many thinkers who followed Descartes to attempt to find new and original means to either answer or at least resolve the question and thus fulfilling a Cartesian ideal of achieving a unity for all our knowledge. As the "Preliminary Discourse" by d'Alembert in the famed *Encyclopédie* reiterates: "…the infinitely varied branches of human knowledge into a unified system."[15] A new road to a world without uncertainty was believed to be found even though there were some serious unanswered questions yet to resolve. Moreover, this was one of the more important steps in the creation of a sense of a secular self by way of a given *cogito* that is personally one's own, an early realization that there was something of an individuation for one's ideas. Several important thinkers were to carry this issue even further and in doing so would contribute to the rise of English empiricism, French rationalism and even eventually German idealism.

Locke was one of the first to note that one relatively simple way to avoid this inherent problem within the walls of dualism was to deny the innateness component of Cartesianism. Locke saw no reason to assume there was something innately fixed within us that must somehow first be present and that must commune without external experiences. There were sensations that created simple ideas which then could be developed in varied combinations into more complex ideas. From a causal point of view this was a beginning of an empiricism well beyond any immediate implications in the thought found in the earlier writings of Aristotle. It was a basic tenet to suggest that being human from this tradition was now to be seen as experiential rather than innate, someone with sensations and memory and thus with the ability to consciously make choices. At least that was the implication of Locke's thought and was, of course, but one of the modern definitions that would replace *homo spiritus*. The question is simply that if there is nothing as a given, where and in what manner is there any interpretive, constructive force or place where these thoughts grow into complex ideas or even a philosophy? This remains an issue for contemporary empiricists today.

Along with the Lockean response of an anti-innate stance to Cartesian dualistic humanity, there were others more sympathetic, notably Nicolas Malebranche (1638–1715), a French philosopher and theologian and an important if unorthodox proponent of Cartesian philosophy. Among the most famous doctrines that developed from his pen was the introduction of a central role for God in dualism, an idea referred to as occasionalism. These ideas were motivated in part—as they were for Descartes—as an act of anti-skepticism, a growing attitude that worried many. There had to be cohesion for life to have order, but in this case, by reverting to divine intervention. If God is nothing he is consistent, at least that is how the argument goes. Thus, the idea of an arm rising is transmitted to God who, because of consistency, will make certain that the arm does rise and you do not fall down instead. The converse would equally apply. God, like all ideas, was central while at the same time well beyond any limits of any idea that would involve matter. Thus the bridge, the tie of consistent unity between the two separate and distinct forms of the real, the *res cogitans* and the *res extensa*, was divine intervention. While this theory had appeal for many, especially for the more religious, it did not match well with the clock-maker thesis most inaccurately associated with Newton. Nevertheless the clock-maker metaphor became commonplace: God had created the universe and then left this phenomenological world of substance to operate on its own without divine intervention, possibly with an occasional tinkering. The clock-maker is involved in the construction of the clock on your mantel but has little to with it after its creation. The desire for a uniformed rational order can be demonstrated by this metaphor:

> How intimately the clock image was connected with the French Enlightenment's conception of order emerges in the remarkable entries for 'system' and 'harmony' in Diderot's *Encyclopédie* (the question of their authorship, which is uncertain, is not crucial; if not written by Diderot himself, they must have met his and his coeditor's approval). Both entries deal with the rationally ordered integration of the parts into a complex whole, and both illustrate their arguments with clock imagery. The entry for system begins: 'System is nothing more than the disposition of the different parts of an art or a science into a state where they all mutually support each other and where the last ones are explained through the first. Those that account for the others are called *principles*, and the *system* is all the more perfect as the principles are fewer in number: indeed, it is desirable that they should be reduced to a single one. For, just as there is one main spring in a clock upon which all others depend, there is also in all *systems* one first principle to which the different parts that make it up are subordinated.'[16]

The power of the clock as a metaphor for knowledge and understanding offered a new set of assumptions for continental Europe prior to the mid-eighteenth century. In fact, it was "…virtually impossible to find metaphors or any other comments on the mechanical clock that were in any sense negative."

Of those who would confront immediately the Cartesian legacy, besides Locke and Malebranche, was the brilliant and influential Gottfried Wilhelm Leibniz (1646–1716), a resident the German-speaking world (Leipzig and Hanover) and a significant contributor to the creation of the clock metaphor: God is the great clockmaker. It was Leibniz "who introduced the clockwork metaphor. He did so in a strongly worded challenge of Newton's views on God's way of governing the universe."[17] It was precisely the desire for a role for God in his system that led him to create this metaphor, explicating the natural order of the universe tied to God's role, since contemporary thinkers were not prepared to remove God from the stage altogether even if placed in the wings.

> What Leibniz offered in place of Newton's alleged errors was the intellectualist image of the clockwork universe with God as its infallible clockmaker, an image that Leibniz had made the basis of his system of the preestablished harmony. Clarke answered with the familiar voluntarist argument that God's unlimited ability to exercise his power and his sovereign will were his most important characteristics and that to deny this would be to approach atheism. If someone claimed that a kingdom was so well governed that the king had nothing to do, that person should rightly be suspected of wanted to depose the king.[18]

Like Malebranche, Leibniz also followed in the footsteps of the Cartesians, insisting that soul and body were separate and distinct. Thus, if there was no action between the two, then how to explain the, "…complete congruity of their actions and experiences…" It was the conclusion of Leibniz, "…that both body and soul were programmed ('preformed') at their creation, like automata, to such perfection that their actions would always be coordinated in perfect harmony." To illustrate his scheme of occasionalism, he used the "…image of two orchestras playing the same music in perfect harmony but having no connection with each other, and by the analogy of two clocks whose running is completely synchronous."[19]

Actually, Leibniz was a very serious and deep thinking philosopher who made seminal contributions in geology, linguistics, historiography, mathematics, and physics. His creation of what he called "monads" was remarkably unique and an extremely complicated concept. He also deserves credit for his own contribution to the creation of calculus which Newton independently had also created. Rather then being concerned, as contemporaries were, as to who was first to develop this branch of mathematics to correspond to the expanding concepts of motion, it is more important for this study that the issue of time and motion as a secular phenomena had grown so great an issue that a new mathematics to deal with this abstraction of time and mechanistic clocks was required. As for the subjects of the self, individuality and consciousness, while he clearly had relatively positive if primitive attitudes to these new topics he was more preoccupied with keeping God active in the new world system. This is not to say he didn't place a great amount of stock on the principle of perceptual knowledge. As Leibniz put it "'*Nihil est in intellectu, quod no fuerit in sensu, excipe: nisi ipse intellectus*,' roughly, 'Nothing is in the understanding that was not [first] in the senses, except the understanding (or the 'I') itself.'"[20] As for his rather unique idea that the universe is made of 'monads,' an idea expressed in his *Monadolgy* (1714), and which is not in need of extensive analysis here, we may allow a more adept thinker on this subject to offer a brief summation with the following: "Monads are absolute points, centers exclusive of one another; these individual substances cannot in any way impinge or exert direct influence upon one another. Yet at the same time each Monad is a 'living mirror' that reflects the universe from its own finite point of view. Every part is, in its own way, the whole. Consciously or unconsciously it contains everything else: the state, the Church, the world and its history."[21] The closest he came to our topic discussed here is his following in the footsteps of the *cogito* (ergo the point of individuality's beginnings) since he would, "...start with the cogito, which they [Locke and Leibniz] distinguish from substance or the 'real self'..."[22] In an expanded form he held that, "...there are three kinds of self-knowledge: 1) immediate awareness of the pre-reflective 'I'; 2) reflective knowledge of the simple and substantial subject of thoughts; and 3) knowledge of myself gathered from observing my experiential encounters."[23] This dovetails with his analysis of, "...the concept of the self at three levels, and both see that the problem of personal identity arises in conjunction with the question of the relation between these levels."[24] In this he calls for us to understand, "It is not enough in order to understand what the me is that I am sensible of a subject which thinks, I must also conceive distinctly of all that which distinguishes me from other possible spirits and of this latter I have only a confused experience."[25] It would be a mistake therefore to assume that a rationalist such as Leibniz was not capable of retaining the Lockean force of sensations applicable to knowledge. Much like the metaphor of the clock, the mechanics is relevant only in so far as it is applicable to our understanding and our learning, moving us in the direction of a more materialistic view of the world, notwithstanding the existence of a God. This question of a growing fondness for retaining God with the rising nascent materialism will continue to haunt thinkers.

While the issue of the clock will be retained as an important topic in the eighteenth century move towards a more analytic view of the world, of nature and of humanity, it is useful to look at two other thinkers who were very drawn to the issue of this Cartesian dualism as well as the ideas of empiricism so inherent in any discussion regarding the creation of modern thought. The first of these was the Jewish-born, Baruch de Spinoza (1632–1677), a Dutch genius, metaphysician, epistemologist, psychologist, moral philosopher, political theorist, and philosopher of religion. He clearly was one of the more important thinkers of the seventeenth century since, among other contributions, he

Enlightenment | 319

offered an important legacy for the future. It is important to note that he lived and died in Holland, a fact of great importance since Holland was the one place in all of Europe that allowed the printing press to be used for a relatively free flow of ideas. Holland, as a Protestant country, was outside the scope of Rome's *imprimatur*: everywhere else censorship could be and usually was very extreme. Here, Locke as well as Descartes found enough open mindedness—particularly among publishers that were willing to publish some of their more controversial projects—to spend some of their time living, studying and writing.

A serious philosophical division was beginning. The English were relying more and more upon empiricism for knowledge; the Germans relied on the power of ideas unto themselves; while the French took a middle road as rationalists. When examining the thoughts of those who followed Descartes and Locke, Spinoza most likely would belong to that group called rationalists in the tradition of Descartes as would so many later French thinkers like Jean-Paul Sartre. Leibniz, however, placed so much stock on the power of ideas—including that of God—that he represents the beginnings of the tradition that we now think of as German idealism. Spinoza, despite his rationalism, leaned in that latter direction. His epistemology and psychology centered upon distinguishing between two fundamental and representational faculties, one of imagination and the other the intellect. Spinoza who was also willing to keep God as a central force, much like Malebranche and Leibniz, was also willing to enter the world of secular thought without denying a continuance of the role for some divine force. This 'secularization of theology' has proven to be an excellent description for the scientific and philosophic transformations of these late seventeenth century thinkers.

> The mind, says Spinoza, is actually the mental expression of the body's states, so that 'the object of the idea constituting the human mind is the body.' Knowledge is in the first place a matter of the mental characterization of bodily modifications (=sense perceptions), yielding 'confused experiences;' only in terms of 'reflexive' knowledge (*ratio*) can 'adequate ideas' be formulated which capture formal essences that are clearly and distinctly conceived. Yet this reflection is not clearly *a priori* but involves the development of 'common notions' out of an awareness of bodily modifications. And in both cases knowledge of the 'I' is subject: Spinoza says that 'The mind does not know itself, except in so far as it perceives the ideas of the modifications of the body.'[26]

Much as in the case of these earliest giants, Spinoza had an interest in the 'I' or self which was just beginning to emerge. It is possible that when Spinoza was expelled from his Sephardic congregation of Amsterdam at the age of twenty-four it could have occurred in part because he could or would not conform, at least not with the ideas he sought to explore, not unlike Galileo who also pushed against establishment assumptions. Most important for the story here, however, was the beginnings of both a serious sense of, as well as a defense of, a singular self separate (although not independent) from community definitions. As for those few centuries to be covered yet, it may be helpful to review the self in the seventeenth century as more a preface rather than an introduction. For any real and meaningful introduction of first, the self followed by the issue and questions of individuality, we must wait well into the eighteenth and more importantly the nineteenth centuries where one can find both the beginnings of such an exploration which will mature in the twentieth where their full implications come to life. This applies especially for a very reflective consciousness where introspection can expand far enough that there can sometimes be a state of estrangement as a by-product. For now, the example here suggested, is that as in the case of, "Leibniz, Spinoza's account of the self is grounded in *a priori* reasoning; also like Leibniz, however, he recognizes that there is a vacuity in the concept of the self considered apart from its role as mere experiencing subject."[27] This is a product in part of the ideas and writings of John Locke as noted by the Lockean scholar, John Yolton. From his interest in empiricism, Locke suggested some sort of, "Self, where the self represents the non-corporeal aspect of the live organism. The duality of this vital union of particles, with the body and with the self, indicates Locke's recognition of the tight relation between mind and body."[28] From Descartes' *cogito* to Locke's Personal Identity, a perceptible shift reminiscent of the Shakespearean tragic figure in the modern world, standing alone within his private soliloquy and personal issues, begins to point to modern angst.

The final commentator in the tradition of analysis of this recently discovered human condition, especially drawn from Locke's empiricism, is the Irish philosopher and Bishop of the Anglican Church in Ireland, George Berkeley (1685–1753). Berkeley was not prepared to advocate the idea of a self but was willing to accept the idea that one could have a notion of the self by way of a *reflex act*; that is, that in the act of perception we are conscious that there is something that is engaged in this perception. Because he was a reductionist, his thinking would not allow much more than this. It is in his contribution to perception, however, that has led to limited conclusions on the existence of external objects since Berkeley concluded that *"esse est percepi,"* that is, "to be is to be perceived." While perception is a fundamental issue for contemporary thinkers regarding the subject of consciousness and Bishop Berkeley is certainly making something of a contribution, he does appear to have gone further than others in his turn towards the world of idealism—i.e., for something to exist we must have a perception (idea) of it. At the time, Samuel Johnson's (1709–84) famed derision of this theory followed when upon responding to the arguments for idealism he is said to have kicked a stone, stubbing his toe and exclaiming, "I refute it thus." For Locke, materialism was not a issue since objects retained both primary and secondary qualities, i.e., the qualities inherent in things and those derived from our experience of them. Berkeley was simply following his own creative version of a set of responses to these beginnings by continuing a struggle against modern skepticism and in doing so creating a guaranteed role for God, the one answer that when it is made to work, is for philosophers an answer that would work, unfortunately, for everything and therefore nothing. Uncertainty would remain a major problem throughout the Age of Reason, notwithstanding the powers of and belief in scientific and applied thinking. Death was certain and without an agreed upon and satisfactory answer from the religious community, no one had yet found an answer in the secular world of natural philosophy—that is to say, not at least offering an alternative certitude to that of death until the end of the following century. It is true, however, that, "...with changing attitudes toward the future, even the concept of death underwent a transformation. Previously, ritual functioned as a preparation for the dying; it enabled the dying person to undertake the passage from this world to the next. But in bourgeois society, there was more concern for the ones left behind."[29] These were beginnings that would be explored in the next two centuries when there will be an even greater transformation drawn from some of the more contemporary and revolutionary thinkers and artists of our own era. All that need be said here is that there was something of a birthing of an interior being where there could reside something of a sense of a self where it could grow into maturity and where a cogito could develop, followed by a consciousness and be given a role in recognition of an expansion into new meaning. As one analysis put it: "...thought 'structures,' such as those of Leibniz, Descartes and Spinoza, bear within themselves the same spaces.... They, too, are searching from one interior space to the next."[30] Once objectivity is established as existing it followed that something of a subjective state must also have made an appearance, and there, a new understanding of that objectivity can be explored. While this can hardly be called dialectic it certainly is a step in that direction.

The replacement of the Stoic-Christian interior soul with the inner self that began with the paradigms of Descartes and of Locke signified a revolution. This is indicative of a variety of changes such as the growth of an even more secularistic and materialistic view in the following years, along with increased mercantilism, a new national identity as well as a corollary sense of one's own importance in being a singular self with an interior voice —something that thinkers all too often today erroneously equate with an expansion of the ancient idea of egoism. As an example, one scholar has observed that, "Descartes' influence was perhaps greatest in transmitting egocentrism to the eighteenth century. It was he who offered the world its first secular framework for total comprehension and, concomitantly, the most unequivocally secular conception of human dignity ever asserted in the West."[31] Granted that it is easy to attribute to a variety of earlier thinkers the development of a grander sense of the self when they are in fact describing the ancient concept of ego. Earlier we discussed that the ego as a Latin term does little other than to give a heightened sense or indicator of the person who is at that time doing the speaking. This is no more a traditional view of a strong sense of an independent being, a self, any more than it is an explication of a self-conscious being. The ontologically external being that we had been throughout our pre-modern lives was no more than our living with an identity that belonged to the group. "Previously that people were members of a community went without saying. It didn't need to be justified relative to a more basic situation. But now [in the seventeenth century] the theory starts from the individual on his own. Membership of a community with common power of decision is now something which needs to be explained by the individual's prior consent."[32] This is as succinct and a complete summation of the situation as could be made here. The idea of the ego and the self being one and the same is not only a confusion of language but is equally a very confusing use of both ancient Latin and modern English.

That there is something new arriving out of the age of Locke cannot be denied. His political theory is about as early as one can find a defense of the unheard concept of rights. It is this concept that can and should be considered as an important early contribution in the creation a legal definition and defense of the rights of the individual. This would be, of course, a very long process as are all major changes in history since rights once granted possess the additional dilemma of definition. Again as exemplifying this change of attitude from a member of a community to standing alone there is this: "Enlightenment thinkers had inherited an egocentric anthropology from the seventeenth-century predecessors who appeared impervious to their ideals of civility. Unleashed, perhaps, by the Reformation and secularized by laymen such as Montaigne and the libertines, egocentrism had gradually come to been shrined on all secular fronts."[33] Community had meant and still means for people that they were members of a collective faith and order, a church, and it is one of the reasons why something more like a 'secularized theology' is such a revealing attitude. "Analysis of the types of ritual devotions permitted by the Counter-Reformation Catholic Church reveals that most were structured in such a way as to de-emphasize collective experiences of *communitas*. The discrepancy between the psychic rewards for participation in the two types of devotional experiences is at the heart of the eighteenth-century decline in lay participation in church sponsored devotions."[34]

As for Protestant sects there is the example of Benjamin Whichcote (1609–83), a member of that remarkable group known as the Cambridge Platonists, an informal gathering of a few members from the Cambridge University community defending the Anglican faith in a growing sea of rationality while at the same time equally defending of the idea of innateness. Little wonder that as defenders of reason and of faith we end with an observation that, "…careful reading of Whichcote's sermons reveals the inexorable drift of this principle of Protestantism towards rational religion and secularization."[35] This really made little or no difference since faith was for the first time in our Western history in retreat with reason in the ascendancy; even the faithful were learning how to rationalize their faith. One last comment on this decline or at least alteration of faith during this period should be suggestive:

> During the sixteenth and seventeenth centuries, prompted by the threat of Protestant competition and guided by the mandates of the Council of Trent, the clerical hierarchy of the Catholic Church sought to change and reform the nature of lay Catholic devotional life. The success the hierarchy experienced in this endeavor was tempered after 1750 by the Enlightenment which brought an attack on the many tenets of Catholic faith from secular and secularized intellectuals, and—I would argue more important—a widespread decline in lay participation in Church-sponsored rites and rituals. These twin processes—intellectual alienation from Church teaching and lay alienation from Church ritual have been studied collectively by historians as dechristianization.[36]

While the soul had dominated the human condition for so many centuries, an alternative, the self, began first to match it in defining our being and, in time, eventually replacing it, not for all, but for at least the few more learned and thoughtful. After all, if you have a soul then you are the child of God; but if you have a self as well, or even the possibility of a self in addition or even instead of a soul then you are not only a child of your heritage and of nature but you are also a child with potential choices. At least this will eventually become something of a recognizable reality.

There were two conceptual components being created for a new ontological structure, one increasingly dominated by the idea of consciousness, while the other was a sense of self and individuality. Descartes had aided in the creation of an argument for the *cogito* which established the early basis for an internal self and while he did not pursue this implication, he did, nevertheless, create, by the nature of his reasoning, something of an ontology of self-reflection. Locke is a bit more complicated, for he as well as Leibniz were at least willing to, "…start with the cogito, which they distinguish from substance or the 'real self'…"[37] Moreover, Locke also makes, "…it clear that the vital union of particles of matter also includes the self where the self represents the non-corporeal aspect of the live organism. The duality of this vital union of particles, with the body and with the self, indicates Locke's recognition of the inherent relationship between mind and body."[38] One had to subscribe, then, to a Cartesian dualism in order to retain a fundamental sense of the self. The replacement of the spiritual—a conscience tied to an analytic partner—with a conscious self, was not simply a matter of the materialization and mechanization of nature, although for many this was the key event in this particular revolution in thinking. Locke, in harmony with technical changes, rejected innate ideas while retaining the self, demonstrating how powerful the forces of secular thought were growing as specifically applied to nature as a new guide to understanding. This revolutionary voice of the natural order was expressed so clearly in Bacon's understanding of the distance that must exist between the mechanism of the universe and the observer. The establishment of a new mental approach became the critical component in the development and operation of modern science. Culturally, one could now think in terms of a clock with hours, minutes and chimes, a world of business and the practical sense in the use of time instead of an efficacious deity, a unified organism and a fixed universe and all that is in it. Nature was still assumed to be an orderly experience that required embracing, discovery and disengagement from a traditional, fixed set of attitudes, habits, dispositions, assumptions and emotional prejudices and, in the end, perhaps even what had been a way of life. You step back from the observed and then into it, with the means of the 'cogito;' you then put space between various time frames in recognition of both organized and indifferent action. From now on, there will always be a compound dualism involved in any scientific or similarly objectifized observation: the observed which remains something to be observed in its own right, and the observer, the mind, the perception and perceiver as well as the beginnings of a self as engaged; one the subject, the other the object. This is why modern science requires a methodology that allows for and implies what we call being 'objective.'

Obviously it follows that one cannot only objectify what one is observing, but one may learn how to also objectify the self, a self that would be the observer and observed; at the least that has been one of the fundamentals of modern thought as expressed, for example, in psychoanalysis. This was a larger problem for the earlier thinkers (and many today) who wished to retain a deity, a fixed universe and orderly and uniform humanity, even if they were willing to abandon traditional and effective social roles while at the same time participating in the new mechanistic and analytic world:

> The move to self-objectification requires more than a belief in a mechanistic physics. Certain thinkers of the late seventeenth century, like Cudworth and Leibniz, each in his own way, took on board mechanism while trying to retain or rebuild a teleological view of the subject. The further step in disengagement from self involved a rejection of all such attempts. It was powered by a radical rejection of teleology, of definitions of the human subject in terms of some inherent bent to the truth or to the good, which might give justification to an engaged exploration of the true tendencies of our nature. Locke took the really uncompromising stance, the one which set the terms in which the punctual self was to be defined through the Enlightenment and beyond. He went beyond Descartes and rejected any form of the doctrine of innate ideas.[39]

Locke did not struggle to find some central replacement for the soul, breaking with a tradition from the days of Zeno and the Stoics. But he believed that the self existed as an interior experiencing being without having a defined structure of innate ideas, although having innate capacities and rather favoring experience and memory for some sense of consciousness. Leibniz took this a step further when he argued, "'It is not enough in order to understand what the me is that I am sensible of a subject which thinks, I must also conceive distinctly of all that which distinguishes me from other possible spirits and of this latter I have only a confused experience.'"[40] This sense of an 'I' without reflection may not have been that uncommon in the previous decades but it is this reflective activity that will in the end remain with us as an important component for the exercise of this internal phenomena of a modern (and even more so post-modern) conscious self.

This gathering of a stronger and more developed self through comparison (experimental encounters?) will also play an important role in the discussions of a self found in the later writings of Rousseau. Leibniz's triadic [triune] definitions of selves is seen in his, "...distinction between the self, the apparent of phenomenal self, and consciousness (*consciosité*), and the correlative distinction between real and apparent identity."[41] Rather than anticipate a proto-Freudian or an Anglicized distortion of these selves, credit is due to Locke who had himself drawn the distinction between apparent and real selves. He knew what appeared was not necessarily what was the real self since only the genuine self had its true memories which we who are on the outside would not be privy to. Spinoza, not surprisingly, follows closely behind and in relative attunement with Leibniz, since his account of the self is also, "...grounded in *a priori* reasoning; also like Leibniz, however, he recognizes that there is a vacuity in the concept of the self considered apart from its role as mere experiencing subject."[42] Again, Lockean empiricism will come to dominate so much of the thinking in the eighteenth century, especially in France among the *philosophes*. Even Berkeley appeared to follow this lead since he was somewhat in harmony with Leibniz and Spinoza when he denied any, "...clear conception of the self apart from its experiences."[43] For Berkeley, the center of the universe remained, to the end, in the hands of God, notwithstanding the Scientific Revolution and the rise of a modern philosophical attitude, leaving him with the conundrum of wanting, on the one hand, to hold onto the concept of Lockean experiences but on the other, being unable to accept the implications of such a position. For him the problem with a universe dominated by matter was precisely that, matter, and Lockean qualities within that matter could not be given any credence by him. One way to illustrate this point is when Berkeley asks in *The Principles of Human Knowledge* (1710) why "...primary qualities, any more than secondary qualities, should inhere in matter. He concludes, of course, that they do not: the external world does not exist as matter but only as mental perceptions that God infuses into the self. Except for its dependence on the Deity, the self, in Berkeley's theory, may be regarded as solipsistic."[44] Berkeley recognized the potential danger and inherent difficulties in a sensationalist-based definition of human nature. However, Berkeley ends by being more an historic anomaly on this topic while the implications of Locke's empiricism became increasingly the more accepted position.

During the Age of Reason there were several thinkers who found it worthy to continue this path of study, one of whom being the extremely unusual and interesting thinker, Julien Offroy de La Mettrie (1709–51), a French physician and philosopher. A thoroughly committed materialist and thus amenable to the Lockean position regarding sensations, de la Mettrie was also an avowed hedonist in a time when such activities, while rare, were becoming increasingly more common. As an example, there was in England the famous Hell Fire Club with weekly orgies and which starred an early defender of the freedom of the press to match something of a growing sense of a free and sensuous self, John Wilkes. There were the newly developing novels of the early self such as *The History of Tom Jones* by Henry Fielding (1707–54) or *Moll Flanders* by Daniel Defoe (1660–1731) and many other risqué works. In France there was the famous, or better stated, the infamous, Marquis de Sade for whom little need to be said. De la Mettrie's most famous work and one that got him into a great deal of trouble with the authorities was his *L'Homme machine* (1747) (*Man a Machine*). De la Mettrie demonstrates a new Enlightenment idea, one intrinsic to our own day, that we were basically born to be happy: "…in order to be happy, nature has given us natural law, 'a feeling that teaches us what we should not do, because we would not wish it be done to us.'"[45] To see man as a machine, although still something of an organic machine, should not seem surprising when one considers the impact of the mechanistic revolutions that these 'enlightened' persons of reason were living with as a part of nature, a nature that was increasingly being explored and compared with machines. As for this principle of happiness, it will become an increasingly important issue in particular with the famed model that will arrive from across the ocean and the coming of the American Revolution which transformed Locke's famous dictum of "Life, Liberty and Property" into "Life, Liberty and the Pursuit of Happiness." What a difference a century of growing reason, a sense of a personal self and its implications can make.

Once the self is placed at the center in place of some abstract and assumed divine force, the issue of how to function in an orderly society becomes very central. A key issue for Hobbes had centered upon what he saw as a major danger undermining the social order by way of the growing number of independent thinkers. How can we keep people and their vices in check was answered in his *Leviathan* which exemplified of what was thought necessary for law and order: fear. From divergence of religious proclivities and expanding market places to the new independent natural philosophers, Hobbes saw danger everywhere and the chaos that could follow. After all, he did witness the beheading of a legitimate king, Charles I in 1648, and this did not create a very promising precedent in his mind. If you can get away with beheading one legitimate king what is to stop others from doing the same with any government leader? Where are the restraints? For de la Mettrie it was natural law, this new force of nature that would govern, "...moral behavior in the strictest sense of the word, for he is compelled to obey its dictates. This law cannot be destroyed, even by the most ferocious outbursts of passion." In other words, the immutable laws of God are now replaced by the immutable laws of nature. He continues that, "One obeys, not from any sense of obligation, but rather to avoid self-torment, for one experiences suffering as a result of inflicting it."[46] But the rebel in de la Mettrie remained constant for he considered that, "...discipline thus becomes a form of gentle, though ineluctable, oppression, a systematic extirpation of nascent spontaneity..." His pleasure in shocking the establishment was demonstrated by his suggestion that, "...a child subjected to such a regimen, the soul would be, no doubt, an 'empty word.'"[47] The irony is that there is more truth than fiction here, for we now know that, "A human child growing up in social isolation will fail to attain a full consciousness of self." In fact no child will develop a sense of self at all if unable to make humanized comparisons.[48] In this sense Adam Smith (1723–90), made a provocative observation when he offered that,

> ...the idea that society is a 'mirror' which enables the individual to see and to 'think of his own character, of the propriety of demerit of his own sentiments and conduct, of the beauty of deformity of his own mind,' which suggests that if it were 'possible that a human creature could grow up to manhood in some solitary place, without any communication with his own species' then he could not develop a self.[49]

This speaks to the problem inherent in the failure of a child hidden too long from the community unable to learn language or even pursuing their humanity. As will be seen, however, the opposite occurs where there is a behavioral opportunity for those who would push the envelope in attempting to achieve something that one could call a self, a genuine identity where the distinction of the growing interiority of the self and the external individualized being observed can clash in one's search of authenticity. When this finally happens —and it will by the end of the following century —consciousness began to blossom.

The idea of awakening into a interior self within the bounds of nature is a thought explored by one of the more telling books written on the rise of the self (mentioned in the last chapter) by Charles Taylor who had argued effectively that as far as the eighteenth century is concerned:

A quite different sense of human identity is operative here. Nature that can move us and awaken our feelings is no longer tied to us by a notion of substantive reason. It is no longer seen as the order which defines our rationality. Rather we are defined by purposes and capacities which we discover within ourselves. What nature can now do is awaken these: it can awaken us to feeling against the too pressing regulative control of an analytic, disengaging, order-imposing reason, now understood as a subjective, procedural power.[50]

It is by way of this subjectivity that the literary world was equally changing and this introduces another French *philosophe* who also found this new subject of the self interesting. This thinker was the novelist, dramatist, philosopher and satirist, Denis Diderot (1713–1784). It is within the dynamic forces that were so important in the creation of the famed *Encyclopédie* that Diderot was and is best known. One of the more famous personal works by him is *Rameau's Nephew* (*Le Neveu de Rameau*, 1821), a work where three qualities are developed: that of style, the creation of character, and pursuit of intellectual substance. But of equal note is that these new, or if you prefer, modern, novels stand, "…out against all previous literature in its portrayal of the particular. [It] departs from traditional plots and archetypical stories and breaks with the classical preference for the general and the universal." These works, Diderot's included, possessed a capacity to narrate, "…the lives of particular people in their detail." These are works where, "…its characters have ordinary proper names—unlike those of Bunyan, for instance, which are personified qualities."[51] The words of the ordinary have entered modernity and have proven to be wider in breadth of understanding, clearer in depth of meaning and longer lived in evolving a mature development of our own thinking than one might have expected. While this was not the novel of the late nineteenth and twentieth centuries, we see the beginnings of a new language and attitude beyond the older archetypes typical of a Chaucer, and to even a lesser extent our first western novel, Cervantes' *Don Quixote* (1605).

There is a parallel story here in the form of the increasing appearance of various dictionaries in France and England, dictionaries that further support this new and more modern language of the novel and an issue that is a central consideration for anyone interested in the terms that dominate this essay. This was a by-product of the interiorization that had grown to some extent, out of the work of Descartes and empirical ideas of John Locke. From this ground, a new vision developed, one discussing, "…self-emancipation and self-imprisonment," and with this, "…a studied ambivalence, echoing the open question of Diderot's final drama, *Est-il bon? Est-il méchant?*" While one could dispute whatever concluding line is taken, there was now a conviction, "...to know the world it was vital first to know the knower; to look within man was to grasp his faculties, dispositions, and potentialities..."[52] The self with a consciousness was a revolutionary idea growing immediately out of the scientific, political, economic, religious and cultural instability that had marked the end of the Medieval hegemony. What was released was a new dynamism that has led us to be increasingly expansive in our curiosity regarding this early wonderment of a sense of being, the uncertainty and meaning of a consciousness and eventually the ability to stand with the inner self as an alone and even isolated individual.

Diderot's contributions to our world have yet to be fully documented but his significance can still be seen in what was becoming a linguistically strange land: "In a century things had become topsy-turvy. It began with the proper study of man being Man; it ended with the proper study of man being himself."[53] To be true to one's self tells us nothing of being a self. Words are only representative and always demand interpretation. This opening of the issues of a self tied to consciousness placed the eighteenth century in the middle of a massive pandora's box, the implications of which will take a great deal of time for thinkers to come to grips with. As one observer has noted, "In one sense this change, this turn, this invention of the self occurred suddenly; in another it was a long time coming, and the discovery is still to come to remote parts of the world and mind."[54] There is nothing simple about the idea of a self just as it is difficult to establish an acceptable definition of consciousness. We have been referring here to what has been thought of as indicative but from now on there will be an increasing rush into the realizations of this triad of terms: *self*, *individual* and *consciousness* which are anything but indicators. It is along these lines that Diderot becomes more modern than some of our own contemporaries may appear, since he, "...was convinced that even while we are awake, we are not always equally conscious of ourselves, our thoughts and actions."[55] The idea that one's consciousness may make itself present only in degrees and that it is not always active in some completed state is not an idea very popular for many yesterday or today. This understanding of Diderot's works has been greatly enhanced by a study by Catherine Glyn Davies in her *Conscience as Consciousness*. She suggests that, "Diderot was convinced of the frequency and generally of these states of minimal consciousness, even during the hours of wakefulness."[56] If it is understandable to suggest that if there is a self and with it a conscious state then it must also follow that either it does have an active presence or it simply cannot be. Any other position would appear to be fudging for most of the thinkers of the eighteenth century, and, not surprisingly, it became something of a serious topic of the age. As the English writer Edward Young in his *Conjectures on Original Composition* of 1759, offered to fellow authors: "'*Know thyself*...learn the depth, extent, biass, and full fort of thy mind; contract full intimacy with the Stranger within thee.'"[57] Considering when this was written it is a remarkably modern notion of turning inward and establishing a personal identity; and again, one is inclined to say thank you, Descartes and Locke!

To speak of consciousness in the eighteenth century is to open up a great many issues and eventually those same issues will point to our own difficulties including a school of thought that denies the existence of consciousness. In addition to the work by Davies there is a somewhat earlier study dealing with this new-found and discussed self, especially in England and among several other authors who should be added to this discussion. Davies, at least indirectly, seems to recognizes this association when she stated that, "Literary figures have been described as 'the basic architecture of Diderot's thought,' and a study of the models with which eighteenth century thinkers strove to illuminate the concepts of the self and self-consciousness may profitably be constructed by reference to the products of Diderot's tumultuous imagination."[58] The work which strikes this topic treated here most relevant is by Stephen D. Cox in his study, *"The Stranger Within Thee": Concepts of the Self in Late-Eighteenth Century Literature*. As in the case of Davies, Cox is very useful in illustrating the unique interest that began to appear in the subject of both the early self and contemporary discussions regarding consciousness. For the first time these become central topics for both writers and philosophers, topics that not only were explored in fiction and narratives but also proved to be inherently problematic issues for these thinkers. For example, Cox suggests a very simple and interesting question: "What is the self?" While on the surface this appears straight forward enough, is not only a definition but qualification:

> Is it merely an obstacle to spiritual growth, or is it something to be valued for its own sake? Is it the same in nature and in dignity as the soul, or is it merely a reflection of sense experience and social conditioning? Does each person possess an essential and consistent identity, or may the self be expected to change under the influence of its environment and, perhaps, multiply into various and competing selves? Where lie its sources of creativity? The list might be extended indefinitely. All of these questions are, in one way or another, related; and each of them may easily evoke all the rest.[59]

In as much as this is not an essay seeking a definitive definition for consciousness, it is equally not intended to offer the same for the terms *self* or *individuality*. The interest here is in an historical view from the earliest roots to the eventual maturation (assuming we have even arrived at a fully developed stage), and thus is suggestive and indicative rather than definitive. However, if the self is to be seen as tied as it was in the Enlightenment to that of consciousness, we must pay some heed to this fact without concern for today's contemporary thinkers many of whom may wish understandably to disassociate these two difficult ideas. The French *philosophes* certainly did not make that kind of delineation. Diderot recognized that a state of isolation within one's state of consciousness just as there is within the self.[60] This inherent state of subjectivity was noted when Diderot remarked that, "No-one...can think or dream himself to be another; the soul or self....The condition of being confined within its own consciousness, unable to share the subjective status of any other person, is the distinguishing mark of a self."[61]

This recognition of a subjective state of being had its immediate beginnings in the previous century, found its roots in that irony of the Roman church's confessional and its creation of a conscience. This creation was ironic since it was meant to strengthen the power of the church over the members of a congregation, especially over the noble lords. If the local priest were to know the local lord's best kept secrets he would have something to blackmail them with. After centuries the Enlightenment thinkers held a variety of views regarding both the nature and content of conscience, which can be considered as one of the earliest expression of privacy and which is, after all, at the root of consciousness and therefore a contributor to the rise of the modern self. One example of a summation of this diversity of views regarding the concept of conscience was:

> ...diversely considered to be a conviction of force, action, or liberty, an awareness of mere existence or being, or of a substantial self (referred to as *le moi, le soi, le nous*). Often it included the body, since it was associated with the physical senses and also with an independent inner sense, whose object was itself alone. It could be a momentary apprehension, or the holding together in memory of the whole series of inner and outer experiences which go to make up the individual self. Always its reference was to a personal, private kind of knowledge, only with difficulty expressed and shared with others by means of language.[62]

And in addition to this relevant observations in this regard the thoughtful reader should also look at Patricia Spacks' fine study, *Privacy: Concealing the 18th Century Self* which gives support for the idea of a privacy finding its

Enlightenment | 333

beginnings in the eighteenth century. And like the issue of privacy, the distinction between the inner being and society has also been slow to evolve for, of the many significant components within this analysis, it is the one inherent disparity that lies between the inner and the outer being and has only increased. To put it another way, one can technically turn as far back as the thirteenth century for the first hints of a distinction to be drawn between objective and subjective states of mind, but its immediate presence in the modern world arrives at the hands of Bacon and Descartes. Moreover, what should be recognized is that the idea of conscience will eventually leave students more confused by its meaning and this confusion will only increase with the development of attempts to develop a more modern and contemporary definition.

It is not surprising, therefore, especially in French that the term *consciousness* presented a very special problem: the inherent Latin roots of the language. For English, as has been noted, there were two distinct and separate terms which resolved the question as to whether one was speaking of conscience or of consciousness. Since this delineation did not exist across the channel, the French had to find their own ingenious methods of communicating new meanings with one ancient word. As difficult as any translation is, and additionally unique for these new and central terms and it may be added that our understanding has not been greatly improved. It was in 1700 that John Locke's *Essay* was translated—interpreted—into French by Pierre Coste, a young Protestant exile in Amsterdam. This work for the French would contribute to, "…the new usage of conscience and philosophically to redirect the notion of self-knowledge it had come to contain."[63] This point cannot be overstated since the original moral dimensions in French will take some time to be transformed into something of a modern meaning with a more secular frame, one which will be especially applied to Descartes' revolutionary thinking. Even Diderot found this implication, this sense of a spiritual interior being, still efficacious even as he joined the ranks of commitment to the new natural philosophy:

> …he [Diderot] describes experimental scientists as passing on to their disciples 'cet esprit de divination par lequel on subodore, pour ainsi dire, des procèdes inconnus, des expériences nouvelles, des resultats ignorés.' This suggestion of divine inspiration suggests that the ancient habit of *divinatio* (the interpretation of significant marks placed in the fabric of things by the hand of God) had not been as completely ousted from the structures of western thought…[64]

While it is not uncommon to see this in the era birthing secular perceptions, the application of a religious orientation was still powerful enough to retain the confusions of meaning inherent in an originally Medieval term now transposed into a modern context. The problem had become one of avoiding oversimplification, however, since to function without some certainty is far too strong a psychological condition for most people to embrace. If God is not central, and God is not dead, then where *is* God's role in stabilizing a fixed order for both the universe and the human condition? Death is still the great nemesis. With the beginnings of doubt regarding the certainty of The Word, the need grew beyond a few simply outgrown traditional rituals and an antiquarian language. The results were various modern religious revivals such as Unitarians and Quakers. While science is the mark of the future, and the new revival of faith is more rational, the desire for a pure and secure spiritual faith still retained a strong appeal for most people who turned to their religion and to where there still was felt to be some good sense and natural order yet to be dissected and understood. Faith and reason should not be incompatible since both come from the unity of all: God. If there is any confusion, it is a matter of not thinking through the forces of nature at work in this static world. It is in this context that the discussion of consciousness took on new meaning. Lockean sensationalism was neither intended nor interpreted as the end of the old order but rather as a new construct and addition to that order. There is little or no evidence that Locke any more than Descartes did not retain a belief in some divine force, only that they were primarily attracted to the new world of natural philosophy. This is not to say that there was not a great increase in a secular mindedness if we think in terms of degrees, not an either/or proposition. God, it is true, is not only not on the center stage for most of the intellectuals, but he only occasionally and incidentally would appear as was needed, to be brought back in order to explain where there may appear to be a problem, much as prayer during a crisis. For example, Locke had been accused of being a Socinian or Deist. And when reading Descartes' sections on God it leaves one wondering how sincere he was besides the fact that a deity really plays no significant role in the rest of his revolutionary writings and thoughts. His whole thesis can be seen standing alone as a secular structure. It is as if a deity is a convenience rather than central. In this, yes, there is more secularism—even for some who consider themselves religious—than any time before. Changes in assumptions always need a great deal more time to establish and grow than simple historical events.[65]

Diderot considered consciousness as "the most 'spiritual'" of our attributes. In this he placed, "...reason and the soul, on exactly the same footing as awareness of physical qualities..."[66] This melange of the rational and spiritual, ironically, remained ingrained in the Age of Reason that still sought certainty even if it was now being reduced to a capacity for reasoning rather than a leap of faith. As Diderot pointed out, "...true self-consciousness...appertains only to the head. It is not the affected part of the body that knows when it is hurt, it merely suffers the pain."[67] From now on, the human head and with it, the issue of the brain and the mind would dominate discussions regarding these questions. Again this is not to negate the importance of 'proper behavior' which was a natural concern even if we place some of the emphasis on the self and not exclusively on the community, its mores and customs. "In the history of philosophy, a defense of the self has not always been considered inseparable from a defense of moral values, but in the eighteenth century the two issues were becoming difficult to distinguish."[68] It would be foolish to think that the implications of a highly developed self with one's own interior identity and conscious thoughts could not possibly lead to a corruption of community standards, a position that the *philosophes* were not prepared to entertain. This may account for the rather peculiar and interesting translation into French by Pierre Coste which enjoyed such popularity that his term for Lockean consciousness was *sentiment*. Consciousness would continue to be translated as *sentiment* regularly also with various other French writers. As Davies points out: "It is difficult to determine the exact significance of sentiment in Coste's translation of these passages dealing with consciousness." This is an inherited issue where there is an "...ambivalence of the term at the end of the seventeenth century, especially in a philosophic context in which the clear and distinct evidence of the intellectual *cogito* had faded into the vague obscurity of a *sentiment intérieur*."[69]

This particular use of a new language can be traced back to the previous century and the work of Malebranche who announced a, "...'third way of knowledge' which was 'by *conscience*, or by internal sentiment' or *sentiment intérieur* also referred to as 'internal sentiment,' 'internal senses' and 'inward sensation.'"[70] 'Internal sentiments' was a phrase that Locke also used and, in fact, thus was not as surprising as some might think for becoming a very typical French expression for consciousness, but one with a clear implication of ethical guidance in the tradition of Descartes as well Locke. So now conscience reappears in the guise of our sentiment. This sense of some moral imperative—sentiment—some conscience within one's community or some sense of group responsibility, was mandatory in a world that was no longer part of the Medieval structure or holy word but yet without the open and private, even psychologically unstable, modern world. The idea of a sentiment which means other than it does today, is, as Cox explains:

> To the eighteenth century, sensibility meant many things. It was simultaneously an ethical and a psychological concept. It was used to refer both to the self's internal order of benevolent impulses and to the medium of nervous 'feeling' through which the self is affected by the outside world. The eighteenth-century concept of sensibility was a peculiar conflation of ideas and attitudes whose origins can be traced to a variety of sources in moral philosophy, theology, psychological theory, and literary practice.[71]

The value system of conscience—the moral imperative inherent in a value-oriented community—remained even with the rise of consciousness and the early stages of a growing sense of the self. Its justifications were very central to eighteenth century thinkers; which is to say that it was not that long of a walk from the previous century of religious wars, what the Age of Reason referred to as the era of 'enthusiasm.' The full force of secularism would have to wait until the end of the next century to have an impact upon the psyche of Western humanity.

> The modern identity arose because changes in the self- understandings connected with a wide range of practices—religious, political, economic, familial, intellectual, artistic—converged and reinforced each other to produce it [self]: the practices, for instance, of religious prayer and ritual, of spiritual discipline as a member of a Christian congregation, of self-scrutiny as one of the regenerate, of the politics of consent, of the family life of the companionate marriage, of the new child-rearing which develops from the eighteenth century, of artistic creation under the demands of originality, of the demarcation and defense of privacy, of markets and contracts, of voluntary associations, of the cultivation and display of sentiment, of the pursuit of scientific knowledge.[72]

This quote from Charles Taylor's study regarding the history of the self makes it very clear that the historical dynamics of this era with its contradictions and varied changes were conducive for the introduction of the question of what is meant when we speak of our identity, especially as applied in a more modern sense. It was precisely the political, economic, religious and cultural changes already briefly discussed that placed the sense of order no longer upon only forces outside oneself but by implication also placed it upon the very self that had been long dormant since there had been little reason for such an independence of attitude unless of course one were a genius and simply took their own counsel.

Even with these changes and with the offerings of such brilliant thinkers as Descartes and Locke, there were still (as today) very serious reservations regarding any discussion of a sense of self and consciousness. This can most easily be seen in the brilliant writings of a remarkably significant English philosopher, historian and critic, David Hume (1711–76), a man who was prepared to follow the implications of Lockean empiricism to its most logical, if also, most dangerous ends. Still, when all is said and done, Hume will unintentionally contribute to the growing vocabulary that further explicates our own understanding and sense of the conscious self. This was first given credence in the world of Lockean empiricism which, while leading Berkeley to a kind of theological idealism, also will eventually, "…lead David Hume to an urban scepticism and agnosticism." It was within the genius of his *Treatise of Human Nature* (1739–40) that Hume adopted the Lockean principle that "…nothing is ever really present with the mind but its perceptions or impressions and ideas, and that external objects become known to us only by those perceptions they occasion."[73] To apply this principle without the varied caveats that Locke also added would take Hume to the absolute wall of empiricism that had, in its limited manner, proved to be the *leit motif* of a century's re-workings. He was the first (and last) to take empiricism as far as one could and in so doing proved that this was not enough of a basis for what we have been calling a self; rather this was only a basis for our singular experiences which is appropriate for the world of theorizing and scientific research but not applicable for our understanding of our own inner being. The famous, if not the infamous, quote from Hume states it very clearly and succinctly:

> For my part, when I enter most intimately into what I call *myself*, I always stumble on some particular perception or other, of heat or cold, light or shade, love or hatred, pain or pleasure. I never can catch *myself* at any time without a perception, and never can observe any thing but the perception. When my perceptions are remov'd for any time, as by sound sleep; so long am I insensible of *myself*, and may truly be said not to exist. And were all my perceptions remov'd by death, and cou'd I neither think, nor feel, nor see, nor love, nor hate after the dissolution of my body, I shou'd be entirely annihilated…[74]

What makes this all the more problematic for those who want to argue for an absolute certainty of a fixed and certain self, an authentic individual and therefore, the evolution and development of a fully developed consciousness with an operational introspection, is the eighteenth century assumption following the tradition that all peoples are the same in all places and at all times. We will find a way out of this psychological conundrum in a more mature modern world, and even more importantly, post-modern world, but for now there were only two exceptions in this century of reason to this idea of a fixed and universal human nature, one by Montesquieu, the other by Rousseau. For even Hume cannot accept diversities of peoples as somehow normative, since as he stated:

> Mankind are so much the same, in all times and places, that history informs us of nothing new or strange in this particular. Its chief use if only to discover the constant and universal principles of human nature by showing men in all varieties of circumstances and situations, and furnishing us with materials from which we may form our observations and become acquainted with the regular springs of human action and behavior.[75]

The sensationistic school of thought in its search for certainty—that is being without doubt—contributed a great deal to the increased secularization of our world, while the desire for uniformity (i.e., Lockean sameness) continued the tradition of both classical and religious assumptions regarding human nature. While following in the footsteps regarding the importance of motion as articulated by the thinking in the new philosophy from Hobbes and Bacon and beyond, David Hume also offered that humans, "…are nothing but a bundle or collection of different perceptions, which succeed each other with an inconceivable rapidity, and are in a perpetual flux and movement."[76] We are what we experience but nothing more. It is this revolution in our thinking regarding motion as natural rather than needing to be explained that for Hume may have locked him into the sense that there cannot be a constant self in an ever changing landscape. How can one know that which is both inside but not fixed? Certainly one can argue that the, "…skin, pores, muscles, and nerves of a day-laborer are different from those of a man of quality: So are his sentiments, actions and manners." But this is an *ex post facto* deduction from externals much as any ancient Greek may be seen shorter or fatter than another Greek. That there are, "…different stations of life [that] influence the whole fabric, external and internal; and these different stations arise necessarily, because uniformly, from the necessary and uniform principles of human nature,"[77] follows the same principle—a noble knight appears different than a peasant, but both are basically the same expression of our humanity for those believing in the judgement of God's eyes and, it could be added, those of your neighbors.

One of the reasons for Hume, who was not a Christian, reaching this conclusion is that impressions are universal and thus constant. We can experience being burned by a flame, but none of us experience what a bird might experience of flight. There is a significant difference, however, between the first time one has the impression of being burned and a later but similar experience since there is a frame of reference for the second time by way of memory. As we acquire experiences we change our selves. And if change occurs regularly, there cannot be a given and constant self to have those experiences. "If any impression gives rise to the idea of self, that impression must continue invariably the same, thro' the whole course of our lives; since self is suppos'd to exist after that manner. But there is no impression constant and invariable."[78] Thus impressions and experiences cannot account for a self any more than a rapids of a river can offer us a fixed and unchanging entity defining the river. Motion is more than mere water.

There was another troubling issue that Hume found he had to confront: the role of causation, specifically that of the act of making a judgement regarding the cause and effect of experience. This had never been an issue: from the beginning, Aristotle gave us a certainty of causation. Since Hobbes, however, the four causes had been reduced to only one.[79] But this proved to be only a beginning for Hume since he also had something to say from an empirical point of view about causation. If one follows the empirical approach it raises the interesting question of why we do not use sense data to organize all our data into one singular, unified whole, one that would result from the stimulants that could now be converted into a cohesive self—that individualized conscious being. He certainly seems to have thought he did. But it was Hume's judgement that the pure experiential philosopher who would speak in terms of cause and effect, specifically the empirical idea of causation, was living an illusion. This rather unique idea has many implications from the dismissal of a First Cause to an ending of the Great Chain of Being. Hume made his famous case for treating cause and effect as nothing more than a mental habit rather than an empirical certainty.[80] While Hume extensively discusses the nature of causation from an empirical point of view, especially arguing that it is more a matter of habit and imagination and offers a long list of qualifiers, he is clear that causation cannot be empirically proven. His example: suppose a billiard ball is hit against another billiard ball and the second ball proceeds to move. Now let us grant you have watched this phenomena occur some 500 times. Question: If I hit the billiard ball against the other ball will it move on the 501st attempt? The only way to know empirically is after the ball is hit the

501st time and you watch it move or not move. If it HAD happened, empirically you know that it did happen. But to predict is not empirical knowledge, a position not that far from a conclusion that Aristotle had, on occasion, suggested. Another way to look at this is to simply state that A is seen (sensed) to touch ball B. Thus A is prior to B in time. Now the constant connection of A and B is concluded. This is not sensed, not an empirical fact, but only a leap to a conclusion for David Hume. You see ball A hit ball B but you do not 'see' cause and effect. If that which is real is only that which is empirical then it follows, for Hume, that since there is no sensed causation but rather only deduced causation, you are now not acting as an empiricist. In other words, for empirical knowledge to be empirical, it is always past knowledge, leaving you 'guessing' that there is a certain pattern that you can rely upon in the future. The actual proof is only in the act and one's own reflection after the act. This would not give an absolute certainty of reliable predictability, although it would give what today would be considered a statistical probability (thank you, Pascal). Perhaps this is why one of Hume's masterpieces of literature was his six-volume *History of England*, a history which, of course, offers facts, (after the events). This would also account for what he had to say about the self: "In order to justify to ourselves this absurdity, we often feign some new and unintelligible principle, that connects the objects together, and prevents their interruption or variation. Thus we feign the continu'd existence of the perceptions of our senses, to remove the interruption; and run into the notion of a *soul*, and *self*, and *substance*, to disguise the variation."[81] Even the idea of a constant self therefore, is an illusion, an act of self-deception that gives coherence to perceptions and therefore our existence. This is not to suggest that Hume was adamantly opposed to the 'possibility' for some others to believe that they possess a constant and fixed self: "If any one upon serious and unprejudic'd reflexion, thinks he has a different notion of *himself*, I must confess I can reason no longer with him. All I can allow him is, that he may be in the right as well as I, and that we are essentially different in this particular. He may, perhaps, perceive something simple and continu'd, which he calls *himself*; tho' I am certain there is no such principle in me."[82] Hume could accept that the argument developed over the century that some possessed in their mind a self, it was just not possible with his own introspection to find such a self. Perception was important to him as an empiricist, but he added that, "…identity is nothing really belonging to these different perceptions, and uniting them together; but is merely a quality, which we attribute to them, because of the union of their ideas in the imagination, when we reflect upon them."[83] The magic word for the future of the concept, interesting enough, is imagination, a word earlier mentioned that will be a key component for mental and creative activities for future thoughtful and artistic minds.

It is of some interest that the term *imagination* appeared so often when the thinkers of this century discuss the self. Imagination ties into those theorists who most favored exploring the ideas of sympathy and especially sensibility.[84] What was being established—and was not favored by Hume— was an attempt at creating the self as a barometer for moral imperatives. Feeling no need to keep any ties with that 'old-time religion' and those absolutes that are there implied, Hume could accept to a far larger degree the absence of meaning but only a limited sense of that identity which, as he stated, "...we ascribe to the mind of man," and, "...is only a fictitious one....It cannot, therefore, have a different origin, but must proceed from a like operation of the imagination upon like objects."[85] In part, Hume's position can be explained by the simple conclusion that he did not accept the argument of those like Diderot who believed that through the process of reasoning one could establish a conscience; what he saw was the rationalization of moral behavior. To project one's own values and assumptions upon others is not that unusual even though it makes little or no empirical sense. After all, if "reason is wholly inactive," then it would follow that it, "...can never be the source of so active a principle as conscience, or a sense of morals,"[86] and further, it would be impossible to argue for a rational basis for moral behavior. Here Hume would agree with his contemporary Edmund Burke (1729–97) who also argued against such rationalized behavior, and instead, in the tradition of Hobbes and conservative values, defended the political principles of tradition, prejudice and habits. In the end, without a clarity or a certainty of an existing self, Hume would spent much of his time working on the dilemmas inherent in those questions of causation and personal identity, all without success. This may be one of the reasons why some of these eighteenth century thinkers, including Hume, felt the need to introduce the term *imagination* into the discussion: "...we must distinguish betwixt personal identity, as it regards our thought or imagination, and as it regards our passions or the concern we take in ourselves. The first is our present subject; and to explain it perfectly we must take the matter pretty deep, and account for that identity, which we attribute to plants and animals; there being a great analogy betwixt it, and the identity of a self or person."[87] This application of imagination to our thoughts further supports the common assumption at the time that reasoning thoughts, or equally our imagination, are an interior or subjective states of being. As Hume put it: "Tis evident, that as we are at all times intimately conscious of ourselves, our sentiments and passions, their ideas must strike upon us with greater vivacity than the ideas of the sentiments and passions of any other person."[88] This will prove to be a very important argument for those recent thinkers who maintain that there is no such thing as consciousness since it is an interior, subjective and completely private act that cannot be documented. And it certainly must follow that those who have never experienced a conscious reflection would believe that there is, in fact, no such phenomena. From the point of view of Hume's ontology, however, there can be no sense of being without consciousness: "Tis evident, that the idea, or rather impression of ourselves is always intimately present with us, and that our consciousness gives us so lively a conception of our own person, that 'tis not possible to imagine, that anything can in the particular go beyond it."[89] It is interesting to read this language of Hume and not sense an anticipation of a more modern or even the implications of an existential attitude. Still the eighteenth century is not the modern world and this itself is an important lesson of history, at least when looking at the history of mentality.

Where a serious problem arises for us in understanding Hume's position is that he is not simply summarizing and editing Lockean empiricism but pointing to implications to be explored later. For example, in addition to a hint of the existential moment, there is an implication of nihilism in a world made only of sense data. "It would appear that Hume recognized this and wrote his *Dialogues* not least of all to disclose the dangers of nihilism lurking behind the ruins of dogmatism."[90] Along with this sense of nihilism, there is also an equal sense of the importance of the immediate present, and the insecurity inherent in skepticism (which Hume is famous for) and to a certain degree of relativism which Kant in Germany found unacceptable. In *The Romantic Enlightenment*, Geoffrey Clive offered: "The Enlightenment was as much the critic of reason and its apostle. Hume and Kant especially by questioning the foundations of traditional metaphysics became instrumental in opening the floodgates to the varieties of skepticism, relativism, and general anti-intellectualism."[91] Arguably a major stumbling block for these new alternating and diverse attitudes in place of a fixed sense experience and a rather gloomy vision of the human condition would have been to reject the tendency at the time to see all people as alike, in all times and all places, although Hume did seem to believe that there were some people who were worthy of slavery, an attitude that is hard to square with a view of the universality of all humans. But it should be remembered that 'sameness' was Locke's attempt to establish how a constant self—one always the same— could exist. That assumption will dominate all thought until the impacts of more revolutionary minds of the following century. Real diversity was needed with another approach and another group of thinkers beyond the pure age of reason, someone who could break free from not only the English but also somewhat French exclusionary thinking: someone like a Rousseau.

Jean Jacques Rousseau (1712–78), a man of many minds who was a Swiss-born (but thought of as French) philosopher, novelist, essayist, musician and autobiographer was the voice more of the future rather than someone who would re-work the inherited ideas of the past. Even more so than Hume, the secondary sources regarding his thought are extremely diverse, contradictory and occasionally very original. He wrote operas that saw production, a study on education, a serious piece on language in the tradition of Locke and Condillac, an important novel as well as religious works. His political philosophy was so central to his thinking that a variety of his ideas can be found impacting upon future political and social thinkers. There is nothing particularly simple in his philosophy. Additionally, there is an irony that he was more aligned with a Cartesian than a Lockean position. He was attracted especially to Cartesian dualism which he makes central to his fundamental concepts: an interior (*cogito*) and an exterior (*sum*) reality. For Rousseau this distinction manifested itself in a dualism between what he labeled an *amour propre* and an *amour de soi*, a private versus a public, or a personal versus a political ontology. As one interpreter of his works has observed, Rousseau had a concern with "…contrasts and connections between the natural and the social; between the good and the corrupt; between *amour-de-soi* and *amour propre*." A student of Rousseau's psychology, N. J. H. Dent, additionally suggests that there were in his ideas other forms of dualism: "…those to do with independence and dependence; freedom and enslavement (both external and 'internal'); power and servitude; integrity and self-alienation or self-estrangement."[92] He took an approach that would make him independent of others of the period, particularly those who had supported the Leibnizian idea, "this is the best of all possible worlds." Voltaire will reject Rousseau eventually while also attacking this Leibnizian thinking now associated with his student, Christian Wolf (1679–1754), in his masterpiece *Candide* through the voice of Pangloss, a book that sold some 20,000 copies when first it appeared in 1760. Rousseau, a popular writer, additionally left behind his compatriots at the *Encyclopédie* and their optimism after he had written several of the important pieces which established his reputation.

He went to Paris as a young author and eventually would become too unpopular to remain. His reputation began with his literary attack against the popular Enlightenment idea of progress in his *Discourse on the Origin and Foundation of Inequality Among Mankind* (1735). He theorized that in the movement away from our original primitive state into a social and political society and with it the invention of private property with its division of labor and where humans also find themselves alienated from each other by class divisions, positive results were not to be found. As Dent notes, "...one of Rousseau's major ideas was that actual human history is not a history of progress, liberation, enlightenment and increasing happiness—quite the opposite."[93] This was an early beginning, in fact, of a romantic state of mind which would take the ideas of the self and individuality into a new and modern realm of actualization, one that was ontologically very real but not one that was a necessarily progressively expansive of our understanding of a healthy life. But it is within the uniqueness of his ideas appearing at the end of the Enlightenment that we see a contribution to our modern understanding of a more viable consciousness. Yet dualism remains a key component in these ideas, both in the world of Rousseau and with the Romantics who will continue this discussion into the next century. And while this is an opening to a new approach it does not prove to be a resolution of the issue of certainty. Reason turns out to not be a gimmick or set formula to replace the 'Good Book's' certainty, particularly regarding the issues of living and our mortality.

Rousseau demonstrated an interest in education, built upon a Lockean foundation. Rousseau subscribed to the belief that, "...the education of man begins at his birth; before speaking, before understanding, he is already learning. Experience anticipates lessons." It is not surprising that he had a sympathy for Lockean empiricism. As he put it, "...plants are shaped by cultivation, and men by education."[94] Even when he speaks in dualistic terms he retains respect for the importance of experience: "We are born weak, we need strength; we are born totally unprovided, we need aid; we are born stupid, we need judgment. Everything we do not have at our birth and which we need when we are grown is given us by education."[95] Upon entering the end of the Enlightenment, the idea of being either a Cartesian dualist or a Lockean empiricist—the latter being the more popular—continued while it also became an increasingly common one for most thinkers not only to subscribe to, but more importantly, to also move beyond, to attempt new and expanded paradigms.

What made Rousseau's thought so different from others of his age may have been that he appeared to face himself more honestly than just about anyone else at the time. True, Montaigne had written personal notes and recorded memoirs which appear to be self-honest but he lacked the inner intimacy demonstrated in Rousseau's *Confessions* (1766–67). The differences have been noted by a variety of scholars, one of which put it as follows: "The psychological realism is absent from the *Confessions*, for Rousseau's language obeys a more ideal rhythm. His periods throughout are delicate and harmonious. Whereas Montaigne can change his voice several times on the same page, Rousseau has only one voice which we recognize alike in the *Confessions*, in *Emile*, in the *Nouvelle Heloise*."[96] J. M. Cohen in his introduction to *The Confessions* writes: "It was possible for the first time, therefore, for a man to write his life in terms only of his worldly experience, and to advance views on his place in the Universe that bore only a distant relationship to the truths of revealed religion."[97] This is not to argue that his personal revelations are in the true sense a modern version of an autobiography in that there is a tone from the beginning of *The Confessions* where he perceives himself as speaking for only himself and yet for all humanity—especially with such comments as, "I have resolved on an enterprise which has no precedent…" Followed by his desire "…to display to my kind a portrait in every way true to nature." It can rightly be added that his "…statement about *The Confessions* is, then, a statement about man."[98] While modern in some ways, it is somewhat difficult to see the beginnings of a modern autobiography when he attempts to elucidate fundamentals regarding the human condition rather than his own personal journey through his own life. For this study it is enough to know that as personal as his works are—and they are very personal—he still speaks with the voice of a philosopher seeking what he considers to be basic universal truths. He was a true transitional figure between the Age of Reason and the Romantics.

For Rousseau, the truth centered entirely around feelings, our driving passions, something long considered (and by some even today) as the basis of all that is wrong or even evil. This was the century of reason, but reason has its limits and those limits are now just beginning to be discovered. As a reminder, it was Blaise Pascal, almost one hundred years earlier, who noted: "The heart has its reasons which reason knows nothing of."[99] It is little wonder then that Rousseau was one of the first defenders of the importance of our feelings, of the positive use of our passions: "…the whole *Confessions* is an attempt to prove that the feelings convey a man's apprehension of truth more faithful than does the brain."[100] And the ultimate feeling was that of love, beginning with a love of self. This was contrary to the official Western Christian position: "According to Augustine, the man who dwelled too much upon the phantasms of past delight fell into the sin of pride, preferring himself to the better presence of God. But according to Rousseau, there was no question of sin. As with Spinoza, to prefer and love oneself was the most 'natural,' most 'necessary' pleasure known to man."[101] Moreover, to love oneself would be the height of not only vanity but the deadliest of all the seven deadly sins. It is in this self-preference that we find the now ubiquitous imagination making its appearance as a key component of his psychological position that could be thought of as separate from the sins of pride or vanity.

> From this point of view, the *Confessions* represent a tragic attempt to reconcile in imagination the natural virtue of self-love with the civilizing vice of vanity; to close the gap, somehow, between *l'enfance du monde*, when men lived in harmony with himself, and *la jeunesse du monde*, when men had already begun the perilous effort to live in harmony with others. Rousseau often dreamed of a society where the healthful solitude of *amour de soi* would be preserved, uncorrupted by the passion to see and be seen, and yet enriched by it. In such a society, to *be* and to *seem* would be one, and the need for recognition would give rise, not to pretense and hostile vanities, but to a truly open revelation of self, a mutual transparency between souls schooled in the only true morality: self-love.[102]

This again introduces us to his very unique and rather odd concept of *amour propre* and *amour de soi*, one being a condition of natural man and the other a byproduct of socialized man. Granted, he recognized that there were dangers in these loves (*amour*) in that they were easily perverted (as confusing as this is, the details are not appropriate for our brief discussion). Part of the problem is that Rousseau sought to find a means of bringing people together in a nontraditional manner but would nevertheless attempt to keep the best of our natural disposition while still perceiving us to be something more than simply individuals. As the unique study, *The Heresy of Self-Love* by Paul Zweig, has pointed out:

> 'It is quite natural that a man who loves himself should try to extend his being and his pleasures, and to possess by attachment whatever he feels to be good for him: it is a simple question of the emotions...' Rousseau contradicts the orthodox opinion that human nature is corrupt because man has lost sight of God and loves himself. Instead he sets the energy of *amour de soi* at the center of our humanity. For Rousseau, as for Leibniz and Spinoza, our best experience grows of this central passion, which is then deflected—sublimated—and most often perverted by life in society.[103]

He who would love himself would be capable of loving others. "Rather, we obtain for ourselves full personal stature and completion, meaning and value in ourselves and our lives, and 'the supreme happiness of life' (which is to love and be loved in return…)."[104] Rousseau never flinched from this commitment even though he was able to offend most of his earlier friends and compatriots, making them into enemies who would in the end reject him. In fact, "Throughout his life Rousseau was to argue that man's best nature lay, as he wrote in *Emile*, in 'the only natural passion of man…self-love'; years after writing *Emile*, harried by paranoia, he still insisted, 'All positive feeling derives immediately from self-love.'"[105]

This commitment to retaining some of what Rousseau found to be qualities in the natural human condition occurred from the discovery of so many different peoples around the world that had such an increasingly powerful impact on his thinking which were the results inherent in the age of discovery. Rousseau, after all, was a firm believer in what he called the 'noble savage' and that geographic differences made for psychological differences. Here we see the first signs of accepting that perhaps not all people are precisely alike. As Rousseau put it in discussing the influence of geography and one's climate: "The disadvantage of extreme climate is obvious. A man is not planted like at tree in a country to remain there forever; and he who leaves one extreme to get to the other is forced to travel a road double the length of that traveled by him who leaves from the middle point for the same destination."[106] He was not alone to argue for a geo-political psychological pre-disposition. He even went so far as to suggest that, "…cold air, far from doing children harm, strengthens them and that hot air weakens them, gives them fever, and kills them."[107] The contemporary French political philosopher, Charles-Louis de Secondat Montesquieu (1689–1755), made the same sort of geographic determinism a central component of his theory; the heated south produced indolence and acquiescent citizens more comfortable in a dictatorship while the north with, a colder climate, made for a more industrious and particpatory population. In addition to anticipating the discipline of sociology in the next century, as Emile Durkheim noted,[108] this attitude was also problematic for both thinkers since it encouraged analytic study of society and the human psyche while at attempting to belong to the world of an Enlightenment reformist. Both thinkers can be confusing for today's readers since they are arguing for an objective analysis in the new scientific tradition while calling for political reforms in the tradition of the *philosophes* who became associated with the French Revolution of 1789. In either case, Rousseau (like Montesquieu) did take note of climate and geographic differences when discussing the human condition and saw humanity on a much larger and more conflicting tableau.

The passions remained central to Rousseau's point of view and in all his writings, since only emotions, "…impelled him to wonderment and thought." For him and his work there was, "…no permanent distinctions between his reflective work, his fiction, and his autobiography."[109] The development of the self, therefore, was not simply a version of Locke and external forces forming one's identify, but rather an interior state that predetermined personal development. And in his most personal study, his *Confessions*, one can find the, "uncovering of the 'inner self' as the latent presupposition of contemporary thinking about ourselves."[110] Self meant inner, the interior, and not an external image. It has even been suggested that he may have faced a sense of isolation from others since, "…by the time he wrote his *Confessions*, Rousseau had come to feel an elusive barrier, a 'difference,' which separated him, he felt, from other men, locking him more and more into a life of painful isolation."[111] Another commentator has found that Rousseau had suggested a reflectivity in his *amour-de-soi*, therefore offering, "…that there were various kinds of self-appraisal, judgements about the character, attributes, qualities of oneself," as well, "…certain other forms of self-assessment…"[112] Dent in his study is very adamant in his interpretation that there were three characteristics in Rousseau's natural man and his concept of *Amour-de-soi*: "perfectability, free will and reflection."[113] But it is the emotional ties to others that makes possible the construction of the self. One cannot maximize the potential of one's own interior self alone. It is in contrast with others that we gain a more complete picture of the uniqueness of our interior self. As Paul Zweig put it: "It is true, Rousseau agrees, that we need the 'help of others' in order to complete our self-delight; but that is so, he adds, only 'in this life.' If man were more perfectly conceived, he could do without this 'help of others'; he would be autonomous and self-delighting, like God himself."[114] Without the aid of others, the result would be, "…the sad prison of isolation, or the subhuman simplicity of animals."[115] The forces that make us human, the power of speech specifically and language in general gives the human a distinction from the animals, and was recognized and discussed by the likes of Locke, some of the *philosophes* and later by Condillac and would only increase interest in an important subject for understanding personal identity. It has been further suggested by Dent that the roots for this phenomenal development were to be found in what has been labeled, "'reflective' *amour-de-soi*…" As he stated, "…it may generally be objected that the elaborations of awareness and agency involved could only be available to someone through his mastery of language."[116] The reason offered for this is that man is a social animal, one who evolves within the context of social institutions (as exemplified in written language) as well as the maximization of an interior potential.

This complexity of thought may in part account for his rather unique attitude regarding both the individual's willfulness and their actualized exercise in the world of politics. It is here that Rousseau breaks free from his dualism and proves capable of a triadic thought pattern, one that would deal with the inherent problem of pursuing the inner life of the self and doing so in a public realm. It was Hobbes who first recognized the dangers and conflicts that could grow out of any sense of individuality arising out of the changes of economics and religion. Thus he was a defender of the state and of more authoritarian governance. Edmund Burke, as we have noted, a contemporary of Rousseau, carried this intrinsic assumption of conservative politics to an expanded level. Rousseau, on the other hand, arrives with a much more complex thought that has to be, in the history of political ideas, one of the more remarkable theories—one centering on the issue of the will, and does so by recognizing and offering three very different and distinct forms of will. On the surface this may seem very confusing but in fact the summation of this triune of wills is not imponderable, starting with first, the General Will with the others being a Private and finally the third, Corporate Will.[117] Although there is no easy way to exemplify Rousseau's meaning, the following is a fairly clear if minor attempt to make some sense of what he may have meant in his distinctions.

The first, the Private Will, also known as a Personal Will, is simply what a single citizen would want when they, for example, would vote. Thus, if they are going to raise taxes and it would cost you more, you would more than likely vote for your own interest and against the increase in your taxes even if they may help the schools since you have no children. This is a position that Rousseau most feared for it is inherently selfish and anti-social. The Corporate Will, on the other hand, would be more a matter of belonging to a group of people with some mutual interest, as in the case of the a private club. Some clubs would encourage its individual members to vote for the tax increase because of some perceived benefit for that group while others would not. As for the General Will, where Rousseau is the least clear and yet it proves to be the most significant for him, he means more than one's personal or group interests, and would seek out how the individual and member of a group would vote for the greater good of the community. Thus if the vote for more taxes was for the school system while you were without children, you would personally walk into the booth on behalf of yourself but in the end vote for an increase in your taxes for the good of the society as a whole. Your personal will would give way to the general will. This would make it possible for the growing individualized person to actually continue to support the good of the community. In this he suggests that we all wear three hats: private, group and general. While this must be seen as an extremely simplified explanation it does give something of an idea of what he meant. Rousseau was seeking the best not just for the self, but of necessity, for the community as a whole. In this Rousseau would have to be listed as a radical thinker. As Rousseau put it, "…our species does not admit of being formed halfway."[118] There was no way that Rousseau could be seen as supportive of 'halfway' measures of any sort. Radical is not an easy word and is not here used in a cavalier manner. Radical as applied to the thinking of Rousseau is here understood to mean that one is primarily concerned with the causes regarding the issues at hand as well as the essence of any issue.[119] Another example may help explicate. Assume there is slow leak in your bicycle tire. The traditional (conservative) would say that when you start the day you fill the tire with air and leave well enough alone. If you are more inclined to being a liberal, you would take the tube out of the tire, and though there may be 20 patches already on the tube, you would nevertheless add another and put it back on the bike. If your attitude is more along the lines of more radical thinking, you would see the problem for what it is and buy a new inner tube. Rousseau was clearly much closer to the latter.

Perhaps the issue centering on the fundamental theme of this work, the historical appearance of the self, reflectivity, individuality and consciousness, that grew out of the discovery of death and our evolutionary process of attempting to give ourselves a certainty, must be looked at in terms of our new understanding of motion. Rousseau lived in an historically more secular framework while still offering lines of thought out of Bacon, Galileo and Newton: "It is only by movement that we learn that there are things which are not us, and it is only by our own movement that we acquire the idea of extension."[120] As the world turned to a more rational and natural order, (call it a radicalization of thinking) this secular characteristic could already be found in Rousseau: "The return to nature, the turning inward in oneself to find an uncorrupted self, is a return to an earthly paradise, the naturally good self, from which 'man's man' has turned away—a secular equivalent to the Christian fall of man. This view of man is at the basis of much subsequent political history, and its importance cannot be overstated."[121] In other words, for Rousseau, the secular separation from the strengths that had been gained by way of a natural

Enlightenment | 351

order was a result of our creation and participation in society. It was not a matter of believing in God but rather in believing in human capacities. Fear remained, especially of death, but a new attitude made its appearance as expressed by Rousseau: "I am not able to teach living to one who thinks of nothing but how to keep himself from dying."[122] While Rousseau spends a great deal of time in *The Confessions* on the subject of death and fear, he was capable of going rationally beyond it. He offered, for example, regarding the question of a child's facing the inevitable: "One thinks only of preserving one's child. That is not enough. One ought to teach him to preserve himself as a man, to bear the blows of fate, in brave opulence and poverty, to live, if he has to, in freezing Iceland or on Malta's burning rocks. You may very well take precautions against his dying. He will nevertheless have to die."[123] The point of education is to draw out the potential for not only facing the hard edge of living but equally of making possible to rationality in facing death through our ability in making intelligent and conscious choices. After all, the Latin word *education* means to lead out.

The thinkers dealing with this issue are just beginning to discover at the end of the this century of rationality that intelligent precautions and the application of ordinary good sense, is the only certainty left to mankind. Rousseau also recognized and understood the relation of fear to the issue of death when he stated that, "I have noticed that children are rarely afraid of thunder, unless the claps are terrible and really wound the organ of hearing. Otherwise, this fear comes to them only when they have learned that thunder sometimes wounds or kills. When reason begins to frighten them, make habit reassure them. With a slow and carefully arranged gradiation [sic] man and child are made intrepid in everything."[124] Fear is a prerequisite for all of life and once learned it can make the difference between a completely lived life and one where people simply pass through. As Rousseau so eloquently put it: "The man who has lived the most is not he who has counted the most years but he who has most felt life. Men have been buried at one hundred who died at their birth."[125] The only addendum to the issue of death offered by Rousseau was pain, for it is pain before the revelation of death that is most inherent in living: "Could not so cruel a constraint have an influence on their disposition as well as on their constitution? Their first sentiment is a sentiment of pain and suffering."[126] As Dent pointed out, Rousseau, "...stresses the obtrusiveness of the experience of pain in the infant's first introduction to the world, his introduction to what it 'feels like' to be a creature set loose from his mother's womb."[127] To be born is to discover pain which in turn will be nothing more than an introduction to the fact that you are first alive and then terminal.

> When an animal is sick, it suffers in silence and keeps quiet. Now one does not see more sickly animals than men. How many people whose disease would have spared them and whom time by itself would have cured have been killed by impatience, fear, anxiety, and, above all, remedies? I will be told that animals, living in a way that conforms more to nature, ought to be subject to fewer ills than we are. Well, their way of life is precisely the one I want to give to my pupil. He ought, therefore, to get the same advantage from it.[128]

The animal that does not know that it is sick is thus an animal that seeks no doctor to muddle up the animal's condition and therefore is nature's example of a strong being. This naturalness is man's future if he is to be strong—not without pain or the reality of being eventually terminal—but as one who endures. Rousseau had very little good to say about doctors in an age when such attitudes were common. With an eloquence that generally marked Rousseau's writing, he stated: "Do you want to find men of a true courage? Look for them in the places where there are no doctors, where they are ignorant of the consequences of illness, where they hardly think of death. Naturally man knows how to suffer with consistence and dies in peace."[129] To stand alone, even in a necessary social setting, still means to endure and avoid the excuses that mark an unlived life.

It is this all too common a possible situation of giving in at all cost to our hunger for avoidance of death, fear and pain that is so inhibiting of the full realization of an unique self. And this has been called by Rousseau a primitive condition: "It is the primitive character of these tears and cries to be *protests*, aggrieved remonstrance and rage against at what is inchoately apprehended as an outrage of affluence inflicted on him. Cries are not mere yelps of pain; they are expressions of *grievance*, at being ill-used or abused." And as Dent continues in quoting from *Emile*: "Since the first condition of man is want and weakness, his first voices are complaint and tears....From these tears that we might think so little worthy of attention is born man's first relation to all that surrounds him; here is formed the first link in that long chain of which the social order is formed."[130]

Considering the comments of both Rousseau and such commentators as Dent, there is little doubt that there clearly is a beginning recognition that self-inflicted limits are those that inhibit the self that is potentially capable of becoming an individual and who can freely make their own conscious choices. In this Rousseau sees the problem as one of slavery: "All our wisdom consists in servile prejudices. All our practices are only subjection, impediment, and constrained. Civil man is born, lives, and dies in slavery."[131]

It will take the next century and others such as artists-thinkers like Goethe to open the doors beyond this point to create a self-reflective conscious individual and modern humanity.

IV

Modernity and Beyond

CHAPTER NINE

ROMANTICS, THE SELF AND INDIVIDUALISM

The heart has its reasons which the reason does not at all perceive. [1]

FROM REASON TO FEELINGS

In 1866 *Crime and Punishment* by Fyodor Dostoevsky (1821–81) was published. Neither sympathy nor sensibility are operational for its protagonist, Raskolnikov. The implications of the ideas expressed in that novel and in the late nineteenth century are only now being fully realized for their significance for the development of self-consciousness. The key for this journey resides in the collapse of a traditional certainty and with it the security of a moral or/and ethical certainty. With the diminution of traditional moral rules to guide certainty for eternal life, a more rational mental structure, a commitment to reasoning began to replace it, leaving the question of eternal life—one of salvation—behind. Where there was an after-life to stabilize human activity one could hope for less fear in the choices made. The ultimate police guarding traditional values and behavior was a church now undermined by decades of religious conflicts.

It would be new intellectual theories, especially those of Locke, that would create a new parameter, a rational guide, a *sentiment intérieur*, to act for the Age of Reason as a secular and rational guide for society's moral imperative. There were some very serious inadequacies, however, that began to appear late in the Enlightenment. Locke, who gave us this sense of rational sentiment, had also made time central to his definition of consciousness when he favored adding memory to Cartesian awareness. In a fine scholarly study, Stephen D. Cox has suggested that "…in the ideas of a literature and aesthetics of sensibility, we see clearly the early stages of development of what might be called a mystique of the individual self," a position beginning to appear as we drift toward the modern world. Cox may have expanded this idea too far, however, when he suggests that a, "…mystique that gained additional complexity in Romantic literature and persists, despite attempts to dispel it, in much of the literature of the twentieth century."[2] The 'mystique' of being an individual self in modern (and post-modern) Europe is one that would leave many contemporary students of the subject at a loss since most people tend to take the contemporary sense of our individuality so for granted that it is not unusual for most to assume that individuality has always been the norm. Of course, by the end of the nineteenth century there were many people who still held to the old moral order—whether by way of religion or secular reasoning. In the hands of a Dostoevsky, however, the assumptions and desire for a fixed and moral universe through good sense and reasoning, Lockean sentiment had clearly fallen out of favor. Religion, long the source of a fixed universe, moral standards and the certainty of an afterlife, had been losing its control for increasing numbers since the wars of the Reformation. In the end the Enlightenment will also fail to offer a new paradigm of security. This transformation now manifests itself in what is loosely referred to as the Romantic movement, an important aspect of which can be partially revealed in the life and work of Johann Wolfgang von Goethe (1746–1832).

It was from the writings of Jean-Jacques Rousseau in France, William Blake (1757–1827) in England and Goethe in the Germanies that historians suggest gave form to a new era commonly referred to as "Romantic." Arthur Lovejoy, the scholar who originated the discipline of the History of Ideas, suggested however, that, "The first step...is that we should learn to use the word 'Romanticism' in the plural."[3] The reason for this is not difficult to find given that:

> ...the simple and obvious fact that there are various historic episodes or movements to which different historians of our own or other periods have, for one reason or another, given the name. There is a movement which began in Germany in the seventeen-nineties—the only one which has an indisputable title to be called Romanticism, since it invented the term for its own use. There is another movement which began pretty definitely in England in the seventeen-forties. There is a movement which began in France in 1801. There is another movement which began in France in the second decade of the century, is linked with German movement, and took over the German name. There is the rich and incongruous collection of ideas to be found in Rousseau.[4]

There are a variety of components that contribute to any definition of Romantic: the elevation of emotions; a fondness for medieval rather than classical models; and an early development of liberalism. The problem remains that, "...there may be some common denominator of them all; but if so, it has never yet been clearly exhibited, and its presence is not to be assumed *a priori*."[5] One agreement is that, "...the Romantics were the first to argue that the

Enlightenment had failed—and not for adventitious reasons but because its program was fundamentally flawed."[6] While neither Goethe (at the beginning) nor Nietzsche (at the end) would ever appreciate the use of the term, there is enough general commonality, especially with the German Romantics, to allow both to be included. What is most significant, however, is the arrival of a new language, one with a modern tone that has been accurately described as: "The crucial formative role assigned to the language of action [which] caused a shift in the conception of the nature of art from imitation to expression..."[7] But this description is not wholly adequate. Whatever term we use, *individual* and *self*, as well as *consciousness*, all three began developing into more contemporary usage. This is because Romanticism recognized that any increase in consciousness also meant an increase in the self and therefore self-consciousness.[8] Part of this developed out of the Scientific Revolution and its expanding definitions of space and time. From the Baconian detachment necessary for the act of scientific observation, and the further interiorization of the Cartesian metaphysical *cogito* as well as Lockean empiricism, a more diverse approach for both our understanding and expanded discussions appeared in an ever expanding library of published works that marked the doorway to modernity. As one fine study on the rise of the modern self has stated:

> This recognition is of great importance, because it appears that the new moral consciousness has been inseparable from a certain sense of our place in history. Once again notions of the good are interwoven with modes of narrative. The imperative of benevolence carries with it the sense that this age has brought about something unprecedented in history, precisely in its recognition of this imperative. We feel that our civilization has made a qualitative leap, and all previous ages seem to us somewhat shocking, even barbarous, in their apparently unruffled acceptance of inflicted or easily avoidable suffering and death, even of cruelty, torture, to the point of reveling in their display.[9]

This statement was motivated in part by an earlier observation regarding the desire of the Liverpool Society for Abolition of Slavery to achieve some, "moral 'improvement'...by attaining some certain, defined, and acknowledged good..."[10] i.e., by committed action rather than by a passive state of optimistic sentiment. Participation within the system became, for some, more important than philosophizing. Goethe was an outstanding example of this new mind set: among his activities besides a genius of a poet, he spent a lifetime as the adviser to the Duke of Weimar and was an early and creative biological scientist.

The importance of historical and linguistic developments again depends on the thesis that there is a direct correlation between the expansion of our understanding of time (public history/ private memory) and our changing sense of language (space/reflection). Both are necessary for the maturation of individualization and the eventual reflective conscious self. In other words, it is not an accident that the occurrence of the interior being, the appearance of an historical perceptiveness and correlative linguistic capacity occurred during approximately the same historical period. Moreover, this congruence of a change in our mentality developed as a companion to the new acknowledgment of diversity, turning away from the traditional concepts of universality for all humanity where everyone is trapped within a static, unchanging and immutable ontology. This transformation from the end of eighteenth century and the beginning of the next is a period well-described by Professor Lovejoy. It was his conclusion, "There have, in the entire history of thought, been few changes in standards of value more profound and more momentous than that which took place…when it came to be believed not only that in many, or in all, phases of human life there are diverse excellences, but that diversity itself is of the essence of excellence…"[11] While we cannot deny the significance of these dramatic changes, it is the changes in thinking, the way we perceive, our assumptions regarding our being and the maintenance of given beliefs which is where the greatest changes have occurred. It is not what occurs around us but rather our interpretations that are most significant.

Rousseau's contribution to the genre of autobiography had taken the format to a new but not yet mature level. His expansion of autobiography was governed by his idea of the general rather than the private will of the individual. It was not the self that drove Rousseau but rather the general will, the society and the collective, that energy of the past represented by the tribe, the clan, at least exemplified by the *demes* of Athens and which at most interested him as a *philosophe*. He attempted to make what he construed to be a healthy and humane community, making whole a unity from separate individuals while keeping these beings somehow distinct; this is what drove his thinking. His intellectual achievements cannot be denied.

It was Goethe who took the next major step with his understanding of an inner and individualized being. Perhaps the term Romantic applies here since when we think of the singular individual and Goethe, as one serious student of the genre of autobiography has noted, possessed such a style: "Goethe found that he had his own way of speaking, his own way of dressing, as he had his own way of loving, and as he had his very own religion. No single element coming to him from the world was accessible only to him and not accessible to others; it might just as equally be building material for another. Every object 'appropriated' became marked, however, by the specificity of his individual style."[12]

While modern individuality began its appearance and the subject of dress may appear to be less than relevant, a short discussion regarding the issue of clothing at the end of the eighteenth century as well as throughout the next could be very revealing. A younger contemporary of Goethe's, the Englishman, Thomas Carlyle (1795–1881), while something of a conservative and clearly associated with Victorian literature wrote in his early years a satirical piece on the relationship of clothing and the appearance of the self entitled *Sartor Resartus* (c.1831). One scholar has observed that "…clothes had become 'unspeakably significant,' because appearances made in the world are not veils but guides to the authentic self of the wearer."[13] The issue of authenticity will become a key component for those who would either seek or claim to possess a self or be an individual. Carlyle, more than that, takes pains to make the point that such a preoccupation with appearance is instinctual:

> Nevertheless, the pains of Hunger and Revenge once satisfied, his next care was not Comfort but Decoration.…Warmth he found in the toils of her chase; or amid dried leaves in his hollow tree, in his bark shed, or natural grotto: but for Decoration he must have Clothes. Nay, among wild people, we find tattooing and painting even prior to Clothes. The first spiritual want of a barbarous man is Decoration, as indeed we still see among the barbarous classes in civilized countries.[14]

Distinguishing oneself from others is more ancient than society and could be considered even primitive. Standing out of the crowd is not necessarily a mark of individuality, however, any more than male birds using their plumage to attract the female. Dressing and decoration originally were more a matter of sexual selection than any singularity or sense of a self. That Carlyle understood this sense of differentiation in some manner is revealed by his comment that, "In all speculations they have tacitly figured man as a *Clothed Animal*; whereas he is by nature a *Naked Animal*…"[15] Here he proves he could be looking in two directions at one time, one towards the past and tradition, the other pointing to the future, especially with his contribution to a new literature, in this case, an essay on the role of clothing. Carlyle also understood something of a post-Hegelian idea that, "…the curtains of Yesterday drop down, the curtains of Tomorrow roll up; but Yesterday and Tomorrow both *are*."[16] The historic past had first been rationally confronted as Early Modern Europe unfolded and the following centuries gave further credence to a more modern perspective of a world built on the past that included a future. This was partially a result of the implications inherent in Enlightenment assumptions regarding the idea of progress. Perceptions of space and time along with that of ontology were transformed. This was followed by the "...Romantics [who] were moved by the vision of the future, of human possibilities, rather than of the past; of what man might become rather than of what he actually was or had been."[17] A root for these changes regarding the understanding of cultural time began with the Italian Renaissance and their newfound sense of a secular history which achieved a realizable maturation within the Romantic world with a future for secular thought. The final, third mental development will occur when the significance of the immediacy of a 'now' will be added to a maturing sense of the past and the future.

For the early part of the nineteenth century the new attitude regarding appearances, as one scholar pointed out, was developed in Carlyle's *Sartor Resartus*, the first written philosophy of dress. This same author, Richard Sennett, makes the case that, "...once the reader is ready to laugh at him, Carlyle begins to introduce, step by step little pieces of common public belief, like the virtue of order and stability, the importance of piety, and so on, so that the reader is drawn into laughing at himself." Self-humor is certainly an important component in the growth of a mature self-consciousness and is best expressed in Carlyle's use of his fictional figure, Professor Teufelsdröckh, as his spokesperson. "Gradually, also, Teufelsdröckh begins to say serious things which are not arrant nonsense, but radical ideas—like his belief in an agnosticism untinged with public ritual. As the reader begins to see himself in Teufelsdröckh, he also sees a new Teufelsdröckh, a man becoming a philosophical radical."[18] From Shakespeare's Falstaff[19] to Carlyle's Teufelsdröckh, we can discover the growing importance of humor towards that which is being given a life. The birthing of the self and this appearance of radical ideas coming from a Victorian Protestant is even more revealing. In part this may have possibly been the result of the influence of Goethe upon the young Englishman. Another commentator, Philip Rosenberg, further suggests that *Sartor Resartus* was: "… [a] sort of *jeu d'espirit* but it is the *jeu d'espirit* of a man in very bad spirits."[20] Sennett continues: "The book appeared at a time in Carlyle's life when he despaired of himself and the burden of the self that each person carried—a dark moment of a hatred of the web of desire in men now become so transparent, so immanent in their appearances. That clothes will reveal a self unbearable to contemplate—this abyss: Carlyle can write about it only with the aid of irony."[21]

That Goethe was individualized by his dress and rhetoric is not what marks his singularity, however. When he explored his ideas through poetry, including his great epic, Faust, he also was exploring his own inner being. It would be the later German philosopher, Wilhelm Dilthey (1835–1911) who would further contribute to the sense that knowledge and meaning are drawn from our past since it is as historical beings that we gain our understanding. As Dilthey put it, "Autobiography is the highest and most instructive form in which understanding of life confronts us."[22] Goethe was also well read in history although he was not particularly attracted to it as a discipline. "The cult of facts meant nothing to him; the history of institutions and abstractions had no appeal; mere events left him uninterested; the cadaverous smell of the sepulcher that clung to all history held him off." Goethe possessed an attraction to the human condition, to life lived rather than a life abstracted from the past. It was, "the meaning of a personal experience," that most interested him and it was in this regard that, "…autobiography was thus a very important genre for him, and he was well read in it."[23] But then he treated autobiography in a manner that was very different than the confession in the tradition of Augustine or specifically, Rousseau. It was in the world of poetry where he could suggest instead, that a "…poet should use the gift entrusted to him for comforting, elevating, and enriching human life. Goethe, it has been noted, admonished an ever-dissatisfied, ever-complaining friend: 'It is always better to enchant friends a little with the results of our existence than to sadden or to worry them with confessions of how we feel.'"[24] Not surprisingly, if there were those who could be enchanted by the writings of Goethe, it especially was the younger readers. The Romantic Germanic Sturm und Drang movement owes a portion of its roots to Goethe as it was his "Storm and Stress" play, Götz von Berlichingen (1773) that made him the hero of the younger generation. A year later his first novel, The Sorrows of Young Werther (1774), "…inspired a wave of suicides not only in Germany but also…in France."[25] The new challenges were not just a simple challenges of the new world in opposition to the old, but, rather, they were challenges of the youth against the traditions of the past; with their freshly unleashed feelings, dreams and imagination often being repeated in the following century. Another characteristic of the word "Romantic," therefore, is the role of youth and a feeling that, "…what is clear is that it is, in every case, a drive toward that fullness and naturalness of Being that the modern world threatens to let sink into oblivion."[26] This passionate sense of emotions has been associated with that aspect of the romantic activities known as romantic love which has, "…important implications for the changing relationships between the sexes and for shifts in the way in which people related to the masculine and feminine. We might characterize its essence as the glorification or idealization of an individual human other..."[27] To make the other so important requires that one would first make a major commitment to strongly defining the self. Thus the Rousseauean use of contrasting with others (general will) as an aid in the developing of the self (particular will) is carried on by Goethe to include the very act of overwhelming romantic love which can create a singular distinction, not unlike the impact of fashion as a distinguishing characteristic. This is not to say that Goethe was deprecating those who preceded him, it is only to make it clear that he felt no more limited by the work of the *philosophes* than did Rousseau although there existed a clearly different perspective.

Traditionally historians have dated the beginnings of the modern Western world with the appearance of Napoleon Bonaparte, but this study will avoid that political issue altogether. Historic dating is always precarious. For this study, Goethe is more than an early and adequate example of the developing modern self. With the appearance of an economic middle class, there clearly were more people, especially younger people, with more leisure that would make for new opportunities to explore and discover the distinguishing marks of a singular self. While many factors apply to the rise of this individuality, Goethe offered several additional unique components especially within the walls of his great masterpiece, his epic and scholarly poem, *Faust*.

Goethe began working on the plot of *Faust* (1808) very early in life when as a child he received a puppet set which he used to explore the Faust legend (first popularized by Christopher Marlowe, 1564–93). This was an unending project, one that apparently for Goethe never saw satisfactory completion since his second volume was only relatively completed in 1831, the year before his death. The actual plot is fairly self-evident and not very complicated: An ageing Faust is offered, by Mephistopheles, his youth now that he is very old and looking back on his life with regrets for not having lived a more active and participatory life. As an elderly scholar who devoted his entire life to the world of books, he knew a great deal about so very much except the actual activity of living. He accepts the offer from Mephistopheles knowing that if he accepts, his part of the bargain will be to relinquish his soul to the underworld upon his death. Simple, straight forward and often appearing in other formats over the centuries, including an opera: the theme has had a long life. Now death is not only being accepted but so too, apparently, damnation. The problem is that notwithstanding this summation, the story, ironically, is more complex than presented here, for it is in the fine tuning of Goethe's language that the plot is revealed. An important first point must be established: Mephistopheles can tempt Faust but only before he visits, converses and asks permission from the Lord. There is therefore, an agreement necessary for this temptation with the caveat that Mephistopheles' efforts can only be directed toward Faust. That Mephistopheles needs permission from God is not to be found in any traditional Christian theology. Moreover, this is not an accident of language as revealed later in the century with the announcement of God's demise, moving the West further toward an increased acceptance of a more secular view. And Goethe was not unattuned to this new perception. In Faust's own words:

> The God who dwells within my breast,
> Who can shake my soul to its depths, who sits
>   enthroned
> Over all my powers—outside me he is powerless.
> And, therefore, Being is a burden,
> Death longed for, Life detestable. [28]

The central importance of God is explicit: permission not only is granted but also moves the plot. The implication could be symbolically interpreted in that he is the source of choices that first began with the fruit of knowledge in Eden. But the Medieval transcending force of omnipotent, omniscient, and omnipresent deities has been removed from Goethe's stage. In response to the demand of the Witch, "To see Squire Satan here again!" Mephistopheles offers the following:

> These days it's only something in a fable
> But you human beings are no better off:
> You may have got rid of the Evil One,
> The evil ones have stayed right on.
> Just call me Baron [29]

While this has been a slow process, the role of deity is simply moved further from the center, first with Shakespeare, now with Goethe, where this change offers room for an individual's life to take shape regardless of a deity. Goethe's tendencies towards pantheism allows him to still subscribe some semblance of a supreme deity (more typically Germanic than Gallic or Anglo-Saxon) and is revealed in his earlier interest in occult philosophy when at the university. Still, with the diminution of the roles of both God and Mephistopheles in everyday choices, there is the parallel story of the growing presence and power of the living self and importance of one's own word. The contract that Faust agrees to is one where the future tense is clear and the purpose, a singular interior one, for Faust suggests that if at any time after being made young again, he cannot find action and activity, motion and movement, change and even the construction of value in both his living and his becoming it would mean little to him should he lose his soul. If he decides to quit and (to stand still) and no longer continue in motion, then what would be the point? If you are living, you are moving: keep on trucking or die (damnation). Thus the commitment to language which is central to Goethe is also a loophole in the contract, one that you would think Mephistopheles would have understood given his response to the 'Student' who queried: "But there has to be a thought with the word." Mephistopheles replies:

> All right! But you needn't let that worry you:
> It's exactly where a thought is lacking
> That, just in time, a word shows up instead.
> With words you can argue beautifully,
> With words you can make up a system,
> A word is a beautiful thing to believe in,
> Not one iota can be taken from a word.[30]

It is Goethe's commitment to language that separates him in part from one of the more well established German philosophers, specifically his somewhat older contemporary, Immanuel Kant (1724–1804). Although Kant is considered very significant because of the detailed organization of his thoughts and his contributions to a ponderous metaphysics, his views are more in harmony with the tradition of Descartes, especially in regard to the desire if not the need for a certainty and the necessity of metaphysical universal order. Kant was, after all, one of the earliest of the modern philosophers who was also a committed academician and as part of the German religious revival known as Pietism. He also wanted all the heavens back in their traditional place. In this, Kant's thoughts do not add that much to the subject of the modern (or post-modern) individual and self. However, in comparison to Goethe, some rather important contrasts appear. For example, Walter Kaufmann noted that, "Goethe was a poet and Kant a philosopher." This is not to say that, "Goethe, unlike Kant, should not be taken seriously in matters of this sort," for, "…both men were also scientists, and Kant's name is still associated with a theory in astronomy while Goethe made a biological discovery and wrote extensively, in prose as well as poetry, on the metamorphosis of plants."[31] But more importantly, "…unlike Kant, [Goethe] says what he means so well that it would be the height of presumption to try to improve on it."[32] Goethe had that clarity of language that one would expect from a poet just as a philosopher might literally use language all too often to obfuscate as well as clarify. But Kaufmann offers two more important reasons why Goethe was so much the clearer thinker than Kant. What Goethe wrote about he *saw* in concrete detail, and therefore was able to find the words to effectively communicate. "One might call the approach he embodied visual and concrete, and Kant conceptual and abstract."[33] Again the difference between the poet and the metaphysician, especially one who tries to make all thought united into a comprehensive whole and fit then into his own preset assumptions as was Kant's proclivity, is transparent. But the second reason Kaufmann offers is that, "…he did not write to please others or to enhance his status but to satisfy himself."[34] Kant had a reputation that he spent a career developing. Moreover he was following in the footsteps of the past, that of Plato, et al., who sought to put together a unified and comprehensive philosophical order of the world, a world that was clearly losing coherence. Goethe on the other hand, was concerned with what would become more and more of significance for future thinkers, i.e., the dynamics of our ontology, and an expansion of an inner self and individuality that so increasingly marks today's ontological understanding. As Kaufmann further notes, "Faust's first monologue begins with a curse on Kant's kind of existence—a life without development, a life of routine, a death in life." This introduces us to a key component to Goethean thought—evolution, not only as he found in his studies of biology where he anticipated Darwin, but equally as well, in our changing psychology.

To stand alone became part of the thinking that is present in the ideas of Goethe, and what is revealing is a remark Goethe made in a conversation on 2 May 1831, "Thus one also finds in life a mass of people who do not have enough character to stand alone; they throw themselves at a party, and that makes them feel stronger and allows them to be somebody."[35] Unlike Rousseau who sought to bring together varied peoples into a cohesive social order, Goethe was one of the first who sought to find the basis for standing alone as an individual with a strong sense of an inner being or self. This commitment was continued later in the century by Kierkegaard who would, when speaking, "…of 'becoming the individual' [had] …in effect sided with Goethe against Kant."[36] Kant and Goethe were in agreement, however, in their commitment to science, but it was Kant and not Goethe who looked back to Newton. This is a clear contrast to the English Romantics like Blake who saw a trilogy of evil thinking in Bacon, Locke and especially Newton with what he called, "mind-forged manacles." Goethe had disagreements with Newton, specifically regarding the subject of color. As is well known, color was one of the more important studies and conclusions Newton offered. But this was not acceptable to Goethe. While they both, "...developed theories of color: Newton's was purely quantitative; Goethe's dealt with the sensuous perception of color, including such phenomena as complimentary colors and clashing colors."[37] In other words, the subjective component, the element of actually perceiving color, the human response to the stimuli, must be included in any definition of color, a position now accepted by neurophysiologists and also part of any discussion of consciousness: the question that is so often asked today is what does the color yellow appear to look like to different observers?

Goethe also demonstrates in a variety of other ways his commitment to the importance of the individual. In contrast to Kant who, "...associated morality with universality, and autonomy with universal laws that are binding for all rational beings, not with individuality. Goethe taught by example that autonomy involves going it alone."[38] It was no longer in the group or collective that the best expression of humanity is found. It is, rather, in individual acts of decency where rational choices may be expressed. The idea of a universal reasoning tied somehow to laws of nature was slowly fading from the intellectual map as the individuality of one's own reasoning and personal life came to the fore. The slow shift away from the public and collective as an exclusive basis for both living and for making judgements grew most clearly in the nineteenth century. Hobbes' earlier fears of individuality, however, were also becoming increasingly supported which can be seen with the appearance of a modern version of a collective identity found in Karl Marx. For Goethe, it wasn't the defense of the collective but the defense of the individual which saves him:

> If ever I stretch myself upon a bed of ease,
> My heart at peace, then let that be the end of me!
> If ever you can fool me with your flattery
> Till I am satisfied with what I am—
> If ever you can swindle me with pleasure,
> May that day be my last! I make you that bet! [39]

That the 'I' in these poetic lines is a dominant theme is to be expected from the century that gave us the earliest preoccupation with the self. 'I' make the bet, 'I' being satisfied, 'I' on a bed of ease, 'I' am; and then we have the 'me,' the end of, 'me' flattered, 'me' swindled; and 'myself,' 'my' last and 'my' heart. 'I' appears five times, 'me' three and 'my' an additional three, all this in only six short lines. To have the self dominate your language this way was once an example of the sin of pride. But the commandments had begun to replace the deadly sins during the Reformation so now reason, art and feelings were carrying this phenomenon of prideful self further.

Goethe was clearly adept with the future tense. It has been suggested that "…the Devil is cheated of his apparently well-deserved prey by the feeble trick of a future tense…and by the intervention of divine grace called down upon him by the only human love Faust ever received and experienced."[40] Dante's love theme with Beatrice as guide through heaven now reappears in Goethe. That is, to care for another, an undeveloped idea in Rousseau, is developed in Goethe, considering love to be a process and not a fixed phenomenon. The certitude of divine intervention or of natural law is not being replaced by a passion of love but rather love as a process for growth, change and development: there is a massive difference between falling in love and growing in one's love of another. The Scientific Revolution's ideas of motion in Goethe are now so natural as to see motion as inherent in all life. Faust will give up his soul when "…he would content himself, even anticipate the enjoyment of peace…in his vision of the contented future."[41] As Faust tells Mephistopheles, "As soon as I stand still I'm a slave: Yours, someone else's, what's the difference?"[42] Those who would want a fixed and secure life, where certainty for all possible future contingencies is a given, are slaves to that need. With death they will spend an eternity at the hands of Mephistopheles, secure and unchanging, time without motion, which they had already practiced during their static existence. What, in the end, is the difference between security, therefore, and death? One interesting way of stating the issue in the eyes of Faust is found in a commentary of Erich Heller's *The Disinherited Mind*: "What is Faust's sin? Restlessness of spirit. What is Faust's salvation? Restlessness of spirit.…criss-crossing of restless strivings of different qualities: the striving for peace, and the striving for sensation; or, to put it differently, and in terms of the quality of the contentment sought, the striving for that peace that passeth all understanding, and the striving for a state of calm, an 'enough' which is merely a state of emotional exhaustion."[43] The idea here is to always be on the move, for Mephistopheles can only catch those without motion, the corpse. *Rigor mortis* is a condition that the future cannot correct, and Goethe was committed to the idea of a future, a living future.

It was this desire for a future marked by activity that drove his story line. The point of the contract is that it gives him back his youth, i.e., a future. It is here where individuality can develop. "Romantics were moved by the vision of the future, of human possibilities, rather than of the past; of what man might become rather than of what he actually was or had been."[44] While the Enlightenment placed a great deal of stock on the earlier discoveries of those who had changed our understanding of nature, the newness of the world around the nineteenth century thinkers was a greater attraction because of this more dynamic view of change. This newer post-Enlightenment view can be found explicated in the writings of another German philosopher of the time, Friedrich Hegel (1770–1831), who also understood the principle that life, "…is characterized by its 'sheer restlessness' and by its absolute and inherent *process of differentiation*…"[45]

Hegel is both a remarkable and difficult thinker to understand. It has been said that if you cannot understand his writings you will equally not understand any works written by those who claim understand him. And if you do understand a monograph on Hegel while not understanding Hegel it is probably because that author does not understand him.[46] While this may be little more than hyperbole, it nevertheless introduces several basic thoughts relative to consciousness as well as offering an alternative perspective that differentiates these revolutionary modern ideas from those of the Enlightenment. What follows is an interpretation Hegel. Part of the limitations in Enlightenment thought had been that it was drawn either from Descartes' rationalism or Lockean empiricism. For the historian of ideas, the Enlightenment split the inner (subject) and outer (substance) worlds from each other. Historically, the English followed the logic of empiricism (sensation) while the French will eventually follow a more Cartesian rationalistic approach (*cogito*). The Germans tended towards positions held by Berkeley and Leibniz, defending ideas and more loosely associated with 'idealism.' Goethe as well as Hegel follow this Germanic path expanding it for future German thinkers. As for consciousness, in Hegelian terms, "…'truth' includes the consciousness which understands and which is partly produced by the dialectical link between substance and subject."[47] Therefore consciousness comes closer to Lockean 'knowledge' rather than Lockean memory or Descartes' 'awareness.' But it is more than that since with such a consciousness one becomes capable of grasping a deeper if not also paradoxical understanding of both phenomena (objects as they appear to us) and noumena (things as they are in themselves) as well as a unity of both. A student of Victorian poetry puts it as follows:

> Substance and subject, essence and form, object and consciousness, being and knowing, become concepts that incorporate each other, subsume each other, turn into each other in acts of mind which at the same time distinguish them from each

other. Such paradoxical propositions are perhaps at the heart of what is so difficult to grasp in Hegel's dialectical thinking, since they disobey the formal conventions of non-contradiction which require that A cannot be both *a* and *not-a*.[48]

While this is not the place to resolve the inherent conflicts within those genuinely unique schemes that reside within Hegelian ideas (and incidentally, Kant's), it is important to point out that a more unified set of assumptions began to appear in place of the fragmented views of a Cartesian versus Lockean Enlightenment. For all their insights, the understanding of self with a corollary individuality supporting consciousness had not been fully developed by these earlier thinkers. Theirs tended to remain a more collective, community-driven set of social-political and economic thoughts. Some of these Romantic geniuses were attempting—and failing—to create a more unified picture.

It is through the new mind set associated with the nineteenth century Romantics that the long road to a contemporary self-conscious reflective individuality received encouragement. To complicate this earlier picture of varied and often contradictory definitions of the relationship of the rational and irrational, the intellectual and passionate, we can now see the development in the nineteenth century of key components of some the assumptions of our own era. As one commentator put it: "What is needed is a more fundamental kind of thinking that will cut under both opposites."[49] While Hegel's thought is elliptic and often confusing and also has been used to advocate varied and even contradictory intellectual and interpretive positions, the concern for this study is his offer of a more complete and integrative study of the term consciousness. Although he offers a no more clearer definition than now in our possession.

This shift in the understanding of time and space played an indispensable role in the creation of our modern thinking that allows for a sense of a self. Time had been understood as being under divine control, then rationalized in the Renaissance while still only concerned with our sense of the past. And while it was further rationalized during the Scientific Revolution and Enlightenment, it only took on a more modern pattern when the future was humanized with the arrival of the modern mind: past, present and future were becoming especially efficacious if not somehow blended. The picture is not always what many might want to embrace, as was demonstrated by the English poet, William Blake's significant *The Marriage of Heaven and Hell*. Blake anticipates later thinkers in his offering a "...particular significance here because...it anticipates Nietzsche, as it also anticipates a good deal of the psychologist Jung in our century....If man marries his hell to his heaven, his evil to his good, he will become a creature such as the earth has not yet seen." Nietzsche supposedly noted a similar paradox: "Mankind must become better and more evil."[50] This introduces a special caveat for how much more complicated the world and our understanding of ourselves was becoming. The simple world of certainty, or of moral comfort or of a saved life begins to fail for the thoughtful observer. From the Enlightenment through the Romantics, the power of death had diminished. This was a world where, "'Daring to know' implied the possibility of an anxiety of consciousness, of the necessity of doubt: in ontology the Enlightenment gave up the supernatural props of human certitude; in epistemology it cut its mooring to the absolute."[51] This was the opening of an intellectual and cultural revolution creating an historically unique and open mentality. Walter Kaufmann suggests that the goal "...was Goethean autonomy—not to live according to rules or maxims à la Kant, not to break through determinism by performing uncaused acts that sprang solely from respect for reason, à la Kant, but to become self-reliant and to live independent and creative lives."[52] Kant represented the past looking for answers of the self in old structural thinking, while Hegel offered an updated dialectic for a certainty of individuality, and Goethe, the poet, left most doors wide open.

When speaking of an ever opening society with an even freer style in thinking, living and creating, it is in part because of a growing sense of individuality with an ability to wallow inside that inner self that further contributed to an expanding ontology of consciousness. Another contemporary of this transformation is found in the writings of Samuel Taylor Coleridge (1772–1834), a significant contributor to the English language as well to our modern identity. He appears at a time when that the idea of genius that Mill had pointed to was critical for our understanding of the arrival of individuality.[53] It was in *Culture and Society* that the author Raymond Williams demonstrated how the words associated with creative activity changed in the 1820's:

> The emphasis on skill, in the word, was gradually replaced by an emphasis on sensibility; and this replacement was supported by the parallel changes in such words as *creative*,... *original*...and *genius*....From *artist* in the new sense there were formed *artistic* and *artistical*, and these, by the end of the nineteenth century, had certainly more reference to 'temperament' than to skill or practice. *Aesthetics*, itself a new word, and a product of the specialization, similarly stood parent to *aesthete*, which again indicated 'a special kind of person.'[54]

This "special kind of person" arrived out of the creative artists and scientists we think of as unique and authentic. Their burden centers upon their authenticity to an evolving sense of self. *Unique* and *authentic* are new words now being explored. Also: "At the dawn of the nineteenth century, the possibilities of consciousness were enormous; and so were the consequences." Writing in his *Notebooks*, Coleridge found that it was in the new world of psychology where he found consciousness: "...the problem, the solution of which cannot too variously be re-worded, too manifoldly be illustrated....Almost all is yet to be achieved."[55] In his view of a resolution, the traditional dualism drawn from Plato, Stoics, Christians and Descartes had not abated but had been transformed by Romantic explorations. Coleridge acknowledged the dilemma concerning mental capacity and its risks: "Man must be *free*; or to what purpose was he made a spirit of reason, and not a machine of instinct? Man must *obey*; or wherefore has he a conscience?"[56] Adding confusion to traditional dualism which Coleridge contributed to with his delineation of our older conscience and the youthful consciousness he further implied a conflict between acts of obedience *and* of freedom. This untraveled road is one when confronted will undermine older thinking regarding death and its certitude.

Death and the desire to be moral had held mastery over our thinking and it was only at the end of the eighteenth century that we find an early example of shifting modes of thinking. This is well illustrated when Boswell asked David Hume, then on his deathbed, whether Hume was in fact a closet Christian since he had been such a very good model of a moral being. Hume replied with his own simple question: why to you suppose only a Christian can be a good? It is not only surprising that he had been known as *le bon David*, he was also an arrow pointing to the modern world of the a modern skeptic, nonbeliever and decent human.

Slowly, that sense of dualism which implies conflict is eclipsed. We could take as an example the famous lines from a modern novel: "It was the best of times, it was the worst of times."[57] Reaching beyond the dualism of life or death or the best versus the worst of times, one moves to a certainty of being alive and so, having time. For most people the act of living is too demanding to leave much room for active thinking, reflection or despair. Life versus death slowing is being recognized as inherently antithetical since, as Hegel would point out, both positions are needed to complete a picture of existence. It is the time and space you have that makes an indisputable fact that can at least offer some resolution of any implied conflict. Alive, there is motion and where there is motion there is time and space: death only magnifies the quality of living for those who still have motion. For Coleridge it was the motion between conscience and consciousness, rather than any contradiction, that interested him. For him as with Goethe and Hegel and others to follow, motion and process were the key to living, growth and knowledge. One way to put it is as follows:

> Coleridge, wisely I think, placed emphasis on the process of reaching an act, not on the act itself: 'The more consciousness in our Thoughts and Words,' he felt, 'and the less in our Impulses and general Actions, the better and more healthful the state both of head and heart.'(*IS*, 95) Morality, he believed, should be 'grounded' in both 'conscience and the common sense'(*F*, 314); and 'the conditional cause of Conscience' is reason 'applied to motives of our conduct' which correspond with our 'sense of moral responsibility.'(*F*, 159) Clearly the process of arriving at 'moral responsibility' was a carefully guided tour, aided by reason, through the stages of consciousness, until we were brought face to face with conscience. That arbiter would then decide in its role as judge whence we had come from and wither we were headed.[58]

There is nothing in the these ideas of what could be labeled an either/or issue that inhibited moral actions for Coleridge. For him one can have both freedom and duty, conscience and consciousness, not one or the other. He held that:

> Like consciousness, duty needs to be redefined to make clearer how it responds authentically to man's actions. Still it seems scarcely conceivable that the concepts of duty are divisible from the newly emerging conceptions of consciousness. However we try, we come back to King Conscience holding court. It was a dilemma that Coleridge confronted all his life, desiring always the freedom of will he considered *sine qua non* for existence but bowing (always) to a certain *primum mobile* which, in his case, tended to emanate from divine sources (Kant acted much too often the role of God) in the shape of duty or conscience.[59]

The implication here is that there is no certainty but only a variety of choices. In some ways Coleridge could remind us that we, ourselves are outsiders especially within the confines of our own century since he, like others today, was among other things an (opium) addict.

It is not surprising that the Surrealist through the Beats—many who were also users of hallucinogens—also admired the life and writings of Coleridge. This hint of modernity, even post-modernity, can be found in a variety of places throughout the nineteenth century. If, "...a foolish consistency is a hobgoblin of little minds,"[60] as Ralph Waldo Emerson stated, a comparable thought also is found in William Wordsworth (1770–1850), who appeared capable of embracing what would appear, at the time, a paradox: "Our meddling intellect / Misshapes the beauteous forms of things: / We murder to dissect."[61] Taking things apart has many important advantages, as in science, but it also can be destructive to the pristine whole. As with Goethe, rather than Kant, it is the poet who often stands against the academic scientist and metaphysician. Modern man, mechanical man, empirical man, specialized man and man as the power driver, all were coming into dominance just as questions were beginning to appear about the unity of living, nature, society and knowledge. Hegel had also recognized the importance of our knowledge of death and how it distinguishes us from the animal kingdom. In doing so he made our knowledge of death more important and central to our uniqueness than our creation of language.[62]

While the idea of death had changed as a central dynamic in the psyche of the deeper and more serious thinkers, in a limited way there is more acceptance of it for the average citizen in many metropolitan areas. An example can be found in the following observation by Jean Delumeau:

> ...the European tradition was based neither on a morbid attraction nor on a lugubrious fascination, but rather on a certain complicity and familiarity with the dead combined with an apparent insensitivity and indifference to the banal reality of someone else's death....In cities, cemeteries doubled as parks, marketplaces, fairgrounds, and dance halls. In seventeenth-century Paris, the famous *Cimitière des Innocents* served as a public shopping center, featuring bookstores, haberdashers, and drapers.[63]

As prosperity increased in Western Europe with the expansion of world trade, increasing numbers of entrepreneurs and the growth of a middle class, life's pleasures began to overtake life's miseries. Perspectives, like insights, changed with circumstances. The inherited class structures, the aristocracy (and peasants) had slowly declined as an exclusive power block while the newer bourgeois and proletariat social groups began making their presence felt throughout Modern Europe. It may very well be that with the weakened sense of traditional classes and the continuous decline of traditional class values and attitudes associated with the aristocracy, as well the growth of a bourgeois and Marxist class-consciousness together, contributed to an increase in the diversity, openness and the possibility for personal consciousness and self-consciousness. For now, the divisions in all economic and geographic categories of a Western culture, as well as the separation of the *literati* from the growing population, need only be noted here as opening the doors to opportunity, diversity, individuality and fresh thinking.

There is little disagreement that the Western view of the world, especially as applied to our understanding of space, time, motion, singularity, diversity, authenticity, reflection, introspection and ideas of the future had gone through extremely dramatic changes. The accumulation of literature, knowledge, information and new scientific theories also contributed to the expansion of academic inquiry in new disciplines of study. The first half of the nineteenth century witnessed the creation of geology as a legitimate scientific study which introduced serious questions regarding the Bible as a source of analytic knowledge, specifically, as applied to the beginnings of the Earth. For the second half of the century, the early impact of Darwin and the biological sciences changed our understanding of what we physically had been, are and may become. Perhaps that is why Blake insisted on making imagination an "…instrument of self-knowledge." However, "…what must be grasped about Blake's conception is that imagination is not purely emotional or intellectual; for Blake, knowledge involved the whole being, body, emotions, intellect."[64] The words *imagination* and *wholeness* are offered in place of the Kantian drive for absolute rational certainty, order, truth and prestige. Furthermore, there is at least a corollary to these new sciences in the qualitative and quantitative expansion of language, especially in the growth of the popular novel and new experiments in modern poetry that increasingly appeared: language supports imagination. These historic changes contributed to a new perspective regarding certainty, to a different and fundamentally modern approach to making space our own even though on the path to death. The poet was expanding beyond the *philosophe* as arbiter in our understanding of an ontologic self: a new post-philosophic and metaphysical reality. Writing was now becoming deeply introspective. It was a new space for images and possibilities that broke through antiquated patterns of what was perceived as real. If the poet could write it, could it not be true, even if for no one other than the one who had imagined it? This is neither a scientific nor a philosophical search for truth. But it can be part of a truth—as is all art. Where there is great art, there is a truth for the future to catch up to. Kant was summarizing the past while the creative artist/writers like Goethe, Blake, Hegel and Coleridge, were opening and encouraging the future. And not an opening by way of rationalization as in the previous century. No, this was a passion and a reason both tandem and separate, a sense of being beyond the constraints of traditional dualism and a recognition that the subject separated from the observed (Bacon) and the object internalized by thought (Descartes) and by empirical experiences (Locke), were only beginnings not a conclusion. Language regarding our individuality is fundamental and it is on this that Alexis de Tocqueville (1805–59) reflected:

> *Individualism* is a novel expression, to which a novel idea has given birth. Our fathers were only acquainted with *egoïsme* (selfishness). Selfishness is a passionate and exaggerated love of self, which leads a man to connect everything with himself, and to prefer himself to everything in the world. Individualism is a mature and calm feeling, which disposes each member of the community to sever himself from the mass of his fellows, and to draw apart with his family and his friends; so that, after he has thus formed a little circle of his own, he willingly leaves society at large to itself.[65]

While expressing this new-found sense of individuality suspended from the classical *ego*, it has proven to be less than a complementary term in France since there it was considered (and still tends to be) unacceptable behavior since it is perceived as conflicting with the cohesion of society. The other language of the age was and still is dominated by the power of the individuality of silence since, "Silence is order, because silence is the absence of social interaction."[66] Social interaction after the centuries of failures in finding security (certainty?) in societal conformity was beginning to wear as thin as biblical imperatives. It may have worked for most but it would not work for those seeking a greater certainty in understanding the natural ontology of our existence rather than those based on the platitudes of the past. Something new in defining the life of the individual was needed and it proved to be forthcoming.

Friedrich Nietzsche (1844–1900) was a philologist, writer and poet who at one point taught the classics until he realized that there was no one left in his classroom who was "hungry." (The history of curiosity and its landscape has yet to be written.) As a student of classical philology, he took language and syntax seriously. The theme of language representing space, and memory representing time, are two of the most fundamental components contributing to the creation of both a modern self and individuality, the twin dynamic components upon which consciousness can stand and to which Nietzsche devoted his life. But language and history are now perceived as less passive than in the past because of the new sense of the power of motion, or action for the sake of action. All the rhetoric of the post-Cartesian and Lockean world increasingly appeared—at least to nineteenth century Romantics—to be little more than talk since it was devoid of passion, imagination or immediate active application. Nietzsche both subscribed to as well as quoted the Goethean perception: "I hate everything that merely instructs me without increasing or directly quickening my activity."[67] To learn and expand our understanding and yet not to fundamentally change in our assumptions and perceptions made little or no sense to Nietzsche. The existence of the self was predicated on the actions, the dynamic choices manifest within our individual, active responsibility.

This new attitude which grew in part out of Romantic views of love as an act of engagement, motion and passion can be found and expressed by a great number of nineteenth century philosophers, poets and novelists. Hegel stated, "...nothing great in the world has been accomplished without passion."[68] For many of the writers of this era, passion and motion were handmaidens. One is brought to mind, for instance, of those scenes in Emile Zola's (1840–1902) *Germinal* (1885) where Etienne Lantier, the reformist-minded voyager who is literally propelled by the winds into a mining town where the story takes place only to reach the end of the story literally with him again being propelled out of town by the those same winds. Imagination is seen as natural as the wind. The additional theme of conflict between proletariat workers, the miners working underground and the bourgeois stock owner was heightened by the forces and energy of a dynamics within nature, something increasingly admired now in part for its unpredictability. These were times of massive change, in economic and social structures, in the maturation of nationalism, technological developments, population growth, and diverse social changes that proved ironically compatible to those who were drawn to the opposite, towards their individualistic tendency. They could now explore a new art by those revolutionary painters and poets at the end of the century as well as new thinking arriving in the sciences that would increasingly dominate their personal road of exploration, hammering out an authentic voice to call their own. *Motion, action, passion* and *imagination* were common terms of the Romantic era. Nietzsche like Dostoevsky went beyond these terms although many Romantic attitudes continued, just as the Enlightenment faith in reason and progress remained a common theme.

What now becomes an intellectual concern, a linguistic issue beyond those terms of *self, individual* and *consciousness*, were more recent components of the psyche: self-consciousness and existential, two extremely complex terms to this day. One of the more challenging metaphors for consciousness was offered by Coleridge: "...the narrow *Neck* of the bottle." To the question, "Whither Consciousness?" he responded recognizing the difficulty of the question: "...the lowest depth that the light of our Consciousness can visit," which would still be short of our understanding being as it was, "...at an unknown distance from the Ground."[69] Coleridge did not have a very optimistic attitude when it came to the concept of consciousness. When Coleridge wrote that the problem for our psyche was consciousness, he had recognized correctly that any solution in dealing with this would have to wait for the future which was as optimistic as he could be. He clearly held a view—opposite to Hegel—that this unknown phenomena is too difficult in part because he retained with it a powerful sense of conscience. "Coleridge was much tormented by the prick of conscience, by guilt, by remorse, which became the title of one of his plays."[70] Freedom is always problematic but not recognized until it becomes an issue. The tradition of the search for an absolute and for certainty did not disappear in this century of change and for some still retained a universal place notwithstanding the singular desire of achieving one's own individual identity. Coleridge,

> ...read Kant, and though he quarreled with that mercilessly strict master, he remained nevertheless a good pupil—most of the time. However his conjunction of conscience and consciousness, he made not so much a Kantian as a Christian *in extremis*, the fall of dark upon him, grim and dreadful: 'Few are so obdurate, few have sufficient strength of character, to be able to draw forth an evil tendency or immoral practice into distinct *consciousness*, without bringing it in the same moment before an awaking *conscience*. But for this very reason it becomes a duty of conscience to form the mind to a habit of distinct consciousness.' Such a habit was in fact more remorseless than opium. Frail man, frail Christian, Coleridge observed sadly, who walks among 'snares' and 'pitfalls,' asking God not to tempt him and yet positioning himself 'on the very edge of [temptation]' because he failed to 'kindle the torch'—the light, the conscience itself, which might prevent disaster.[71]

Sounding a little like Goethe in a desire to push to the very edge of a lived life, he stands alone because he appears on this issue like a reactionary in that he equates not only, "conscience and reason," but further suggests that, "Consciousness itself...of which all reasoning is the varied modification, is but the Reflex of Conscience."[72] Of course consciousness, especially self-consciousness, can be seen as something that "inhibits spontaneity of expression," spontaneity of thought now seen as admirable.[73] There is this potential contradiction for some arguments regarding self-consciousness.

Hegel equates consciousness with knowledge, an extension of a Lockean view.[74] And while he also appears to make self-consciousness important in some of his thinking, he is always problematic particularly when one attempts to understand the full implications of any systematization of his meaning. One approach is to argue that, "...consciousness for Hegel is in effect simply a metaphor, that it has no substantive referent in any metaphysical or even material sense, no signification outside the contextual implications of Hegel's own text."[75] And as one commentator has put it:

'Self'—'one's own'—is the defining element of the Hegelian Subject—*Geist*. Absolute Knowledge is where this 'self-ness'—although 'selfishness' would not be entirely out of order, either—achieves its full, absolute measure and where it can be possible only in full measure. The self thus determines Hegelian subjectivity as the economy of self-engagement, leading to the general problem of the inhibition and delay of reflection...[76]

Additionally, "...the concept of the self has acquired considerable disseminating power during its history since Hegel."[77] Moreover, "...in Hegel's language, the mind produces what we call culture and civilization."[78] This is an interesting comment since, "If Hegel is right, if language represents a specific mode of self-estrangement, then we have to ask ourselves whether the preoccupation with language as language, so prevalent in our time, is not an expression of the very estrangement which we are discussing."[79] Given the difficulty in reading Hegel, it is not surprising to suspect that he wants to create a fluid system or fluid certainty and yet will speak in static terms of a matter that he perceives as pure process. Is this a problem of the limits of his language? Whether it is his language or his thinking, this is not inconsistent with a general overall understanding regarding his views. Hegel was clearly influenced by Goethe's life and certainly understood the power of diversity and action, but he appears to want Goethe's motion while retaining Kant's absolutes.[80] The self was real and central for both. For the purpose of this work, however, it need only be noted that consciousness in general and now self-consciousness in particular became important issues to several nineteenth century writers, and even Nietzsche was anything but an exception.

Whatever problems one would have in working with the writings of Hegel they cannot be compared with Nietzsche who is relatively accessible even if he is not systematic or optimistic in his thinking. His intellectual interests were as broad as his understandings were deep and he should be thought of as much as a poet as a philosopher, more in the tradition of Goethe whom he admired more. One serious concern for Nietzsche, as it had been with Goethe and Hegel, was the issue of a self, especially a self as a learning and changing being. Here the ontology is fluid. The influence of Hegelian thought is demonstrated by the following: "Whenever one speaks of self-knowledge, the shadow of Hegel begins to grow. It may never fully disappear. It is perhaps shortest in Nietzsche when *Zarathustra* begins—the 'moment of the briefest shadow.' It may still be the longest in the last long paragraph of the *Phenomenology*—a shadow the length of History."[81] Nietzsche of course knew something of Hegelian parameters. While he was very impressed by Goethe, he "...did not take his cue from Faust, as the popular misinterpretation of his philosophy would imply, but from the old Goethe." Actually "...he disparaged *Faust* and emphasized, like no major interpreter before him, the surpassing greatness of the ever popular old Goethe."[82] One important factor in his admiration is that Nietzsche was a student of the classical world and his one and only admirable ancient figure was Dionysus, a figure of action and passion. Not surprising, therefore, he said of Goethe:

> He created himself [as] the man of tolerance, not from weakness but from strength, because he knows how to use to his advantage even that from which the average nature would perish....Such a spirit who has *become free* stands amid the cosmos with a joyous and trusting fatalism, in the *faith* that only the particular is loathsome, and that all is redeemed and affirmed in the whole—*he does not negate any more*. Such a faith, however, is the highest of all possible faiths: I have baptized it with the name of *Dionysus*.[83]

In some ways Nietzsche can appear as an optimized Faust. One commentator, in discussing the Nietzsche masterpiece, *Thus Spoke Zarathustra*, noted that both, "... *Faust* and *Zarathustra* are in fact brothers among books. Both attempt to elaborate in symbols the process by which the superior individual—whole, intact, and healthy—is to be formed; and both are identically 'immoral' in their content, if morality is measured in its usual conventional terms."[84] He was in this sense a transitional figure, a fresh mind that most clearly looked toward the future. However, the picture that can be drawn regarding his vision is not salutary. "As regards the future, Nietzsche felt that the next two centuries would be characterized by cataclysmic events, such as great wars and revolutions, as well as a further advance of spiritual nihilism."[85] That he was so accurate in anticipating our future offers little if nothing in the way of comfort either. To add to his insights Nietzsche suggested in his brilliant *Human, All-Too-Human* presaged that the phenomenon of "nationalism" was a serious danger. He went so far as to express his hope that some day there would be a more, "...mixed race, that of the European man," that would develop from national identities. This may not be so surprising if one remembers that he also considered himself to be more likely Polish than German.[86] As we look back at the twentieth century it is easy to see how accurate a picture he painted since the great wars of nationalism that dominated the landscape and decimated the planet with the unheard number of dead leads to the conclusion that an accurate label for this world could be The Century of Annihilation. A concern for the future was as new for the nineteenth century as the rationalizing of the past had been for the Renaissance. An important point regarding chronology is that a contemporary of Nietzsche in France, Jules Verne (1828–1905) created the literary genre of science fiction. And to add to his unique and growing new sense of time, not only past but now future, Nietzsche will add the importance of a new guide for life, one that will call for a domination of the present; i.e., a beginnings of an existential attitude.

While Nietzsche was broad in his thinking and understanding, he could be confusing in some of his conclusions, many of which were sometimes negative. His ability to be very opaque and poetic with his aphorisms was one of his unique characteristics. In a certain sense this is not surprising since he was clear in his aversion towards those would be his followers. Since he views history as the story of brutality and senseless conflicts he is at least in this sense, consistent.[87] But it was in the classical world that he found his greatest comfort. From his philological studies of antiquity to the edge of the new madness that would be labeled nationalism and materialism, Nietzsche addressed the times that would challenge all our humanity. He was a defender of the first Dionysus, and a chronicler for any new Dionysus who might appear, a figure that he also related to his concept of an *Übermensch*. This Germanic term for his "overman" demonstrates the problem for those attempting to put some logical coherent scheme to this period of history: a constant increase of a creatively changing, challenging and unique languages with sometimes confused meanings. In addition popular words, syntax and meaning appear with the recently developed penny press and explosion of popular literacy. Additionally, there was another new idea, nihilism, that will join hands with that of existential. This is not work intended to offer conclusive definitions but rather a working understanding of the context of various meanings that are generally used, some of which arrived partially, out of Nietzsche's vision of a doomed Europe where, "…an eclipse of all traditional values was at hand, and that modern European man, this pampered child of the optimistically rational eighteenth century, would needs go astray in a wilderness without path or guidance."[88] For those of this past century and those considered late Romantics and those loosely associated with the term existential, the sense of nihilistic foreboding clearly impacted. For example, "…many Romantics passed, often more than once, through a stage which, following Nietzsche's terminology, we have become accustomed to define as nihilism; but already in contemporary usage 'Nihiliste' meant, according to L.S. Mercier's *Néologie* of 1801: "*Un homme qui ne croit a rien.*" The new term first appeared in 1796. In German, '*Nihilismus*' was used in the same sense for the first time, apparently by Novalis."[89]

It was these traditions and their decay Nietzsche often confronted in his writings. "Nietzsche described his own age, and the two centuries to come, as the era of 'nihilism'—a word he used, in a complex and idiosyncratic way, to refer to various consequences, personal and cultural, of an exaggerated subjectivism." The *cogito* of Descartes had quietly grown into a powerful voice of the inner, subjective, and personal guide in place of tradition for whatever knowledge was to be acquired and given value. While Nietzsche was no friend of religion he did note a key component to this mentality set since the "…one central element of this nihilism was the disappearance of a sense of external grounding of values…"[90] Nietzsche had held religion in general to be a crutch and specifically, the Christian religion as a negative force, a denial of an assertive and active disposition. He found himself in a dilemma, however, one that "…appeared to be complete: without a return to Christianity—which Nietzsche rejected—man's spiritual essence would wither away." Given this situation one could expect the possibility that he would capitulate and grant the tradition of turning to God and the Church for life's securing certainty, at least for those he labeled the "herd." Given the opening of the world, the lack of a secure mental framework and the new bourgeois economics of prosperity and materialism, the role of God for Nietzsche was more important than ever since he had such a low opinion of people even as he personally rejected religion. This is all the more remarkable, since "…the other half of Nietzsche's personality refused to surrender to gloom and despondency. Even though human lives were becoming empty and meaningless, could not Life itself be glorified? If no other Gods remained, Life would have to be declared divine."[91]

The completion of the story of the demise of the divine in general and on behalf of a certainty beyond death can be summarized around one singular Nietzschean concept—The Death of God. It was in his famous, *Zarathustra*, where Nietzsche spoke of the this death.[92] When we think back to the evolution of our hunger for certainty, first regarding death, and then immortality, from the use of language, writing, a born-again religion, and then the collapse of the authentic "Word" and the remaining answers of Cartesian and Lockean paradigms and it is rather startling to see the growing secular mind reach a point of an acceptance of a decomposition of divine answers. For that reason and because of its importance we should include Nietzsche's full comment in section 125 of *The Madman*, in *Gay Science* (1882) regarding this revolutionary transformation:

> Have you ever heard of that madman who lit a lantern in the bright morning hours, ran to the market-place called out uncessantly: 'I seek God! I seek God!'...
>
> ... 'Whither is God?' he cried. 'I will tell you! *We have killed him*—you and I! All of us are his murderers! But how did we do this? How could we drink up the sea? Who gave us the sponge to wipe away the entire horizon? What did we do when we loosened this earth from its sun? Whither does it now move? Whither do we move? What were we doing when we unchained this earth from its sun? Whither is it moving now? Whither are we moving? Away from all suns? Are we not plunging continually? Backwards, sideways, forwards, in all directions? Is there still any up or down? Are we not straying as thorugh an infinite nothing? Do we not feel the breath of empty space? Has it not become colder? Is not night continually closing in on us? Do we not need to light lanterns in the morning? Do we hear nothing as yet of the noise of the gravediggers who are burying God? Do we not smell the divine decomposition? Gods, too, decompose. God is dead. God remains dead. And we have killed him.
>
> 'How shall we console ourselves, the murderous of all murderer? The holiest and mightiest of all that the world has yet owned has bled to death under our knives: who will wipe the blood off us? What water is there for us to clean ourselves? What festivals of atonement, what sacred games shall we have to invent? Is not the greatness of this deed too great for us? Must we ourselves not become gods simply to appear worth of it? There has never been a greater deed; and whoever is born after us—for the sake of this deed he will belong to a higher history than all history hitherto.'[93]

Nietzsche blamed the rise of modern science for this circumstance rather than any particular philosopher or philosophy.[94] Moreover, he implied that the very act of modernization and varied social changes including the rising bourgeois, democratic governments and increasing pluralism had to be considered as factors also, especially since he believed that these were negative for man's development. In *The Gay Science* he also noted that the world was now without sanctuary or holiness. It had become an empty world.[95] There are those who would suggest that this transformation of such a fundamental idea was chronologically particular and politically specific as when one confronts that idea that, "The truly modern aspect of individual consciousness dates from the proclamation of the death of God ..."[96] Or that divine intervention was no longer an impediment for human growth since, "...what God's death meant epistemologically—namely, the elimination of His authority over the universe and over human consciousness."[97] For historians of ideas such dating is at best problematic if not dubious, but whatever dating one might choose, the impact has truly been significant. Another scholarly study, for example, has suggested that, "...Nietzsche metaphorically link[s] positive negative space...by suggesting that the death of god had forced man to feel 'the breath of empty space.'"[98] This transformation of our sense of space, of even spacelessness, contributed to the earlier changes of our understanding that time was also now being completely humanized. Changes in views of time and space only increase our expanding and discombobulated state of mind for the next century leading to new forms of materialism, doubt and depression.

This expansion of a newly secularized perception of the world, one without a god or religious faith, continued to add to our sense of self, our individuality and ability to make conscious choices. More importantly, these changes contributed directly to a feeling in the Western world of a growing state of doom and gloom, not only with Nietzsche but with a famous acquaintance of his, discussed earlier, regarding the idea of Renaissance individuality: Jacob Burckhardt. It was he who,

> ...knew, as certainly as Nietzsche, that the civilization of Europe which he loved was doomed. To one of his German Friends, who placed high hopes in the pre-1848 revolutionary and nationalist movement, he wrote—to quote only one example out of a very great number of similar statements: 'None of you has any idea yet what a people is and how easily it deteriorates in to a barbarous mob. You do not know yet what a tyrannical rule is to be set up over the spirit.... We may all perish; but I for one shall choose the cause for which I am going to perish: the culture of old Europe.'[99]

As with Nietzsche, Burckhardt had lost his religious faith, even though he was not an iconoclast.[100] The two had met at the University of Basel where Burckhardt was a professor. They developed a mutual admiration where Nietzsche "...described him in a letter as, '...that elderly, highly original man, given, not to distorting truth, but to passing it over in silence.'" In addition he appears to have enjoyed, "...listening to Burckhardt's lectures 'with their profound thoughts and their strangely abrupt breaks and twists as soon as they touch the danger point...'" and continued to suggest that Burckhardt was, "...more of a rebel than he is inclined to show..."[101] While such a judgement may be or may not be accurate, it is nevertheless correct to suggest that for Nietzsche, "...despair [was] reconciled to life through beauty: this is Nietzsche's interpretation of the Greek view of the world," and it can further be suggested that this view is, "...identical with the view of Greek antiquity which pervades the pages of Burckhardt's *History of Greek Culture*..."[102] The closeness of their thinking can be demonstrated in a rather interesting story where Burckhardt reveals that he understood that Nietzsche was not a Romantic but actually closer in some ways to the Enlightenment especially when reading his *Human, All-Too-Human* that Nietzsche had dedicated to Voltaire. Burckhardt observed that it was a brilliant collection of aphorisms, and he considered to be in the tradition of that particular aphorist, Voltaire.[103] But then, Nietzsche cannot be categorized, even when their closeness can be further documented by way of Schopenhauer, Nietzsche's teacher who, "...pervades the whole of the work of Jacob Burckhardt."[104] It is not an accident that the two most influential thinkers to impact upon Nietzsche's life whom he, "...intellectually...had abandoned, but whom he continued to love, respect and admire," were Burckhardt and Schopenhauer.[105] Burckhardt was the first to make an historical argument for the recent development of individuality in his study of the Renaissance.[106] Since today's Renaissance scholars would argue that he very much overstated his case, it can again be suggested that he may have projected more of his own experiences and his own era (as with his contact with the highly individualized Nietzsche) into the past, a mistake sometimes still made by professional historians. Nietzsche himself offered commentary regarding this problem, although he was actually thinking of philosophers when he explored in *Human, All-too-Human*, under the title, "Original error of the philosopher,"

> All philosophers share this common error: they proceed from contemporary man and think they can reach their goal through an analysis of this man. Automatically they think of 'man' as an eternal verity, as something abiding in the whirlpool, as a sure measure of things. Everything that the philosopher says about man, however is at bottom no more than a testimony about the man of a very *limited p*eriod. Lack of a historical sense is the original error of all philosophers...[107]

If one were to replace the word *philosopher* with that of *historian* we would find a clearly expressed problem that today's students of history would understand. As for Nietzschean individuality, "...his program is more individual than political—he is more interested in the development of men who are noble than in the return of the nobles themselves, whom he castigates for their decadence."[108] Politics did not interest Nietzsche as it did Burckhardt. When Tocqueville used the term individualism it was understood that this was to distinguish it, "...from egotism, or the plain selfishness."[109] Again, the *ego* is an ancient Latin indicator, a term that should not be confused with the actual act of being an individual.

To draw a distinction between the terms *individual, ego* and the *self* was precisely one of the issues that Nietzsche addressed. Before exploring his ideas in this regard it is important to understand the distinction between those who would possess a self and the great majority of people whom he referred to as "the herd" and of which he said: "Consider the herds that are feeding yonder: they know not the meaning of yesterday or today; they graze and ruminate, move or rest, from morning to night, from day to day, taken up with their little loves and hates, and the mercy of the moment, feeling neither melancholy nor satiety."[110] These are not the people that Nietzsche would consider capable of meaningful action, other than that which was structured by the church and its power to control them by way of the concept of sin. "An inhibitive and repressive religion, intent on self-flagellation in the name of 'sin,' has, as Nietzsche sees it, destroyed men by denying life itself."[111] He is unequivocal regarding the nature of "the herd" being perhaps as old as mankind when he noted that, "The delight in the herd is more ancient than the delight in the ego; and as long as the good conscience is identified with the herd, only the bad conscience says: I."[112] The singular and efficacious 'I' was not a we-established concept for him any more than it has been for this analysis. In the first chapter, it was argued, as did Nietzsche also suggest, that when we speak of a truly alone self, an individualized ontology, we are not speaking of a very deep past. Rather, he notes:

> ...once 'there was nothing more terrible to a person than to feel himself independent.' Independence, 'neither to obey nor to rule,' was an aloneness which was considered 'punishment'; one was ' condemned "to be an individual,"' and though modern man feels laws as constraint and loss against his freedom, in former times laws protected and 'egoism,' that is, independence, was felt to be painful: 'For a person to be himself, to value himself according to his own measure and weight—that was then quite distasteful...All miseries and terrors were associated with being alone. At that time the "free will" had bad conscience in close proximity to it; and the less independently a person acted, the more the herd-instinct, and not his personal character, expressed itself in his conduct, so much the more moral did he esteem himself.'[113]

In place of speaking of a self when discussing "the herd" he chooses the more ancient term, *ego*, to describe their nature. In other words, there is no self in antiquity, only ego. When such beings, whether in the past, or more contemporaneously, speak of their individuality, they are either in error or less than honest, which Nietzsche believed to be very common; the act of self-deception is more offensive and self-destructive than any other lie. Of the various ways he expressed this thought the following is very appropriate: "In the theater one is honest only in the mass; as an individual one lies, one lies to oneself."[114] One can only shout fire on the stage when it is part of a script, while would be illegal for an audience member to do the same unless there really were a fire. The law exists because members of the "herd" cannot draw such a distinction.

It should not be a surprise, then, that in drawing a distinction those capable of being free and those not capable (the "herd") he is also drawing a distinction between possessing an ego and a self. Thus, the self in Nietzsche is seen as a "...willed openness to interpretation..."[115] While he can be difficult to interpret as Hegel is difficult in his philosophic system, the issue is that Nietzsche does not consider himself—and we should not contradict—a philosopher. He holds more to an attitude than to a scheme of thought, which in truth can be deduced as one of the intentions in his writing—perhaps one of the reason his work is filled with aphorisms. The self and its implications, nevertheless dominate a great deal of his thought. For instance, in *The Gay Science, Thus Spoke Zarathustra, Beyond Good and Evil, On the Genealogy of Morals*, and *The Will to Power*, Nietzsche did produce an answer to the question, "What is the self?"[116] It is the ego in opposition to the self: "...Nietzsche finds an ego that must be surpassed, must go under..."[117] The ego may be present in our youth (as we were all once young) but as we have evolved over the centuries we have acquired the ability to overcome the ego as we developed the self. This liberation will come about, therefore, only when the deleterious effects of Christianity are finally addressed, the "...denying life itself,"[118] and the phenomenon is expunged from our inherited value system. This perceived negativity inherent in the early Church, the idea of sin and with it damnation—opposed to a certainty of an after-life—played a major role in Nietzsche's view of its inhibition of the growth of, if not the active suppression of mankind's potential. To grow, one must be mentally free, and in this case, free from the hunger to find simple patterns of existence. As he succinctly put it: "The Christian belief in a life after death had reduced life's value on earth. Man has put his hope in the future instead of perfecting himself here and now. Death is final, and nothing follows it."[119] The idea of death (a fundamental driving force of this work's thesis) has driven many of the attitudes and actions of the West, and while it has lost some of its influence starting in the seventeenth century it only becomes more relevant, granting Nietzsche's thesis. However, in our own era only, it is only addressed by a limited number of thinkers and artists. With this change he sees the birth of a new man, one we have already noted he called the over-man (*Übermensch*), one living by direction of the inner self: "Behind your thoughts and feelings, my brother, there stands a mighty ruler, an unknown sage—whose name is self. In your body he dwells; he is your body."[120] He made it clear in a variety of notes that there has been this negative force that had led to the denial of potential selves. "They [Christians] have lived in fear of life, anxious to attain heaven....The fear of death is a 'European disease' identical with the fear of hell. It weakens the will to live fully and in exaltation."[121] This disease is for him an antihumane force which has been a dark nemesis for mankind's development since "...it is in Christianity, against the background of belief in original sin, that we first find this wallowing in man's depravity and this uncompromising concentration on the dark side of man's inner life."[122] It would be futile to make an attempt to find any thinker prior to Nietzsche who had ever made such harsh and condemning statements regarding this Christian component of Western civilization.

What made this possible for someone like Nietzsche was his attitude towards death: "Only life matters; it is absolute, whereas death is irrelevant."[123] Rather than deny death he was prepared to embrace it and not only as a matter of necessity but rather as an inherent part of the very nature of living: "One must pay dearly for immortality: one has to die several times while still alive."[124] It may very well be this attitude that made his understanding of the self so powerfully positive in contrast to his negative view of the common man. He admits that the subject of the individual is very problematic and not simple, as "...individuality is not retouched, idealized, or holy; it is wretched and revolting, and yet, for all its misery, the highest good."[125] But for all the wretchedness of this individual, he retains the self in enough esteem to pursue this positive judgement in so many of his works. In part this is done by rejecting a simple dualistic approach to man's being: "Not the efficacy of consciousness, but the 'popular' dualism of flesh and spirit, is denied."[126] The long tradition of Platonic, Christian and Cartesian dualism is rejected as too simplistic and negative to deserve consideration as a guide for living a full life while recognizing the difficulty of identifying what makes a self worth merit. Part of his difficulty centers on the human weakness of not listening to their own inner (authentic) voice and two fundamental human characteristics that are universal in inhibiting most all humanity: fear and laziness. "Both keep man from heeding the call to achieve culture and thus to realize himself."[127] For it is not just the body but a special characteristic that drives his view of the self, a self that is basically creative.[128] Here is man in the making, the creative self bringing forth the fullness of his own potential. In a passage from what is arguably one of his most self-explicating works he states it in a lengthy but very clear manner: "Who am I? I await the worthier one; I am not worthy even of being broken by it?"[129]

> But the awakened and knowing say: body am I entirely, and nothing else; and soul is only a word for something about the body.
>
> ...Instruments and toys are sense and spirit: behind them still lies the self. The self also seeks with the eyes of the senses; it also listens with the ears of the spirit. Always the self listens and seeks: it compares, overpowers, conquers, destroys. It controls, and it is in control of the ego too.
>
> Behind your thoughts and feelings, my brother, there stands a mighty ruler, an unknown sage—whose name is self. In your body he dwells; he is your body.
>
> ...Your self laughs at your ego and at its bold leaps. 'What are these leaps and flights of thought to me?' it says to itself. 'A detour to my end. I am the leading strings of the ego and the prompter of its concepts.'
>
> The self says to the ego, 'Feel pain here!' Then the ego suffers and thinks how it might suffer no more —and that is why it is *made* to think.
>
> The self says to the ego, 'Feel pleasure here!' Then the ego is pleased and thinks how it might often be pleased again —and that is why it is *made* to think.
>
> ...The creative self created respect and contempt; it created pleasure and pain. The creative body created the spirit as a hand for its will. [130]

The word spirit (*geist*) here is usually meant to be read as mind and what is described is a state of mind seeking liberation from one's naturally lazy and frightened condition. These are not to be seen as not a reason for defeat but a reason for overcoming and is also recognized as a serious challenge and not to be treated lightly. The reason is self-evident in that one cannot be detached from one's own being. "It [self] cannot at once stand inside itself and give a full description of itself. But certainly there has never been only one fold in our self-knowledge, a single system of the self: the articulation of difference within that system always engenders a history."[131] The Baconian argument for a detached observation for operation of a scientific methodology does not necessarily or automatically work for the human psyche. However, he does suggest that:

> ...in the celebrated creation in *Beyond Good and Evil* of the noble type, the self is constituted by an initial act of reflection. 'The noble type of man experiences itself as determining values.' The self arises within a feeling (the *Selbtgefühl* of the account of 'thought as such' in the *Genealogy*). 'Everything it knows as part of itself it honors; such amorality is self-glorification. In the foreground there is the feeling of fullness, of power that seeks to overflow, the happiness of high tension, the consciousness of wealth that would give and bestow....The noble human being honors himself as one who is powerful.'[132]

These ideas were rooted in a variety of sources which were also given additional substance by another influential writer who Nietzsche studied and admired when only sixteen years old, Ralph Waldo Emerson whose classics, "Self-reliance'"and "The Oversoul," both tinged with a Stoicism that he retained all his life.[133] For "...Nietzsche puts us on the track of our genuine, our 'creative' selves."[134] After all, it is possible—although Nietzsche never makes this point—that because we begin life with an ego and since we are completely dependent upon others, at a certain point in our maturation we achieve the capacity to build an interior being, an inner center, where the self separate from others and society can flourish. He offers, however, an interesting theory as to why more people do not develop their creative selves: "...if we have missed ourselves, it is because we have not 'had time for,' or 'given our hearts' to, the venture, and not because the self is a deception."[135] For those who must struggle with the very fundamentals of supporting one's existence it is not to be expected that a self is of any particular value. This has been one of the historic characteristics of the fine arts where leisure has always been a key component in establishing aesthetic judgement and taste. This idea, at the least, is a compelling suggestion worthy of studied analysis and raises the question of whether one should consider consciousness itself as a particularly positive phenomenon.[136] It also implies another question raised by Nietzsche who noted that, "As we thus reject the Christian interpretation and condemn its 'meaning' like counterfeit, *Schopenhauer's* question immediately comes to us in a terrifying way: *Has existence any meaning at all?*"[137] This is not a question for this historical review but it is a question that will remain central, notwithstanding varied attempts at explanations for those interested in the relation between leisure and consciousness.

Nietzsche also confronted the issue of consciousness and conscience, again offering a rather clear ambiguity as he did with the self:

> He...speaks of intersubjective communication (herd behavior) as the chief refiner of self-consciousness and language. Under the pressure of the need to communicate, 'consciousness...has developed subtlety.' 'The ultimate result is an excess of this strength and art of communication,' whose 'heirs are those who are called artists.' Moreover, if 'consciousness...[is] at first the furthest distance from the biological center of the individual,...[it] deepens and intensifies itself, and continually draws nearer to that center.'[138]

Part of the intellectual problem stems from a confusion between consciousness and its origins in conscience. Coleridge, as noted, drew on this relationship to make his point clearly when speaking of consciousness as a "reflex of Conscience." Of note also is that "This reciprocity between consciousness and conscience becomes the illustrative thesis of what Kant came to call the 'judicial conscience dramas' of modern man."[139] In addition there are those thoughts that are less than clear regarding Hegel's use of consciousness and self-consciousness, particularly, that can leave the reader in doubt. Part of the difficulty comes from the uniqueness of such a language for this German philosopher, since, "Hegel debatably, was the first serious and widely read philosopher of the modern age to shift the emphasis in Western thought from traditional categories of mind and substance to a more overriding concern called 'consciousness.'"[140] That this conscious state was associated with his sense of a dialectic history and the spirit (*geist*) of the Germanic peoples (*volk*) and institutionalized in the state again leads us to more confusion than clarification.[141] As odd as it may seem, Hegel appears to think that his continuous dialectic change will actually end within the framework of the creation of the German state. There are those, additionally, who in attempting to understand Hegel's thinking take a very different approach, one even suggesting that, "…it can certainly be argued that consciousness for Hegel is in effect simply a metaphor, that it has no substantive referent in any metaphysical or even material sense, no signification outside the contextual implications of Hegel's own text."[142] The problems with the use of these terms are very noticeable today in their lack of clarity. But then, even Nietzsche has proven to be not be as clear as we might like: some intellectuals tend to be more descriptive than analytic.

Whatever is to be said regarding Nietzsche's view of consciousness he does not think in terms of metaphor. He is explicit in his *Gay Science* where he suggests that, "Consciousness is the last and latest development of the organic and hence also what is most unfinished and unstrong. Consciousness gives rise to countless errors that lead an animal or man to perish sooner than necessary…"[143] As this book began and has consistently argued, consciousness is not an Ancient or even Medieval phenomenon, but rather it is a modern psychological development that has been discussed more recently only because of its more recent and dominating presence. Nietzsche also appears to have understood that traditionally there has been little or no reason for consciousness appear or mature until recently. While somewhat lengthy, he offers clearly his understanding of the reasons for this late appearance, again stating it in *Gay Science*, "Over the Footbridge":

> In our relations with people who are bashful about their feelings, we must be capable of dissimulation; they feel a sudden hatred against anyone who catches them in a tender, enthusiastic, or elevated feeling, as if he had seen their secrets. If you want

to make them feel good at such movements, you have to make them laugh or voice some cold but witty sarcasm; then their felling freezes and they regain power over themselves.

There was a time in our lives when we were so close that nothing seemed to obstruct our friendship and brotherhood, and only a small footbridge separated us. Just as you were about to step on it, I asked you: "Do you want to cross the footbridge to me?'—Immediately, you did not want to any more; and when I asked you again, you remained silent. Since then mountains and torrential rivers and whatever separates and alienates have been cast between us, and even if we wanted to get together, we couldn't. But when you now think of that little footbridge, words fail you and you and sob and marvel.[144]

The sense of community that made our social identities possible was once so powerful that anything like a conscious being would have been such an extreme anomaly and, one would think, at the least, potentially dangerous unless in a creative artist or thinker. It was precisely what Nietzsche considered to be "the personal past" that was indispensable as a "necessary component of consciousness."[145] This suggests the need for a memory which returns us to Locke's theory of the correlation between memory and consciousness. However, Locke is not his mentor or part of his analysis since he disavows the idea that knowledge or thought should be considered as part of consciousness. "For the longest time, conscious thought was considered thought itself. Only now does the truth dawn on us that by far the greatest part of our spirit's activity remains unconscious and unfelt."[146] Well before Freud, therefore, Nietzsche recognized that much of our thinking is not particularly conscious:

> The problem of consciousness (more precisely, of becoming conscious of something) confronts us only when we begin to comprehend how we could dispense with it; and now physiology and the history of animals place us at the beginning of such comprehension (it took them two centuries to catch up with *Leibniz's* suspicion which soared ahead). For we could think, feel, will, and remember, and we could also 'act' in every sense of that word, and yet none of all this would have to 'enter our consciousness' (as one says metaphorically). The whole of life would be possible without, as it were, seeing itself in a mirror. Even now, for that matter, by far the greatest portion of our life would be possible without this mirror effect; and this is true even of our thinking, feeling, and willing life, however offensive this may sound to older philosophers. *For what purpose*, then, any consciousness at all when it is in the main *superfluous*?[147]

One of his more interesting thoughts is his willingness to imply that animals, along with humanity, are evolving into conscious beings. "Consciousness gives rise to countless errors," wrote Nietzsche, "that lead an animal or man to perish sooner than necessary, 'exceeding destiny,' as Homer puts it."[148] This is all the more interesting since he appears to believe that consciousness is also dependent upon communication and language. Perhaps this is because he perceived consciousness and social activity as somehow tied together.

> My ideas is, as you see, that consciousness does not really belong to man's individual existence but rather to his social or herd nature; that, as follows from this, it has developed subtlety only insofar as this is required by social and herd utility. Consequently, given the best will in the world to understand ourselves as individually as possible, 'to know ourselves,' each of us will always succeed in becoming conscious only of what is not individual but 'average.' Our thoughts themselves are continually governed by the character of consciousness—by the 'genius of the species' that commands it—and translated back into the perspective of the herd. Fundamentally, all our actions are altogether incomparably personal, unique, and infinitely individual; there is no doubt of that. But as soon as we translate them into consciousness *they no longer seem to be*.[149]

That he would on one hand claim that there was no need for consciousness in a more communal setting, a view held to some degree more recently by Julian Jaynes, and then turn to argue that consciousness begins with the language of the community, may seem less than consistent unless we assume that the first steps toward a conscious being begins with language even if there is little need or even an exercise of a conscious self at that time. Again there is less than an absolute of consistency here since he even can appear to return to a more Lockean position, in this case regarding the importance of language when he states: "The emergence of our sense impressions into our own consciousness, the ability to fix them and, as it were, exhibit them externally, increased proportionately with the need to communicate them to *others* by means of signs." It is in this communicative ability that a human being, "…becomes ever more keenly conscious of himself. It was only as a social animal that man acquired self-consciousness—which he is still in the process of doing, more and more."[150] This is an important argument since it demonstrates that his concept of self-consciousness is predicated by what is referred to here as a form of self-awareness and the insecurity that can follow.

As the "Footbridge" quote above notes, there is an inherent self-awareness that is natural to a social life; from the ancient Greek *aretē* to the medieval saint, society historically determines to some extent a member's identity. Additionally, there is the issue of the sense of shame which is another social response. Carl D. Schneider who wrote a seminal work on shame and guilt referred specifically to Nietzsche in this regard: "...both the second and the third of *The Gay Science* conclude with the question of shame. The second book ends with this challenge: '...as long as you are in any way ashamed before yourselves, you do not yet belong with us.'"[151]

The aphorisms that end Book Three (273-75) are perhaps Nietzsche's most well-known on shame: "*Whom do you call bad?*—Those who always want to put to shame./*What do you consider most human?*—To spare someone shame./*What is the seal of liberation?*—No longer being ashamed in front of oneself."[152] It is the force of shame that contributes to the tie between consciousness and conscience, especially regarding what he calls, "bad consciousness" (associated with "the herd"). Like Schopenhauer, he demonstrates he can, "be impatient with consciousness" which is to be taken here as the same in this case as with self-consciousness, and "...blames the *maladie du siècle*, 'nihilism,' *taedium vitae*, and the general enervating state of European man on the consequences of consciousness."[153] Like conscience, memory and consciousness, "...he finds self accusation almost effortless: 'I accuse myself up and down. It's not hard.'" All this is but prologue to his conclusion that these psychological factors are used to keep people in bondage. "'In short,...the essential is to cease being free and to obey, in repentance, a greater rogue than oneself.'"[154] Still the positive force in consciousness remains present as when he notes that, "...it seems to me as if the subtlety and strength of consciousness always were proportionate to man's (or animal's) *capacity for communication*, and as if this capacity in turn were proportionate to the *need for communication*."[155]

This complexity is only enhanced by his desire to condemn consciousness as little more than a disease. As he stated at one point, "...the growth of consciousness becomes a danger, and anyone who lives among the most conscious Europeans even knows that it is a disease."[156] The idea of members of "the herd" becoming conscious is a topic for another work, but this idea may have been learned from Dostoevsky's Underground Man.[157] One likely contributing factor leading to this negativity towards a conscious state besides it being attached to conscience and bad for "the herd" while possibly a good conscience for those who would go beyond socially limiting systems is that Nietzsche developed another important and very relevant concept, i.e., the will to power. "According to Nietzsche, no structure will save us; only men who are 'self-overcoming' and who know truth is hard, yet crave it, will avail."[158] The *Übermensch*, those with a will to power, are not interested in power over others, but rather only power over the self: the making of the creative self. One introductory way to begin to understand his viewpoint might be suggested in the chapter, "Personality in Public," in Sennett's book, *Fall of Public Man*:

> ...personality, unlike natural character, is controlled by self-consciousness. The control of an individual practiced in relation to his natural character was the moderation of his desires....Personality cannot be controlled by action: circumstances may force different appearances and so destabilize the self. The only form of control can be the constant attempt to formulate what it is one feels. This sense of controlling the self is mostly retrospective; one understands what one has done after the experience is over. Consciousness always follows emotional expression in this scheme....personality is also the capacity to 'recover' one's emotions. Longing, regret, and nostalgia acquire an importance....His [19th Century bourgeois] personal self-consciousness is not so much an attempt to contrast his feelings with those of others as to take known and finished feelings, whatever they once were, as a definition of who he is.[159]

The idea of a personality returns us again from Nietzsche's classical training where the "mask" one wears is more important than the inner and creative self, an individual unencumbered by religion or social standards. But as a contrast, an interesting alternative to the public being is found in the tie between the will to power and his conceptional frames of consciousness which was noted by Walter Kaufmann in his opus *Nietzsche: Philosopher, Psychologist, Antichrist*

> Nietzsche's argument would prove the inferiority of the pleasure standard only if he were prepared to deny the efficacy of consciousness altogether. His view, however, precludes any deprecation of consciousness, which cannot be disentangled from the totality of human behavior. Nietzsche, moreover, makes much of the efficacy of consciousness. It has been seen how his very doctrine of the will to power encompassed the insight that this striving could never achieve ultimate fulfillment without availing itself of reason.[160]

Kaufmann is clearly subscribing to a rather supportive and even positive view regarding Nietzsche's understanding of consciousness. For it is this will to overcome one's own weakness and step away from the crowd and dominance of personality that finally makes it possible to achieve that relatively new concept called happiness. Stated simply: "Happiness is envisaged less as a state of consciousness than it is a state of being: as power."[161] Obviously this ties a 'creative self' with the "will to power" in addition to being conscious, i.e., without inhibition. This view includes spontaneity which is necessary for the growth of a true self.[162] In the end, this transcends Sennett's understanding of feelings applied to self-consciousness except in one particular mode to be discussed later.

The idea of growth is central in Nietzsche's thinking, especially in the importance placed on the idea of process for this is not a thinker building static philosophies for a static, fixed ontology. This is the error too many people make, thinking that consciousness is something to have, a static state which is fixed and always certain much like one's pre-established emotions, rather than it being an evolving state, one where someone is in the state of becoming conscious. This static state of consciousness was intolerable for Nietzsche:

> One of the misconceptions about consciousness, Nietzsche complains, is that men have tended to treat it as an accomplished state 'accepted as the "unity of the organism,"' so that no chance for growth and development, no option for maturation was open: 'Because men believed that they already possessed consciousness, they gave themselves very little trouble to acquire it.' [163]

To have consciousness is to have nothing but to seek and work at becoming conscious is fulfilling. He recognizes that this process can only occur when we accept that, "The belief in authority,...is the source of conscience"; but this is "...not the voice of God in the heart of man, but the voice of some men in man."[164] Thus the voices we hear when we are young, what your mother tells you is your conscience is, in fact, your own voice and therefore has the potential to become what it can become, an act of consciousness. It is for this reason that the argument could be made that Nietzsche is suggesting, "...we tend blindly to accept the reproaches of conscience without ever really questioning: 'But why do you *listen* to the voice of your conscience? And in how far are you justified in regarding such a judgment as true and infallible?'"[165] This struggle between conscience and consciousness can free the mind to open itself to all possibilities. That is why, "...there are parts of...Nietzsche's *Genealogy of Morals* which advocate not only a divorce between conscience and consciousness but an opposition between them, perhaps even a dialectic."[166] While Nietzsche does seem at times ambiguous on the role of consciousness he does have one very clear purpose besides his commitment to language and communication, for he sees this but as an aid to the exercise of our own good sense. "Oblivion, says Nietzsche, is a screening device, keeping from our consciousness the flood of all experience: oblivion acts like a 'concierge,' only letting up those visitors we give permission to enter....Conscience, then, becomes initially an enforcer, who sees to it that forgetful man remembers wherein lies the root of torture and pain as mnemonic devices to stir the memory."[167] Nietzsche makes his point salient by way of this "concierge." The point of the early conscience was a matter of control of actions of those ruled.[168] Much the same can be said of the rule of God over man, again the restriction of any development of potential.

It is the potential, the process, the movement and the activity that drives such thinkers like Nietzsche. Change becomes something not only normal but expected. After all, "it cannot be denied that *The Use and Abuse of History* contains—as an antidote against historicist intellectualism—a glorification of action for its own sake, 'activism,' and an ensuing tendency toward treating historical writing and education as an instrument for mobilizing 'action.'"[169] This is a thought that also can be found in Dostoevsky, especially from his *Notes From the Underground*. Nietzsche was acquainted with some of the writings of this Russian novelist and he recognized that they both possessed a healthy degree of skepticism. What it was that Nietzsche sought was nothing less than the ultimate creative self or artist: "But Nietzsche dreamt—and dreamt in vain—of an artist of the future who would reach in his art that turning-point where the highest degree of consciousness and self-consciousness transform itself into a new spontaneity, primitivity and innocence—just as he strove to realize the utmost of nihilistic despair to arrive at a new faith, and mobilized all forces of negation to defeat all denial."[170] In arguing for a "degree of consciousness and self-consciousness" he reveals his understanding that consciousness, the self both alone and in combination with consciousness as well as our understandings, are reducible to a matter of degree. Therefore it is not hard to understand his desire to fight, inch by inch, to overcome the pessimism that is inherent in the unlived life. He states his case clearly in one of the last paragraphs of *The Will to Power*: "To have paced out the whole circumference of modern consciousness, to have explored every one of its recesses—this is my ambition, my torture, and my bliss. Really to overcome pessimism…"[171] It could very well be in part this attitude which partially accounts for his response upon reading the *Notes From the Underground* by Dostoevsky in 1887:

> 'I did not even know the name of Dostoevsky just a few weeks ago…. An accidental reach of the arm in a bookstore brought to my attention *L'esprit souterrain*, a work just translated into French….The instinct of kinship (or how should I name it?) spoke up immediately; my joy was extraordinary.' [part one] Nietzsche characterizes as 'really a piece of music, very strange, very un-Germanic music' and goes on to speak of 'a kind of self-derision of the [know thyself].'[172]

It is by degrees, therefore, that he does find one of his promising artists when he discovered this Russian novelist.

Rightly or not, both of these writers have been associated with the term existential. As with the conundrum of defining self-consciousness, existentialism should be seen as, "... not a philosophy but a label for several widely different revolts against traditional philosophy."[173] And, moreover, since it is not a philosophy it is equally not to be seen as, "... a movement or a set of ideas or an established list of authors."[174] There are other names associated with this movement, but they will prove more problematic than "Romantic" because, "...existentialism is but a growing series of expressions of a set of attitudes which can be recognized only in a series of portraits."[175] Arguably the term 'attitude' might be one of the better descriptions. And while Kaufmann has spent most of his intellectual life working with Nietzsche, in particular, and the term existential, in general, he adds that he, "... can see no reason for calling Dostoevsky an existentialist, but I do think that Part One of *Notes from Underground* is the best overture for existentialism ever written."[176] He then continues, "This book, [*Notes*...] published in 1864, is one of the most revolutionary and original works of world literature."[177] However one labels his work, Dostoevsky is a remarkable talent, significant for the study of nihilism and existentialism. If there is a problem, it is his tendency to lump existential together with self-consciousness, for within, "... the existential syndrome every tension increases self-consciousness, every increase in self-consciousness exaggerates the irresolvable tension with the world that is always there."[178] Two undefinable terms may not add clarity to our understanding, but there is something here that is more than just a little remarkable about the transformation of Western thought that significantly expands at the end of the nineteenth century and flows into the following century in an even more extreme state of reflection and confusion.

An attitude, yes, but one singularly marked by a change in the relationship one has with the world and all life in it, changes that some of the most talented artists and brilliant writers have ever embraced. It is not inaccurate to conclude with that idea: "The existential attitude is first of all an attitude of self-consciousness. One feels himself separated from the world, from other people. In isolation, one feels threatened, insignificant, meaningless, and in response demands significance through a bloated view of self. One constitutes himself as a hero, as an offense, as a prophet or anti-Christ, as a revolutionary, as unique."[179]

Isolation, estrangement and the unknown beyond what had yet been imagined followed out of this most remarkable century of transition, a transition into what could be eventually called the Century of Annihilation.

CHAPTER TEN

THE FRACTURED AGE: TWENTIETH CENTURY TRANSFORMATION

The world has changed less since Jesus Christ than it has in the last thirty years.
—Charles Peguy (1913)[1]

FROM ORDER TO DISORDER

The history which leads to the doorsteps of our own world has been given a clarity as a frame for the background of the rise of consciousness. However, when we enter our own era we are immersed in a remarkably dark room. "Once expressed, the existential attitude appears as a universal condition, but only to those who can understand it. It is a peculiarly Western attitude, and talk of 'the human condition' is presumption as it is over dramatic."[2] This darkness exists notwithstanding all of our inventions, technologies and materialistic achievements. There is a certain clarity for the political and economic components of our world's expansion and complexity although not enough to let through a great deal of light even on these accomplishments. The coming of age of the nation state and nationalism as well as capital-driven competition, reached a maturation with the Great War, World War II and the Cold War and with it many yet unrecognized implications and problems. Just as this work has taken as its lead from the Western component of consciousness, so too it can be said that these terms and the attitude toward them, have a peculiar Western ring. The problem resides in finding agreed upon definitions. And the terms self-consciousness and individuality have retained a certain malleability. In fact, "...nothing could be further from the existential attitude than attempts to define existentialism, except perhaps a discussion *about* the attempt to define existentialism."[3] We therefore enter our own world, trapped with ill-defined terms.

The path taken by the West has been exceptional with its emphasis on an unresolved dualism that has traditionally been confronted only by conflict. Compounding our difficulty in understanding is the arrival of what has been called the second industrial revolution with its powerful alteration of our sense of time and space. This and much more, tied to what it means to be self-consciousness and existential, makes for a rare historic congruence filled with massive complexities and confusion. For historians of culture, ideas and mentalities, it is always important to consider the historical relationship between such varied but potentially correlative events, partially, one of hardware and the other, our psyche. In such a short work on such a massive subject only a few suggestive interpretations will be offered for our own world.

With the first revolution of coal and iron, both industry and factory-driven economies begin to impact everyday lives. The second stage of steel and electricity gave rise to oil and chemical corporations. The third and final transformation was the information revolution with the arrival of computers and technocrats. Since about 1867 we can trace the beginnings of a transportation revolution with the railroad that will span the American continent by 1869 followed by the internal combustion engines offering even newer independence for travelers. The acquisition of information was also transformed with the arrival of the wireless telegraph, gramaphone, telephone and microphone. Then there is the electric lamp, which made night into day, and new mechanical forms of public transportation, pneumatic tires and bicycles, methods of motion, again altering dramatically our relationship to time and space. To the printing press we add the typewriter and penny press which carried this information revolution into the twentieth century. As for new economics, the appearance of synthetic fibers, artificial silk, synthetic plastics and bakelite further contributed to making mass produced goods more available and less expensive. Literacy as well as consumerism were becoming common. The radio, television and computers, and both alienation and estrangement are increasingly made manifest. This alteration of our sense of time and space away from the intimacy and traditional stability of a community contributed to high anxiety which is still problematic for citizens of our world.[4] At the end of the nineteenth century London achieved for the first time in the Western world, since ancient Rome, a population of about one million citizens. With continued demographic changes and massive growth of population depersonalization expanded along with urbanization.

After 1914 with the arrival of aircraft, radios and telephones the very nature of making of war was decidedly changed. For modern warfare, information on the status of the battle front was radically and quickly acquired. The top brass need not lead the troops to know the situation, but rather, they could sit well behind the lines in order to direct the war from a more secure distance.

And the changes in the weapons used made for even more impersonalization during actual combat. Killing became a less personal act, more mechanical, undermining the psychological consequences for many.

All this and more continued to an increased sense of isolation and a growing turning inward towards an independence and expanded sense of the self. "One of the reasons why we in our society can tolerate variance in human behavior, which is far more differentiated than it was in early non-technological societies, is that we are more organized. We can find where people are. We know their addresses. We know their phone numbers. We know their social security numbers."[5] We live in a more impersonal world with corollary technical changes that make for a smaller planet. Yes, we have passports and visas, but we also have internet communication to most places on the planet. True, Big Brother may be more effectively watching, but the irony (a favorite term for the last century) is that in some ways intended results are opposite since any tightening of the "…organization of society enables individuals to be more individualistic," at least in ways different than ever existed before. We have noted that the earlier Hegelian idea of a "…dialectic going on here between the community and the individual…"[6] was now expanding. One can only take as an appropriate example the story of the authoritarian dictatorship of Adolph Hitler and his Gestapo, which, for all its power, could be remarkably inefficient as the number of Jews who survived living in occupied territories at the end of the war prove.

There has been a string of disorientating and confusing events in our history which can be seen as "…by-products of the Renaissance, the Reformation, the growth of science, the decline of the Church authority, the French Revolution, and the growth of mass militarism and technocracy." Little wonder then that the idea of 'the individual' made its first major significant appearance by the end of the Enlightenment.[7] This occurred while the role of divine intervention as well the assumption of a universal order with people still being driven by a 'sentiment' of decency that was to create a secular moralization was dissolving under the weight of an attack arising from materialism and indifference. The nineteenth century was of course the beginning of the end of that order for many. The first recognition of an abyss can be found in Rousseauean reconstructions, Goethean motion, Hegelian alienation, technological changes and governments fighting over the myth of nationalism. Nietzsche was one of the earliest and most important thinkers to call attention to these changes in both social order and in any sense of decency. It was for the twentieth century to live up to the collapsing Western order of the previous century where those dedicated to these new "-isms" could continue their destructive activities. Here is where the possession of a conscious self was not some simple neutral event but rather more likely, at least for some, a necessary positive act for psychological survival.

The singular event that transformed the pessimistic world views so clearly expressed by Nietzsche and Dostoevsky occurred on the 10th of August 1914, with the outbreak of "the war to end all wars," an outbreak that does not appear to have been completely resolved even now. When one considers all of the changes prior to the outbreak of the Great War plus the immediate impact of those destructive years, this was truly one of the most significant and revolutionary transformational periods in all Western and global history. Those who went through and marked this period are the some of the earliest to been seen as having a post-modern mind set. While this both is a debatable term and concept for historians, if it is to be used, it is probably best associated first with that period of changes that occurred somewhere between 1890 and 1914. This was the end of a relatively closed yet dynamic Western Civilization with the first steps towards a global and technologically driven planetary culture, although we will continue to mark this particular essay with the specific label *West* because of the concern with consciousness.

Of the many transformational events regarding the creation of a post-modern world, one of the most significant is the expansion of the inner self:

> Human beings are highly social animals. For most of our existence, we have been embedded in immediate relationships and functions, particularly those involving kinship, communal ritual, and cultural custom. For all but a tiny portion of the one hundred thousand years since the emergence of Neanderthal man (or the million years since the appearance of species *Homo*), one behaved in certain ways toward the people around one, according to status, role or occupation, and geographic place. One did so because one was required to (and would be shamed or punished if one did not) and because one wished to (had internalized these requirements and made them one's own). That has changed during the past two centuries or so in connection with three historical forces that have brought about the release of proteanism. These forces —historical dislocation, the mass media revolution, and the threat of extinction—are inseparable from the modern and postmodern state and are related to our surging technologies and our equally surging ideas and feelings of self. [8]

This issue of the self in the contemporary world is tied directly to our consciousness, especially as it applies to our modern (and post-modern) self-consciousness. This in turn is part of the larger culture that has changed and still is changing at an ever more increasing rate of speed and diversity. That the planet gets smaller and the people become more divided is a great irony. The end of the nineteenth century left a legacy to which we in our confusions are now trying to give coherence. Part of the problem particularly prevalent in the West is the massive diversity not only in politics and economics but in the nature of our being that keeps changing. The very functional world of economics, social classes, technology and politics has gone through massive upheaval, turmoil and even confusion. And we must not neglect the new power of '-isms:' capitalism, socialism, communism, behavioralism, materialism, creationism, conservatism, liberalism, fascism, humanism, commercialism, patriotism, naturalism, et al. It is as if that with the end of traditional absolutes we offer in its place the absolutes of any and all these '-isms.' This is a story of conflicting assumptions and perspectives that has yet been given proper attention.

For better or worse we now have an explosion of information and knowledge in newly created scholarly disciplines. Biblical efficacy was greatly undermined by the new discipline of geology beginning in the nineteenth century with the discovery that the planet was older than ever dreamed. Darwin and biology, we noted, challenged our understanding of physical nature. With the creation of modern physics, nuclear physics was born. And with modern psychology, the land of the brain, mind and consciousness was finally beginning to be explored. This knowledge is still being digested as it expands our understanding.

While the immediate story of our own age can be dated from 1914 when the Great War broke out with Kaiser Wilhelm II reviewing his troops (July 18) commenting that he was looking forward to a lovely ten week war, there were several other important incidents that should be noted and discussed. As an antecedent, we should note that by the time of that war the Western world, culturally had become closed. One hallmark of the Western world has been its inherent, if not compulsive, drive to expand. The story of this movement is in the direction of the north and the west from its beginnings in Asia minor evolving from Babylon and northern Africa, through Crete, Athens towards Rome and finally Renaissance Florence. This direction of geographic growth was followed by great cultural revolutions in Paris and London, carried on in the New World and in the final ending of this movement when arriving on the shores of the Pacific Ocean. The Census Bureau of the United States government in 1890 finally declared that the West was closed and since then we have moved into a global civilization. To give credence to this observation, Virginia Woolf in 1924, made her famous observation: "In or about December 1910 human nature changed." She further elaborated: "All human relations have shifted—those between masters and servants, husbands and wives, parents and children. And when human relations change there is at the same time a change in religion, conduct, politics, and literature."[9] This can be expounded upon by an observation of a very traditional and thoughtful Victorian, C. S. Lewis, who offered on behalf of many of his contemporaries, "…that any previous age produced work which was, in its own time, as shatteringly and bewilderingly new as that of the Cubists, the Dadaists, the Surrealists, and Picasso has been in ours."[10] To this it can be added that, "Along with such critics as George Steiner and Roland Barthes, he [Lewis] saw the decades preceding World War I as marking the greatest rupture in the entire history of Western art and culture…"[11] What is most pertinent here is that Woolf also suggested, regarding the subject of the self, essentially in the context of biography that: "A biography is considered complete if it merely accounts for six or seven selves, whereas a person may well have as many as a thousand."[12] While the changes brought about by the war were continuous throughout the twentieth century one of the most important factors to consider here is that certainty so long sought even in the more secular visions of a Descartes or a Locke, as well as those following in the Age of Reason, eventually led to one and only one certainty for so many in our own era—i.e., the certainty that all is uncertain.

Through the work of Ernst Karl Heisenberg (1901–76) we are forced to confront the "Uncertainty Principle", which should perhaps be applied to a much larger realm than just physics. The following quote is as succinct an explanation of what he had realized:

> Heisenberg…pointed out that for the presumption of predictability to be carried out, it is necessary *to observe* the position and momentum of this tiny particle [photon]. And to observe it we must throw light on it—right? But the wavelength of ordinary light (10–5 centimeter) is a million times greater than the diameter of the particle you are observing; so it won't provide any accuracy (a difficulty that limits the resolving power of optical microscopes to three-thousand-fold).
>
> Very well, let's use shorter-wavelength light. But since this shorter-wavelength light (x-rays) is in the form of photons which carry enormous energy, their impact upon the particle will knock it out of the picture.
>
> Hence the predicament: the observation of position and momentum required for prediction *cannot be carried out*, and the determinism we were led to expect at the level of molar aggregates (objects made of billions of particles) does not hold for elementary particles; their position and momentum are indeterminate.[13]

According to Heisenberg, to observe is to disturb, and once something is observed it is altered, leaving the human parameter with the central and only component in life with any meaning now a matter of uncertainty. In a universe inherently filled with a degree of uncertainty, it is not unnatural to see an increasingly large number of fascinating studies that suggest that the universe itself is in fact chaotic rather than smooth and orderly. It could be suggested that it is in the projective genius of the observer where order is created not in the stars or neutrons. This is not particularly satisfying for most.

Not surprisingly, the primary relationship with death in our world is now becoming one of denial. Avoid, do not see, and it is not. We live in a world without death and thus without anything real—let them go to the hospital to die. This could help in part to explain the rise of the counter-culture. Here the position is not simply an affirmation of being an active living moving being, but an affirmation that death in fact does sit on everyone's shoulders, so let's get on with living. This happened to an extent during the Great Plague as well as other times of great crises filled with serious threats to life. As has become common, denial becomes part of a society's daily routine. There has occurred increasingly for artists and thinkers an acceptance of a *carpe diem* attitude, retaining a capacity in extending themselves beyond the inevitable phenomenon of death. In the movie M*A*S*H the theme is "suicide is painless; it brings on many changes." In 1956, Samuel Beckett (1908–89) offered us his *Waiting for Godot*, which was at best a statement regarding absurdity, one built upon a tradition established earlier with the writings of Franz Kafka (1883–1924). When Beckett's play in which "Nothingness circulates through every line from beginning to end—runs for more than sixteen months to packed houses in the capitals of Europe, we can only conclude that something is at work in the European mind against which its traditions cannot wholly guard it and which it will have to live through to the bitter end."[14] They wait, but for what? Are others also waiting, and again, for what? We are not only fortunate to possess Beckett's insights but also Kafka's work since Kafka asked that his writings be destroyed upon his death.

Walter Kaufmann has suggested that, "Kafka stands between Nietzsche and the existentialists: he pictures the world into which Heidegger's man, in *Sein und Zeit*, is 'thrown,' the godless world of Sartre, the 'absurd' world of Camus."[15] And in his translation and analysis of *The Castle* one could see an anticipation of the Uncertainty Principle of Heisenberg where he states that one particularly important sentence in German: "*Die Lüge wird zur Weltordnung gemacht*: 'The world-order is based upon a lie.'"[16] This accounts in part for some of Kafka's ambiguity that attracted Kaufmann as well as many others. As he succinctly put it, "...ambiguity is of the essence of his [Kafka] art."[17] Are earlier modern thinkers like Hegel and Nietzsche the first to construct brilliant ideas that leave us with an ambiguity, especially concerning the very nature of our world? In any case, we should add that this is a characteristic in some degree of the art in our own modern (post-modern) world: an art that demands interpretation. The 'Law' in *The Trial* introduces this issue for Kaufmann in his comparison with Kafka's style and of the *Book of Genesis*, where, "...he fashions stories which, like those of Genesis, invite a multitude of different interpretations; and he does not want to be reduced to one exclusive meaning,"[18] a position comparable with that of Nietzsche.

It was Virginia Woolf who was well aware of these changes. She believed that human character changed somewhere around 1910.[19] But more important for the study of the appearance of the self, she noted the rise of a very modern and unique being in the Western world which resolved to some extent the conundrum regarding the knowledge of the self that had confused David Hume and his empiricist perspective. Woolf understood that what Hume addressed in not knowing what self it is that is walking through a door could be addressed by the theory of multiple selves. It is not an accident that this position can be found as well in the writings of James Joyce.[20] Human language, the self and consciousness are all dynamic and, therefore, in flux; they are attuned to an existential attitude. In such a world, interpretations will depend upon the conscious self existing at a particular moment and will, however, change in time, eventually allowing for different interpretations or selves. Perhaps people are seen here as not nouns but as verbs, a process without a fixity. Today's readers of even older works, in the case of Shakespeare's plays, for example, often find that when they are re-read *Hamlet*, for example, they usually find another Hamlet than the one first discovered, and perhaps even another plot, especially as our thinking moves us into a new world. This is more unique to us now than at any other time in our history because of the variety, complexity, speed, of both personal and public events that require individual adjustments which for many become a full time occupation. As Kaufmann put it: "The world that confronts us and our life in it defy every attempt at a compelling exegesis: that life lends to many different interpretations is of its essence."[21] Two other notes should further round out these changes in the way we perceive and mark the twentieth century, first, Kafka, a significant post-modern genius, made the following note in 1922 that stated: "It's impossible to sleep, impossible to wake, impossible to bear life or, more precisely, the successiveness of life. The clocks don't agree. The inner one rushes along in a devilish or demonic—in any case, inhuman—way while the outer one goes, falteringly, its accustomed pace."[22] Secondly, from *The Trial*, he further offers us Josef K. informing his employer about the summons to his first hearing: "I have been rung up and asked to go somewhere, but they forgot to tell me when." He assumes he should arrive at nine but oversleeps and arrives over an hour late. The Examining Magistrate reproaches him: "You should have been here an hour and five minutes ago." The next week when he returns he is on time but no one shows up.[23] In a study of the modern mind and madness by Louis A Sass, the issue of alienation and isolation becomes central. The argument is simple and sharp suggesting that, "...human action in our time...lacks 'shape and measure' and is 'veined with currents of inertia.'"[24] All of which leads to, "...a burgeoning of a certain introversion and alienation, the acceleration of an inner process that Kafka, a figure representative of the age, described in his diary as the 'wild tempo' of an 'introspection [that] will suffer no idea to sink tranquilly to rest but must pursue each one into consciousness, only itself to become an idea, in turn to be pursued by renewed introspection.'"[25] The issue to consider is the relationship of introspective thinking; the hearing of inner voices and the rise of schizophrenia, which is very new at least as diagnostically recognized.

This characteristic of multiple interpretations of time and space, of events and of our understanding, by various artist, thinkers and even members of the audience is now a generally accepted practice. People are not told what to see, read and understand by the church, an aristocracy or the state with their arbitrary standards. If the individual is to have something of an understanding of modern art and thought they are reduced to their own insights drawn from their own interior selves. It is within the consciousness of the observer that the voice of painters and poets are completed, not in the artist's intent. Time and space, memory and language, history and thought have all become increasingly personal, subjective and mostly, that very special twentieth century word, private. James Joyce (1882–1941), a contemporary of Kafka, catches this modern sense as well as anyone. In *Ulysses*, "Joyce created a dramatic interruption in the forward movement of narrative time. As Bloom approaches a brothel he steps back to avoid a street cleaner and resumes his course forty pages and a few seconds later."[26] There would later be many others from Alain Robbe-Grillet in his novel the *Voyeur* to Jorge Luis Borges' œuvre which is replete with this new attitude. Time is not simply a matter of a mechanism, a clock, or even an atomic clock, but rather a point of view, a set of assumptions, depending upon where you are and how you are existing at any given moment.

As Stephen Kern in his fascinating study of time and space in the construction of the modern world has pointed out: "Joyce's reminder that time is relative to the system by which it is measured also points to Einstein's theory that all temporal coordinates are relative to a specific reference system. In a textbook of 1883 Ernst Mach raised new questions about classical physics....Mach rejected Newton's views of absolute space and absolute motion and dismissed his absolute time as an 'idle metaphysical conception.'"[27] It was specifically the fascinating character of Molly Bloom that offers one of the best examples of the malleability of time. The scene is described by another observer and needs no help from this writer:

> As Molly Bloom lies sleepless, she is the landscape of Gibraltar, its flowers, hills, streets and houses as she is caressed by them as she caressed them, with her hands, with her eyes, and with her body rolling on a hill later with Leopold Bloom, for both these times and others have wound into *a time* for Molly, a time in which the yes goes back and forth, shuttlelike from Molly to landscape, from Bloom to Molly, from now to Gibraltar, to another time on a hill, and further into other interlacings of things and Molly, within a time itself a chasm. Here is a fever pitch of the manifestation of reversibility, but that is Molly's genius.[28]

The last chapter of this classic work runs some 44 pages in the Modern Library edition and is a continuous sentence without punctuation or capitalization![29] This clearly is one of the earliest and most excellent examples of what William James called "streams of consciousness."[30] And this ending also gives us the, "...fullest expansion of the time of Molly's world as it is experienced in her consciousness. It is the only episode to which Joyce assigned no particular hour of the day and it symbolizes that of eternity and infinity..."[31] For Molly there is a power of living, one where she can, "...enter and articulate what Merleau-Ponty called in *Eye and Mind* the 'deflagration of Being' [*déflagration de l'Etre*] ....Time burns itself up in the phoenix fire of its renewal and becoming. Its kindling is the bodily enmeshment in things, in the landscape, in the life lived with others as gestural, embodied beings."[32] Joyce was both of his time and beyond time as authentic individuals (genius) which our age must be prepared to embrace. Separation from the conformity of a technical and destructive society is paramount in asserting life over death and this has been seen and subscribed to by many artists and thinkers.

William James (1842–1910), a brilliant contemporary of these writers, developed one of the more interesting and instructive concepts regarding consciousness with his stream of consciousness theory. In 1890, the year the American West was closed, he built part of his reputation with a popular textbook of psychology and added his formulation that subsequently became famous: "Consciousness does not appear to itself chopped up in bits. Such words as in 'chain' or 'train' do not describe it fitly...It is nothing jointed; it flows. A 'river' or a 'stream' are the metaphors by which it is most naturally described. In talking of it here-after, let us call it the stream of thought, or consciousness."[33] The implication again is that consciousness is not static but in motion which supports a conclusion made by Nietzsche that there was no being behind the becoming or a doer behind the doing. The laws of motion now are applied to our identities as well as to the universe. For awareness there is a certain consistency as when you are aware of a magnificent tree you are observing in the forest. For consciousness, there is no necessarily fixed time, no absolute certainty of observation, no time standing still, for consciousness is always in motion, which also can be said of the self. The Lockean use of 'same' used as part of his defining personal identity—which signified fixity—and used as an adjective for consciousness in his famous Chapter XXVII has simply not held up over the years.[34] "*Self* can mean process; self as experience and self as process overlap. *Self* is usefully understood as process....Both James's stream, in which each succeeding segment encompasses the preceding segments and represents all the others, and Whitehead's 'objective immortality,' in which the past is comprehended by the present, are illuminating accounts of the self as a process."[35] It is possible that an aware state is pre-oriented, i.e., fixed towards objects in materialistic terms, while consciousness is more a conceptual and transitory activity. Thus the individual, or *persona* in the Latin sense, is a fixed perceptive entity ordained by the public while the self is more a matter of flux, a matter of constant change and dynamism. As Kern stated: "William James saw the...fluid nature of human consciousness..."[36] He also noted that not all of our actions are a matter of conscious choices, but rather, not unlike Hume and Julian Jaynes noted, he saw much of our activity as little more than habits. The truth is that, "...our actions originally prompted by conscious intelligence may grow so automatic by dint of habit as to be apparently unconsciously performed. Standing, walking, buttoning and unbuttoning, piano-playing, talking, even saying one's prayers, may be done when the mind is absorbed in other things."[37] The basketball player who is in a 'groove,' the concert pianist who is completely lost in his performance, and the poet who knows not where words are coming from, all represent an actualization of this theory. And as long as the poet and artists don't pay attention to that fact, the words and music can continue to flow. Nothing here is conscious and, if anything, it requires that one should not always be consciously engaged. James understood this. It is possible that this fact occurs because, "...he demolishes the notion that consciousness is a thing, some kind of stuff, different from material stuff. What it is is one way of organizing the only stuff there is."[38] The key here is the 'one way of organizing' but not necessarily the only way.

Once death is simply accepted as a fact of life and is lived as fully as possible then the real issue becomes one's ability to make conscious choices. There is, of course, such a thing as too much interiority, for it is possible, according to James, that the, "...person who stares intently at his own stream of experience is unlikely to discover any concrete evidence of his own identity, innerness, or volition. Even his own bodily sensations will seem separate from him, since the very fact of scrutinizing will make them seem out there, apart."[39] This is unfortunately so subjective a condition, so interiorized, that this thesis, while compelling, is not one that can be given a great deal of documentation. What is certain, however, is that the role of suicide, that historically unacceptable activity, has become acceptable, even for James who, "...found himself forced to accept the conclusion that man is nothing but a physical object among other objects doomed to purposeless conditioned action and reaction within a closed mechanistic universe. Suicide or madness seemed the only possible response to this bleak world view." He does, however, offer a resolution for this issue of free will when in one of his entries in his diary he noted that: "I think that yesterday was a crisis in my life. I finished the first part of Renouvier's second 'Essais' and see no reason why his definition of Free Will —'the sustaining of a thought *because I choose to* when I might have other thoughts'—need be the definition of an illusion... My first act of free will shall be to believe in free will."[40] In this he offers an anticipatory response to the materialistic position which is best expressed by Daniel C. Dennett in his *Consciousness Explained* which denies free will. For any one who can achieve an interior voice can also convince themselves by the power of an existential and thus self-conscious choice to advocate a freedom of will. This does not prove there is a will, but then this does not prove consciousness either. This is, in part, the result of the history of logical positivism and its legacy, specifically the work of another contemporary of James, John B. Watson (1878–1958), the founder of behaviorism in the United States:

> Psychology as the behaviorist views it is a purely objective experimental branch of natural science. Its theoretical goal is the prediction and control of behavior. Introspection forms no essential part of its methods, nor is the scientific value of its data dependent upon the readiness with which they lend themselves to the interpretation in terms of consciousness. The behaviorist, in his efforts to get a unitary scheme of

animal response, recognizes no dividing line between man and brute. The behavior of man, with all of its refinement and complexity, forms only a part of the behaviorist's total scheme of investigation.[41]

While this certainly was a major set-back for the consideration, study and examination of consciousness and with it the self and reflectivity, its extreme influence only lasted until after WW II when this position came under increasing attack from many quarters including neurophysiology, philosophy, literary studies and psychology. Because it is unmeasurable does not necessarily mean it does not exist any more than dreams or hopes do not exist.

But William James noted other critical aspects regarding the functioning of consciousness that has proven to retain applicability to this day. As he states in his *Principles of Psychology*:

> The proposition that within each personal consciousness thought feels continuous, means two things:
> 1. That even where there is a time-gap the consciousness after it feels as if it belonged together with the consciousness before it, as another part of the same self;
> 2. That the changes from one moment to another in the quality of the consciousness are never absolutely abrupt.[42]

What is of interest is again how James anticipates a more current understanding, in this particular case, regarding modern physics. Fred Alan Wolf discussing quantum mechanics in relation to consciousness suggests that in a physical setting the idea of the "now" is limited since, "To say 'now' and to know I am experiencing 'now' requires something beyond now; it requires both past and future. The word *now* cannot even be heard now because to hear 'now' requires the length of time it takes for the consonant and vowel sounds to register in our brains. Thus 'now' is also a phantom! 'Now' is not here. It cannot be experienced as time."[43] This brings to mind the view that the self cannot be singularized, that like the term 'now' there is a plurality and not one monolithic phenomena even if it is our tendency to obey our senses as though there is a recognized immediacy in all cases. This not to deny that any given responses is inappropriate. On the contrary, the immediacy of a situation can and often does demand immediacy of response. It is only the assumptions that are being called into question regarding this word 'now.' Much like an explanation of a self requires that once you what have explained that self, what you have actually explained is now in the past and therefore the self explained is a past self, one that technically no longer is current. Any explanation of the self becomes quickly part of the past. Part of the phenomena that Wolf expresses is done so by way of the example of the ringing of a telephone. The phone rings, and several people in the room hear it, but do they all hear the same ringing at the same time? Not according to the laws of physics for while "each recognition that you have is yours" the fact is that "no one else in the room 'reads' that ring at exactly the same time you do." The unique self is so unique that what appears to be a same experience is rather only a similar experience with variations generally un-noted: "The phone has rung and I have heard it. I had to project my 'hearing' 'out there' to the phone back in time when the phone rang." What makes this so interesting to Wolf is that he can conclude that "My mind is a time machine." When we speak of out there, the mind must first internalize that out there before it can become an inner phenomena which can now be recognized as an exterior phenomenon. As Wolf puts it: "It is a self-referential process in which the physical event A and the mental event B connect. That is why we hear the phone at the phone. That is why external events appear external. Our minds are not in our heads, although that is where the time-reversed process begins. Our minds are 'out there.'"[44] And the idea of an existing mind that has been rejected by the behaviorists leaves more questions than answers. There is nothing simple about the self, consciousness, freedom, or our understanding.

William James offers a recognition of the complexity of the self, "...*in its widest possible sense, however, a man's Self is the sum total of all that he* CAN *call his.*"[45] This makes the self a cumulative sport where each addition changes the sum of the whole, reminiscent of an Hegelian structure. To state it directly: "This is a completely new notion in our history of theories of the self."[46] The idea of a new notion of self was expanded by others with a new notion of consciousness and sense of time which can be found in the writings of the poet T.S. Eliot (1888–1965). In his 1942 essay "The Music of Poetry" he stated that: "...the poet is occupied with frontiers of consciousness beyond which words fail, though meanings still exist."[47] A clarification can be found in some of his earlier works, specifically early lines from the first of his *Four Quartets* (1944):

> Time past and time future
> Allow but a little consciousness.
> To be conscious is not to be in time
> But only in time can the moment in the rose-garden,
> The moment in the arbour where the rain beat,
> The moment in the draughty church at smokefall
> Be remembered, involved with the past and future.

>   Only through time time is conquered.[48]

The potential for varied interpretations of a poem are great. However, with modern poetry the difficulties can be massive. And with the poet who Yeats has called "the greatest poet,"[49] any interpretation is compounded by the existence of multitude of other interpretations. Yeats understood in his unforgettable lines (1916):

> Turning and turning in the widening gyre
> The falcon cannot hear the falconer;
> Things fall apart; the center cannot hold;
> Mere anarchy is loosed, and everywhere
> The ceremony of innocence is drowned;
> The best lack all conviction, while the worst
> Are full of passionate intensity.[50]

Besides being prophetic this is less than a salutary judgement. The issue centers around that of time—like space—being so transformed from our preconceived notions. Time can lock one in and yet it can also be emancipating. The issue is not time or space in this case, it is more a matter of the mind, the self and what can be called an existential attitude. Eliot in the *Quartets*, "...examines the qualitative aspects of the experience of time. He distinguishes between the schematic time as a meaningless sequence of events and the 'timeless moment' at which consciousness touches the deeper patterns of order and meaning embedded in the tissues of experience."[51]

The role of our understanding of time is indispensable in aiding in the creation, development and maturation of our consciousness. Where there is a sense of more time, it follows that there will follow more memory, more reflection and the potential for more consciousness. Rightly observed: "...it is only 'through time' (the actuality of experience) that we enter the higher ground where time as limitation is 'conquered.'"[52] Consider the growing love affair with imagination at the end of the Enlightenment along with its maturation as part of the romantic perception followed by its dominance in our own era, time becomes a malleable phenomenon, much as language, which is clearly seen as open-ended. The adage was to learn the rules of grammar first before attempting to break them. The less sense of history one has then the less developed one's consciousness likely will be; an indication that not all people have the same degree of consciousness, or for some, perhaps, no consciousness at all. This may be on of the reasons we find consciousness first making some hint of an appearance after the Renaissance discovery of what today would be considered a knowledge of Western history. And history, moreover, must be learned in order to be free of it. In *Little Gidding* Eliot offered that:

> A people without a history
> Is not redeemed from time, for history is a pattern
> Of timeless moments.[53]

It is not unlikely, however, that in studying and learning history we become emancipated from it much as when we admit that our memories make it possible to find a certain degree of freedom in facing up to them. That is, if we do not know our own personal history to have knowledge of our past and be set free from any of our pre-judgmental understandings and any myths that were fed to us, we will remain enslaved to those misunderstandings and prejudices that hide behind the walls of our youthful experiences. To some extent Eliot touches upon this point in what some would consider his masterpiece, "The Waste Land"" (1922) where one of his favorite lines is "HURRY UP PLEASE ITS TIME."[54] [sic] In a footnote he further offers from his reading of a work by F. H. Bradley that: "My external sensations are no less private to myself than are my thoughts or my feelings. In either case my experience falls within my own circle, a circle closed on the outside; and…In brief…the whole world for each is peculiar and private to that soul."[55] This sense of privacy is very important as it reflects back upon the inner and therefore unknown individual that society can only wonder about. This was what worried the French (and others) in the nineteenth century when questions were raised regarding what was going on behind the public facade. There is very little evidence of a concern with privacy until we enter the our own modern and post-modern world, (or at the earliest the nineteenth century).

It is in this sense of time that takes on new and original dimensions beyond the world of physics. The past—memoirs and autobiography—plus the future—science fiction, are combined into new forms of a sense of a reality of time. Our perceptions dictate our physical experiences. How many thoughts, sights and sounds can you experience and discern? "There is also a desire to occupy, if only for a moment, as many points of view as possible, an impulse clearly present in the multi-perspectivism of analytic cubist painting, in portraits by Picasso, as well as in poems like T. S. Eliot's 'The Wasteland' and Wallace Stevens's 'Thirteen Ways of Looking at a Blackbird'—works in which a multiplicity of perspectives conveys the realization that reality includes our attempts to see it."[56] The very act of thinking basically alters that experience. For Eliot as for so many other contemporary creative thinkers the inter-relationships are far greater than the parts. When Eliot speaks of "time past and time future," he is as one commentator put it noting that there are "limited conceptions of past and future," which in turn, "'allow but a little consciousness,' for they permit an awareness of time only as a succession of isolated (and for that reason meaningless) moments." After all, "moving out of a time-orienated experience suggests living in terms of a universal rather than a limited and personal standpoint."[57] As the physicist Wolf noted we actually perceive only bits but immediately put them together to create a consistency for our senses and so to appear to experience very coherent moments.[58] Order is a creation of our imagination rather than given for Eliot, since he, "...diagnosed the modern condition as a 'dissociation of sensibility' a widening rift between thought and emotion, intellect and sensation, and a general failure to achieve 'unification of sensibility.'"[59]

This was not unlike a perception found in the writing of Robert Musil (1880–1942). In his *The Man Without Qualities* he makes a remarkable suggestion that prior to WW II that people in the United States were preoccupied with movement not as an abstraction but as an activity:

> For some time now such a social *idée fixe* has been a kind of super-American city where everyone rushes about, or stands still, with a stop-watch in his hand. Air and earth form an ant-hill, veined by channels of traffic, rising storey upon storey. Overhead-trains, overground-trains, underground-trains, pneumatic express-mails carrying consignments of human beings, chains of motor-vehicles all racing along horizontally. Express lifts vertically pumping crowds from one traffic-level to another...At the junctions one leaps from one means of transport to another, is instantly sucked in and snatched away by the rhythm of it, which makes a syncope, a pause, a little gap of twenty seconds between two roaring outbursts of speed, and in these intervals in the general rhythm one hastily exchanges a few words with others.[60]

Such movement leaves one not only exhausted but also alienated and estranged from all others as well as from one's own potential self. And where there is enough alienation, there can be no self, but only a paradox. As we move ever closer to our own world with all its marvels of technology, we become another cog in the wheel of industry where an authentic self becomes that much more problematic. Ulrich's self-consciousness, Musil's voice in his leading figure, immature and stunted regardless of its existence. The characters in Eliot's "The Hollow Men" and "The Wasteland" are filled with a "...rueful mockery of the timorous hesitations and paralyses of self-consciousness..." Musil, "...experiences reality as fragmentary and merely subjective while at the same time losing a sense of his own subjective being." Experiences for Ulrich are of, "…the world going in and out, aspects of the world falling into shape inside a head…"[61] And here we find, "…the belief that the most important thing about experience is the experiencing of it, and about deeds the doing of them."[62] While there are hints of Nietzsche here we also can find something close to Camus' *The Stranger* where Mersault does not come to life until the very end of the novel after telling the priest he has no need for comforting. Life comes into focus once he accepts his death and its implications which are powerful since now for the first time Mersault is totally alive waiting for his execution. As Musil stated it, "Ulrich was a man whom something compelled to live against his own grain, although he seemed to let himself float alone without a constraint."[63] In another passage he again makes it clear that the self seems almost to be struggling to come out in spite of his indifference and narrow self-conscious state of mind: "…Ulrich has to confess to himself, smiling, that for all he was, after all, a 'character,' even without having one."[64] There is additionally a recognition of the emptiness implied in specialization, seeking meaning in an alienating industrial world, when he notes that: "For the inhabitant of a country has at least nine characters: a professional one, a national one, a civic one, a class one, a geographical one, a sex one, a conscious, and unconscious and perhaps even too a private one; he combines them all in himself, but they dissolve him, and he is really nothing but a little channel washed out by all these trickling streams, which flow into and drain out of it again in order to join other little streams filling another channel."[65]

The specialization process which removes most people from the tools of a trade or direct means of a finished product was noted by a contemporary of Musil, José Ortega y Gasset, who in his *Revolt of the Masses*, (1930) entitled chapter twelve, "The Barbarism of 'Specialization.'" On one day we wear a golfing cap, another a bowling cap, another a bridge cap and on and on until there is simply no one home except at a given moment. There can sometimes appear to be many selves when there is in fact no self at all. This raises the question of the dangers of advocating many selves since it could mean no centering of any self from which all others flowed, interacted with or impacted upon. But this was not what Woolf meant. While the novel regarding this non-qualitative man is anything but optimistic about the human condition it does open doors to a thinking all too common. The fact is that both Ortega y Gasset and the earlier Nietzsche had, "…developed a philosophy of 'perspectivism' which implied that there are as many different spaces as there are points of view."[66] The question that should be considered is this: is there nothing but varied perspectives without any center or is there in fact something of a constant to the self that experiences these variations?

This is not to say that the growing pluralism of the past century has only been detrimental to the growth of the self even if the power of an existential attitude tied to a mature self-consciousness raises more questions than answers, especially regarding that key component of action for the sake of action. The exception to this confusion comes from the more common responses which have their own inherent life via the arts, for here the fully developed self-conscious reflective individual does make more than an occasional appearances, in both its positive and its burdensome state of mind. Arguably, no one makes a better case in the world of visual arts and plurality of selves than Pablo Picasso (1881-1973). He went through a neo-impression period followed by a blue-period, then helped to create cubism (analytic, synthetic, hermetic and Rococo), spending a life time as a sculptor, then entered a pink period followed by a brief period returning to realism and continued to be arguably the most original and creative artists of the twentieth century. When Picasso stated that, "'I do not search, I find,'" he simply, "...implied that his freedom of approach was unlimited."[67] This comes close to the modernists who claimed that they didn't paint what was but rather what they saw. The same can be observed when listening to the strikingly new music of our world which can be exemplified by Stravinsky, a composer of great diversity who applied a similar principle to music as Picasso to painting: "...both Picasso and Stravinsky have repeatedly demonstrated that a new work can be based on an aesthetic theory diametrically opposed to the one that preceded it."[68] Starting with the Impressionists in the previous century as well as the revolutionary art of Cézanne, one can argue that the Cubism that followed created an impact that was so elusive that, "perspectival world broke up as if an earthquake had struck..."[69] Cézanne clearly understood the changes that had taken place when he remarked, "Monet, he's only an eye, but my God what an eye!"[70] It isn't what is but what is perceived that mattered to these artists. What made Cézanne's work so revolutionary—as well as contributing to the post-impressionists—was his desire, as he put it, "...to make of impressionism something solid like the art of the museums."[71] It is very possible that the modern self-conscious state of mind makes for the individual something solid about the 'now,' that moment when the existential attitude exists beyond any continuous theme.

Cézanne known as, "the father of 'modern art,'"[72] also was a significant contributor to the revolution among the creative geniuses who brought about a radical change in our understanding of time and space. In his mature years he acknowledged that his efforts were only a beginning and he remarked that he would "...forever be the primitive of the method he had discovered."[73] This was only matched by his desire to see, "...each of his pictures as a type of visual-research problem." At the same time, the sculptor, Auguste Rodin (1840–1917) was exploring new syntheses of matter and form while the "literacy realists"—the writers—were cultivating a "...scientific detachment in their writing and developing a technique that would enable them to record the details of their minute observations of everyday life with accuracy and precision. Zola, by means of his experimental novel, introduced a modified social-scientific technique to fiction....Debussy, when writing to a friend, spoke about some of his compositions as his 'latest discoveries in musical chemistry.'"[74]

The arts like the world of science have been going through a dramatic transformation that many still find impossible to understand or accept. The problem for so many observers was that the traditional standards of commissioned art were vanishing and artists were appearing out of non-artistic backgrounds with little or no formal training: the post-impressionist, Vincent Van Gogh (1853–90) was trained to be a Methodist preacher while his friend, the famed expressionist (synthesism) Paul Gauguin (1848–1903) began his career as a successful stockbroker; and the primitivist painter Henri Rousseau (1844–1910), nicknamed *le Douanier* was a retired customs collector who had started to paint in his middle age with no training. He was, "...that paradox, a folk artist of genius."[75] It was Picasso and his compatriots who were the earliest to recognize the brilliance of this untrained artist's work and, "...revered him quite justifiably, as the god-father of twentieth-century painting,"[76] and who has also been considered a forerunner of the Surrealists.[77] This was an expansion of horizons for all who would enter into the arts, whether they were literary, visual or musical. These were the results of the end of the age of commissions for portraitures or for additions to buildings or string quartets for members of the royalty, nobility or the idle rich. "When commissions of this kind became rarer, artists had to choose their own subjects."[78] Perhaps it was this opportunity to explore their own inner voices and visions that had attracted modern artists to the creative process. Pluralism and openness meant freedom in many categories for those willing to make such choices and engage in the risks while those who were trapped remained in the system of factories or offices. It meant mostly that the creative minds of this modern world was building an age of genius, i.e., the individual was becoming manifest.

The mental orientation of a Picasso for example was one with no preconceived views of order, time or space. It was the well-known art historian

Helen Gombrich who acknowledged a new reality: "Why not be consistent and accept the fact that our real aim is rather to construct something than to copy something."[79] If Cézanne could construct out of patterns found in nature and Picasso could be the one who could paint what he sees and not what is, then one could mock, as Picasso did: "...those who want to understand his art. 'Everyone wants to understand art. Why not try to understand the song of a bird?'"[80] Not surprisingly, Gombrich believed, "...that the situation which led Picasso to his different 'finds' is very typical of modern art."[81] While this does not necessarily explain his brilliant *Les Demoiselles d'Avignon*, (1907), this masterpiece did incorporate, "...so many of the ideas of the early 20th century that it became a landmark of the modern-art movement."[82] In literature we find the French poet Arthur Rimbaud (1854–91), creative and unorthodox in his life style, would offer the, "...claim that the true artist is a visionary."[83] As a precursor of the symbolists and favored of Surrealists, it has been suggested in regard to, "...the preface to his *Illuminations*, poems that had great influence on the artistic community, to go so far as to suggest that the artist, in order to achieve the seer's insight, must become deranged or, as he says in effect, must systematically unhinge and confuse the everyday faculties of sense and of reason, which serve only to blur his vision."[84] That this French poet was held in high regard by Picasso and his fellow painters is given emphasis by way of his *Les Demoiselles d'Avignon* which challenges the "...traditional concept of an orderly, constructed, unified pictorial space that mirrors the world..."[85]

If we remind ourselves of the changes in the world of physics that had been occurring at this time, we find a fragmenting of time and space. In the world of quantum mechanics our relationships to space and time are forever altered and where an Albert Einstein (1879–1955) can describe a new physical world where space and time merged. "Time is 'assimilated' to the three dimensions of space in such a way that measurements of space and time, especially where astronomical distances are involved, are functions of each other, and never independent."[86] Thus experimentation in physics becomes more complicated and more demanding along with often being more abstract.

It is this drive for exploration that also appears in the art community, and in this, "Picasso is characteristic of the modern age in his constant experimentation, in his sudden shifts from one kind of painting to another, and in his startling innovations in painting and even sculpture."[87] As unique as the impressionists, post-impressionists and expressionists have been it is in cubism that the real break from the mold of traditional order occurs.

> Perspective space in Western painting since Massacio assumes a continuous, unbroken space fixed from a single point of view. We can say of this rigid, geometric space that all the represented objects in it are *simultaneous*; the single *scene* constitutes a single *event*. Cubism, with its new kind of simultaneity, the simultaneity of different viewpoints, destroyed consistency of image and appearance and yielded in its place 'abstract' form. The process is well begun in Les Demoiselles d'Avignon.[88]

It is in the eye of the beholder that order is created and not in the preconceived assumptions of a pre-ordained structure. If one's consciousness is predicated in part by the operation of a particular self or of some self-conscious choice then it can be also suggested that the deeper meaning of any perception may not always be apparent at first glance. Cubism explores and exploits this condition of multiple perspectives as well as if not better than any other art at this time. It is also filled with a degree of reflective judgements. It has been stated that, "…being no longer restricted to a single viewpoint, the artist might see any given object in the world not as a fixed appearance or shape, but as a universe of possible lines, planes and colors."[89] Once the self is perceived as possibly multiple and non-static, an open-ended and non-fixed state of being, one dominated by a quantifying or qualifying inner drive, then it can actualize events and judgements on its own. There is little doubt that if this principle is valid, it technically could be applied to a variety of phenomena. "The proliferation of perspectives and the breakup of a homogeneous three-dimensional space in art seemed to many to be a visible representation of the pluralism and confusion of the modern age."[90] And the relationship between the Cubists and the new science has also been noted by a variety of thinkers. One such example was the French poet in the tradition of Rimbaud and the symbolist school, Guillaume Apollinaire (1880–1918), a major supporter of Cubist forms and highly favored of the later American Beat writers. In 1913 Apollinaire commented in his *Cubist Painters* that Cubists have followed scientists beyond the third dimension and "have been led quite naturally…to preoccupy themselves with new possibilities of spatial measurement which, in the language of the modern studies are designated by the term: the fourth dimension."[91] But it is precisely the writers and poets that find it more difficult to follow the axioms of Cubism. Dwight McDonaled, the author of a set of essays called *Against the American Grain*, once told this writer that the post-impressionist artist's ability to go beyond forms was impossible in the written arts given the limits of the very structure inherent in language. Obviously Appolinaire was one who gave it an effort and there would follow many others from the Surrealists to the Beat writers and beyond. There has been something of a heritage in writing that has already been introduced from Eliot to Borges: "...writers, limited to a series of single settings, used multiple perspective to depict different views of objects in space." Obviously it was necessary to experiment as these painters and physicists had been doing. This attitude can be found in both Proust and Joyce who experimented in such a way as they "...used the technique [of varied perspectives] in several ways."[92]

While the painters and sculptors experimented with perceptions of space, writers could manipulate time. And they did in ways not seen before. Joyce's continuous narrative at the end of *Ulysses* and Marcel Proust's (1871–1922) *Remembrance of Times Past*, are excellent examples. Proust had been influenced by Henri Bergson (1859–1941) and his philosophic considerations regarding our idea of time. The art historian William Fleming offers the following to demonstrate Bergson's view: "Time, therefore, is 'the continuous progress of the past, which gnaws into the future and which swells as it advances.'" While this does have the sound of an Hegelian dialectic version of time, "...Bergson's concept of time is neither Hegelian nor clock time with its divisions into seconds, minutes, and hours, nor is it concerned with the usual groupings of past, present, and future."[93] Time is so critical to Bergson that he had even placed his, "...theory of knowledge on the way we know ourselves in time."[94] Time was moving beyond its secular definition. It was becoming the most fundamental component in our understanding and claims to knowledge. Another perspective is offered in an addenda with an enlargement of the thesis into music: "...in visual impression, the eye mixes the colors; in a symbolist poem, the mind supplies the connecting verbs for the nominal fragments...and in Debussy's music, the ear bridges over the silences."[95] We see and hear by way of a series of mental combinations that give separate bits of sound a completeness. Everything can be perceived as an integration of all the various sounds or colors; it is the mental creation of what we think of as a unity much as we mentally unify the universe. But this is the result of a self-conscious reflective act of individual choices rather than a necessary assumption of a preconceived notion of a given universal order.

From the Hobbesian fear that rose out of the emerging individuality to the later French doubts regarding the word 'individualism,' the tide began to turn towards a growing sense of our unique and singular means of understanding, This became the direction for the more intellectually creative. In that period at the end of the nineteenth century and even before Watson and behaviorism became an agreed and unquestioned certainty for some scholars, writers like

Proust and Joyce and Eliot and the post-impressionist artists saw a world that was dominated by only the certainty of motion, time and space. At the end of Proust's *Remembrance of Things Past*: "...all stable relationships of character and situations are suddenly revealed as transmuted beyond recognition."[96] And it can be found in Proust as in Bergson that, "'...the recollection of single, unique, unrepeatable experiences...was assigned a special function in the quest for the recovery of time and the self,' and thus recollection became 'an activity, an operation—not the passive reproduction of habitual memory responses.'"[97] Flux takes command over the static, even if most people are unwilling to see it as such. The discovery of the malleability of our experience of time is partly the reason for this expanding view of time and space.

It was in his *Introduction to Metaphysics* (1903) that Bergson approached

> ...time by distinguishing two ways of knowing: relative and absolute. The former, impoverished kind is achieved by moving around an object or by coming to know it through symbols or words that fail to render its true nature. Absolute...achieved by experiencing something as it is from within. This absolute knowledge can only be given by intuition, which he defined as 'the kind of intellectual sympathy by which one places oneself within an object in order to coincide with what is unique in it and consequently inexpressible.'[98]

The relativism of time was, of course, a very modern approach to the physical world and thus was also applied freely by philosophers. This was significant for Bergson because he "...based his theory of knowledge on the way we know ourselves in time."[99] As Virginia Woolf and others had come to believe that the self was not a singular phenomena, but rather a unique expression of a specific self of selves, the specific moment of experience was paramount. It was in 1889 when Bergson produced *Time and Free Will: Essay on the Immediate Data of Consciousness* in which, "...he wrote of a self whose former states 'permeate,' 'melt,' or 'dissolve' into one another as do notes in a tune. Another metaphor has the conscious states of our inner self effecting a 'mutual penetration, an interconnection.'"[100] What he was attempting in this early work was, "...to distinguish between a 'superficial psychic life' to which the scientific logic of space and number could properly be applied, and a life in the 'depths of consciousness' in which 'the deep-seated self followed a logic of its own...'"[101] The idea of a 'deep-seated self' raises the question as to whether he sees one or many although consciousness itself appears to be multiple depending upon the question of a specific time. For Bergson, time was now a positive force and not a "...mere source of 'change and decay' that poets and thinkers had" for so long held onto.[102] His view was dominated by the idea that time-as-experienced was in fact duration which for him had implications for consciousness: "Duration ... could be sensed and understood only through introspection: only through a concentration on one's own consciousness could one arrive at a realization of human experience in its fullness and actuality—not as it was customarily chopped up into discrete portions. And this process of sympathetic comprehension was what was commonly called intuition."[103] The idea of introspection, therefore, has appeared along with reflection to be seminal terms to any meaningful discussion of both consciousness and self-consciousness. The immature form of self-consciousness, the awkwardness felt inherently in our youth, can encourage a certain degree of both reflection and introspection. And unlike being simply aware (Cartesian consciousness) this is not an automatic condition. Action when conscious, especially a more mature self-conscious, brings to the fore the sense of an existential choice involving the power of the 'now' or the present moment. As Bergson stated in his essay "An Introduction to Metaphysics" published in 1903, "...there is one reality, at least, which we all seize from within, by intuition and not by simple analysis. It is our own personality in its flowing through time—our self which endures. We may sympathize intellectually with nothing else, but we certainly sympathize with our own selves..."[104] That he uses both the singular and plural of self indicates that he himself had a mixed perception of both the self and any potential multiplicity.

There have been and remains today many attempts to analyze the very subjective experience of what—because of its subjective nature—has been treated by some as a complete waste of time. In the world of logical positivism, if it cannot be measured it cannot be given veracity. As for the flow of the conscious mind, Bergson, in opposition to such thinking, wrote the following conclusion:

> I find, first, that I pass from state to state. I am hot or cold. I am gay or I am sad. I work or I do nothing. I look around me or I think of something else. Sensations, feelings, volitions representations, these are the modifications among which my existence divides itself and which color it, each in turn. I am changing, then, ceaselessly. ...
>
> ...My state of mind, advancing along the highway of time, inflates itself continually with the duration it picks up; it snowballs, as it were. So it is even more strongly with the more profoundly interior states, sensations, affects, desires, etc., which do not correspond like interior states, sensations, affects, desires, etc., which do not correspond like a simple visual perception, to some invariable exterior object.

...The truth is that one changes ceaselessly, and that the state itself is already change.[105]

For those who subscribe to a potential of selves there also is the, "...best known descriptions of the flow of consciousness [which] are those by James Joyce and Virginia Woolf. ... Their accounts tried to include everything—'sensations and memories, feelings and conceptions, fancies and imaginations, intuitions, visions, insights, processes of association.'" It was thinkers like these who attempted, "...to record passages of an individual's entire psychic life."[106] Moreover, there is a legacy of Bergsonion thinkers that have carried on some of his ideas. One example is the work of Henri Hubert and Marcel Mauss in 'Etude sommaire de la représentation du temps dans la réligion et la magie,' which appears in their *Mélanges d'histoire de réligions* (Paris, 1909), where they, "...believed that there is dynamic...the concept of time as an 'active tension by which consciousness realizes the harmony of independent durations and different rhythms.'"[107] Here again we se the beginnings of the very modern notion that consciousness is a capacity for a construct of creative organization. That it is not passive any more than time or space is passive and that it is active at the moment of choices being made by way of an expression of the self helps explain the dynamics of conscious states.

For an historian of ideas and mentalities it is not very often we discuss political let alone military events. Such an exception, however, clearly occurs with the beginnings of this past century which could well be called the Century of Annihilation. Although there are precedents to the Great War, the Napoleonic Wars, for example, which introduced conscription, and the U. S. Civil War, with its massive slaughter, there were still too many radical and technical changes which occurred in the war years between 1914 and 1918 to make it comparable. There are the new weapons such as tanks, submarines, depth charges, airplanes, poison gas, etc. During the war there were at least some ten million deaths. Among these there were arguably some of the most promising and talented young people that society would produce. The first and most obvious change that clearly impacted negatively on this period was the idea of the nation state, especially as an absolute in the form of nationalism. Before 1914 most western European countries, "...had limited or no passport requirements and allowed almost everyone to travel freely."[108] The borders that have been increasingly undermined with the European Union has been an attempt to resolve a very modern (post-modern) problem—politically narrow specialization. Three countries, "...Germany, Austria, and Italy could only glance back two generations to the wars that brought them into being as modern nation states."[109] This was for some a very new political phenomena stamped upon the very old order of seven medieval royal houses that had traditionally governed what was becoming seven modern nation states. Those seven houses would also be victims of the war. The Germans especially felt that they had to catch up with the symbols of a nation state with products and colonies like the older Dutch, English and French governments had clearly mastered.[110]

The tie between the newer nationalist states and the nascent capitalistic economies became a powerful driving force for a major alteration in western culture. Earlier, after Napoleon reduced the 500 German political administrations to about 50 and the Napoleonic wars ended, the German business communities in these 50 communities actually took the most significant step towards political union through an agreed upon economic cooperative called the Zollverein. Bismark only sometime later had to finish the project of political unification with the blood of warriors (Blood and Iron). But Germany also had another, a geographic problem: it was bordered by aggressive states on all sides. Therefore, for the new organized peoples of Germany, there was the experience of being, "...surrounded by countries with older and more highly developed cultures. Germany was thus cramped in time as well as in space, vulnerable in the infancy of its nationhood and in being at the geographic center of Europe."[111] Just consider how important a nationalistic political order with a strong economy at the outbreak of World War I and the complexity achieved by both the French and Germans moving some three million troops by way of some 4,278 trains. And, "...the German mobilization timetable was even more precise, for it led immediately to war on two fronts and required the element of surprise to succeed."[112]

Hardware, economics and nationalism came together in a congruence that helped to bring about this remarkable madness of politics and war and an end to the traditions of Western culture. What a perfect age for those with a self to turn toward the fresh challenges of the sciences, arts and literature. It was Marshall McLuhan in his *Understanding Media* who made the interesting observation about modern warfare: "War is never anything less than accelerated technological change. It begins when some notable disequilibrium among existing structures has been brought about by inequality of rates of growth. The very late industrialization and unification of Germany had left her out of the race for staples and colonies for many years. As the Napoleonic wars were technologically a sort of catching-up of France with England, the First World War was itself a major phase of the final industrialization of Germany and America."[113] An interesting irony in all this is offered by an American military analyst who had, "...thought that the very possibility of aerial bombings would be a deterrent to war. He argued that wars must cease because no ruler would dare to undertake them, since all were equally vulnerable."[114] Unfortunately, even advent of atomic bombs has not seen the attainment of this optimistic dream. The major problem was a dichotomy that grew between the leadership and the circumstances encountered. Generals themselves had not come to appreciate the, "...significance of long-range artillery and machine guns and continued to think in terms of the glory of the cavalry charge and the 'terror of cold steel'..." Additionally, it was the diplomats who, "...failed to understand the full impact of instantaneous communications without the ameliorating effects of delay. They still counted in the ultimate effectiveness of 'spoken words of a decent man' in fact-to-face encounters but were forced to negotiate many important issues over copper wire."[115] One of the characteristics of multiple and dramatic engineering changes is that they take time before the impact can be absorbed. Whenever major changes occur the last thing to change are the assumptions that people bring to the table.

For the first time war was declared by a telegram and almost instantly Austria declared war on Serbia, 28 July 28 1914. A contributing factor for accuracy was that in 1890 (again that interesting date) Standard Time had been created. The issue of time and its mechanization can be demonstrated in several ways. Before the war, wrist watches had been considered rather unmanly. When war broke out it became standard military equipment. On 1 July 1916 at 7:30 a.m. the Battle of the Somme began.[116] Unheard of control was in the hands of the officers in the structuring of varied activities for such large numbers of troops. Whatever private time that had existed up to this time had to be bridged into a coherent unit. Coordination of all activity according to a single public time reversed the dominant cultural thrust of the prewar years and expanded the multiplicity of one's own sense of time. "The delicate sensitivity to private time of Bergson and Proust had no place in the war. It was obliterated by the overwhelming force of mass movements that regimented the lives of millions of men by the public time of clocks and wrist watches..."[117] As Stephen Kern points out, "...preparation for fighting divided time into discrete units as neat as the lines of position and advance on the commanding officer's maps, from which the planners attempted to construct the sequence of events in battle."[118] With the new communications network officers far from the front could know the situation almost immediately. War had become a paradox with improved centralized control from a distance and an indifference and randomness never seen before. And, perhaps more significantly, war was now taken to the non-combatant citizens. "This form of war blurred the distinction between soldier and civilian, front and home, safety and danger."[119] With heavy artillery having a range of more than 4,000 to 5,000 yards and planes dropping bombs indiscriminately, the war had become mechanical and impersonal. The Great War also experienced both accuracy and lethal distances of up to 2,000 yards for small-caliber arms.[120] The face to face implications of a killing even if it was the enemy, was now removed. There were no longer any distinctions of class, rank, and profession for muddied solders in the trenches. It is important to emphasize that, "there was an eerie anonymity about this fighting..."[121]

The issue that needs be understood was that the sense of order for both time and space was being shattered. One of the more significant mental aspects of any story regarding this era, "...was that the present moment could be filled with many distant events. As one historian concluded boldly, because of these changes, on the eve of the war 'succession gave way to simultaneity.'"[122] A private secretary to the German Chancellor at this time of crisis kept a diary which gave an idea of how quickly the declaration and action of war seemed to overcome a traditional sense of time. As quoted in Kern, this gentleman responded on July 24th with a sense of the "...feverish tempo after the delivery of the Austrian ultimatum: '...What will our destiny be? But destiny is for the most part completely stupid and uncertain and all entangled in pure chance. Whoever grabs it, gets it. This damn crazy world had gotten too confused to comprehend or predict. Too many factors all at once.'"[123] The need for a strong sense of self much like an ability for self-reflective consciousness, to introspect and thus make personal choices increased in a world, especially in the Western world, clearly exponentially increasing anonymity and violence as this new century began to bumble along. A very succinct and clear expression of this circumstance is found in that "...time seemed to burn brightly in the war, riveting consciousness in an eternal present."[124] The existential now and self-consciousness to come were coupled to those artists and thinkers who had to create a world that could be worked with and lived in. Gertrude Stein on looking back on the war saw a Cubist war: "Really the composition of this war, 1914-1918, was not the composition of all previous wars, the composition was not a composition in which there was one man in the center surrounded by a lot of other men but a composition that had neither a beginning nor an end, a composition of which one corner was as important as another corner, in fact the composition of cubism."[125]

The multiplicity of events that occur in such paintings as *Nude Descending a Staircase* by Marcel Duchamp (1887–1968) can be overwhelming, but then so could twentieth century warfare. And yet by the simple act of editing one's focus and therefore what one perceives, notes and constructs, then the work can made sensible. For example, during the World War I, soldiers had learned to only hear what they chose to and not necessarily to all that was happening, immediately perceiving only what was relevant to them.[126] Many of the generals came to know this truth since to fight such a war, leaders like Schlieffen, Le Bon, and Stein would have to adjust to the fact, "…that comprehension of modern war required a multiplicity of perspectives."[127] If necessity is the mother of invention as historians are wont to suggest, then it would be possible to suggest that this may very well be an exception to the necessity of human survival. One thing is certain and can be documented: "World War I was THE simultaneous drama of the age of simultaneity." Moreover, since the communications network at the time was so elaborate that it made it possible for both the military and citizens to be cognizant of more disparate events,[128] it is no surprise that after these technological changes, the issue of 'simultaneity' had only increased. Kern puts it succinctly:

> It is possible to interpret how class structure, modes of production, patterns of diplomacy, or means of waging war were manifested historically in terms of changing experiences of time and space. Thus class conflict is viewed as a function of social distance, assembly lines are interrupted in conjunction with Taylorism and time management studies the diplomatic crisis of July 1914 is seen to have a historically unique temporality, and World War I can be interpreted under a Cubist metaphor. The phonograph and cinema are evaluated in terms of the way they modified the sense of the past, the telephone and World Standard Time are seen restructuring the experience of the present, the steamship and the Schlieffen Plan reflect a desire to control the future, urbanism is viewed as a process of diminishing living space, the politics of imperialism is seen as a universal impulse to claim more space, wealth is conceived as the power to control time and space.[129]

Art, technology and war were intertwined in an almost bizarre manner as in the famous story of Stein and Picasso walking down a Parisian boulevard during the war and encountering a camouflage for the first time. Picasso is supposed to have observed: "It is we who have created that."[130] It is no surprise that, "…further inquiry revealed that the man who invented camouflage was inspired by the Cubists and explicitly acknowledged that debt."[131] Cubism and war, a curious but revealing marriage tied on the surface but separated by the presence of consciousness on one side and the trap of political systems on the other. For better or worse, the absolute faith in systems is one of the many characteristics of a post-modern Europe. It is no accident that gestalt psychology emerged just before the Great War and suggested an evaluation of the relation between the subject of perception and the background that frames it. The pioneers of Gestalt psychology, "…elaborated laws explaining how the 'ground' and the 'figure' create each other in perception, but they also maintained that the figure was more prominent. Their theory rejected the associationist view that complex perceptions are built up out of a simple, discrete elements. They argued rather that perception is an experienced whole…"[132]

It is with the arrival of the War that we can find that there were two distinct directions that would be taken, one being that of the world of finance, capital, nations and wars and massive, expanding demographics, and the other a cultural elite that stood outside the systems in order to observe, think, create and evolve. Interestingly enough, on occasion the artist-poets might visit the former. One of the more interesting creative artistic movements that in retrospect seemed so natural in growing out of and after the War was that of Surrealism. It was, after all, this war that offered, "…a surrealistic sense of history that comes from confrontation with the grotesque newness of everything."[133] In one sense, one of irony, one could think of the surrealists as those attempting to replace the past that seemed to have so drastically failed with a revolutionary perspective that transcended systemic order. It is hard if not impossible to not agree: "…the war ripped up the historical fabric and cut everyone off from the past suddenly and irretrievably."[134] In a certain sense, the West was already closed (1890) which meant the traditional culture that could trace its continuum to early Greece (Crete) some 5,000 years earlier was also coming to an end. Consciousness was not a large part of the Western canon of thought until it began to fail. It may be possible that the explosive growth of consciousness as well as that of the self and an existential attitude gained a great impetus in the first two decades of the twentieth-century. At least this would follow if it is also true that any, "…belief in evolution, progress, and history itself was wiped out as Europeans were separated from the 'pre-historic days' of the prewar years by the violence of war," for then it must also be true that it would be for many the demise of any faith, "…in evolution, progress and history itself…"[135] At the least there was a major transformation from a blind faith to one that was predicated on social and economic convenience and necessity. Dostoevski's Raskolnikov may have been a literary character who did not make much sense except for a very small number of people, but the idea appears somewhat less striking than the updated concrete example found in the real life story of Leopold and Loeb in Chicago. Perhaps that partially explains the following thought about traditional morality that Kern offered: "Cut off from the past by the enormous contrast between prewar civilian life and morality and wartime violence and killing, the front-line soldier experienced panic in a world that justified the most bizarre paranoid fears."[136] Just as fear was not a stranger, so death had become an immediacy of life in a foxhole. It is inherently understandable in such a circumstance that any preoccupation with the present was a very sensible "…response to the imminence of death…"[137] These were rather common reactions to a crisis so great that the abstraction of faith of any type began to appear unnatural since luck made more sense than simple prayers. The desire for a mythic past expressed by nostalgia and the belief in the cult of the anti-hero would both develop in such destructive soil. This also could help explain why the subject of history that got its most modern development at the end of the nineteenth century has not faired well under the aegis of the even more contemporary love affair with the 'social sciences,' the land of statistics and data (Marc Twain's "lies, damned lies, and statistics") rather than interpretation and exploration. If it can be measured it is real, if it is an art it is only imagined. The idea of the, "…past as a continuous source of meaning for the present," has not done well in retaining an intellectual place as we enter the new millennium of war, materialism and the illusion of technique.[138]

One certainty we have perceived in our own world is the dashing against the wall of cubism the older rational and romantic assumptions. The problem for the rational world can be found in the terrible irrational characterization of the Great War.[139] As for any romantic paradigm, the issue had changed in such a manner that the simple drive for emotional and aesthetic conclusions seemed inadequate. Politics appeared too emotional and the aesthetics of war too destructive. True, romantic painting survived into the next century, but only, "…until the cubists, following Cézanne, attempted to think through the problem of man's relation to the world in a new way," especially in the sense of being isolated. "Cubism was theoretical; romantic painting was not. The cubists were impersonal as the romantic painters were not. Systematically the cubists restudied how consciousness dealt with the actualities outside of consciousness; and in so doing they ended romanticism."[140] Even in the more popular literature of the day, from penny novels of the Old West to the later cheap detective stories as exemplified by Micky Spillane, they too sounded the same theme of being singular and isolated. Thus the cowboy and the detective both shared the same unique stature of independence: The cowboy as in the case of *Shane*, for example, comes into town, alone, does his heroic action, and then leaves alone; the same for the Mike Hammer sitting alone in his office, the neon sign blinking outside, at the beginning and again at the end after having saved the day. Being outside the mainstream was now considered a potentially admirable position. These have become very contemporary and popular archetypes. The detachment concept that has come to dominate so much of our thinking can be traced back to the Galilean and Pascalian transformation of science as an act of objectification: now both the observed and the observer. Out of the past century, time became an object much as the clock 'tells' us the time. This objectification, some four centuries in development made it difficult to have a time that is personal. Futurists and science fiction fans look to the future for time. Those who work with memories (psychologists, for example) and historians, of course look to the past.[141] Only it is for the more the existential to grasp the ambiguous "now."

Bergson was not the only thinker of this era to have worked with this question of time. It also proved to be a central concern in the writings of Martin Heidegger (1859–1941), sometimes described as a founder of existentialism or existential phenomenology[142] although he is on record as stating that he was not an existentialist.[143] He will also be remembered for better or worse for his pro-Hitler views. He did continue the work of Husserl and phenomenology and influenced the ideas of Jean-Paul Sartre (1905–80). The idea of time that is of most interest to the existentialist is that of the present and Heidegger has on occasion been, While Sartre would accept this label, his fellow French writer, Albert Camus, would reject it. If one considers that existentialism is first an attitude and secondarily anti-systems and metaphysics, it is rather problematic to think that there could be anything called existentialism at all, at least that part called an "-ism." Nevertheless, however the more contemporary term and its meanings are used, it has been influenced by the writings of Heidegger as well as those of Karl Jaspers (1883–1969).[144] One way to define the term and apply it to the rise of the reflective self would be to consider Heidegger's suggestion that, "He is in the world because, existing, he is involved in it totally." This unique attitude offers that a being exists in the world while at the same time within the self, and he continues that, "…existence itself…means to stand outside oneself, to be beyond oneself. My Being is not something that takes place inside my skin… my Being, rather, is spread over a field or region which is the world of its care and concern."[145] This gives us some sense of how existentialism and self-consciousness can be related. Heidegger does use the term existential in certain contexts, "...human existence is marked by three general traits: (1) mood or feeling; (2) understanding; (3) speech. Heidegger calls these *existentialia* and intends them as basic categories of existence."[146] A more serious discussion arrived less than ten years after the War—in 1927—when he published what has been described as, "...a somber and rigorous meditation on human finitude" in his *Being and Time (Sein und Zeit)*. The explosion of brilliant insights only continued any desire for a better understanding of both people and the world. In 1927, Heisenberg added to our insights when he published his "Principle of Indeterminacy" which suggests that there is always a change, a tranformation or alteration in the observed by the very act of the observation.

This intellectual revolution and discovery is also reflected in the field of mathematics:

> In 1929 the mathematician Skolem published a theorem which some mathematicians now think almost as remarkable as Gödel's that even the elementary number system cannot be categorically formalized. In 1931 appeared Gödel's epoch-making discovery. ...we are tempted to conclude that they are not mere 'meaningless' coincidences but very meaningful symptoms. The whole mind of the time seems to be inclining in one direction. What emerges from these separate strands of history is an image of man himself that bears a new, stark, more nearly naked, and more questionable aspect.[147]

When the world of mathematics becomes the property of a very exclusive club of pure abstract thinkers, pure mathematicians, conflicting interpretations are no longer sustainable and the only certainty appears to have become uncertainty.

Within this confusion Heidegger actually attempts to address the question of the self in several of his works. One of the most important questions he addresses and has already appeared at the end of the previous century was that of authenticity of self, that is a self whose identity is not determined by external forces. For him, "...inauthenticity denotes the prevalence of an undifferentiated, quasi-collective life-form, where *Dasein* (German meaning literally Being-there) appears as interchangeable and 'one among other'; the notion of 'the They' is said to answer the question regarding the 'who' of everyday existence.'" However, "...what needs to be considered is the ontological, more that the ontic or empirical, status of 'the They.' The term implies an ontological-existential condition..."[148] The notion of a *Dasein* in Heidegger can be compared to something of an ontological self, or a distinctively human mode of existence characterized by participation or involvement in the world of objects, although most readers may find his use of this term, as well as his writings, somewhat more confusing than enlightening. It may be of some help for the reader to remember where we inherited the beginnings of this modern sense of self and of consciousness. The followers of Descartes make the self central for their philosophizing while others, like Locke and Hume, regard the self as either a construction (Locke) or an illusion (Hume). This division continues into the twentieth century with its modern incarnations and protagonists of either "...the logical positivists and analytic philosophers who have maintained either that the questions 'Does the self exist?' and 'What is the nature of the self?' are meaningless, or that the self is an illusion, and the phenomenologists and existentialists who, in one way or another, place self at the center of their philosophizing, treating it as that which is indubitably known and the one certainty." While Heidegger, and his mentor Edmund Husserl followed by Sartre, represent the side of the phenomenologists and existentialists, the positivists are represented by Bertrand Russell, Alfred Ayer, and Gilbert Ryle.[149] It is worth noting, therefore, that there are those today who deny not only the existence of a self, but also the existence of consciousness and even the mind. None of these thinkers mentioned, it should be noted, however, would likely argue for the modern development of an anti-mind. Philosophers have a tendency all too often to not want to think historically which is an old complaint clearly articulated by Nietzsche. Heidegger did contribute along with Sigmund Freud to the issue which started this book, the certainty of death which parallels *thanatos*, Freud's theory of the death instinct. As one commentator noted, it is no accident that both wrote soon after the, carnage of World War I.[150] As for Heideggerian definitions of the structure of the self he offered the following delineation: "...as embedded, encompassed, attuned, comprehending, linguistic, in contact with the unconcealed and the hidden, anxious, finite, concerned, thrown, contingent, dialectically authentic and inauthentic, temporal, and historical."[151] This does little to clarify the meaning of the self and additionally his comments regarding consciousness offer little if any help.

Heidegger does not use the term consciousness at first when analyzing the nature of existence. The reason is understandable since he does not want to reintroduce Cartesian dualism of mind and body into a discussion of the self.[152] And this has increasingly been a more popular position. Gilbert Ryle went so far in his *Concept of the Mind* to argue that there is not only no inner conscious state but that this is little more than an argument for a "Ghost in the Machine" as he stated it: "Such in outline is the official theory. I shall often speak of it, with deliberate abusiveness, as 'the dogma of the Ghost in the Machine.' I hope to prove that it [the concept of the mind] is entirely false, and false not in detail but in principle....It is one big mistake and a mistake of a special kind. It is, namely, a category-mistake. It represents the facts of mental life as if they belonged to one logical type or category (or range of types or categories), when they actually belong to another. The dogma is therefore a philosopher's myth."[153] What is of most interest is that in a sense, Heidegger returns to Cartesian doubt. If he doubts his own consciousness then he would be conscious of his doubt and so would prove the existence of consciousness.[154] This works for Descartes but not for Ryle. And this may very well be the most common argument for consciousness notwithstanding its dated appearance. There is a very real sense that consciousness may be what some like the brilliant British philosopher, Ludwig Wittgenstein (1889–1951), considered to be little more than an active mind: "Why should I deny there are mental processes?"[155] He admits it only as a fact of our mentality. Heidegger, on the other hand, explores it further by suggesting that, "...what is true of consciousness is also true of Being. Being is not to be apprehended as an object to be controlled or a problem to be solved. It is, rather, a mystery and to believe otherwise is to confuse Being with 'be-ings.'"[156] Thus we return to the very beginnings of consciousness as a mystery. The subjective state cannot be objectively knowable. His conclusion regarding the issue of Western dualism is that it is the source of Western humanism where the, "...pre-dominance of the subject-object polarity..." and which makes possible the, "...proclivity to treat the entire world as assembly objects or phenomena amenable to inspection by a detached mind or consciousness."[157] It is not simply intellect or computer phenomena that leads to scientific or artistic discoveries. On the contrary, it is by way of introspective and reflective capacities that our curiosity receives fuel. This is not to say, however, that the phenomenon of a dynamic intellect is inherent. Heidegger, while not the only one, raises this interesting question, especially for a philosopher. He takes the position that, "Nothingness is a presence within our own Being, always there, in the inner quaking." [158]

The twentieth century for all its economic benefits including mobility and prosperity must be repeatedly noted as very destructive. It results in part from the dominance of the power of continuous change, and additionally, an unheard of amount of openness and diversity, leaving behind the stable or the closed world that it had been. Those technical gains have cost us dearly. The same could also be applied to language. With the explosion of dictionaries and encyclopedias in the centuries since the printing press, language exploded not only in the rise of new art forms (the novel) but also in the growth of post-modern theater and post-lineal poetry. When the French *Encyclopedia* of the Enlightenment was written it was understood that this was probably the last time when all of our knowledge could be so expressed and controlled. Technological developments, from the radio and movies to televison and computers only expand our world as they exacerbate the old world sense of consistency and meaning. In such a situation, "...this change from closed to open language is also a passage from a closed to an open world, for our world...."[159] It is in this openness of language, "...that we have to use for the purpose of life means that the world of our experience is correspondingly open. And that the world should lie open to us is the real and concrete meaning of freedom..."[160] Freedom, and with it individuality, self, consciousness, reflection, introspection and privacy which are very recent concepts still seeking a specific and clear place in our vocabulary. William Barrett, is less than sanguine about this run-away belief in technique (or systems). It should not surprise us, therefore, that concepts like deconstruction and phenomenology should find a home in this new world. Heidegger, in the tradition of Husserl, contributed to the later concept, one drawn from the, "...word 'phenomenon'—a word in ordinary usage, by this time, in all modern European languages—means in Greek 'that which reveals itself.'" Thus for Heidegger the term phenomenology means, "...the attempt to let the thing speak for itself."[161] Not surprisingly, he understood the recent development (in the nineteenth-century) of the power of silence since it, "...is only because man is capable of such silence that he is capable of authentic speech."[162] The rule of authenticity is clearly, then, an interior space where privacy, silence and language reign. But he does not accept private speech since he subscribed to the theory that 'private' language is an oxymoron as, "...he argues that any conceivable language must refer to categories that are public in nature, tied in with shared and observable criteria; it follows that language, by its very nature, is incapable of referring to the private and unique sensations of a single individual."[163]

Self-consciousness is more than a single phenomenological condition, that there are no less than two participants, an observer and an act of reflection, leads to a more complex understanding of inner mental activity. This ties together the idea of a meaningless world where at the same time those more existentially inclined are capable of creating meaning by way of conscious and self-conscious choices. While this is not a position that everyone would accept, it does appear to be particularly true of Ryle's condemnation of the Cartesian "Ghost in the Machine" and the idea of an interior self. Clearly influenced by Hume, Ryle too doubts—in the skeptical tradition of Hume—that any self can be found walking into a room, even one's own self. As he stated, "…even Hume confesses that, when he has tried to sketch all the items of his experience, he has found nothing there to answer to the word 'I,' and yet he is not satisfied that there does not remain something more and something important, without which his sketch fails to describe his experience."[164] Ryle is adamant in his condemnation of dualism and belongs to a relatively large (if shrinking) number of contemporary scholars who might basically agree. As he says of the Ghost: "It maintains that there exist both bodies and minds; that there occur physical processes and mental processes; that there are mechanical causes of corporeal movements and mental causes of corporeal movements. I shall argue that these and other analogous conjunctions are absurd …"[165] Like the mind, therefore, the inner voices are not valid because they are not measurable. After all, the only reason we are able to talk to ourselves in silence is because, "…it is a necessary condition for our acquiring it that we should have previously learned to talk intelligently aloud and have heard and understood other people doing so."[166] Thus an introspective inner voice is only a result of nothing more than our public speech, and therefore demonstrates that it is not of any special significance. For Ryle and others who argue against the presence of an inner, existential or self-conscious position, consciousness, "is a myth," our, "…mental processes are, in some mortifying sense, unconscious, perhaps in the sort of way in which I often cannot tell of my own habitual and reflex movements."[167] His language suggests that he recognizes that it is common for people to believe that the, "…intelligent execution of an operation must embody two processes, one of doing and another of theorizing." But his major complaint is that there is some sort of causal relationship between the two, the mind (abstraction) and the body (physical).[168] The assumption of a "link" as he calls it, or bridge ("vortices" for Descartes) has always been a major problem much as calling consciousness nothing more than awareness to which both Descartes and Ryle would agree. This language is inadequate as expressed and leaves our understanding the poorer. It is precisely the question of language and definitions that must still be addressed.

The clearest point to draw is that our language has changed so dramatically since the time of Descartes and Locke that the literary critic and scholar George Steiner (1929–) would be able to claim "…that until the end of the seventeenth century language had a capacity to refer to reality and to represent experience by words. But the new mathematics, like abstract painting or the new music, cannot be verbalized. Mathematics has so deeply invaded all the sciences, as well as philosophy, that language no longer serves to express the range of reality when the world we live in is like a game played by topologists, whose mathematic is able to erect structures so far beyond the boundaries of the old logic…"[169] Perhaps the language that Ryle is using is too trapped by a language that is dated. There is in his thoughts a belief in a language that many today might find much too simple and lineal. His discussion of attending to several various mental events at the same time for example offers that:

> …an act of inner perception would require that the observer could attend to two things at the same time. He would, for example, be both resolving to get up early and concomitantly observing his act of resolving; attending to the programme of rising bedtimes and perceptually attending to his attending to this programme. This objection is not, perhaps, logically fatal, since it might be argued that some people can, anyhow after practice combine attention to the control of a car with attention to the conversation. The fact that we speak of undivided attention suggests that the division of attention is a possibility, thought some people would describe the division of attention as a rapid to-and-fro switch of attention, rather than as a synchronous distribution of it.[170]

Simple logic would agree with this statement if it is true that all inner voices and thoughts and consciousness are simply lineal much as a newspaper article is—without metaphors, implications and without leaps of logic, insights or any such thing as "bizarre" reasoning. The story of the discovery of the pattern of DNA by way of a dream would not sit well with Ryle's reasoning except as an exception. Is this an unquestionably valid position or is there in fact an alternate way to look at language? To understand this position one need but turn to the nonsense written by Lewis Carroll which is "anti-poetry; and in our day Eliot once wrote that the 'poetry does not matter' since words slip, crack, and perish …"[171] T. S. Eliot is a very fine example of the poet who genuinely loves language and yet can bridge into a more abstract, even cubist, framework. In his poem "Ash Wednesday," "…he turned from the actualities of time and place, and from the infirm glory of nature, to a more abstract… language…" This can be seen in the statement: "Or say that the end precedes the beginning, and all is always now."[172] This early transition is marked by a change in the language of the sciences as well, especially regarding the issue that seems to haunt Ryle, that of cause and effect. It was the mathematician, poet, and humanist, Jacob Bronowsky (1906–74) who noted that there was a tie between the changes in the periods of literature which often coincided with that in science. He also observed that what we call the laws of cause and effect had become, "...so nearly identical with scientific thinking that the Victorians had a compulsion to deal with all their experiences, ethical and psychological as well as scientific, in these categories." The problem is that sometimes the language changes but the categories retain their tradition. To state that the mind of the Victorian is extremely irrelevant to our world is too much of an understatement that it should not have to be made. As the argument continues, the Victorian, "...universe was a machine run by infallible logic—the logic of physics.... They never paused to ask whether Newton was extending to the universe under the guise of mathematical equations the operations of his own psyche."[173] As for an alternative approach towards language in the our own world, it was the physicist and philosopher, Ernst Mach (1836–1916) who "...invoked a principle of economy: we must exclude from our accounts of nature every feature not needed to deal with the observations at hand. Such economy would dispense with a Greek logic that had persisted under plausible terms like *how, because, so, in order to, suppose, as a result, although, when*, and so on. Schroedinger, making an effort to limit the vocabulary of a science by dropping such terms, calls upon us to speak a language that is not Greek."[174] Language in the world of literature and art had proved to be the cutting edge in not just the joy of sound but also in both the freedom of and from our tradition of seeking meaning.

In the world of modern (or post-modern) literature, the transformation of methods and understanding is every bit as extreme as it has been in the world of mathematics. It is not an exaggeration for the French playwright, Eugene Ionesseco (1912–94) to recognize that art and science have done far more than politics to change any of our attitudes. As he expressed it, the only "...true revolution has occurred in scientific laboratories, in artists' studios. Einstein, Oppenheimer, Breton, Kandinsky, Picasso, Pavlov—these are the genuine innovators. They widen the field of our awareness, review our vision of the world, change us."[175] It would appear that, "Ionesco seems to know that our science has affected the nature of our literature, making all verbal language a cliché, and a rather crude cliché at that."[176] It would be a remarkable event to see politics begin to attempt to match the revolutionary changes in thinking demonstrated in the arts and the sciences. Lineal language may make sense on the surface, in systems such as governance but it is not of much help to getting into the heart of living without a certainty—including any creative confrontation with death. Science for some, and on some levels, may be the door to a type of certainty, but for the certainty on the level of existence, of the existential and conscious components of living, it also has proven less than sufficient. The French artist, Jean Dubuffet (1901–85), once sharing his observation regarding traditional language in a speech he gave to the Arts Club of Chicago in 1951 stated that he thought the, "...culture of the Occident is a coat which does not fit him; which, in any case, doesn't fit him any more. I think this culture is very much like a dead language, without anything in common with the language spoken in the street. This cultural drifts further and further from daily life."[177] His suggestions were already recognized before the end of the nineteenth century by the precursors of the surrealists, Baudelaire, Mallarmé, and Rimbaud who, "...describe their use of language indiscriminately as a *sorcellerie évocatoire*, a magic operation, or an *alchimie du verbe*."[178] This tradition has been carried on by the Beats and especially in their ties to the new musical art form called jazz. "Jazz is the vernacular of the beat communion, in which beatitude does not take the form of silence before nothingness, but of feeling joy in groups." This new musical attitude can be traced back to the view that "...ecstasy is democratic, like Whitman's.... The hipster does not, he says, feel any need to talk, but above all he wants a sense of togetherness; and his simplification of language is a way of reassuring his fellow hipster that 'I'm with you, I've got you.'"[179] For the people of the Beat age there was a love for the sounds in music with few if any words exchanged. When words were exchanged, the form was generally referred to as rapping, which if one looks to the ancient world they will find an early version of it in the form similar to what has been called Socratic dialectic. This change in musical language had an earlier root in the recent past in Vienna where there was, "...produced two of the most powerful and symptomatic movements of modern culture—psychoanalysis and atonal music—both voices that speak of the homelessness of modern man."[180] While atonal music is not everyone's choice it has had a powerful impact much as the new visual arts has had.

There may be something absurd in all this and rightly so; however, it is in language that one can find the self, the inner part of our being that Ryle—like Hume—questioned. While, "...language is the natural medium for self-analysis; the idea of a 'way back to himself' cannot be expressed in any other medium...," it is nevertheless, "...not a matter for *words*, but a matter for action."[181] Here is a key suggestion to add as a component of consciousness as it has matured in the past three plus centuries; it is not simply a matter of memory, awareness, thought, reflection or introspection, but more a matter of doing, of becoming, of expanding oneself in living and in action; here consciousness can both lead and respond to. It is possible that in the creative life that Nietzsche sought, consciousness when expanded into a self-reflective individuality becomes manifest in the art of living and expresses both our wonder and confusions rather than reducing everything to some simple formula or scheme for living.

What occurred in the creation of this modern western world now growing into a global (and post-modern) world was the development of an inner self with a sense of space and time different than anything found in traditional communities. To say that there is something absurd in all this from a social point of view is transparently obvious. The community that dominates all social and personal development finds itself in conflict with the appearance of the individual. Hobbes and Burke were correct as are their fellow conservatives in the view that no one knows how it is possible to sustain a society of individuals since this appears to be a contradiction of terms. Is a self-conscious state to take precedent over the good of the community? This was the issue in its more primitive state that Rousseau had confronted. The corollary ideas that developed along with these changes, that of privacy, the inner life remains in conflict with the modern and especially, the totalitarian state. And what of the relationship between the existential singularity with the numerically superior collective? History does not offer an answer, but it does give hints about what it is to become conscious. Only those who achieve a high level of self-conscious confidence can embrace uncertainty for what it is: opportunity. As William Butler Yeats stated: "'Out of the argument with ourselves we make poetry, out of the argument with others, rhetoric.'" It is no accident that we can now seriously consider a position stating that, "...the hero and the poet have become inseparable,"[182] at least as we now are coming of a conscious age.

One novel that may offer an introduction to the idea of coming of age, i.e. of 'becoming' consciousness, was written by Ray Bradbury (1920–), *Dandelion Wine* (1957). On the surface it is a simple story of two young brothers, one of them who is coming of age, that is, discovering his mortality: that he will eventually die. Funerals are found to be a closure and there is a murderer loose in this plot. The two lads enjoy the fear of uncertainty since it is exciting and stimulating, for here they have found a certain type of authenticity—inner feelings. Douglas, the 12 year old, is given the world: "I'm *really* alive! he thought. I never knew it before, or if I did I don't remember!" He then yells it loudly, "...but silent a dozen times. Think of it, think of it! Twelve years old and only now! Now discovering this rare timepiece, this clock gold-bright and guaranteed to run threescore and then, left under a tree and found while wrestling."[183] Time and space become real and eminent because of the edge they feel. The younger brother, "…was only ten years old. He knew little of death, fear, or dread. Death was the waxen effigy in the coffin when he was six, and Great-grandfather passed away…"[184] The discovery of death and being of an age where the titillation through fear begins to alter the boys' perception of life.

As happened so often for those in the Great War, there was a discovery that in a crisis situation as with anyone who has faced death, there is no other time in one's life more completely filled with the certainty of one's sensing, feeling or even knowing one is alive. As the younger brother, John noted: "Some nights it happens to me in my own house; scares the heck out of me. I got to go in my folks' room and look at their faces while they sleep, to be sure; And I go back to my room and lose it again. Gosh, Doug, oh gosh! He held on to his knees tight. Promise me just one thing, Doug. Promise you'll remember me, promise you'll remember my face and everything. Will you promise?"[185] As he notes, if you can see me, or remember me, or recognize my existence then I must be. This theme is offered in a somewhat different form, as we noted, regarding Sartre in his play *No Exit* where the one male character of the three deceased, Garçin, can see those still alive below on earth only as long as they think or speak of him. His name being remembered gives him the ability to defy death, but only, again, as long as they continue to keep active his memory. When that ends he loses the ability and see anything going on on earth and of course then does not exist for others or himself.

Perspective was coming to dominate our thinking in that era of powerful destruction.

CHAPTER ELEVEN

❧❧

A TIME AND SPACE FOR CONSCIOUSNESS

Closely related to the problem of consciousness was the question of the meaning of time and duration in psychology, philosophy, literature, and history.[1]

FROM DISORDER TO CREATIVITY

For those who remember their youth with an innocence or even naiveté, there is that point in time where each of us comes to recognize our terminal condition, that mortality that rests upon our shoulders. So often it is easy to be preoccupied, indifferent or just plain filled with fear. At some point, there are those who discover a willingness to look into the face of death without cringing. They discover that where there is life there is time. That our time is limited whether we admit to it or not, supports the most fundamental reality of our existence: we have it. The idea of being here and now as well as an engagement in an enlargement of our sense of space and our control of time, whether physical or metaphoric, operates as a foundation for the existence of a self-individualized consciousness or at least the exploration of its potential.

In the creation of a sense of space and time, credence can be given to the importance we place on the word 'time' by observing some of the contemporary and colloquial uses of it in our daily language: time is money; time and a half; the forty-hour week; an eight-hour day; time is on our side; a good (or bad) time; we are out of time; just in time; *Time Magazine*; time to burn; timelessness; relative time; and the ever infamous, meet you under the clock at noon. As for space, there is being spaced out; space ranger; space ship; empty space; inner space; relative space; outer space; curved space; spatial categories; spatial layouts and many more. Little wonder that consciousness, if related to our sense of time and space, has expanded in our own age. This is especially true when we remember that what is perceived by sight and sound is not necessarily what is, but rather what we construct in our mind's eye. Space and time depend upon perspective as much if not more than any alternate technical, mechanical or philosophical viewpoints.

Another way of putting this into a context is to discuss the modern notion of what we mean by the word 'instantaneous' when speaking of time as it relates to the classical philosophical arguments regarding essence. As the philosopher George Santayana (1863–1952) put it: "A thing that occupied but one point of physical time would be *instantaneous*. No essence is instantaneous, because none occupies any part of physical time or space; and I doubt whether any existence is instantaneous either;…the smallest event has duration in and contains an infinite number of such units; so that one event (though not one instant) can be contiguous to another."[2] One's actual existence has no more essence or substance than the character of Faust, for the force of the individual self is not achieved by the "instantaneous now" but by way of the moment after, the reflection and the introspection regarding that instant, i.e., just a matter of perception.

How large the brain actually is may be far less important than how large the mind is, which is a central and unmeasurable abstraction. The insights of Santayana whose comments on essence and time as discussed here, enlarges our understanding of both: "A given essence containing no specious temporal progression or perspective between its parts would be *timeless*."[3] The traditional argument had been about the essence of human beings which now is seen as a discussion concerning immortality. The key to essence is that it transcends time. If there is no essence there is no 'now' time, and no space means no ontology. To begin creating a point of view or interior space, there needed be a line to draw from, a spot to frame, a moment to note. It is within the motion of self, individuality, consciousness that time and space have found an authentic residence which is increasingly perceived as a normal condition replacing inertia. Time and space can be discussed but not held.

When we originally perceived our tribal selves it was in a fixed universe where we were dependent upon naming each of us and then given solidity by way of the written word followed by The Word of a savior. When this traditional religious construction for certainty began to collapse, an alternative, the new sciences and a new approach to life—reason—began to fill the void. By the end of the nineteenth century the position of faith in reason was called into question and was followed by its being further qualified if not ignored in growing modern and post-modern thinking. With Galileo, Bacon, and Newton there was a new order that could be perceived but only through detachment —objectivity. Such a revolutionary change literally made possible a new Western culture, an alternate set of perceptions and values. This idea of being separate from an object observed is an important contribution to the creation of an alternative certainty based on interiority rather than exclusively upon exterior phenomena. While this idea was not fully appreciated in the seventeenth century it had become so in the twentieth. An interesting discussion of some of these revolutionary figures can be found in *Star Wave* by Fred Wolf who offers some implications of detached observations: "Observables are the consequences of our actions. We 'do' to observe. We must bring out or cause something to occur in order that we observe. We must bring out or cause something to occur in order that we observe anything at all. To even read these words your eyes must do a dance of incessant scanning. If they rest for the smallest instant, the image of the words will vanish from your retinas. Observables are the result of operations."[4] This radical alteration of our assumptions and perceptions was further encouraged by implications in both disengagement and reflexivity. It is this capacity to detach and reflect on what is and what isn't that became the modality for a different type of certainty, one that offered a "...full realization of one's essential being—which is to say, of one's being as a consciousness—and which requires detachment from the body and from the passions rooted in it...." The 'inner eye' was to become even more in our own era, the touch stone of what is and isn't knowable or achievable.[5]

The perception of the open aspect of space in our own era can be traced to several sources, one of the earliest mentioned being Nietzsche who, with Ortega y Gasset in our own century developed a unique thinking in regard to a 'perspectivism' which could mean that there may be as many alternative ideas of space as there are points of view, at least in a humanistic and cultural modality.[6] For our own era, it is arguable that the most famous mind in transforming our understanding of space would have to be Albert Einstein who in 1916 explained: "We entirely shun the vague word 'space,' of which we must honestly acknowledge, we cannot form the slightest conception and replace it by 'motion relative to a practically rigid body of reference.'" He summed up boldly: "...there is an infinite number of spaces, which are in motion with respect to each other."[7] Much like a cubist painting, space is not singular but multiple, dependening on one's perspective. Stephen Kern has remarked that in modern art, "...the multiplication of points of view in painting had an impact far beyond the world of art. It created a new way of seeing and rendering objects in space and challenged the traditional notion of its homogeneity."[8] Whichever came first, the issue centers around diversity rather than order. If one asks when looking at the 1912 *Nude Descending the Staircase*, (Marcel Duchamp) whether the nude is half way up or half way down the staircase, the mandatory answer is now 'yes.' Another example would be when we find ourselves discussing optimism or pessimism with the metaphor of the half-empty or half-full glass, again, the answer for some must be 'yes.' As for favoring a positive view regarding open space, it has been suggested that it was Oswald Spengler (1880–1936), the author of *The Decline of the West* (1926–29), whose "…account of space…parallels his thesis—that the prime symbol of the Faustian soul of the modern age is limitless space. Faust's restless striving, the soaring of Gothic cathedrals, and the proliferations of geometric spaces reflect this sense of infinity."[9] From the beginnings of the nineteenth to the end of the twentieth century the issue of a Faustian life became an increasingly welcomed appeal for many. The theory of multiplicity of space (spaces?) has been presented to suggest that the universe could even be conceived as a hologram, a thesis to be found in a most interesting work by Michael Talbot's *The Holographic Universe* (1991).

This is not to say there is absolutely no certainty in this physical world that we now find ourselves. After all, it is from the revolution in quantum physics we learn that "…light comes in whole units (quanta) which cannot be further divided. Light, moreover, is immaterial; it is without charge, rest mass or other properties. It is outside of space and time—clocks stop at the speed of light and the photon can traverse an unlimited distance without loss."[10] While it is an absolute, it is outside our normative or daily understanding since all that makes up nature is either a particle or a wave, except for light which is both and is altered by the very act of observation, according to Heisenberg. The closest we have come to certainty is outside of time and space and if we introduce time and or space into the phenomenon, it too turns relative to observation. It is worth considering Wolf's other comments regarding space and time: "…we come to the conclusion that time is the observer. Space is the observed. That is why time cannot be observed. The observer is invisible."[11] He continues: "…the observed then equals space. The observer equals time."[12] Perhaps his observations can be applied to the revolution in the arts that match the revolution in science and psychology. He takes the position that, "…the past decides the present to the extent that the world is a machine," he continues, "…the future decides the present to the extent that the world is creative. To create something new, we need the future."[13] We therefore must accept that if this is true then every moment beyond the now is a creative opportunity which both impressionist and post-impressionist artists have embraced. The inherent communion between time and space is considered here a key component in the rise of a sense of self as a creative being as well as necessary for the maturation of that which is most private, our consciousness. We remember that time is, among other things, looked at as personal memory and public history, while space is the key component of language, whether spoken or written. Finally, there cannot be one without the other. Any student of a language is a student of history and thus any student of history is, of necessity, a student of language.

The idea of a private time—space—is, of course, a very modern (and postmodern) concept. Privacy did not exist in the political writings of Locke when he articulated the first cohesive argument for rights, specifically those concerning property without the notion of a psychologically privately-driven self. Montesquieu, less than a century after Locke, further contributed to our forms of modern government with his idea of a tripartite system which posits limits on those governing. Again the modern argument for privacy was absent just as its absence is conspicuous in the U. S. Constitution. While there are hints of privacy in the eighteenth century the fully-developed idea does not become part of our vocabulary until the nineteenth century, the age of the Romantics and the century of the early expression of individuality and the self. But space like self is as multiple as our sense of time. The idea that time is in flux and not static can, of course, be found in the writings of Hegel who suggested that the future determines both our present and our past since we anticipate and so construct our actions to reach that anticipation and then construct a memory conducive to that goal. Modern theory of memory, of course, would support the idea that memory is anything but infallible.[14] While one may not find Hegelian thought appealing—or even understandable—it was he, nevertheless, who noted that a "…reversal of the ordinary time sequence—past-present-future —is caused by man's denying his present: he 'says *no* to his Now' and thus creates his own future."[15] A very simple example of this phenomenon can be demonstrated when people make plans for their education and career as a guide for today's choices and actions thus making the anticipated future contingent on today's choices. In addition, this pre-occupation with what will happen, whether it be a career or an upcoming vacation tends to color the memory of our experiences in similar circumstances. And since we can make our memory conform to our wishes rather than the actual event, it too can prove to be unreliable. The newer studies on memory have been more revealing about assumptions rather than the knowledge of the facts. Part of the difficulty could be a matter of our understanding the machinations and varieties of time. Hegel did offer some of the first insights as to how we understand the psychological elements of time:

...for him, above all, 'human time' whose flux man first, as it were, unthinkingly experiences as sheer motion, until he happens to reflect on the meaning of outside events. It then turns out that the mind's attention is primarily directed toward the future, namely, toward the time that is in the process of coming toward us (indicated...in the German *Zukunft*, from *zu kommen*, like the French *avenir* from *à venir*), and this anticipated future negates the mind's 'enduring present,' which it transforms into an anticipated future negates the mind's 'enduring present,' which it transforms into and anticipated 'no-more.' In this context, 'the dominant dimension of time is the future, which takes priority over the past.' 'Time finds its truth in the future since it is the future that will finish and accomplish Being. But Being, finished and accomplished, belongs as such to the Past.'[16]

The Italian Futurists of the recent past agreed in principle with Hegel as has the new genre of literature known as science fiction. And any philosophical discussion of private time, for our era, returns us to the thinking of Bergson. There were many thinkers who have advocated a variety of private times to match the idea of many selves. Bergson himself went so far as to "...come to question whether the fixed and spatially represented public time was really time at all or some metaphysical interloper from the realm of space."[17] Far less important for this book is the issue of public time, however, since it is in the realm of the private: self, consciousness, reflection that is here of interest. There is something curious that while time like space was becoming a studied phenomenon in physics and art, both time and space were also becoming meaningful for the individual.

It is in literature and the arts that this new language of space tied to a matured sense of memory and history would draw its clearest lines. The objectification of the world and empty space has in physics created events that are, "...related diachronically purely by efficient causal relations, and synchronically by mutual conditioning."[18] Meanwhile philosophers from Bergson to Heidegger have offered 'innovative philosophy' that attempts to answer the question of how we could function if we were to recognize an inherent emptiness in living, while the creative artists have addressed that very challenge.[19] A very clear if lengthy explication of this transformation of our own language is expressed in the following:

> The classic statement of the relevant view regarding modernism is Joseph Frank's seminal essay of 1945, 'Spatial Form in Modern Literature,' which describes a widespread attempt in modern literature to deny time and thereby to achieve a sense of simultaneity at a deep level of response....Such writers dwell, for example, on the description of static objects rather than on the recounting of processes or action, or

may engage in a reflexive turn ('a space-logic of reflexive reference,' as Frank calls it), focusing attention not on the narrated events but on certain formal or structural aspects of the literary act and product —such as the act of writing itself, the sound or graphic appearance of the words, literary conventions, the merely fictional nature of the characters, or the presence of a perspective or standpoint that informs, even to a large extent creates the story. Both tendencies have the effect of breaking down the reader's sense of the causal coherence and purposive thrust of the story as a sequence of real events in time.[20]

Narrative requires a lineality of the sounds in a comprehensive manner that allow for the possibility of a certain level of understanding. The problem is in the assumptions regarding causation when increasingly it is recognized that causation since David Hume is often seen as little more than a contrivance and that the appearance of accuracy does not necessarily provide a precise picture. When we speak of language we certainly are not speaking of causation just as the arts by definition are beyond causation. A sentence is a sentence is a sentence and only a cause when it is an interpretation. When someone puts a gun to your head and says, "Your money or your life," the fear experienced is the cause of anxiety which is based not on the language used but the gun in your face. If science had not failed to offer certainty when introducing quantum mechanics and relativism then it is possible that this could have been different:

> ...science is faced with a breakdown in the logic of cause and effect, for this illogicality in mathematic is supported by evidence of illogical behavior in the atom and light. According to the quantum theory, energy is emitted in certain units, or at certain levels, and there seems to be no way of predicting accurately which units will be emitted in any one instance at any given time. Particles behave with a logic of discontinuity. And light behaves both like waves and particles. To complicate matters, we can locate the position of a particle at any instant, or we can determine its speed; but we cannot do both at the same time, apparently because in measuring very small quantities the observer by his very observing somehow gets between what is being measured and the measurement he makes. Thus there is always a margin of uncertainty...[21]

This is not to suggest that the study of the sciences is not an objective activity nor that it is not often very successful in its discoveries; its dilemma is for those who would seek an absolute and agreed upon certainty that once was assumed in the pre-modern world of Western beliefs. Time and space are still objectified, even if there is only limited agreement among students of the subject, while in the arts any objectification is so creatively manipulated that it becomes subjective. This applies equally to the observers. For the reader, narratives often are made, "...part of the simultaneously in the same story- space. The reader is made into an omniscient observer, able to hold these independently unfolding trains of events together."[22]

The picture is both explicated and made rather confusing with the arrival of film and its very unique abilities of manipulating space and time: "Like modern art, the cinema offered some new and varied spatial possibilities."[23] In relation to our understanding of conscious relationships of both space and time, the camera has proven to be a powerful altering force exemplified through the angle of the lens, close-ups, panning, accelerated speed, slow-motion, and other techniques. Because the voice of the artist exists within the confines of the camera, the point of view or distance could be shifted and the space in view could move continuously with a pan and could be augmented by editing.[24] Understanding by way of a visual certainty requires a new vocabulary and with it new perspectives. Both Nietzsche and Ortega y Gasset argued for a new philosophy, one of 'perspectivism' in which it was suggested that there are more than one viewpoint: what one sees depends, as it were, on the person.[25] This was a revolutionary attitude appearing only very recently in the age of the second industrial revolution and in the twentieth century particularly, with the post-impressionistic theater of the absurd and invention of film. For example, a close-up could create intimacy while a quick cut could create a "...dramatic sense of separation and of distance spanned."[26] These 'perspectivisms' contributed to a new cultural sense of time and space after World War II and during that period that was called the counterculture. This new cultural sense coined the term, 'happening' which reflects perspectivisms in both experiences as well as in a finely constructed art. *The Cabinet of Dr. Caligari (Das Kabinett des Doktor Caligari*, 1918) is a great example of disconcerting visual narrative. It is here where the axiom can be established that both time and space are but different camera angles (or different lenses) of the same phenomenon. Just as a word is a word because of its historicity, so a scene has an inherent comprehension because of what immediately precedes and follows it as well its relationship to all other varied scenes and elements. There is indeed a, "...continuance, our wish for the continuity, that glues us to our destinies."[27]

Given the nature of the universe, it has been suggested that "...underneath it all we are all quite 'nuts.' No one alive can really take life seriously with its myriads of kaleidoscopic paradoxes; but we do."[28] This may seem extreme even from a professional physicist but for Professor Wolf there is such a commitment to this view that he feels compelled to repeat the point on the next page of his book with the following: "Like us, the physical world is also a little 'nuts.'"[29]

Humanity and the universe could be, and in this case, is construed to be off the edge: while the desire for continuity and certainty is pursued by the average individual, our understanding of the universe, in fact, has been altered by such discoveries as that of Heisenberg in physics or Gödel in mathematics. What is of interest in Heisenberg's Uncertainty Principle is the possibility of consciousness in such an uncertain universe where the activities of our brains require a continuous adjustment to changing discoveries: "Maybe we've got this all reversed. Perhaps our brains evolved the way they did because of the universal requirement of the uncertainty principle. Our 'geological' brain layers may be required in order to allow doubt and conflict, which are sensed forms of the uncertainty principle, the 'space' needed for correlation that is necessary for evolved brain functioning and intelligence. Like the whole universe, our brains are quantum mechanical not classical mechanical."[30] While, it is true, that this is a matter of conjecture it exists in a world where conjecture has become increasing central to our understanding of both the human and the natural order. It may be circumstantial that the century that gave us an end to the traditional search for a certainty to counter the certainty of death, (the central drive for those who find our inherent termination too overwhelming), also gave us the ability to realize conscious and self-conscious capacities. Any discussion of consciousness is, by definition, one of conjecture which allows the possibility that the rise of consciousness occurs in part as a means for dealing with an ever-evolving uncertainty in our society while self-consciousness may be the means for the more existentially inclined to cope with the uncertainty of life's experiences. This would suggest that consciousness and the self are necessary human developments that aid those of us so inclined, to outgrow the confusing and dipole conditions that result from the historic changes we have and are now experiencing. If the world has become much more complex it follows that those tools for coping from the distant past would be inadequate for the realities of our own era. A relevant point to consider regarding the role of contemporary physics comes from the Danish physicist and Noble Prize winner, Niels Bohr (1885–1962):

> Bohr called his discovery the correspondence principle because he realized that our normal, or classical, world view is continuous. Yet his discovery of the quantum within the atom showed that atoms were fundamentally discontinuous in any transaction involving observers. How could the 'atomic inmates' be so erratic while the 'villages of atoms' that make up the macroscopic universe appear so normal and orderly? Bohr's discovery showed how the 'quantum insane asylum' *corresponded* with the 'normal atomic village' i.e., the orderly classical world of continuous motion.[31]

This may be a 'nut house,' but it is ours for better and worse, and those best prepared psychologically to find the challenges are not trapped by a sense of despair, alienation or estrangement.

The discontinuity that often appears in modern music, films, plays, novels, poems, paintings and sculptures are part of a singular cloth of modern (and in some cases, post-modern) culture. The only order guaranteed arrives from our inner processes: "...we don't feel what we feel; we feel what we think we feel."[32] Consistency is more a matter of the orderliness of our thoughts than any necessarily inherent or preestablished social order. The issue is a matter of perspective, a highly evolved byproduct of the growing post-Cartesian and post-Lockean understanding of our mind. As has been pointed out, when we say, 'now,' it is not the 'here' we think we perceive we are experiencing but rather the "experiencing what we have come to call 'space.'"[33] It is the combination of what we perceive of as time with that of space that gives us a basis for our mental continuity. It is the physicists point of view that even our "... 'here' is not an observable; we cannot observe 'here' because the act of observation requires an observer and an observed. It needs separation to exist. That is why 'here' cannot be experienced without there being a 'there'—in other words, a 'now.'"[34] The nature of modern thought is a matter of detachment—the scientific mind-set that asks us to separate the observer from the object, a classical dualistic tradition reconstructed into a modern secular mode. It was this transformation—amongst other things—that eventually led to a sense of privacy in the nineteenth century and the issue of a private living in the following. Little wonder that someone noted for deep understanding as Nietzsche held the position that no one was entitled to his opinions since they were a private matter for which he alone would determine with whom he might share them. Space and time become hereafter, in a very important and psychological sense, a private matter and, as such, it is recognized as an inner life separated from the world around it. Marcel Proust's *Remembrance of Things Past* takes place in a clearly identifiable public time from the Dreyfus Affair to World War I. "But the private time of its narrator, Marcel, moves at an irregular pace that is repeatedly out of phase with that of the other characters and defies reckoning by any standard system."[35] The arts again reflect the changes in understanding of the world of physics and the mingling of the two with their unique but respective openness that increasingly appear more and more the norm; we detach in order to maximize an inner self.

Much of this transformation is a result of the brilliant work of Einstein who when describing the physical world noted that, "...there is a similar merger of space and time. Since he held that time is a matter of assimilation to the inherent three dimensions that we find in space and in a way that any measurements of space and time, and most especially where astronomical distances are of concern, they function together and can not be perceived as independent of each other."[36] This can explain in part that for our own world there is a consistent delineation between what is thought of as private and what is given to us as public time. "The popular idea that time is made up of discrete parts as sharply separated as boxed days on a calendar continued to dominate popular thinking about public time, whereas the most innovative speculation was that private time was the real time and that its texture was fluid."[37] Bergson had, like others later, "...argued for a plurality of private times..." He also raised the question, "...whether the fixed and spatially represented public time was really time at all or some metaphysical interloper from the realm of space."[38] If our sense of time becomes a contributor to the self and the exploration of our varied selves, then space and time as well as language and memory must be understood in the end as primarily a personal and private matter. Moreover the driving force of time in the new world was to, "...affirm the reality of private time against that of a single public time and to define its nature as heterogeneous, fluid, and reversible."[39] Time in and of public life did not of course, come to an end. Rather, the power of the private, the individual self's own sense of a personal clock and territory, came to first compete, and, for many, eventually master a personal sense of the real.

A fine expression of the internal experiences drawn from a personal time can be found in many works of art, including an example of the French New Novel specifically, *The Voyeur* by Alain Robbe-Grillet (1922–).[40] The plot of his remarkable novel centers around the main figure, Mathias, who successively disembarks a ship. The first scene is with a boat whistling while docking. This beginning is repeated again and again with Mathias going further and further into the story, first down the gang-plank and eventually to his destination in the city. Part of the irony is that his intention was to sell watches. The movement of demarcation from the ship and going through this repetition again and again, each time a little further, illustrates the subjective nature of time:

> ...external reality loses not its substantiality and otherness but its human resonance or significance, thus bringing about what Heidegger called the 'unworlding of the (human) world.' One extreme manifestation of this is what has been called the 'white style' or 'zero degree of literature'—exemplified by the novelist Alain Robbe-Grillet's *chosisme* ('thingism'), his aspiration to depict a world 'neither

meaningful nor absurd, [that] quite simply *is*,' a world where 'all around us defying our pack of animistic or domesticating adjectives things *are there*...without false glamour, without transparency.' "[41]

Absurdity in the eye of the beholder, or is it the nature of reality?

In a crisis situation while waiting for a doctor's report, time for that patient can appear to move very slowly. But if involved in a deeply enjoyable activity that demands great involvement, time can appear to move very quickly. "What are we observing in all of the above? The answer is motion. We infer time as a result of motion."[42] It is not here and there but from here to there that establishes a parameter. It was in 1920 when Einstein explained that there was in fact an infinite number of spaces, all of which are moving in respect to one another. It was from this ability stemming from the revolutionary thinking of Newton that the modern idea of motion was born and given momentum. "In Newton's time, force was the cause that created motion....That was called having momentum....With the recognition that more work meant more speed, the idea of conservation of energy became apparent."[43] There are those, today, who feel their real achievement is the conservation of the potential selves in order to expand horizons yet to be imagined. How many conscious experiences can one have and how many selves in a conscious state can one be part of? Of course not all spaces in all time are necessarily in motion relative to each other. Robbe-Grillet includes in the middle of his novel a blank page that reminds us of those unremembered events that we cannot always recall. It has been suggested for some time now that there is a plurality of times to match Woolf's plurality of selves. And Bergson like others has questioned, "...whether the fixed and spatially represented public time was really time at all or some metaphysical interloper from the realm of space."[44]

Private time allows a great deal of leverage and diversity in how we perceive. The Argentine writer, Jorge Luis Borges (1899–1986), exemplifies these thoughts with a startling amount of Beckett-type characteristics from a "A Dialog About a Dialog" to "A Dialog Between Dead Men."[45] This also brings to mind the works of Maurits Escher (1898–1972), especially the print of a hand drawing a hand drawing a hand, *ad infinitum*. This element of the redundancy of time and narration in terms of the unknowable was clearly stated earlier in the century with the picture that Joyce drew of Molly Bloom quoted in the last chapter.[46] Add to this the poet T. S. Eliot who, intrigued with motion, offered in one of his *Quartets*:

> Words move, music moves,

> Only in time; but that which is only living
> Can only die. Words, after speech, reach
> Into the silence. Only by the form, the pattern,
> Can words or music reach
> The stillness, as a Chinese jar still
> Moves perpetually in its stillness.
> Not the stillness of the violin, while the note lasts,
> Not that only, but the co-existence,
> Or say that the end precedes the beginning,
> And the end and the beginning were always there
> Before the beginning and after the end.
> And all is always now.[47]

It is not a matter of time as often as it is a matter of motion. But then, if there is a difference how would one draw it? As has already been well expressed: "The experience of time is the experience of 'hereness.' Time has nothing to do with movement. Things move, but time stands still."[48] Part of the problem is that "…time experience is *not* an observable!"[49] We can observe a ball in motion but we deduce the time it takes to transverse its distance unless we supplement the observation with technical aides. In other words, what we take for real is the space between the positions of the ball, the beginning and the end, from which we draw a time frame. Even the 'now' can be recognized as nothing more than a contrivance of time in the form of past and future, for, as has been noted, without a past and a future there is no 'now.' We had noted that "the word *now* cannot even be heard" for the simple reason that there is a time lag between the making and the hearing of a sound.[50] Joyce's Molly Bloom transverses space and time because of openness. A genuinely lived experience can often be lost within a moment where the movements of living are neither held or even noted because of a presupposed frame of unconsciously held assumptions. It is natural enough, of course, for at least most people, to hold to a set of functional assumptions in order to get on with the making of a structure of living. Perhaps that is why fiction often gives us a closer look at life than the daily routines that can trap so many people in the simple but necessary world of the functional. Molly Bloom could be considered an early literary example of a character breaking out from the more mundane aspects of every day life since she was a woman able to give voice "…to haltings, discontinuities, to circularities, to the urgings and openings of the body alive to the world and itself."[51] Add to this the wonderful example, the end of

Waiting for Godot where Vladimir asks "Shall we go?" and then Estragon answers "Yes, let's go," for the important point to this final scene is the stage direction, the last line of the play: "They do not move." Motion can be a very private matter and for some it can be even impossible.

Private time is as personal as one's private memory and own cogito even though there is a public and collective time within which we all live. There is, after all, a public memory in the form of the art of historiography. Moreover, memory is now a difficult subject for researchers since we now know that memory is not held simply in some storage compartment in the brain. "Where is memory stored? The amazing answer is, nowhere and everywhere. Another way to put this is to say that memory is holographic, with the universe playing the part of the complete hologram."[52] And the cogito can be seen as public in the form of our mutual understanding and encyclopedic knowledge and academic achievements. In the end it is the uncertainty that most dominates one's inner and personal life. Heisenberg, as much as any other, if not more, is significant in guiding us to this conclusion: "When he says that one cannot observe both the position and momentum of any object at the same time, he really means 'observe.' He doesn't mean that one cannot interact with an object such that both its position and momentum are determined simultaneously. Albeit, this is a subtle distinction. It is the act of observing that disrupts the pattern so severely. Interaction does not cause such an acausal effect. It is always 'causality-preserving.'"[53] This makes the personal observation an altering observation, and in this Heisenberg offers not merely principles of physics but also something of a philosophic conundrum, especially in the arts, as a contrarian example, since this uncertainty is not unusual. What is the Fellini film 8½ about? One of the best answers might well be that it is about 90 minutes long. What does a Mondrian painting mean, but the painting itself. A Schöenberg composition is precisely what it sounds like and what you hear, no more or less, unless the listener can be inventive enough to go beyond, a position that modern art generally encourages. One of the best demonstrations of the idea that the key for the artist is motion can be found in the work of Jackson Pollock and his 'action paintings.' In poetry, an example of this tendency can be found in what is called 'free verse.' It was in the 1880's when, "… French symbolists began to experiment with 'free verse' stretched across consciously shaped white spaces on the page…This technique was most fully developed by Stéphane Mallarmé who…believed that poetry should be evocative urging, in an often-quoted instruction, 'Paint not the thing, but the effect it produces.'"[54] More recently one of the more interesting poets to enjoy the freedom of blank pages and the placing of letters and words in a unique and original manner was the poetry of E. E. Cummings (1894–1962) although there have been many others.[55]

To think, according to Santayana, is to effectively practice a discourse.[56] This can lead to an independence of thought which could allow each one of us to interpret our own language in our own way. The need for an hierarchical pre-established authority in regard to any growth of understanding is far less the requirement it once was.[57] We should remember that to read is to translate which is to interpret, a personal act for each one alone who resides within their own conscious perceptions. And it is a tradition of the great authors to, "…have never written in any standard language."[58] Being an artist requires originality in the expressions of whatever the art form. Aeschylus or Shakespeare or, "…the student who reads them each has his own language."[59] Only the most brilliant writers and interpreters have made the most significant difference in our existence. And the more we move toward our own world we find reading to be increasingly an act of interpretation, especially if the work is worthy of being considered serious. Wonder, therefore, is very much another characteristic of our world and appears appropriate along with curiosity for the exercise of our potential conscious states; many of us today are actually more attracted to the questions and challenges than to the answers or a definition of success. Audience participation has also increased to where members of the audience today have to be something of an artist themselves: "Much of modern poetry works in this way. There may not be a succession of clearly defined images, but the very disruption and tension in what is evoked sets up an epiphanic field. This poetry has strong analogies to contemporary non-representative visual art."[60] From post-impressionism to the new novels, plays and films, members of the audience are so often left in a state of wonder. Of course, classical Greek theater, as an example, was also to have an impact in the form of a catharsis. But it possessed a clear direction and therefore without the inherent challenge that appears so often for contemporary audiences. Here, aesthetics and meaning can literally part company for the aesthetic is not a given but deduced.

> Aesthetic response is…to be analyzed in terms of a dialectic relationship between text, reader, and their interaction. It is called aesthetic response because, although it is brought about by the text, it brings into play the imaginative and perceptive faculties of the reader, in order to make him adjust and even differentiate his own focus. This approach implies that the book is to be regarded as a theory of aesthetic

response (*Wirkungstheorie*) and not as a theory of the aesthetics of reception (*Rezeptionstheorie*).[61]

The study of history became a profession as well as a humanistic art at the end of the nineteenth century, notwithstanding its ancient roots and Renaissance re-birth.[62] The reason for its modernity is, again, a matter of the necessity and the acceptance of detachment. (This should be kept in mind when discussing American historical writing since it has an additional characteristic influenced by the rise of logical positivism and thus is too often seen more as a social science rather than as part of the humanities.) All aesthetics can be, in some cases, removed and replaced with statistical analysis; being so exact that it is something of an artless art. The tradition of historical narrative, however, should have at least one foot in the aesthetic (or at least the creative); writers of history notwithstanding its many concerns, are often drawn to the ironic, arguably one of the more curious aspects of historical construction. If all language including historical analysis (detection), therefore, potentially contributes to the growth of consciousness, then language and its topics must be cherished and not treated with indifference. It is through reading that we become emancipated and thus it is not an accident that the slave owners of the Old South would not allow slaves to learn to read. One of the recent examples occurred in prison where freedom can, ironically, be often found more readily than in the suburbs. The following statement says it all: "Malcolm X studied the dictionary, writing out each entry from A to Z in longhand. He soon graduated to reading American history and then philosophy—Socrates, Schopenhauer, Kant, Nietzsche. 'Months passed without my even thinking about being imprisoned. In fact, up to then, I had never been so truly free in my life.' The story of Malcolm X is an archetypal example of the way in which literacy redeems what is most vital in us from the chaos of ignorance."[63] Conscious raising may be a possibility through reading although the evidence from Malcolm X to Helen Keller is too little to make any absolute judgement. Still, there is enough evidence to indicate that the acquisition and expansion of literacy appears to contribute one element in the creation and expansion of the self and the development of a more self-consciously reflective individual.

Having noted that there may be a correlation between reading and the growth of an individual is not to say that consciousness will necessarily arrive at the door of a reader. One scholar on the subject of literacy has even suggested that, "…literacy did not—does not ever by itself—awaken the passion of the mind…" This reasoning is clear in that, "…literacy is always a combination of consciousness about language and technical skill in the manipulation of the technologies of language."[64] To say literacy contributes to the creation of a conscious being is to say that literacy fully forms conscious itself, which would be a slippery slope. For the author of this same reservation also stated: "The act that begins to lead us out of the prison of our ignorance is not reading or writing or any other technology of language, but some more primitive initiative toward consciousness." And, "This act may not even be verbal, thought words are finally its manifestation. The impulse toward consciousness underlies all literacy but is not itself literacy. It is the mysterious act of the mind in discovering itself." This not to say that literacy is irrelevant since he adds that, "Once awakened, consciousness may turn to literacy for fulfillment, but the awakening itself occurs beyond literacy."[65] As has been noted, the complex act of consciousness and with it, silent reading and appearance of a strong sense of self is not given a fixed definition but rather is being offered as suggestive directions for further thought and research. Additionally, there are those who would take a more sympathetic position regarding the role of language and consciousness suggesting that "…every language is a vast pattern-system, different from others, in which are culturally ordained the forms and categories by which the personality not only communicates, but also analyses nature, notices or neglects types of relationship and phenomena, channels his reasoning, and builds the house of his consciousness."[66] There is little doubt that Descartes who began the language of consciousness was an extremely literate thinker in both Latin and in his own French. Locke was equally literate and owned a large personal library of more than 5,000 volumes. Perhaps it is possible to be illiterate and very conscious but there has been no evidence found yet to support this position. Until evidence to the contrary, how we look at space, time, language, and history should be considered as at least, for the purpose of discussion, as some of the key ingredients for any understanding of this nemesis called consciousness.

Of all the contemporary writers who have discussed consciousness in this light, one of the most interesting and significant is Jean-Paul Sartre who revealed in his own life the difference between literacy and an existential attitude with conscious choices. This brilliant thinker fought during World War II as a partisan against the Nazi occupation and is best known as a playwright, novelist and philosopher. First, it should be noted, however, that there were two important contemporary thinkers who were influential on Sartre and his ideas, thinkers we have neither the space or time to pursue in great detail. The first, Edmund Husserl (1859–1938), lectured in phenomenology, a philosophy concerned with describing personal experience without seeking to arrive at metaphysical explanation of them. The other, the German philosopher, Martin Heidegger, followed Husserl and developed his own views that influenced Sartre and his own existential thinking. This said, Sartre should be remembered as a thinker complete onto his own since his thoughts stand as a singular and unique statement, especially on the subject of consciousness. His significant writing on this subject has been translated as *The Transcendence of the Ego: An Existentialist Theory of Consciousness*. However, the reader should be aware that the subtitle, *Esquisse d'une description phénoménologique*, would be strictly translated as a "Study of a Phenomenological Description." This only reminds us of the difficulties inherent in translations and interpretations which is a subjective activity in itself. It is this subjective state that Sartre adopts as his philosophical center. Following Husserl's lead, he agreed that philosophy should not concern itself with "…theoretical debates about the existence of things and accept the world in all its qualitative richness."[67] This is a position that is consistent with Sartre's being correctly called "…quintessentially existential." Rather than metaphysical systems, "…he is wholly absorbed in the concrete experience of human beings."[68] Ontological pursuits left him cold. Perhaps this explains why he held to a position that unified his humanism with his existentialism.[69] A key concept of the existentialists in general and in the writings of Sartre specifically, is that "existence precedes essence." Another way to put it is that man, "…makes himself to be what he is; his individual essence or nature comes to be out of his existence…" And one could add what Ortega y Gasset had noted, "…man has no nature, only a history."[70]

From the historian's point of view it is of some interest that the great age of modern historiography and the rise of existential thinking (a topic worth further pursuit for future scholars) grew parallel to each other. Especially in the world of arts, the correlation between varied events and the mind-set (*Zeitgeist*) of the time are tied together in such a way that even when artists are not close to the philosophical theories of the day, they nevertheless live in a climate, "…determined by that thought, because, by virtue of their sensibility, they are interpreters of their epoch…"[71] Historians today approach the past openly and without pre-suppositions from political to social and from intellectual to cultural; it is appropriate that in a similar fashion this has, or at least should, also apply to the discipline of philosophy. This is particularly true in that philosophy has moved away from an exclusive or traditional dependence upon metaphysics, turning towards the newer fields of psychology, physics and even the post-modern theory of chaos (randomness). But the concept *existential* means something different. As Walter Kaufmann has noted: "Existentialism is not a philosophy but a label for several widely different revolts against traditional philosophy."[72] And while the Great War contributed to this circumstance it was the atomic bomb that truly revealed the "dreadful and total contingency of human existence." Therefore it is not difficult stating that "Existentialism is the philosophy of the atomic age."[73] It is also a philosophical (anti-philosophical?) position that belongs to the streets much like the new literature and poetry of the Beats who removed writing from the Ivory Tower and brought it back to every day life. For if existentialism is not a given set of doctrines, it is a manner of "...philosophizing and a way of looking at the world that emphasizes extreme states, estrangement, singularity, and the limitations of reason. It is the philosophy of the privy, not of the castle."[74]

Beat literature like Sartre's thinking is essentially accessible. But Beats are very much American just as Sartre's work along with his fellow writer Albert Camus is essentially French. It again, is easy to make this comparison since the roots of the Beat movement grew, in part grown out of the earlier French movement known as Surrealists: the latter arriving after the Great War and the former after Chapter II, World War II. If the World War I was destructive then, "...the sabotage of reason, painting, and poetry continued after the First World War in the antics of Dada and Surrealism. Anti-painting and the anti-literature are not new."[75] And the concepts associated with the Dada branch of surrealism also influenced Beat poetry.[76] This may make the Beats no more comprehensible than the existential and modern or post-modern artists. But Beats were "...wise enough to see that terms like insanity, psychosis, and a-social conduct are only sophisms useful to those whose emotional life is run by *Time* [Magazine], and who in effect are far madder than the Beats."[77] Where does insanity leave off and where does modernity and post-modernity take over? This is not a question often asked because of problematic implications. Whatever else one says about them, however, "...one must admit that the Beats are authentically [post-]modern in their wish to get out from under the burden of our apparatus."[78]

If there were any unifying concept for those involved in any of these mental activities from existential to Beat, it could be suggested that it would be the principle of authenticity. When it comes to terms like *surreal, existential, consciousness, self* or *Beat* it is appropriate that the issue here is with an historical view, placing them into an historic context. For the mind that demands clear and concise definitions, this has not been a very friendly century. But there is a commonality in these terms since, in seeking authenticity, they do not see society possessing a satisfactory certainty or even order. Andy Warhol found only one certainty and that was in the future everyone will be famous for 15 minutes. Those who are actively conscious and who possess powerful and evolving sense of the self (selves?) are like the Beats in that they "...witness that we do grow up absurd." While this is "...uniquely American because they reject a society that makes more and more useless goods which more and more thoughtless persons are persuaded to buy," the existential component has remained tied to its European roots.[79] Even Jack Kerouac, who was born a French Canadian, found it necessary to eventually visit Brittany in search for his roots, even if it was less than a satisfying experience. And if one is looking for live performances of that music which is most associated with the Beats, i.e., jazz, there is no problem finding a performance on the Left Bank of Paris, as it has become universal art form.

There is between Sartre and existentialism at the very least an empathetic communion if not an always clear analytic understanding. This is said in part because there really is no valid '-ism' to existentialism, although it is commonly used. And the idea of anyone actually being an 'existentialist' is difficult to comprehend. Indeed, Camus—a writer classified as existentialist—denied that the term applied to him. The counterculture of the 1950's and 1960's, however, could be called an exercise in existential attittudes, however. In fact, there was an existential variant associated with Zen and which was given a limited definition in a book called *Be Here Now*.[80] Defining and interpreting in an uncertain world leaves more doors open to misunderstandings. One thing is certain: "...since the nineteenth century the colloquy with self has widened and become more desperate."[81] As we look to the beginnings of the term *consciousness* to find a hint of meaningful understanding we can do the same with that of *existential* and several other terms here mentioned. Rather than closing the circle on these terms, such as Dada in art, absurd in theater and progressive in jazz, they leave us with more questions than clarification.

For those looking for an etymological understanding of the term *existential*, the word, from Latin, *existēre*, means 'to stand out.' "The English verb, unlike the French and German, is intransitive and connotes the passivity of 'mere existence.' The idea is better conveyed by saying that persons are centers radiating or exuding meaning. While existentialists recognize objects, they deny that the human being is just an object among others."[82] The subjective center in the Cartesian cogito now travels beyond the inner world to extend into any place that the inner world perceives as being significant. *Solipsism* is but one other very modern term to apply to the lonely, alienated and self-conscious, post-modernist. "Existentialism emerged as a protest against the displacement of individual consciousness from the centre of life's stage by a depersonalized nature, a transcendent deity, and or the collectivized state. Three centuries of rapid advance and compartmentalization of sciences, based on Newtonian mechanism, had shattered the human image."[83] This would be in opposition to those who would argue for a direct foundation in Descartes for a Sartrean understanding of consciousness.[84]

Sartre's position on consciousness is at times fairly clear and at others less than revealing. Unable to speak as to why this is, it will have to be enough to point out some of the more salient points regarding his views for it cannot be doubted that he did take the subject seriously and in some ways was one of the last in a history of significant philosophical discussions addressing this issue. Correctly stated, "The most radical break with empiricism occurs in transcendental-philosophical arguments; drawing in part on Cartesian and Kantian notions of subjectivity, these arguments depict man as basically a fugitive or intangible creature capable through his consciousness to negate and transcend contingent conditions."[85] In his essay, "Existentialism is a Humanism" we can find an early and succinct formulation of this view. Sartre is radical thinker for our own age much as the most interesting arts and thoughts of this century must be considered radical—i.e., possessing a modern and post-modern state of mind and an ability and willingness to face any and all basic assumptions. There is one problem to be noted before discussing Sartre's views regarding consciousness and therefore his existential attitude and this is the question of our ablity to give coherence to his varied ideas. Sartre is somewhat reminiscent of Nietzsche who not only lacked a coherent system but also rejected such an idea. What makes Nietzsche's writings coherent but not systematic is that he can and should be approached more as a poet than a philosopher. Sartre too is best approached in this manner although he is not a poet as much as a playwright who favored short works rather than long ponderous studies, *Being and Nothingness*, excepted. Even such important works as his *Transcendence of the Ego* and his *Existentialism is a Humanism* are relatively short works. In addition, there are his short stories that are very revealing: *No Exit, The Flies, The Wall* and *The Childhood of a Leader*. His *Being and Nothingness*, is the exception in that only students of philosophy are inclined to study this very difficult and ponderous work. Since he may be better understood in his plays, his philosophical works pose the greatest problems for understanding. Fortunately for this work, we are considering the historical and so the conundrum raised by the complexity and opaque nature of this work are not a primary concern. What should be understood, however is that if one is to speak of Sartre on consciousness they will find they also are speaking of the existential.

One of the themes running throughout this study has been the hunger for certainty. It has been suggested that this was the first step towards the early appearance of a self, of consciousness, and of an inner being, especially with the idea of the necessary appearance of a god who will defeat death. The end of a role for gtod is the end of that hope. With thinkers like Nietzsche, a new role for the inner self begins to offer an alternative approach. Sartre further notes another contributor to this new attitude when he stated that "Dostoevsky once wrote 'If God did not exist, everything would be permitted'; and that, for existentialism, is the starting point."[86] It is precisely in this awareness that there are no answers nor any certainty except being here and alive which is the basis not only for an existential existence but very possibly a component in the appearance of modern consciousness. As Sartre concludes: "Thus, there is no human nature, because there is no God to have a conception of it."[87] The fixed view of being, a conclusive metaphysical ontology, once removed from our living map, allows us to become our authentic inner self in our alone and estranged state separated from any fixed order. As one commentator put it: "...actually a major effort was made by existentialist writers to strip man of substantive connotations and to replace human nature with the notion of the human condition or human reality,"[88] a position that did not please Sartre. Many conservative religious leaders argue that non-believers attempt to destroy faith which is farthest from the truth since, "The existentialist...finds it extremely embarrassing that God does not exist, for there disappears with Him all possibility of finding values in an intelligible heaven. There can no longer be any good *a priori*, since there is no infinite and perfect consciousness to think it."[89] Despair and anguish may not be part of a life lived (by many who spend their time functioning in a very difficult environment or even those who live by myths), but are appropriate for those seeking to live a life of reasoned engagement and freedom. Note that this viewpoint is not a cause for celebration. For most people a designed universe, a natural order for all life and all of nature is a necessary ingredient for direction. Masses of people without direction can be as frightening a thought as when they are given purpose: Russia under the Soviets or Germany under the Fascists. Meanwhile, individuals, those who seek to make conscious choices without a road map or grand design, are reduced to living without guidance, on their own, each day as uncertain as the last. As Sartre stated it, "...but I cannot count upon men whom I do not know, I cannot base my confidence upon human goodness or upon man's interest in the good of society, seeing that man is free and that there is no human nature which I can take as foundational."[90]

As we enter the world of the existential, Sartre makes a very important point that it was not necessary to be anti-religious to embrace an existential stance. As he stated in *Existentialism as a Humanism*: "The question [defining existentialism] is only complicated because there are two kinds of existentialists. There are, on the one hand, the Christians,...on the other the existential atheists, amongst whom we must place Heidegger as well as the French existentialist and myself. What they have in common is simply the fact that they believe that *existence* comes before *essence*..."[91] The theory that there is no God is the position called 'atheistic existentialism,' which as Sartre noted "...declares with greater consistency that if God does not exist there is at least one being whose existence comes before its essence, a being which exists before it can be defined by any conception of it. That being is man..."[92] This is a critical point since it supports another theory of his regarding the definition of man since any attempt must follow a sensible pattern in creating any useful definition. "We mean that man first of all exists, encountered himself, surges up in the world—and defines himself afterwards."[93] There cannot be an *a priori* definition of a person until the person has not only existed but more importantly actually "encountered himself." This is but one aspect in any attempt to understand the concept of being existential as well the fact that this is an attitude that can, in principle, be embraced by anyone. There is something original in the way the West has been preoccupied with a dualism marked by conflicts unlike other civilizations which, while granting a dualism, see an appropriate response in reaching for a resolution, a harmony, rather than an inherently unresolvable conflict. The Western mind, in contrast, is marked by this continuous struggle for dominance of one over the other in a continuous and unresolved *modus vivendi*.

The idea that Sartre expresses regarding this struggle is defined by his view that, "Man is nothing else but that which he makes of himself that is the first principle of existentialism."[94] In this sense man is always in the making, his history is his doing and that which precedes is a past on which he is not necessarily dependent. Thus the argument earlier in the century that held that we are but behavioral responses now has been countered by an alternate view. This is partly because one must make for themselves their own choices, choices that can make of their life an experience of despair and anguish; as Sartre put: "...in making decisions, he cannot but feel a certain anguish."[95] Although he also speaks of man living as well in despair and with a sense of abandonment he does on occasion favor the term *anguish* to describe mankind's condition: "The existentialist frankly states that man is in anguish. His meaning is as follows—'When a man commits himself to anything, fully realizing that he is only choosing what he will be, but is thereby at the same time a legislator deciding for the whole of mankind—in such a moment a man cannot escape from the sense of complete and profound responsibility.'"[96] And with abandonment Sartre ties the two together: "...that is what 'abandonment' implies, that we ourselves decide our being. And with this abandonment goes anguish."[97] To a certain extent one must let go of presuppositions about the order of nature and humanity and it is no accident that Sartre made these discoveries with the arrival of World War II and Nazi occupation. According to Sartre, it was the "...situation after the fall of France in June 1940 [which] condensed the issue of freedom and individual authenticity...as Sartre points out, never were certain individuals, who in consciousness could grasp what the genuine situation was, more free than at that very time."[98] This is a common theme for those who have experienced such defining moments as death and combat. For Sartre, whether working in the Underground resistance, writing plays or handing out political pamphlets, he remained an activist who saw that, "...man is condemned to be free. Condemned, because he did not create himself, yet is nevertheless at liberty, and from the moment that is thrown into this world he is responsible for everything he does."[99] This could be considered an extension of Rousseau's idea of being forced to be free although freedom now exists by way of existential choices. This, of course, raises questions of meaning for the term freedom since it too has had different meanings over time.

Whatever position one would take on this matter, there is little doubt that after two world wars and the dropping of two atomic bombs there was little left of a civilized social order worthy of a great deal of admiration or trust. This partially explains how, "Sartre's later formulation...is 'Freedom of Terror,'"[100] again demonstrating that where death, sits freedom can be found most clearly. It follows that to be free is in itself a personal and individual achievement since no one can give it to you. As Sartre himself had observed: "...it was during the war, working in the Underground resistance, in constant danger of betrayal and death, that he felt most free and alive."[101] As for freedom, it "...is not simply being allowed to do what you like; it is *intensity of will*, and it appears under any circumstances that limit man and arouse his will to more life."[102] It is through the psychological doorway to freedom, rather than some sociological, political or economic entrance that freedom is discovered. Since so many people work at a functional life, the word freedom is limited to the absence of authoritarian control—that is the knock in the middle of the night by an official in a uniform. And freedom is important especially for Sartre who realized that, "A threat of imminent death—or even a passing thought of out own mortality—is sufficient to wrench us out of current involvements—even if but for a moment—and force us to look at our lives."[103]

The subject of death has been a major theme in this review and so we end our discussion with it as a central theme. In Sartre's short story, *The Wall*, the subject of death is central. But it is the burden of living and not the issue of death that pre-occupies Sartre who once noted in *The Flies* that, "…human life begins on the far side of despair."[104] All this is background to his existential orientation regarding any commitment to the world of choice. His story of Lucien coming of age in *The Childhood of a Leader*, for example, is reminiscent of Bradbury's *Dandelion Wine* with the difference being that for Sartre there is much less of an innocent tone. Moreover, in Bradbury the coming of age possesses both some charm and humor whereas Sartre portrays it as a much more bitter experience: "He thought, 'I'm Lucien Fleurier, I'm in my room, I'm doing a problem in physics, it's Sunday.' But his thoughts melted into banks of white fog. He shook himself and began counting the cretonne characters, two shepherdesses, two shepherds and Cupid. Then suddenly he told himself, 'I am and there was a slight click: he had awakened from his long somnolence." After this thought he adds, "It was not pleasant."[105] The desire to hold on to youth and avoid the burden of freedom can and often is too much to resist. It is immediately after this that Lucien declares "'Now I have it!' he thought, 'now I have it! I was sure of it: *I don't exist!*'"[106] Not existing is surely easier than to exist, or it is easier to die than to live, which is one reason why suicide is not that uncommon, especially among a variety of artists in this past century.[107] What Lucien must do is to avoid the inner self, all reflection and his conscious self. So Sartre has Lucien "…turn himself away from a sterile and dangerous contemplation of self:… he must apply himself to human geography and history."[108] Yet the confusion that is a mark of his leading character is partly a metaphor for France in the post-war years. Vacillation was unappealing for Sartre and his Lucien demonstrates this after having decided not to exist when he then turns around and announces that, "'I exist…because I have the right to exist.'"[109] Again he exists not because he exists but because he has a right to exist in a world without a God carrying his burdens and without any cultural demand to exist. He exists because he exists just as being conscious is a matter of being conscious. Both the literal and figurative metaphor that applies at the very end of the work occurs with the scene where Lucien finally accepts growing up: "A clock struck noon; Lucien rose. The metamorphosis was complete: a graceful, uncertain adolescent had entered this café one hour earlier; now a man left, a leader among Frenchmen."[110] But rather than achieving an existential and conscious existence, Lucien continues the primitive and ancient pattern (his ego) of seeking a definition for himself from the outside world as the play ends with the following: "…he would have liked to find on his own face the impenetrable look he admired on Lemordant's. But the mirror only reflected a pretty, headstrong little face that was not yet terrible. 'I'll grow a moustache,' he decided."[111] In the beginning of the play he appeared as a "little angel" and by the end his appearance still pre-occupied him. The only choices that are supposed to be made are those that fit you into the society that you find yourself living in:

> 'First maxim,' Lucien said, 'not to try and see inside yourself; there is no mistake more dangerous.' The real Lucien —he knew now—had to be sought in the eyes of others, in the frightened obedience of Pierrette and Guigard, the hopeful waiting of all those beings who grew and ripened for him, these young apprentice girls who would become *his* workers, people of Ferolles, great and small, of whom he would one day be the master. Lucien was almost afraid, he felt almost too great for himself. So many people were waiting for him, at attention: and he was and always would be this immense waiting of others. 'That's a leader,' he thought.[112]

To make a choice, whether it is existential or conscious, becomes a key component to twentieth century thinking. It is for Sartre the closest thing to being: "Life is nothing until it is lived; but it is yours to make sense of, and the value of it is nothing else but the sense that you choose."[113] Our personal histories are nothing more than a reflection of our choices—or possibly of our not choosing, for Sartre also makes clear, "I can always choose, but I must know that if I do not choose, that is still a choice."[114] While this is an idea that can be found earlier in the writings of William James it is Sartre who was not afraid to employ the principle of an absolute regarding choice, and it should not be surprising, therefore, that for all the destruction experienced in this past century there has also been a rebirth, even a redesigned humanism, flowing from the heritage of the Renaissances. "This is humanism, because we remind man that there is no legislator but himself; also because we show that it is not by turning back upon himself, but always by seeking, beyond himself, an aim which is one of liberation or of some particular realization, that man can realize himself as truly human."[115] In being human the exercise of humanism is through choices. To choose not to choose and let a human life float beyond an interior and reflective reasoning as well as chosen relationships, even if this is to choose to die, one is still displacing space. That we have a capacity to be reflectively conscious of our choices is part of the burden of existence and any denial leads to a belief in nothing—or nihilism. "Man is all the time outside of himself: it is in projecting and losing himself beyond himself that he makes man to exist; and, on the other hand, it is by pursuing transcendent aims that he himself is able to exist. Since man is thus self-surpassing, he is himself the heart and center of his transcendence. There is no other universe except the human universe, the universe of human subjectivity."[116] Here Sartre comes close enough to a solipsisitic position which understandably has disturbed some thinkers. Ego is in some ways for Sartre the I or the individualized self. Thus consciousness and *ego* (or I) must be seen as having a relationship, but only with Sartre. As he put it, "It is thanks to the ego, indeed, that a distinction can be make between the possible and the real, between appearance and being, between the willed and the undergone."[117] There is a judgmental component with the ego for Sartre and while this would not fit the classical view of the term it is appropriate in Sartre's world which is especially marked by reflection. "But it can happen that consciousness suddenly produces itself on the pure reflective level. Perhaps not without the ego, yet as escaping from the ego outside the consciousness by a continued creation. On this level, there is no distinction between the possible and the real, since appearance is the absolute."[118] He continues and avoids the serious dilemma of solipsism when he states in his work on ego: "This conception of the ego seems to us the only possible refutation of solipsism."[119]

There is a price to pay for implications within the confines of the simple Cartesian position of the cogito. It is much simpler, and for many, more appealing, to take a more behavioral, materialistic and logically positivistic position than to attempt discussions about that which is not only immeasurable but non-sensible. This has always been a problem for Lockean empiricism: what can we actually experience may be part but not necessarily all of the human phenomena we perceive. Modern artists have illustrated this phenomenon well. On the same note, the idea of John Stuart Mill comes to mind where to be an individual is to be a genius. This is extremely fitting for today's artists who consider each and every one of their works to be authentic and unique; Sartre said it: "…there is no genius other than that which is expressed in works of art."[120]

There is one more important point to draw regarding Sartre's concept of choice which he applies to all people. As he states it "…one chooses in view of others, and in view of others one chooses himself."[121] The reason for this conclusion is that it is impossible to make a choice, whether speaking existentially and/or consciously, and not make that choice for all humans. Since to choose is a unique act demonstrative of our humanity, when we make any choice it is inherently an expression of all of humanity. As he stated in another passage:

> When we say that man chooses himself, we do mean that every one of us must choose himself; but by that we also mean that in choosing for himself he chooses for all men. For in effect, of all the actions a man may take in order to create himself as he wills to be, there is not one which is not creative, at the same time, of an image of man such as he believes he ought to be. To choose between this or that is at the same time to affirm the value of that which is chosen; for we are unable ever to choose the worse. What we choose is always the better; and nothing can be better for unless it is better for all.[122]

His analysis can be viewed as an answer to an implied question in Dostoevsky's *Crime and Punishment*: If one were to argue that God were dead and all things are possible then why not see what it feels like to kill someone? Sartre's answer resolves any problem simply by stating that when you make a choice you are saying to all the world that as a living human being this choice of mine is appropriate and worthy of any and all other humans to exercise. If I choose to kill someone then I am simply stating that being human is killing another human. Another way to think of it is in traditional pre-existential thinking pattern where the essence of humankind is a philosophical issue. This is perfectly understandable for there is a great deal of room, as history has taught, for many divergent positions to exist. But if one were to kill all opponents then there would be no one to disagree with or debate. This clearly is nonsense since differences are required for a variety of views to gain light of day, or better still, for differing ways of being a particular self at a particular time in a unique given space.

This is not to say that history and literature are not necessary ingredients for the development of a community of individuals. In the past, the society and with it, the community were assumed for obvious reasons to be absolutely fundamental for all to have a secure space. In this world where the self-conscious becomes increasingly common, choices for a gathering as a group, for example, will have to be made by enough people for them to find means to live together. I can choose to jump from an airplane at 5,000 feet without a parachute—but only once. For all humans to do so would mean no discussion as to whether one could or should make such a jump. You are free to choose whatever but that freedom has a frame of reality and existence that is called responsibility. To choose is to be responsible because when you make a choice you lose some of the options you had before you make that choice. If I choose to turn right I have taken away the possible choice of turning left. Choices are an exercise of freedom that is immediately diminished when any choice is made.

To be is to become, but beyond this Nietzscheian view, the being is an *I* or, as Sartre prefers it, the 'ego.' However, having an ego does not determine possession of consciousness. In this he retains the more classical Latin understanding of ego where consciousness was at best too rare and meager to note. His view is simply that he would, "…like to show here that the ego is neither formally nor materially in consciousness: it is outside, in the world. It is a being of the world, like the ego of another."[123] Ego in antiquity, as noted, is a public word without any private elements that our modern 'self' (or 'I') possesses and in this he remains true to the root meaning. It has also been suggested here that it is the word individuality, unlike self, that is the public side of our lives after all. Sartre notes this public sense of the I: "The I is the ego as the unity of actions. The me is the ego as the unity of states and of qualities."[124] Consciousness, on the other hand, is not dependent upon our ego, for it is in our actions where this "unity" occurs and where existentialism is manifest for Sartre. In fact, he goes so far as to suggest that the "…doctrine I am presenting…declares that there is no reality except in action."[125] Moreover, his ego, "…is not the owner of consciousness; it is the object of consciousness."[126] The determining forum for consciousness is therefore the ability for the ego (self) to exercise consciousness but at the same time the ego (self) is revealed to us by way of our consciousness. That this is important to his understanding of the existential is noted: "…at the very heart and center of existentialism, is the absolute character of the free commitment, by which every man realizes himself in realizing a type of humanity—a commitment always understandable, to no matter whom in no matter what epoch…"[127] Hence there is the implication that our existential side is the more public while the conscious side would be seen as more private. Whatever his thinking may have been specifically he is very clear in his support of a given type of consciousness, one that is transcending. As he understands it, "We may…formulate our thesis: transcendental consciousness is an impersonal spontaneity. It determines its existence at each instant, without our being able to conceive anything *before* it. Thus each instant of our conscious life reveals to us a creation *ex nihilo*. Not a new *arrangement*, but a new existence."[128] This is not a matter of choices but a matter of living on the edge with the potential for choices but without a preconceived notion of action. Here the term *spontaneity* appears in his writings with some regularity. Additionally, he is struggling to offer an alternative to relativism in living. "This transcendental sphere is a sphere of *absolute* existence, that is to say, a sphere of pure spontaneities which never objects and which determine their own existence."[129] Thus spontaneity and absolute can be brought together under the heading of transcendental consciousness as a matter of its exercise rather than by way of contrivance.

Sartre's arguments are not always clear, especially in his essays rather than his more creative artistic expressions. Part of this may be attributable to the French language and in part may arrive from one of his mentors from whom he drew ideas and language, Husserl who he noted had, "…reverted…to the classic position of a transcendental *I*. This *I* would be…behind each consciousness, a necessary structure of consciousness…"[130] Husserl's influential concepts regarding phenomenology, his rejection of empiricism and belief in seeing philosophy as fundamentally an *a priori* discipline was very influential in psychology, in general and Gestalt psychology, in particular. Sartre drew extensively on his ideas which are still being interpreted and digested, since it has been properly observed that the French phenomenologists, like Sartre and other leading representatives, "…managed to blend Husserlian teachings with existentialist and Hegelian conceptions, as well as the powerful indigenous legacy of Cartesianism."[131] One could be reminded of Rousseau and Goethe: in the need for freedom for Rousseau and Goethe's need for action as roots for this transformation.

Reflection is an important idea tied to consciousness for both Husserl and Sartre. It was Sartre who stated, "…unreflected consciousness must be considered autonomous. It is a totality which needs no completing at all…"[132] As for reflection, he holds that, "…it is on the reflected level that the ego-life has its place, and on the unreflected level that the impersonal life has its place."[133] Unreflective consciousness is therefore one that has an "ontological priority" since it "…does not need to be reflected in order to exist, and because reflection presupposes the intervention of a second-degree consciousness."[134] The place of the directness of unreflective consciousness is demonstrated for him when he suggests, "…in the case of reflection, and only in the case, affectivity is posited for itself, as desire, fear, etc. Only in the case of reflection can I think 'I hate Peter,' 'I pity Paul,' etc."[135]

The link between the conscious mind and the existential is not always clear for there is no reason to necessarily tie the two together, even though there are interesting ideas in this regard. The history of this link can be traced back to the end of World War II. "The existential perspective on individual consciousness became serious, widespread, and for a time nearly definitive of individual consciousness in Western Europe only right after 1945."[136] Paul Monaco who makes this suggestion in his *Modern European Culture and Consciousness* also offers, "…the existential point of view appears to be a matter more of temperament than of intellect," a position that further supports the idea that there is no philosophy to existentialism.[137] Another writer suggests the following association between consciousness and existentialism:

> One's consciousness is one's way of taking up the ontological question; it contains within it one's unique way of having the world in which to live, of being a self in that world, and of giving meaning to the self-world relationship one lives or is. One's consciousness is structured; it is not random or chaotic. That structure, which enables life's events to be experienced, which enables them to have a meaning, is never the object of our attention. It is the way we have of paying attention. It is the place of our standing as we interpret; it is not itself capable of being interpreted, for interpretation always assumes it. It is the 'existential platform' on which we stand when we experience anything at all, as meaningful at all.[138]

Here the association occurs in that existential which is an attitude, acts as a foundation for the exercise of cataloging the meaning of our experiences; in other words, it stands before consciousness. This creates a problem if we look at the chronological foundation of consciousness since no matter how late we date it, it occurs, at the earliest, within the confines of the seventeenth century where it is not possible to find an existential attitude. However, the self is not a fixed phenomenon since it is in constant state of flux: "…man is not a constant, unchanging being: he is one person one day, another person the next. He forgets easily, lives in the moment, seldom exerts will-power, and even when he does, gives up the effort after a short time, or forgets his original aim and turns to something else. No wonder that poets feel such despair when they seem to catch a glimpse of some intense state of consciousness, and know with absolute certainty that *nothing* they can do can hold it fast."[139] Sartre certainly would agree that there is a dynamic of action and motion of the self through experience when he chose 1940 for the beginnings of his own optimum freedom of choice and authenticity. As for Sartre's creation of a definition of consciousness, he offers the following: "In our introduction we defined consciousness as 'a being, the nature of which is to question its own being, that being implying a being other than itself.' But now that we have examined the meaning of 'the question,' we can at present also write the formula thus: 'Consciousness is a being, the nature of which is to be conscious of the nothingness of its being.'"[140] To accept—to be conscious, that we are born an ontological nothing and thus must make our being by choices is the only means Sartre can see to fill a life. "Man is nothing else but that which makes of himself. That is the first principle of existentialism."[141] Nothing is a given other than the capacity for consciousness and choice.

In the discussion of self-consciousness, the very problematic issue of consciousness becomes an even more confusing concern. From one point of view, "...self-consciousness does not add anything to the world or to consciousness," because, according to Robert Solomon, "...it is neither a Lockean 'turning back on itself' nor a Cartesian reflective substance. Self-consciousness robs the world of its authority, its given values, and it robs consciousness of its innocence."[142] This is significant since there has been a tendency among a few scholars as well as Sartre himself to suggest that self-consciousness—like consciousness—was an important issue for Descartes. It has been suggested that it was from Sartre's point of view that, "...the Cartesian formula...still provides the crucial yardstick for assessing the validity of theoretical assertions: 'At the point of departure there cannot be any other truth than this, I think, therefore I am... which is the absolute truth of consciousness as it attains to itself.'"[143] In terms of a Cartesian point of view, Sartre added, "...outside of the Cartesian *cogito*, all objects are no more than probable, and any doctrine of probabilities which is not attached to a truth will crumble into nothing."[144] It is in this understanding that Sartre, although seeing so much in terms of the creative self through choices, still could not completely leave the Cartesian tradition, or reject the concept of certainty. There is something fixed in the transition of choices for him. As for going beyond the Cartesian position, Sartre also suggested that the notion that, "man primarily exists," signifies, "...that man is, before all else, something which propels itself towards a future and is aware that it is doing so. Man is, indeed, a project which possesses a subjective life, instead of being a king of moss, or a fungus or a cauliflower. Before the projection of the self nothing exists, not even in the heaven of intelligence: man will only attain existence when he is what he purposes to be."[145] It is here that something of a certainty appears specifically in the form of the ego, the I and the self and is thus applicable to consciousness. As he stated, "...there must be an absolute, and...it consists in one's immediate sense of one's self."[146] The interesting component for self-consciousness in Sartre's comment, therefore, is the question of the self rather than simply consciousness. Solomon already discussed this issue in his analysis of existential as something more complex than simply consciousness since, "...according to some recent existentialists, there is no *self* as such." This is the result to some extent that each individual would make their own choices and consider themselves as existential would therefore be specifically in a 'one of a kind' and unique situation, without any "-ism." As for consciousness itself, Solomon continues, "'It is nothing,' Sartre tells us, and for Heidegger it is scarcely worth mentioning."

There is "the other" or the embarrassed state of youthful 'immature' self-consciousness as Solomon notes: "One is self-conscious because of the camera, he is embarrassed, to be ill-at-ease...Descartes sees self-consciousness as a propositional attitude; consciousness of one's own existence seems in the light of reason to be not much different from a mathematical postulate."[147] Pushing this component of self back into the seventeenth century and the world of Descartes is at the least very questionable even though there are those who *would* put the presence of self-consciousness as far back as Descartes' *cogito*.[148] The problem for that argument is that the ancient Latin word *ego* that Husserl and Sartre used extensively was at best, in fact, only a grammatical indicator for an I. The development of the self, the foundation for individuality can trace its immediate roots to the nineteenth century which is about the earliest presence of self-consciousness. The world was always perceived as a reality to adjust to rather than the world adjusting to the self. As is well put: "The realization that 'I am the world' is a necessary step in the awakening of self-consciousness. In the existentialists' self-conscious sense, perhaps one has never existed if he has never once seen himself as everything."[149] This existential position ties the two concepts, that of existential and that of self-consciousness, into a tenuous but mutually supportive grouping of ideas. It may be that historically, the eventual maturation of consciousness to a higher level of introspectivity has added to the creation of an existential attitude. This is further supported with the appearance of industrialization as well as the technological and demographic changes of the recent decades where the terms alienation and estrangement have become increasingly common. In such an environment the individual is left to their own resources for the definition of meaning. Again, Solomon adds: "The existential attitude is first of all an attitude of self-consciousness. One feels himself separated from the world, from other people. In isolation, one feels threatened, insignificant, meaningless, and in response demands significance through a bloated view of self. One constitutes himself as a hero, as an offense, as a prophet or anti-Christ, as a revolutionary, as unique."[150] The idea of a hero in this role is not as far-fetched as some might believe. Paul Zweig defends the thesis that today's artists are also heros: "There is no society of heroes." And like J. S. Mill's genius as the true individual, Zweig suggests that those who would stand outside the mainstream as poets and artists have the opportunity to explore the inner self but on occasion may find the desire to re-enter the world from their "radical solitude." The thesis continues with the proposition that a poet's, "...adventure is not complete until he has returned home, or has at least seen to it that his deed becomes known to those who remained behind.... What the hero has done for himself, by changing his life, is truly done only if it is done for others." [151]

Sartre could also be added to this picture with his view that, "It is because I can say my consciousness, and because Peter and Paul can also speak of their consciousness, these consciousness distinguish themselves from each other. The I is the producer of inwardness."[152] It is from this 'inwardness' that not only certainty but a universality is achieved. Sartre has clearly perpetuated his view: "In every purpose there is universality, in this sense that every purpose is comprehensible to every man. Not that this or that purpose defines man for ever, but that it may be entertained again and again."[153] Here the commitment to any universal structure by way of an individual choice is clearly exemplified, as his additional thinking indicates, "...every purpose, however individual it may be, is of universal value. Every purpose, even that of a Chinese, an Indian or a Negro, can be understood by a European."[154] In this case, his views apply to all people and not to any given culture or political order. Moreover, this ability to create value through the power of consciousness and existential choices is further demonstrated when he suggests that "...we may say that there is a human universality, but it is not something given; it is perpetually made."[155] It remains, therefore, in process, an absolute of change and choice.

The existential hero who accepts and lives by his conscious choices can be found in Sartre's *The Flies*, a modern adaptation on the classical theme of *Oresteia* by Aeschylus, and which had reappeared and been elaborated upon by Shakespeare in *Hamlet*. The fundamental differences in the renderings, from Ancient to Renaissance to modern is that the story constructs a progressively greater dilemma for the hero avenging a father's death. The story of Hamlet having a sense of modernity that no other of Shakespeare's plays would appear to possess.[156] For Sartre's version, however, the shame and guilt for a murderous act of revenge arrives in the form of the flies. Of the many important works by Walter Kauffman, his book *Without Guilt and Justice* is a brilliant explication of a somewhat existential approach to life. He contrasts this experience of choice with dependence upon some super natural or spiritual order guiding mankind, a fixed guilt or justice given to us by nature in the form of our conscience. Justice can now be seen as a social contrivance, while guilt can be perceived as psychological conditioning. The subjects of both shame and guilt and their relationship to consciousness and modernity has received attention by a variety of contemporary thinkers. One insightful example deals with our understanding of the issue of guilt: "Guilt, or self-reproach, is based on internalization of values, notably parental values—in contrast to shame, which is based upon disapproval coming from outside, from other persons... [i.e.] guilt, a failure to live up to one's own picture of oneself (based on parental values), with shame, a reaction to criticism by other people."[157] While guilt is usually associated with a public state of mind, shame is more of a personal state and mental, as such, there has been a decline in our sense of shame. Part of this is a result of the assumptions regarding the order of the universe. For example, "A sense of place in relationship to the cosmos has been lost in the modern world. We are caught up in limitless self-assertion—that is, shamelessness —and thus fail to see the connection between shame and awe."[158] The burden then, of self-consciousness is that in reflectiveness one can transcend the shame of the self in terms of others' opinions and embrace the burden of one's conscious choices: a self and individuality.

Where there is freedom there is a burden and no one knows this more than those who achieve a reflective consciousness. To reiterate Sartre: "We mean that man first of all exists, encountered himself, surges up in the world—and defines himself afterwards."[159] And, in Solomon's words: "...self-consciousness in the existential sense is this very recognition that there is no self. The self is an ideal, a chosen course of action and values."[160] This is a very modern, perhaps post-modern view that should not be projected very far back in time. It is his humanity that, "... he makes of himself. That is the first principle of existentialism."[161] The problem for many students of the subject is that, "Self-consciousness is not a premise or an object for study. It is rather the perspective within which existentialism attempts to focus itself."[162] Yet for all anyone would notice, those feelings—from despair to alienation—that are not uncommon today is not what is important since a feeling does "...not have an identity or a direction before it is already made self-conscious. For anyone who is not yet self-conscious, a feeling can be a cause of behavior. In one who is self-conscious, a feeling is but an obscure text which requires an interpretation, and that presupposes a set of values."[163] In this world of increasingly self-conscious existential behavior, values are a result of choices not fixed entities that somehow exist out there in some mystical place filled with metaphysical certainty. Death alone is the absolute reality and all else is editorial.

An acquaintance of Sartre, Albert Camus (1913–60), also understood this principle regarding consciousness:

> ...existential revolt as more fundamentally human than—and implicitly superior to—what Camus labels as historical revolt. Camus saw historical revolt, the modern materialist revolutionary project, as only a surface reflection of one aspect of rebellion, which is inherent in the human condition. For all humans are endowed with a propensity to rebel against that paradox that is fundamental to life. On the one hand, we can never know enough about the 'others' in whose company we find ourselves, and we can never...make sense out of the world of the 'others' in which we find ourselves, namely society. In contrast...we all know something we might wish to purge from awareness, and that is that we shall die. [164]

This view represents how Camus in one sense joined Sartre; for unlike Kierkegaard and Nietzsche who wrote only for the few, Camus and Sartre wrote to generations.[165] While Camus had rejected the title existential which Sartre had embraced, these writers clearly demonstrated the modern conscious mind in action.[166] One fairly popular metaphor for consciousness is the idea of light used by Julian Jaynes as well as others, including C. Humphreys who used this metaphor in an interesting manner:

> The searchlight of consciousness when directed to a given field of attention has, as it were, two qualities, extension and intensity. When playing on a distant landscape, for example, the light may either be diffused over a whole village or concentrated on a church tower, and the intensity of the light will vary with the extension of the field of view. As the whole object of concentration is to learn to focus the attention on a single point and to hold it there at will, it follows that the more simple the object chosen the more intense will be the concentration upon it. [167]

The question regarding this metaphor is that if consciousness is focused on a particular phenomenon and therefore not on others then is there a unity of being? This question was somewhat confronted by Sartre when he noted: "The ego is a virtual locus of unity, and consciousness constitutes it in *a direction contrary to* that actually taken by the production: *really*, consciousness are first; through these are constituted states; and then, through the latter, the ego is constituted."[168] This is an unusual sequence when the evidence of history would indicate that the ego exists prior to consciousness. Moreover, light is not an appealing metaphor for some readers when the discussion turns toward self-consciousness. Gilbert Ryle, the opponent of Descartes' dualism, argued that, "Self-consciousness, if the word is to be used at all, must not be described on the hallowed para-optical model, as a torch that illuminates itself by beams of its own light reflected from a mirror in its own insides. On the contrary it is simply a special case of an ordinary more or less efficient handling of a less or more honest and intelligent witness."[169] The light and mirror metaphors work for some when consciousness is the issue but not so easily applied to self-consciousness, again in part because of the meaning and understanding of the word 'self.' A more clear explication of consciousness is offered by Ernest Keen in *Psychology and the New Consciousness*.

> One's consciousness is one's way of taking up the ontological question; it contains within it one's unique way of having the world in which to live, of being a self in that world, and of giving meaning to the self-world relationship one lives or is. One's consciousness is structured; it is not random or chaotic. That structure, which enables life's events to be experienced, which enables them to have a meaning, is never the object of our attention. It is the way we have of paying attention. It is the place of our standing as we interpret; it is not itself capable of being interpreted, for interpretation always assumes it. It is the 'existential platform' on which we stand when we experience anything at all, as meaningful at all.[170]

There is, of course, a massive body of work attempting to define consciousness to which this work, given its historical orientation, could never have done justice. Appendix III which offers authors and the terms they use to modify consciousness also gives evidence to a great deal of plurality of meanings (hence uncertainty), from psychological types to those of sociology. There has been of late a great body of scholarly writings also on the self, individuality as well consciousness, self-conscious and their fellow travelers. There are several schools one can introduce that may be of some help regarding recent research and theories. One such example represented by a fairly popular writer on the subject is Daniel C. Dennett in his *Consciousness Explained* that offers a materialist view favoring the idea that even computers will some day become capable of being conscious and, perhaps, more importantly, that free will is an illusion. He agrees with Julian Jaynes and this writer, however, that consciousness is a later development rather than existing in our original natural state.

As for the problem of offering definitions, there is Colin McGinn who stated his case well when he offered: "Somehow, we feel, the water of the physical brain is turned into the wine of consciousness, but we draw a total blank on the nature of this conversion. Neural transmissions just seem like the wrong kind of materials with which to bring consciousness into the world."[171] This represents a recognition of the difficulty that resides in any attempt to give shape and meaning to the term, and he is explicit in such works as *Problems in Philosophy* where the doubts that consciousness will ever or can ever be defined. There are others who hold to the rather extreme position that the term *consciousness* is meaningless. While some will marvel at the existence of consciousness: "...consciousness is the greatest invention in the history of life; it has allowed life to become aware of itself," a view expressed by the award winning scientist, Stephen J. Gould, it has not changed the mind of the sceptics. Another reservation is: "In all the contexts in which it tends to be deployed, the term 'conscious' and its cognates are for *scientific* purposes both unhelpful and unnecessary."[172] This particular writer who is clear in his reservations, Nicholas Humphrey in *A History of Mind*, states additionally that, "I find that I have no clear conception what people are talking about when they talk about 'consciousness' or 'phenomenal awareness.'"[173] For so many serious and honest thinkers the question asked is a simple but not an easily answered one: "Consciousness presents us with puzzle after puzzle. How can a neural events cause consciousness to happen. What good is consciousness."[174] The problem only increases as you give thought to the question of usefulness for, "...if consciousness is useless—if a creature without it could negotiate the world as well as a creature with it—why would natural selection have favored the conscious one?"[175]

Is it little wonder then that consciousness has become, especially in the second half of the twentieth century, such a complex and confusing intellectual concern? As Steven Pinker thoughtfully put it: "Consciousness has recently become the circle that everyone wants to square. Almost every month an article announces that consciousness has been explained at last, often with a raspberry blown at the theologians and humanists who would put boundaries on science and another one for the scientist and philosophers who dismiss the topic as too subjective or muddled to be studyable"[176] He continues with an incident that can further demonstrate the problem of using this ubiquitous term of *consciousness* at all: "I have just received in the mail a manifesto for a forthcoming workshop on consciousness. The author of it, Aaron Sloman, opens his remarks: "...the noun 'consciousness' as used by most academics (philosophers, psychologists, biologists...) does not refer to anything in particular. This implies for example that you cannot ask how it evolved, or which organisms do and which do not have it."[177]

The more traditional approach was begun in our own era by William James, arguably one of the most important as well as earliest of modern students of this question. As he noted in 1904: "'Consciousness'...is the name of a nonentity, and has no right to a place among first principles. Those who still cling to it are clinging to a mere echo, the faint rumor left behind by the disappearing 'soul,' upon the air of philosophy....It seems to me that the hour is ripe for it to be openly and universally discarded."[178] Humphrey continues his own observations regarding James' contributions with the following: "James actually went further. 'Breath,' he wrote, 'moving outwards, between the glottis and nostrils, is, I am persuaded, the essence out of which philosophers have constructed the entity known the them as consciousness.' That the man who a few years earlier had popularized the idea of the 'stream of consciousness' in his *Principles of Psychology* should have become so hostile to the very term suggests an unusual degree of disillusionment."[179]

There are a great many additional views that can be studied by the serious student without the necessary clarification of our understanding of what is meant by consciousness. There is even the position that consciousness is not a singular monolithic and absolute force since there is no reason to conclude that consciousness cannot appear in small amounts or occasionally. The story of being in 'the groove' or 'the zone' whether playing a sport or music has been rightly noted by Julian Jaynes as well as anyone who has performed demanding athletic or creative tasks requiring no consciousness.[180] A concert pianist in performance, in fact, must not be conscious any more than a basketball player who is on a scoring run. There is nothing necessarily good about being very conscious or self-conscious, it simply may be a condition of some degree at some particular time for some people.[181] One can find both a solid summation of a multiple expression of consciousness, its meanings and a variation of Lockean thinking in *How the Mind Works* by Steven Pinker. It is his position that consciousness can be seen as a sentient activity: "Sentience without access might occur when you are engrossed in a conversation and suddenly realize that there is a jackhammer outside the window and that you have been hearing it, but not noticing it, for some time."[182] People driving on the highway for a long distance can sometimes forget where they are, especially if they use the route regularly and thus are in their own way 'in this groove.' Sometimes a person is conscious and at other times not. Such a subjective state is not something that everyone is prepared to exercise, argue for, exercise at all times, or even argue for its existence as a complete operation. While we have noted that there are those who would ask if there is anything good about being conscious,[183] Julian Jaynes will raise the same question but nevertheless conclude it does exists even if of no particular use. And Sartre noted this to some extent when he observed: "…consciousness is not for itself its own object. Its object is by nature outside of it, and that is why consciousness *posits* and *grasps* the object in the same act. Consciousness knows itself only as absolute inwardness. We shall call such a consciousness: consciousness in the first degree, or *unreflected* consciousness."[184]

That consciousness could be a matter of degree, as in "first degree", appears to be a fairly obvious conclusion for some, and a position of the biologist Stephen Jay Gould who wrote that, "*Homo sapiens* is one small twig [on the tree of life]....Yet our twig, for better or worse, has developed the most extraordinary new quality in all the history of multicellular life since the Cambrian explosion. We have invented consciousness with all its sequelae from Hamlet to Hiroshima."[185] In addition, Gould also denies "...consciousness to all nonhuman animals; [while] other scientists grant it to some animals but not all."[186] There are those who "...are even more restrictive than Gould: not even all people are conscious."[187] Thus, it can be argued that a conscious state of mind is occasional, singular, of a certain type and normally a matter of degrees in its appearance. Given its history there is little wonder that there are a rather large number of interpretations among these many scholars. Whatever stance one takes, however, the principle is the same since consciousness is not and has not been defined. Even the lesser mental state of awareness is not always present although there are other implied meanings in a literature replete with theories.

A representation of a variety of views has been given us by Pinker when he summarizes some of the positions taken:

> Sometimes 'consciousness' is just used as a lofty synonym for 'intelligence.' Gould, for example, must have been using it in this way. But there are three more-specialized meanings
>
> One is *self-knowledge*....including the ability to use a mirror, is no more mysterious than any other topic in perception and memory. ...
>
> A second sense is *sense of information*....This sense of consciousness...also embraces Freud's distinction between the conscious and the unconscious mind....
>
> Finally,...*sentience*: subjective experience, phenomenal awareness, raw fells, first-person present tense, 'what it is life' to be or do something, if you have to ask you'll never know.[188]

This is not to negate the larger picture that Pinker makes, especially in regard to the reservation offered by Colin McGinn:

> I am partial to a different solution, defended by McGinn and based on speculations by Noam Chomsky, the biologist Gunther Stent, and before them David Hume. Maybe philosophical problems are had not because they are divine or irreducible or meaningless or workday science, but because the mind of *Homo sapiens* lacks the cognitive equipment to solve them. We are organisms, not angels, and our minds are organs, not pipelines to the truth. Our minds evolved by natural selection to solve problems that were life-and-death matters of our ancestors, not to commune with

correctness or to answer any question we are capable of asking. We cannot hold ten thousand words in short-term memory. We cannot see in ultraviolet light. We cannot mentally rotate an object in the fourth dimension. And perhaps we cannot solve conundrums like free will and sentience.[189]

While this is but an introduction to the literature and should not be construed as being anywhere near copious, it does demonstrate a massive literary confusion seeking resolution.

As a conclusion for this work, there is one potential aspect of consciousness not yet given much exploration that should be noted; the idea of being capable of being more than singularly conscious and therefore the possibility— for want of a description—could be labeled as a poly-conscious mental state. While this can compound our problem of understanding it should still be at least indicated. The suggestion here is that perhaps it is possible for some to achieve an even 'higher' level or more complex expression of consciousness. Even Sartre—who agreed with the idea of consciousness by degree—also thought there was a multilevel consciousness when he states a view peculiar to the postmodern mind: "There is a well-known and much discussed link between modernism, understood as the reaction against instrumental civilization and co-opted Romanticism, multilevelled consciousness, and framing epiphanies, on one hand; and political reaction, on the other. The ascendancy of Pound and Eliot, with a partial assist from Yeats and Stevens, have made this very obtrusive. It is the amalgam we find in Hulme."[190] William James suggests an interpretation that, at the least, offers the idea of more than one consciousness operational around our sense of time and space:

> In short, the practically cognized present is no knife-edge, but a saddle-back, with a certain breadth of its own on which we sit perched, and from which we look in two directions into time. The unit of composition of our perception of time is a *duration*, with a bow and a stern, as it were—a rearward—and a forward-looking end. It is only as parts of this *duration-block* that the relation of *succession* of one end and the other is perceived. We do not feel one end and then feel the other after it, and from the perception of the succession infer an interval of time between, but we seem to feel the interval of time as a whole with its two ends embedded in it.[191]

The problem with any time interval is that the mind (consciousness?) is capable and often functioning outside of a fixed (clock or solar) time sequence. This idea was explicated earlier by both Robbe-Grillet and Borges in their fiction. Another writer from England, Penelope Lively (1933–), also demonstrated this mind set in her *City of the Mind*, discussing the experience of simultaneity of images and handled more or less successfully by her architect-protagonist:

> He is in London, on a May morning of the late twentieth century, but is also in many other places, and at other times. He twitches the knob of his radio: New York speaks to him, five hours ago, is superseded by Australia tomorrow and presently by India this evening. He learns of events that have not yet taken place, of deaths that have not yet occurred. He is...an English architect stuck in a traffic jam, a person of no great significance, and yet omniscient. For him, the world no longer turns; there is no day or night, everything and everywhere are instantaneous....He is told so much, and from so many sources, that he has learned to disregard, to let information filter through the mind and vanish, leaving impressions—a phrase, a fact, an image....He is an intelligent man, a man of compassion, but he can hear of a massacre on the other side of the globe and wonder as he listens if he remembered to switch on his answering machine. He is aware of this, and is disturbed. [192]

The German novelist Ernst Junger (1895–) is said to have subscribed to the theory of a "splitting of consciousness" in his brilliant essay *Uber den Schmerz* (On Pain).[193] One last writer who has confronted this question is Morton Hunt:

> Metacognition is thus the monitoring and guiding of one's own thought processes; it is mind observing itself and correcting itself. Even as I write this sentence, I am observing the thoughts and words that come next, am dissatisfied with them, change them, observe and judge the product, and finally declare myself content. (In doing so, just now, it seemed to me that I experienced yet a higher level of mind, for I watched my metamind watching my mind—a dizzying experience.
>
> I wonder, indeed, it this is not the reason we all sense our own freedom of will, even though, aside from those who believe in it on religious grounds, we consider free will an impossibility—an effect without a cause, an event that owes nothing to the past. But if it is an impossibility—why do we all experience it every day in countless ways? [194]

Recognizing that this is not an established thesis it is nevertheless something that appears to be a possibility according to some thinking and certainly worth further consideration. Even the anti-Cartesian dualism and ghost in the machine thinker, Gilbert Ryle, has at least implied that more than a singular and monolithic consciousness was possible, especially in regard to our inner self tied to external events:

> ...the occurrence of such an act of inner perception would require that the observer could attend to two things at the same time. He would, for example, be both resolving to get up early and concomitantly observing his act of resolving; attending to the programme of rising betimes and perceptually attending to his attending to

this programme. This objection is not, perhaps, logically fatal, since it might be argued that some people can, anyhow after practice combine attention to the control of a car with attention to the conversation. The fact that we speak of undivided attention suggests that the division of attention is a possibility, though some people would describe the division of attention as a rapid to-and-fro switch of attention, rather than as a synchronous distribution of it.[195]

Interestingly enough, Ryle also ties the multi-component of conscious states with that of both being awake and also of being capable to some extent in controlling one's dreams when asleep, an activity that may be known by more than a just a few.[196] There is one other example even if very hypothetical. This is the capacity of teenagers to do more than one mental activity at a time such as studying in front of a television, while listening to music and talking on the phone.

There has been one study that suggests the issue may be even more extreme than has been suggested: "A figure—it may not be reliable, but it sounds as if it's pretty near the truth—suggest that almost 80% of American *literate* teenagers, educated teenagers, and particularly in universities, can no longer read without an attendant noise, without music or a record player or a very complicated phenomenon which needs thinking about—a television screen, not looked at, but flickering at the corner of the field of perception."[197] As unique as this situation is of what may be considered a transformation of our conscious capacities to unexplored levels, there is at least some thought being given to an even more complex state, a triune (triadic) state of mind. Again Ryle suggests a category for a triune mind-set that at the least implies something more than a monothematic or even dualistic functional schema. "It has for a long time been taken for an indisputable axiom that the Mind is in some important sense tripartite, that is, that there are just three ultimate classes of mental processes. The Mind, or Soul, we are often told, has three parts, namely, Thought, Feeling and Will; or, more solemnly, the Mind or Soul functions in three irreducibly different modes, the Cognitive mode, the Emotional mode and the Cognative mode. This traditional dogma is not only self-evident, it is such a welter of confusions and false inferences that it is best to give up any attempt to refashion it."[198]

To argue that thought, feeling and will are part and parcel of the mental process, of course, may not sit well with many thinkers who would argue that while thought is a cognitive activity, emotions may not be. As for willfulness, Dennett denies freedom of choice, and others, especially those in the logical positivist school, would also deny the existence of the mind itself. Another writer on the subject, however, Stanely L. Scott has offered additional support for the potential for a more triune conscious state. He suggests: "The individual is always confronted with a choice between a dyadic and a triadic orientation to any fact, whether it is a text, a molecule, or a neighbor. But triadic interpretation, as in the discovery or invention of a philosophical idea to interpret a text, has a peculiar power to extend consciousness."[199]

There is additionally the work of an earlier thinker of the twentieth-century, the idealist Josiah Royce (1855–1916), a thinker influenced by Charles Pierce. This was a time when again the poet and the philosopher were not necessarily antithetical in their interests and orientations. It was Royce that "...drew the conclusion that the fundamental structure of all experience is triadic. The elements of the triad may exist within a single human consciousness, as in the act of interpreting my own idea to myself. More typically, according to Royce, consciousness is engaged in social encounters between individuals in a community of interpretation, and between persons and objective facts."[200] To speak of consciousness beyond some narrow clinical context where the whole of the real is an interior (and often mechanical) state had yet to take hold with our contemporary neurophysiological approaches. For Royce there were interpretative, perspective and conceptional parts in a conscious act and no reason to believe any one of the three would take precedence. As Scott put it "...Royce claims that the interpretive process 'transcends both perception and conception'...yet 'touches the heart of reality.'"[201] Yet, the interpretive must lie within the experiences of perceptions and conceptions. We do not see a forest without a preconceived concept of where we are going and what we are doing. Is there an absolute objective perception? Not in the arts or even in the physics of the twentieth century. Again we are thrown up against the wall of modernity and post-modernity, words themselves that are as likely to confuse as to enlighten.

For the historian there are two problems demonstrated particularly with this and the previous chapters—closeness. The more attached to the condition described the more problematic is the discussion. What will future historians say of the term *consciousness* in its setting of the twentieth century cannot be guessed. Being conscious, introspective, reflective and a self are inner conditions that perhaps are best explored by the creative mind rather than that of the scholar unless the scholar can be equally creative. After all, the century began with a three dimensional world. With Einstein there was a shift, "...in world view. 'It appears therefore more natural to think of physical reality as a four-dimensional existence, instead of, as hitherto, the evolution of a three-dimensional existence.'"[202] Perhaps consciousness is a multi-faceted phenomenon where many components once thought exclusive of each other are part and parcel of any integrated definition or understanding: awareness, memory, thought, knowledge, introspection or more. If all forms of time and space can be made interchangeable, it is possible that our definitions and interpretations have been far too exclusionary.[203]

And perhaps even here there is a serious role in all of this for curiosity.

Conclusion

Chemically speaking, fear is close to curiosity—hence many so-called terrors have an eerie attraction.[1]

That death is an absolute certainty is ironically its own certainty. From death, certainty, to language and faith, and finally the soul and conscience, we have traveled an extremely long road that leads to the first plateau of our interior existence. It is from here that we gained a secular space and time since the sword of salvation proved and inadequate answer to fundamental questions regarding our ontology. With the failure of a certainty of an after-life, conscience was replaced by consciousness as the soul metamorphosed into a primitive self (psyche) where salvation eventually became the act and art of an authentic life.

It has been said that historians are detectives, not unlike research scientists, although in a different manner.[2] Where there is such a search there are always some discoveries and some failures. To compound this difficulty, the writing of history is an art which only makes it that much more problematic. Thus the topic studied here is one of discovery and hypothesis from the best that data can offer, while disengagement, as Bacon suggested, is of primary concern. The implications of this study have grown out of sources and suggestions and are only meant as a guide for further study. Given these circumstances, therefore, this has proven to be a work not with a fixed conclusion since much of any conclusion has simply offered more questions. The German term *nachwort* would be somewhat more appropriate since this is really a matter of an afterthought for those so inclined to continue an historic analysis of our evolution into conscious beings.

Fear, so central to that certainty we live with, is a natural force in our mental and emotional makeup, thus offering Nietzsche an opportunity again to note his famed analysis that we are all born in fear and laziness. This human condition must eventually be itself considered as part of the panorama and component in any significant transformation of our psyche. Not being static beings implies far more than this work is prepared to venture into. And that we are never finished until after it matters only adds to the difficulties for our understanding. This is not to imply that it follows necessarily that there is any one cause for the existence of consciousness assuming that there is any cause at all other than the historic circumstances. Context, our history, is the necessary ingredient for expanding any critical examination of a conscious self in its development, expansion and confusion. And even this is but a beginning, for the difficulties as has been noted by some are insurmountable although this writer is not prepared to discontinue the search.

As for dating there is no doubt that the earliest date for consciousness would have to be the seventeenth century although that it was then more an introduction than a satisfactory explication. Consciousness like self and individuality are very modern conditions that have only appeared more recently. Ego was early and now can be perceived as a potential hindrance to becoming a self and if I were to offer some metaphoric expression for that meaning it would be as follows: We can think of a teeter totter of individuality where we place the ego on one side and the self on the other. For most people it is the ego side, our youthful emotions and mentality, that dominates while for some it can be that the teeter-totter moves back and forth with one side at any given moment dominating more than the other. The self begins to come to the fore occasionally and for some, those going beyond their ego, even a great deal. It is here, not in the ego, but in the self that consciousness becomes activated. One could imagine that where that side of the teeter totter where the self takes hold is where consciousness grows and the whole process becomes simply irrelevant, much like certainty and death. Here is where curiosity takes hold and the creative side of our being comes to dominate.

The introduction offered several questions which appeared given the nature of the work and would are an appropriate way to close this study, especially as most have one way or the other already been at least implied. The questions here suggested are meant to encourage further thought and perhaps eventually additional studies that could offer further clarification:

1. What is the difference between awareness and consciousness?
2. What is the difference between self and individuality?
3. What if anything is the difference between being a self-conscious reflective individual and a self-reflective conscious individual?
4. Is the creation of consciousness a matter of historical accident or by way of some natural order as in fulfilling both some purpose of order and or of structure?

5. Is the appearance, growth and maturation a result of an accident of nature that in the end creates a self-conscious reflective individual?
6. Does an ego need to exist within someone before that person can begin to develop into individuality, into a self capable of consciousness?
7. Is it an offense against structure to object to competitiveness that requires a matrix of construction prior to activity?
8. If consciousness is not necessary for our existence than why has it developed, and then so slowly, over millennium, and the appears only among a minority of people?
9. If there are relatively lower and higher stages of consciousness, then what is the mark for drawing such a distinction?
10. What is, if it is, the fundamental difference between consciousness as an interior experience devoid of objects and consciousness of objects?
11. Is consciousness an absolute or does it appear only in *degrees* from a very little consciousness to a very full consciousness?
12. Is consciousness singular or is there in fact a variety of differing types of consciousness?
13. What if anything is the correlation, similarity and differences, between having an ego and having a self?
14. Is mature self-consciousness an evolutionary development that grows out of our possessing an immature self-consciousness as a child or teen, one of awkwardness and discomfort; or are these two entirely different species?
15. If cognition and fear of death is part of a beginning of consciousness could a more mature developed consciousness mitigate this fear for those who face this situation?
16. Is the ego with which we are born with something that we hold onto when we first discover our mortality at approximately the age of 6 or 7 years (depending on the genetics of a particular person) and thus can be stuck for the rest of their lives with the 'camera on me' version of self-consciousness?
17. Is there a correlation between the maturation of consciousness in our day with that of the appearance of existential?

18. Is it possible to yet achieve a higher level of consciousness than already experienced?
19. Is possible that there is a poly-conscious state of mind that has been occasionally realized and which may appear even more in the future?

APPENDIX I

Quasi-Essentialistic Characterizations

Terms Associated with Consciousness

Alienation	Freedom	Predetermined
Awareness	Future	Private
Authenticity	Genius	Reflective
Authority	Happiness	Reflection
Conscience	Humor	Relative
Control	Imagination	Rights
Curiosity	History	Secular
Degree	Individuality	Self
Developmental	Inner	Self-consciousness
Disengagement	Insight	Self-humor
Diversity	Interiority	Singularity
Dynamic	Introspection	Solipsism
Evolutionary	Knowledge	Space
Estrangement	Language	Static
Existential	Literacy	Subjective
Fantasy	Maturation	Time
Fear	Memory	Variable
Fixed	Open	Will
Focus	Post-modernism	

Some of these varied terms could possibly be applied to a given specific individual at a specific moment when consciousness is applicable and possibly contribute to what is meant when one is exercising one's consciousness. For any one person's specific experience of consciousness it is possible that any combination and/or degree of presence of any of these (and some not noted) terms may very well be part of that experience we label conscious.

Appendix II

Contrastive Terms

List of Terms reflective of Western historic mental and social changes drawn from past to present assumptions.

Past	Present
Absolute	Relative
Aware	Conscious
Belief	Skepticism
Class	Mass
Closed	Open
Collective	Singular
Communal	Individualistic
Community	Isolation
Consistent	Change
Dependence	Autonomy
Determinism	Freedom
Divine	Human
Egoism	Self
External	Introduction
Faith	Rational
Family	Alone
Fate	Free Will
Female	Masculine
Fixed	Evolution
Generalized	Particularistic
Hierarchical	Lineal
Historic	Existential
Holistic	Systems
Homo Sapiens	Homo Economics
Integrated	Alienation
Local	Planetary
Meaning	Nihilism
Mystery	Science
Natural	Contrived

PAST	PRESENT
Oral	Written
Organic	Mechanistic
Prejudice	Reflective
Pre-Modern	Post-Modern
Public	Private
Qualifying	Quantifying
Quiet	Noisy
Religion	Secular
Rural	Urban
Sensible	Absurdity
Shame	Pride
Societal	Personal
Sociological	Psychological
Spiritual	Materialistic
Universal	Specialization

These terms of contrast are intended not as absolutes but only as indicators. Example: An organic attitude and assumption tended to dominate more than a mechanistic attitude in antiquity but that does not mean a Pythagorean, Aristotelean or Heron of Alexandria would be uninterested, indifferent or incompetent regarding the mechanistic any more than an engineer today has no sense of an organic approach, notwithstanding the orientation towards the technical, mechanical and electrical. These too, are teeter-totters.

Appendix III

Cross-References

Varied Adjectives Applied to Consciousness by various authors in this work.

Term	Author, Page #
Absolute Cons.	Sass, 328.
Access-Cons.	Pinker, 136.
Alienated Cons.	Berman, 17.
Altered Cons.	Weil, 51; Wolf, 327.
Altered States of Cons.	Pelletier, 11; Wilber, 301; Wolf, 269.
Alternate States of Con.	Pribram, 10.
Anticonsciousness	Arguelle, 208.
Area-Cons.	Janson, 506.
Augmented Cons.	Coan, 68.
Authentic Cons.	Aquila, 177.
Body Cons.	Aquila, 555.
Capacious Cons.	Bloom (2002), 5.
Causal Cons.	Pearce, 80.
Class Cons.	Dallymar, 119; Kerrigan, 47.
Co-Consciousness.	Mackie, 178.
Coconsciousness	Hilgard, 209.
Collective Cons.	Coan, 126; Kahler, 90–91.
Concerned Cons.	Behan, 65, 68–70.
Conservative Cons.	Lowe, 29.
Contemporary Cons.	Monaco, 72.
Cosmic Cons.	Arquelle, 6; Merrill, 5.
Core Cons.	Damasio, 82–106.
Controlled Cons.	Coan, 51.
Creative Cons.	May, 120.
Degree of Cons.	Damasio, 4, 55, 122; Sartre (1957) 45, 58.
Different States of Cons.	Wilber, 64.

Differentiated Cons.   Slinn, 27; Webb, 73, 79, 80.
Dream Cons.   Levin, 99; Pearce, 80.
Dreaming Cons.   Shattuck, 35.
Discrete States of Cons.   Tart, 215.
Doubt Cons.   Sass, 347.
Ecological Cons.   Arguelles, 102.
Ego Cons.   Gablick, 178; Monaco, 96–97; Neumann, xvii, 26, 33, 275, 294; Wilber, 186.

Egotistical Cons.   Engleberg, 102.
Embodied Cons.   Lowe, 168.
Emotional Cons.   Lowe, 99.
Empirical Cons.   Caton, 35, 53ff, 169, 185.
Essential Cons.   Webb, 232.
European Cons.   Arguelle, 250; Weintraub, 58,
Excessive Cons.   Sass, 173.
Exclusive States of Cons.   Wilber, 304.
Explicit Cons.   Pearce, 80.
Extended Cons.   Damasio, 195–233.
False Cons.   Hunter, 40; Monaco, 94; Schneider, 41

Flowing Cons.   William James, passim.
Feminine Cons.   Coan, 133.
Foreshortened Cons.   Keen, 65–66.
Formless Cons.   Wilber, 97.
Fragmented Cons.   Ingram, 176.
Global Cons.   Pelletier, 12.
Half-Cons.   Burckhardt, 245.
Heightened Cons.   Dennett, passim; Eistenstein, 432; Mitchell, 640; O'Kelley, 60; Sypher, 76.

Hierarchy Cons.   Wilber, 272–74.
Higher State of Cons.   Wilber, 64.
Historical Cons.   Wilber, 203; Mazzeo, 39, 49–50; Stromberg, 303.

Holistic Cons.   Berman, 23; Hunter, 13.
Human Cons.   Lowe, 90; Rossman, 24; Wilber, 7.
Hyperconsciousness   Solomon, 32.

Hypostatized Cons. Iser, 154–55.
Image Cons. Barfield, 124; Burrow, xiv.
Implicate Cons. Pearce, 80.
Increasing Cons. Wilber, 7.
Individual Cons. Coan, 126; Monaco, 4.
Impersonal Cons. Hayman, 101.
Integral Cons. Kramer, xxxiv, xxviii.
Intentional Cons. Lauer, 81; Webb, 96.
Intra-mundaine Sartre, (1957) 59.
Introspective Cons. Churchland, 74.
Invented Cons. Pinker, 133.
Lowered Cons. Leonard, 33.
Magical Cons. Kramer, xxii.
Matriarchal Cons. Coan, 133.
Masculine Cons. Coan, 133.
Methodological Self-Cons. Caton, 55.
Moral Cons. Taylor, 333.
Multileveled Cons. Taylor, 483.
Mythical Cons. Richter, 29; Cassirer, xvi.
National Cons. Ferguson, 8, 17; Monaco, 100.
Naturalistic Cons. Taylor, 5.
New Consciousness. Hunter, 31; Keen, 1; Singh, 144.
Non-divided Cons. Rossman, 60.
Non-disciplinary Cons. Keen, 1.
Non-human animal Cons. Rossman, 24.
Nonparticipating Cons. Berman, 71, 91, 143.
Non-reflective Cons Rossman, 60.
Normal Cons. Pirandello, 138.
Objective Cons. Wilson, 265.
Occasional Cons. Jaynes (1976), 22.
Operational Cons. Wilber, 273.
Ordered Cons. Coan, 51.
Original Cons. Lauer, 71.
Ordinary Cons. Ornstein, 459.
Ontological Cons. Keen, 7, 134.
Overacute Cons. Engleberg, 99.
Participating Barfield, 81, 87, 109; Berman, 16, 23, 65, 145.

Particular Cons.	Berger, 15.
Particular State Cons.	Wilber, 303.
Patrirachal Cons.	Coan, 133.
Paying Attention Cons.	Wolf, 211.
Perceptual Cons.	Churchland, 74; Collins, 86; Reid.
Pre-Homeric Cons.	Berman, 73.
Permanent Cons.	Engleberg, 244.
Premodern Cons.	Berman, 73.
Pre-refective Cons.	Rossman, 60.
Personal Cons.	Ornstein, 170.
Perspectival Cons.	Lowe, 75.
Physical Cons.	Pearce, 80.
Planetary Cons.	Dallymar, 266.
Political Cons.	Chabod, 53.
Polycons.	Baars, 61f; Hunt, 231; Miller, 330, [this term implied].
Post Cons.	Neuman, 23.
Post-modern Cons.	Berman, 73.
Post-resurrection Cons.	Behan, 75.
Post-war Cons.	Hunter, 13.
Precons.	Dennet, 126; Hampden-Turner, 10; Lowe, 168; Wolf, 116.
Pre-Homeric Cons.	Berman, 73.
Present State of Cons.	Wilber, 303.
Pre-reflective Cons.	Rossman, 6, 100–1, 128, 149, 162.
Pre-resurrection Cons.	Behan, 75.
Presentational Cons.	Brown, 153.
Pre-theoretical Cons.	Berger, 12, 204.
Primal Cons.	Leonard, 20.
Primary Cons.	Burrow, 33; Merrell, 24.
Primordial Cons.	Merrill, 181, 192.
Protocons.	Eccles, 14; Pettletier, 242–3.
Protoplasmic Cons.	Wilber, 25.
Pure Cons.	Iser, 154; Merrill, 263.
Quale Cons.	Flanagan, 63.
Rational Cons.	Merrill, 184.
Reactionary Cons.	Monaco, 4, 91, 100.
Receptive Cons.	Monaco, 4.

Reflective Cons.	Rossman, 6, 7, 23, 24, 177.
Reflexive Cons.	Hariman, 14; Humphrey, 7; Lowe, 116.
Relative Cons.	Merrill, 43.
Representation Cons.	Brown, 153.
Resurrection Cons.	Behan, 75.
Revolutionary Cons.	Ingram, 176; Monaco, 4, 53, 67.
Schizophrenic Cons.	Sass, 40.
Scientific Cons.	Berman, 17.
Second-Degree Cons.	Sartre, (1957) 58.
Self-determined Cons.	Errol, 260.
Sensor-motor Cons.	Brown, 153.
Sleep Cons.	Pearce, 80.
Social Cons.	Errol, 239.
Solipsitic Cons.	Collins, 74; Karl, 17; Monaco, 37; Sass, 330.
Streams of Cons.	Dennett, 67; Furst, 141; Humphrey, 35; James, 239; Kern, 1, 24; Popper-Eccles, 89; Scott, 61, 64.
Sub-Cons.	Taylor, 107.
Subjective Cons.	Berger, 11; Engelberg, 96; Flanagan, 134; Scott, 106.
Super Cons.	Coan, 126; Wilber, 86; Wilber, 8, 31, 59, 70, 181.
Supra-implicate Cons.	Pearce, 80.
Subtle Cons.	Pearce, 80.
Symbolic Cons.	Brown, 153.
Theoretical Cons.	Berger, 12; Lowe, 57.
Time Consciousness.	Kern, 257; Lowe, 41, 112; Taylor, 463.
Transcendent Cons.	Merrill, 24, 39.
Transcendental Cons.	Dallymar, 2; Pribram, 11.
Transformed Cons.	Coan, 68.
Unachoring Cons.	Sass, 347.
Unconscious Cons.	Plotnitsky, 166; Dennett, 126.
Undifferentiated Cons.	d'Aquili, 130; Webb, 73, 78–79.
Unhappy Cons.	Engleberg, 91, 99, 100.
Universal Cons.	Engleberg, 95, 104; Slinn, 27, 32.

Unreflective Cons.　　　　　　Sartre, 58.
Ultimate State of Cons.　　　　Wilber, 128, 294, 300–3.
Visual Imagery Cons.　　　　　Hofstader, 364.
Wake Cons.　　　　　　　　　Pearce, 80; Wilson, 265.

ADVERBIAL/ADJECTIVAL REPRESENTATION

Consciousness Gap　　　　　　Leonard, 111.
Cons. Perception　　　　　　　Kissin, 144, 154.
Cons. Plane　　　　　　　　　McCrone, 135.
Cons. Pecognition　　　　　　　Kissin, 154.
Cons. Paising　　　　　　　　　Monaco, 70.
Cons. Thought　　　　　　　　Monaco, 22.

SELF-CONSCIOUSNESS

Self-Consciousness is so ubiquitous among these and so many other authors that the list would simply be too long to include.

This list is, like all else, is an indication and anything but copious for there are many others not listed from racial consciousness to plastic consciousness which are not listed.

Notes

Abbreviations
JHI=Journal of the History of Ideas
OED=Oxford English Dictionary

Introduction

1. Steven Runciman, "Preface," *A History of the Crusades*, (1951; repr., London: Folio Society, 1994), xii-xiii.
2. See Appendix II.
3. A larger list of questions is suggested in the Conclusion
4. Special thanks is offered to Dr. Harold Walsh for his contribution of the phrase "quasi-essentialistic characterizations," and aiding in translations of classical Greek and Latin.
5. Nils Kvastad, "Semantics in the Methodology of the History of Ideas," JHI, 38:1 (1977), 157-74:157. Also see the following footnote.
6. Donald R. Kelley, "What is Happening to the History of Ideas?" JHI, 51:1 (1990), 3-25. Also see in the same article, 11-12 for a perusal of varied Lovejoy's rubrics for the discipline of the history of ideas. Also see Arthur Lovejoy, "Reflections on the History of Ideas," JHI 1:1 (1940), 3- 29.

Chapter One

1. Jacquetta & Sir Leonard Wooley Hawkes, *History of Mankind: Prehistory and the Beginnings of Civilization*, (NY: Harper & Row, 1963), 104.
2. Hannah Arendt, *The Life of the Mind, Willing*, 2 volumes, (NY: Harcourt Brace Jovanovich, 1978), II, 43.
3. Robert Hunter, *The Storming of the Mind: Inside the Consciousness Revolution*, (NY: Doubleday & Co., Inc., 1972), 212.
4. Morton Hunt, *The Universe Within: A New Science Explores the Human Mind*, (NY: Simon and Schuster, 1982), 46.
5. Hunt, 46.
6. John Pfeiffer, *The Emergence of Man*, (NY: Harper & Row, 1972), 192–93.
7. Richard W. Coan, *Human Consciousness And Its Evolution: A Multidimensional View*, (New York: Greenwood Press, 1987,) 46.
8. Coan, 46.
9. Coan, 46.
10. Philip Leiberman, *Uniquely Human: The Evolution of Speech, Thought, and Selfless Behavior*, (Cambridge: Harvard University Press, 1991), 38.
11. Leiberman, 38.
12. Walter J. Ong, "Communications and the Rise of Individualism," *Views on Individualism: Presentation by Israel M.Kirzner, Walter J.Ong, Mancur Olson, and Kurt Baier*, ed. by Danna Card Charron, (St. Louis Humanities Forum, Missouri Committee for the Humanities, 1986), 30–31.

13. Parry, 6.
14. Parry, 7.
15. Parry, 5–6.
16. See Herodotus, *Histories*.
17. See Thucydides, *The Peloponnesian War*.
18. Kurt von Fritz, "Nooz and Noein in the Homeric Poems." *Classical Philology*, 38, no. 2 (1943), 79.
19. Jaynes, *Origins*, 22.
20. Jaynes, *Origins*, 24.
21. Jaynes, *Origins*, 89.
22. Jaynes, *Origins*, 72.
23. Jaynes, *Origins*, 228.
24. Jaynes, *Origins*, 13.
25. Jaynes, *Origins*, 22.
26. Jaynes, *Origins*, 22.
27. Jaynes, *Origins*, 24.
28. Jaynes, *Origins*, 28.
29. Jaynes, *Origins*, 47.
30. Jaynes, *Origins*, 48–66.
31. Jaynes, *Origins*, 2.
32. Jaynes, *Origins*, 69.
33. Jaynes, *Origins*, 69.
34. Jaynes, *Origins*, 79.
35. Jaynes, *Origins*, 273.
36. Jaynes, *Origins*, 276.
37. Jaynes, *Origins*, 45.
38. Whittemore, *Pure Lives*, 6.
39. Deborah K. Modrak, *Aristotle: The Power of Perception*, (Chicago: University of Chicago Press, 1997), 8. See also W. Hardie, "Concepts of Consciousness in Aristotle," *Mind* 85: 388–411; and C. Kahn, "Sensation and Consciousness in Aristotle's Psychology," *Archiv fur Geschechte der Philosophie* 43–81: 48.
40. Modrak, 8.
41. Whittemore, *Pure Lives*, 6.
42. Modrak, 134.
43. Modrak, 151.
44. Modrak, 152.
45. Modrak, 133.
46. Modrak, 133.
47. Modrak, 133.
48. Modrak, 133.
49. See Chapter Six.
50. Modrak, 11.
51. Modrak, 151.
52. Modrak, 151.
53. Modrak, 151.
54. Modrak, 53.
55. Modrak, 152.
56. Whittemore, *Pure Lives*, 5.

57. Geoffrey Parrinder, ed., *World Religions. From Ancient History to the Present*, (NY: Facts on File, 1973), 161.
58. Anthony Long, "Ethics of Stoicism," *Dictionary of the History of Ideas*, ed. Philip P. Wiener, (NY: Charles Scribner's Sons, 1973), vol. 3, 319.
59. Long, 322.
60. Long, 319.
61. Long, 322.
62. Marcus Aurelius, *Marcus Aurelius: Meditations*, trans Maxwell Stanifort, (Baltimore: Penguin Books, 1964), 4: 3.
63. Delumeau, 190.
64. Delumeau, 375.
65. John Bowker, ed., *Dictionary of World Religions*, (Oxford: Oxford University Press, 1997), 965.
66. Delumeau, 193.
67. Kaufmann, *Religions*, 61. See also Paul Newman, *A History of Terror. Fear & Dread Through the Ages*, (Stroud: Sutton Publishing, 2000).
68. Charles Hampden-Turner, *Maps of the Mind*, (London: Mitchell Beazley Publishers Ltd., 1981), 67. See also Ernest Becker, *Denial of Death*, (NY: Free Press, 1973).
69. Carl D. Schneider, *Shame Exposure and Privacy*, (Boston: Beacon Press, 1977), 111. In regard to the questions of reason on of faith in the west, the reader may want to turn to Charles Freeman, *The Closing of the Western Mind: The Rise of Faith and Fall of Reason*, (NY:Alfred A. Knopf, 2003).
70. Schneider, 78.

Chapter Two

1. Paul Saenger, *Space Between Words: The Origins of Silent Reading*, (Stanford: Stanford University Press, 1997), 1.
2. Owen Barfield, *Saving Appearances: A Study in Idolatry*, (London: Faber and Faber, 1957), 98. For those interested in the question of uncertainty and doubt see Jennifer Michael Hecht, *Doubt: A History. The Great Doubters and Their Legacy of Innovation from Socrates and Jesus to Thomas Jefferson and Emily Dickenson*, (San Francisco: Harper San Francisco), 2003.
3. Augustine, Bishop of Hippo, *City of God*, trans. Gerald G. Walsh et al., (Garden City, NY: Image Books, 1958), 413–26.
4. For Einstein this view was expressed in regard to the discovery of the atom. There is an unpublished dissertation that documents this conclusion that assumptions are the last thing to change: See Walter R. Martin, "Ideas in the Political Life of England, 1760–1783," (University of Missouri, 1966).
5. Wolfgang Iser, *The Range of Interpretation*, (NY: Columbia University Press, 2000), 5. The two most common mistakes people can make about history is that: 1) it repeats itself; or 2) that history is a singular and continuous narrative thread.
6. Augustine, Bishop of Hippo, *Confessions*, trans by D. S. Pine-Coffin, (Baltimore: Penguin Books, 1964), 397.
7. Reed Whittemore, *Pure Lives: The Early Biographers*, (Baltimore: Johns Hopkins University Press, 1988), 36.
8. Gary Wills, *Saint Augustine*, (NY: Penguin Books, 1999).

9. Harold Bloom, *A Map of Misreading*, (NY: Oxford University Press, 1980), 85 cited in Iser, *Range*, 5.
10. Long, George. "Forward," *The Meditations of the Emperor Marcus Aurelius Antoninus*, by Marcus Aurelius Antoninus, trans. George Long [1873], (Garden City: Doubleday & Company, Inc.1960) i.
11. Whittemore, *Pure Lives*, 2.
12. Iser, *Range*, 5.
13. Benjamin Jowett, *Works of Plato*, (NY: The Jefferson Press, 1892).
14. Willis Barnstone, *The Poetics of Translation: History, Theory, Practice*, (New Haven: Yale University Press, 1993), 18.
15. Iser, *Range*, 5.
16. Jerome David Levin, *Theories of the Self*, (Washington: Hemisphere Pub. Corp., 1992), 5.
17. Whittemore, *Pure Lives*, 36.
18. Whittemore, *Pure Lives*, 7.
19. Stephen Bertman, *Handbook to life in Ancient Mesopotamia*, (NY: Facts on File, 2002).
20. Wills, passim.
21. Whittemore, *Pure Lives*, 39.
22. Whittemore, *Pure Lives*, 36.
23. Whittemore, *Pure Lives*, 39.
24. Whittemore, *Pure Lives*, 38.
25. Whittemore, *Pure Lives*, 38.
26. Whittemore, *Pure Lives*, 37.
27. Whittemore, *Pure Lives*, 37.
28. Whittemore, *Pure Lives*, 11.
29. Whittemore, *Pure Lives*, 3.
30. Whittemore, *Pure Lives*, 3.
31. Whittemore, *Pure Lives*, 6.
32. Reed Whittemore, *Whole Lives: Shapers of Modern Biography*, (Baltimore: Johns Hopkins University Press, 1989), 6, 105.
33. Whittemore, *Pure Lives*, 105.
34. Whittemore, *Pure Lives*, 12.
35. Whittemore, *Pure Lives*, 12.
36. Whittemore, *Pure Lives*, 11.
37. Whittemore, *Pure Lives*, 5.
38. Whittemore, *Pure Lives*, 2.
39. Whittemore, *Pure Lives*, 38–39.
40. Whittemore, *Pure Lives*, 40.
41. Whittemore, *Pure Lives*, 40.
42. Whittemore, *Pure Lives*, 6.
43. Whittemore, *Pure Lives*, 4.
44. Whittemore, *Pure Lives*, 38.
45. Augustine, Bishop of Hippo, *De Trinitatae*, X, iii, 5 and VIII, vi, 9, trans. by and cited in E. M. Curley, *Descartes Against the Skeptics*, (Cambridge: Harvard University Press, 1978), 173.
46. Gareth B. Matthews, *Thought's Ego in Augustine and Descartes*, (Ithaca, NY: Cornell University Press, 1992), 189.
47. Curley, 172–73.

Notes to pp. 65–77 | 509

48. Charles Taylor, Sources of the Self: The Making of the Modern Identity, (Cambridge: Harvard University Press, 1989), 131.
49. Taylor, 156.
50. Matthews, ix.
51. Levin, 5.
52. Levin, 5.
53. See Karl Joachim Weintraub, The Value of the Individual: Self and Circumstance in Autobiography, (Chicago: University of Chicago Press, 1978). Also see Whittemore, Pure Lives.
54. Timothy David Barnes, Tertullian. A Historical and Literary Study, (Oxford: Clarendon Press, 1971), 114.
55. Taylor, 143
56. Taylor, 143.
57. Matthews, 142.
58. Whittemore, Pure Lives, 37.
59. Whittemore, Whole Lives, 5.
60. Whittemore, Pure Lives, 45.
61. Whittemore, Pure Lives, 40–41.
62. Taylor, 143.
63. Ong, 33.
64. Paul Saenger, "Silent Reading: Its Impact on Late Medieval Script and Society," Viator: Medieval and Renaissance Studies, 13, (1982), 372.
65. See Charles Homer Haskins, The Renaissance of the Twelfth Century, (NY: Meridian Books, 1962). Also see Thomas Cahill, How the Irish Saved Civilization: The Untold Story of Ireland's Heroic Role from the Fall of Rome to the Rise of Medieval Europe, (NY: Doubleday, 1995).
66. Cahill, passim.
67. See Richard E. Sullivan, ed., The Gentle Voices of Teachers. Aspects of Learning in the Carolingian Age, (Columbus: Ohio State University Press, 1995). Cahill, passim.
68. Barfield, 88–89.
69. Ong, 33.
70. Augustine, Confessions, Bk.VI, 114.
71. Saenger, 370.
72. Saenger, 370.
73. Saenger, 370.
74. Saenger, 370–71.
75. Saenger, 371.
76. Saenger, 371.
77. Saenger, 371.
78. Saenger, 371.
79. Saenger, 372–73.
80. Saenger, 373.
81. Saenger, 373.
82. Saenger, 373–74.
83. Saenger, 337.
84. Saenger, 373–74.
85. Saenger, 382–83.
86. Saenger, 378–89.

87. G. Waitz, ed., *Hermanni liber de restauratione S. Martini Tornacensis*, MGH Scriptores 14 (Hanover 1893) 313, trans. John Willis Clark, *The Care of Books* (Cambridge 1904) 268, cited in Saenger, 379.
88. Saenger, 379.
89. Saenger, 379.
90. Saenger, 372.
91. Saenger, 378.
92. Saenger, 378.
93. Saenger, 390. This 'intimacy' for the author would eventually contribute to the idea of solitude, much as Dostoevski's *The Death of Ivan Illiach*.
94. Saenger, 383–84.
95. Saenger, 386.
96. Isidore of Seville, *Sententiae*, 3.14.9, trans. and cited in Saenger, 383–84.
97. Saenger, 405.
98. Saenger, 397.
99. Saenger, 391.
100. Saenger, 385.
101. Saenger, 385.
102. Saenger, 390.
103. Saenger, 410.
104. Saenger, 399.
105. Saenger, 399.
106. Saenger, 401.
107. Thomas à Kempis *The Imitation of Christ*, (c.1415–1429).
108. Saenger, 399-400.
109. See Elizabeth Eisenstein, *The Printing Press as Agent of Change: Communications and Cultural Transformations in Early Modern Europe*, (Cambridge: Cambridge University Press, 1979), opening chapter title and chapter 4, footnote 41.
110. Saenger, 399–400.
111. See Sean Desmond Healy, *Boredom, Self, and Culture*, (London: Fairleigh Dickinson University Press, 1984).
112. Saenger, 414.
113. Saenger, 414.
114. Saenger, 386 for a discussion on the other Gothic, that of "Gothic cursive script."
115. Baldassare Castiglione, *The Book of the Courtier* (1528).
116. John Aberth, *From the Brink of the Apocalypse. Confronting Famine, War, Plague, and Death in the Later Middle Ages*, (NY: Routledge, 2001), 182.
117. Aberth, 183.
118. Aberth, 232.
119. Aberth, 234.
120. Jean Delumeau, *Sin and Fear: The Emergence of a Western Guilt Culture 13th–18th Centuries*, trans. Eric Nicholson, (NY: St. Martin's Press, 1989), 198.
121. William J. Courtenay, *Schools and Scholars in Fourteenth-Century England*, (Princeton: Princeton University Press, 1987), 5, footnote 5.
122. Saenger, 410–11.
123. Saenger, 71–77.
124. Alberto Manguel, *History of Reading*, (NY: Viking Books, 1996), 49.
125. Saenger, 411.

Notes to pp. 91–104 | 511

126. Saenger, 411.
127. Saenger, 411.

Chapter Three

1. Hans Nachod, "Petrarca: Introduction," *The Renaissance Philosophy of Man*, eds. Ernst Cassirer, P. O. Kristeller and T. H. Randall, (Chicago: University of Chicago Press, 1948), 23.
2. Theodore E. Mommsen, "Petrarch's Conception of the 'Dark Ages,'" *Mommsen, Medieval and Renaissance Studies*, ed. Eugene F. Rice, Jr., (Ithaca, NY: Cornell University Press, 1959), 121–22.
3. Peter Burke, *The Italian Renaissance. Culture and Society in Italy*, (1972; Princeton: Princeton University Press, 1986), 178.
4. Burke, 178–79.
5. Burke, 179.
6. Burke, 179.
7. See Peter W. Juszyk, *The Discovery of Spoken Language*, (Cambridge: MIT Press, 1997).
8. Richter, 3.
9. Roberto Weiss, *The Renaissance Discovery of Classical Antiquity*, (London: Blackwell 1969), 16.
10. Burke, 179. Two representative views of the very few who would make of Dante more than a Renaissance figure than Medieval are Weiss, 563 and Mommsen, Petrarch, 109.
11. Mommsen, Petrarch, 114–15.
12. Mommsen, Petrarch, 112.
13. Weiss, 16.
14. Theodore E. Mommsen, "The Last Will: A Personal Document of Petrarch's Old Age," *Mommsen, Medieval and Renaissance Studies*, ed., Eugene F. Rice, Jr., (Ithaca, NY: Cornell University Press, 1959), 233.
15. Mommsen, Last Will, 231.
16. Mommsen, Last Will, 231.
17. Christopher S. Celenza, "Late Antiquity and the Florentine Renaissance: Historiographical Parallels," *JHI*, 62: 1 (2001), 34 and *passim*.
18. Weiss, 3.
19. L. Varga, *Das Schlagwort vom "finsteren Mittelalter,"* (Vienna-Leipzig, 1932), III, 169f trans. and cited in Mommsen, Petrarch, 108.
20. Franco Simone, "La Coscienza della Rinascita negli Umanisti," *La Rinascita*, III, (1940), III: 182f, trans and cited in Mommsen, Petrarch, 109.
21. Mommsen, Petrarch, 123.
22. Benedetto Croce, *History: Its Theory and Practice*, trans. Douglas Ainslie, (NY: Russell and Russell, 1960), 206.
23. Mommsen, Petrarch, 123–24.
24. Mommsen, Petrarch, 124.
25. Mommsen, Petrarch, 125.
26. Myron P. Gilmore, "The Renaissance Conception of the Lessons of History," *Facets of the Renaissance*, ed. William H. Werkmeister, (NY: Harper Torchbooks, 1963), 74.
27. Mommsen, Petrarch, 128 and fn 81.
28. Petrarch, *Africa*, IX, 451–457 (ed. Festa, 278) trans, and cited Mommsen, Petrarch, 127.
29. Petrarch, *Epist. metr.*, III, 33 (ed. D. Rossetti, *F. Petrarchae poëmata minora*, II [Milan,

1831], 262), trans. and cited Mommsen, Petrarch, 127–28.
30. P. Joachimsen, *Geschichtsauffassung und Geschichtschreibung in Deutschland unter dem Einfluss des Humanismus*, (Leipzig-Berlin, 1910), 24, trans. and cited Mommsen, Petrarch, 129.
31. Mommsen, Petrarch, 129. Also see Lynn Thordike and J. Huizinga for examples of rejection of the idea of an existence of a major Italian Renaissance
32. Erwin Panofsky, "Artist, Scientist, Genius: Notes on the 'Renaissance-Dammerung,'" *The Renaissance: Six Essays*, (NY: Metropolitan Museum of Art, 1953), 169.
33. Theodore Mommsen, "Petrarch and the Story of the Choice of Hercules," *Mommsen, Medieval and Renaissance Studies*, ed. Eugene F. Rice, Jr., (Ithaca, NY: Cornell University Press, 1959), 193.
34. Eric Fromm, *Escape From Freedom*, (1941; NY: Discus Books/ Avon Pub., 1969), 111.
35. Mommsen, Hercules, 194.
36. Karl Joachim Weintraub, *The Value of the Individual: Self and Circumstance in Autobiography*, (Chicago: University of Chicago Press, 1978), 99.
37. Paul Oskar Kristeller, *Renaissance Thought II. Papers on Humanism and the Arts*, (NY: Harper & Row, 1961), 39, 71, 176. See also Denys Hay, *The Italian Renaissance in its Historical Background*, (Cambridge University Press, 1966), 36. See also Lynn Thorndike, "Renaissance or Prenaissance?" *JHI*, 3, (1943), 65–74.
38. Thorndike, *passim*.
39. Fromm, Escape, 59.
40. Jacob Burckhardt, *The Civilization of The Renaissance in Italy*, trans S. G. C. Middlemore, (NY: Random House, 1954), 100.
41. Werner Kaegi, "Introduction," *Gesammelte Schriften* by E. Walser, (Basel, 1932), xxxvii, trans. and cited in Burke, 193.
42. Mommsen, Last Will, 214.
43. Theodore E. Mommsen, "Petrarch and the Decoration of the Sala Virorum Illustrium in Padua in Mommsen," *Medieval and Renaissance Studies*, ed Eugene F. Rice, Jr., (Ithaca, NY: Cornell University Press, 1959), 167.
44. Burke, 193.
45. Burke, 193–94.
46. See Erwin Panofsky, *Gothic Architecture and Scholasticism*, (NY: World Publishing Co., 1962).
47. John Stuart Mill, *On Liberty*, (NY: Appleton-Century-Crofts, Inc., 1947), 64. See also Harold Bloom, *Genius. A Mosaic of One Hundred Exemplary Creative Minds*, (NY: Warner Books, 2002).
48. John O. Lyons, *The Invention of The Self: The Hinge of Consciousness in The Eighteenth Century*, (Carbondale, Ind.: Southern University Press, 1978), 43.
49. H. W. Janson, *History of Art. A Survey of the Major Visual Arts from the Dawn of History to the Present Day*, (Englewood Cliffs, NJ: Prentice-Hall, 1965), 289.
50. Kristeller, 10.
51. Burke, 178.
52. Francesco Petrarca, "On His Own Ignorance and That of Many Others," trans. Hans Nachod, *Renaissance Philosophy of Man*, eds. Ernst Cassirer, et al., (Chicago: University of Chicago Press, 1948), 103.
53. Paul Oskar Kristeller and John Herman Randall, Jr., "General Introduction," *Renaissance Philosophy of Man*, eds. Ernst Cassirer, et al., (Chicago: University of Chicago Press, 1948), 18.

54. Pietro Pomponazzi, "On the Immortality of the Soul," trans. William Henry Hay II, 280–381 cited in Ernst Cassirer *Renaissance Philosophy of Man*, 361.
55. John Aberth, *From the Brink of the Apocalypse: Confronting Famine, War, Plague, and Death in the Later Middle Ages*, (NY: Routledge, 2001), 2.
56. Aberth, 2.
57. For an outstanding rendering of flagellants see the film by Igmar Bergman, *Seventh Seal* (1956).
58. Donald R. Howard, *Chaucer and the Medieval World*, (London: Weidenfeld and Nicolson, 1987), 17.
59. Wallace K. Ferguson, *Europe in Transition 1300–1520*, (Boston: Houghton Mifflin Co., 1962), 338. See also J. Huizinga, *The Waning of the Middle Ages*, (Garden City: Doubleday Anchor Books, 1954), chs 11, 12.
60. Aberth, 2.
61. Huizinga, 322.
62. Pomponazzi, 362.
63. Huizinga, 335.
64. Burke, passim.
65. Burke, 199.
66. Gilmore, 75–76.
67. Gilmore, 78.
68. Gilmore, 78.
69. Gilmore, 79.
70. Gilmore, 79.
71. Paul Oskar Kristeller, *Renaissance Thought II. Papers on Humanism and the Arts*, (NY: Harper and Row, 1961), 11.
72. Burke, 195.
73. Burke, 192.
74. Lyons, 43, fn 10.
75. Ferguson, 248.
76. Ferguson, 248–49.
77. Burke, 196.
78. Kristeller, 65.
79. Kristeller, 66.
80. Kristeller, 95.
81. Gilmore, 76.
82. Ferguson, 249.
83. Max Weber, *Protestant Ethic and the Spirit of Capitalism* (1930) and R. H. Tawney, *Religion and the Rise of Capitalism* (1926).
84. Niccolò Machiavelli, *The Prince and Selected Discourses*, trans. Daniel Donno, (NY: Bantam Books, 1960), 121.
85. Machiavelli, 60.
86. Machiavelli, 60.
87. Machiavelli, 60.
88. Aberth, 154.
89. Aberth, 261.
90. Franklin L. Baumer, *Modern European Thought: Continuity and Change in Ideas, 1600–1950*, (NY: Macmillan Publishing Co., Inc., 1977) 63.
91. Henry S. Lucas, *The Renaissance and the Reformation*, (NY: Harper and Brothers Pub.,

1934), 476.
92. William Shakespeare, *Hamlet*, III. ii. 207–209.
93. See Garrett Mattingly, *The Spanish Armada*, (Boston: Houghton Mifflin Co., 1959).
94. Aberth, 205.
95. Aberth, 256.

Chapter Four

1. M. D. Feld, "Revolution and Reaction in Early Modern Europe," *JHI*, 38, no. 1 (1977), 175.
2. Feld, 175.
3. John O. Lyons, *The Invention of The Self: The Hinge of Consciousness in The Eighteenth Century*, 67.
4. Baumer, 63.
5. See Michel Montaigne, *The Complete Essays of Montaigne*, trans. Donald M. Frame, (Stanford, CA: Stanford University Press, 1965). On Montaigne as an individual by way of genius see Bloom, *Genius*.
6. Harold Bloom, *Shakespeare: The Invention of the Human*. (NY: Riverhead Books, Penguin Putman Inc., 1998), 741. This is a reference to Bloom's comment in regard to Luther's discourse "Christian Freedom."
7. Harold J. Grimm, *The Reformation Era. 1500–1650*, (NY: Macmillan Corp., 1954), 103.
8. See R. H. Bainton, *Here I Stand: A Life of Martin Luther* (NY: New American Library, 1950).
9. Grimm, 103.
10. Grimm, 104.
11. Grimm, 103.
12. Grimm, 104.
13. Grimm, 103.
14. Grimm, 58.
15. Grimm, 58.
16. Grimm, 58–59.
17. Grimm, 59.
18. Grimm, 104.
19. Lucas, 476.
20. Baumer, 26.
21. See C. V. Wedgewood, *The Thirty Years War*, (New Haven: Yale University Press, 1939).
22. See Mattingly.
23. See Tawney.
24. Burke, 189–90.
25. Baldassare Castiglione, *The Book of the Courtier*, (1528).
26. William Shakespeare, *Hamlet*, III, ii, 183–209.
27. Bloom, *Genius*, 18.
28. Donald Lowe, *History of Bourgeois Perception*, (Chicago: University of Chicago Press, 1982), 48.
29. Lowe, 48.
30. Lowe, 48.
31. Aberth, 205.
32. Aberth, 205.

33. Bloom, *Shakespeare*, 721.
34. Bloom, *Shakespeare*, 721.
35. See Dwight Macdonald, *Against the American Grain* (NY: Random House, 1962).
36. Saenger, 414.
37. Saenger, 414.
38. See Frank Kermode, *Shakespeare's Language*, (NY: Farrar, Straus and Giroux, 2000).
39. Bloom, *Shakespeare*, xvii.
40. Frances and Joseph Gies, *Cathedral, Forge, and Waterwheel. Technology and Invention in the Middle Ages*, (NY: Harper Collins, 1994), 291.
41. A. R. Hall, *The Scientific Revolution 1500–1800: The Foundation of the Modern Scientific Attitude*, (Boston: Beacon Press, 1956), 29.
42. Hall, 33.
43. David S. Landes, *Revolution in Time. Clocks and the Making of the Modern World*, (NY: Barnes and Noble, 1983), 77.
44. Hall, 11.
45. Hall, 12.
46. Hall, 12–13.
47. Hall, 13. See also A. C. Crombie, *Medieval and Early Modern Science, Science in the Later Middle Ages and Early Modern Times: XIII–XVII Centuries*, vol. 2, (NY: Doubleday Anchor Books, 1959).
48. Crombie, 30.
49. Crombie, 30.
50. Crombie, 30.
51. Crombie, 64–65.
52. Crombie, 66.
53. Crombie, 67.
54. Crombie, 67.
55. Crombie, 167.
56. Crombie, 167–68.
57. Crombie, 169.
58. Hall, 387.
59. Hall, 73.
60. Hall, 132.
61. Charles Nauert, *Agrippa and the Crisis of Renaissance Thought*, (Urbana: University of Illinois Press, 1965).
62. Gies, 95.
63. W. P. D. Wightman, *Science in a Renaissance Society*, (London: Hutchinson University Library, 1982), 57.
64. Gies, 1–2.
65. Gies, 3.
66. Lewis, Mumford, *Technics and Civilization*, (NY: Harcourt, Brace and Co., 1934), 15.
67. Landes, 16.
68. Landes, 3.
69. Landes, 3.
70. Landes, 7.
71. Landes, 3.
72. Landes, 6.

73. For inventive uses of language by More and Machiavelli see Burke, 189. See also J. H. Hexter, *The Vision of Politics on the Eve of the Reformation. More, Machiavelli and Seyssel*, (NY: Basic Books, 1973).
74. Desiderius Erasmus, "The Praise of Folly," *Essential Erasmus*, (NY: Bantam Books), 103.
75. Erasmus, 140.
76. Erasmus, 141.
77. Erasmus, 141.
78. Erasmus, 141.
79. Bloom, *Shakespeare*, xvii.
80. Bloom, *Shakespeare*, 720.
81. Bloom, *Shakespeare*, 721.
82. Bloom, *Shakespeare*, 720.
83. Harry Berger, Jr., *Imaginary Audition*, (1939) cited in Bloom, *Shakespeare*, 720.
84. Bloom, *Shakespeare*, 720.
85. See Kermode.
86. Bloom, *Shakespeare*, 721.
87. Bloom, *Shakespeare*, 725.
88. Bloom, *Shakespeare*, 733.
89. Kermode, 5.
90. For a discussion of Plato and language see Eric A. Havelock, *Preface to Plato*, (Cambridge: The Belknap Press of Harvard University Press, 1963).
91. Bloom, *Shakespeare*, 715.
92. Bloom, *Shakespeare*, 725.
93. Bloom, *Shakespeare*, 727.
94. Bloom, *Shakespeare*, 726.
95. Bloom, *Shakespeare*, 722.
96. Bloom, *Shakespeare*, 715, 722, 715.
97. Bloom, *Shakespeare*, 718.
98. Bloom, *Shakespeare*, 726.
99. Bloom, *Shakespeare*, 733–34.
100. Bloom, *Shakespeare*, xviii–xix.
101. Kermode, 12.
102. Kermode, 12.

Chapter Five

1. Paul Hazard, *The European Mind (1680–1715)*, trans. J. Lewis May, (1935; Cleveland: Meridian Books, 1963), xv.
2. Geoffrey Barraclough, *Turning Points in World History*, (London: Thames and Hudson, 1977), 26.
3. Blaise Pascal, *Pensées*, trans. Martin Turnell, Lafuma ed., no. 13, cited in Baumer, 65.
4. Hazard, xvii.
5. See Daniel Ogden, *Magic, Witchcraft, and Ghosts in the Greek and Roman Worlds: A Sourcebook*, (NY: Oxford University Press, 2002). The literature on this subject is expansive.
6. Carl J. Friedrich, *The Age of Baroque 1610–1660*, (NY: Harper Torchbooks, Harper and Row, 1952), 41.
7. Friedrich, 39–49.

8. Friedrich, 42.
9. Baumer, 39–41.
10. Helen Gardner, *Art Through the Ages*, 6th ed., (1926; NY: Harcourt Brace Jovanich, Inc., 1975), 561.
11. Baumer, 34.
12. Friedrich, 43.
13. Friedrich, 50. That Shakespeare and Cervantes' *Don Quixote* can be associated with the modern is not an issue. The Baroque had a tendency to embellish for no other reason than the embellishment and can be highlighted (out of context) by the automobiles of the past century, especially those with fins or other unnecessary decorations like the Pontiac Thunderbird.
14. Friedrich, 65.
15. Friedrich, 65.
16. Friedrich, 47.
17. Hazard, 3.
18. Hazard, xvi.
19. Peters, Richard. *Hobbes*, (Baltimore: Penquin Books, 1956), 191.
20. Bloom, *Shakespeare*, xix.
21. John Locke, *Essay on Human Understanding*, Bk. III, Chap. XI, Sect. 16 and Bk. IV, Chap. XII, Sect. 11. See also Baumer, 74.
22. Baumer, 74
23. Baumer, 71.
24. Richard Foster Jones, *Ancients and Moderns: A Study of the Rise of the Scientific Movement in Seventeenth-Century*, second ed., (Berkeley: University of California Press, 1965) 5.
25. Gustav Jahoda, *Crossroads Between Culture and Mind: Continuities and Change in Theories of Human Nature*, (Cambridge: Harvard University Press, 1993), 15. Also see Jahoda, 19, the discussion of Park and Daston (1981) on the significance of 'monsters' in medieval discourse, and the changes in the connotations of the term between the Renaissance and the seventeenth century (from marvels to medical pathology).
26. Jahoda, 15.
27. Jahoda, 15.
28. Jahoda, 16.
29. Jahoda, 16.
30. Margaret Hodgen, *Early Anthropology in the Sixteenth and Seventeenth Centuries*, (Philadelphia: University of Pennsylvania Press, 1971), 243, cited in Jahoda, 15.
31. Jahoda, 15–16.
32. A. R. Hall, *The Scientific Revolution 1500–1800: The Foundation of the Modern Scientific Attitude*, (Boston: Beacon Press, 1956), 74.
33. A. C. Crombie, *Medieval and Early Modern Science. Science in the Middle Ages: V–XIII Centuries*, (NY:Doubleday Anchor Books, 1959), vol. 1, 159.
34. Giordano Bruno, *On the Infinite Universe and World*, trans. Dorthy Singer, (NY: Henry Schuman, 1950) 245–46, cited in Baumer, 55.
35. Bruno, 246, cited in Baumer, 55.
36. Herbert Butterfield, *The Origins of Modern Science. 1300–1800*, rev. ed., (NY: Collier Books, 1962), 29 and chapter 2.
37. Butterfield, 36.
38. Baumer, 54.
39. Baumer, 54.

40. Baumer, 54.
41. Baumer, 54.
42. Butterfield, 7.
43. Bruno, 249 cited in Baumer, 58.
44. Baumer 54.
45. Baumer 56. Also note fn 44 of the same page.
46. Blaise Pascal, *Pensées*, trans. W. F. Trotter, Brunschvieg ed., no. 72, cited in Baumer, 56.
47. Jerome David Levin, *Theories of the Self*, (Washington: Hemisphere Pub. Corp., 1992), 15. Also see Bayard Rankin, "The History of Probability and the Changing Concept of the Individual," *JHI*, 27, no, 4 (1966), 491.
48. Hall, 20.
49. Hall, 19.
50. Hall, 21.
51. Hall, 114.
52. Blaise Pascal, *Pensées sur la religion et sur quelques autre sujets*, (Paris: Lafuma, 1951), i. 374, (Fragment 597), cited in Catherine Glyn Davies, *'Conscience' as Consciousness: The Idea of Self-Awarness in French Philosophical Writing from Descartes to Diderot*, (Oxford: Oxford University Press, 1990), 5.
53. Pascal, *Pensées*, cited in Pierre Hadot, *The Inner Citadel. The Meditations of Marcus Aurelius*, trans. Michael Chase, (Cambridge: Harvard University Press, 1998), 181.
54. Hall, 138–39.
55. Galileo Galilei, "The Assayer," *Discoveries and Opinions of Galileo*, trans. Stillman Drake, (Garden City, NY: Doubleday and Co., 1957), 237–38, cited in Baumer, 50.
56. Baumer, 50.
57. Baumer, 50.
58. Galileo Galilei, *Dialogue Concerning the Two Chief World Systems*, trans. Stillman Drake, (Berkeley: University of California Press, 1953), 58, cited in Baumer, 54.
59. Butterfield, 226.
60. Jones, viii.
61. Jones, ix.
62. Julie Robin Solomon, *Objectivity in the Making: Francis Bacon and the Politics of Inquiry*, (Baltimore: John Hopkins University Press, 1998), xv.
63. This discussion can be found in Crombie, 139–62.
64. Francis Bacon, *The New Organon and Related Writings*, (NY: Library Arts Press, 1960), no. XLV, 62.
65. Baumer, 67.
66. Baumer, 51–52.
67. Baumer, 57, 66.
68. Francis Bacon, *The New Atlantis*, (London, 1626) cited in Barraclough, 25.
69. Baumer, 93.
70. Bacon, *New Organon*, Aphorism no. XLI, Bk I, 48.
71. Bacon, *New Organon*, Aphorism no. XLIV, Bk I, 49.
72. Bacon, *New Organon*, Aphorism no. XLV, Bk I, 50.
73. Bacon, *New Organon*, Aphorism no. XLIII, Bk I, 49.
74. Richard Peters, "Introduction," in Thomas Hobbes, *Leviathan Or the Matter, Forme and Power of a Commonwealth Ecclesiastical and Civil*, ed. Michael Oakeshott, (NY: Collier-Macmillan Ltd., 1970), 8–9.

75. Ong, 30.
76. Ong, 39.
77. Bacon, *New Organon*, Aphorism no. XLII, Bk I, 48.
78. Baumer, 31.
79. Jahoda, 5. Also see Francois H. Lapointe, "The origin and evolution of the term 'psychology,'" *American Psychologist*, 25 (1970), 640–6.
80. Jahoda, 8.
81. Jahoda, ix.
82. Baumer, 27.
83. Ong, 29.
84. John Stuart Mill, *On Liberty*, (NY: Appleton-Century-Crofts, Inc., 1947), 64–65.
85. Mill, (391–400), 65. Also see Bloom, *Genius*, 500–9 for a discussion on Homer as genius (individual).
86. Bloom, *Genius*, 12.
87. Mill, 64.
88. Mill, 64–65. See Bloom's discussion of Socrates as a genius (and individual?).
89. Mill, 64.
90. Bloom, *Genius*, 8.
91. Mill, 64.
92. Bloom, *Genius*, 12.
93. Peter Gay, *Schnizler's Century: The Making of Middle-Class Culture, 1815–1914*, (NY: W.W. Norton and Co., 2002), xxiv.
94. Bloom, *Genius*, 12.
95. Jorge Luis Borges, "Pierre Menard, Author of the Quixote," *Collected Fictions*, trans. Andrew Hurley, (NY: Viking, 1998), 94.
96. Solomon, xvi.
97. Solomon, xiv–xv.
98. Solomon, xv.
99. Solomon, xi.
100. Solomon, xi–xiii.
101. Solomon, xvi–xvii.
102. Solomon, xviii.
103. Solomon, xii.
104. Herschel Baker, *The Image of Man. A Study of the Idea of Human Dignity in Classical, Antiquity, the Middle Ages, and the Renaissance*, (1947; NY: Harper and Row, 1961), 132.
105. Solomon, xii.
106. Solomon, xii.
107. Solomon, xv.
108. Solomon, xiv.
109. Solomon, xiv.
110. Solomon, xv. The reader might want to refer to Pierre Bourdieu, *Outline of a Theory of Practice*, trans. Richard Nice, (Cambridge: Cambridge Univ. Press, 1977), 164–71. "...orthodoxy—or the need to establish what is authoritative—arises only when traditional *doxa*, or modes of belief, are under threat from competitors.
111. Solomon, xii.
112. Hobbes, 7.
113. Genevieve Rodis-Lewis, *Descartes: His Life and Thought*, trans. Jane Marie Todd, (Ithaca: Cornell University Press, 1998), 133.

114. Richard Peters, *Hobbes*, (Baltimore: Penguin Books, 1956), 53.
115. Peters, 136.
116. Hobbes, 31.
117. Hobbes, 33.
118. Hobbes, 34.
119. Hobbes, 33.
120. Peters, 17.
121. Peters, 240.

Chapter Six

1. Hiram Caton, *The Origin of Subjectivity: An Essay on Descartes*, (New Haven: Yale University Press, 1973), 32.
2. Blair Campbell, "La Mettrie: The Robot and the Automaton," *JHI*, 31, no. 4, 558.
3. Louis Sass, *Madness and Modernism: Insanity in the Light of Modern Art, Literature, and Thought*, (NY: Harper Collins, 1992), 91.
4. Baumer, 42. Also see Stephen Gaukroger, *Descartes, An Intellectual Biography*, (Oxford: Clarendon Press, 1995). Although not as helpful, the student may also wish to consult Rodis-Lewis.
5. Ben-Ami Scharfstein, *The Philosophers: Their Lives and the Nature of Their Thought*, (NY: Oxford University Press, 1980), 49, 134.
6. Crombie, 64–65, 67. Also see Hall, 13; Barfield, 51; and Baumer, 54–55, 56–255. For an interesting introduction to the subject of inertia, motion and Descartes' positions (and laws thereof) see Daniel Garber, *Descartes' Metaphysical Physics*, (Chicago: University of Chicago Press, 1992), 156–255.
7. See Edwin Arthur Burtt, *The Metaphysical Foundations of Modern Physical Science*, rev. ed., (1924; Garden City, NY: Doubleday Anchor Books, 1954).
8. Basil Willey, *Seventeenth Century Background: Studies in the Thought of the Age in Relation to Poetry and Religion* (NY: Columbia University Press, 1962).
9. Alexandre Koyre, *From the Closed World to the Infinite Universe*, (Baltimore: Johns Hopkins Press, 1957), 1.
10. Bloom, *Genius*, ix.
11. Bloom, *Genius*, 28.
12. Richard Rorty, *Philosophy and the Nature of the Mind*, (Princeton, NJ: Princeton University Press, 1980), 48–49. Also see Emily and Fred S. Michael, "Corporeal Ideas in Seventeenth-Century Psychology," *JHI*, 50, no. 1 (1989), 31–48.
13. David B. Morris, "The Marquis de Sade and the Discourses of Pain: Literature and Medicine at the Revolution," *The Languages of Psyche: Mind and Body in Enlightenment Thought, Clark Library Lectures 1985–1986*, ed. G. S. Rousseau, (Berkeley: University of California Press, 1990), 294.
14. Leonora D. Cohen, "Descartes and Henry More on the Beast Machine: A Translation of their Correspondence Pertaining to Animal Automation," *Annals of Science 1* (1936), 49–50, cited in Otto Mayr, *Authority, Liberty and Automatic Machinery In Early Modern Europe*, (Baltimore: Johns Hopkins University Press, 1986), 90–1.
15. Mayr, 95.
16. See Chapter Five.

17. All quotes from Descartes, unless otherwise noted, are from *The Philosophical Works of Descartes*, ed. and trans. Elizabeth S. Haldane and G. R. T. Ross, (1911; NY: Dover Publications, Inc., 1955), *Meditation II*, v.1, 157.
18. Descartes, Arguments, vol. 2, 52.
19. Descartes, *Meditation II*, vol. 1, 152, 153. See also Georges Rey, "A Reason for Doubting the Existence of Consciousness," *Consciousness and Self-Regulation: Advances in Research and Theory*, vol. 3, ed. by Richard J. Davidson, Gary E. Schwartz and David Shapiro, (NY: Plenum Press, 1983), 3–4.
20. Rey, 3–4.
21. Also a worthwhile discussion of Descartes's continued relationship with Aristotlian 'essences' can be found in Antonio Damasio, *Descartes' Error: The Feelings of What Happens: Body and Emotion in the Making of Consciousness*, (NY: Harcourt Brace and Company, 1999).
22. Robert McRae, "Descartes' Definition of Thought," *Cartesian Studies*, (Oxford, Basil Blackwell, 1972), 55. Descartees, *Reply II*, def. IATVII, 160, HR II, 52. The Latin "*ut ejus immediate conscii simus*," is given in the French translation as "*...que nous en sommes immediatement connaissants.*" AT IX, 124. See also *Principles* I, ix, AT VII,7. HR I, 222. In the French translations of Descartes' Latin which he approved, the word *conscience* is avoided, with this exception in *Reply III*: "*Entendre, vouloir, imaginer, sentir, etc., conviennent entre eux en ce qu'ils ne peuvent etre sans pensée, ou perception, ou conscience et connaissance.*" AT IX, 137. G. Lewis remarks that this is perhaps from the first use in French of the word *conscience* in a non-moral sense. *Le problème de l'inconscient et le cartésianisme*, (Paris 1950), 39.
23. Descartes, *Arguments*, vol. 2, 52.
24. For such distinguished Cartesian scholars as Gilson, Laporte and Alquie, this definition asserts that thought is simply a synonym for consciousness. See E. Gilson, *Discours de la méthode, Commentaire*, (Paris, 1947), 293; J. Laporte, *Le rationalisme de Descartes*, (Paris 1950), 78; *Descartes, Œuvres philosophiques*, ed. F. Alquie, (Paris, 1967), vol. II, 586n. The passage from *Reply III* in the previous note makes *conscience* a synonym of *pensée*, as does also Descartes' phrase, '*ma propre pensée ou conscience*,' AT III, 474. It may, however, be questionable whether the *definitions* of thought given in *Reply II* and *Principles I*, ix, make the two terms synonymous.
25. David P. Behan, "Locke on Persons and Personal Identity," *Canadian Journal of Philosophy*, 9, no. 1, (1979), 53–75.
26. Richard E. Aquila, "The Cartesian and a Certain 'Poetic' Notion of Consciousness," *JHI*, 49, no. 4 (1988), 543.
27. Aquila, 534.
28. For a discussion and attempt to make Aristotle somehow the parent of consciousness, see Modrak.
29. For a discussion of the role rise of the confessional see Delumeau .
30. Aquila, 543.
31. Aquila, 543.
32. Aquila, 544.
33. C. Thomas Powell, *Kant's Theory of Self-Consciousness*, (Oxford: Clarendon Press, 1990), 212.
34. Hobbes, 57.
35. For the reader interested in an earlier expression in the *OED*, see Aquila, 549: "...the earliest occurrence from *The Rape of the Lock*, 'Some o'er her Lap their careful Plumes

522 | Notes to pp. 232–238

        display'd/Trembling, and conscious of the rich Brocade.' (III, 116) Apart from the difference in preposition (*to* as opposed to *of*), it may be useful to ask why the following, from Dryden's *Aeneis*, is not cited: 'And, in a Heav'n serene, refulgent arms appear;.../ The temper'd metals clash, and yield a silver sound.../ Aeneas only conscious to the sign, Presag'd th' event.' (VIII, 697–702)."

36. Cited in Rodis-Lewis, 133.
37. Hobbes, 57.
38. Damasio, 27 states the case as such: "Consciousness and conscience are in fact distinguishable: consciousness pertains to the knowing of any object or action attributed to a self, while conscience pertains tot he good or evil to be found in actions or objects." Also see Damasio 230–233. The role of 'self ' will be dealt with later.
39. Leslie Stephens, *Historian of European Thought in the Eighteenth Century* (London, 1876), I, 3, cited in Donald R. Kelley, "What is Happening to the History of Ideas?" *JHI*, 51, no. 1 (1990), 6.
40. Arguably one of the most interesting discussions of the rise of the self in the Romantic Age and the question of authenticity can be found in: Wylie Sypher, *Loss of the Self in Modern Literature and Art*, (NY: Vintage Books, 1964).
41. Rey, 3.
42. Neil Rossman, *Consciousness: Separation and Integration*, (Albany: State University of N.Y. Press, 1991), 1.
43. There are at least three exceptions that can be found where Descartes' use of consciousness receives treatment: E. M. Curley, *Descartes Against the Skeptics*, (Cambridge: Harvard University Press, 1978); Aquila; and McRae "Descartes' Definition." This contrasts sharply with the work of and works on Locke and consciousness.
44. Without straying from the subject at hand, our understanding of the terms 'subjective' and 'objective' were transformed into a meaning much closer for the first time to our (modern) understanding than the Medieval scholastic definitions. See Caton.
45. The difficulty for today's student of consciousness is precisely the issue of where and what parameters are to be inclusive in any working definition. It is the vagueness of meanings kicking around today that makes understanding so convoluted.
46. Walter J. Ong, *The Presence of the Word*, (Minneapolis: University of Minnesota Press, 1981), 211, cited in Sass 91.
47. Lowe, 87.
48. Jahoda, 17.
49. Popper and Eccles, 177.
50. Sean Desmond Healy, *Boredom, Self, and Culture*, (London: Fairleigh Dickinson University Press, 1984), 77.
51. Blaise Pascal, *Pensées* (Baltimore: Penguin Books, 1966), 47.
52. Montaigne, 83.
53. Gilbert Ryle, *The Concept of Mind*, (London: Hutchinson's University Library, 1949), 1. For a more recent and equally anti-Cartesian 'theater' see Daniel C. Dennett, *Consciousness Explained*, (Boston: Little, Brown and Company, 1991).
54. Rossman, 1. The reflexivity to match the subjective in Descartes has been suggested by Rossman: "…it is rather mentality as grasped and experienced self-reflectively. Indeed it is largely through the writings of Descartes that this has occurred, for it is he who explicitly and systemically directed the gaze of awareness inwardly and in so doing

helped create a world, the world of self-reflective consciousness or self, within the larger non-self-reflective world."
55. Arnold H. Modell, *The Private Self*, (Cambridge: Harvard University Press, 1995), 26.
56. Bloom, *Genius*, 30.
57. Phillipe Ariès, *Centuries of Childhood: A Social History of Childhood*, trans. R. Baldick, (NY: Knopf, 1962), 398.
58. Augustine, *Confessions*. For the basic subject of biography and autobiography see Whittemore, *Pure Lives*.
59. Curley, 172.
60. Charles Taylor, *Sources of the Self: The Making of the Modern Identity*, (Cambridge: Harvard University Press, 1989), 31.
61. Taylor, 143.
62. Taylor, 143.
63. Bloom, *Genius*, 29.
64. Or as Robert Boyle (1627–91), who established 'Boyle's law' and contributed to the primitive science of chemistry, noted in his *Skeptical Chymist* (1661): "It has long seemed to me none of the least impediments of true natural philosophy, that men have been so forward to write systems of it, and have thought themselves obliged either to be altogether silent, or not write less than an entire body of physiology," cited in William H. Brock, *The Chemical Tree*, (London: Norton, 1992), 65.
65. For a more detailed discussion see Chapter Two.
66. Levin, 5.
67. Levin, 5.
68. Taylor, 141. For a more detailed discussion, see Chapter Two.
69. Gareth B. Matthews, *Thought's Ego in Augustine and Descartes*, (Ithaca: Cornell University Press, 1992), 142.
70. Matthews, ix.
71. See Montaigne. Also see Bloom, *Genius*, 40–46 regarding Montaigne.
72. Bloom, *Genius*, 20.
73. Matthews, 189, 29. See also Augustine, *City of God*, "How can I be mistaken [in thinking] that I[*] am?" Other translations use "ponder" for "turning over in my mind." See Gerard Watson.
74. Cited in Mathews, 29. The actual Augustine argument from the *Concerning The City of God Against the Pagans*, trans. Henry Bettenson, (NY: Penguin Books, 1984), 459, reads as follows: "…we know that we exist,…the certainty that I exist, that I know it, and that I am glad of it, is independent of any imaginary and deceptive fantasies." (XI, 26) Augustine, 460 finishes with a reminder of the roots of the Cartesian cogito argument stating that, "They [Academics] say, 'Suppose you are mistaken?' I reply, 'If I am mistaken, I exist.' A non-existent being cannot be mistaken; therefore I must exist, if I am mistaken. Then since my being mistaken proves that I exist, how can I be mistaken in thinking that I exist, seeing that my mistake establishes my existance? Since therefore I must exist in order to be mistaken, then even if I am mistaken, there can be no doubt that I am not mistaken in my knowledge that I exist."
75. Stanley L Scott, *Frontiers of Consciousness: Interdisciplinary Studies in American Philosophy and Poetry*, (NY: Fordham University Press, 1991), 13.
76. Taylor, 141.
77. Matthews, 141–2.

78. Jonathan Green, *Chasing the Sun. Dictionary Makers and the Dictionaries They Made*, (NY: Henry Holt and Co., 1996).
79. See *JHI*, 64, no. 1 (2003), 1–72.
80. Ann Blair, "Reading Strategies for Coping With Information Overload ca. 1550– 1700." *JHI*, 64, no. 1 (2003), 15.
81. Blair, 15.
82. *Oxford English Dictionary*, (Oxford: Oxford University Press, 1971), 847.
83. Edward Engelberg, *The Unknown Distance: From Consciousness to Conscience Goethe to Camus*, (Cambridge, Mass.: Harvard University Press, 1972), 10–11.
84. Engelberg, 11.
85. Hans Kurath, et al., eds., *Middle English Dictionary*, (Ann Arbor, University of Michigan Press, 1952).
86. Robert A. Greene, "Synderesis, the Spark of Conscience, in the English Renaissance," *JHI*, 52, no. 2 (1991), 196.
87. Greene, 196.
88. Greene, 218.
89. Greene, 218.
90. Engelberg, 11–2.
91. OED, 847.
92. Thomas Reid, "Essays on the Intellectual Powers," *Works*, 5th ed., ed. W. Hamilton, (Edinburgh, 1858), Essay I, Ch. 5, cited in Norman Malcolm, *Problems of Mind: Descartes to Wittgenstein*. (NY: Harper and Row, 1971) 1.
93. Sass, 45. The quote "logic of private inquiry" is from Ong, 211. Sass, 91, also offers two notes regarding Descartes' use of the interior: "…consciousness is assumed to have direct access not only to the external world but only to inner 'ideas'…," Sass, 91: "The achievement of certainty in knowledge also requires disengagement disengagement from the naive acceptance of the existence of the external world in favor of an introspection, by the 'inner Eye' of the Mind, of those 'clear and distinct ideas that can be found within'…," 91. Also see R. Rorty, *Philosophy and the Mirror of Nature*, (Princeton, N.J.: Princeton University Press, 1979), 45ff.
94. There is no meaningful argument that can be offered in attempting to deny the historic significance of Burckarhdt's *Civilization of the Renaissance in Italy*. It is this author's conviction that much of what Burckhardt thought and wrote of the Renaissance was a matter of simple projection —for he attempted to image a world being created that would eventually offer up a contemporary like Nietzsche in roots of the Quattrecento. In some ways this classic speaks to us more of the Germanies Burckhardt experienced more than the city-states of Renaissance Italy.
95. For a solid general work on the historic development of the individual see: Steven Lukes, *Individualism*, (Oxford: Basil Blackwell,1973); and Steven Lukes, "The Meanings of 'Individualism.,'" *JHI*, 32, no. 1, (1971), 45–66. Additionally, for the earliest but unconvincing attempt to deal with the subject see Colin Morris, *The Discovery of the Individual 1050–1200*, (London: S. P. C. K. for the Church Historical Society, 1972). For the Renaissance, Norman Nelson, "Individualism as a Criterion of the Renaissance," *The Journal of English and German Philology*, 32 (1933), 16–334. A somewhat more relevant work dealing with England is Alan Macfarlane, *The Origins of English Individualism: The Family, Property and Social Transition*, (NY: Cambridge University Press, 1979). Also see John G. Weiger, *The Individuated Self: Cervantes and the Emergence of the Individual*, (Athens: Ohio University Press, 1979). A more general work is G. V.

Notes to pp. 248–253 | 525

Plekhanov, *The Role of The Individual in History*, (1898; Lawrence and Wishart Ltd., 1940).
96. Saenger, 410.
97. Saenger, 371–72: "...a mark specifically employed to give a graphic representation of the aside, a device of ancient oratorical eloquence." See Chapter Two for more detail on silent reading.
98. Saenger, 410.
99. Eisenstein, 304. Also for the rhetorical and its historical development and role see Walter J. Ong, *Interface of the Word*; and *Orality and Literacy: The Technologizing of the Word*, (London: Methuen, 1982); and Walter J. Ong, *Rhetoric, Romance and Technology: Studies in the Interaction of Expression and Culture*, (Ithaca: Cornell University Press, 1971).
100. The French idea of a history of "mentality" is best reflected perhaps by Delumeau.
101. Taylor, 153; see his fn 29 for the full statement.
102. William Barrett, *The Illusion of Technique: A Search for Meaning in a Technological Civilization*, (NY: Doubleday, 1978), 22.
103. Barrett, 22.
104. See Caton.
105. Campbell, 558. In footnote 9 he refers to the comment regarding secularization and Descartes in Jacques Maritain's *Three Reformers: Luther, Descartes and Rousseau*, (NY: Crowell, 1929), chapter two.
106. Taylor, 141.
107. Sass, 91.
108. Julian Jaynes, "How Old is Consciousness," *Exploring the Concept of Mind*, ed. Richard M. Caplan, (Iowa City: University of Iowa Press, 1986), 53.
109. G. B. Madison, "Did Merleau-Ponty Have a Theory of Perception?" *Merleau-Ponty, Hermeneutics, and Postmodernism*, ed. by Thomas W. Busch and Shaun Gallagher, (Albany: State University of New York Press, 1992), 84.
110. Descartes, *Reply II* def I AT VII, 160 HR II, 52. See also Aquila, 558.
111. For Augustine's unique contribution to the creation of an interior existence one could begin with *Confessions*, (XII.16) where he states: "Truth tells me inwardly in my mind." Additional commentators on this subject include Curley, 173, 177; Lyons, 39; Mathews, 3, 29, 37, 40, 166–67, 192, 199; Taylor 113, 129, 131, 133, 143, 156, 177; Saenger, 383; Lukes, 60f; Levin, 5, 16. Also worth looking at are Ivan Illich, *In the Vineyard of the Text: A Commentary to Hugh's Didascalicon*, (Chicago: University of Chicago Press, 1993) 82, 120. Wilhelm Windelband, *History of Philosohpy*, vol.2: *Renassiance, Enlightenment and Modern*, (NY: Harper Torchbooks), 391, speaks of Augustine's "inner perception." Weintraub, 26; Mazzeo, 152; and Robert J. O'Connell, *St. Augustine's Confessions* cited in Lyons, 25: "the real 'I' is the soul" of Augustine. And P. Brown, *Augustine of Hippo* cited in Lukes, 60: "Confessions have justly been called a 'manifesto of the inner world.'" Gareth Matthews, "Consciousness and Life," *Philosophy*, 52 (1977), 13–26 cited in Rorty, 51, has noted that one can find the idea of a, "human being as having...both an 'inside' and an 'outside'...in Augustine, but not much earlier, and not much between the time of Augustine and that of Descartes."
112. Robert McRae, "'Idea' as a Philosophical Term in the Seventeenth Century," *JHI*, 26, no. 2, (1965), 178.
113. McRae, Definition, 56. Also see MacRae, 'Idea,' 182; and Descartes, I, 52, fn96.
114. McRae, Definition, 56.

115. McRae, "Definition," 56, fn 12.
116. McRae, "Definition," 56.
117. The argument for machine consciousness is most prevalent with those involved with 'artificial intelligence' (for this writer, an oxymoron). As examples, Ray Kurzwell, *The Age of Spiritual Machines. When Computers Exceed Human Intelligence*, (NY: Viking 1999), or for a more intellectual adventure, Hans Moravec, *Robot. Mere Machine to Transcendent Mind*, (Oxford: Oxford University Press, 1999). There are others but the arguments and principles are the same.
118. McRae, Idea, 182, fn 101.
119. McRae, Definition, 57.
120. McRae, Definition, 57.
121. McRae, Definition, 58.
122. McRae, Definition, 59.
123. Descartes, I, *Principles*, ix, 222.
124. McRae, Definition, 59.
125. McRae, Definition, 59. The topic of consciousness is certainly not one on which Descartes can be accused of offering a foolish consistency. See Curley, 181, 179–80; or Kathleen V. Wilkes, "Is Consciousness Important?" *British Journal for the Philosophy of Science*, 35 (1984), 224: "Nobody, I assume, would wish to argue that 'conscious,' or its nominalisation 'consciousness,' are clear notions." The issue of using antiquated language to express revolutionary is explored in Havelock 's, *Preface to Plato*.
126. Descartes, *Principles*, vol. I, xlviii, 238. See also McRae, "Definition," 59. For an introduction on the history of the self one could begin with a psychoanalytic approach with Arnold Modell, *The Private Self*, (Boston: Harvard University Press, 1993).
127. See Havelock.
128. See Kathleen Wider, *The Bodily Nature of Consciousness. Sartre and Contemporary Philosophy of Mind*, (Ithaca: Cornell University Press, 1997).
129. Descartes, *Reply to Objections IV*, vol. II, 115 .
130. Descartes, *Reply IV*, (AT VII), 246, cited in McRae, "Definition," 62.
131. McRae, Definition, 67. Also see Curley, 180.
132. McRae, Definition, 67.
133. Robert McRae, "Innate Ideas," *Cartesian Studies*, ed. R.J.Butler, (New York: Barnes and Noble, 1972), 37–39 cited in McRae, Definition, 67.
134. McRae, Definition, 5.
135. McRae, Definition, 67–68.
136. McRae, Definition, 64–65.
137. McRae, Definition, 66.
138. Descartes, AT V, 149, cited in McRae, Definition, 67.
139. Descartes, vol. 1, *Principles*, part 1, xlv, 237.
140. McRae, Definition, 68.
141. Descartes, vol. 1, *Discourse*, part III, 95.
142. McRae, Definition, 68.
143. McRae, Definition, 61.
144. Descartes cited in McRae, Definition, 61.
145. Friedrich, 47.
146. McRae, Definition, 68. And Descartes, *Principles I*, xlv, 237.
147. McRae, Definition, 68. And Descartes, *Principles I*, xlv, 237.
148. Descartes, *Principles I*, XLV p, 237.

149. Curley, 181. Descartes AT VII, 246 HR II, 115
150. Curley, 178, footnote 11: "The Latin is: '*Cogitationis nomine complector illud omne quod sic in nobis est, ut ijus immediate conscii simus.*' (AT VII, 160; HR II, 52). The French reads: '*Par le nom de* penséee, *je comprend tout ce qui est tellement en nous, que nous en sommes immediatement connaissants.*' (AT IX, 124). This raises an interesting linguistic point. Alquie, *Œuvres,* 586, remarks that '*Au lieu de* connaissants, *nous dirions mieux:* conscients.' Apparently prior to Descartes, conscience and its cognates were not used in the psychological sense they can have in modern French, but only in a moral sense."
151. McRae, Definition, 55–56, 57.
152. McRae, Definition, 56.
153. Daisie Radner, "Thought and Consciousness in Descartes," *Journal of the History of Philosophy,* 26, vol. 3 (1988), 439.
154. Campbell, 558.
155. Campbell, 558.
156. Radner, 444.
157. Radner, 444.
158. Radner, 451.
159. Aquila, 560.
160. McRae, Definition, 57. "Apparently misreading both Descartes and Locke, the author of the *Encyclopédie* article '*Conscience,*' (M. Le Chevalier de Jaucourt) reverses the judgement. Since for Locke but not for 'the Cartesians' there are no unconscious perceptions, for the former but not for the later '*la perception and la* conscience *doivent être prises pour une seule and même opération.*'" Denis Diderot et al., eds., *Encyclopédie ou Dictionnaire Raisonné des Sciences, des Arts et des Métiers* (Paris, 1751–1780), v.III, 902." See also Aquila, 547.
161. Aquila, 547. The reader may want to also look at Sass, 23.
162. Sass, 23.
163. Sass, 23.
164. Sass, 23.
165. Descartes, vol. II, *Reply to Objections IV,* 115.
166. Dennis L. Sepper, *Descartes's Imagination: Proportion, Images, and the Activity of Thinking,* (NY: University of California Press, 1996), 295.
167. Malcolm, 10, also see Malcolm, 10, fn 13. Descartes, vol. 1, 163, *Meditation III*.

Chapter Seven

1. Hans Aarsleff, "Locke's influence," *The Cambridge Companion to Locke,* ed. Vere Chappell, (Cambridge: Cambridge University Press, 1994), 252.
2. Alfred North Whitehead, *Science and the Modern World,* Lowell Lectures, 1925, (NY: Pelican Mentor Books, 1948), 40–41. Chapter three is "The Century of Genius."
3. Aarsleff, 252.
4. John Yolton, *John Locke and Education,* (NY: Randon House, 1971), 5.
5. Lyons, 8.
6. Lyons, 8.
7. Bloom, *Shakespeare,* xvii.
8. John Locke, "The Epistle to the Reader," *An Essay Concerning Human Understanding,* ed. Peter H. Nidditch, (Oxford: Clarendon Press, 1975), 10. The Nidditch edition will be favored over the Fraser (unless noted) because it is a more recent edition. In addition

there are occasionally uncertainties as to pagination of sections, especially in the important Book II, Chapter XVII, "On Identity and Diversity." However the Fraser footnotes will be used as a primary source. See also Maurice Cranston, *John Locke: A Biography*, (London: Longmans, Green and Co. Ltd., 1959), 264.
9. Locke, Bk. I, Ch. IV, 25, 102.
10. Locke, John. *An Essay Concerning Human Understanding*, 2 volumes, collated and annotated Alexander Campbell Fraser, (NY: Dover Publication, Inc., 1959), v. I, 37. See Descartes, vol. I, *Meditation III*, 160: "But among these ideas, some appear to me to be innate, some adventitious, and others to be formed [or invented] by myself..."
11. Douglas Greenlee, "Locke and the Controversy over Innate Ideas," *JHI*, 33, no. 2 (1972), 260.
12. John Yolton, *Perceptual Acquaintance from Descartes to Reid*, (Minneapolis: University of Minnesota Press, 1984), 210.
13. John Yolton, *John Locke and the Way of Ideas*, (1956; Oxford: Clarendon Press, 1968), 205.
14. Whitehead, 39–40.
15. Yolton, *Ideas*, 111.
16. Yolton, *Education*, 56.
17. Kenneth MacLean, *John Locke and English Literature of the Eighteenth Century*, (NY: Russell and Russell, 1962), 85, referring here to II.XIII.10.
18. MacLean, 85.
19. Yolton, *Perceptual Acquaintance*, 90, referring to II.I.3.
20. Yolton, *Perceptual Acquaintance*, 147.
21. Yolton, *Perceptual Acquaintance*, 147–8.
22. Yolton, *Education*, 55.
23. Yolton, *Perceptual Acquaintance*, 90.
24. Yolton, *Perceptual Acquaintance*, 89.
25. Yolton, *Perceptual Acquaintance*, 221.
26. Dennett, 229 speaking of a "Cartesian Theater."
27. Greenlee, 251. The cited passage, "the perception...of our Ideas." is IV.I.2
28. Aarsleff, 262–63. Also see MacLean, passim.
29. Ryle, 159.
30. Ryle, 15–16.
31. This particular reference, II.I.19, is so fundamental it should be noted and will reappear throughout this work, even though it is not part of the infamous Book II, Chapter XXVII "Identity and Diversity."
32. Julian Jaynes, "How Old is Consciousness," 5–6. A poignant question yet asked is what would have happened to modern radio dramas where the reality of action is hidden from view and thus must of necessity be a product of the interior of the mind where the unseen *Shadow*, for example, comes to life? Put another way, could radio drama have existed with no pretense of an interior space from whence to 'see' the world? Drama and imagination will be dealt with at a later time in this work.
33. On language see Yolton, *Perceptual Acquaintance*, 218–19; and Yolton *Ideas*, 44–45, 46, 47.
34. Lyons, 204.
35. C. S. Lewis, *Studies in Words*, (Cambridge: Cambridge University Press, 1960), 181.
36. See Green.
37. Lewis, 181.

38. Lewis, 181.
39. This is in the final edition of Nidditch's 1975 paperback. Thirty-two pages exist in the Fraser paperback, volume I because, in part, of his lengthy footnotes.
40. At II.XXVII.17 he states that "*Self* is that conscious thinking thing,…which is sensible, or conscious of Pleasure and Pain, capable of Happiness or Misery, and so is concern'd for it *Self*, as far as that consciousness extends." And again at II.XXVII.23 with "*Self*…not determined by Identity or Diversity of Substance,…but only by Identity of consciousness."
41. Locke's discussion can be found in II.XIV.7, 8, 9, 10, 11.
42. For an example of this truism see Albert Einstein. Assumptions are the last thing to change as applied to England and radicalism in the eighteenth-century. Also see Walter R. Martin.
43. Baumer, 59.
44. See Patricia Meyer Spacks, *Imagining a Self. Autobiography and Novel in Eighteenth-Century England,* (Cambridge: Harvard University Press, 1976).
45. Taylor, 49. Also see II.XXVII.9.
46. Maurice Ashley, *England in the Seventeenth Century (1603–1714),* (Baltimore: Pelican Books, 1961), 108.
47. Sir William Smith and Sir John Lockwood, *Chambers Murray Latin-English Dictionary,* (1933; London: Chambers, Edinburgh and John Murray, 1999), II, b, a, 146.
48. R. C. Tennant, "The Anglican Response to Locke's Theory of Personal Identity," *JHI,* 43, no. 1 (1982), 81. Also see John Yolton. *Locke and the Compass of Human Understanding: A Selective Commentary on the 'Essays,'* (Cambridge University Press, 1970), 141 and passim.
49. Locke's comments here regarding consciousness can be compared with those in defense of conscience when he stated: "Perhaps *Conscience* will be urged as checking us for such Breaches, and so the internal Obligation and Establishment of the Rule be preserved." I.III.7
50. Taylor, 173.
51. Maclean, 100.
52. Locke continued this line of reasoning concerning the *same self* with the argument that this consistency was, "…appropriated to me now by this self-consciousness." Thus self-consciousness like consciousness and self itself is always the *same.*
53. Taylor, 172.
54. Taylor, 172 referring to II.XXVI.12ff. See also Derek Parfit, *Reasons and Persons,* (Oxford: Oxford University Press, 1984), chapters 10–13.
55. Taylor, 49. Clarity regarding the term *consciousness* will only come when we clarify the distinct separate and unique features of this term in opposition to these others too often and freely used as synonyms. Even Locke understood this: "I think, it is agreed, that *a Definition is nothing else, but the shewing the meaning of one Word by several other not synonymous Terms.*" [III.IV.6] Also see Wider as well as Chapter Eleven of this work.
56. Aquila, 544.
57. Aquila, 544.
58. See Cox.
59. Levin, 21.
60. Levin, 21. Locke stated that, "Only as to things whose Existence is in succession, such as are the Actions of finite Beings, *v.g. Motion* and *Thought,* both which consist in a continued train of Succession, concerning their Diversity there can be no question:

Because each perishing the moment it begins, they cannot exist in different times, or in different places, as permanent Beings can at different times exist in distant places..." [II. XXVII. 2]

61. Levin, 21.
62. Levin, 21–22.
63. See also Fraser, 129–30, footnote 3. In addition to noting here that this quote was added (along with Section XXVII) to the second edition of the *Essay* (and is primarily concerned with consciousness) Fraser here observes "That there may be ideas with without any consciousness of them—that thoughts of which the individual is unconconscious may influence that individual—that principles may exist potentially, in the nature of things, explaining our experience of things—all this seems impossible to Locke."
64. Fraser, 130, footnote 2, referring to II.I.11.
65. See Fraser, 448–49, footnote 3: "The term 'consciousness,' in the sense of apprehension by the *ego* of its operations and other states as its own, came into use in the seventeenth century, among the Cartesians and in Locke, who sometimes confuses direct consciousness with the reflex act in which self is *explicitly* recognised. Although recently in almost as constant use with some psychologists as the term 'idea' is with Locke, 'consciousness,' so often introduced in this chapter [XXVII], hardly occurs in any other part of the *Essay*. See however, ch. I. 10–19."
66. Fraser, 127 footnote 2: "The argument against constant 'thinking,' or constant consciousness in the human soul, 'as long as it exists,' elaborated in this and the ten following sections, looks like a digression, interpolated without reason in the exposition of Locke's thesis—that our original ideas are phenomena of sensation and reflection. It is really meant to clear the ground."
67. Fraser, 459, footnote 2: There is an implication of regressing to a medieval viewpoint here if one takes seriously what Fraser pointed out here: "What is this but a definition of a *spiritual substance?*"
68. Fraser, 452, footnote 3. For Fraser the issue of morals and of memory make an appearance with this passage. "When Locke makes pesonal, i.e., moral identity depend on memory, this may include *potential* memory, in which our whole past conscious experience is possibly retained; and when he suggests that transmigration of one man's memory into the bodies of other men, or even of brutes, this may be taken as an emphatic illustration of the essential dependence of the idea of our personality upon self-consciousness *only*, but not as affirming that this transmigration actually occurs under the present order of things." Without a clarity of meaning for such diverse terms as *memory, personality, conscious* and *self-consciousness* it is difficult to confront the essence of this late nineteenth century reasoning.
69. Fraser, 454, footnote 3: "According to Mr. Locke, we may always be sure that we are the same persons, that is, the same accountable agents or beings, now which we were as far back as our remembrance reaches..."
70. Fraser, 139.
71. That Locke continued this thought on the limits of philosophy with the following: "...and it cannot be less than Revelation, that discovers to another, Thoughts in my mind, when I can find none there myself," demonstrates this philosopher still could occasionally hold onto thoughts more appropriate for preceding centuries earlier than for those to come.

72. Fraser, 450–51, footnote 3: "In thus pressing a distinction between identity of *substance* and identity of *person*, he seeks to show that the latter is independent of the former, and that the personality is continuous as far as memory (latent as well as patent?) can go, whatever changes of annexed bodily or spiritual substances may take place..." While this is of some interest again regarding the medieval idea of spiritual, what follows is very revealing regarding consciousness, for Fraser continued that "...the substance of a man is perhaps 'material'— as it may 'have pleased God to make' consciousness one of the qualities of powers or organized matter."
73. For memory today, see Daniel L. Schacter, *The Seven Sins of Memory*, (Boston: Houghton Mifflin, 2001). For history of memory, see James McConkey, ed., *Anatomy of Memory: An Anthology*, (NY: Oxford University Press, 1996).
74. Fraser, 453, footnote 2: Fraser's contention is that Locke believed "...that we have as clear (or as obscure) an idea of what spiritual substances are as of material substances."
75. Fraser, 453, footnote 2; 455, footnote 2.
76. Fraser, 465, footnote 1: Fraser rejects the idea that Locke is thinking of "...a double personality in the same body...which would be a fatal error."
77. Fraser, 454, footnote 2. It is unfortunate that Locke should find it necessary to fall back on a God who in answering issues as this could, after all, answer all issues making all reasoning unnecessary. Not surprising, Fraser, the Victorian Englishman, finds this acceptable: "Under the natural order of things, which we are obliged to accept in faith, the identity apparent to the persons who feels himself the same, with its implied moral responsibility, is intransferable in fact."
78. Fraser, 467, footnote 1. Fraser is referring to II.XXVII.26.
79. For discussions regarding Locke and memory see: Jeffrey Wieand, "Locke on Memory," *Locke Newsletter* II (1980), 63–75. For works specifically dealing with personal identity see D. Perry, ed., *Personal Identity*, (Berkeley: University of California Press, 1975). This discussion on personal identity necessarily requires a discussion of Locke on memory.
80. Fraser, 467, footnote 1. Fraser is referring to II.XXVII.26.
81. Fraser, 451 footnote 3: As Fraser notes, this passage II.XXVII.10 has the sound of "Making itself the same by its memory *creating*, and not merely discovering, are strictly interpreted; the thinking substance 'contributing to the production' of the successive acts, which acts memory 'unites' in one person."
82. Fraser, 466, footnote 2: Fraser offers in light of Locke's comment "...of all its memory or consciousness of past Actions" at the beginning of this citation, that this makes "...its past actions were all *incapable* being recollected—neither patent nor latent in memory."
83. Steven Pinker, *How the Mind Works*, (NY: W.W.Norton and Company, 1997), 132, 136.
84. Yolton, *Ideas*, 97–98.
85. Yolton, *Ideas*, 90.
86. Antony Flew, "Locke and the Problem of Personal Identity," *Locke and Berkeley: A Collection of Critical Essays*, ed. C.B. Martin and D.M. Armstrong, (Notre Dame: University of Notre Dame Press, 1968), 172.
87. Hans Aarsleff, "Locke's Influence," *The Cambridge Companion to Locke*, ed. Vere Chappell, (Cambridge: Cambridge University Press, 1994), 277.
88. Malcolm, 12–13, referring to III.IX.1.
89. See Havelock.
90. Henry Lee, D. D., *Anti-Scepticism: Or, Notes upon each Chapter of Mr. Lock's Essay concerning Humane Understanding*, (London: Clavel and C. Harper, 1702), 1, 48, cited

in Yolton, *Ideas*, 87. See also Vere Chappell, "Locke's Theory of Ideas," *The Cambridge Companion to Locke*, ed. Vere Chappell, (Cambridge: Cambridge University Press, 1994), 48.
91. Yolton, *Ideas*, 87.
92. John Milner, *An Account of Mr. Locke's Religion*, (1700), 14–15 cited in Yolton, *Ideas*, 89–90.
93. Robert Pattison, *On Literacy: The Politics of the Word from Homer to the Age of Rock*, (NY: Oxford University Press, 1982), 146.
94. Malcolm, 13.
95. For discussion of this phrase see David B. Paxman, "Language and Difference: The Problem of Abstraction in Eighteenth-Century Language Study," *JHI*, 54, no. 1, (1993), 23. Also see Taylor, 38 and Aarsleff, 274–75 for additional discussions. Because of the newness of dictionaries of vernacular language and the difficulty with terms used, as noted, the following may be of some clarification. Aarsleff, 274, notes that Locke's admiration of "Richelet's acclaimed monolingual French dictionary (1680), which Locke (writing in French to Toinard) thought had 'found the true secret of good diztionary-making, for the usual manner of rendering the words of one language by those of another is no more reasonable than sending to France for a case for an English instrument that is unknown in France both in regard to form and use, for the words of different languages do not agree any better than that.' " (Letter 596: C II: 310)
96. Greenlee, 258.
97. Aarsleff, 257.
98. Aarsleff, 257, referring to III.II.8.
99. Aarsleff, 273.
100. Aarsleff, 273.
101. Kenneth MacLean, *John Locke and English Literature of the Eighteenth Century*, (NY: Russell and Russell, 1962), 150.
102. Fraser, 378, footnote 3: " 'capricios'—caprices from *caper*, a goat—the waywardness of a goat."
103. MacLean, 150.
104. Aarsleff, 252–53.
105. Aarsleff, 274.
106. Herbert Weisinger, "The Self-Awareness of the Renaissance as a Criterion of the Renaissance," *Papers of the Michigan Academy of Science, Art and Letters*, 29, (1943), 566.
107. Lowe, 40.
108. See Green, passim.
109. Lowe, 39.
110. Flew, 159.
111. Flew, 159.
112. Barraclough, 25.
113. Aarsleff, 275.
114. Anne-Robert-Jacques, "Etymologie," *Encyclopédie*, (1756) 108 a–b. cited in Aarsleff, 275.
115. Aarsleff, 275.
116. Aarsleff, 273.
117. See Jaynes, *Origins*.
118. Lowe, 43.
119. Lowe, 43.

120. Lowe, 43.
121. Howard, 63.
122. Suzi Gablik, *Progress in Art*, (London: Thames and Hudson, 1976), 33. Also see J. B. Bury, *The Idea of Progress: An Inquiry into its Origin and Growth*, (NY: Dover Publications, Inc., 1955), 175.
123. R. C. Tennant, "The Anglican Response to Locke's Theory of Personal Identity," *JHI*, 43, no. 1 (1982), 73.
124. Sass, 99.
125. Frances Yates, "Bacon and the Menace of English Literature," *New York Review of Books*, 27 March 1969, 37.
126. Sass, 99.
127. Taylor, 185.
128. David Ingram, *Habermas and the Dialectic of Reason*, (New Haven: Yale University Press, 1987), 179.
129. Denis Diderot, "Encyclopédie," *Enclyclopédie*, (1755), 638va, cited in Aarsleff, 276.
130. David J Chalmers, *The Conscious Mind. In Search of a Fundamental Theory*, (NY: Oxford University Press, 1996), ix.

Chapter Eight

1. Frederick L. Nussbaum, *The Triumph of Science and Reason: 1660–1685*. (NY: Harper Torchbooks, Harper and Row, Publishers, 1962), 24.
2. Richard Peters, *Hobbes*. (Baltimore: Penguin Books, 1956), 136.
3. Peters, 191.
4. Peters, 192.
5. Peters, 192.
6. Peters, 192–93.
7. See John Neville Figgis, *The Divine Right of Kings*, (1914; NY: Harper Torchbooks, 1965).
8. Blair Campbell, "La Mettrie: The Robot and the Automaton," *JHI*, 31, no. 4 (1970), 555.
9. Campbell, 555. Also see Lester G. Crocker, *An Age of Crisis*, (Baltimore: Johns Hopkins Press, 1959), xv.
10. Henry Vyverberg, *Human Nature, Cultural Diversity, and the French Enlightenment*, (NY: Oxford University Press, 1989), 205.
11. See Emile Durkheim, *Montesquieu and Rousseau. Forerunners of Sociology*, trans. by Ralph Manheim, (Ann Arbor: University of Michigan Press, 1960).
12. Vyverberg, 155. Also see Durkheim
13. Campbell, 555. Also see Davies.
14. Dennett, 250. And in contradiction see Sass. Also see Jaynes, How Old is Consciousness, and Jaynes, *Origins*.
15. Jean Le Rond d'Alembert, *Preliminary Discourse to the Encyclopedia of Diderot*, trans. Richard N. Schwab, (NY: Library of Liberal Arts, 1963), 1.
16. Denis Diderot and Jean Le Rond d'Alembert, *Encyclopédie*, (Paris, 1751–66) 15:777, s.v. "*Système*," cited and trans. in Mayr, 79.
17. Mayr, 49, 99.
18. Mayr, 100.
19. Mayer, 71.
20. Powell, C. Thomas. *Kant's Theory of Self-Consciousness*. (Oxford: Clarendon Press, 1990),

2. See also Leibniz, *Human Understanding*.
21. Don Parry Norford, "Microcosm and Macrocosm in Seventeenth-Century Literature," *JHI*, 38, no. 3, (1977), 428.
22. Henry E. Allison, "Locke's Theory of Personal Identity: A Re-Examination," *JHI*, 27, no. 1, (1966), 53.
23. Powell, 2.
24. Allison, 52.
25. Gottfried Leibniz, *Discourse on Metaphysics/**Correspondence with Arnauld**/ Monadology*, trans. G. R. Montgomery (LaSalle, IL: Open Court Pub., 1973) 126, cited in Powell, 2
26. Benedictus Spinoza, "Ethics," *Chief Works of Spinoza*, trans. R. H. M. Elwes, (NY: 1951), Proposition xiii, cited in Powell, 3.
27. Powell, 3.
28. John Yolton, "Locke's Man," *JHI*, 62, no. 4, (2001), 683.
29. Lowe, 48.
30. Richter, 217.
31. Campbell, 558.
32. Taylor, 193.
33. Campbell, 558.
34. Andrew E. Barnes, "*Ces Sortes de Pénitences Imaginaires*": The Counter-Reformation Assault on Communitas," *Social History and Issues In Human Consciousness: Some Interdisciplinary Connections*, Andrew E. Barnes and Peter N. Stearns, eds. (NY: New York University Press, 1989), 68.
35. Robert A. Greene, "Whichcote, the Candle of the Lord, and Synderesis," *JHI*, 52, no. 4, (1991), 629.
36. Barnes, 67.
37. Allison, 53.
38. Yolton, 683.
39. Taylor, 164.
40. Gottfried Leibniz, *Correspondence with Arnauld*, 126 cited in Powell, 2.
41. Powell, 3.
42. Powell, 4.
43. Cox, 15.
44. Campbell, 564. For the rise of privacy and more intimate readings of novels at this times see Spacks, *Privacy*.
45. Campbell, 565.
46. Campbell, 562.
47. Popper and Eccles, 111, fn7.
48. Smith, Adam [1759] Part III, Section II; Part III, chapter I in the sixth and later editions cited in Popper and Eccles, 111, fn7.
49. Taylor, 301.
50. Taylor, 287.
51. G. S. Rousseau and Roy Porter, "Introduction: Toward a Natural History of Mind and Body," *The Languages of Psyche: Mind and Body in Enlightenment Thought*, *Clark Library Lectures 1985–1986*, ed. G. S. Rousseau, (Berkeley, Cal.: University of California Press, 1990), 31.
52. Lyons, 7.
53. Lyons, 7.

54. Davies, 101.
55. Davies, 101.
56. Edward Young, *Conjectures on Original Composition*, (1759; Leeds: Scholar Press, 1966), 52–53 cited in Cox, 3.
57. J. Robert Loy, review of *Order and Chance: The Pattern of Diderot's Thought*, by Geoffrey Bremner, *Eighteenth Century Studies*, 19, no. 1, (1985), 124.
58. Cox, 4.
59. Davies, 93.
60. Davies, 93.
61. Davies, 70.
62. Davies, 22.
63. Davies, 113.
64. See Walter R. Martin.
65. Davies, 85.
66. Davies, 91.
67. Cox, 21,
68. Davies, 33–4.
69. Davies, 30.
70. Cox, 25.
71. Taylor, 206.
72. Cox, 15.
73. David Hume, *An Inquiry Concerning Human Understanding*, (NY: Library of Liberal Arts, Bobbs-Merrill, 1955), 252.
74. Hume, *Human Understanding*, 93.
75. David Hume, *A Treatise of Human Nature*, second edition with text revised and variant readings by P. H. Nidditch, (Oxford:Clarendon Press, 1978), 252.
76. Hume, *Human Nature*, 402, II.III.I.
77. Hume, *Human Nature*, 251, I.IV.VI.
78. See Chapter Five of this work.
79. Hume, *Human Nature*, 77 and index. For his billiards analogy see Hume, *Human Understanding*, 62, 187–8.
80. Hume, *Human Nature*, 254.
81. Hume, *Human Nature*, 252.
82. Hume, *Human Nature*, 260, I.IV.VI.
83. Cox, 27.
84. Hume, *Human Nature*, 259.
85. Hume, *Human Nature*, 458, III.I.I.
86. Hume, *Human Nature*, 253, I.IV.VI.
87. Hume, *Human Nature*, 339 II.II.II.
88. Hume, *Human Nature*, 317, II.I.XI.
89. Geoffrey Clive, *The Romantic Enlightenment*, (NY: Meridian Books, Inc., 1960), 59.
90. Clive, 30.
91. N. J. H. Dent, *Rousseau. An Introduction to his Psychological, Social and Political Theory*, (Oxford: Blackwell, 1989), 31.
92. Dent, 33–34.
93. Rousseau, *Emile*, 38.
94. Rousseau, *Emile*, 38.
95. Paul Zweig, *The Heresy of Self-Love. A Study of Subversive Individualism*, (NY: Harper

Colophon Books, 1968), 147.
96. J. M. Cohen, "Introduction," *Confessions of Jean Jacques Rousseau*, trans. by J. M. Cohen, (Baltimore: Penguin Books, 1953), 7.
97. Ann Hartle, *The Modern Self in Rousseau's Confessions: A Reply to St. Augustine*, (Notre Dame: University of Notre Dame Press, 1983), 10.
98. Blaise Pascal, *Selections from The Thoughts*, ed. and trans. Arthur H. Beattie. (NY: Appleton-Century-Crofts, 1965), 96 (no. 277).
99. Cohen, 10.
100. Zweig, 149.
101. Zweig, 155.
102. Zweig, 151.
103. Dent, 113. See Rousseau, *Emile*, 4. For a similar view the reader may wish to look at Eric Fromm's *The Art of Loving*, (NY: Harper, 1956).
104. Zweig, 151.
105. Rousseau, *Emile*, 52.
106. Rousseau, *Emile*, 60.
107. See Durkheim. Also see Dent.
108. Zweig, 144.
109. Hartle, 157.
110. Zweig, 146.
111. Dent, 98.
112. Dent, 97.
113. Zweig, 163.
114. Zweig, 152. This subject will reappear in the last chapter and specifically in regard to the thoughts of Sartre.
115. Dent, 96.
116. Dent, 173; 203f.
117. Rousseau, *Emile*, 37.
118. See Martin.
119. Rousseau, *Emile*, 64.
120. Hartle, 157.
121. Rousseau, *Emile*, 53.
122. Rousseau, *Emile*, 42.
123. Rousseau, *Emile*, 64.
124. Rousseau, *Emile*, 42.
125. Rousseau, *Emile*, 42.
126. Dent, 71.
127. Rousseau, *Emile*, 55.
128. Rousseau, *Emile*, 55.
129. Rousseau, Emile, 1, 65; IV, 286 cited in Dent, 71.
130. Rousseau, *Emile*, 42.

Chapter Nine

1. Pascal, 277.
2. Cox, 37.
3. Arthur Lovejoy, *Essays in the History of Ideas*, (1948; NY: G.P. Putman's Sons,1960), 235.

4. Lovejoy, *Essays*, 235–36.
5. Lovejoy, *Essays*, 236.
6. Allan Megill, *Prophets of Extremity: Nietzsche, Heidegger, Foucault, Derrida*, (Berkley: University of California Press, 1980), 5.
7. Aarsleff, 276.
8. Edward Engelberg, *The Unkown Distance: From Consciousness to Conscience: Goethe to Camus*, (Cambridge: Harvard University Press, 1972), 32.
9. Taylor, 396.
10. Taylor, 396.
11. Arthur Lovejoy, *The Great Chain of Being. A Study of an Idea*, (1936; NY: Harper and Row, 1960), 293.
12. Weintraub, 373, fn 46.
13. Sennett, 153.
14. Thomas Carlyle, *Sartor Resartus: The Life and Opinions of Herr Teufelsdröckh*, (NY: Odyssey Press 1937), 39.
15. Carlyle, 39.
16. Carlyle, 260.
17. William Barrett, *Irrational Man: A Study in Existential Philosophy*, (NY: Doubleday, 1962), 125.
18. Sennett, 170.
19. See Bloom, *Shakespeare*.
20. Philip Rosenberg, *The Seventh Hero*, (Cambridge: Harvard University Press, 1974), 46, cited in Sennett, 171.
21. Sennett, 171.
22. Wilhelm Dilthey, *Pattern and Meaning in History*, (New York: Harper and Row, 1961), 85.
23. Weintraub, 344.
24. Weintraub, 345, fn 18. See also Weintraub, chapter 13.
25. Kaufmann, *Discovery of the Mind*, 4 volumes (NY: McGraw-Hill Book Co., 1980), I, 53.
26. Barrett, *Irrational*, 123.
27. Coan, 89.
28. Johann Wolfgang Von Goethe, *Faust, Part I*, trans. Randall Jarrell, (1976; NY: Farrar, Straus and Giroux, 2000), 80.
29. Goethe, 140.
30. Goethe, 100–1.
31. Kaufmann, *Discovery*, I, 46.
32. Kaufmann, *Discovery*, I, 42.
33. Kaufmann, *Discovery*, I, 42.
34. Kaufmann, *Discovery*, I, 42–43.
35. Kaufmann, *Discovery*, I, 29. Goethe's phrase, "throw themselves at a party," brings to mind Groucho Marx's maxim of not belonging to an organization that would have him as a member.
36. Kaufmann, *Discovery*, I, 16.
37. Barrett, 37.
38. Kaufmann, *Discovery*, I, 17.
39. Goethe, 85.
40. Erich Heller, *The Disinherited Mind. Essays in Modern German Literature and Thought*, (NY: Harcourt Brace, 1975), 59.

41. Heller, 59.
42. Goethe, 86.
43. Heller, 61.
44. Barrett, 125.
45. Georg Hegel, "Preface," Phenomenology of Mind cited in E. Warwick Slinn, *The Discourse of Self in Victorian Poetry*, (Charlottesville: University Press of Virginia, 1991), 23.
46. This comment was made by a professor of political philosophy at Columbia in 1962.
47. Slinn, 22.
48. Slinn, 22.
49. Barrett, 206.
50. Barrett, 124–5. Also see Dostoyesvsky's Roskolnikov from *Crime and Punishment* noted at the beginning of the chapter
51. Daniel Roche, *France in the Enlightenment*, trans. Arthur Goldhammer, (Cambridge: Harvard University Press, 1998), 602.
52. Kaufmann, *Discovery*, III, 79.
53. See Chapter Five of this work for a discussion of J. S. Mill, genius and individuality.
54. Raymond Williams, *Culture and Society: 1780–1950*, (NY: Harper and Row, Publishers, 1958), 44.
55. Samuel Taylor Coleridge, *Inquiring Spirit: A New Presentation of Coleridge from his Published and Unpublished Prose Writings*, ed. Kathleen Coburn, (NY: Pantheon, 1951), 25.
56. Coleridge, 411.
57. Charles Dickens, *Tale of Two Cities*, (1859), 1.
58. Engelberg, 243–44. "IS" refers to Colderidge, *Inquiring Spirit*. "F" refers to Coleridge, *The Friend, Collected Work of Samuel Taylor Coleridge*, vol. 1, ed. Barbara E. Rooke, (Princeton: Princeton University Press, 1969).
59. Engelberg, 243.
60. Ralph Waldo Emerson, "Self-Reliance," *Selections from Ralph Waldo Emerson*, ed. Stephen E. Whicher, (Boston: Riverside Press, 1960), 153.
61. William Wordsworth, "The Tables Turned," (1798), cited in Barrett, 125.
62. Arendt, *Mind*, II, 43. Also see discussion in Chapter One of this work.
63. Delumeau, 38.
64. Colin Wilson, *The Outsider*, (Boston: Riverside Press, 1956), 237.
65. Alexis de Tocqueville, *Democracy in America*, ed. Richard D. Heffner, (NY: New American Library, 1956), II, 27, 192–93.
66. Sennett, 215.
67. Friedrich Nietzsche, *The Use and Abuse of History*, trans. Adrian Collins, (NY: Library Arts Press, 1949), 11.
68. Georg Hegel, *Die Vernunft in der Geschichte* trans. and cited in Walter Kaufmann, *Hegel: A Reinterpretation*, (NY: Doubleday Anchor Book 1966), 4–5.
69. Coleridge *Inquiring Spirit*, 31, 45.
70. Engelberg, 37.
71. Coleridge, *Inquiring Spirit*, 35 cited in Engelberg, 38.
72. Coleridge, *Friend*, 523 cited in Engelberg, 38.
73. Sennett, 153.
74. Aarkady Plotnitsky, *In the Shadow of Hegel: Complementarity, History, and the Unconscious*, (Gainsville: University of Florida Press, 1993), 165.

75. Slinn, 41–2.
76. Plotnitsky, 286.
77. Plotnitsky, 288.
78. F. H. Heinemann, *Existentialism and the Modern Predicament*, (NY: Harper and Brothers, 1958), 10.
79. Heinemann, 10–11.
80. Walter Kaufmann, *From Shakespeare to Existentialism*, (NY: Anchor Books Ed, 1960), 57.
81. Plotnitsky, 288.
82. Kaufmann, *Shakespeare*, 57–58.
83. Kaufmann, *Shakespeare*, 73.
84. Barrett, 189–90.
85. H. G. Schenk, *The Mind of the European Romantics: An Essay in Cultural History*, (London: Constable, 1966), 238.
86. Walter Kaufmann, *Nietzsche. Philosopher, Psychologist, Antichrist*, 4th ed., (Princeton: Princeton University Press, 1974), 288.
87. William Hubben, *Dostoevsky, Kierkegaard, Nietzsche and Kafka: Four Prophets of our Destiny*, (NY: Collier Books, 1972), 115.
88. Heller, 116.
89. Schenk, 49.
90. Sass, 94.
91. Schenk, 238.
92. Friedrich Wilhelm Nietzsche, "Thus Spoke Zarathustra: A Book for All and None," *The Portable Nietzsche*, ed. and trans. Walter Kaufmann, (NY: Penguin Books, 1985), 115. Also see Friedrich Nietzsche, *The Gay Science with a prelude in rhymes and an appendix of songs*, trans. Walter Kaufmann, (NY:Vintage Books, 1974).
93. Nietzsche, *Gay Science*, 181.
94. Paul Monaco, *Modern European Culture and Consciousness, 1870–1980*, (Albany, NY: State University of New York Press, 1983), 25, 178–9.
95. Kern, 178–79.
96. Monaco, 63.
97. Monaco, 28.
98. Kern, 179.
99. Heller, 81. Quote from Burckhardt is a letter to Schaunberg 5 March 1846. Also see discussion on Burckhardt in Chapter Three of this work.
100. Heller, 81.
101. Heller, 80.
102. Heller, 83–4.
103. Schenk, 233. Also see Schenk, 248, fn 3.
104. Heller, 77.
105. Heller, 83.
106. Heller, 77. See discussion of Burchkart and Nietzsche in Chapter Three of this work.
107. Friedrich Wilhelm Nietzsche, "Human, All-Too-Human," *Portable Nietzsche*, 51.
108. Carl D. Schneider, *Shame Exposure and Privacy*, (Boston: Beacon Press, 1977), 9.
109. Ralph Ketcham, *Individualism and Public Life: A Modern Dilemma*, (Oxford: Blackwell, 1987), ix. See Tocqueville, Section 27, "Of Individualism in Democratic Countries."
110. Nietzsche, *History*, 13.
111. Engelbert, 198.

112. Nietzsche, *Zarathustra*, 171–72.
113. Nietzsche, *The Joyful Wisdom*, cited in Engelberg, 217–18. Kaufman's translation of this work goes by the title *Gay Science*. For a discussion of this distinction see Kaufman's introduction to *Gay Science*.
114. Nietzsche, *Gay Science*, 325.
115. Stanley Corngold, *The Fate of the Self: German Writers and French Theory*, (New York: Columbia University Press, 1986), 10.
116. Corngold, 97.
117. Corngold, 10.
118. Engleberg, 198.
119. Hubben, 120.
120. Nietzsche, *Zarathustra*, 146.
121. Hubben, 120.
122. Walter Kaufmann, "Existentialism from Dostoevsky to Sartre," *Existentialism from Dostoevsky to Sartre*, ed. with prefaces and translations Walter Kaufmann, (Cleveland: Meridian Books, 1970), 13.
123. Hubben, 120.
124. Friedrich Wilhelm Nietzsche, "Ecce Homo," *The Portable Nietzsche*, 660.
125. Kaufmann, "Existentialism," 12.
126. Kaufmann, *Nietzsche*, 268.
127. Kaufmann, *Nietzsche*, 158.
128. Corngold, 11.
129. Nietzsche, *Zarathustra*, 258.
130. Nietzsche, *Zarathustra*, 146–47.
131. Corngold, 6.
132. Corngold, 121.
133. Wilson, 123.
134. Corngold, 98.
135. Corngold, 98. Citations are from *Nietzsche, Beyond Good and Evil*.
136. Jaynes, *Origins*.
137. Nietzsche, *Gay Science*, 308.
138. Corngold, 98–99.
139. Engelberg, 38.
140. Monaco, 22.
141. Monaco, 22.
142. Stinn, 41–42.
143. Nietzsche, *Gay Science*, 84–85.
144. Nietzsche, *Gay Science*, 90.
145. Kern, 62–63.
146. Nietzsche, *Gay Science*, 262.
147. Nietzsche, *Gay Science*, 297.
148. Nietzsche, *Gay Science*, 84.
149. Nietzsche, *Gay Science*, 299.
150. Nietzsche, *Gay Science*, 299.
151. Nietzsche, *Gay Science*, 107.
152. Nietzsche, *Gay Science*, 220.
153. Engelberg, 193.
154. Engelberg, 236.

155. Nietzsche, *Gay Science*, 297–98.
156. Nietzsche, *Gay Science*, 300.
157. Engelberg, 194. Also see Sass, xi.
158. Schneider, 9.
159. Sennett, 152.
160. Kaufmann, *Nietzsche*, 267.
161. Kaufmann, *Nietzsche*, 266.
162. Engelberg, 193–94. Also see Heller, 119 and Kaufmann, *Nietzsche*, 232–33.
163. Nietzsche, *Joyful Wisdom* cited in Engelberg, 69.
164. Nietzsche, *Human, All-Too-Human, Works*, VII, pt. II, 224 cited in Engelberg, 208–9.
165. Engelberg, 194.
166. Engelberg, 10.
167. Engelberg, 200–1.
168. Nietzsche, *Gay Science*, 299.
169. Julius Kraft, "Introduction," *The Use and Abuse of History*, by Friedrich Nietzsche, trans. by Adrian Collins, (NY: Library Arts Press, 1949), 8–9.
170. Heller, 119.
171. Friedrich Nietzsche, *Will to Power*, trans. Walter Kaufmann and R. J. Hollingdale, (NY: Random House, 1967), 549.
172. Walter Kaufmann, Preface to Notes from the Underground from *Existentialism from Dostoevsky to Sartre*, 52.
173. Kaufmann, "Existentialism," 11.
174. Schenk, xviii.
175. Schenk, xviii.
176. Kaufmann, "Existentialism," 14.
177. Kaufmann, "Existentialism," 13.
178. Schenk, xi.
179. Schenk, xi.

Chapter Ten

1. Roger Shattuck, *The Banquet Years: The Origins of the Avante Garde In France, 1885 to World War I*, rev. ed., (NY: Vintage Books, 1968), 1.
2. Robert C. Soloman, "Introduction," *Existentialism*, ed., Robert C. Solomon, (NY: Modern Library, 1974), xii.
3. Solomon, xix.
4. Barraclough, 45.
5. Ong, Communications, 29.
6. Ong, Communications, 29.
7. Solomon, ix.
8. Herbert Jay Lifton, *The Protean Self: Human Resilience in an Age of Fragmentation*, (NY: Basic Books, 1993), 14.
9. Woolf, Virginia, "Mr. Barrett and Mrs. Brown," *The Captain's Deathbed, and other Essays*, (NY: Harcourt Brace and Company, 1950), 96–97. For a discussion of plurality of selves see Whittemore, *Whole Lives*.
10. C. S. Lewis, "*De Descriptione Temporum*: An Inaugral Lecture," *They Asked for a Paper: Papers and Addresses*, (1954; London: Geoffrey Bles, 1962), 18.
11. Sass, 28.

12. Arthur M. Young, *The Reflexive Universe: Evolution of Consciousness*, (NY: Delacorte Press, 1976), 5–6.
13. Barrett, *Irrational*, 63.
14. Walter Kaufmann, "Preface to Kafka," *Existentialism from Dostoevsky to Sartre*, trans. and ed. Walter Kaufmann, (Cleveland: Meridian Books, 1970), 122.
15. Kaufmann, "Kafka," 121.
16. Kaufmann, "Kafka," 122.
17. Kaufmann, "Kafka," 122.
18. Woolf, "Mr. Barrett and Mrs. Brown," 96.
19. Virginia Woolf, *Orlando: A Biography*, (NY: Harcourt Brace Jovanovich, 1958), 309.
20. Caryl Marsh, "A Framework for Describing Subjective States of Consciousness," *Alternate States of Consciousness*, ed. Norman E. Zinberg, (NY: The Free Press, 1977), 128–29. Marsh also adds Woolf, Joyce and Bergson who also argue that there is more than one self. Regarding Woolf also see Wittemore, 125; and Jerome L Singer, "Ongoing Thought: The Normative Baseline for Alternate States of Consciousness," *Alternate States of Consciousness*, 90.
21. Kaufmann, "Kafka," 122–23.
22. Franz Kafka, *Tagebucher, 1910–23* (Frankfurt, 1951), 552, cited in Kern, 17.
23. Franz Kafka, *The Trial*, trans. Willa and Edwin Muir and E. M. Butler, (NY: Modern Library, 1956), 48–49.
24. H. Rosenberg, *Act and the Actor: Making the Self*, (1970; Chicago: University of Chicago Press, 1983), 9, cited in Sass, 8.
25. Kafka's diary, 16 Jan 1922, cited in Sass, 8.
26. Kern, 31.
27. Kern, 18.
28. Glen A. Mazis, "Merleau-Ponty and the 'Backward Flow' of Time: The Reversibility of Temporality and the Temporality of Reversibility," *Merleau-Ponty, Hermeneutics, and Postmodernism*, ed. Thomas W. Busch and Shaun Gallagher, (Albany: State University of New York Press, 1992), 66.
29. The reader can also compare the 41 pages in Vintage edition of the book from 1980 edition.
30. See William James *Principles of Psychology*, (Cambridge: Harvard University Press, 1983); and William James, *The Varieties of Religious Experience*, (NY: Collier Books, 1961).
31. Kern, 28. Also see Richard Ellmann, *Ulysses on the Liffey*, (NY: Oxford University Press, 1972), 163; and Rayner Banham, *The Architecture of the Well-Tempered Environment*, (Chicago: University of Chicago Press, 1969), 64.
32. Mazis, 67.
33. James, *Principles*, I, 233. Also see Kern, 24: "Although James and Bergson tended to use somewhat different metaphors to characterize thought, they agreed that it was not composed of discrete parts, that any moment of consciousness was a synthesis of an ever changing past and future, and that it flowed."
34. Levin, 20–21.
35. Levin, 207.
36. Kern, 43.
37. James, *Principles*, I, 19.
38. Levin, 82.
39. Sass, 226–27.

40. William James, *The Letters of Williams James*, ed. Henry James, (Boston: Atlantic Monthly Press, 1920) vol. 1, 147.
41. John B. Watson, "Psychology as the Behaviorist Views It," *Psychological Review*, 20, (1913), 158.
42. James, *Principles*, 231.
43. Wolf, 20.
44. Wolf, 194
45. James, *Principles*, 279.
46. Levin, 74.
47. T. S. Eliot, "Music of Poetry," *On Poetry and Poets*, (NY: Farrar, Straus, and Cudahy, 1957), 21–22.
48. T. S. Eliot, "Burnt Norton," *Four Quartets*, II, 83–90.
49. Richard Ellmann and Robert O'Clair, eds., *Norton Anthology of Modern Poetry*, (NY: Norton, 1973), 445.
50. W. B. Yeats, *The Second Coming*, 1–7.
51. Scott, 45.
52. Scott, 46.
53. T. S. Eliot, *Little Gidding*, IV, 235–237
54. T. S. Eliot, *The Waste Land*, II, 152.
55. F. H. Bradley, *Appearance and Reality*, (Oxford: Clarendon Press, 1946), 39 cited by Eliot in *Norton*, 471, fn5.
56. Sass, 137.
57. Scott, 46.
58. Wolf, 99, 187, 357.
59. Sass, 357. And see cited in Sass, 335–36, fn2: T. S. Eliot, "The metaphysical poets," *Criticism: The Major Texts*, ed. W. J. Bate, (1921; NY: Harcourt, Brace and World, 1952), 529–34: Eliot describes the new poet as able only to think *or* feel, 'by fits, unbalanced.'
60. Robert Musil, *The Man Without Qualities*, trans. E. Wilkins and E. Kaiser, (NY: Perigee, 1980), 30. See also, Sass, 129, 175.
61. Musil, 129.
62. Musil, 175. See also Sass.
63. Musil, 176.
64. Musil, 175.
65. Musil, 34.
66. Kern, 132.
67. William Fleming, *Art and Ideas*, third ed., (NY: Holt, Rinehart and Winston, Inc., 1968), 544.
68. Fleming 544.
69. Kern, 140.
70. Cite in Fleming, 485.
71. Fleming, 486.
72. E. H. Gombrich, *The Story of Art*, (NY: Phaidon Pub. Inc., 1966), 413.
73. Fleming, 488.
74. Fleming, 498
75. H. W. Janson, *History of Art. A Survey of the Major Visual Arts from the Dawn of History to the Present Day*, (Englewood Cliffs, NJ: Prentice-Hall, 1965), 510.
76. Janson, 510.

77. Helen Gardner, *Art Through the Ages*, sixth ed., (1926; NY: Harcourt Brace Jovanich, Inc., 1975), 708.
78. Gombrich, 439.
79. Gombrich, 436.
80. Gombrich, 439.
81. Gombrich, 439.
82. Fleming, 505.
83. Gardner, 727.
84. Gardner, 720.
85. Gardner, 728.
86. Gardner, 730.
87. Gardner, 727.
88. Gardner, 730.
89. Gardner, 730.
90. Kern, 147.
91. Guillaume Apollinaire, *Cubist Painters; Aesthetic Meditations*, trans. Lionel Abel, (1913; NY: Wittenborn, Schultz, 1944), 13.
92. Kern, 148.
93. Fleming, 500.
94. Kern, 45.
95. Fleming, 500.
96. H. Stuart Hughes, *Consciousness and Society: The Reorientation of European Social Thought 1890–1930*, (1958; NY: Vintage Books, 1977), 365–66. Regarding Proust, Hughes, 365-66 : "It is implicit in the brutal unmasking of character that is at the center of Pirandello's dramas. Indeed, it is in Pirandello that we find the most uncompromising assertion of the dubious nature of psychological reality: Proust and Hesse, Gide and Mann, eventually reveal to us their own notion of the truth; Pirandello is content to leave us suspended in eternal doubt." Also see for artist as hero Paul Zweig, *The Heresy of Self-Love: A Study of Subversive Individualism*, (NY: Harper Colophon Books, 1968), 265: "…the hero needs a new language, a style appropriate to what he has shaken loose in his own life. It is surely no accident that our civilization, obsessed with material progress, engaged in perpetual warfare with 'nature' and thereby isolated from it as few civilizations have been, should also have produced a repertory of languages for self-discovery, a 'poetry' on which its very politics have been founded."
97. Hans Meyerhoff, *Time in Literature*, (Berkeley: University of California Press, 1955), 47–48, cited in Hughes, 386.
98. Henri Bergson, *An Introduction to Metaphysics*, (1903), 23–26 cited in Kern, 24–25.
99. Henri Bergson, *Essai sur le données immédiates de la conscience*, (Paris: 1961), 73, 74, trans. and cited in Kern, 45.
100. Kern, 43. See Henri Bergson, *Time and Free Will*, (1889; New York, 1960), 101. See also Hughes
101. Hughes, 63–64.
102. Hughes, 117–18.
103. Hughes, 116–17. See Bergson, *Essay on the Immediate Data of Consciousness* (1889) and *Matter and Memory* (1897).
104. Henri Bergson, *Introduction to Metaphysics*, (1907), cited in Hughes, 117.
105. Henri Bergson, *L'Evolution créatrice*, (1907; Paris: Presses Universitaires de France, 1946), 1–2, trans. and cited in Marsh, 128–29. See also Hughes, 117–18 and R.

Humphrey, *Stream of Consciousness in the Modern Novel*, (Berkeley: University of California Press, 1954), 272.
106. Humphrey, 272 cited in Marsh, 128–29.
107. Cited in Kern, 32. See also Kern, 201, 207, 209, 211–212.
108. Kern, 195.
109. Kern, 277.
110. A rather polemical if not alarmist popular work by Ernest E. Williams, *Made in Germany*, (London, 1896), 10–13, cited in Kern, 247–48, was published in England: "In an inventory of English life Williams pointed out German goods lurking everywhere. 'Made in Germany' could be found stamped on clothing, toys, dolls, embroidery, needlework cottons, leather goods, books, newsprint, china, pencils, prints, engravings, photographs, pianos, mugs, drain pipes, ornaments, wall hangings, iron goods, electrical appliances, German opera, instruments, and sheet music dominated the English musical world. He completed this litany of commercial doom with the most terrifying fact of all—that in 1893 the port of Hamburg surpassed Liverpool for the first time in total tonnage of shipping."
111. Kern, 250–51.
112. Kern, 247–48. The dichotomy between the German society and its intellectuals as exemplified by Nietzsche could not be more clear—any wonder he claimed he was Polish and not a German and spend his post-university years in Switzerland.
113. Marshall McLuhan, *Understanding Media*. (New York, 1964), 101 cited in Kern, 275.
114. Kern, 246.
115. Kern, 276.
116. Kern, 288.
117. Kern, 288.
118. Kern, 289.
119. Kern, 311.
120. Kern, 308.
121. Kern, 307.
122. Pär Bergman, *"Modernolatria" et "Simultaneità": Recherches sur deux tendances dans l'avant-gard littéraire en Italie et en France à la veille de la première guerre mondiale*, (Uppsala, Sweden, 1962), x, cited and trans. in Kern, 81.
123. Karl Dietrich Erdmann, *Kurt Riezler: Tagebücher, Aufsätze, Documente*, (Göttingen, 1972), 190–91, trans. and cited in Kern, 276–77.
124. Kern, 293.
125. Gertrude Stein, *Picasso*, (1938; NY: B. T. Batesford, Ltd., 1949), 11.
126. Kern, 291.
127. Kern, 300.
128. Kern, 295.
129. Kern, 4.
130. Stein, 11.
131. Kern, 8.
132. Kern, 176.
133. Kern, 291.
134. Kern, 290.
135. Kern, 291.
136. Kern, 292.
137. Kern, 293.

138. Kern, 293. See also Barrett's *Illusion of Technique*
139. See Stanley Kubrick's film, *Paths of Glory*, (1957).
140. Wylie Sypher, *Loss of the Self in Modern Literature and Art*, (NY: Random House, 1964), 57.
141. Taylor, 288.
142. Fred R. Dallmayr, *Twilight of Subjectivity: Contributions to a Post-Individualist Theory of Politics*, (Amherst, Mass.: The University of Massachusetts Press, 1981), 31
143. Barrett, *Illusion*, xvi.
144. Barrett, *Irrational*, 11.
145. Barrett, *Irrational*, 217.
146. Barrett, *Irrational*, 220.
147. Barrett, *Irrational*, 40.
148. Dallymar, 67.
149. Levin, 125.
150. Levin, 155.
151. Levin, 157.
152. Barrett, *Irrational*, 218.
153. Ryle, 15–16.
154. Barrett, *Irrational*, 243.
155. Barrett, *Illusion*, 69.
156. David and Marjorie Haigt, "The Country of Consciousness," *Monist: An International Quarterly Journal of General Philosophical Inquiry*, 61, no. 1 (1978), 131.
157. Dallymar, 32.
158. Barrett, *Irrational*, 226.
159. Barrett, *Illusion*, 75.
160. Barrett, *Illusion*, 76.
161. Barrett, *Irrational*, 214.
162. Barrett, *Irrational*, 223.
163. Sass, 186. That language becomes such a critical issue in an age of growing self-consciousness is to be expected. One philologist and literary critic, Paul de Man (1919–1983), influenced by Heidegger and deconstructionism gave us a description of self-consciousness that is at the least unusual. See Paul De Man, "Rhetoric of temporality," cited in Sass, 349: "De Man...describes self-consciousness as the act of self-duplication or self- multiplication by which one divides oneself in two (into an empirical self and a disinterested spectator) and differentiates oneself from the external world. He associates this explicitly with the 'reflective activity' of the philosopher...in contrast with 'the activity of the ordinary self caught in everyday concerns.' But, unlike Merleau-Ponty or Heidegger, de Man treats the latter, prereflective mode as a 'self-mystification,' while praising the much rarer philosophical attitude for its 'lucidity'—its ability 'authentically' to capture the 'inauthenticity' at our core." See also Sass, 211, 212, 208.
164. Ryle, 186–87.
165. Ryle, 22.
166. Ryle, 27.
167. Ryle, 161.
168. Ryle, 32.
169. Sypher, 97. See also George Steiner, "Retreat from the Word," *Kenyon Review*, Spring, 1961.

170. Ryle, 164–65.
171. Sypher, 68.
172. Sypher, 134. Eliot, T.S. *Ash Wednesday*.
173. Sypher, 80.
174. Sypher, 79–80.
175. Eugene Ionesco, *The Killer and Other Stories*, (NY: Grove Press, 1960), 82.
176. Sypher, 96.
177. Jean Dubuffet, "Anticultural Positions," excerpted in Sypher, 171. "Anticultural Positions" was a lecture given to the Arts Club of Chicago, December 1951.
178. Zweig, 219.
179. Sypher, 144.
180. Barrett, *Illusion*, 29. This writer was part of that movement in the 1950's in America known as the Beats.
181. Wilson, 147.
182. Cited in Zweig, 265: "...style appropriate to what he has shaken loose in his own life. It is surely no accident that our civilization, obsessed with material progress, engaged in perpetual warfare with 'nature' and thereby isolated from it as few civilizations have been, should also have produced a repertory of languages for self-discovery, a 'poetry' on which its very politics have been founded."
183. Ray Bradbury, *Dandelion Wine*, (London: Grafton Books, 1977), 14.
184. Bradbury, 35.
185. Bradbury, 85.

Chapter Eleven

1. H. Stuart Hughes, *Consciousness and Society: The Reorientation of European Social Thought 1890–1930*, (1958; NY: Vintage Books, 1977), 64.
2. George Santayana, *Scepticism and Animal Faith: Introduction to a System of Philosophy*, (1923; NY: Dover Publications Inc., 1955), 270.
3. Santayana, 270.
4. Wolf, 67.
5. Sass, 91.
6. Kern, 132. See also Chapter Ten.
7. Albert Einstein, *Relativity*, trans. Robert W. Lawson, (1920; Amherst, NY: Prometheus Books, 1995), 9.
8. Kern, 140.
9. Kern, 139.
10. Arthur M. Young, *The Foundations of Science: The Missing Parameter*, (San Francisco: Robert Briggs Association, 1985), 12.
11. Wolf, 23.
12. Wolf, 23.
13. Wolf, 102.
14. For a discussion of memory see Matt K. Matsudo, *The Memory of the Modern*, (NY: Oxford University Press, 1996); James McConkey, *The Anatomy of Memory. An Anthology*, (NY: Oxford University Press, 1996); Douwe Draaisma, *Metaphors of Memory. A History of Ideas About the Mind*, (NY: Cambridge University Press, 1995). For a more historical analysis see Mary J. Carruthers, *The Book of Memory. A Study of Memory in Medieval Culture*, (NY: Cambridge University Press,1990).

15. Hannah Arendt, *The Life of the Mind: Willing*, (NY: Harcourt Brace Jovanovich, 1978), vol. 2, 41.
16. Georg Hegel, *Philosophy of Right*, Preface; *Encyclopedia*, 2nd ed., #465, 177, 185 cited in Arendt, 40–1.
17. Kern, 21.
18. Taylor, 188.
19. Taylor, 188.
20. Sass, 159. Also see J. Frank, "Spatial Form in Modern Literature," *The Widening Gyre: Crisis and Mastery in Modern Literature*, (Bloomington: Indiana University Press, 1968), 13. Also see J. Frank, "Spatial Form: Thirty years after," *Spatial Form in Narrative*, eds J.R. Smitten and A. Daghistany, (Ithaca: Cornell University Press, 1981), 204.
21. Sypher, 102–3.
22. Taylor, 288.
23. Kern, 142. Also see Suzanne Bernard, "Le 'Coup des des' de Mallarmé replacé dans la perspective historique," *Revue D'Histoire Litteraire de la France*, (April-June, 1951), 183.
24. See Kern, 143.
25. Kern, 132.
26. Kern, 219.
27. Wolf, 74.
28. Wolf, 74.
29. Wolf, 75.
30. Wolf, 208.
31. Wolf, 75.
32. Wolf, 163.
33. Wolf, 22.
34. Wolf, 22.
35. Kern, 16.
36. Gardner, 730.
37. Kern 33–34.
38. Kern, 33.
39. Kern, 34.
40. Alain Robbe-Grillet, *Le Voyeur*, 1955.
41. Alain Robbe-Grillet, *For a New Novel*, trans R. Howard, (NY: Grove Press, 1965) cited in Sass, 31.
42. Wolf, 22.
43. Wolf, 72–73.
44. Kern, 33.
45. Jorge Luis Borges, *Collected Fictions*, trans. Andrew Hurley, (NY: Viking, 1998).
46. See Chapter Ten.
47. T. S. Eliot, *Quartets*, (1944).
48. Wolf, 20.
49. Wolf, 20.
50. See Chapter Ten.
51. Mazis, 67.
52. Wolf, 175. Also the reader may want to look at Michael Talbot, *The Holographic Universe*, (NY: Harper Perennial, 1992); and Stanislav Grof, *The Holotropic Mind*, (San Francisco, HarperSanFrancisco, 1992). For memory one could start with McConkey.
53. Wolf, 64.

54. Kern, 172.
55. E. E. Cummings, *100 Selected Poems*, (NY: Grove Press, Inc., 1959).
56. Santayana, 291.
57. Robert Pattison, *On Literacy: The Politics of the Word from Homer to the Age of Rock*, (NY: Oxford University Press, 1982), 101.
58. Pattison, 210–11.
59. Pattison, 211.
60. Taylor, 477. Also see Frank, 588: "…has shown the link between what I have been calling a framing epiphany, with its revelation by juxtaposition, often of elements widely separated in time, and the rise of the time-consciousness…which denies linearity, and unites widely separated moments either in a timeless present or through the archetypes of myth. Both reflect a move away from ordinary narration to a 'spatialization'.…Unlike this, the spatializing of time in modernist literature is very much situated. It grows out of and does not cancel our situation in time."
61. Wolfgang Iser, *A Theory of Aesthetic Response*, (Baltimore: Johns Hopkins University Press, 1978), x.
62. The earliest stage modernity's understanding of the basics of the art of historical research has been explored in a recent issue of *JHI*, 24, no. 2 (2003). The topic is "The Uses of Historical Evidence in Early Modern Europe," with an introduction by Jacob Soll, 57: "…if we look at the Renaissance in part as a practice—that of the critical assessment of historically evidence —its scope expands."
63. Pattison, 135.
64. Pattison, 136–37.
65. Pattison, 137.
66. Benjamin Lee Whorf, *Language, Thought, and Reality*, (NY: Technology Press of MIT and John Wiley and Sons, Inc., 1956), 252.
67. Joseph S. Catalano, *A Commentary on Jean-Paul Sartre's Critique of Dialectical Reason: Theory of Practical Ensembles*, (Chicago: University Chicago Press, 1986), vol. 1, 11.
68. Levin, 159.
69. Levin, 161.
70. Barrett, *Irrational*, 102.
71. Marcel Brion, et al., eds., *Art Since 1954*, (NY: Abrams, 1958), cited in Barrett, *Irrational*, 103.
72. Walter Kaufmann, "Existentialism from Dostoevsky to Sartre," *Existentialism from Dostoevsky to Sartre*, ed. Walter Kaufmann, (Cleveland, OH: World Publishing Corp., 1956), 11.
73. Barrett, 65.
74. Levin, 60.
75. Sypher, 70.
76. Sypher, 141.
77. Sypher, 143.
78. Sypher, 142.
79. Sypher, 143
80. Richard Alpert, (aka Baba Ram Dass), *Be Here Now*, (Albuquerque, NM: Hanuman Foundation, 1978).
81. Zweig, 265.
82. Hampden-Turner, 52.
83. Hampden-Turner, 52.

84. Kathleen Wider, *The Bodily Nature of Consciousness. Sartre and Contemporary Philosophy of Mind*, (Ithaca: Cornell University Press, 1997), 7.
85. Dallmayr, 17.
86. Jean-Paul Sartre, "Existentialism is a Humanism," *Existentialism from Dostoevsky to Sartre*, ed. Walter Kaufmann, trans. Philip Mairet, (Cleveland, OH: World Publishing Corp., 1956), 294–95.
87. Sartre, Existentialism, 290–91.
88. Dallmayr, 28.
89. Sartre, Existentialism, 294.
90. Sartre, Existentialism, 299.
91. Sartre, Existentialism, 289.
92. Sartre, Existentialism, 290.
93. Sartre, Existentialism, 290.
94. Sartre, Existentialism, 291.
95. Sartre, Existentialism, 294.
96. Sartre, Existentialism, 292.
97. Sartre, Existentialism, 298.
98. Monaco, 46.
99. Sartre, Existentialism, 295.
100. Wilson, 30.
101. Wilson, 30.
102. Wilson, 30.
103. Solomon, xiii.
104. Jean-Paul Sartre, "The Flies," *No Exit and Three Other Plays*, trans Stuart Gilbert, (NY: Vintage Books, 1948), 123.
105. Jean-Paul Sartre, "The Childhood of a Leader," *The Wall*, trans. Lloyd Alexander, (NY: New Directions Publishing, 1969), 99.
106. Sartre, Childhood, 99.
107. The reference to survival is indirectly noted in a passage in Sartre, Childhood, 103, where the Jewish homosexual, Berliac, notes how he uses in writings the "new technique called automatic writings."
108. Sartre, Childhood, 131–32.
109. Sartre, Childhood, 143.
110. Sartre, Childhood, 144.
111. Sartre, Childhood, 144.
112. Sartre, Childhood, 142–43.
113. Sartre, Existentialism, 309.
114. Sartre, Existentialism, 305.
115. Sartre, Existentialism, 310.
116. Sartre, Existentialism, 310.
117. Jean-Paul Sartre, *The Transcendence of the Ego: An Existentialist Theory of Consciousness*, trans. and annotated Forrest Williams and Robert Kirkpatrick, (1936; NY: Noonday Press, 1957), 101.
118. Sartre, *Ego*, 101.
119. Sartre, *Ego*, 103.
120. Sartre, Existentialism, 300.
121. Sartre, Existentialism, 307.
122. Sartre, Existentialism, 291–92.

123. Sartre, *Ego*, 31.
124. Sartre, *Ego*, 60.
125. Sartre, Existentialism, 300.
126. Sartre, *Ego*, 97.
127. Sartre, Existentialism, 304.
128. Sartre, *Ego*, 98–99.
129. Sartre, *Ego*, 96.
130. Sartre, *Ego*, 37.
131. Dallmayr, 71.
132. Sartre, *Ego*, 58.
133. Sartre, *Ego*, 58.
134. Sartre, *Ego*, 58.
135. Sartre, *Ego*, 58.
136. Monaco, 45.
137. Monaco, 45.
138. Ernest Keen, *Psychology and the New Consciousness*, (Monterey, Ca.: Brooks/Cole Publishing Co., 1972), 136.
139. Wilson, 46.
140. Jean-Paul Sartre, "Self-Deception," *Existentialism from Dostoevsky to Sartre*, ed. Walter Kaufmann, trans. Hazel Barnes, (Cleveland, Oh.: World Publishing Corp., 1956), 241.
141. Sartre, Existentialism, 291.
142. Solomon, xvi.
143. Dallmayr, 18.
144. Sartre, Existentialism, 291.
145. Sartre, Existentialism, 291.
146. Sartre, Existentialism, 302.
147. Solomon, xv.
148. Wider, 153.
149. Solomon, xv.
150. Solomon, xi.
151. Zweig, 171.
152. Sartre, *Ego*, 37–38.
153. Sartre, Existentialism, 304.
154. Sartre, Existentialism, 304.
155. Sartre, Existentialism, 304.
156. See Bloom, *Hamlet*.
157. Helen Merrell Lynd, *On Shame and the Search for Identity*, (NY: Harcourt, Brace and Co., 1958), 21. See also Robert Karen, "Shame," *The Atlantic Monthly*, Feburary 1992, 40; Carl D. Schneider, *Shame Exposure and Privacy*, (Boston: Beacon Press, 1977); and Ruth Benedict, *The Chrysanthemum and the Sword: Patterns of Japanese Culture*, (Boston: Houghton Mifflin, 1946), 222.
158. Schneider, 111.
159. Sartre, Existentialism, 290.
160. Solomon, xvi.
161. Sartre, Existentialism, 291.
162. Solomon, xvi.
163. Solomon, xvii.
164. Monaco, 74–75.

165. See Solomon, xviii.
166. See Chapter Ten on the subject of Camus.
167. Nicolas Humphrey, *Consciousness Regained: Chapters in the Development of Mind*, (Oxford: Oxford University Press, 1983), 50.
168. Sartre, *Ego*, 81.
169. Ryle, 194–95.
170. Keen, 136.
171. Colin McGinn, "Can we Solve the Mind-Body Problem," *Mind*, 98, 349–366, cited in Pinker, 132.
172. Humphrey, 34. See also Wilkes, "Is Consciousness Important?" 223–243; and Kathleen V. Wilkes, "—,Yishi, Duh, Um, and Consciousness," *Consciousness in Contemporary Science*, eds. A. J. Marcel and E. Bisiach (Oxford: Clarendon Press, 1988), 38.
173. Humphrey, 35. See also Alan Allport, "What Concept of Consciousness," *Consciousness in Contemporary Science*, eds. A. J. Marcel and E. Bisiach (Oxford: Clarendon Press, 1988), 159. Stephen J. Gould's comment which is originally from a conversation with Colin Tudge, BBC Radio 3, *The Listener*, (20 September 1984), 19, cited in Humphrey, 34.
174. Pinker, 132.
175. Pinker, 132.
176. Pinker, 132–33.
177. Humphrey, 117. Consciousness workshop convened by Daniel Dennett, Bellagio, May 1990.
178. William James, Consciousness, *Journal of Psychology and Scientific Method I*, 1904 cited in Humphrey, 35.
179. James, Consciousness, cited in Humphrey, 35.
180. See Julian Jaynes on the need for no consciousness when playing the piano.
181. It is this author's thesis, not explored here, that there may very well be a correlation between authentic creativity and the capacity of being occasionally very conscious.
182. Pinker, 145.
183. Pinker, 132.
184. Sartre, *Ego*, 41.
185. Stephen Gould, *Eight Little Piggies*, (NY: W.W. Norton and Co., 1993), 294–95.
186. Pinker, 133.
187. Pinker, 133.
188. Pinker, 134–35. See also Ray Jackendoff, *Consciousness and that Computational Mind*, (Cambridge: MIT Press, 1995); and Ned Block, "On a Confusion about a Function of Consciousness," *Behavioral and Brain Sciences*, 18, 227–87.
189. Pinker, 561.
190. Taylor, 483.
191. William James, *Principles*, 574.
192. Lifton, 20–21.
193. See Erich Kahler, *The Tower and the Abyss: An Inquiry Into the Transformation of Man*, (NY: Viking Press, 1967), 85.
194. Hunt, 231.
195. Ryle, 164–65.
196. Ryle, 190.
197. Steiner, George, "Books in an Age of Post-Literacy," *Publishers Weekly*, 25 May 1985, 46.

198. Ryle, 62.
199. Scott, 34.
200. Scott, 32.
201. Scott, 33.
202. Albert Einstein, *Relativity: The Special and General Theory*, (1916; NY, 1952) 150 cited in Kern, 206.
203. Kern, 206.

Conclusion

1. Newman, xiv.
2. This definition of an historian was offered by Dr. Maurice Crane, a fellow faculty member in the Humanities program at Michigan State University.

BIBLIOGRAPHY

ABBREVIATIONS
JHI=Journal of the History of Ideas
Monist=The Monist: *An International Quarterly Journal of General Philosophical Inquiry*

Aberth, John. *From the Brink of the Apocalypse. Confronting Famine, War, Plague, and Death in the Later Middle Ages*. NY: Routledge, 2001.

Abram, David. *The Spell of the Sensuous. Perception and Language in More-Than-Human World*. NY: Pantheon Books, 1996.

Acton, John Emerich Edward Dalberg. *Essays on Freedom and Power*. Cleveland: Meridian Books, 1964.

Addison & Steele, et. al. *The Spectator*. 4 vols. Ed. by Gregory Smith. London: J.M. Dent & Son Ltd., 1958/

Alexander, S. *Space, Time, and Deity: The Gifford Lectures at Glasgow 1916–1918*. NY: Dover Publications, Inc., 1966.

Alembert, Jean Le Rond d'. *Preliminary Discourse to the Encyclopedia of Diderot*. Trans. by Richard N. Schwab. NY: Library of Liberal Arts, 1963

Allison, Henry E., "Locke's Theory of Personal Identity: A Re-Examination,' *JHI* 27 (1966): 41–58.

Allison, Henry E. and Nicholas Jolley, "Locke's Pyrrhic Victory," *JHI* 42 (1981): 672–74.

Altman, Gerry T. M. *The Ascent of Babel. An Exploration of Language, Mind, and Understanding*. Oxford: Oxford University Press, 1997.

Ames, Roger T. and Wimal Dissanayake, eds. *Self and Deception. A Cross-Cultural Philosophical Enquiry*. NY: State University of New York Press, 1996.

Anderson, William. *The Face of Glory. Creativity, Consciousness and Civilization*. London: Bloomsbury, 1996.

Anderson, Susan Leigh. "The Substantive Center Theory Versus the Bundle Theory." *Monist* 61 (1978): 96–108.

Apollinaire, Guillaume. *The Cubist Painters. Aesthetic Meditations 1913*. Trans. by Lionel Abel. NY: Wittenborn, Schultz, 1944.

Aquila, Richard. "The Cartesian and a Certain 'Poetic' Notion of Consciousness." *JHI* 49, 1988, 543–562.

Archard, David. *Consciousness and the Unconscious*. La Salle, Ill.: Open Court Publishing Co., 1984.

Arden, John Boghosian. *Consciousness, Dreams, and Self: A Transdiciplinary Approach*. Madison, Conn.: Psychosocial Press, 1996.

Arendt, Hannah. *The Life of the Mind*. 2 vols. NY: Harcourt Brace Jovanovich, 1978.

Argüelles, José A. *The Transformative Vision: Reflections on the Nature and History of Human Expression*. Berkeley: Shambhala, 1975.

Ariès, Philippe. *Centuries of Childhood: A Social History of Family Life*. Trans. by Robert Baldick. NY: Knopf 1962.

Ariès, Philippe and Georges Duby, general eds. *History of Private Live*. 5 vols. Cambridge Mass.: Belknap Press of Harvard University, 1987–1991.

Ariew, Roger and Marjorie Greene, eds. *Descartes and His Contemporaries: Meditations, Objections, and Replies*. Chicago: University of Chicago Press, 1995.
Ariew, Roger and Marjorie Grene. "Ideas, In and Before Descartes," *JHI* 56 (1995): 87–106.
Aristotle. *The Works of Aristotle*, 3 vols. Edited by W. D. Ross. Oxford: Clarendon Press, 1963.
Arkle, William. *A Geography of Consciousness*. Introduction by Colin Wilson. London: Neville Spearman, 1974.
Ashley, Maurice. *England in the Seventeenth Century (1603–1714)*. Baltimore: Penguin Books, 1961.
Augustine, Bishop of Hippo. *City of God*, Trans. by Gerald G. Walsh et al. Garden City, NY: Image Books, 1958.
———. *Confessions*. Trans by R.S. Pine-Coffin. Baltimore: Penguin, 1964.
———. *Saint Augustine*. Translated by Thomas F. Gilligan. NY: CIMA Pub. Inc., 1948
———. *Introduction to the Philosophy of Saint Augustine. Selected Readings and Commentaries*. Edited by John A. Mourant. University Park: Pennsylvania State University Press, 1964
Aurelius, Marcus Antoninus. *The Meditations of the Emperor Marcus Aurelius Antoninus*. Translated by George Long. Garden City: Doubleday and Company, Inc., 1960.
Avineri, Shlomo. *Hegel's Theory of the Modern State*. London: Cambridge University Press, 1972.
Baars, Bernard J. *A Cognitive Theory of Consciousness*. Cambridge: Cambridge University Press, 1988.
Baars, Bernard J. *In the Theater of Consciousness. The Workplace of the Mind*. NY: Oxford University Press, 1997.
Babbitt, Irving. *Rousseau and Romanticism*. Cleveland: Meridian Books, 1964.
Bacon, Francis. *Essays or Councils, Civil and Moral of Francis Bacon*. Edited by Brian Vickers; London: Folio Society, 2002.
Bacon, Francis. *The New Organon and Related Writings*. NY: Library Arts Press, 1960.
Baghramian, Maria, ed. *Modern Philosophy of Language*. Washington: Counter Point, Washington 1999 (1st ed. England 1998)
Bainton, R. H. *Here I Stand: A Life of Martin Luther*. NY: Adingdon-Cokesbury Press, 1950.
Baker, Herschel. *The Image of Man. A Study of the Idea of Human Dignity in Classical, Antiquity, the Middle Ages, and the Renaissance*. NY: Harper and Row, 1961.
Balaban, Owen. *Subject and Consciousness: A Philosophical Inquire into Self-Consciousness*. Savage, Md.: Rowman & Littefield, 1990.
Balakian, Anna. *Surrealism: The Road to the Absolute*. Rev. ed. NY: Dutton, 1970 .
Balz, Albert G. A. *Descartes and the Modern Mind*. New Haven: Yale University Press, 1952.
Banham, Rayner. *The Architecture of the Well-Tempered Environment*. Chicago: University of Chicago Press, 1969.
Barber, Charles L. *The Story of Speech and Language*. NY: Thomas Y. Crowell Co., 1965.
Barfield, Owen. *History of the English Word*. Great Barrington, Mass.: Lindisfarne Press, 1988.
———. *Saving Appearances: A Study in Idolatry*. London: Faber and Faber, 1957.
Barksdale, E. C. *Cosmolgies of Consciousness: Science and Literary Myth in an Exploration of the Beginnings and Development of Mind*. Cambridge: Schenkman Pub., 1980.
Barlow, Stanley J. *The Fall into Consciousness*. Philadelphia: Fortress Press, 1973.
Barnes, Andrew E. and Peter N. Stearns, eds. *Social History and Issues in Human Consciousness: Some Interdisciplinary Connections*. NY: New York University Press. 1989.
Barnes, Annette. *Seeing Through Self-Deception*. Cambridge: Cambridge University Press, 1997.
Barnes, Timothy David. *Tertullian. A Historical and Literary Study*. Oxford: Clarendon Press, 1971.

Barnstone, Willis. *The Poetics of Translation: History, Theory, Practice*. New Haven: Yale University Press, 1993.
Baron, Hans. *From Petrarch to Leonardo Bruni: Studies in Humanistic and Political Literature*. Chicago: University of Chicago Press, 1968.
Barraclough, Geoffrey. *An Introduction to Contemporary History*. Harmondsworth: Penguin Books, 1975.
———. *Turning Points in World History*. London: Thames and Hudson, 1977.
Barrett, William. *The Illusion of Technique: A Search for Meaning in a Technological Civilization*. NY: Doubleday, 1978.
———. *Irrational Man: A Study in Existential Philosophy*. NY: Doubleday, 1962.
Baruss, Imants. *The Personal Nature of Notions of Consciousness. A Theoretical and Empirical Examination of the Role of Consciousness*. Lanham: University Press of America, 1990.
Bateson, Gregory. *Steps to an Ecology of Mind*. NY: Ballantine Books, 1972.
Bauer, Robert J. "A Phenomenon of Epistemology in the Renaissance." *JHI* 31 (1970): 281–8.
Baumer, Franklin L. *Modern European Thought. Continuity and Change in Ideas, 1600–1950*. NY: Macmillan Pub. Co. Inc., 1977.
Beakley, Brian and Peter Ludlow, eds. *The Philosophy of Mind: Classical Problems/Contemporary Issues*. Cambridge: MIT Press, 1992.
Beck Lewis White. "Secondary Qualities." *Journal of Philosophy*, 43 (1946): 599–609.
Becker, Carl. *The Heavenly City of the Eighteenth-Century Philosophers*. New Haven: Yale University Press, 1962.
Becker, Ernest. *The Denial of Death*. NY: Simon and Schuster, 1973.
Behan, David P. "Locke on Persons and Personal Identity." *Canadian Journal of Philosophy*, 9 (1979): 53–75.
Bellah, Robert N., et al., *Habits of the Heart: Individualism and Commitment in American Life*. NY: Harper & Row, 1986.
Bennedict, Barbara M. *Curiosity. A Cultural History of Early Modern Inquiry*. Chicago: University of Chicago Press, 2001.
Berenson, Bernard. *Italian Painters of the Renaissance*. NY: World Publishing Co., 1962.
Berg, J. H. Van den. *The Changing Nature of Man. An Introduction to a Historical Psychological (Metabletica)*. NY: W.W. Nortron & Co., 1961.
Berger, Peter L, Brigitte Berger and Hansfried Kellner. *The Homeless Mind: Modernization and Consciousness*. NY: Vintage Books, 1974.
Berger, Ralph. *Psyclosis*. San Francisco: W. H. Freeman and Company, 1977.
Berlin, Isaiah. *The Crooked Timber of Humanity. Chapters in the History of Ideas*. Edited by Henry Hardy. NY: Knopf, 1991.
———. *Vico and Herder: Two Studies in the History of Ideas*. NY: Viking Press, 1976
Berman, Morris. *Coming to Our Senses. Body & Spirit in the Hidden History of the West*. NY: Simon & Schuster, 1989.
———. *The Reenchantment of the World*. Ithaca: Cornell University Press, 1981.
Bernstein, Alan E. *The Formation of Hell. Death and Retribution in the Ancient and Early Christian Worlds*. Ithaca: Cornell University Press, 1993.
Bertocci, Peter A. "The Essence of a Person." *The Monist* 61 (1978): 28–41.
Biro, J. I. and Robert W. Shahan. *Mind, Brain, and Function. Essays in the Philosophy of Mind*. Norman: University of Oklahoma Press, 1982.
Blackmore, Susan. *The Meme Machine*. Oxford: Oxford University Press, 1999.
Bloch, R. Howard and Stephen G. Nichols, eds. *Medievalism and the Modernist Temper*. Baltimore: Johns Hopkins University Press, 1996.

Block, Ned, Owen Flanagan, and Güven Güzeldere, eds. *The Nature of Consciousness: Philosophical Debates*. Cambridge: MIT Press, 1997.

Bloom, Edward and Lillian D. *Educating the Audience: Addison, Steele, & Eighteenth-Century Culture*. Papers presented at a Clark Library Seminar 15 November 1980. University of California, Los Angeles, 1984.

Bloom, Harold. *Genius. A Mosaic of One Hundred Exemplary Creative Minds*. NY: Warner Books, 2002.

———. *A Map of Misreading*. NY: Oxford University Press, 1975.

———. *Shakespeare: The Invention of the Human*. NY: Riverhead Books, 1998.

Bobrick, Benson. *Wide as the Waters. The Story of the English Bible and the Revolution It Inspired*. NY: Simon & Schuster, 2001.

Bolles, Edmund Blair. *A Second Way of Knowing: The Riddle of Human Perception*. New York: Prentice Hall Press, 1990.

Borchard, Frank L., "Etymology in Tradition and in the Northern Renaissance," *JHI* 29 (1968): 415–29.

Borges, Jorge Luis. *Collected Fictions*. Trans. by Andrew Hurley. NY: Viking 1998.

Boulding, Kenneth E. *The Meaning of The 20th Century: The Great Transition*. NY: Harper Torchbooks, 1964.

Bourdieu, Pierre. *In Other Words: Essays Towards a Reflective Sociology*. Trans. Matthew Adamson. Stanford: Stanford University Press, 1990.

———. *Outline of a Theory of Practice*. Trans. Richard Nice. Cambridge: Cambridge University Press, 1977.

Bouwsma, William J., "Work on Blumenberg" review of *Work on Myth* by Hans Blumenberg. *JHI* 58 (1987): 347–54.

Bowen, Catherine Drinker. *Francis Bacon. The Temper of a Man*. Boston: Little, Brown and Co., 1963.

Bowler, Peter. "The Changing Meaning of 'Evolution' " *JHI* 36 (1975): 95–114.

Bradbury, Ray. *Dandelion Wine*. London: Grafton Books, 1977.

Brann, Eva. *What, Then, is Time?* NY: Rowman & Littlefield Pub., Inc., 1999.

Bremmer Jan, N. *The Early Greek Concept of the Soul*. Princeton: Princeton University Press, 1983.

Brinton, Crane. *The Shaping of Modern Thought*. Englewood Cliffs: Prentice-Hall, 1963.

Brock, William H. *The Chemical Tree*. London: Norton, 1992.

Bronowski, Jacob. *The Origin of Knowledge and Imagination*. New Haven: Yale University Press, 1978.

Bronowski, Jacob and Bruce Mazlish. *The Western Intellectual Tradition. From Leonardo to Hegel*. NY: Harper and Row, 1962.

Brown, Gillian. *Domestic Individualism. Imagining Self in Nineteenth-Century America*. Berkeley: University of California Press, 1990.

Brouwer, L. E. J. *Philosophy and Foundations of Mathematics*, vol. 1 of *Collected Works*. Edited by A. Heyting. NY: North-Holland Pub. Company, 1975.

Brown, Jason. *Mind, Brain, and Consciousness: The Neuropsychology of Cognition*. NY: Academic Press, 1977.

Bruno, Frank J. *Dictionary of Key Words in Psychology*. London: Routledge & Kegan Paul, 1886.

Bryson, Bill. *The Mother Tongue: English and How It Got That Way*. NY: William Morrow & Co. Inc., 1990.

Bucombe, Matthew. *The Substance of Consciousness: An Argument for Interactionism*. Brookfield, Vt.: Avebury, 1995.

Buickerood, James G. "'The Whole exercise of reason': Charles Mein's Account of Rationality," *JHI* 63 (2002): 639–58.

Bullock, Alan and Oliver Stallybrass, eds. *The Harper Dictionary of Modern Thought.* NY: Harper & Row, 1977.

Burckhardt, Jacob. *The Civilization of The Renaissance in Italy.* Trans by S. G. C. Middlemore. NY: Random House, 1954.

———. *The Greeks and Greek Civilization.* Edited by Oswyn Murray. Trans. by Sheila Stern. NY: St. Martin's Press, 2001.

Burge, Tyler. "Individualism and the Mental," *Studies in Metaphysics*, vol. 4 of *Midwest Studies in Philosophy*. Morris, Minn.: University of Minnesota Press, 1979.

Burke, James. *The Knowledge Web: From Electronic Agents to Stonehenge and Back—and Other Journeys Through Knowledge.* NY: Simon & Schuster, 1999.

Burke, Peter. *The Italian Renaissance. Culture and Society in Italy.* Princeton: Princeton University Press, 1986.

Burke, Peter. "The Renaissance" *Perceptions of the Ancient Greeks.* Ed. by K. J. Dover, Oxford: Blackwell, 1992.

Burrow, J. W. *The Crises of Reason. European Thought, 1848–1914.* New Haven: Yale University Press, 2000.

Burrow, Trigant. *The Neurosis of Man: An Introduction to a Science of Human Behavior.* London: Harcourt, Brace and Co., 1950.

———. *Preconscious Foundations of Human Experience.* Edited by William E. Galt. NY: Basic Books, Inc., 1964.

———. *The Social Basis of Consciousness: A Study in Organic Psychology Based upon a Synthetic and Societal Concept of the Neuroses.* London: Harcourt, Brace & Co., 1927.

Burtt, Edwin Arthur. *The Metaphysical Foundations of Modern Physical Science*, revised edition. Garden City, NY: Doubleday, 1954.

Bury, J. B. *The Idea of Progress: An Inquiry into its Growth and Origin.* NY: Dover Publications, Inc., 1955.

Busch, Thomas and Shaun Gallagher. eds. *Merleau-Ponty, Hermeneutics, and Postmodernism.* NY: State University of New York Press, 1992.

Butler, Judith P. *Subjects of Desire: Hegelian Reflections in Twentieth-Century France.* NY: Columbia University Press, 1987.

Butler, R. J. *Cartesian Studies.* Oxford: B. Blackwell, 1972.

Butterfield, Herbert. *The Origins of Modern Science. 1300–1800.* Rev. Ed. NY: Collier Books, 1962.

Cahill, Thomas. *How the Irish Saved Civilization: The Untold Story of Ireland's Heroic Role from the Fall of Rome to the Rise of Medieval Europe.* NY: Doubleday, 1995.

Calvin, John. *On God and Political Duty.* NY: Bobbs-Merrill Co., 1956.

Calvin, William H. *The Cerebral Symphony. Seashore Reflections on the Structure of Consciousness.* NY: Bantam Books, 1990.

———. *How Brains Think: Evolving Intelligence, Then and Now.* NY: Harper Collins, 1996.

Campbell, Blair. "La Mettrie: The Robot and the Automaton." *JHI* 31 (1970): 555–72

Campbell, Joseph. *The Inner Reaches of Outer Space: Metaphor as Myth and as Religion.* New York: Harper & Row, 1986.

Camus, Albert. *Caligula and Three Other Plays.* Translated by Stuart Gilbert. NY: Vintage Books, 1958.

———. *The Myth of Sisyphus and Other Essays.* Trans. by Justin O'Brien. NY: Vintage Books 1959,

———. *The Stranger*. Trans. by Stuart Gilbert. NY: Vintage Books, 1945
Caplan, Richard M., ed. *Exploring the Concept of Mind*. Iowa City: University of Iowa Press, 1986.
Carlyle, Thomas. *Sartor Resartus. The Life and Opinions of Herr Teufelsdröckh*. Ed. by Charles Frederick Harrold. NY: Odyssey Press, 1937.
Carruthers, Peter. *The Book of Memory. A Study of Memory in Medieval Culture*. Cambridge: Cambridge University Press, 1990.
———. *Phenomenal Consciousness. A Naturalist Theory*. Cambridge: Cambridge University Press, Cambridge, 2000.
Carter, Rita. *Exploring Consciousness*. Berkeley: University of California Press, 2002.
Cassam, Quassim. *Self and World*. NY: Oxford University Press, 1997.
Cassirer, Ernst. *The Philosophy of the Enlightenment*. Boston: Beacon Press, 1960.
———. *The Philosophy of Symbolic Forms*. 4 vols. Trans. by Ralph Manheim. New Haven: Yale University Press, 1953.
———. *Rousseau, Kant Goethe: Two Essays*. Trans. by James Gutmann, Paul Oskar Kristeller, and John Herman Randall, Jr. NY: Harper Torchbooks, 1965.
Cassirer, Ernst, P.O. Kristeller and T. H. Randall eds. *The Renaissance Philosophy of Man*. Chicago: University of Chicago Press, 1948.
Casson, Lionel. *Libraries in the Ancient World*. New Haven: Yale University Press, 2001.
Castaneda, Hector-neri. " 'He': A Study in the Logic of Self-Consciousness " *Ratio*, 8 (1966): 130–57.
———. "On the Logic of Attributions of Self–Knowledge to Others." *Journal of Philosophy*, 65 (1968): 439–56.
Castiglione, Baldesar. *The Book of the Courtier*. Trans. by Charles S. Singleton. NY: Anchor Books, 1959.
Catalano, Joseph S. *A Commentary on Jean-Paul Sartre's Critique of Dialectical Reason*. Vol. 1, *Theory of Practical Ensembles*. Chicago: University Chicago Press, 1986.
Caton, Hiran. *The Origin of Subjectivity: An Essay on Descartes*. New Haven: Yale University Press, 1973.
Celenza, Christopher S. "Late Antiquity and the Florentine Renaissance: Historiographical Parallels." *JHI* 62 (2001): 17–35.
Cesare, Mario A. di, ed. *Reconsidering The Renaissance: Papers From the Twenty-First Annual Conference*. Binghamton, NY: Medieval and Rensiassance Texts & Studies, 1992.
Chabod, Frederico. *Machiavelli and the Renaissance*. London: Bowes & Bowes. 1958.
Chalmers, David J. *The Conscious Mind: In Search of a Fundamental Theory*. NY: Oxford University Press, 1996.
Changeux, Jean-Pierre. *Neuronal Man: The Biology of Mind*. Trans. by Laurence Garey. NY: Oxford University Press, 1985.
Chappell, Vere, ed. *Locke*. NY: Oxford University Press, 1998 .
Ching, Julia. "'Authentic Selfhood': Wang Yang-ming and Heidegger." *Monist* 61 (1978): 3–27.
Chisholm, Roderick M. *The First Person: An Essay on Reference and Intentionality*. Minneapolis: University of Minnesota Press, 1981.
Choron, Jacques. *Death and Western Thought*. NY: Macmillan Co., 1963.
Churchland, Paul M. *Matter and Consciousness: A Contemporary Introduction to the Philosophy of Mind*. Cambridge, Mass.: MIT Press, 1984
Cladis, Mark S. "Durkheim's Individual in Society: A Sacred Marriage?" *JHI* 53 (1992) 71–90.
Clancy, M. T. *From Memory to Written Record: England, 1066–1307*. Cambridge, Mass.: Harvard University Press, 1979.

Clark, George N. *The Seventeenth Century*. Second edition. NY: Oxford University Press, 1961.
Clark, S. H. "'The Whole Internal World His Own': Locke and Metaphor Reconsidered.' *JHI* 59 (1998): 241–65.
Clatterbaugh, Kenneth. *The Causation Debate in Modern Philosophy, 1637–1739*. NY: Routledge, 1999.
Clive, Geoffrey. *The Romantic Enlightenment*. NY: Meridian Books, Inc., 1960.
Close, A.J. "Commonplace Theories of Art and Nature in Classical Antiquity and in the Renaissance." *JHI* 30 (1969): 467–486.
Coan, Richard W. *Human Consciousness And Its Evolution: A Multidimensional View*. New York: Greenwood Press, 1987.
Cobban, Alan B. *The Medieval English Universities: Oxford and Cambridge to c.1500*. Berkeley: University of California Press, 1988.
Coleridge, Samuel Taylor. *Inquiring Spirit: A New Presentation of Coleridge from His Published and Unpublished Prose Writings*. Rev. ed. Ed. by KathleenCoburn. Toronto: University of Toronto Press, 1979.
Collingwood, R.G. *The Idea of History*. NY: Oxford University Press, 1962.
Collins, Arthur W. *The Nature of Mental Things*. Notre Dame: University of Notre Dame, 1987
Copleston, Frederick. *A History of Things*. Vol. IV, *Descartes to Liebniz*. NY: Doubleday & Co., 1963.
Corngold, Stanly. *The Fate of the Self: German Writers and French Theory*. NY: Columbia University Press, 1986.
Cottingham, John. ed. *Descartes*. NY: Oxford University Press, 1998.
Coulanges, Fustel de. *The Ancient City: A Study on the Religion, Laws, and Institutions of Greece and Rome*. Garden City, NY: Doubleday Anchor Books, 1956.
Courant, Richard and Robbins, Herbert. *What Is Mathematics? An Elementary Approach to Ideas and Methods*. London: Oxford University Press, 1941.
Courtenay, William J. *Schools & Scholars in Fourteenth-Century England*. Princeton: Princeton University Press, 1987.
Cox, Stephen D. *"The Stranger Within Thee" Concepts of the Self in Late-Eighteenth Century Literature*. Pittsburgh: University of Pittsburgh Press, 1980.
Craig, Edward. *The Mind of God and the Works of Man* . Oxford: Clarendon Press, 1987.
Cranston, Maurice. *Jean-Jacques. The Early Life and Work of Jean-Jacques Rousseau 1712–1754*. Chicago: University of Chicago Press, 1982.
———. *John Locke: A Biography*. London: Longmans, Green and Co. Ltd., 1958.
———. *The Noble Savage. Jean-Jacques Rousseau 1754–1762*. Chicago University of Chicago Press, 1991.
———. *The Solitary Self. Jean–Jacques Rousseau in Exile and Adversity*. Chicago: University of Chicago Press, 1997.
Crawshay-Williams, Rupert. *The Comforts of Unreason: A Study of the Motives Behind Irrational Thought*. London: Kegan Paul, Tranch, Trubner, Ltd., 1947.
Crick, F. H. C. "Thinking about the Brain." *The Brain* a Scientific Americana Offprint, (1984): 13–20.
Crocker, Lester G., ed. *The Age of Enlightenment*. NY: Harper & Row, 1969.
Crombie, A. C. *Medieval and Early Modern Science*. 2 vols. NY: Doubleday Anchor Books, 1959.
———. *Robert Grosseteste and the Origins of Experimental Science 1100–1700*. Oxford: Clarendon Press, 1953.
Cummings, E. E. *100 Selected Poems*. NY: Grove Press, Inc., 1959.
Curley, E. M. *Descartes Against the Skeptics*. Cambridge, Mass.: Harvard University Press, 1978.

Dallmayr, Fred R. *Twilight of Subjectivity: Contributions to a Post-Individualist Theory of Politics.* Amherst: University of Massachusetts Press, 1981.
Damasio, Antonio. *The Feeling of What Happens. Body and Emotion in the Making of Consciousness.* NY: Harcourt Brace & Company, 1999.
Dampier, William Cecil. *A History of Science and its Relations With Philosophy & Religion.* 4th ed. Trans. by I. Bernard Cohen. Cambridge: Cambridge University Press, 1966.
Daniels, Norman. *Thomas Reid's Inquiry: The Geometry of Visibles And The Case For Realism.* NY: Burt Franklin & Co., 1974.
Darnton, Robert. *The Great Cat Massacre and Other Episodes in French Cultural History.* NY: Basic Books, Inc., 1984.
Davies, Catherine Glyn. *'Conscience' as Consciousness: The Idea of Self-Awareness in French Philosophical Writing from Descartes to Diderot.* Oxford: Oxford University Press, 1990.
Deese, James Earl. *Thought Into Speech.* Englewood Cliffs: Prentice-Hall, Inc., 1984.
Delany, Paul. *British Autobiography in the Seventeenth Century.* London: Routledge & Kegan Paul, 1969.
Delumeau, Jean. *La Peur en Occident (XIVc – XVIIIc siècles) Une cité assiégée.* Paris: Librairie Artmeme, Fayard, 1978.
———. *Sin and Fear: The Emergence of a Western Guilt Culture 13th–18th Centuries.* NY: St. Martin's Press, 1989.
Dennett, Daniel C. *Consciousness Explained.* Boston: Little, Brown and Company, 1991.
Dent, N. J. H. *Rousseau. An Introduction to his Psychological, Social and Political Theory.* Oxford: Blackwell, 1989.
Denton, Derek. *The Pinnacle of Life: Consciousness and Self-Awareness in Humans and Animals.* San Francisco: Harper, 1993.
Descartes, René. *The Philosophical Works of Descartes.* Two vols. Edited and Translated by Elizabeth Haldane and G. R. T. Ross. NY: Dover Publications, Inc. 1931.
———. *The Philosophical Writings of Descartes.* Two Vols. Translated by John Cottingham, Robert Stoothoff and Dugald Murdoch. NY: Cambridge University Press, 1985.
Diderot, Denis. *Selected Writings.* Ed. by Lester G. Crocker. Trans. by Derek Coltman. NY: Macmillan Co., 1966.
Dilman, Ilham. "The Unconscious: A Theoretical Construct?" *Monist* 56 (1972).
Dilthy, Wilhelm. *Pattern & Meaning in History. Thoughts on History and Society.* Ed. by H. P. Rickman. NY: Harper Torchbooks, 1961.
Dilworth, David A. and Hugh J. Silverman. "A Cross-Cultural Approach to the De-Ontological Self Paradigm." *Monist* 61 (1978) 82–95.
Dodds, E. R. *The Greeks and the Irrational.* Berkeley: University of California Press, 1973.
Donald, Merlin. *A Mind so Rare. The Evolution of Human Consciousness.* NY: W. W. Norton & Co., 2001.
Dostoevsky. *Thre Short Novels.* Trans. by Andrew R. MacAndrew. NY: Bantam Books, 1970.
Draaisma, Douwe. *Metaphors of Memory. A History of Ideas About the Mind.* Trans. by Paul Vincent. Cambridge: Cambridge University Press. 1995.
Duffin, Kathleen E. "Arthur O. Lovejoy and the Emergence of Novelty," *JHI* 41 (1980): 267–81.
Dunbar, Robin. *Grooming, Gossip, and the Evolution of Language.* Cambridge, Mass.: Harvard University Press, 1996.
Durkheim, Emile. *Montesquieu And Rousseau. Forerunners of Sociology.* Foreword by Henri Peye. Ann Arbor: University of Michigan Press, 1960.

Eccles, John ed. *Mind and Brain: The Many-Faceted Problems: Selected readings from the Proceedings of the international Conferences on the Unity of the Sciences* . Washington: Paragon House, 1982.
Eccles, John and Daniel N. Robinson. *The Wonder of Being Human: Our Brain and Our Mind*. NY: Free Press, Macmillan, 1984.
Edelman, Gerald M. and Giulio Tononi. *A Universe of Consciousness. How Matter Becomes Imagination*. NY: Basic Books, 2000.
Edelman, Gerald M. *Wider Than the Sky: The Phenomenal Gift of Consciousness*. New Haven: Yale University Press, 2004.
Edwards, Paul, editor in chief. *Encyclopedia of Philosophy*. 8 vols. NY: Macmillan Pub. Co., Inc. and Free Press, 1972
Einstein, Albert. *Relativity*. Trans. by Robert W. Lawson. NY: Prometheus Books, 1995.
Eisenstein, Elizabeth L. *The Printing Press as An Agent of Change*. 2 vols. NY: Cambridge University Press, 1979.
Eliot, T. S. *Collected Poems 1909–1962* NY: Harcourt, Brace & World, Inc., 1963.
———. *On Poet and Poetry*. NY: Farrar, Straus and Cudahy, 1957.
Elkins, James, "Renaissance Perspectives," *JHI* 53 (1992): 209–30.
Ellmann, Richard and Robert O'Clair, eds. *The Norton Anthology of Modern Poetry*. NY: Norton Co., 1973.
Ellmann, Maud. *The Poetic of Impersonality: T. S. Eliot and Ezra Pound*. Cambridge, Mass.: Harvard University Press, 1987.
Ellmann, Richard. *Ulysses on the Liffey*. NY: Oxford University Press, 1972.
Emerson, Ralph Waldo. *Selections from Ralph Waldo Emerson*. Ed. Stephen E. Whicher. Boston: Riverside Press, 1960.
Engelberg, Edward. *The Unknown Distance: From Consciousness to Conscience: Goethe to Camus*. Cambridge: Harvard University Press, 1972.
Enright, D. J., ed. *The Oxford Book of Death*. NY: Oxford University Press, 1983.
Enzensberger, Hans Magnus. *The Consciousness Industry: On Liturature, Politics, and the Media*. NY: Seabury Press, 1974.
Erasmus, Desiderius. *Essential Erasmus*, NY: Bantam Books, 1964.
Evans, Fred J. *Psychology and Nihilism. A Genealogical Critique of the Computational Model of Mind*. Albany: State University of New York Press, 1993.
Evans, Richard I. *Jean Piaget: The Man and His Ideas*. NY: E. P. Dutton & Co., 1973.
Everdell, William R. *The First Moderns. Profiles in the Origins of Twentieth-Century Thought*. Chicago: Chicago University Press, 1997.
Ey, Henri. *Consciousness: A Phenomenological Study of Being Conscious and Becoming Conscious*. Trans. by John H. Flodstrom. Bloomington: Indiana University Press, 1978.
Faas, Ekbert. *Retreat into the Mind: Victorian Poetry and the Rise of Psychiatry*. Princeton: Princeton University Press, 1988.
Farb, Peter. *Humankind*. Boston: Houghton Mifflin, 1978.
Feifel, Herman. *The Meaning of Death*. NY: McGraw-Hill Book Co., 1959.
Feinberg, Joel. *Reason and Responsibility: Readings in Some Basic Problems of Philosophy*. 6th ed. Belmont, Calif.: Dickenson Pub. Co., 1985
Feld, M.D., "Revolution and Reaction in Early Modern Europe," *JHI* 38 (1977): 175–194.
Ferguson, Arthur B. "The Historical Thought of Samuel Daniel: A Study in Renaissance Ambivalence," *JHI* 32 (1971): 185–202.
———. "Humanist Views of the Renaissance." *The American Historical Review* 46 (1939): 1–28.
———. *Europe in Transition 1300–1520*. Boston: Houghton Mifflin Co., 1962.

———. *The Renaissance in Historical Thought*. Cambridge: Riverside Press, 1948.
———. *Renaissance Studies*. NY: Harper Torchbooks, 1970.
Ferris, Timothy. "Belly Laughs." *MindField: A Quarterly Source Journal for Consciousness*, 1 (1992): 7–20.
Ferry, Anne. *The "Inward" Language: Sonnets of Wyatt, Sidney, Shakespeare, Donne*. Chicago: University of Chicago Press, 1983.
Feyerabend, Paul. *Conquest of Abundance: A Tale of Abstractions Versus the Richness of Being*. Ed. by Bert Terpstra. Chicago: University of Chicago Press, 1999.
Feyerabend, Paul K. and Grover Maxwell. *Mind, Matter, and Method: Essays in Philosophy and Science in Honor of Herbert Feigl*. Minneapolis: University of Minnesota Press, 1966.
Figgis, John Neville. *The Divine Right of Kings*. NY: Harper Torchbooks, 1965.
Finley, M. I. *The World Of Odysseus*. Rev. ed. NY: Penguin Books, 1982.
Fischer, Steven Roger. *A History of Language*. London: Reaktion Books, 1999.
Fischer, Klaus P., "John Locke in the German Enlightenment: An Interpretation," *JHI* 36 (1975): 431–46.
Flanagan, Owen. "Consciousness" *A Companion to Cognitive Science*. Ed. by William Bechtal and George Graham. Malden, Mass.: Blackwell, 1998.
———. *Consciousness Reconsidered*. Cambridge, Mass.: MIT Press, 1992.
———. *Dreaming Souls. Sleep, Dreams, and the Evolution of the Conscious Mind*. Oxford: Oxford University Press, 2000.
———. *The Problem of the Soul: Two Visions of Mind and How to Reconcile Them*. NY: Basic Books, 2003.
———. *The Science of the Mind*. 2nd ed. Cambridge, Mass.: MIT Press, 1991.
Flemming, William. *Arts and Ideas*. 3rd ed. NY: Holt, Rinehart and Winston, Inc., 1968.
Flew, Antony. "Locke and the Problem of Personal Identity." *Locke and Berkeley: A Collection of Critical Essays*. Ed. by C. B. Martin and D. M. Armstrong. Notre Dame: University of Notre Dame Press, 1968.
Fodor, Jerry A. "The Mind-Body Problem." *Scientific America*, Jan. 1981, 114–123.
———. *The Problem of Meaning in the Philosophy of Mind*. Cambridge, Mass.: MIT Press, 1987.
———. *Psychological Explanation: An Introduction to the Philosophy of Psychology*. NY: Random House, 1968.
———. *Radiant Cool: A Novel Theory of Consciousness*. Cambridge, Mass.: MIT Press, 2004.
———. *A Theory of Content and Other Essays*. Cambridge, Mass.: MIT Press, 1990.
Foucault, Michel. *The Order of Things*. NY: Pantheon Books, 1970.
France, Peter. *Hermits. The Insight of Solitude*. NY: St. Martin's Press, 1996.
Frankl, Viktor. *Man's Search for Meaning: An Introduction to Logotherapy*. Trans. by Ilse Lasch. NY: Pocket Books, 1972.
Fraser, Alexander Campbell. *Locke*. Port Washington: Kennikat Press, 1970.
Friedland, Roger and Deidre Boden, eds. *Now Here. Space, Time and Modernity*. Berkeley: University of California Press, 1994.
Friedrich, Carl J. *The Age of Baroque 1610–1660*. NY: Harper & Row, 1952.
Frijda, Nico H. *The Emotions*. New Haven: Cambridge University Press, 1986.
Fritz, von K. "Nooz and Noein in the Homeric Poems." *Classical Philology* 39 (1943): 79–93.
Fromm, Eric. *Escape From Freedom*. NY: Discus Books/ Avon Pub., 1969.
Fromm, Eric. *Art of Loving*. NY: Harper, 1956.
Funkenstein, Amos. *Theology and the Scientific Imagination from the Middle Ages to the Seventeenth Century*. Princeton: Princeton University Press, 1986.

Furst, Charles. *Origins of the Mind: Mind-Brain Connections*. Englewood Cliffs: Prentice-Hall, 1979.
Gablik, Suzi. *Progress in Art*. London: Thames and Hudson, 1976.
———. *The Reenchantment of Art*. NY:Thames and Hudson, 1991.
Galileo Galilei. *Discoveries and Opinions of Galileo*. Ed. and trans. by Stillman Drake. Garden City: Doubleday Anchor Books, 1957.
Garber, Daniel. *Descartes' Metaphyscial Physics*. Chicago: University of Chicago Press, 1992.
Gardiner, Judith Kegan, "Elizabethan Psychology and Burton's Anatomy of Melancholy," *JHI* 38 (1977): 373–388.
Gardner, Helen. *Art Through the Ages*. 6th ed. Revised by Horst de La Croix and Richard G. Tansey. NY: Harcourt Brace Jovanich, Inc., 1975.
Gardner, John. *Grendel*. NY: Ballantine Books, 1971.
Garber, Daniel. *Descartes' Metaphysical Physics*. Chicago: University of Chicago Press, 1992.
Gaukroger, Stephen. *Descartes, An Intellectual Biography*. Oxford: Clarendon Press, 1995.
Gay, Peter. *The Enlightenment: An Interpretation. The Rise of Modern Paganism*. NY: Vintage Books, 1968.
———. *The Enlightenment: An Interpretation. The Science of Freedom*. NY: W.W. Norton & Co., 1969.
———. *Schnizler's Century. The Making of Middle-Class Culture 1815–1914*. NY: W.W. Norton & Co., 2002.
Gazzaniga, Michael S. *The Mind's Past*. Berkeley: University of California Press, 1998.
Gebser, Jean. *Consciousness and Culture: An Introduction to the Thought of Jean Gebser*. Contributions in Sociology, no. 101. Ed. by Mark Kramer. Trans. by Eveline Lang. Westport, Conn.: Greenwood Press, 1992.
———. *The Ever-Present Origin*. Trans. by Noel Barstad with Algis Mickunas. Athens: Ohio University Press, 1985.
Geiger, Moritz. *The Significance of Art; A Phenomenological Approach of Aesthetics*. Current Continental Research, no. 402. Edited and translated by Klaus Berger. Washington, D. C.: Center for Advanced Research in Phenomenology and University Press of America, 1986.
Gelb, I. J., *A Study of Writing*. Rev. ed. Chicago: University of Chicago Press, 1965.
Gell, Alfred. *The Anthropology of Time: Cultural Constructions of Temporal Maps and Images*. Oxford: Berg, 1992.
Gianni, Vattimo. *The End of Modernity: Nihilism and Hermeneutics in Post-Modern Culture*. Baltimore: Johns Hopkins University Press, 1991.
Gibbon, Edward. *The History of the Decline and Fall of the Roman Empire*. 7 vols. Ed. by J. B. Bury. London: Methuen & Co., 1909.
Giles, Frances and Joseph. *Cathedral, Forge, and Waterwheel. Technology and Invention in the Middle Ages*. NY: Harper Collins, 1994.
Gilmore, Myron P. *The World of Humanism, 1453–1517*. NY: Harper & Row, 1952.
Giustiniani, Vito R. "Homo, Humanus, and the Meanings of 'Humanism'" *JHI* 46 (1985): 167–95.
Goethe, Johann Wolfgang Von, *Faust, Part I*. Translated by Randall Jarrell. NY: Farrar, Straus and Giroux, 2000.
Goldberg, Hillel, "An Early Psychologist of the Unconscious," *JHI* 43 (1982): 269–84.
Goldman, Harvey. *Max Weber and Thomas Mann. Calling and the Shaping of the Self*. Berkeley: University of California Press, 1988.

Goleman, Daniel. *Vital Lies, Simple Truths: The Psychology of Self-Deception.* NY: Simon and Schuster, 1986.
Gombrich, E. H. *The Story of Art.* NY: Phaidon Pub. Inc., 1966.
Gonzalez, Justo L. *Faith and Wealth. A History of Early Christian Ideas on the Origin, Significance, and Use of Money.* San Francisco: Harper & Row, 1990.
Good, Irving John ed. *The Scientist Speculates: An Anthology of Partly-Baked Ideas.* NY: Basics Books, 1962.
Gorham, Geoffrey. "Mind-Body Dualism and the Harvey-Descartes Controversy." *JHI* 55 (1994): 211–34.
Gould, Stephen. *Eight Little Piggies.* NY: W.W. Norton and Co., 1993.
Grazia, Margreta de, "Secularization of Language in the Seventeenth Century." *JHI* 41 (1980): 319–29.
Green, Janathon. *Chasing the Sun. Dictionary Makers and the Dictionaries They Made.* NY: Henry Holt & Co., 1996.
Greenblatt, Stephen Jay. *Hamlet in Purgatory.* Princeton: Princeton University Press, 2001
———. *Renaissance Self–Fashioning From More to Shakespeare.* Chicago: University of Chicago Press, 1980.
Greene, Robert A. "Synderesis, the Spark of Conscience, in the English Renaissance." *JHI* 52 (1991): 195–219.
Greene, Robert A. "Whichcote, the Candle of the Lord, and Synderesis," *JHI* 52 (1991): 617–644.
Greene, Thomas. "The Flexibility of the Self in Renaissance Literature." *The Disciplines of Criticism: Essays in Literary Theory, Interpretation, and History.* Ed. by Peter Demetz, Thomas Greene, and Lowry Nelson, Jr. New Haven: Yale University Press, 1968.
Greenfield, Susan. *Brain Power. Working Out The Human Mind.* Shaftesbury, Boston: Dorset, 1999.
———. *The Private Live of the Brain. Emotions, Consciousness, and the Secret of the Self.* NY: John Wiley & Sons, Inc., 2000.
Greenlee, Douglas, "Locke and the Controversy over Innate Ideas." *JHI* 33 (1972): 251–264.
Gregory, Richard L. ed. *The Oxford Companion to the Mind.* NY: Oxford University Press, 1987.
Grimm, Harold J. *The Reformation Era. 1500–1650.* NY: Macmillan Co., 1954.
Grof, Stanislav. *Holotropic Mind. The Three Levels of Human Consciousness and How They Shape Our Lives.* San Francisco: Harper, 1992.
———, ed. *Human Survival and Consciousness Evolution.* Albany: State University of New York Press, 1988.
Grossinger, Richard, ed. *Ecology and Consciousness: Tradition Wisdom on the Environment.* Berkeley: North Atlantic Books, 1978.
Grundlehner, Philip. *The Poetry of Friedrich Nietzsche.* NY: Oxford University Press, 1986.
Guttenplan, Samuel, ed. *Mind and Language.* Oxford: Clarendon Press, 1975.
Hadot, Pierre. *The Inner Citadel. The Meditations of Marcus Aurelius.* Translated by Michael Chase. Cambridge: Harvard University Press, 1998.
Haigt, David and Marjorie. "The Country of Consciousness." *Monist* 61 (1978).
Hall, A. R. *The Scientific Revolution 1500–1800: The Foundation of the Modern Scientific Attitude.* Boston: Beacon Press, 1956.
Hampden-Turner, Charles. *Maps of the Mind.* London: Mitchell Beazley Publishers Ltd., 1981.
Hankins, James, "The 'Baron Thesis' after Forty Years and Some Recent Studies of Leonardo Bruni," *JHI* 56 (1995): 309–338.
Thomas Hanna, ed. *Explorers of Humankind.* NY: Harper and Row, 1979.

Hariman, Robert, "Composing Modernity in Machiavelli's *Prince*," *JHI* 50 (1989): 3–29.
Harrington, Anne. *Medicine, Mind, and the Double Brain: A Study in Nineteenth-Century Thought.* Princeton: Princeton University Press, 1987.
Harris, Errol E. *Formal Trancendental, and Dialectical Thinking; Logic and Reality.* SUNY Series in Philosophy. Edited by Robert Cummings Newville. Albany: State University Press, of New York, 1987.
Harris, William V. *Ancient Literacy.* Cambridge: Harvard University Press, 1989.
Harrison, E. L. "Notes on Homeric Psychology." *Phoenix*, 14 (1960).
Hartle, Ann. *The Modern Self in Rousseau's Confessions: A Reply to St. Augustine.* Notre Dame: University of Notre Dame Press, 1983.
Haskins, Charles Homer. *The Renaissance of the Twelfth Century.* NY: Meridian Books, 1962.
Hatch, Ronald B. "Joseph Priestley: An Addition to Hartley's *Observations*." *JHI* 36 (1975): 548–50.
Havelock, Eric A. *Preface to Plato.* Cambridge: The Belknap Press of Harvard University Press, 1963.
Haven, George R. *The Age of Ideas. From Reaction to Revolution in Eighteenth-Century France.* NY: Collier Books, 1962.
Hawkes, Jacquetta & Sir Leonard Wooley. *History of Mankind: Prehistory and the Beginnings of Civilization.* NY: Harper & Row, 1963.
Hay, Denys. *The Italian Renaissance in its Historical Background.* Cambridge: Cambridge University Press, 1966.
Hayman, Ronald. *Sartre: A Life.* NY: Simon & Schuster, 1987.
Hazard, Paul. *The European Mind. 1680–1715.* Translated by J. Lewis May. Cleveland: Meridian Books, 1963.
———. *European Thought in the Eighteenth Century: From Montesquieu to Lessing.* Translated by J. Lewis May. Cleveland: Meridian Books, 1963.
Healy, Sean Desmond. *Boredom, Self, and Culture.* London: Fairleigh Dickinson University Press, 1984.
Heidegger, Martin. *The Question Concerning Technology and Other Essays.* Trans. by William Lovitt. NY: Harper Colophon Books, 1977.
Heinemann, F. H. *Existentialism and the Modern Predicament.* NY: Harper & Brothers, 1958.
Heimann, P. M., "Voluntarism and Immanence: Conceptions of Nature in Eighteenth-Century Thought," *JHI* 39 (1978): 271–83.
Heller, Erich. *The Disinherited Mind. Essays in Modern German Literature and Thought.* NY: Harcourt Brace, 1977.
Helm, Paul, "Did Locke Capitulate to Molyneux?" *JHI* 42 (1981): 669–71.
Henle, Mary, Julian Jaynes and John J. Sullivan, eds. *Historical Conceptions of Psychology.* NY: Springer, 1973.
Henry, Michel. *The Genealogy of Psychoanalysis.* Stanford: Stanford University Press, 1993
Herbert, Nick. *Elemental Mind. Human Consciousness and the New Physics.* NY: Penguin Group, 1994.
Herlihy, David. *The Black Death and the Transformation of the West.* Ed. by Samuel K. Cohn. Jr. Cambridge: Harvard University Press. 1999.
Hersh, Reuben. *What Is Mathematics, Really?* NY: Oxford University Press, 1997.
Hesse, Herman. *From Stories of Five Decades.* Ed. by Theodore Ziolkowski. Trans. by Ralph Manheim and Denver Lindley. NY: Triad/Panther Books, Granada Pub. Ltd., 1976.
Hexter, J. H. *Reappraisals in History: New Views on History and Society in Early Modern Europe.* 2nd ed. Chicago: University of Chicago Press, 1979.

———. *The Visions of Politics on the Eve of the Reformation. More, Machiavelli, and Seyssel.* NY: Basic Books, 1973.
Higgens, Kathleen Marie. *Comic Relief. Nietzsche's Gay Science.* Oxford: Oxford University Press, 2000.
Hill, Christopher. *The Century of Revolution. 1603–1714.* NY: W. W. Norton & Co., 1966.
———. *Intellectual Origins of the English Revolution.* Oxford: Clarendon Press, 1980.
———. *Some Intellectual Consequences of the English Revolution.* Madison: University of Wisconsin Press, 1980.
Hobbes, Thomas. *Leviathan: Parts I and II.* NY: Library of Liberal Arts, 1958.
———. *Leviathan Or the Matter, Forme and Power of a Commonwealth Ecclesiastical and Civil.* Ed. by Michael Oakeshott. NY: Collier-Macmillan Ltd. 1970.
Hofstadter, Douglas R. *Godel, Escher, Bach: an Eternal Golden Braid.* NY: Vintage Books, 1980.
Horgan, John. *The Undiscovered Mind. How the Human Brain Defies Replication, Medication, and Explanation.* NY: Free Press, 1999.
Horkheimer, Max and Theodor W. Adorno. *Dialective of Enlightenment.* Trans. by John Cumming. NY: Continuum, 1993.
Howard, Donald R. *Chaucer and the Medieval World.* London: Weidenfeld and Nicolson, 1987.
Hubben, William. *Dostoyevsky, Kierkegaard, Nietzsche, and Kafka. Four Prophets of our Destiny.* NY: Collier Books, 1972.
Hubel, David H. "The Brain." *The Brain* a Scientific American Offprint, 1984, 3–12.
Hughes, H. Stuart. *Consciousness and Society: The Reorientation of European Social Thought 1890–1930.* NY: Vintage Books, 1977.
Huizinga, Johan. *Men and Ideas* Trans. by James S. Holmes and Hans van Marle. NY: Meridian Books, 1965.
———. *The Waning of the Middle Ages.* Garden City: Doubleday Anchor Books, 1954.
Hume, David. *An Inquiry Concerning Human Understanding,* with a supplement *An Abstract of A Treatise of Human Nature.* Ed. by Charles W. Hendel. NY: Library of Liberal Arts, 1955.
———. *Essential Works of David Hume.* Ed. by Ralph Cohen. NY: Bantam Books, 1965.
———. *A Treatise of Human Nature.* Edited, with an Analytical Index, by L.A. Selby-Bigge. Second Edition with text revised and variant readings by P. H. Nidditch. Oxford: Clarendon Press, 1978.
Humphrey, Nicholas. *Concentration and Meditation: A Manual of Mind Development.* Baltimore: Penguin Books, 1971.
———. *Consciousness Regained: Chapters in the Development of Mind.* Oxford: Oxford University Press, 1983.
———. *A History of Mind.* NY: Simon & Schuster, 1992.
Humphrey, R. *Stream of Consciousness in the Modern Novel.* Berkeley: University of California Press, 1954.
Hunt, Morton. *The Universe Within: A New Science Explores the Human Mind.* NY: Simon and Schuster, 1982.
Hunter, Robert. *The Storming of the Mind: Inside the Consciousness Revolution.* NY: Doubleday & Co., 1972.
Hurley, S. L. *Consciousness in Action.* Cambridge: Harvard University Press, 1998.
Illich, Ivan. *In the Vineyard of the Text: A Commentary to Hugh's Didascalicon.* Chicago: University of Chicago Press, 1993.
Ingram, David. *Habermas and the Dialectic of Reason.* New Haven: Yale University Press, 1987.
Inhelder, Barbel and Jean Piaget. *The Growth of Logical Thinking: From Childhood to Adolescence An Essay on the Construction of Formal Operational Structures.* NY: Basic Books, Inc., 1958.

Innis, Robert E. *Consciousness and Play of Signs*. Bloomington: Indiana University Press, 1994.
Inwood, Michael. *Hegel Dictionary*. Cambridge, Mass.: Basil Blackwell Inc., 1992.
Ionesco, Eugene. *The Killer and Other Plays*. Trans. by Donald Watson. NY: Grove Press, 1960.
Iser, Wolfgang. *The Act of Reading: A Theory of Aesthetic Response*. Baltimore: Johns Hopkins University Press, 1978.
———. *The Range of Interpretation*. NY: Columbia University Press, 2000.
———. *A Theory of Aesthetic Response*. Baltimore: Johns Hopkins University Press, 1978.
Ito, Masao. *Cognition, Computation and Consciousness*. Ed. by Masao Ito, Yasushi Miyashita and Edmund T. Rolls. Oxford: Oxford University Press, 1997.
Jackendoff, Ray. *Consciousness and that Computational Mind*. Cambridge, Mass.: MIT Press, 1995.
Jacob, Margaret C. *The Radical Enlightenment: Pantheists, Freemasons, and Republicans*. London: George Allen & Unwin, 1981.
Jahn, Robert G. and Brenda J. Dunne, *Margins of Reality: The Role of Consciousness in the Physical World*. San Diego: Harcourt Brace Jovanovich, 1987.
Jahoda, Gustav. *Crossroads Between Culture and Mind. Continuities and Change in Theories of Human Nature*. Cambridge: Harvard University Press, 1993.
James, William. *Principles of Psychology*. Cambridge: Harvard University Press, 1983.
———. *The Varieties of Religious Experience: A Study in Human Nature*. Introduction by Reinhold Niebuhr. NY: Collier Books, 1961.
Jammer, Max. *Concepts of Space. The History of Theories of Space in Physics*. Foreword by Albert Einstein. NY: Harper Torchbooks, 1960.
Janson, H. W. *History of Art. A Survey of the Major Visual Arts from the Dawn of History to the Present Day*. Englewood Cliffs, NJ: Prentice-Hall, Ind., 1963.
Jansson, Gunnar, Sten Sture Bergestrom and William Epstein, eds. *Perceiving Events and Objects*. Hillsdale, N.J.: Lawrence Erlbaum Associates, Pub., 1994.
Jaynes, Julian. *Origins of Consciousness in The Breakdown of the Bicameral Mind*. Boston: Houghton Mifflin, 1976.
Johns, Adrian. *The Nature of the Book: Print and Knowledge in the Making*. Chicago: University of Chicago Press, 1998.
Johnson, Mark. *The Body in the Mind: The Bodily Basis of Meaning, Imagination, and Reason*. Chicago: University of Chicago Press, 1987.
———. *Philosophical Perspectives on Metaphor*. Minneapolis: University of Minnesota Press, 1981.
Jolley, Nicholas. *Locke. His Philosophical Thought*. NY: Oxford University Press, 1999.
Jones. Richard Foster. *Ancients and Moderns: A Study of the Rise of the Scientific Movement in Seventeenth-Century*. 2nd ed. Berkeley: University of California Press, 1965.
Joseph, Rhawn. *The Naked Neuron. Evolution and the Languages of the Body and Brain*. NY: Plenum Press. 1993.
Juszyk, Peter W. *The Discovery of Spoken Language*. Cambridge Mass.: MIT Press, 1997.
Kafka, Franz. *The Trial*. Trans. Willa and Edwin Muir and E. M. Butler. NY: Modern Library, 1956.
Kahler, Erich. *Man the Measure, A New Approach to History*. New York: George Braziller, Inc., 1956.
———. *The Tower and the Abyss: An Inquiry Into the Transformation of Man*. NY: Viking Press, 1967.
Karen, Robert. "Shame." *The Atlantic Monthly*, February 1992, 40–50.
Karl, Frederick R. *Modern and Modernism: The Sovereignty of the Artist 1885–1925*. NY: Atheneum, 1985.

Kaufmann, Walter. *Discovery of the Mind*. 3 vols. NY: McGraw-Hill, 1980.
———. *Existentialism from Dostoyevsky to Sartre*. Edited, translated, introduced by Walter Kaufmann. Cleveland: Meridian Books, 1970.
———. *Existentialism, Religion and Death: Thirteen Essays*. NY: Meridian Books, 1976.
———. *From Shakespeare to Existentialism*. NY: Anchor Books, 1960.
———. *Hegel. A Reinterpretation*. NY: Doubleday Anchor Books, 1966.
———. *Nietzsche. Philosopher, Psychologist, Antichrist*. 4th ed. Princeton: Princeton University Press, 1974.
———, ed. *Portable Nietzsche*. NY: Penguin Books, 1985.
———. *Tragedy and Philosophy*. NY: Anchor Books 1969.
Kateb, George. *The Inner Ocean. Individualism and Democratic Culture*. Ithaca: Cornell University Press, 1992.
Katz, Michael, William P. Marsh and Gail Gordon Thompson, eds. *Earth's Answer: Exploration of Planetary Culture at the Lindisfarne Conferences*. NY: Lindisfarne Books, 1977.
Kearns, Michael S. *Metaphors of Mind: In Fiction and Psychology*. Lexington: University Press of Kentucky, 1987.
Keen, Ernest. *Psychology and the New Consciousness*. Monterey, Cal.: Brooks/Cole Pub. Co., 1972.
———. *A Primer in Phenomenological Psychology*. NY: University Press of America, 1982.
Kelley, Donald R. "Horizons of Intellectual History: Retrospect, Circumspect, Prospect." *JHI* 48 (1987): 143–69.
———. "What is Happening to the History of Ideas?" *JHI* 51 (1990): 3–25.
Kenny, Anthony. *Descartes: A Study of His Philosophy*. NY: Random House, 1968.
Keohane, Nannerl O. "The Radical Humanism of Etienne de La Boétie," *JHI* 38 (1977): 119–30.
Kermode, Frank. *Shakespeare's Language*. NY: Farrar, Straus & Giroux, 2000.
Kern, Stephen. *The Culture of Time and Space: 1880–1918*. Cambridge: Harvard University Press, 1983.
Kerrigan, William and Gordon Braden. *The Idea of the Renaissance*. Baltimore: Johns Hopkins University Press, 1989.
Kessel, Frank S., Pamela A. Cole and Dale L. Johnson, eds. *Self and Consciousness: Multiple Perspectives*. Hillsdale, N.J.: Lawrence Erlbaum Ass. Pub., 1992.
Ketcham, Ralph. *Individualism and Public Life. A Modern Dilemma*. Oxford: Blackwell, 1987.
Kierkegaard, Søren. *Fear and Trembling / The Sickness Unto Death*. NY: Doubleday Anchor, 1954.
King, Adele. *Camus*. NY: Capricon Books, 1969.
King-Farlow, John and Roger A. Shiner eds. *New Essays in the Philosophy of Mind*. Guelph, Ont.: Canadian Ass. for Pub. in Philosophy, 1975.
Kintgen, Eugene R. *Reading in Tudor England*. Pittsburgh: University of Pittsburgh Press, 1996.
Kirk, G. S., ed. *Language and Background of Homer, Some Recent Studies and Controversies*. NY: Barnes & Noble, 1964.
Kirk, Robert. *Raw Feeling: A Philosophical Account of the Essence of Consciousness*. Oxford: Clarendon Press, 1994.
Kissin, Benjamin. *Conscious and Unconscious Programs in the Brain*. NY: Plenum Medical Book Co., 1986.
Kitto, H. D. F. *The Greeks*. Baltimore: Penguin Books, 1965.
Kivy, Peter. *The Seventh Sense: A Study of Francis Hutcheson's Aesthetics And Its Influence in Eighteenth-Century Britain*. NY: Burt Franklin & Co., 1976.

Klein, D. B. *The Unconscious: Invention or Discovery? A Historico-Critical Inquiry.* Santa Monica, Ca.: Goodyear Pub. Co., 1977.
Knight, James A. *Conscience and Guilt.* NY: Appelton-Century-Crofts, 1969.
Knowles, David. *The Evolution of Medieval Thought.* NY: Vintage Books, 1962.
Koestler, Arthur. *The Ghost in the Machine.* NY: MacMillan Co., 1968.
———. *The Sleepwalkers: A History of Man's Changing Vision of the Universe.* NY: Grosset & Dunlap, 1963.
Korshin, Paul J. "Johnson and the Renaissance Dictionary." *JHI* 35 (1974): 300–12.
Koyre, Alexandre. *From the Closed World to the Infinite Universe.* Baltimore: Johns Hopkins University Press, 1957.
Krieger, Leonard. "The Autonomy of Intellectual History." *JHI* 34 (1973): 499–517.
Kristeller, Paul Oskar. " 'Creativity' and 'Tradition.' " *JHI* 44,(1983): 105–13.
———. *Renaissance Thought: The Classic, Scholastic, and Humanistic Strains.* NY: Harper, 1961.
———. *Renaissance Thought II. Papers on Humanism and the Arts.* NY: Harper & Row, 1961.
Kubler-Ross, Elisabeth. *Death. The Final Stage of Growth.* Englewood Cliffs: Prentice-Hall, Inc., 1975.
Kuhn, Thomas S. *The Copernican Revolution. Planetary Astronomy in the Development of Western Thought.* NY: Random House, 1959.
Kvastad, Nils B., "Semantics in the Methodology of the History of Ideas." *JHI* 38 (1977): 157–74.
LaCapra, Dominick. "A Review of a Review." *JHI* 49 (1988): 677–87.
Lakoff, George and Mark Johnson. *Metaphors We Live By.* Chicago: University of Chicago Press, 1980.
———. *Philosophy in the Flesh: The Embodied Mind and Its Challenge to Western Thought.* NY: Basic Books, 1999.
Land, Stephen K. "Universalism and Relativism: A Philosophical Problem of Translation of the Eighteenth Century." *JHI* 35 (1974): 597–611.
Landes, David S. *Revolution in Time. Clocks and the Making of the Modern World.* NY: Barnes & Noble, 1983.
Langbaum, Robert *The Mysteries of Identity: A Theme of Modern Literature.* NY: Oxford University Press, 1977.
Langer, Susanne K. *Feeling and Form: A Theory of Art.* NY: Scribner's Sons, 1953.
———. *Mind: An Essay on Human Feeling.* 3 vols. Baltimore: Johns Hopkins University Press, 1967–1982.
Langford, Peter. *Modern Philosophies of Human Nature: Their Emergence from Christian Thought.* Dordrecht: Martinus Nijhoff Pub., 1986.
Lasch, Christopher. *The Minimal Self: Psychic Survival in Troubled Times.* NY: W. W. Norton, 1984.
Lauer, Quentin. *The Triumph of Subjectivity: An Introduction to Transcendental Phenomenology.* NY: Fordham University Press, 1978.
Leaky, Richard E. and Roger Lewin. *Origins.* NY: E. P. Hutton, 1977.
Leavis, F. R. *The Living Principle. 'English' as a Discipline of Thought.* London: Chatto & Windus, 1975.
Lederer, Richard. *The Miracle of Language.* NY: Pocket Books, 1991.
LeDoux, Joseph. *Synaptic Self. How Our Brains Become Who We Are.* NY: Penguin, 2002.
Lieberman, Philip. *Uniquely Human: The Evolution of Speech, Thought, and Selfless Behavior.* Cambridge: Harvard University Press, 1991.

Leites, Edmund, ed. *Conscience and Casuistry in Early Modern Europe*. Cambridge: Cambridge University Press, 1988.

Leites, Edmund. "Conscience, Leisure, and Learning: Locke and the Levellers." Sociological Analysis, 39 (1978): 36–61.

Leonard, George B. *The Transformation: A Guide to the Inevitable Changes in Humankind*. NY: Delacorte Press, 1972.

Leslie, Margaret, "Mysticism Misunderstood: David Hartley and the Idea of Progress," *JHI* 34 (1972): 625–32.

Levin, Jerome David. *Theories of the Self*. Washington: Hemisphere Pub. Corp., 1992.

Levin, Joseph. *Purple Haze. The Puzzle of Consciousness*. Oxford: Oxford University Press, 2001.

Levy-Bruhl, Lucien. *The Notebooks on Primitive Mentality*. Oxford: Basil Blackwell, 1975.

———. *Primitive Mentality*. Boston: Beacon Press, 1966.

Lewis, C. S. *They Asked for a Paper: Papers and Addresses*, London: Geoffrey Bles, 1962.

———. *Studies in Words*. Cambridge: Cambridge University Press, 1960.

Lewontin, R. C. Steven Rose and Leon J. Kamin. *Not in Our Genes: Biology, Ideology and Human Nature*. NY: Pantheon Books, 1984.

Lifton, Herbert Jay. *The Protean Self. Human Resilience in an Age of Fragmentation*. NY: Basic Books, Harper Collins, Pub., 1993.

Lippincott, Kristen, et al., eds. *The Story of Time*. London: Merrell Holberton with National Maritime Museum, 1999.

Locke, John. *An Essay Concerning Human Understanding*. 2 vols. Collated and Annotated by Alexander Campbell Fraser. NY: Dover Publications Inc., 1959.

———. *Essays on the Law of Nature. The Latin Text with a Translation, Introduction and Notes, Together with Transcripts of Locke's Shorthand in His Journal for 1676*. Ed. by W. von Leyden. Oxford: Clarendon Press, 1970.

Locke, John. *Of the Conduct of the Understanding*. Ed. and intro. by John Yolton. Bristol England: Key Texts, Thoemmes Press, 1996.

Logan, George M., "The Relation of Montaigne to Renaissance Humanism." *JHI* 36 (1975): 613–32.

Lohrey, Andrew. *The Meaning of Consciousness*. Ann Arbor: University of Michigan Press, 1997.

Lomas, David. *The Haunted Self: Surrealism, Psychoanalysis Subjectivity*. New Haven: Yale University Press, 2000.

Longuet-Higgins, H. C. "Is Consciousness a Phenomenon?" *Consciousness and the Physical World*. Edited proceedings of an interdisciplinary symposium on consciousness held at the University of Cambridge, Jan 1978. Edited by B. D. Josephson and V. S. Ramachandran. Oxford: Pergamon Press, 1980.

Lovejoy, Arthur. *Essays in the History of Ideas*. NY: G. P. Putman's Sons, 1960.

———. *The Great Chain of Being. A Study of an Idea*. NY: Harper & Row, 1960.

———. "Reflections on the History of Ideas," *JHI* 1 (1940): 3–23.

Lowe, Donald. *History of Bourgeois Perception*. Chicago: University of Chicago Press, 1982.

Loy, J. Robert, Review of *Order and Chance: The Pattern of Diderot's Thought*, by Geoffrey Bremner. *Eighteenth Century Studies* 19 (1985).

Lucas, Henry S. *The Renaissance and the Reformation*. NY: Harper & Brothers Pub., 1934.

Ludwig, Arnold M. *How Do We Know We Are? A Biography of the Self*. Oxford: Oxford University Press, 1997.

Lukacher, Ned. *Daemonic Figures. Shakespeare and the Question of Conscience*. Ithaca: Cornell University Press, 1994.

Lukes, Steven. *Individualism*. Oxford: Basil Blackwell, 1973.

———. "The Meanings of 'Individualism.'" *JHI* 32 (1971): 45–66.
Lumsden, Charles J. and Edward O. Wilson. *Genes, Mind, and Culture: The Coevolutionary Process*. Cambridge: Harvard University Press, 1981.
Lycan, William G. *Consciousness and Experience*. Cambridge Mass.: MIT Press, 1996.
———. *Consciousness*. Cambridge, Mass.: MIT Press, 1987.
Lynd, Helen Merrell. *On Shame and the Search for Identity*. NY: Harcourt, Brace and Co., 1958.
Lyons, Joseph. *Ecology of the Body: Styles of Behavior in Human Life*. Durham: Duke University Press, 1987.
Lyons, John O. *The Invention of The Self: The Hinge of Consciousness in The Eighteenth Century*. Carbondale: Southern University Press, 1978.
Macfarlane, Alan. *The Origins of English Individualism: The Family, Property and Social Transition*. NY: Cambridge University Press, 1979.
Machiavelli, Niccolò. *The Art of War*. Rev. ed. of Ellis Farneworth translation. NY: Library of Liberal Arts, 1966.
———. *The Prince and Selected Discourses: Machiavelli*. Ed. and trans. by Daniel Donno. NY: Bantam Books, 1965.
Mackie, J. L. *Problems from Locke*. Oxford: Clarendon Press, 1976.
MacLean, Kenneth. *John Locke and English Literature of the Eighteenth Century*. NY: Russell & Russell, 1962.
MacPhail, Eric. "The Plot of History from Antiquity to the Renaissance." *JHI* 62 (2001): 1–35.
Macphail, Euan M. *The Evolution of Consciousness*. Oxford: Oxford University Press, 1998.
MacPherson, C. B. *The Political Theory of Possessive Individualism: Hobbes to Locke*. Oxford: Oxford University Press, 1985.
Malcolm, Norman. *Problems of Mind: Descartes to Wittgenstein*. NY: Harper & Row, 1971.
Mandelbaum, Maurice. *Philosophy, Science, and Sense Perception*. Baltimore: John Hopkins University Press, 1964.
Manguel, Alberto. *A History of Reading*. NY: Viking Books, 1996.
Mann, David W. *A Simple Theory of the Self*. NY: W.W. Norton & Company, 1994.
Manuel, Frank E. *The Age of Reason*. Ithaca: Cornell University Press, 1965.
Marcel, A. J. and E. Bisiach. eds. *Consciousness in Contemporary Science*. Oxford: Clarendon Press, 1988.
Marshall, Louise H. and Horace W. Magoun. *Discoveries in the Human Brain. Neuroscience Prehistory, Brain Structure, and Function*. Totowa, N.J.: Humana Press, 1998.
Martin, Raymond & John Barrest. "Hazlett on the Future of the Self." *JHI* 56 (1995): 463–81.
Martin, Walter R. "Ideas in the Political Life of England, 1760–1783." Ph.D. diss. University of Missouri, 1966.
Martin, Wayne M. *Idealism and Objectivity: Understanding Fichte's Jena Project*. Stanford: Stanford University Press, 1997.
Martinich, A. P. *Hobbes Dictionary*. Cambridge, Mass.: Blackwell Publishers Inc., 1995.
Maslow, Abraham H. *Toward a Psychology of Being*. 2nd ed. NY: Van Nostrand Reinhard Co., 1962.
———. *The Farther Reaches of Human Nature*. NY: Penguin Books, 1971.
Matsudo, Matt K. *The Memory of the Modern*. NY: Oxford University Press, 1996.
Matsuo, Hōsaku. *The Logic of Unity: The Discovery of Zero and Emptiness in Prajñāpāramitā Thought*. Trans. by Kenneth K. Inada. Albany: State University of New York Press, 1987.
Matthews, Gareth B. "Consciousness and Life." *Nature of the Mind*. Ed. by David M. Rosenthal. NY, Oxford: Oxford University Press, 1991.
———. *Thought's Ego in Augustine and Descartes*. Ithaca: Cornell University Press, 1992.

Mattingly, Garrett. *Renaissance Diplomacy*. NY: Penguin Books, 1964.
———. *The Spanish Armada*. Boston: Houghton Mifflin Co., 1959.
May, Rollo. *Man's Search for Himself*. NY: New American Lib., 1967.
———, ed. *Existential Psychology*. NY: Random House, 1961.
Mayr, Otto. *Authority, Liberty & Automatic Machinery In Early Modern Europe*. Baltimore: Johns Hopkins University Press, 1986.
Mazzeo, Joseph Anthony. *Renaissance and Revolution: The Remaking of European Thought*. London: Secker & Warburg, 1967.
McCamm, Edwin. "Cartesian Selves and Lockean Substances." *Monist*, 69 (July 1986): 458–82.
McConkey, James. ed. *The Anatomy of Memory. An Anthology*. NY: Oxford University Press, 1996.
McCrone, John. *The Ape That Spoke: Language and the Evolution of the Human Mind*. NY: William Morrow and Co., Inc., 1990.
———. *Going Inside. A Tour Round a Single Moment of Consciousness*. NY: Fromm International, 1999.
McFarland, Thomas. *Romanticism and the Heritage of Rousseau*. Oxford: Clarendon Press, 1995.
McGinn, Colin. *Minds and Bodies: Philosophers and Their Ideas*. NY: Oxford University Press, 1997.
———. *Problems in Philosophy: The Limits of Inquiry*. Cambridge, Mass.: Blackwell, 1993.
McLaverty, James. "From Definition to Explanation: Locke's Influence on Johnson's *Dictionary*." *JHI* 47 (1987): 377–94.
McLuhan, Marshall. *The Gutenberg Galaxy: The Making of Typographic Man*. Toronto: University of Toronto Press, 1962.
McKnight, Stephen A. *The Modern and the Recovery of Ancient Wisdom. A Reconsideration of Historical Conscious, 1450–1650*. Columbia: University of Missouri Press, 1991.
McMahon, Darrin M. *Enemies of the Enlightenment. The French Counter-Enlightenment and the Making of Modernity*. Oxford: Oxford University Press, 2001.
McRae, Robert. "'Idea' as a Philosophical Term in the Seventeenth Century," *JHI* 26 (1965): 175–190.
McGill, Allan. *Prophets of Extemity. Nietzche, Heidgger, Foucalt, Derrida*. Berkeley: University of California Press, 1980.
Menand, Louis. *The Metaphysical Club*. NY: Farrar, Straus and Giroux, 2001.
Merleau-Ponty, Maurice. *Phenomenology of Perception*. Trans. by Colin Smith. London: Routledge & Kegan Paul, 1962.
Merrell-Wolff, Franklin. *The Philosophy of Consciousness Without an Object: Reflections on the Nature of Transcendental Consciousness*. NY: Julian Press, Inc., 1973.
Messer, Stanley, Louis A. Sass and Robert L. Woolfolk. *Hermeneutics and Psychological Theory: Interpretive Perspectives on Personality, Psychotherapy, and Psychopathology*. Vol. 2. Rutgers Symposia on applied psychology. New Brunswick: Rutgers University Press, 1988.
Metropolitan Museum of Art. *Renaissance: Six Essays by Wallace K. Ferguson and others*. NY: Harper & Row, 1962.
Michael, Emily and Fred S. "Corporeal Ideas in Seventeenth-Century Psychology." *JHI* 50 (1989): 31–48.
Miel, Jan, "Pascal, Port-Royal, and Cartesian Linguistics." *JHI* 30 (1969): 261–71.
Mill, John Stewart. *On Liberty*. Ed. by Alburey Castell. NY: Appleton-Century-Crofts, Inc., 1947.
Mishlove, Jeffrey. *The Roots of Consciousness. The Classic Encyclopedia of Consciousness Studies Revised and Expanded*. Tulsa: Council Oak Books, 1993.

Mitchell, Harvey, "Reclaiming the Self: The Pascal-Rousseau Connection." *JHI* 54 (1993): 637–58.
Mithen, Steven. *The Prehistory of the Mind. The Cognitive Origins of Art, Religion and Science.* London: Thames and Hudson, 1996.
Modell, Arnold H. *The Private Self.* Cambridge: Harvard University Press, 1993.
Modrak, Deborah K. *Aristotle: The Power of Perception.* Chicago: University of Chicago Press, 1997.
Mommsen, Theodor E. *Medieval and Renaissance Studies.* Ed. by Eugene F. Rice Jr. Ithaca: Cornell University Press, 1959.
Monaco, Paul. *Modern European Culture and Consciousness, 1870–1980.* Albany: State University of New York Press, 1983.
Montaigne, Michel Eyquem de. *The Complete Essays of Montaigne.* Trans. by Donald M. Frame. Stanford: Stanford University Press, 1965.
Moore, J. T. "Locke's Analysis of Language and the Assent to Scripture." *JHI* 37 (1976): 707–14.
Moran, John H. and Alexander Gode. *On the Origin of Language.* Jean-Jacques Rousseau, *Essay on the Origin of Languages* and Johann Gottfried Herder, *Essay on the Origin of Language.* Trans. by John H. Moran and Alexander Gode. Chicago: University of Chicago Press, 1986.
Moran, Richard. *Authority and Estrangement. An Essay on Self-Knowledge.* Princeton: Princeton University Press, 2001.
Moravia, Sergio. "From *Homme Machine* to *Homme Sensible*: Changing Eighteenth-Century Models of Man's Image." *JHI* 39 (1978): 45–60.
Morgenstein, Mira. *Rousseau and the Politics of Ambiguity. Self, Culture, and Society.* University Park: Pennsylvania State University Press, 1996.
Morris, Colin. *The Discovery of the Individual 1050–1200.* London: S. P. C. K. for the Church Historical Society, 1972.
Morris, John N. *Versions of the Self: Studies in English Autobiography from John Bunyan to John Stuart Mill.* NY: Basic Books, 1966.
Morris, Richard. *Time's Arrows. Scientific Attitudes Toward Time.* NY: Simon and Schuster, 1985.
Mumford, Lewis. *Technics and Civilization.* NY: Harcourt, Brace and Co., 1934.
Munitz, Milton Karl. *The Moral Philosophy of Santayana.* NY: Columbia University Press, 1939.
Muses, Charles and Arthur M. Young. eds. *Consciousness and Reality: The Human Pivot Point.* NY: Avon Books, 1972.
Musil, Robert. *The Man Without Qualities.* Vol. I: *A Sort of Introduction the Like of it Now Happens.* Translated with a forward by Eithne Wilkins and Ernst Kaiser. NY: Perigee Book 1980.
Nadeau, Maurice. *The History of Surrealism.* Translated by Richard Howard with and Introduction by Roger Shattuck. Cambridge, Mass.: Belknap Press of Harvard University Press, 1989.
Nadler, Steven, ed. *Causation in Early Modern Philosophy: Cartesianism, Occasionalism, and Preestablished Harmony.* University Park: Pennsylvania State University Press, 1993.
Nagel, Thomas. *Mortal Questions.* NY: Cambridge University Press, 1979.
———. *The View from Nowhere.* NY: Oxford University Press, 1986.
Nardo, Anna K. *The Ludic Self in 17th Century English Literature.* Ithaca: State University of New York Press, 1991.
Nauert, Charles. *Agrippa and the Crisis of Renaissance Thought.* Urbana: University of Illinois Press, 1965.

Nehamas, Alexander. *The Art of Living. Socratic Reflections From Plato to Foucault.* Berkeley: University of California Press, 1998.

Nelson, Norman. "Individualism as a Criterion of the Renaissance." *The Journal of English and German Philology* 32 (1933): 16–334.

Neumann, Erich. *The Origins and History of Consciousness.* Princeton: Princeton University Press, 1973.

Newman, Paul. *A History of Terror. Fear & Dread Through the Ages.* Phoenix Mill: Sutton Publishing, 2000.

Newcombe, Nora S. and Janellen Huttenlocher. *Making Space. The Development of Spatial Representation and Reasoning.* Cambridge Mass.: MIT Press, Cambridge 2000.

Nicolson, Marjorie Hope. *The Breaking of the Circle: Studies in the Effect of the 'New Science' upon Seventeenth Century Poetry.* Evanston: Northwestern University Press, 1950.

Nietzsche, Friedrich. *The Birth of Tragedy.* Trans. by Francis Golffing. NY: Doubleday Anchor Books, 1956.

———. *The Gay Science with a prelude in rhymes and an appendix of songs.* Trans. with Commentary by Walter Kaufmann. NY: Vintage Books, 1974.

———. *The Genealogy of Morals.* Trans. by Francis Golffing. NY: Doubleday Anchor Books, 1956.

———. *Hammer of the Gods. Selected Writings.* Ed. and trans. by Stephen Metcalf. London: Creation Books, 1996.

———. *New Nietzsche. Contemporary Styles of Interpretation.* Edited David B. Allison. NY: Dell Pub. Co, 1977.

———. *Philosophy of Nietzsche.* Translated by Thomas Common et al. NY: Modern Library, 1937.

———. *Schopenhauer as Educator.* Trans. by James W. Hillesheim and Malcolm R. Simpson. South Bend, Ill.: Regency/Gateway, 1965.

———. *The Use and Abuse of History.* Trans. by Adrian Collins, NY: Library Arts Press, 1949.

Nisbet, Robert. *History of the Idea of Progress.* NY: Basic Books, Inc., 1980.

Norford, Don Parry. "Microcosm and Macrocosm in Seventeenth-Century Literature," *JHI* 38 (1977): 409–28.

Norretranders, Tor. *The User Illusion.* Trans. by Jonathan Sydenham. NY: Viking Penguin, 1998.

Nussbaum, Fredrick L. *The Triumph of Science and Reason: 1660–1685.* NY: Harper & Row, Publishers, 1962.

Oberg, Barbara Bowen, "David Hartley and the Association of Ideas." *JHI* 37 (1976): 441–54.

O'Kelly, Bernard, ed. *Renaissance Image of Man and The World.* Columbus: Ohio State University Press, 1961.

Olney, James. *Memory & Narrative. The Weave of Life-Writing.* Chicago: University of Chicago Press, 1998.

Ong, Walter J. "Communications and the Rise of Individualism." *Views on Individualism: Presentation by Israel M.Kirzner, Walter J.Ong, Mancur Olson, and Kurt Baier,* ed. by Danna Card Charron, St. Louis Humanities Forum, Missouri Committee for the Humanities, 1986.

———. *Interface of the Word: Studies in the Evolution of Consciousness and Culture.* Ithaca: Cornell University Press, 1977.

———. *Orality and Literacy: The Technologizing of the Word.* London: Methuen, 1982.

———. *Presence of the Word.* Minneapolis: University of Minnesota Press, 1981.

———. *Rhetoric, Romance and Technology: Studies in the Interaction of Expression and Culture.* Ithaca: Cornell University Press, 1971.

Ornstein, Robert. *Evolution of Consciousness. Of Darwin, Freud, and Cranial Fire: The Origins of the Way We Think*. NY: Simon & Schuster, 1991.
———, ed. *Nature of Human Consciousness: A Book of Readings*. NY: Viking, 1974.
———. *The Psychology of Consciousness*. NY: Viking Press, 1972.
Ortega y Gasset, José. *The Appearance of Art and Other Essays on Art, Culture, and Literature*. Princeton: Princeton University Press, 1968.
———. *The Revolt of the Masses*. NY: W. W. Norton, 1957.
Oxford English Dictionary. Compact ed. NY: Oxford University Press, 1971
Pagden, Anthony. "Rethinking the Linguistic Turn: Current Anxieties in Intellectual History." *JHI* 49 (1988): 519-29.
Palmer, Helen, ed. *Inner Knowing. Consciousness, Creativity, Insight, and Intuition*. NY: Jeremy P. Tarcher/Putnam, 1998.
Panofsky, Erwin. *Gothic Architecture and Scholasticism*. NY: World Publishing Co., 1962.
———. *Studies in Iconology: Humanistic Themes in the Art of the Renaissance*. NY: Harper & Row, 1972
Parfit, Derek. *Reasons and Persons*. Oxford: Oxford University Press, 1986.
Parker, Geoffrey. *Europe in Crisis. 1598-1648*. NY: Cornell University Press, 1979.
Parrinder, Geoffrey, ed. *World Religions. From Ancient History to the Present*. NY: Facts on File, 1973.
Pascal, Blaise. *Thoughts*. Tran. by W. F. Trotter et al. NY: P.F. Collier & Son Corp., 1959.
Pastoureau, Michel. *The Devil's Cloth. A History of Stripes and Striped Fabric*. Trans. by Jody Gladding. NY: Columbia University Press, 2001.
Pattison, Robert. *On Literacy: The Politics of the Word from Homer to the Age of Rock*. NY: Oxford University Press, 1982.
Paxman, David B. "Language and Difference: The Problem of Abstraction in Eighteenth-Century Language Study." *JHI* 54 (1993): 19-36.
Pearce, Joseph Chilton. *Evolution's End: Claiming the Potential of Our Intelligence*. NY: Harper Collins Pub., 1992.
Pelletier Kenneth R. *Toward A Science of Consciousness*. New York: Dell Publishing Co., Inc., 1978.
Penrose. Roger. *Emperor's New Mind Concerning Computers, Minds, and The Laws of Physics*. Oxford: Oxford University Press, 1989.
———, et al. *Large, The Small and the Human Mind*. Ed. by Malcolm Longhair. NY: Cambridge University Press, 1997.
———. *Shadows of the Mind: A Search for the Missing Science of Consciousness*. Oxford: Oxford University Press, 1994.
Perez-Higuera, Teresa. *Medieval Calendars*. London: Weidenfeld & Nicolson, 1998.
Perkins, Jean. *The Concept of Self in the French Enlightenment*. Librairie Droz, Geneve 1969
Perkins, Merle L. *Jean-Jacques Rousseau on the Individual and Society*. Lexington: University Press of Kentucky, 1974.
Peters, Richard. *Hobbes*. Baltimore: Penguin Books, 1956.
Petrarca, Francesco. "The Ascent of Mount Ventoux," *The Renaissance Philosophy of Man* Translated by Hans E. Nachod. Ed. by E. Cassirer, et al. Chicago: Chicago University Press, 1948.
Pfeiffer, John. *The Emergence of Man*. 2nd ed. NY: Harper & Row, 1972.
———. *The Emergence of Society: A Prehistory of the Establishment*. NY: McGraw-Hill, 1977.
Piaget, Jean. *Biology and Knowledge: An Essay on the Relations between Organic Regulations and Cognitive Processes*. Trans. by Beatrix Walsh. Chicago: University of Chicago Press, 1971.

———. *The Grasp of Consciousness: Action and Concept in the Young Child.* Trans. by Susan Wedgwood. Cambridge, Mass.: Harvard University Press. 1976.
Pickering, John and Martin Skinner, eds. *From Sentience to Symbols. Readings on Consciousness.* Toronto: University of Toronto Press, 1990.
Pico, Richard M. *Consciousness in Four Dimensions. Biological Relativity and the Origins of Thought.* NY: McGraw-Hill, 2002.
Piers, Gerhart and Milton Singer. *Shame and Guilt: A Psychoanalytic and a Culture Study.* Springfield, Ill.: Charles C. Thomas, Pub., 1953.
Pinker, Steven. *How the Mind Works.* NY: W.W.Norton & Company, 1997.
———. *The Language Instinct.* NY: William Morrow and Co., 1994.
———. *Words and Rules. The Ingredients of Language.* NY: Basic Books, 1999.
Plekhanov, G.V. *The Role of The Individual in History.* London: Lawrence and Wishart Ltd., 1940.
Pletsch, Carl. *Young Nietzsche. Becoming a Genius.* NY: Free Press, 1991.
Plotnitsky, Aarkady. *In the Shadow of Hegel. Complementarity, History, and the Unconscious.* Gainsville: University of Florida Press, 1993.
Pool, Roger. *Towards Deep Subjectivity.* NY: Harper & Row, 1972.
Popkin, Richard H. ed. *The Columbia History of Western Philosophy.* NY: MJG Books, 1999.
Popper, Karl R. and John C. Eccles. *The Self and Its Brain.* NY: Springer International, 1977.
Porter, Roy. *The Creation of the Modern World. The Untold Story of the British Enlightenment.* NY: W. W. Norton, 2000.
Postan, M. "Why Was Science Backward in the Middle Ages." *A Short History of Science. Origins and Results of the Scientific Revolution: A Symposium.* NY: Doubleday Anchor Books, 1959.
Powell, C. Thomas. *Kant's Theory of Self-Consciousness.* Oxford: Clarendon Press, 1990.
Price, Huw. *Time's Arrow and Archimedes' Point New Directions for the Physics of Time.* Oxford: Oxford University Press, 1996.
Putman, Hilary. *The Threefold Cord: Mind, Body, and the World.* NY: Columbia University Press, 1999.
Radin, Paul. *The World of Primitive Man.* NY: E.P. Dutton & Co., Inc., 1971.
Radner, Daisie. "Thought and Consciousness in Descartes." *Journal of the History of Philosophy* 26 (July 1988): 439–452.
Radner, Daisie and Michael Radner. *Animal Consciousness.* Amherst, NY: Prometheus Books, 1996.
Ramachandran, V. S. and Sandra Blakeslee. *Phantoms in the Brain. Probing the Mysteries of the Human Mind.* NY: William Morrow & Co., 1998.
Randall, John Herman, Jr. *The Making of the Modern Mind. A Survey of the Intellectual Background of the Present Age.* Revised ed. Cambridge: Houghton Mifflin Co., 1954.
Rankin, Bayard, "The History of Probability and the Changing Concept of the Individual," *JHI* 27 (1966): 483–505.
Rapaczynski, Andrzej. *Nature and Politics. Liberalism in the Philosophy of Hobbes, Locke, and Rousseau.* Ithaca: Cornell University Press, 1987.
Reid, Thomas. *An Enquiry Into the Human Mind,* Edited with introduction by Timothy Duggan. Chicago: University of Chicago Press, 1970.
———. *Essays on the Intellectual Powers of Man.* Ed. and Abridged by A. D. Woozley. Macmillan and Co. St. Martin's Street, London 1941
———. *Thomas Reid's 'Inquiry.' The Geometry of Visibles and the Case for Realism.* Forward by Hilary Putnam. Stanford: Stanford University Press, 1989.

Reiss, Timothy J. "Denying the Body? Memory and the Dilemmas of History in Descartes." *JHI* 57 (1996): 587–607.
Richards, Glyn. "Conceptions of the Self in Wittgenstein, Hume, and Buddhism: An Analysis and Comparison." *Monist* 61 (Jan. 1978): 42–55.
Richard, Robert J. *The Meaning of Evolution. The Morphological Construction and Ideological Reconstruction of Darwin's Theory*. Chicago: University of Chicago Press, 1992.
Richter, Gottfried. *Art and Human Consciousness*. Trans. by Burley Channer and Margaret Frohlich. Forward by Konard Oberhuber. Spring Valley, NY: Anthroposophic Press, 1982.
Robert, Paul. *Grand Robert de la Langue Française*. 9 vols. Paris: Le Robert, 1986.
Roche, Daniel. *France in the Enlightenment*. Trans. by Arthur Goldhammer. Cambridge: Harvard University Press, 1998.
Rockmore, Tom. "Marxian Man." *Monist* 61 (Jan. 1978): 56–71.
Rodis-Lewis, Genevieve. *Descartes: His Life and Thought*. Trans. by Jane Marie Todd. Ithaca: Cornell University Press, 1998.
Rogers, G. A. J., "Locke, Newton, and the Cambridge Platonists on Innate Ideas." *JHI* 40 (1979): 191–204.
Rogers, G. A. J. and Alan Ryan, eds. *Perspectives on Thomas Hobbes*. Oxford: Clarendon Press, 1988.
Rohmann, Chris. *A World of Ideas. A Dictionary of Important Theories, Concepts, Beliefs, and Thinkers*. NY: Ballantine Books 1999.
Rowland, Ingrid D. *The Culture of the High Renaissance. Ancients and Moderns in Sixteenth-Century Rome*. Cambridge: Cambridge University Press, 1998.
Rorty, Richard. *Philosophy and the Mirror of Nature*. Princeton: Princeton University Press, 1979.
———. *Philosophy and the Nature of the Mind*. Princeton: Princeton University Press, 1980.
Rosenfield, Israel. *The Strange, Familiar and Forgotten: Anatomy of Consciousness*. NY: Alfred A. Knopf, 1992.
Rosenthal, D., ed. *Materialism and the Mind-Body Problem*. Indianapolis: Hackett Pub. Co., 1971.
Roslansky, John D. ed. *The Human Mind: A Discussion at the Nobel Conference*, 1967. Amsterdam: North-Holland Pub. Co., 1967.
Rossi, Ernest Lawrence. *Dreams, Consciousness, Spirit. The Quantum Experience of Self-Reflection and Co-Creation*. Third ed. Malibu, Cal.: Palisades Gateway Pub., 2000.
Rossman, Neil. *Consciousness: Separation and Integration*. Albany: State University of New York Press, 1991.
Roszak, Theodore. *Unfinished Animal: The Aquarian Frontier and the Evolution of Consciousness*. New York: Harper & Row, 1975.
Roubiczek, Paul. *Existentialism For and Against*. Cambridge: Cambridge University Press, 1966.
Rousseau, G. S., ed. *The Languages of Psyche: Mind and Body in Enlightenment Thought Clark Library Lectures 1985–1986*. Berkeley: University of California Press, 1990.
Rousseau, Jean-Jacques. *Collected Writings of Rousseau*. 2 vols. Ed. by Roger D. Masters and Christopher Kelly. Trans. by Judith R. Bus, Roger D. Masters, and Christopher Kelly. Hanover: Published for Dartmouth College by University Press of New England, 1990.
———. *Confessions of Jean-Jacques Rousseau*. Trans. w. intro. by J. M. Cohen. Baltimore: Penguin Books, 1963,
———. *Emile. Julie and Other Writings*. Ed. by R.L. Archer. Woodbury: Barron's Educational Series, 1964.
———. *Emile or On Education*. Trans. and notes by Alan Bloom. NY: Basic Books, 1979.
———. *On the Social Contract* with *Geneva Manuscript* and *Political Economy*. Ed. by Roger D. Masters. Trans. by Judith R. Masters. NY: St. Martin's Press, 1978.

Rudavsky, T. M. "Galileo and Spinoza: Heroes, Heretics, and Hermeneutics." *JHI* 62 (2001): 611–31.

Rudner, Richard and Israel Scheffler. *Logic & Art: Essays in Honor of Nelson Goodman*. NY: Bobbs-Merrill Co., 1972.

Russo, Joseph and Bennett Siman. "Homeric Psychology and the Oral Tradition." *JHI* 29 (1968): 483–98.

Rycroft, Charles. *Rycroft on Analysis and Creativity*. NY: New York University Press, 1992.

Ryle, Gilbert. *Concept of Mind*. London: Hutchinson's University Library, 1949.

Saenger, Paul. "Silent Reading: Its Impact on Late Medieval Script and Society." *Viator: Medieval and Renaissance Studies* 13 (1982): 367–414.

Saenger, Paul. *Space Between Words: The Origins of Silent Reading*. Stanford, Stanford University Press, 1997.

Sagan, Carl. *Dragons of Eden: Speculations on the Evolution of Intelligence*. NY: Random House, 1977.

Santayna, George. *Life of Reason or the Phases of Human Progress. Reason in Art*. NY: Charles Scribner's Sons, 1917.

———. *Scepticism and Animal Faith: Introduction to a System of Philosophy*. NY: Dover Publications Inc., 1955.

———. *Winds of Doctrine* and *Platonism and Spiritual Life*. NY: Harper Torchbooks, 1957.

Sartre, Jean-Paul. *The Condemned of Altona, A Play in Five Acts*. Trans. by Sylvia and George Leeson. NY: Vintage Books, 1963.

———. *Literary and Philosophical Essays*. Trans. by Annette Michelson. NY: Collier Books, 1962.

———. *Literature and Existentialism*. Trans. by Bernard Frechtman. NY: Citadel Press, 1962.

———. *Les Mouches, Drame en trois actes*. Paris: Gallimard, 1943.

———. *No Exit and Three Other Plays*. NY: Vintage Books, 1959.

———. *The Psychology of Imagination*. Trans. by Bernard Frechtman. NY: Washington Square Press, 1966.

———. *The Transcendence of the Ego: An Existentialist Theory of Consciousness*. Trans. and Annotated by Forrest Williams and Robert Kirkpatrick. NY: Noonday Press, 1957.

———. *The Wall and Other Stories*. Trans. by Lloyd Alexander NY: New Directions 1975

Sass, Louis. *Madness and Modernism: Insanity in the Light of Modern Art, Literature, and Thought*. NY: Basic Books, 1992.

Scharfstein, Ben-Ami. *The Philosophers: Their Lives and the Nature of Their Thought*. NY: Oxford University Press, 1980.

Schechtman, Marya. "The Same and the Same: Two Views of Psychological Continuity." *American Philosophical Quarterly* 31 (1994).

Schenk, H. G. *The Mind of the European Romantics: An Essay in Cultural History*. Preface by Isaiah Berlin. NY: Anchor Books Editions, 1969.

Schiffer, Fredric. *Of Two Minds: The Revolution of Dual-Brain Psychology*. NY: Free Press, 1998.

Schlipp, Paul Arthur, ed. *The Philosophy of Ernst Cassirer*. Evanston, Ill.: Open Court Pub. Co., 1973.

Schmaltz, Tad M. "What Has Cartesianism To Do With Jansenism." *JHI* 60 (1999): 37–56.

Schneider, Carl D. *Shame Exposure and Privacy*. Boston: Beacon Press, 1977.

Schwartz, Gary E. and David Shapiro, eds. *Consciousness and Self-Regulation: Advances in Research*. 4 vols. NY: Plenum Press, 1976.

Schulkin, Jay. *The Pursuit of Inquiry*. Albany: State University of New York Press, 1992.

Scott, Stanley L. *Frontiers of Consciousness: Interdisciplinary Studies in American Philosophy and Poetry*. NY: Fordham University Press, 1991.
Searle, John R. *Intentionality: An Essay in The Philosophy of Mind*. Cambridge: Cambridge University Press, 1983.
———. *Minds, Brains and Science*. Cambridge: Harvard University Press, 1984.
Segal, Alan F. *Life After Death. A History of the Afterlife in Western Religion*. NY: Doubleday, 2004.
Seigel, Jules Paul, "Enlightenment and the Evolution of a Language of Signs in France and England." *JHI* 30 (1969): 96–115.
Sennett, Richard. *The Fall of Public Man*. NY: W. W. Norton, 1992.
Sepper, Dennis L. *Descartes's Imagination: Proportion, Images, and the Activity of Thinking*. NY: University of California Press, 1996.
Shaffer, Jerome A. "The Subject of Consciousness," *The Philosophy of Mind*. Englewood Cliffs, NJ: Prentice-Hall, 1968.
Shanor, Karen Nesbitt. *The Emerging Mind*. Los Angeles: Renaissance Books, 1999.
Shattuck, Roger. *The Banquet Years: The Origins of the Avante Garde In France 1885 to World War I*. Rev. ed. NY: Vintage Books, 1968.
Shear, Jonathan, ed. *Explaining Consciousness: The Hard Problem*. Cambridge, Mass.: MIT Press, 1997.
Sheldrake, Ruppert. *A New Science of Life: The Hypothesis of a Formative Causation*. Los Angeles: J.P. Tarcher, Inc., 1981.
Shepard, Paul. *Nature and Madness*. San Francisco: Sierra Club Books, 1982.
Siewert, Charles P. *The Significance of Consciousness*. Princeton: Princeton University Press, 1998.
Silver, Bruce. "Berkeley and the Principle of Inertia." *JHI* 34 (1973): 599–608.
Simon, Bennett and Herbert Weiner. "Models of Mind Illness in Ancient Greece: I. The Homeric Model of Mind." *Journal of the History of the Behavioral Sciences* 2 (1966): 303–14.
Slinn, E. Warwick. *The Discourse of Self in Victorian Poetry*. Charlottesville: University Press of Virginia, 1991.
Smith, Curtis G. *Ancestral Voices: Language and the Evolution of Human Consciousness*. NY: Prentice-Hall, Inc., 1985.
Smith, Peter and O. R. Jones. *The Philosophy of Mind: An Introduction*. Cambridge: Cambridge University Press, 1986.
Smith, Robert. *Ben Franklin's Web Site: Privacy and Curiosity from Plymouth Rock to the Internet*. Providence: Privacy Journal, 2000.
Smith, Sir William, and John Lockwood. *Chambers Murray Latin-English Dictionary*. London: Chambers, Edinburgh & John Murray, 1999.
Smyth, Thomas W. "Unconscious Desires and the Meaning of Desire." *Monist* 56 (1972): 413–25.
Snell, Bruno. *The Discovery of Mind*. Trans. by T. G. Rosenmeyer. NY: Dover, 1982.
Solomon, Julie Robin. *Objectivity in the Making: Francis Bacon and the Politics of Inquiry*. Baltimore: Johns Hopkins University Press, 1998.
Solomon, Robert C., ed. *Existentialism*. NY: Modern Library, 1974.
———. *Introducing the Existentialists. Imaginary Interviews with Sartre, Heidegger and Camus*. Indianapolis: Hackett Pub. Co., 1981.
Spacks, Patricia Meyer. *Boredom. The Literary History of a State of Mind*. Chicago: University of Chicago Press, 1995.

———. *Desire and Truth. Functions of Plot in Eighteenth-Century English Novels*. Chicago: University of Chicago Press, 1990.

———. *Imagining a Self. Autobiography and Novel in Eighteenth-Century England*. Cambridge: Harvard University Press, 1976.

———. *Privacy: Concealing the Eighteenth-Century Self*. Chicago: University of Chicago Press, 2003.

Sprinker, Michael. "Gerard Manley Hopkins on the Origin of Language." *JHI* 41 (1980): 113–50.

Stafford, Barbara Maria. *Body Criticism: Imaging the Unseen in Enlightenment Art and Medicine*. Cambridge Mass.: MIT Press, 1991.

Steer Jr., Alfred G. *Goethe's Social Philosophy as Revealed in Campagne in Frankreich and Belagerung von Mainz*. University of North Carolina Studies in the Germanic Languages and Literatures, no. 15. Chapel Hill: University of North Carolina, 1955.

Stein, Gertrude. *Picasso*. London: B.T. Batsford, Ltd., 1948.

Steiner, George. "Books in an Age of Post-Literacy." *Publishers Weekly*, 25 May 1985.

———. *Grammars of Creation. Originating in the Gifford Lectures for 1990*. New Haven: University Press, 2001.

Steiner, Rudolf. *The Essential Steiner: Basic Writings of Rudolf Steiner*. Ed. and intro. by Robert A. McDermott. San Francisco: Harper & Row, 1984.

Stelzig, Eugene L. *The Romantic Subject in Autobiography. Rousseau and Goethe*. Charlottesville: University Press of Virginia, 2000.

Stern Laurent. "Hermeneutics and Intellectual History." *JHI* 46 (1985): 287–96.

Stich, Stephen P. *Deconstructing the Mind*. NY: Oxford University Press, 1996.

Stock, Brian. *The Implications of Literacy: Written Language and Models of Interpretation in the Eleventh and Twelfth Centuries*. Princeton: Princeton University Press, 1983.

Stocking, George W. *Race, Culture, and Evolution: Essays in the History of Anthropology*. Chicago: University of Chicago Press, 1982.

Stone, Michael H. *Healing the Mind. A History of Psychiatry from Antiquity to the Present*. NY: W. W. Norton, 1997.

Stout, Martha. *The Myth of Sanity. Divided Consciousness and the Promise of Awareness*. NY: Viking, 2001.

Stromberg, R. N. "History in the Eighteenth Century." *JHI* 12 (1951): 295–304.

Strongman, K.T. *The Psychology of Emotion*. 3rd ed. NY: John Wiley & Sons, 1978.

Stuurman, Siep. "Social Cartesianism: François Poulain de la Barre and the Origins of the Enlightenment." *JHI* 58 (1997): 617–40.

Sugerman, Shirley, ed. *Evolution of Consciousness: Studies in Polarity*. Middletown, Conn.: Wesleyan University Press, 1976.

Sullivan, Richard E., ed. *The Gentle Voices of Teachers. Aspects of Learning in the Carolingian Age*. Columbus: Ohio State University Press, 1995.

Sypher, Wylie. *Loss of the Self in Modern Literature and Art*. NY: Vintage Books, 1964.

———. "Similarities Between the Scientific and the Historical Revolutions at the End of the Renaissance." *JHI* 26 (1965): 353–68.

Talbot, Michael. *The Holographic Universe*. NY: Harper Collins Pub., 1991.

Tattersall, Ian. *Becoming Human. Evolution and Human Uniqueness*. NY: Harcourt Brace & Co., 1998.

Tawney, R. H. *Religion and the Rise of Capitalism. A Historical Study*. NY: New American Library, 1961.

Taylor, Beverly and Robert Bain, ed. *The Cast of Consciousness: Concepts of the Mind in British and American Romanticism*. NY: Greenwood Press, 1987.
Taylor, Charles. *Sources of the Self: The Making of the Modern Identity*. Cambridge: Harvard University Press, 1989.
Taylor, David A. *Mind*. NY: Simon and Schuster, 1982.
Taylor, Eugene. *William James on Consciousness Beyond the Margin*. Princeton: Princeton University Press, 1996.
Taylor, Gordon Rattray. *The Natural History of the Mind*. NY: E. P. Dutton, 1979.
Taylor, John H. *Death and the Afterlife in Ancient Egypt*. Chicago: University of Chicago Press, 2001.
Tennant, R. C. "The Anglican Response to Locke's Theory of Personal Identity." *JHI* 43 (1982): 73–90.
Thorndike, Lynn. *History of Magic and Experimental Science during the First Thirteen Centuries of Our Era*. 8 vols. NY: Columbia University Press, 1924.
———. "Renaissance or Prenaissance?" *JHI* 4 (1943): 65–74.
Tobach, Ethel. *Historical Perspectives and the International Status of Comparative Psychology*. Hillsdale, NJ: Lawrence Erlbaum, 1987.
Tocqueville, Alexis de. *Democracy in America*. Ed. by Richard D. Heffner. NY: New American Library: 1956.
Toulmin, Stephen. *Human Understanding. The Collective Use and Evolution of Concepts*. Princeton: Princeton University Press, 1972.
Trilling, Lionel. *Sincerity and Authenticity*. Cambridge: Harvard University Press, 1972.
Tuan, Yi-Fu. *Escapism*. Baltimore: Johns Hopkins University Press, 1998.
———. *Segmented Worlds and Self: Group Life and Individual Consciousness*. Minneapolis: University of Minnesota Press, 1982.
Tuveson, Ernest Lee. *Millennium and Utopia. A Study in the Background of the Idea of Progress*. NY: Harper Torchbooks, 1964.
Tye, Michael. *Ten Problems of Consciousness: A Representational Theory of the Phenomenal Mind*. Cambridge Mass.: MIT Press, 1995.
Underwood, Geoffrey and Robin Stevens, eds. *Aspects of Consciousness*. 4 vols. NY: Academic Press, 1979.
Van de Castle, Robert L. *Our Dreaming Mind*. NY: Ballantine Books, 1994.
Vartarian, Aram. *Diderot and Descartes: A Study of Scientific Naturalism in the Enlightenment*. Princeton: Princeton University Press, 1953.
Vasari, Giorgio. *Lives of the Artists*. 3 vols. Tran. by George Bull. London: Folio Society, 1998.
Voltaire, Marie Francois Arrouet de. *A Philosophical Dictionary*. NY: Coventry House, 1932.
Vovelle, Michael. *Ideologies and Mentalities*. Trans. by Eamon O'Flaherty Chicago: University of Chicago Press, 1990.
Vygotsky, L. S. *Thought and Language*, Ed. and Trans. by Eugenia Hanfmann and Gertrude Vakar. Cambridge Mass.: MIT Press and Wiley & Sons, 1986
Vyverberg, Henry. *Human Nature, Cultural Diversity, and the French Enlightenment*. NY: Oxford University Press, 1989.
Wagman, Morton. *Cognitive Science and the Mind-Body Problem: From Philosophy to Psychology to Artificial Intelligence to Imaging of the Brain*. Westport, Conn.: Prager, 1998.
Walker, Even Harris. *The Physics of Consciousness. Quantum Minds and the Meaning of Life*. Cambridge: Perseus Books, 2000.
Wallace-Hadrill, J. M. *The Barbarian West. The Early Middle Ages, A.D. 400–1000*. NY: Harper & Row, 1962.

Warden, J. R. "The Mind of Zeus." *JHI* 32 (1971): 3–14.
Watson, Peter. *The Modern Mind. An Intellectual History of the 20th Century.* NY: Harper Collins, 2001.
Webb, Eugene. *Philosophers of Consciousness: Polanyi, Lonergan, Voegelin, Ricoeur, Girard, Kierkegaard.* Seattle: University of Washington Press, 1988.
Webber, Joan. *The Eloquent "I": Style and Self in Seventeenth-Century Prose.* Madison: University of Wisconsin Press, 1968.
Webber, Max. *The Protestant Ethic and the Spirit of Capitalism.* Trans. by Talcott Parsons, Forward by R. H. Tawney. NY: Charles Scribner's Sons, 1958.
Wedgewood, C. V. *The Thirty Years War.* NY: Doubleday & Co., 1961.
Weiger, John G. *The Individuated Self: Cervantes and the Emergence of the Individual.* Athens: Ohio University Press, 1979.
Weil, Andrew T. *The Natural Mind: An Investigation of Drugs and the Higher Consciousness.* Rev. ed. Boston: Houghton Mifflin Co., 1980.
Weinstein, Donald. *Renaissance and Reformation, 1300–1600.* NY: Free Press, 1965.
Weintraub, Karl Joachim. *The Value of the Individual: Self and Circumstance in Autobiography.* Chicago: University of Chicago Press, 1978.
———. "Ideas of History During the Renaissance." *JHI* 6 (1945): 415–35.
———. "Renaissance Accounts of the Revival of Learning." *Studies in Philology* 45 (April 1948): 105–18.
———. "Renaissance Theory of the Reaction Against the Middle Ages as a Cause of the Renaissance." *Speculum* 20 (1945): 461–67.
———. "The Self-Awareness of the Renaissance as a Criterion of the Renaissance." *Papers of the Michigan Academy of Science, Art and Letters* 29 (1943): 561–67.
Weiskrantz, Lawrence. *Consciousness Lost and Found: A Neuropsychological Exploration.* Oxford: Oxford University Press, 1997.
Weiss, Roberto. *The Renaissance Discovery of Classical Antiquity.* Oxford: Blackwell, 1969.
Wertz. D.K. "Hume, History, and Human Nature." *JHI* 36 (1975): 481–96.
Westfall, Carroll W. "Painting and the Liberal Arts: Alberti's View." *JHI* 30 (1969): 487–506.
Whitehead, Alfred North. *Modes of Thought.* NY: Free Press, 1968.
———. *Science and the Modern World.* Lowell Lectures, 1925. NY: Pelican Mentor Book, 1948.
Whittemore, Reed. *Pure Lives: The Early Biographers.* Baltimore: Johns Hopkins University Press, 1988.
———. *Whole Lives: Shapers of Modern Biography.* Baltimore: Johns Hopkins University Press, 1989.
Whorf, Benjamin Lee. *Language, Thought, and Reality: Selected Writings of Benjamin Lee Whorf.* Ed. by John B. Carroll. Cambridge Mass.: MIT Press, 1956.
Wider, Kathleen. *The Bodily Nature of Consciousness. Sartre and Contemporary Philosophy of Mind.* Ithaca: Cornell University Press, 1997.
Wightman, W. P. D. *Science in a Renaissance Society.* London: Hutchinson University Library, 1982.
Wilber, Ken. *Eye to Eye: The Quest for the New Paradigm.* Garden City, NY: Anchor Press/Doubleday, 1983.
———. *Up From Eden: A Transpersonal View of Human Evolution.* Boulder: Shambhala, 1983.
Wilkes, Kathleen V. "Is Consciousness Important?" *British Journal for the Philosophy of Science* 35 (1984): 223–43.
Willey, Basil. *The Seventeenth Century Background. The Thought of the Age in Relation to Religion and Poetry.* NY: Doubleday Anchor Books, 1953.

Williams, Bernard. *Descartes: The Project of Pure Enquiry.* Atlantic Highlands, NJ: Humanities Press, 1978.
Williams, Raymond. *Culture and Society: 1780–1950.* NY: Harper & Row, Pub., 1958.
Wills, Gary. *Saint Augustine.* NY: Penguin Books, 1999.
Wilson, A. N. *God's Funeral.* NY: W. W. Norton & Co., 1999.
Wilson, Colin. *The Outsider.* Cambridge, Mass.: Riverside Press, 1956.
Wilson, Edmund. *Consilience: The Unity of Knowledge.* NY: Alfred A. Knoff, 1998.
———. *Axel's Castle: A Study in the Imaginative Literature of 1870–1930.* NY: Scribner's Sons, 1931.
Windelband, Wilhelm. *History of Ancient Philosophy* Trans. by Herbert Ernest Cushman. NY: Dover Pub. Inc., 1956.
Windelband, Wilhelm. *History of Philosophy.* 2 vols. Trans. by James H. Tufts. NY: Harper, 1958.
Witters, Patricia. *Drugs and Society.* Monterey: Wadsworth Inc., 1983.
Wittkower, Rudolf. "Individualism in Art and Arists: A Renaissance Problem." *JHI* 22 (1961): 291–302.
Wolf, Abraham. *A History of Science, Technology, & Philosophy in the 18th Century.* 2 vols. Rev. ed. NY: Harper Torchbooks, 1961.
Wolf, Fred Alan. *Star Wave: Mind, Consciousness, and Quantum Physics.* NY: Macmillan Pub. Co., 1984.
———. *Taking the Quantum Leap: The New Physics for Nonscientists.* Rev. ed. NY: Harper & Row, 1989.
Woodhouse, Mark B. "Consciousness and Brahman-Arman." *Monist* 61 (1978): 96–124.
Woolf, Virginia. *Captain's Deathbed, and other Essays.* NY: Harcourt Brace and Company, 1950.
———. *Orlando. A Biography.* NY: Harvest Book / Harcourt Brace Jovanovich, 1956.
Yates, Frances. "Bacon and the Menace of English Literature." *New York Review of Books,* 27 March 1969, 37–39.
Yeo, Richard, "Ephraim Chambers's *Cyclopoedia* and the Tradition of Commonplaces." *JHI* 57 (1996): 157–75.
Yolton, John. "As In a Looking-Glass: Perceptual Acquaintance in Eighteenth-Century Britain. *JHI* 40 (1979): 207–34.
———. *John Locke and Education.* NY: Random House, 1971.
———. *John Locke and the Way of Ideas.* Oxford: Clarendon Press, 1968.
———. *Locke and the Compass of Human Understanding: A Selective Commentary on the 'Essays.'* Cambridge: Cambridge University Press, 1970.
———. "Locke's Man." *JHI* 62 (2001): 665–83.
———. *Perceptual Acquaintance from Descartes to Reid.* Minneapolis: University of Minnesota Press, 1984.
———. *Theory of Knowledge.* NY: MacMillan Co., 1965.
———. *Thinking Matter: Materialism in Eighteenth-Century Britain.* Oxford: Blackwell, 1984.
Young, Arthur M. *The Reflexive Universe: Evolution of Consciousness.* NY: Delacorte Press, 1976.
Zack, Naomi. *Bachelors of Science. Seventeenth-Century Identity, Then and Now.* Philadelphia: Temple University Press, 1996.
Zeldin, Theodore. *An Intimate History of Humanity.* NY: Harper Collins, 1994.
Zinberg, Norman E., ed. *Alternate States of Consciousness.* NY: Free Press, 1977.
Zweig, Paul. *The Heresy of Self-Love. A Study of Subversive Individualism.* NY: Harper Colophon Books, 1968.

Index

A

Aarsleff, Hans, 299, 302
Aberth, John, 128
Absolute, 424
Absurd, 407, 456
　See also, Theater of
Achilles, 35–36, 41
Aelfric, 68
Aeschylus, 30, 36, 206, 459, 478
Aeneid, 36
Aesthetics, 32, 112, 115, 183–84, 271, 291
Agamemnon, 36
Agnostic, 337
Agriculture, 165
Agrippa von Netteshein, 164
Alembert, Jean le Rond de, 303, 314
Alexander of Aphrodisias, 49
Alexander the Great, 33, 47, 186, 209
Alienation, 85, 154, 164, 402, 417, 454, 477, 479
Alone, 362
Alphabet, 25, 29, 30, 73
　Greek, 29
Alphonse de Spina, 84
Alquie, F., 320
Ambrose, St., 74
Ambrosia, 35
Anaximander, 38
Anaximenes, 38
Ancient, See Chapter One
Animals, 11, 228, 348, 349, 352, 484
　death, 41
Anguish, 84, 466–68
Annihilation, 20, 174
　Century of, 381, 399, 426
Anthropology, 64, 189, 246, 322
Anti-Hero
　Mickey Spillane, 433
　Shane, 433
Antonioni, Michelangelo, 176
　Blowup, 176
Apocalypse, 88–89
Apperceptual relations, 44
Appolinaire, Guillaume, 422
　See also Surrealism
Aquila, Richard E., 263, 283, 284
Aquinas, Thomas, St., 67, 80, 87–88, 103, 118, 147, 159–60, 194, 210, 212, 215, 282
Archimedes, 196
Arete, 29, 35, 63, 394
Aristarchus, 162
Aristotle, 29–30, 34, 38, 41–45, 61–62, 64, 67, 80, 103, 118, 140, 158–61, 163, 168, 189, 191–93, 199, 208, 212, 215, 218, 220, 225, 227, 230, 236, 257, 280, 282, 291, 315, 337, 340
Arnauld, Antoine, 273
Atomic, bomb, 428, 463, 468
Augustine, St., Bishop of Hippo, 47, 51, 54, 56–59, 62, 64, 65–66, 69–76, 77, 97– 99, 104, 106, 210, 215, 236, 239–44, 251–52, 263, 282, 306, 346, 363
　City of God, 56, 104
　Soliloqies, 65
　Testimony (Confessions), 56–59, 241
Augustus, Emperor, 36, 103
Authentic self, 203, 328, 337, 491
Authenticity, 361, 372–73, 375, 389, 410, 434–35, 437, 463, 466, 475, 491
Autobiography, 56, 58–59, 120, 210, 239, 241, 248, 281, 345, 348, 230, 363, 416
Avant-garde, 264
Averroës (Ibn Rushd), 282
Avicenna, 164
Awake, 40, 286, 330
　not conscious, 40
Aware, 9, 10, 15–16, 22, 37, 44–46, 120, 206, 226, 230, 231, 238, 239, 245–46, 249, 251–54, 255, 274, 278–79, 285–87, 290, 294–95, 319, 348, 357, 370, 417, 441, 466, 475, 480–81, 484, 489, 492
　death, 18

non-conscious, 3
non-human, 10
reflexive, 43
self-, 10, 120
Ayer, Alfred, 435

B

Babylonian Captivity, 129
Bach, 208
Bacon, Francis, 87, 159–60, 179, 181, 186, 198–200, 202–3, 205, 208, 210, 212–18, 220, 267, 235, 238, 250, 309, 311, 314, 324, 333, 350, 359–58, 376, 390, 446, 491
    Lord Chancellor, 214
    First Idol, 201
    Fourth Idol, 203
    Idols of the Tribe, 200
    New Atlantis, 200
    Novum Organum, 204
    self-distancing, 213–215
    Second Idol, 201
    Third Idol, 201
Bacon, Roger, 180, 199
    Doctor Mirabilis, 199
Bainton, R. H., 140
Barbarosso, Friedrick, 103
Barnston, Willis, 58
Baroque, 132, 152, 183–84, 260–61
    motion, 183
    power, 183
Barraclough, Geoffery, 302
Barrett, William, 437
Barrow, Isaac, 195
Barthes, Roland, 406
Battle of the Somme, 406
Baudelaire, Charles Pierre, 441
Beat Movement, 174, 374, 422, 441, 463–64
Beckett, Samuel, 407, 456, 458
    Waiting for Godot, 407
Bede, The Venerable,104
Beethoven, 176
Behavioralism, 253, 471
Behaviorism, 412–14, 423
"Be Here Now", 306, 464
Benedict, St., 76, 79
    monastaries, 68, 124

Berger, Harry Jr., 170
Bergson, Henri, 423–25, 428, 433, 450, 455–56
Berkeley, George, Bishop, 277, 320–21, 326, 337, 370
Bernard of Clairvaux, St., 141
Bernini, Gian Lorenzo, 139, 183–84
Bible, 376, 405
    Compultensian, 145
    King James, 198
    Polyglot, 145
    vernacular, 133, 151
    Vulgate, 145, 151
    Word, The, 76, 79, 249
Biography, 59–62, 120–21, 211, 248, 406
Blake, William, 358, 367, 371, 376
Bloody Revolution, 269
Bloom, Harold, 134–35, 152, 156, 169–70, 173–75, 186, 203, 207–11, 226, 238, 240–41, 243
Boccaccio, Giovanni, 103, 108
Bodin, Jean, 188–89, 220
Boetheus, Anicius Manlius Severinus, 73, 74
Bohr, Niels, 453
Bonaparte, Napoleon, 364
Borges, Jorge Luis, 211, 409, 456, 485
Boswell, James, 373
Boule, Pierre N., 186
Bourbons, 181
Boyle, Robert, 267, 277, 296
Bradbury, Ray, 442, 469
    Dandelion Wine, 442
Bradley, F. H., 416
Braggadocia, 150
Brahe, Tycho, 125, 200, 244, 272
Brain, 258
Brethern of the Common Life, 142
Breton, Andre, 440
Bronowsky, Jacob, 349
Bruce, Lenny, 174
Bruegel, Pieter, 139
Brunelleschi, Felipe, 111
    La Cupola, 111
Bruno, Giordano, 180, 186, 189–92, 198
Bunyon, 329
Burckhardt, Jacob, 90, 107, 112, 120, 122, 124, 248, 300, 385, 386
Buridan, Jean, 161, 193–94

Burdian's Ass, 193
Quaestiones super Octo Librao Physicorum, 161
Questiones de Caelo et Mundo, 161
Burke, Edmund, 341, 349, 442
Butler, Joseph, 246
Buttefield, Herbert, 198
Byzantine, 71

C

Cabinet of Dr. Caligari, 452
Caesar, Augustus, 209
Caesar, Julius, 60, 76, 122
Calculus, 309
Calderón de la Barca, Pedro, 185
Calvin, John, 85, 127, 131, 146–47, 150, 187, 212
Camus, Albert, 406, 418, 433, 463, 480
    The Stranger, 417
Candle of the Lord, 246
Capellanus, Andreas, 87
    De Amore, 87
Capitalism, 124–25, 427
Cardan, Jerome, 165
Carlyle, Thomas, 95, 361–62
    Sartor Resartus, 361–62
Carolingian Renaissance, 71–74
Carroll, Lewis, 439
Castiglione, Baldasar, 149–50
    Book of the Courtier, 149–50
Cathedrals
    Chartres, 86, 100
    Gothic, 70, 85, 448
    Romanesque, 85
    Vezéley, 109
Causation, 273, 308, 339–341, 451
    material, 217
Censorship, 167, 319
Century of Annihilation, 381, 399, 426
Certainty, 3, 9, 47, 52, 88, 96, 144, 148, 155, 176–77, 180, 204, 210, 223, 227, 229, 252–53, 255, 321, 334, 375, 377, 379, 383, 388, 440, 447, 451–53, 464, 479, 491
    See also Locke
Certitude, 3, 50, 54, 69, 255, 321, 369, 372–73

Cervantes, Miguel de, 184, 329
    Don Quixote, 329
Cézanne, Paul, 419, 421, 432
Chalmers, David, 308
Chaos, 4, 200
Charlemagne, 71–73
    dual alphabet, 73
    minuscule, 73
    palace schools, 72
    Palatine schools, 73
Charles I, 144, 327
Charles II, 145
Chaucer, Geoffrey, 98–99, 149, 172, 209, 226, 240, 310, 329
    Canterbury Tales, 98
Chichele, Henry, Archbishop, 88–89
Chomsky, Noam, 24, 484
Christ, 36, 50
Christianity, 48, 50, 64, 69–70, 77, 107, 124, 131, 148, 177, 179, 181, 187, 215, 234, 236, 239, 242, 245, 280, 303, 311, 322, 339, 373, 383, 388–89, 391
    Anglican, 131, 146, 148, 323, 326
    Avignon, 129–30
    Catholic, 187
    damnation, 356, 366, 388
    Garden of Gethsemane, 48
    heresy, 83–84, 182
    killing Christians, 145
    salvation, 124, 144, 148, 187, 234, 239, 310, 357
    Sermon on the Mount, 48, 142
    two swords, 127, 148–49, 211
    Word, see Bible
Churchland, Paul, 308
Cicero, 47–48, 76, 90, 102, 105–6, 170, 249
Clan, 22, 24
Clement of Alexandria, 47, 49
Clive, Geoffrey, 342
Clock, 119, 138, 158, 165, 204, 278, 310, 324, 409, 423, 448, 455, 533
    atomic, 409
    mechanical, 100, 131, 157
    solar, 485
Clock-Maker, 316
Clovis, 72
    Merovingians, 72
Cogito ergo sum, See Descartes

Cohen, J. M., 345
  See also Descartes
Coleridge, Samuel Taylor, 373–74, 376, 378–79, 391
Colie, Rosalie, 170
College, Greshman, 167, 212
Columbus, Christopher, 115, 188, 210, 272
Compass, 119, 130, 156, 164–66, 179, 204, 227
Computers, 255, 436
Condell, 170
Condillac, Etienne de, 303, 343, 348
Confession, 69, 86, 89, 223, 233 237, 293, 332
Conscience, 63, 69, 74, 82, 86, 89, 91, 106, 130, 155, 207, 223, 230, 232–33, 237, 244, 247, 256–57, 260–62, 277, 281, 289, 293–94, 302–3, 307, 324, 330, 332–33, 335, 373–74, 378–79, 387, 392, 394–95, 397, 479, 484, 491
Conscious, 230, 235, 244, 248, 251, 253, 255, 259–60, 262–64, 278, 280, 285–86, 304, 335, 337, 342, 385, 393, 442, 452, 459, 463, 465, 471, 487, 491
Consciousness, 9, 11, 14–18, 20–22, 25, 31–34, 36, 38–40, 42–44, 46–47, 50, 52, 74, 89–91, 96, 107–8, 120, 123, 139, 152, 154, 170–71, 174–76, 180, 195, 204–9, 212, 214, 223–24, 226, 229–32, 234–35, 237–39, 241, 243, 245–47, 249, 251–60, 262–69, 273–82, 285–95, 297, 301, 303, 304, 310, 317, 320–21, 325–26, 328, 330–31, 335, 337, 341–42, 344, 350, 352, 357, 359–60, 370–75, 377–79, 385, 389–94, 396–97, 401, 404, 406, 408, 412, 414–15, 417, 419, 422, 424–26, 431–32, 435–37, 439, 442, 445, 447–48 450, 460–61, 464, 466, 468, 470–33, 475–89, 491
  access, 295
  animals without; 10–11, 40
  aware, 6, 44
  bad, 395
  choices, 219
  class, 375
  death, 14–15, 18
  degrees of, 17, 25, 40
  developmental, 69
  dynamic, 9, 21, 36
  language, 12–13, 17–18, 19–23, 25
  memory, 11
  neutral, 293
  non-conscious, 20, 38, 41
  non-static, 9, 17–18
  potential, 261
  pre-conscious, 39
  reflective, 9
  reflexive, 43–44
  relative, 47
  second-degree, 474
  self-conscious, 9, 16, 72
  stream of, See William James
  sub-conscious, 30
  synthesis, 40, 44
  transcendental, 474
  unreflective, 474, 483
Copernicus, Nicolaus, 125, 151, 162–63, 180, 189–93, 195, 197–98, 280
Corneille, Pierre, 185
Coste, Pierre, 333, 335
  sentiment intérieur, 335–36
Council of Constance, 129
Council of Trent, 145, 323
Counter-culture, 407, 464
Cox, Stephen D., 331, 336, 357
Cranmer, Thomas, 134
Creative, 372, 390–91, 395–96, 448, 451, 478, 488, 492
Crombe, A. C., 161–62
Cromwell, Oliver, 145
Croce, Benedetto, 103
Crusades
  First, 87
  Second, 109
Cubism, 406, 419, 422–23, 429–30
  camouflage, 430
Cudworth, Ralph, 228, 325
Cummings, E. E., 459
Cuneiform, Mesopotamian, 25
Curia, 84
Curiosity, 11, 52, 53, 83, 116, 162, 187, 225, 377, 450, 459, 491, 492, 499
Cusanus, Nicholas, 190

D

Dadaists, 406, 430, 463–64
Dante, Alighieri, 97–99, 101–3, 133, 149, 151, 172, 191, 193, 209, 211, 368
Darwin, Charles Robert, 280, 367, 376
Davies, Catherine Glyn, 330–31
Death, 3, 9–12, 13–6, 17–23, 25–29, 34–35, 47–48, 50, 52–53 64, 66, 69–70, 88–89, 116, 127, 133–34, 148, 152, 157, 162, 175, 179, 210, 321, 334, 350–52, 365, 369, 373, 375–76, 383, 387–89, 407, 435, 440, 443, 453, 465–66, 468–69, 471, 479–80, 484, 491
    See also Religion
    animals, 10–11, 15, 40, 43
    "arrow of life", 26
    Black, 116, 129, 130
    burial, 11, 14–18
    certainty, 6, 21, 27–29, 34, 42, 51
    certitude, 28
    dance of, 117
    danses macabres, 152
    damnation, 51–52, 140
    of God, 383–84
    Jimmy and Kitty, 18–20
        never Fido, 24
    Neanderthal, 11, 13, 14–15, 19, 21
    resurrection, 50
    salvation, 29, 50–51
    savior, 36
    tombs, 27–28, 32, 88–89, 117
    uncertainty, 15, 47, 49
Debussy, Claude, 420, 423
Defoe, Daniel, 327
Degree, 31, 200, 206, 258, 330, 334, 398, 415, 483, 485, 493–94
    stages, 493
Deist, 59, 334
Delumeau, Jean, 19, 69, 375
Democritus, 34, 190
Dennett, Daniel, 273, 412, 481, 487
Dent, N. J. H., 343–44, 348, 351–52
Descartes, René, 42, 44–45, 65–67, 84–85, 91, 132, 139, 151, 153, 155, 171, 186–87, 191, 203, 205, 214, 216–17, 223–66, 267, 271–76, 278–80, 285, 289, 296, 306, 308–9, 311–317, 319, 322, 324–25, 329, 331, 333, 335, 343–44, 357, 359, 370, 373–74, 376–77, 425, 437, 454, 461, 476, 486
    analytic geometry, 268
    aware, 38
    cogitato, 230, 263
    cogito, 229, 236, 256, 259, 260, 264, 324, 334, 337, 343, 359, 370, 383, 389, 406, 435–36, 464–65, 470–71, 474, 476–77
    cogito ergo sum, 234, 255, 258
    conscientia, 230
    homoculus, 238
    ghost in the machine, 275
    idea, 227–28, 252–53, 258, 265
    vortices, 438
Despair, 454, 468–69, 479
Detachment, 454
Devotio moderna, Chapter Two, 83, 84, 142, 154
Dialogue, 250–51
Dictionaries, 171, 226, 232, 244, 278, 301, 437
Dictionary of the History of Ideas, 49
Didactic, 30, 32, 36, 46
Diderot, Denis, 307, 312, 316, 329–33, 335, 341
    Neveu de Rameau, 329
Dilthey, Wilhelm, 363
Dionysus, 74
    See also Nietzsche
Disengagment, 324–25, 247, 251, 359, 433, 491
Diversity, 131, 138, 375
Divine Right of Kings, 129, 311
Dostoevsky, Fyodor, 375, 378, 390, 395, 399, 404, 432, 466, 472
    Crime and Punishment, 357, 358
    Notes from the Underground, 395, 398 399
Donatello, 111
    Gattamelata, 111
Dondi, Giovanni, 100
Double-entry bookeeping, 118, 128–29, 132 144, 165
Doubt, 155, 187, 223, 229, 253–54, 256, 258, 290, 334, 337, 385, 453
Dreyfus Affair, 454

Dualism, 29, 177, 224, 227, 236–37, 259, 275, 315, 318, 320, 324–25, 343–44, 349, 373, 376, 389, 436, 454, 467, 480, 486–87
Dubuffet, Jean, 441
Duchamp, Marcel, 430, 447
   Nude Descending the Staircase, 430, 447
Dürer, Albrecht, 139, 141, 269
Durkheim, Emile, 347
Duty, 60

E

Eccles, John C., 16, 19
Eckermann, Johann Peter, 367
Eckhardt, Master, 141–42
Economics, 179, 186, 188–89, 204, 310
   capitalism, 124–25, 149, 405
   mercantilism, 427
Edict of Nantes, 144, 146
Ego, 16, 22, 26–27, 32–33, 53, 121, 174, 242–43, 262, 322, 377, 386, 388–90, 471, 473–74, 476–77, 480, 492
Egypt, 13, 19, 25–27, 29, 48
   Book of the Dead, 28
   space and time, 9, 24, 26, 37, 41
   tombs, 27
   writing, 22
Einstein, Albert, 56, 210, 280, 400, 410, 421, 440, 447, 454–55, 488
Eisenstein, Elizabeth, 154
Eleanor of Aquitaine, 87, 150
El Greco, 113
Eliot, T. S., 414, 417, 423–24, 439, 457, 485
   Four Quartets, 414–15, 457
   Hollow Men, 417
   Little Gidding, 416
   Wasteland, 416
Elizabeth I, 146–48, 169, 189, 311
Emerson, Ralph Waldo, 374, 391
Empedocles, 34
Empiricism, 268–71, 276–77, 289, 305, 310, 312, 315, 318, 326, 336, 339–40, 342, 344, 359, 370, 375–76, 408, 468
Encyclopedias, 437
Encyclopédie, 199, 303, 315–16, 329, 343
Enlightenment, 179–80, 223–24, 226, 234, 237, 246, 257, 262, 269, 278, 281, 299, 300, 303, 305, 307, 358, 362, 370–72, 378, 406
Enthusiasm, 277
Epic, 98
Epictetus, 49
Epicurean, 47–48
Epicurus, 47
Epicycle, 162, 191
Epistemology, 303, 318
Erasmus, Desiderius, 125, 141, 143, 145, 168–69, 179, 307
   Praise of Folly, 143, 168, 179
Escher, Maurits, 456
Estranged, 35, 66, 417, 466
Estrangment, 66, 164, 320, 380, 399, 402, 454, 463, 477
d'Etables, Lefevre, 141
Etymology, 242, 300, 302–4
   conscientia, 230, 245, 278, 271
Euclidean, 158
Euripides, 31
Eusebius of Cesarea, 104
Evolution, 2, 9–12, 18, 25–26, 32, 37, 40, 45–47, 77, 85, 167, 124 195, 305, 337, 488, 491
Existential, 2, 5, 66, 156, 173, 249, 256, 261, 281, 307, 342, 382–83, 399, 401– 2, 408, 412, 419, 425, 429, 431, 434, 442, 465, 461–69, 472–81, 493
   attitude, 382, 399, 401, 408, 415, 419, 432, 462, 465, 475, 477
   choice, 425
   self, 156
   phenomenology, 433
Experience, 339, 376
Expressionism, 421
Exterior, 271
Eyeglasses, 165

F

Faith, 148–49, 154, 193, 195, 218, 223, 277, 282, 309, 323, 334, 378, 381, 385, 491
Fear, 15, 19, 46–48, 50–51, 60, 62, 69, 89, 116, 132, 152, 179, 202, 216, 220, 351, 432, 451, 474, 491
Feifel, Herman, 16
Fellini, Frederico, 458

8 ½, 458
Feudalism, 87, 121, 128, 185, 204, 309
Fielding, Henry, 327
Film, 4, 452
Firearms, 165
Flagellants, 117
Fleming, William, 423
Fontenelle, Bernard le Bovier de, 191, 305
Foreshortening, 110, 157
Fourth Lateran Council, 86, 129, 138
Francis of Assisi, St., 148, 212
    Franciscans, 149
Franks, 71
Fraser, Alexander Campbell, 287, 289, 291, 293–94
Freedom, 473, 475, 468, 487
Freud, Sigmund, 31, 175, 435, 484
    unconscious, 484
Fromm, Eric, 105–6, 107
    Escape From Freedom, 105
Future, 362, 366, 369–70, 375, 378, 381, 416–17, 448–50, 457, 475, 488
Futurism, 4, 433

G

Galen, 164
Galileo Galilei, 115, 125, 151, 162, 167, 180, 186, 189, 192, 195, 197, 200, 205, 209, 216–17, 244, 267, 272, 280, 320, 350, 433
    The Assayer, 196
    Eppur si muove, 198
Gaugin, Paul, 420
Gay, Peter, 210
Gelli, Giambattisti, 122
Genesis, 198
Genius, 112, 145, 153, 167, 175, 177, 184, 206–11, 226, 246, 265, 267, 300, 307–8, 318, 337, 372, 410, 420, 471
Gerson, 141
Gettysburg Address, 171
Ghiberti, Lorenzo, 103
Ghost in the machine, See Descartes; Ryle
Gilgamish, Epic of, 19, 28
Gilmore, Myron P., 119–20
Gilson, 230

Giotto di Bondone, 103, 108–9, 119, 192–93, 200, 205, 272
    Bewailing of Christ, 110
Globalism, 4
Glorious Revolution, 145, 269, 301
Glosses, 82, 86
Godel, Kurt, 434, 453
    Uncertainty Principle, 453
Goethe, Johann Wolfgang von, 98, 172, 353, 358–63, 365–68, 372, 374, 376, 379–80, 403, 474
    Faust, 363, 364, 381
    Sturm und Drang, 363
Gogh, Vincent van, 420
Gombrich, E. H., 421
Goths, 71
Gothic, 70, 85, 109, 112, 278, 363
Gould, Stephen J., 481, 484
Great Chain of Being, 128–29, 149, 212, 218, 339
Great Clock, 197
Great Famine, 117
Great Plague, 88, 100, 117, 128, 130, 152, 166, 407
Great Schism, 129
Great War, 426, 430–35
    Chapter One, 401, 406, 454
    Chapter Two, 401, 413, 417, 452
Greece, 22, 29–30, 32, 35–36, 37–38, 40–41, 47
    abstract thought, 21–22, 37
    Golden Age, 30, 32, 38
    humanizing, 33, 37
    language, 22, 29, 31–33, 37–38
    theater, 22, 30, 32
    vowels, 29
Greenblatt, Stephen, 134, 152
Greenlee, Douglas, 274, 270
Gregorius Reisch, 158
Grimmelshausen, Hans, 185
Groote, Gerard, 83–84, 142
Guild, 310
Guilt, 152, 237, 246, 379, 394, 479
    See also Shame
Gun powder, 130, 164, 165, 179, 277

H

Hagiography, 63, 68, 212
Hair, 173, 175
Hammurabi, Code of, 28
"Happening", 452
Hardie, 43, 44
  See Modrak
Hartley, David, 277
Harvey, William, 186, 267
Hawkes, J., 26
Hazard, Paul, 180
Hebrews, 19
Hegel, George Wilhelm Friedrich, 10, 307, 361, 370–76, 378–80, 388, 392, 403, 408, 414, 423, 449–50, 474
  Geist, 380, 390, 392
Heidegger, Martin, 175, 251, 406, 433–37, 450, 461–62, 467, 477
Heisenberg, Ernst Karl, 195, 406–7
  Uncertainty Principle, 406–7, 453
Hellenistic, 37, 42, 47, 54, 236
Heller, Erich, 369
Hell Fire Club, 327
Helvetius, 312
Heminges, 170
Henri of Navarre (Henri IV), 144
Henry VII, 311
Henry VIII, 128, 131, 133, 146, 151
Heraclitus, 38, 41
Heresy, 83–84, 143, 145, 154, 163, 182, 197–98
Hero, 35–36, 41, 46, 62, 64, 249
Herodotus, 37
Hesiod, 34
Hexter, J. H., 168
Historians, 57
Historiography, 103, 169, 300, 461
History, 1, 9–11, 14, 20, 24, 32, 37, 43, 50, 59, 95–97, 104, 119, 124, 170, 175, 180, 205, 210–11, 214, 226, 233, 242, 261, 270, 275, 284, 299, 300, 303–4, 306, 360, 372, 377 380, 384, 386, 390, 402, 415–16, 445, 449–50, 452, 458, 460–62, 472, 478, 481, 484
  detective, 491
  ideas, 1, 3, 358
  intellectual, 3, 107, 118, 426
  irony, 107, 227, 328, 460
  mentalities, 4
  modern, 124
  time, 9, 10, 24–26, 30–31, 41
Hobbes, Thomas, 131, 189, 190, 202, 216–20, 224, 229, 232–33, 235, 261–62, 268, 293, 302, 309–10, 327, 339, 349, 368, 423, 442
  Leviathan, 216–17, 232, 327
Holbein, 113
Holland, 244, 319
Hologram, 458
Homer, 12, 19, 31–4, 36, 41, 58, 75, 98, 172, 206, 394
  psyche, 34
  thymos, 34
Homoculus, 45
Hooke, Robert, 186
Hubert, Henri, 426
Huguenots, 127, 131, 144, 146
Huizinga, 117–18
Hulme, T. E., 485
Humanism, 91, 123–24, 126, 128, 164–65, 182, 205, 228, 236, 277, 312, 328, 360, 385, 117, 153, 465, 470, 472–73, 481
  Greek, 30–32, 33
  Renaissance, 90
  studia humanitatus, 114, 150
Humanities, 1, 172, 460
Hume, David, 231, 233, 235, 251, 265, 275, 337–43, 373, 408, 411, 435, 437, 441, 451, 484
  billiards, 339
  causation, 451
Humor, 173–74, 362, 459
Humphreys, C., 480
Hundred Years' War, 117, 129
Hunt, Morton, 10–11, 486
Husserl, Edmund, 433, 435, 461–62, 474, 477
Huygens, Christiaan, 267
Hydrology, 165

I

"I", 32–33, 45, 59–60, 240, 243, 284, 314, 317–19, 325–26, 368, 387, 437, 473
  analog, 40
"I am the door", 190

Idea, 135, 272–73, 276, 279, 288, 294, 297–98, 301, 321, 337, 343, 474
  empirical, 329
Idealism, 315, 321, 337
Identity, 238, 244, 272, 279, 283, 285, 305–6, 320–21, 326, 328, 336, 340–41, 348, 372, 379, 411–12
  See also Locke
  inner, 144
Ignatius of Loyola, See Jesuits
Iliad, 33, 44
Imagination, 9, 253, 265, 272, 276, 331, 340–41, 346, 363, 376, 378, 415, 417, 426
Immortal, 34–35, 37, 69
Impetus, 161–62, 194
Imprimatur, 319
Impressions, 270, 339–40
Impressionism, 419, 448
Innate, 235, 265, 268–69, 271, 275, 298, 303, 310, 313, 323, 325
  anti-innate, 315
Individual, 9–11, 14–18, 20, 26, 30–31, 33, 36, 38–40, 42, 49, 52, 59, 61, 64, 87, 96, 98–99, 107–8, 121–22, 124, 128, 131, 133, 153–54, 164, 175–76, 202, 206, 214, 230–31, 234, 241–44, 247– 48, 256–57, 262, 279, 294, 305, 310, 315, 322, 328, 330, 337, 339, 344, 346, 348–49, 357, 359–60, 363–64, 348, 379, 381, 389, 394, 403, 409, 416, 423, 446, 468, 477, 492
Individualism, 121–22, 205, 215, 220, 305, 307, 310, 377
Individuality, 13, 16, 20, 31, 33, 38–39, 43, 45, 49, 52, 57, 66, 68, 89, 119–20, 122–24, 127, 139, 151–52, 169–70, 180, 189, 195, 202–8, 210–12, 217, 219, 223, 239, 241–43, 247–48, 256, 267, 279, 288, 304–5, 317–18, 320, 322, 324, 358, 361, 367, 369, 371–72, 375–76, 378, 385–86, 437, 442, 473, 477, 492
Individualized, 184, 350
Industrial Revolutions, 167, 452
Industrialization, 427, 477
  aircraft, 426
  artificial silk, 402
  bakelite, 402
  coal, 402
  combustion engine, 402
  computers, 402, 437
  depth charges, 426
  electricity, 402
  iron, 402
  penny press, 382, 402
  plastic, 402
  poison gas, 426
  radio, 402
  steel, 402
  submarine, 426
  synthetic fibers, 402
  tanks, 426
  technocrats, 402
  telephone, 402
  television, 402
  typewriter, 402
Inertia, 161, 225, 409
Infinity, 192–95
Inner, 17, 21, 45, 52, 121, 140, 155, 223–24, 226–27, 233, 235, 238–41, 247, 251, 269, 271, 275, 284, 308, 314, 322, 331, 333, 337, 348, 367, 383, 388–89, 391, 404, 409, 422, 424, 436, 439, 442, 447, 454, 458, 466, 486, 488
  self, 154
  voice, 169
Innocent III, 86
Instinct, natural, 246
Intentionality, 44
Interior, 21–22, 45–46, 52, 233–34, 236–40, 242, 244, 246–48, 251–52, 257–58, 260–61, 263, 268, 271, 273–76, 298, 300, 304, 321–22, 324–25, 328–29, 333, 335, 341–42, 348–49, 359, 366, 391, 409, 412, 471, 488, 491, 493
  conscience, 85
  ontology, 9, 10, 21, 33, 47, 67, 127
  space, 85
  voice, 202
Internal, language, 173
Interpretation, 96, 244, 249, 481, 499
  See also Translation
Introspection, 9, 43, 90, 223, 226, 251, 275, 338, 376, 409, 425, 436–38, 441, 446, 477, 489
Intuition, 426

Invention, 12, 225, 401
Inward, 17, 132, 215, 245, 247, 274, 306, 478
    knowledge, 233, 247
    soul, 215
Inwit, 245
Ioneseco, Eugène, 440
Ireland, monastaries, 72
Irish monks, 71
Isabella and Ferdinand, 127, 145
Isidore of Seville, 80, 104
-isms, 405, 433, 464, 477
Isolation, 154
Italian Renaissance, 95–136

J

James I, 151, 169, 199, 216
James, William, 211, 410–14, 470, 482, 485
    Priniciples of Psychology, 413, 843
    streams of consciousness, 410–11, 483
Jaspers, Karl, 433
Jaynes, Julian, 15, 20, 23, 38–41, 251 275, 394, 411, 480–81, 483
    analog "I", 40
    conciliation, 40
    death, 15
    excerption, 40
    fear, 15
    metaphor "me", 40
    narratization, 40
    spacialization, 40
Jazz, 4, 176, 441, 464
Jerome, St., 103, 246
Jesus, 42, 210
Jesuits, Society of Jesus, 146, 224–25
Jimmy and Kitty, 11–14, 18, 20
Johnson, Samuel, 300, 321
Jowett, Benjamin, 58
Joyce, James, 408–10, 423, 426, 455, 457
    Ulysses, 409, 423
Jung, Karl, 371
Junger, Ernst, 486
Juvenal, 33

K

Kafka, Franz, 407–9
    Castle, 407
    Trial, 408–9

Kahn, 43, 44
    See Modrak
Kaiser Wilhelm II, 405
Kandinski, Wassily, 440
Kant, Immanuel, 233, 313, 342, 366–68, 371–72, 374–76, 379–80, 382, 460, 465
Kaufmann, Walter, 366–67, 372, 396, 399, 407–8, 463, 478
Keen, Ernst, 481
Keller, Helen, 460
Kempis, Thomas à, 84, 129, 142
Kepler, Johannes, 191, 200, 267, 272, 244
Kermode, Frank, 171, 176
Kern, Stephen, 410–11, 428–30, 432
Kerouac, Jack, 464
Kierkegaard, Søren, 480
Knowledge, 274, 279, 287, 292, 294, 296, 319, 375, 370,
Koyre, Alexander, 226
Kristeller, Paul Oskar, 123

L

Lamb, Charles, 170
Landesman, 44
    See Modrak
Language, 3, 10, 12, 17, 20–22, 24, 36–37, 52–53, 56, 63, 72–73, 90, 100, 102–3, 133, 143–44, 153, 155, 167–70, 175, 177, 179–80, 199–200, 203, 210–11, 218, 224, 257–58, 270, 277, 296–98, 300–1, 306, 309, 337, 348–49, 359, 361, 376, 380, 382, 408–9, 415, 437–38, 441, 449–52, 459–61, 474, 491
    concrete, 21, 22, 27
    consonants, 13
    Greek, 29–33, 37
    homonyms, 25–26
    ideographic, 75
    immortality, 20, 28, 34–35, 37, 76
    inflective, 25
    lexography, 57, 123, 302
    linguistics, 71, 298
    literate, 21, 24, 27
    music, 172
    naming, 19–20
    oral, 75
    phonentics, 75

physical gestures, 23
space, 9, 24, 26, 37
static, 17
syntax, 18, 55, 57, 90, 252, 256, 301 377, 382
theater, 22, 24, 30
vocabulary, 36, 256
vowels, 13, 29–30
writing, 17, 21, 23-27, 29–30, 39, 52
Laporte, 230
Last Judgement, 89
Lateen sail, 165
Le Bon, 430
Lee, Henry 297
Leibniz, Gottfried Wilhelm, 197, 235, 267, 278, 316–18, 320–21, 326, 346, 370, 393
   Great Clock-Maker, 278, 280
   monads, 318–19
Leonardo da Vinci, 112, 115, 125, 196, 210
Leopold and Loeb, 432
Levy-Bruhl, Lucien, 20
Lewis, C. S., 278, 406
Libraries, 168, 198, 244, 245, 297
   See also Monasteries
Lieberman, P., 13
Light, speed of, 448
Literacy, 70–73, 244, 249, 461, 487
Lively, Penelope, 485
Locke, John, 44, 84–85, 151, 153, 155, 171, 186–87, 203, 205, 212, 215, 224–25, 233, 235, 238, 246–47, 251, 253, 265, 267–307, 309–10, 312–13, 315–16, 318–22, 324–27, 329, 331, 333–35, 337, 342–44, 348, 357–59, 367, 370–71, 376, 379, 383, 393–94, 406, 435, 438, 449, 454, 461, 476, 483
   blank slate, 274, 305
   complex ideas, 274, 315
   empiricism, 471
   Personal Identity, 85, 155, 212, 238, 253, 268, 281–82, 285, 288, 290–95, 307, 321, 411
   same identity, 279, 281–84, 288–90, 293– 95, 304, 338, 342, 411
   sensations, 270, 277, 287–88, 315
   simple ideas, 274, 315
   tabula rasa, 274, 285, 305
Logos, 49

Lollards, 83–84, 154
Loneliness, 66
Long, George, 57
Louis VII, 109
Louis XIV, 184
   Versailles, 184
Lovejoy, Arthur, 358, 360
Lucretius, 48, 190
Luther, Martin, 131, 139–41, 143, 146–47, 167, 184, 187, 204, 249
   Augustine, 414
   Bible, personalized, 414
   priesthood of all believers, 414
Lowe, Donald, 304

M

Mach, Ernst, 410, 440
Machiavelli, Niccolo, 95, 119, 122, 125–28, 133, 145, 167, 171, 207, 312
Maclean, Kenneth, 271, 299–300
Magnus, Albertus, 80
Malcolm X, 207, 460
Malebranche, Nicholas, 315–17, 319, 335
   occasionalism, 315, 317
Mallarmé, Stéphane, 441, 458
Mannerism, 132
Marcus Aurlieus, 48, 50, 58, 60, 62, 64–65, 67, 69
Marlow, Christopher, 364
Marx, Karl, 175, 212, 368, 375
Mary Magdalen Church, Vézelay, 109
Mary Tudor, 146
M*A*S*H, 407
Maslow, Abraham, 248
   self-actualized, 248
Materialism, 4, 229, 253, 278, 318, 321–22, 324, 382–83, 385, 401, 403, 411, 431, 471, 481
Mathematics, 26, 163, 165, 173, 194–96, 200, 202, 218, 224, 227, 263, 267–68, 270, 277, 301, 309, 434, 439–40, 453, 477
   See also Language; Bacon, Corpernicus; Descartes; Hobbes; Russell
Matthews, Gareth, 242
Mauss, Marcel, 426
McDonald, Dwight, 422

McGinn, Colin, 481, 484
McLean, Kenneth, 271–72, 299–300
Mcluhan, Marshall, 427
McRae, Robert, 253, 255, 258–59, 261–63
Mechanistic, 179, 197, 229, 249, 277–78, 280, 318, 324, 327, 332, 335, 347–48, 375, 438, 445, 488
    See also Clock
    attack on tradition, 193
Medeival, 52, 53–90
Medici, Cosmio de, 128
Memory, 56, 57, 91, 158, 210, 212, 218, 256–57, 264–65, 283, 285, 287, 289–90, 292–96, 304–5, 325, 360, 370, 377, 409, 415–16, 424, 426, 441, 449–50, 458, 484–85, 489
    collective, 10, 24, 37, 210–11
    private, 95
Menard, 211
Mercantile, 125, 204, 322
Mercier, L. S., 382
Mère, Chevalier de, 181
Merleau-Ponty, Maurice, 410
Mesmerism, 278
Metaphysics, 367, 379, 410, 450, 466, 479
Mettrie, Julian de la, 327–28
Michelangelo Buonarroti, 112, 119, 125, 210
Microscopes, 197, 199
Middle English Dictionary (MED), 245
Mill, John Stewart, 112, 206–9, 212, 307, 471, 478
    individual, 206
    genius, 112, 207–9
Milner, John, 297
Milton, John, 185, 269
Mind, 10, 69, 223–24, 227, 239–40, 243, 245, 246–47, 249, 251, 253, 256, 258–61, 264–65, 268, 271–72, 274, 277–79, 294–95, 305, 330, 381, 390, 397, 414–15, 425, 465, 467, 484, 486–87, 492
"mind-forged manacles", 367
Mirrors, 11, 275, 318
    Venice, 112, 122
Mithraism, 48
Mitton, Damien, 181
Modern
    perspectives, 173
    pre-, 451

Modernism, 484
Modernity, 98, 172, 180, 182, 186, 189–90, 203–5, 224–25, 227, 233–34, 236, 240–41, 243, 245, 247–48, 250–51, 253, 256–57, 263, 271, 273, 279, 284, 289, 296, 298, 300, 306–7, 310, 312, 318, 321, 324, 325–26, 329, 332–33, 336–38, 342, 344, 359, 372, 374–75, 377, 384, 392, 416–17, 419, 426, 442, 449–50, 454, 459, 463, 466, 471, 473, 478, 492
    early, 121, 137, 215
Modrak, Deborah K., 42–46
Molyneux, William, 279
Momentum, 456
Monaco, Paul, 475
Monastaries
    chained libraries, 82
    cloistered, 243
    mendicant, 154
    mumbling rooms, 77, 83, 87
    scriptorium, 78, 82
    silence, 78, 82
Mondrian, Piet, 458
Monet, Claude, 419
Monk, Thelonious, 176
Monologue, See Inner voice
Montaigne, Michel Eyquem de, 16, 122–24, 132, 139, 175, 209, 237, 243, 245, 249, 306, 312, 323, 345
Montesquieu, Charles-Louis de Secondat, 245, 313, 337, 347
More, Henry, 191, 228, 280
More, Sir Thomas, 125, 143, 167, 171
Motion, 162, 165, 183, 193–94, 197, 218, 270, 280, 309, 317, 338–39, 366, 375, 378, 380, 405–6, 410–11, 417, 453, 458, 475, 456
    See also Time
    epicycles, 162, 191
    Eppur si muove, 198
    impetus, 161–62, 194
    inertia, 161, 225, 409, 446
    movable type, 138, 157, 165–67
    oscillator, 166
    pictures, 4, 452
    unmoved mover, 159–60
Muenster, Sabastian, 188
Mumbling room, 77, 83, 87

Mumford, Lewis, 165
Musil, Robert, 417–18

N

Nationalism, 4, 401, 403, 462
Natural Law, 327–28, 369
Naturalism, 246
Neanderthal, 11–13, 15, 19, 403
    language, 13
Nectar, 35
Neocortex, 10
Neoplatonism, 55
Neural tansmissions, 481
Newton, Sir Isaac, 157, 161, 195–96, 205, 225, 244, 267, 280, 296, 311, 316–17, 350, 367–68, 410, 440, 446, 465
Nicene Creed, 84, 138
Nietzsche, Friedrich Wilhelm, 48, 64, 173–75, 359, 371–72, 377–78, 380, 382–87, 389, 391, 393–94, 396–99, 403–4, 408, 411, 418, 435, 442, 447, 452, 454, 460, 465–66, 473, 480, 491
    See also Existential
    Beyond Good and Evil, 388, 390
    death of god, 283–84
    Dionysus, 381–82
    fear and laziness, 389–91
    Gay Science, 383–84, 387, 392, 395
    herd 387–88, 395
    Humam-all-too-Human, 381, 385–86
    Geneology of Morals, 397
    Thus Spoke Zarathustra, 381, 383, 388
    Use and Abuse of History, 398
    Übermensch, 382, 388, 395
    Will to Power, 396–98
Nihilism, 342, 381–83, 395, 398, 471
Novalis, Baron Friedrich, 382

O

Objective, 61–62, 200, 202, 211–16, 236, 250–52, 263, 273, 280, 314, 321, 325, 333, 446, 450–51
Ockham, William of, 87, 160–61, 180, 193, 210
    Ockham's Razor, 160, 193
Odyssey, 33, 41
One Flew Over the Cuckoo's Nest, 174

Ong, Walter J., 12, 17, 21, 202, 205
Ontology, 21, 240, 242, 247, 273, 279–80, 284, 294, 301, 322, 344, 346, 360, 362, 372, 377, 397, 462, 466, 475, 491
Optics, 138, 199, 272
Oppenheimer, Robert, 440
Order, see Religion, Science
Oreseme, Nicole, 193–94
Ortega y Gassett, José, 418, 447, 452, 462
    Barbarism of Specialization, 418
    Revolt of the Masses, 418
Oscillator, 166
Osiris, 48
Otto the Freising, 104
Oxford English Dictionary, 232–33, 245, 247, 252

P

Paleolithic, 14
Paracelsus, 163, 188
Paradox, 371, 420, 429, 452, 480
Parmenides, 34, 38
Parthenon, 31
Pascal, Blaise, 181, 193, 195, 237, 261, 340, 345, 433
    Pascal's wager, 199
Past, 362, 417, 432, 448, 450, 454, 457, 486
Paul, St., 50, 140–41, 236, 239
Pavlov, Ian Petrovich, 440
Peace of Augusburg, 132
Peguy, Charles, 401
Penny press, 382, 402
Perceive, 456
Perception, 14, 17, 43, 70, 73, 100, 127, 162, 170, 196, 203, 211, 213, 239, 249, 251, 254, 258–60, 272, 274–75, 284, 287–88, 294, 320–21, 325–26, 334, 337–38, 340, 360, 362, 439, 459, 484–88
Pericles, 31, 37, 122, 209
Persona, 33, 243, 293, 296, 299, 305
    mask, 33
Personal, 90, 234, 237, 240, 247, 345, 347, 449
    See also John Locke, personal identity
Perspective, 49, 110, 224, 375, 422–23, 430–31, 443, 445–46, 451–52, 454, 479
Peter the Venerable, 78

Petrarch, Francesco, 95, 97, 100–1, 103, 105–6, 115, 118, 120, 122, 133, 151, 162, 174, 193, 205, 210
   Africa, 104
   antiquity, 102
   Epistles, 104
   humanist, 104
   library, 102
   Mount Ventoux, 106
   Prince of Humanists, 103
Phenomenology, 380, 433, 437, 461–62, 474
Phillip II, 128, 146
Philology, 102, 377
Philosophers, 386
Philosophes, 312–13, 326, 329, 332, 335, 347–48, 360, 364, 376
Philosophy, 158, 188, 194, 196, 208, 247, 249, 250, 253, 267–68, 275, 277, 284, 299, 312, 318–19, 397, 399, 413, 435–36, 439, 445, 450, 452, 458, 461–62, 472, 481, 489
   analytic, 217
   cognitive, 288
   empiricism, 199
   epistemology, 241, 372
   metaphysics, 123, 255, 227, 269, 270, 313, 318, 342, 461, 462
   natural, 195–96, 198, 200, 223
   transcendental, 465
   theology, 123, 189, 200, 365
Photons, 406
Physics, 4, 194, 406, 410, 413–14, 416, 421, 423, 440, 450, 453, 462, 488
   mechanistic, 325, 410
   nuclear, 406
   quantum, 448
Piccaso, Pablo, 210, 406, 416, 419–21, 440, 460
Pico della Mirandola, 114, 141
Pierce, Charles, 488
Pinker, Steven, 482–84
Plato, 22, 37, 34, 38, 58, 74, 102, 149, 168, 171, 177, 190, 199, 208–10, 227, 236, 239, 263, 275, 297, 303, 367, 373, 389
Platonic, 55, 67, 114, 177, 263, 304, 389
Platonists, Cambridge, 191
Plotinus, 47, 49, 55, 231
Pluralism, 125, 131, 138, 420, 481

Plutarch, 42, 60–61, 63, 67
Pollock, Jackson, 458
Polybius, 126
Poly-consciousness, 259, 485, 494
Pomponazi of Mantua, Pietro, 116, 118
Popper, Karl R., 16, 18
Portraits, 112, 121, 248
Post-impressionism, 448, 459
Postmodern, 4, 173, 404
Post-modern, 4, 257, 326, 358, 374, 404, 408, 416, 426, 431, 440, 442, 449, 462–63, 465, 479, 485, 488
   Hair, 173
Pound, Ezra, 485
Power, 183
Pragmatism, 44
Pride, 65, 184, 346, 369
Printer, 155
   orthography, 155, 248
Printing press, 74, 84, 95, 102, 131, 133, 138, 143, 151, 153–55, 167–68, 170, 177, 179, 219, 225, 227, 248–49, 437
   movable type, 138, 157, 165–67
   rag paper, 240
Privacy, 20, 32, 42, 57, 66, 76, 82, 89, 96, 120, 122, 131, 153–54, 170, 177, 209, 223, 233–35, 237, 239, 240, 242, 247–49, 251, 297, 332, 336, 343–44, 416, 425, 437, 448, 450, 454–55, 458, 473
   See also Space
Progress, 305, 362, 378
Progressive, 199
Protestant Reformation, Chapter Four, 55, 84–85, 137–178
   See also Anglican; Calvin; Luther
Proust, Marcel, 423–24, 428, 454
Psyche, 41, 115, 144, 150, 169, 203–4, 283, 301, 306, 347, 378, 390, 440, 491
Psychology, 41, 97, 119, 126, 137, 149, 156, 185, 205, 241, 248–49, 261, 268, 291, 298, 305, 318, 325, 334, 336–37, 367, 395, 402–403, 406, 411–13, 445, 448, 462, 465, 468, 478, 481, 449
   See also Freud; James
   Gestalt, 431, 474
Ptolemy, 58, 162, 191, 192, 280
Puritan, 144
Putting-out system, 165

Pythagoras, 32

Q

Quadrivium, 114, 150
Quakers, 334
Quattrocento, 162
Quantum Mechanics, 431, 451, 453
Quintillian, 47, 76, 79, 104, 114

R

Radical, 350, 447, 465, 478
Radner, Daisie, 262–63
Raleigh, Sir Walter, 188–89
Rationalism, 315
Reading, 53, 56, 133
    private, 85
    public, 75
    silent, 74–75, 78–79, 81–82, 90–91, 95, 131, 133, 137–39, 143, 151, 155, 171, 177, 179, 195, 219–20, 249, 461
Reason, 54, 186–87, 189, 334, 341, 345, 351, 357, 378–79, 432
Reflection, 20, 168, 238, 255, 259, 275, 285, 295, 299, 331, 340, 342, 348, 360, 375, 380, 437, 441, 470, 474
Reflective, 76, 156, 203, 209, 226, 230, 235, 238, 248, 258, 260–61, 293, 319– 20, 340, 348
    pre-reflective, 259
Reflexive, 319, 371, 433, 451
    aware, 44, 46
Reflexivity, 43, 65, 247, 306, 350, 413, 447
Reformation, 96, 137–178, 358, 368, 403
    Catholic, 97
    counter, 97
    Protestant, 97
Reid, Thomas, 246–47
Reisch, Gregorius, 158
Relativism, 342, 424, 451
Religion
    damnation, 69–70
    personal relationship with, 77
    resurrection, 60
    salvation, 50, 64, 69, 88, 91, 491
    sin, 50, 69, 89, 97
    soul, 67, 491
    two-sided sword, 127, 148–49, 211

Rembrandt, 132, 139, 152, 184, 269
Renaissance, 95–136, 362, 381, 385–86, 403, 406, 415, 460, 470
Reuchlin, Johann, 141
Richelieu, Cardinal, 182
Rimbaud, Arthur, 421, 441
Robbe-Grillet, Alain, 409, 455–56, 485
    Voyeur, 409
Rodin, Auguste, 420
Romanesque, 85, 109, 113
    Mary Magdalen Church, Vezélay, 109
Romantic, 59, 173, 206, 249, 274, 277, 300, 357–99, 415, 432, 449, 485
Rorty, Richard, 45
Rosenberg, Philip, 362
Rousseau, Henri, 420
Rousseau, Jean-Jacques, 66, 227, 326, 337, 343–45, 348–52, 358, 360, 363–64, 368, 442, 468, 474
    amour-de-soi, 343, 346, 348
    amour propre, 343, 346
    autobiography, 58
    Confessions, 345
    corporate will, 349–50
    Emile, 345, 347, 352
    general will, 349–50, 360, 364
    Heloise, 345
    particular will, 349, 350, 364
    private will, 360
Royal Society, 200, 280, 296, 305, 309
Royce, Josiah, 488
Rubens, Peter Paul, 139, 184
Russell, Bertrand, 435
Ryle, Gilbert, 435, 436, 439, 441, 480, 486–87
    Ghost in the Machine, 436, 438, 487

S

Saenger, Paul, 74, 79–81, 90, 155
    See also Reading, silent
Sade, Marquis de, 327
Salutati, Caluccio, 114
Santa Maria del Fiore, 110
Santayana, Geroge, 446, 459
Sartre, Jean Paul, 249, 257, 319, 406, 433, 435, 443, 461, 463–78, 486, 485
    See also Existential

Being and Nothingness, 249, 465
Childhood of a Leader, 469–70
No Exit, 35, 443, 465
Flies, 465, 478
Transcendence of the Ego, 462, 465
Sass, Louis A., 251, 409
Schlieffen plan, 430
Science, Chapter Five, 3, 158–60, 165, 185, 189–81, 193, 196, 198–200, 207, 213–15, 228, 248, 248, 250, 254, 263, 268, 270, 277, 296, 299, 301, 309, 311, 313, 319, 321, 324–25, 334, 336, 374, 376, 384, 390, 420, 433, 436, 439–40, 446, 451, 454, 465, 481
  method, 202
Science fiction, 382, 416, 433, 452
Scientific Revolution, 20, 91, 97, 105, 124–25, 137–38, 156, 167, 177, 179–82, 192, 200, 204, 205, 226, 233, 248, 250, 300, 302, 359, 369, 371
  See Mathematics
  experimental method, 272
  natural philosophy, 223, 225–27, 281–82, 302, 311, 321, 333–34
Schizophrenia, 38–39, 264, 314, 409
Schneider, Carl D., 394
Scholastic, 80, 82, 91, 118, 140–42, 190, 204–5, 212, 224, 226, 271, 282, 296, 309
Schopenhauer, Arthur, 386, 395, 460
Schroedinger, Erwin, 440
Schoenberg, Arnold, 458
Scott, Stanely L. 488
Scotus, John, 74
Scribes, 26–27, 76, 86, 90
  See also Writing
  Benedictine, 78
  dictation, 73, 76, 79, 81, 83
Secularism, 66, 86, 131–32, 137–40, 144–45, 177, 183, 185–86, 195, 199, 223, 226, 228, 233, 238, 244, 250, 261–62, 274, 293, 300–2, 304–5, 315, 317–18, 322–23, 334, 336, 338, 350, 423, 491
Self, 13, 16–18, 20, 22, 31–32, 38–39, 41–43, 50, 52, 57, 61–63, 65–69, 89–91, 96, 102, 107, 108, 120–24, 131, 133–34, 138–40, 155, 170, 174, 176, 180, 189, 193, 202, 204, 206, 209, 212, 214–15, 219, 223, 231, 233–34, 236, 238–41, 244, 247, 249, 251, 256–57, 265, 269, 273–74, 276, 279–85, 288, 290, 292, 294, 297, 300–1, 305–7, 315, 317–18, 320, 322, 324–28, 330–32, 335–37, 339, 341–42, 344–46, 348–50, 352, 358–62, 365–67, 371, 373, 377–78, 380, 385–86, 388–91, 394–96, 398, 403, 408, 411, 414, 417–18, 422, 424, 426–27, 435, 437–38, 446, 448–50, 454, 461, 463–64, 466, 469, 473, 475, 477, 479, 481, 486, 488, 492
  interior, 74
  modern, 55, 171
Self-actualized, 248
Self-alienation, 343
Self-assertive, 108
Self-analysis, 441
Self-aware, 10, 16, 173, 264, 283, 305
Self-communion, 302
Self-consciousness, 16, 18, 43, 108, 121, 124, 242, 256–57, 231, 283–84, 293, 322, 331, 335, 359, 362, 371, 375, 378–80, 392, 394–96, 399, 401–2, 404, 417, 419, 422, 425, 441, 487, 489, 492
  immature, 177, 193
  mature (camera on me), 174, 419, 425, 493
Self-assertion, 479
Self-conscious reflective individual, 9, 250, 353, 460, 493
Self-conscious selves, 164
Self-consistent, 156
Self-contained, 132, 143, 304
Self-control, 306
Self-conversing, 226
Self-critical, 158
Self-deception, 203, 340, 387
Self-delight, 348
Self-destructive, 387
Self-development, 242
Self-dictation, 76
Self-discipline, 310
Self-driven, 208, 304
Self-discovery, 137
Self-distancing, 213–15
Self-emancipation, 329
Self-engagement, 380
Self-estrangement, 343, 380

Self-explicating, 389
Self-flagellation, 387
Self-honest, 345
Self-humor, 174, 362
Self-identity, 312
Self-imprisonment, 329
Self-individualized consciousness, 445
Self-interest, 217
Self-knowledge, 318, 333, 376, 390, 484
Self-love, 346–47
Self-meaning, 61
Self-overcoming, 395
Self-overhearing, 156, 226, 227, 238
Self-portrature, 112
Self-preservation, 13
Self-realization, 247, 297
Self-referential, 414
Self-reflective, 124, 174, 238, 256, 264, 269, 324, 442
Self-reflective conscious individual, 208, 297, 429, 492
Self-reliance, 125, 208
Self-responsible, 307
Self-reticent, 60
Self-revelation, 130
Self-righteousness, 29
Self-scrutiny, 336
Self-surpassing, 471
Self-survival, 288
Self-torment, 328
Self-transparent, 264
Self-understanding, 254, 336
Selves, 156, 173–74, 256, 290, 306, 321, 326, 339, 371, 388, 409, 418, 425, 455, 464
  See Woolf, multiple selves
Seneca, 147
Sennett, Richard, 362, 396
Sensations, 256, 270, 276, 287, 298, 303, 315, 334, 340–41, 370, 426
  See also Locke
Sentiment, 342, 358, 487
Sentiment intérieur, 335
Sepper, Dennis L., 264–65
Seven cardinal virtues, 65
Seven deadly sins, 12, 65, 184, 212
Shakespeare, William, 22, 31, 62, 65, 118, 133, 134, 149, 151, 153, 155–57, 169–72, 174–76, 180, 192, 198, 202–3, 209, 212, 215, 226, 229, 235, 237, 243, 269, 273, 312, 320, 362, 365, 408, 459
  See also Theater, Soliloquies
  Falstaff, 173, 175, 240
  Hamlet, 36, 134, 153, 156, 171, 173–76, 186, 209, 240, 478
    personal identity, 156
Shame, 52, 126, 479, 394, 433
  See also Guilt
Shane, 433
Sheol, 19
Silence, 377
Silent reading, See Saenger; Reading, silent
Sin, 12, 19, 105, 131, 140, 159, 184, 217, 233, 237, 242, 240, 242, 281, 293, 346, 368, 687, 388, 389
  damnation, 51, 140
Signed art, 112, 122
Skepticism, 321, 337, 342, 398
  anti-, 315
Skolen, 434
Sloman, Aaron, 482
Smith, Adam, 212, 328
  homo economicus, 212
Socinianism, 282
Socrates, 14, 20, 22, 70, 74, 76, 207, 209, 236, 287, 441, 460
Solecki, R. S., 15
Solipsism, 464, 471
Soliloquy, 240, 243
Solomon, Julie Robin, 214–16
Solomon, Robert, 477, 479
Sophocles, 30, 31
  Oedipus, 30
Soul, 48, 67, 287, 322
  interior, 239
Sovereignty, See Bodin
Space, 10, 24, 26, 31, 37, 66, 76, 100–1, 115, 124–25, 157, 162, 165, 170, 176, 179, 190–92, 195–97, 205, 212–13, 225–27, 238–40, 248, 258, 261, 270–76, 294, 301–4, 306, 310, 314, 321, 360, 362, 375, 377, 385, 402, 409–10, 415, 418, 420, 422–23, 426, 429, 433, 445–46, 448, 450–56, 461, 470, 472, 485, 499
  Age of Discovery, 95
  categories, 445
  curved, 445

empty, 445
four-dimension, 488
humanized, 108
infinity, 190
inner, 445
internal, 101, 108, 155
Gothic, 85
Greek, 29, 31, 37, 41
language, 37
layouts, 445
New World, 115, 128, 137, 146, 150, 187, 192, 224, 271–72, 310, 406
spaced out, 445
outer, 445
positive negative, 385
private, 82
relative, 445
sense of, 3, 31, 41, 97, 100–1, 125, 153, 192, 205, 271, 304, 306, 385, 442, 445
ship, 445
spaced out, 445
three-dimensional, 422, 488–89
vacuum, 194
Spacks, Patricia, 332
Spanish Armada, 134, 216
Spark, 245, 246
Speech, 12–13, 18, 218, 219
thought, 4, 12
Spengler, Oswald, 448
Spillane, Micky, 433
Spina, Alphonse de, 84
Spinning wheel, 131
Spinoza, Benedict de, 261, 267, 318–21, 326, 346
Spontaneity, 379, 396, 398, 473, 474
Stein, Gertrude, 429–30
Steiner, George, 406, 438
Stephens, Leslie, 233
Stevens, Wallace, 416, 485
Stewarts, 181, 269
Stoic, 47–50, 60, 234, 236, 239, 250, 303 322, 373, 391
Stravinsky, Igor, 419
Studia humanitatus, 114, 150
Sturm und Drang, 363
Subjective, 46, 61, 96, 122–23, 176, 236, 241, 243, 257, 263–264, 273–275, 283, 289, 294, 308, 314, 328, 332–33, 341–
42, 383, 409, 417, 425, 452, 454, 462, 464–65, 470–71, 481, 484
Sumerian, 25–26
syllabic signs, 25
Suicide, 412
Surrealism, 174, 374, 406, 420–21, 431, 441, 463
Sutorius, 62, 69
Syncretistic, 28, 42
Synderesis, 245–46, 257
natural instinct, 245
spark, 231, 239, 245–46

T

Talbot, Michael, 448
Talmud, 76
Tartaglia, Niccolo, 196
Tauler, 141
Tawny, R. H., 125
Taylor, Charles, 240, 244, 282–83, 306, 328, 336
Taylorism, 430
Technique, 4, 249
illusion of, 432
Technology 401
Teleman, Georg Philipp, 208
Telescope, 196
Tertullianus, 67, 69, 141, 210, 237
De Testimonio Animae, 66
hell, 51
Testament
See also Bible
New, 53, 58
Old, 76
Thales of Miletus, 38
Theater, 22, 24, 30, 32, 170–71, 273
See also Shakespeare
absurd, 4, 407, 452, 456, 464
Greece, 30
movies (film), 4, 171–72, 176, 210, 407, 437, 452, 458
television, 171–72, 402, 437, 487
Theodore, St., 111
Theology, 318
Thinking, 21, 27, 30, 32, 34, 37, 43–44, 46, 236, 238, 247, 251–52, 254–60, 263,

Index | 605

277, 287, 290, 292, 301–2, 309, 367, 390, 393, 425, 441
abstract, 4, 21, 37–38, 67, 115, 252, 264, 434
computation, 258
Thirty Years' War, 132, 144, 227
Thorndike, Lynn, 107
Three Graces, 12
Thucydides, 37
Tibetan Book of the Dead, 28
Time, 24–26, 37, 66, 86, 100–1, 105, 115, 124–25, 157, 162, 165–66, 170, 179, 191, 195–97, 205, 225–26, 270, 283, 300, 302–4, 306, 310, 313, 324, 360, 362, 375, 377, 385, 402, 409–11, 414–15, 420, 423–26, 429, 433, 443, 445–46, 448, 450–52, 454–58, 461, 485, 491
See also Bergson
bad, 445
and a half, 445
eight-hour day, 445
forty-hour week, 445
good, 445
history, 24, 37
humanized, 105
instantaneous, 446
is on our side, 445
just in time, 445
Magazine, 445, 463
management, 430
meet you under the clock, 445
is money, 445
motion, 317
out of, 445
relative, 445
standard, 428, 430
timelessness, 445
to burn, 445
relative, 445
universal, 460
wrist watch, 428
Titian, 113
Tocqueville, Alexis de, 376, 386
Translation, 55–58, 244, 459
Trajan, 103
Treadle loom, 131
Triadic, 326, 349

Tribe, 14, 19, 22
Triune, 326
Trivium, 114, 150
Turgot, Anne Robert Jacques, 303
Twain, Mark, 432

U

Unacknowledged Revolution, See Eisenstein
Uncertainty, 29, 48–49, 53, 96, 154, 227, 311, 321, 453, 464, 481
Uncertainty Principle, 406–7, 453
Unconscious, 66, 286, 318, 418, 438, 457
Underground Man, 395
Unintended consequences (U.C.), 179, 213, 223, 237
Unique, 348–49, 352, 372–73, 392, 399, 414, 477
Unitarianism, 282, 334
Unity, 43–44, 47
Universe
  closed, 55
  open, 56, 204
Universities
  Bologna, 86
  Cambridge, 81, 167, 212
  Oxford, 81, 86, 89, 167, 212
  Padua, 198
  Paris, 80–81, 86, 212
  Pisa, 198
  Sorbonne, 81, 212
Utilitarian, 12, 27, 206, 210, 481

V

Vacuum, 204
Vasari, Giorgo, 121
Valesquez, Diego, 184
Valla, Lorenzo, 114, 141
Vandals, 71
Van Eyck, 113
Vega, Lope de, 185
Vermeer, Jan, 184
Vernacular, 82, 86, 95, 132, 137–38, 155, 169–70, 176–77, 179, 249
Verne, Jules, 381
Versailles, 183
Villani, Filippo, 103

Vincent of Beauvais, 104
Virgil, 37, 75, 98–99, 172
    Aeneid, 36
Virtue, 97, 105–6, 126
    active, 105, 115, 117, 184, 346
    passive, 115, 238, 281, 293
Vittorino da Feltra, 114
Volition, 238–39, 251, 253, 256–57, 261, 264, 348, 349, 351–52, 385, 412, 425–26, 437, 461, 467, 469, 471–73, 476–79, 485–88
Voltaire, 225, 311–12, 343, 386
    Candide, 343
Vondell, 185

W

Warhol, Andy, 64, 464
War of the Three Henries, 144
Watermill, 131
Watson, John B., 412, 414, 423
Weber, Max, 125, 149
Whichcote, Benjamin, 323
Wilkes, John, 327
Will to Power, See Nietzsche
Whitehead, Alfred N., 267, 269–70
Whitman, Walt, 441
William the Silent, Prince of Orange, 146
Willis, Thomas, 186
Wills, Gary, 58
Willey, Basil, 225
Williams, Raymond, 372
Windmill, 130
Wittgenstein, Ludwig, 171, 436
Wolf, Christian, 343
Wolf, Fred, 413–14, 417, 447–48, 452
    here, 454
    now, 413, 433, 446, 449, 454
    nuts, 452, 454
Wooley, L. 26
Woolf, Virginia, 405–6, 408, 418, 424, 426, 456
    selves, 456
Word, The, 76, 91, 334, 383, 446
    See also Bible
Wordsworth, William, 374
World War I, see Great War
World War II, see Great War

Wrist watch, 225, 428
Writing, 11, 16, 21–22, 24–27, 53, 70, 74, 76, 96, 98, 108, 202
    censorship, 167, 319
    concrete, 27
    footnotes, 82
    imprimatur, 167
    parenthesis, 90–91
    punctuation, 75, 90–91
    scribes, 26–27
    structure, 80

X

Ximenes, Cardinal, 127, 145
X-Rays, 406

Y

Yeats, William Butler, 415, 442, 484
Yolton, John, 270–73, 296–97, 320
Young, Edward, 331

Z

Zarathustra (Zoraster), 28
    Ahura Mazda, 28
Zeitgeist, 462
Zen, 464
Zeno, 47, 231, 325
Zola, Emile, 378, 420
    Germinal, 378
Zoroastrianism, 177
Zurbaran, Francisco De, 184
Zweig, Paul, 346, 340, 477–78
Zwinglians, 145